STATE
OF THE NATION

South Africa 2007

STATE
OF THE NATION

South Africa 2007

Edited by Sakhela Buhlungu, John Daniel,
Roger Southall & Jessica Lutchman

Published by HSRC Press
Private Bag X9182, Cape Town, 8000, South Africa
www.hsrcpress.ac.za

First published 2007
ISBN 978-0-7969-2166-6

Copyedited by Vaun Cornell and Lee Smith
Typeset by Christabel Hardacre
Cover photograph by Mandla Mnyakama of Iliso Yabantu
Print management by comPress

Distributed in Africa by Blue Weaver
Tel: +27 (0) 21 701 4477; Fax: +27 (0) 21 701 7302
www.oneworldbooks.com

Distributed in Europe and the United Kingdom by Eurospan
Distribution Services (EDS)
Tel: +44 (0) 20 7240 0856; Fax: +44 (0) 20 7379 0609
www.eurospangroup.com/bookstore

Distributed in North America by Independent Publishers
Group (IPG)
Call toll-free: (800) 888 4741; Fax: +1 (312) 337 5985
www.ipgbook.com

Contents

Introduction

Part 1: Politics

List of tables

List of figures

Foreword

In February 2006, a number of researchers from the Human Sciences Research Council (HSRC) and I had the opportunity to participate in the First International Forum on the Social Science–Policy Nexus held under the aegis of Unesco's Management of Social Transformations Programme. The Forum was billed as, and proved to be, an innovative space for dialogue between researchers, policy-makers and policy activists from various parts of the world. In the South African context, the fourth edition of *State of the Nation* continues the tradition of being a regular contribution to such a dialogue, and a stimulus to informed and wide-ranging debate.

The original essays in this edition on South African politics, economy, society and international relations are a testament to the intensity of discussion that swirls around the major challenges that face the government and people of South Africa. The interpretations of our situation that are offered here are hugely diverse, including some which are strongly critical of government policies and state institutions. However, all the authors have sought to interpret their topics based upon both historical understanding and empirical research; and the essays reflect a nuanced take on aspects of the state of the nation. In keeping with its commitment to 'social science that makes a difference' the HSRC is proud to present the selection of views contained in this edition of *State of the Nation*. Neither the introductory editorials nor the perspectives presented in the individual chapters represent the views of the organisation and, as is the case with all publications from the HSRC, the editorial independence of these publications – including the *State of the Nation* – is respected and upheld as a matter of principle.

I would like to record our gratitude to the four donor organisations that continue to provide solid support to our flagship project in the nexus of social science and policy. Atlantic Philanthropies, the Charles Mott Foundation and the Ford Foundation provided the generous financial assistance which enabled the compilation and production of this publication. Equally important has been the contribution of the Konrad Adenauer Foundation which organised and financed the 'launch-workshops' which allow us to engender debate well beyond the academy.

In this regard, an important initiative this year is our launch of the Isolezwe (Eyes of the Nation) Project, whereby our cover photograph is the winner of a competition, conducted this year by Iliso Labantu (Eyes of the People). The latter are a Cape Town-based, informal, self-help group of township street photographers and enthusiasts who for the last four years have been working together to promote their members' technical and business skills, and hence to improve their employment opportunities. The Isolezwe Project presented participants with the challenge of providing a photograph which, in the view of an expert panel of judges, best depicts 'the state of the nation' at the present time and which could hence be used on the cover of the volume. The photographs submitted by the competition's entrants were of a very high quality, and we will be proud to present the best ten to the general public when we conduct the volume's 'launch-workshops' around the country. However, a special word of congratulation is due to Mandla Mnyakama, the winner of our first competition, whose remarkable photograph adorns the cover of the present collection. I would also like to thank the expert judges who provided freely of their time and enthusiasm. On the basis of our encouraging experience this year, we are hoping to widen the competition to other parts of the country in the future.

The success of *State of the Nation* is in large measure due to the commitment and effort of the current editorial team consisting of Sakhela Buhlungu (University of the Witwatersrand) and John Daniel, Roger Southall and Jessica Lutchman of the HSRC. To all of them, I express my sincere gratitude. The fact that John Daniel and Roger Southall are also the founding editors of *State of the Nation* – together with Adam Habib – speaks for itself. Thank you all for a highly successful project. Garry Rosenberg, Mary Ralphs, Karen Bruns, and all of the staff of the HSRC Press have also played their part in ensuring the success of the project and I convey the appreciation of their colleagues.

With an eye focused on both past and future editions of *State of the Nation*, I would like to quote from the Buenos Aires Declaration of the International Forum on the Social Science–Policy Nexus:

> We thus state our conviction that better use of rigorous social science can lead to more effective policies and outcomes. Such use requires strengthening linkages between the social sciences and policies for social and economic development. For the knowledge that the social sciences seek is precisely the knowledge that policy needs. The world needs new forms of interaction between social scientists and policy actors – and innovative spaces to make them possible.

The *State of the Nation* is a mechanism for dialogue and public debate in this space.

Dr Olive Shisana

President and Chief Executive Officer,
HSRC

Acronyms

ACDP	African Christian Democratic Party
Acsa	Airports Company of South Africa
AFDL	Alliance des forces democratiques pour la liberation du Congo
AIC	African Initiated Church
AMP	African Muslim Party
AMWU	African Mineworkers' Union
ANC	African National Congress
AP	assessment panel
APF	Anti-Privatisation Forum
Apla	Azanian People's Liberation Army
APLAMVA	Apla Military Veterans' Association
AQEE	access, quality, efficiency & equity
ART	antiretroviral therapy
ARV	antiretroviral
ASGISA	Accelerated and Shared Growth Initiative for South Africa
BAe	British Aerospace
BEE	black economic empowerment
BIG	basic income grant
CASE	Community Agency for Social Enquiry
CBM	cross-boundary municipality
CCR	Centre for Conflict Resolution
CEO	chief executive officer
CGE	Commission on Gender Equality
CHB	Chris Hani Baragwanath Hospital
CMC	Case Management Committee
Cosatu	Congress of South African Trade Unions
CPLO	Catholic Parliamentary Liaison Office
CPN	chief professional nurse
DA	Democratic Alliance
DBSA	Development Bank of Southern Africa

DCS	Department of Correctional Services
DEAT	Department of Environmental Affairs and Tourism
DHS	district health system
DoD	Department of Defence
DoH	Department of Health
DoHA	Department of Home Affairs
DoJCD	Department of Justice and Constitutional Development
DP	Democratic Party
DPLG	Department of Provincial and Local Government
DRC	Democratic Republic of Congo
DTI	Department of Trade and Industry
DVA	Domestic Violence Act
EDL	essential drugs list
EGS	employment guarantee scheme
FDI	foreign direct investment
FF	Freedom Front
GDP	gross domestic product
GEAR	Growth, Employment and Reconstruction strategy
GM	genetic modification
GNU	Government of National Unity
GSSC	Gauteng Shared Services Centre
HDI	Human Development Index
HMIS	Health and Management Information System
HR	human resources
ICD	Independent Complaints Directorate
IDC	Industrial Development Corporation
IFP	Inkatha Freedom Party
IRB	International Rugby Board
ISP	Industrial Strategy Project
JPOI	Johannesburg Plan of Implementation
KANU	Kenyan African National Union
KZNRU	KwaZulu-Natal Rugby Union
MDC	Movement for Democratic Change
MEC	Minerals-Energy Complex
MK	Umkhonto we Sizwe

MKMVA	Umkhonto we Sizwe Military Veterans' Association
MLA	Monitoring Learning Achievement
MO	medical officer
Naledi	National Labour and Economic Development Institute
NARC	National Rainbow Coalition
NCA	National Co-operation Agreement
NCOP	National Council of Provinces
NDR	national democratic revolution
NEC	National Executive Committee (of the African National Congress)
NMC	National Management Committee (of the Democratic Alliance)
NP	National Party
NNP	New National Party
NRB	Natal Rugby Board
NSDP	National Spatial Development Perspective
NSSD	National Strategy for Sustainable Development
NUM	National Union of Mineworkers
OKM	Operation Khanyisa Movement
PAC	Pan Africanist Congress
PBMR	pebble bed modular reactor
PHC	primary health care
PID	party identification
PMTCT	Prevention of mother-to-child transmission
PTUZ	Progressive Teachers' Union of Zimbabwe
RDP	Reconstruction and Development programme
SAA	South African Airways
SACBC	Southern African Catholic Bishops' Conference
SACC	South African Council of Churches
SACMEQ	Southern African Consortium for Monitoring Education Quality
Sacos	South African Council on Sport
SACP	South African Communist Party
SADF	South African Defence Force
SAHRA	South African Heritage Resources Agency
SANDF	South African National Defence Force
SAPS	South African Police Services
SARB	South African Rugby Board

Sarfu	South African Rugby Football Union
Saru	South African Rugby Union
SCA	Supreme Court of Appeal
Scopa	Standing Committee on Public Accounts
SDU	self-defence unit
SES	socio-economic status
SHI	social health insurance
SOE	state-owned enterprise
SPU	self-protection unit
Stats SA	Statistics South Africa
TAC	Treatment Action Campaign
TRC	Truth and Reconciliation Commission
UDM	United Democratic Movement
UIF	United Independent Front
UNDP	United Nations Development Program
UP	Universal Party
VCT	voluntary counselling and testing
WHO	World Health Organization
Zanu–PF	Zimbabwe African National Union–Patriotic Front
ZCC	Zion Christian Church

Introduction: The ANC state, more dysfunctional than developmental?

Roger Southall

The two preceding volumes of *State of the Nation* have highlighted the aspiration of President Thabo Mbeki's government for South Africa to become a 'developmental state', that is, one which works successfully to combine extensive social redistribution with high economic growth, thereby effectively tackling poverty, overcoming historic racial divides, and generally rendering the economy more dynamic, innovative, just and equitable. Mbeki himself is convinced that remarkable progress is being made towards this objective. His 'State of the Nation' address for 2006 trumpeted a raft of achievements. On a basis of sustained positive economic growth, the government claims to have, *inter alia*, provided access to potable water to some ten million South Africans since 1994; allocated two million housing subsidies to the poor since that year; spent particularly heavily on education (with primary school enrolment having remained steady at 95.5 per cent of the relevant population since 1995 and secondary school enrolments at 85 per cent); and raised the gross annual value of the 'social wage' (transfer payments made by government to eligible recipients) to R88 billion by 2003, with the poor being the principal beneficiaries. Overall, significant numbers of people have been leveraged out of poverty, for whereas in 2001, 4.1 million out of 11.2 million households in South Africa lived on an income of R9 600 or less per year, this decreased to 3.6 million households in 2004, even after taking the negative effect of price increases into account. In short, the government's management of the economy – premised on the broad objectives of increasing investment, lowering the cost of doing business, widening economic inclusion and providing the skills that are required – now ensures that it is able to deliver increased services to the population in a sustainable way (Mbeki 2006).

Although the annual 'State of the Nation' speeches highlight triumphs more than tears, there is widespread agreement that major economic and social progress has been made since 1994. According to a recent review of South Africa's first ten years as a democracy:

> Between 1995 and 2003, real GDP grew at an average of nearly 3 per cent, which was about double the growth rate recorded between 1980 and 1994…the economy [has] experienced a sharp turnaround in productivity performance…[reflecting] the impact of greater integration with the rest of the world following the removal of trade

sanctions in the early 1990s and the implementation of extensive trade reforms. At the same time the incidence of poverty has fallen, and significantly more South Africans have access to improved housing and basic health, sanitation and utility services. (Nowak 2005: 2)

Writing in the *Business Day* (12.04.06), local newspaper columnist John Kane-Berman concurs, noting that South Africa's gross domestic product per head will probably reach its highest level yet in 2006, exceeding the figure of R23 414 (at 2000 prices) achieved in 2005, although also noting that it will have taken a quarter of a century to surpass the previous highest figure of R23 972 (at 2000 prices) attained in 1981, an achievement which has come alongside advances in the spheres of health, sanitation and education.

Yet such commentators also point to the unevenness of delivery, a shared complaint being that gains made have in some instances been overhauled by failures, the most widely cited example being that of the government's flawed approach to the HIV/AIDS pandemic, which has done little to counter increasing mortality rates, and which overall has seen a decline of life expectancy in South Africa. However, perhaps most damning of all is that South Africa's Human Development Index (HDI) rating (as calculated by the United Nations Development Programme) increased from around 0.735 in 1990 to 0.742 in 1995, but thereafter slumped to 0.658 in 2003, and the country's global ranking in this regard is downwards rather than up (from 85th out of 174 countries in 1990 to 120th out of 177 countries in 2003) (UNDP 1995, 2004). Triumphs there are and have been, but if South Africa's overall HDI is plummeting so sharply, something is clearly drastically wrong – raising the question of whether, despite the government's best intentions, the African National Congress's state is more dysfunctional than developmental. It is to grappling with this fundamental issue that this editorial is directed.

We have argued previously that 'state capacity' is a critical aspect of South Africa becoming a developmental state (Southall 2006). The state in post-1994 South Africa was noted as having acquired the political legitimacy which it lacked under apartheid, and as mobilising its new inclusiveness to tackle social inequalities, drive growth, meet social needs and resolve conflicts in a consensual rather than a coercive manner. However, it was also observed that considerable debate attends the capacity of the state to intervene in a constructive manner in the economy, the extent to which such capacity is undermined by policy-driven attempts to achieve 'demographic representivity' within both the public and private sectors given skills deficiencies amongst previously disadvantaged groups, and whether the state is ultimately capable of pursuing its developmental goals democratically.

Following Cummings and Norgaard (2004), the editorial in last year's *State of the Nation* conceptualised 'state capacity' as having four dimensions: ideational, political, implementational and technical (Southall 2006). The controversies concerning how and whether today's South Africa is proving able to meet the formidable challenges that fall under these headings continue, and opinions vary sharply about how they should be met. Even so, it is probably true to say that there is more consensus around implementational and technical dimensions than around ideational and political capacities. This is because there is broad sympathy (albeit disagreement around specific policies) with the major thrusts of what may be termed Mbeki's modernising project.

Mbeki's modernising state

Whereas the presidency of Nelson Mandela was characterised by the drive for national unity and racial reconciliation, that of Thabo Mbeki has sought to give substance to the ANC's perception of its historical role as being to structure a modern democracy out of the backward legacy of apartheid (Daniel et al. 2005). Presently conceptualised in terms of the aspiration towards the 'developmental state' and the modernisation of the continent as a whole, this vision has been founded in significant part around Mbeki's bid to enhance capacity for delivery via the restructuring and centralisation of the governmental machinery under a powerful presidency. This has had both state and party aspects.

The centralising presidency

Mbeki began constructing the machinery that would deliver modernisation as early as 1995. Initially, the different government ministries operated relatively autonomously, yet in practice line functions overlapped and impacted upon each other. Accordingly, when Mbeki became president in 1999, he sought to increase co-ordination by merging the hitherto separate offices of the presidency, deputy president and the Office of the President, under whose effective authority the different ministries were brought together in five overlapping 'clusters' – international relations and trade, social affairs, governance and administration, economic affairs, and investment and employment – in order to deal with 'transversal' issues and to work closely together according to the government's agreed strategies. Within this context, some ministries were definitely more equal than others, with the Treasury undoubtedly reigning supreme in terms of both authority and prestige. By 2004–05, this combined presidency was comprised of an establishment of 469 people with a budget of R170 million (up from R89 million in 2001) (*Sunday Times* 19.09.04).

Central to the presidency's functioning is the policy unit (headed by Joel Netshitenzhe) – the engine room where proposals are most thoroughly scrutinised and key reports on economic and social issues are produced, which are then translated into five-year strategic frameworks. Agreed policy is refined through a complex web of specialised offices and directorates, ranging from the Cabinet

Secretariat and Forums of Directors General (the most senior public servants within ministries) and special advisors through to working groups on issues such as higher education, youth, business, agriculture, black business and trade unions, and Offices with responsibilities for the Status of Women, the Rights of the Child, and Disabled People. Alongside these structures, the deputy president functions as the leader of government business (responsible for securing passage of the government's programme through Parliament), and undertakes other tasks as allocated by the president. For instance, after Jacob Zuma replaced Mbeki as deputy president in 1999, he was appointed to head the Moral Regeneration Movement and the National AIDS Council.

The creation of a powerful presidency was accompanied by the restructuring of the public service. The authority of ministers to manage their own departments, to create and abolish posts and to promote, transfer and discharge employees, was increased; targets were set for national and provincial administrators; and performance management contracts were introduced at senior levels (Picard 2005). Meanwhile, there were concerted attempts to bring greater discipline and coherence to the structure of government established in 1994. The ANC's original hope during the negotiations process had been for a strongly centralised state to replace the previously racially-divided bodies of apartheid governance, but what emerged in the 1994 Interim Constitution (agreed by political elites) was a compromise with federalist positions which saw the establishment of a three-tiered machinery of national, provincial and local authorities. Subsequently, in terms of the Final Constitution of 1996 (adopted by the first democratically-elected Parliament sitting as a National Assembly and which reflected ANC preferences to a considerably greater degree), these different tiers were required to operate within a framework of 'co-operative governance'. In practice, this was underpinned by party discipline (the ANC always being in political control of a minimum of seven out of the nine provinces) and, more fundamentally, by the fact that provincial budgets were almost wholly derived from national government.

The government's attempts to contain the autonomy of provinces, get them singing to the same tune, and centralise state power, were matched by Mbeki's bid to impose stricter discipline on the ANC. After 1994, the ANC's character in the provinces was disparate because of its having incorporated a diversity of political cultures, the provincial party structures drawing in as they did a mix of exiles, internal anti-apartheid United Democratic Front (UDF) activists, homeland politicians and technocrats. This had led to severe tensions between a number of provincial premiers and their local ministers, these often inflamed by resentment at the way the national leadership of the party was felt to have imposed premiers upon provinces in opposition to the preferences of the party's provincial executives and pre-election party primaries (although the actions of the ANC's National Executive Committee [NEC] in this regard were in practice pragmatic and uneven).

These tensions came to a head in Gauteng when, in 1997, delegates from local ANC branches defied the wishes of the national leadership and provincial cabinet by electing Mathole Motshekga to replace Tokyo Sexwale as premier, following the latter's resignation to go into business. Motshekga, whose candidacy built upon the perception of party activists from outside Johannesburg that Soweto had received the major portion of development resources, was deeply distrusted by the party hierarchy for both his independence and his reputation as a 'populist'. Consequently, when allegations of corruption against him were leaked to the press, he became the object of investigation by an internal ANC commission of inquiry. This cleared him of corruption, but so criticised his managerial capacities that it advised that the party should dispatch appropriate persons to assist him to run the province more competently. More pertinently, it also suggested that henceforth provincial premiers should be appointed by the ANC president, this recommendation being endorsed by the NEC in August 1998. This decision in no way resolved intra-provincial tensions, for it de-linked the premiership from the chairperson-ship of the party's provincial executive (distinct posts which henceforth were no longer necessarily filled by the same person). However, in practice it represented a significant shift in authority away from the provinces, allowing the president to exert control more firmly over both the provincial governments and the party organisations. Motshekga, for instance, was displaced by Mbhazima Shilowa as the party's choice for premier for the 1999 elections, even though he managed to retain the provincial chairmanship until May 2000. When this led to confrontations with Shilowa's government, the ANC National Working Committee dissolved the provincial executive, replacing it with an interim body until the next provincial conference, when it structured a formal reconciliation between the conflicting groups (Lodge 1999; 2002). Subsequently, increasing efforts have been made to contain and control regionalism within the party, and to secure 'co-operative gov-ernance' by appointment of the president's men – and women[1] – to the key posi-tions in the provinces. The same approach has been adopted with regard to local government, with the ANC at national level reserving the right to nominate may-ors and council chairpersons. Meanwhile, the government seems bent on reducing the provinces to merely administrative entities and to exerting greater centralised control over municipalities.

The construction of a modernising state is widely hailed as having provided the framework for remarkable achievements: the consolidation of political legitimacy, consistent economic growth, fiscal discipline, delivery of increased social benefits to poorer citizens, and so on. At the same time, however, alongside controversy around major aspects of the government's economic policy (notably its inequalitarian consequences) and widespread criticism concerning alleged policy failures (for instance regarding HIV/AIDS and the kid-gloved treatment of crude-ly anti-democratic regimes in neighbouring Zimbabwe and Swaziland), there is recognition even within government circles that realisation of the modernisation project has been uneven. In particular, the implementational and technical capacities of the state appear to be inhibited by flawed efforts to combine 'representivity' with 'efficiency', and the apparent systematisation of corruption.

Representivity and efficiency: costly or complementary?

Access to education and skills was overwhelmingly skewed in favour of white people during the decades of apartheid. Eventually, of course, the consequences of legislation such as the Bantu Education Act of 1953 (which sought to limit modern education for black people on the grounds that few opportunities would become available to them in a white-dominated economy) were to catch up with the apartheid regime, as employers compensated for a developing shortage of white skilled workers by hiring cheaper black workers and training them on the job. In turn, the growth of the black trade union movement from the early 1970s onward – premised upon the inexorable urbanisation and de facto acquisition of skills by an increasingly militant black working class – was one of the key developments which paved the way to democratisation, even if it was the youthful revolt against the government's attempt to impose Afrikaans as a language of education which provided the spark which lit the conflagration of open black revolt. Yet even though by the early 1990s the economy had become highly reliant upon semi-skilled black labour, the skills deficit amongst the black population was formidable, and a primary cause of extensive poverty. It was therefore inevitable that political liberation was envisaged by black people as providing not only for free and improved access to education and jobs previously denied to them, but also to the redress of racial imbalances in both the state and private sectors.

From 1994, the ANC worked strenuously towards the attainment of 'representivity' within the public sector. Black workers had long formed the majority of workers in the public service and associated institutions. By 1989, for instance, the public sector (comprising central government and provincial administrations, the 'self-governing' states, parastatals, other public entities, universities and technikons but excluding local government and the four 'independent' homelands of Transkei, Bophuthatswana, Venda and Ciskei) was comprised of 337 382 white people (34%), 125 284 coloured people (13%), 36 605 Asians (4%) and 481 051 black people (49%). However, fully 38 per cent of black public servants were located in the 'self-governing states', and there and elsewhere black people were overwhelmingly located in professional categories such as teaching and nursing, where they were poorly remunerated, or in low paid, low status and menial positions. Furthermore, white people occupied 98 per cent of the top four income categories within the public service, and 81 per cent of the top eight (Hugo 1992: 54–6). Initially, the ANC's efforts to 'transform' the public sector were constrained by the so-called 'sunset' clause in the Interim Constitution, whereby white public servants were guaranteed their jobs, or appropriate financial compensation, for a period of five years. However, the new government set out its stall as early as 1995, when its

White Paper on the Transformation of the Public Service established that within four years, 50 per cent of management positions should be staffed by black people (Naidoo 2006), the ANC having indicated as early as 1991 that it intended making the 1 500 most senior posts in the public service 'representative' as soon as possible (Hugo 1992: 58). Subsequently, although the government's fiscal caution meant that there was no substantial growth in the size of the public sector during the first decade of democracy, white departure and proportionately increased black recruitment did lead to it becoming more representative, as indicated by Table 1.

Table 1 *Racial composition of the civil service, 1993 and 2003*

	National 1993	Non-independent homelands 1993	National 2003	Provinces 2003
African	316 929	241 335	195 238	563 300
	41.3%		62.8%	78.6%
Asian	30 453		16 641	21 493
	4.0%		5.4%	30.0%
Coloured	124 711		91 994	65 152
	16.3%		29.6%	9.1%
White	295 429		73 319	66 797
	38.5%		23.6%	9.3%
Total	767 521		310 907	716 742

Source: Southall 2004: 533

Equally importantly, representivity increased markedly at senior levels. In 2000, the Department of Public Services indicated that some 60 per cent of 1 766 senior managers in national departments and 1 175 in the provinces were black (Southall 2004: 533), while according to an independent evaluation, 32 per cent of public service managers were black, 42 per cent coloured, 3.5 per cent Asian and a mere 23 per cent white (Thompson & Woolard 2002: 5). Meanwhile, measures such as the Employment Equity Act of 1998, the Promotion of Equality and Prevention of Unfair Discrimination Act of 2000, the Broad Based Black Empowerment Act of 2003 and the current pressures upon the private sector to adopt ambitious black employment targets are providing for a considerable levelling of the employment field across society as a whole.

For the ANC, the striving towards 'representivity' (including measures to redress gender and disability imbalances) has been simultaneously a bid to extend its control of the state, a strategy to meet the expectations of its constituency, a thrust to redress the social injustices of apartheid and a hope that the commitments to delivery and growing work experience of black employees will compensate for any lack of formal education and training for the jobs they do. Meanwhile, of course, these aspirations have been complemented by major initiatives that the government has undertaken to transform the educational system to achieve both equity and, most particularly, an improved quality of education for black learners. Suffice it to say here that progress towards the meaningful transformation of the education sector has been mixed – well-intentioned policies with regard to resource equalisation, institutional restructuring, curriculum reform and better school governance have been adopted, but the pursuit of equity and excellence has been severely compromised not only by the ravages of HIV/AIDS and the inhibiting effects of poverty and malnutrition upon the capacity of many children to learn, but also by factors such as an unwise (and expensive) loss of experienced teachers from the public sector after 1994, the underqualification and demoralisation of many teachers (especially in rural and township schools), and limited financial and managerial capacity amongst educators (Fiske & Ladd 2004). Indeed, overall, educationists concur that while the government has made considerable strides towards the allocation of educational resources on far more equitable terms, the output in terms of improved learner outcomes remains extremely disappointing. Furthermore, while the deracialisation of the educational system officially provides opportunities for all, in practice benefits accrue mostly to a growing black middle class while the urban and working poor struggle to take advantage (Chisholm 2004). In short, not only has the search for equity in education proved elusive, but the output of schools and universities attended by the majority of black people (especially) remains disappointingly low in both qualitative and quantitative terms. This in turn leads to disconcertingly slow progress towards the evening-out of the skills distribution in the labour market (Moleke 2006).

The principal issue at stake is whether the drive for representativeness is compatible with efficiency and effectiveness. In his recent review of the topic, Picard (2005) acknowledges that the debate about affirmative action is too often crudely simplified. Nonetheless, he strongly criticises the government's focus upon rendering the public service demographically representative as being inadequately accompanied by systematic attention to human resource development, capacity building and training. The ANC opted for a short-term strategy of middle-class replacement through on-the-job affirmative action rather than choosing to invest in human capacity over the long term. The outcome has been a low level of administrative performance and the extensive abuse of their powers and positions by many self-serving public servants.

The systematisation of corruption

There are disturbing indications that corruption in government is becoming systemic, and that it is linked to the drive for representivity. However justifiable and politically necessary, affirmative action appears to have spawned a culture of entitlement amongst some of the beneficiaries of racial preferment. In turn, this has been fostered by the apartheid legacy of lack of formal education, skills and training amongst the majority of black people, for this undermines their competitiveness on the open job market and hence increases the intensity of their scramble for public or political office. Party and state positions are regarded as providing access to private wealth.

Assessing the extent of corruption is always difficult, for by definition much of it is covert and illegal. It is also a highly emotive and sensitive issue, whilst in South Africa there is a tendency for the level of corruption since 1994 to be compared with what went before. Indeed, with liberal and conservative critics of the government tending to propose that the extent of corruption is growing, and the government itself insisting that their claims are exaggerated and nostalgic for supposed better times past, the debate about corruption is also intensely (and unhelpfully) ideological (Hyslop 2005). Yet whether or not present-day corruption is 'better' or 'worse' than under apartheid is in essence a red herring, for under its newly democratic order, South Africa aspires to an unimpeachable level of civic virtue, and numerous institutions have been established and laws passed which require the accountability of politicians and public servants to the citizenry, and indeed, of corporate executives to their shareholders. There is no doubt, too, that at the highest level of government, not least in the person of President Mbeki, there is major determination to combat corruption and to protect the public fiscus. This has found expression in key measures like the Public Finance Management Act of 1999 (which imposes stiff financial requirements upon public managers), the Prevention of Corruption and Combating of Corrupt Activities Act of 2003 (which makes it an offence to receive benefits which have not been earned, in either the public or private sector), the improved professionalisation of the South African Revenue Service and of the Office of the Auditor-General, and the requirement that politicians and senior public servants disclose their private financial interests (Sole 2005). Even so, many would agree with the recent judgement of analyst Richard Calland (*Financial Mail* 21.04.06) that today South Africa stands 'on the edge of an ethical precipice', subject to the 'drip drip accumulation' of evidence that corruption is becoming pervasive. At fault, it appears, is not a lack of formal measures but of political will to combat corruption. This has its roots in the volatile combination of the ANC's erosion of the distinction between party and state, the widespread sense of entitlement amongst many public and ANC functionaries, and a scramble for private wealth within an economy whose advantages have historically been denied to the majority of the population on grounds of race.

Space does not allow for elaboration of the assertion that corruption is becoming pervasive. However, it is not a claim that the majority of South Africans, of whatever colour or background, find far-fetched (see, for example, Orkin & Jowell 2006). Thus, four propositions can be ventured.

First, corruption has been allowed to gain ground because of the mixed messages emitted by the ANC's national leadership. There are strong grounds for asserting that the root of this particular evil lies in the deal whereby in the mid-to-late 1990s contracts to supply South Africa with arms were provided to a mix of European firms. A steady flow of allegations and evidence indicates that a combination of heavy political pressure and bribery was utilised to secure South African agreement. However, the government was to prove reluctant to pursue them, and indeed was to use party discipline to hobble the hitherto independent Standing Committee on Public Accounts (Scopa) and blunt its investigative capacity, while the issue of a report of a joint investigation into the deal by the Auditor-General, Public Protector and National Director of Public Prosecutions released in November 2001 was widely derided as a whitewash (Crawford-Browne 2004). It is precisely the ANC's apparent reluctance to open up the deal to full scrutiny which has fuelled the conviction in some quarters that the recent successful prosecution of Shabir Shaik, a close confidant of Jacob Zuma, for soliciting bribes from a French arms contractor, was part of a conspiracy to deprive the latter of the opportunity to succeed Mbeki in the presidency (discussed later in this chapter). When, in addition, there is only uneven and half-hearted prosecution of members of Parliament accused of misusing their official travel funds (February 2006), 'Travelgate' provides further indication to some that misuse of public resources is a risk worth taking.

Second, there is a particular reluctance to investigate allegations that state positions and resources have been misused to the ANC's advantage. The chief example of this is the 'Oilgate Scandal', publicised by the *Mail & Guardian* (notably 20–26.05.05), whereby the state oil company, PetroSA, irregularly made an advance payment of R15 million to Imvume Management for the supply of oil condensate sourced from a Swiss company, Glencore. However, when Imvume – which had close connections to the party – chose to divert R11 million of this sum to a cash-strapped ANC ahead of the 2004 general elections, Glencore turned for direct payment of the R15 million, and another R3 million owing to it from Imvume, to PetroSA. The latter thereupon paid Glencore the R18 million for fear that its Mossel Bay gas-to-liquid fuel point would run out of feedstock. Although PetroSA made efforts to recover the money and Imvume acknowledged the debt, only a small portion was paid, and Imvume later defaulted upon agreed instalments that would have seen the debt repaid over four-and-a-half years.

A host of questions followed. Not least of these was the extent to which senior members of the ANC might have known of the transaction. These included the party's Secretary-General Kgalema Motlanthe and party treasurer Mendi Msimang, to both of whom Imvume's Chief Executive Officer, Sandi Majali, claimed a close professional and business relationship, as well as the then Minerals and Energy Minister, Pumzile Mlambo-Ngcuka, under whom PetroSA ultimately operated. In addition, it was alleged that even before making the payments to the ANC, Imvume wrote cheques (described as 'loans') of R50 000 and R65 000 respectively to Uluntu Investments, a company wholly owned by Mlambo-Ngcuka's brother, and to Hartkon, a construction company renovating the residence of Zola Skweyiya, the Minister of Social Development (*Mail & Guardian* 10–16.06.05).

The ANC's response to the *Mail & Guardian*'s expose was that there was nothing wrong with a private company making a donation to a political party – as if

Imvume's payment was not sourced from state funding! To the wide dismay of media watchdogs, the ANC also obtained a gagging order from the high court which prevented the *Mail & Guardian* from publishing a sequel to its initial report on the grounds that it invaded Imvume's right to privacy, and this was followed by threats of legal action by the ANC, Motlanthe and Msimang against the *Mail & Guardian, Business Day* and the *Sunday Times* over articles exploring their relationship with Imvume. Worse, it was soon revealed that national police headquarters was investigating the *Mail & Guardian* to find out the sources of its information. Meanwhile, opposition leader Tony Leon and Freedom Front MP Willie Spies had referred the various allegations to the Public Protector, Lawrence Mushwana, whose constitutional function is to report upon possible abuses of power by government. However, in a report which was widely described as kowtowing to his political masters, Mushwana cleared PetroSA of any wrongdoing and stated that his mandate did not allow him to enquire about what happened to the R11 million payment once it was in the hands of a private company, thus sparing the ANC embarrassment. Nor were ANC parliamentarians keen to pursue the matter. The ANC used its majority on the Minerals and Energy Portfolio Committee to endorse Mushwana's report. Meanwhile, although Scopa found that the payment made by PetroSA to Imvume was procedurally irregular, opposition attempts to secure crucial documentation relating to the R15 million payment which might have implicated the ANC were blocked (*Mail & Guardian* 2–8.09.05, 23–29.09.05; *Business Day* 30.03.06).

Unfortunately for the government, the UN published at this time a report which, in detailing how Saddam Hussein's regime had abused its Oil-for-Food programme, showed how a bribe of $60 000 had been paid to the regime on behalf of Imvume and/or a related South African company or companies. Internationally embarrassed, Mbeki appointed a presidential commission of inquiry (*Sunday Times* 12.02.06). Nonetheless, this unfinished story suggests the ANC's preparedness to combine an appropriation of state resources with the subordination of state institutions to the party.

The third proposition is that the ANC is ambivalent about taking determined action against conflicts of interest. Formal recognition that politicians and public servants should not use their state or political office to unfairly further their personal interests is firmly in place. However, a recent report by the Auditor-General (2006) indicates that many individuals, including ministers, deputy ministers, provincial ministers and 'designated' public servants, are failing to publicly declare their business interests as required. Meanwhile, there is considerable public anxiety that, in many instances, contracts are awarded on the basis of political connections rather than according to the officially embraced principles of impartiality, fairness, public accountability, transparency, empowerment and effective use of resources. Public confidence has been further undermined by the reaction of many leading figures in the ANC to the assassination in mid-2005 of mining magnate

Brett Kebble, declaring him a 'patriot' upon the basis of his supposed commitment to black empowerment, which saw him engaged in a web of business interests with, *inter alia*, the ANC Youth League, this despite the fact that it was already well known that he was being pursued for non-payment of taxes. Yet subsequent revelations have already exposed Kebble as having systematically looted his own companies, at a cost of well over R2 billion to their shareholders, and suggest that he saw his close connections to certain ANC politicians, the ANC Youth League and various empowerment figures as a means for securing valuable political favours.[2] Although such mafia-style party–state–business entanglements are exceptional, considerable disquiet attends the government's reluctance to clamp down unambiguously upon political office being used to further business interests, particularly where senior members of the party are involved.

The fourth proposition is that the national leadership's various inconsistencies, as already outlined, weaken its authority to combat corruption at lower levels in government. It is fair to say that the government has launched a number of initiatives designed to complement its formal machinery of financial accountability. In 2005, for instance, the government promised an amnesty from prosecution for those of its employees and members of the public who owned up to defrauding the Department of Social Development (which is responsible for paying an array of pensions and social grants). By early 2006, 80 000 people had taken advantage of the amnesty, yet government still managed to uncover 35 000 new cases of social-grant fraud, with more than 12 000 public servants being found to be receiving social grants for which they were ineligible (*Sowetan* 28.04.06). Similarly, an investigation instigated by the Gauteng government has recently uncovered a scam whereby certain officials are said to have been colluding with nine bus companies contracted to transport children to school to defraud the provincial education department of many millions of rands (*Star* 01.05.06). Numerous other official successes in exposing corruption could be cited from around the country, yet the impression remains that the government's efforts at tackling the issue are half-hearted, in part because it is so extensive, and in part because to do so would be to involve the high political costs of taking on provincial and local ANC elites.

Delivery, dysfunctionality and the poor

Early 2006 saw the ANC approaching the country's second democratic local government elections with some trepidation. Its problem, according to one report, was that it 'had presided over the near collapse of local government over the past five years' (*Business Day* 09.01.06), whilst according to another, the forthcoming contest would come to be remembered as the one where the ANC began to lose its grip on power: 'next time we vote we will have a real race on our hands' (*Sowetan* 27.02.06).

The ANC's anxiety was increased by an upsurge of pre-election anger. One newspaper report recorded 20 waves of popular protest against poor service delivery, the housing crisis, corruption, and water and electricity cut-offs between July 2004 and May 2005 throughout numerous towns in Gauteng, Eastern Cape, Northern Cape, Mpumalanga and Free State, almost all of them supposedly ANC strongholds (*Sunday Times* 29.05.05). As the elections scheduled for 1 March 2006 drew nearer, protests intensified.

One study of the protests in seven Free State towns recorded that in five of them, the level of expenditure upon salaries and emoluments of local officials was well above the provincial average, while the level of capital expenditure tended to be considerably lower than the provincial average. The conclusion drawn was that while the poor were prepared to exercise patience so long as they saw evidence of development, a lack of delivery combined with increased municipal salaries and perceived 'fat-cat' lifestyles of councillors and officials was a prescription for protest (*Business Day* 04.09.06). This finding is consonant with the analyses provided by Doreen Atkinson in her chapter in this volume. She argues that while the sheer pervasiveness of poverty and unemployment in many communities means that not all delivery failures can be laid at government's door, problems have been compounded by clear dysfunction and malpractice at municipal level and the failure of the intergovernmental system to support municipalities adequately.

The government's response to the popular protests was, at times, unwisely heavy-handed, and justified by dark hints that the violence was being orchestrated by sinister forces (*Business Day* 30.05.05). Yet as the elections drew closer it adopted a more measured approach which reflected its acknowledgement of the extent of delivery failures. On the one hand, Mbeki vowed to monitor the performance of local politicians more closely. ANC councillors were required to sign an anti-corruption pledge, live in the areas that they represented, and to adhere to a code of conduct. On the other, the ANC pledged to conduct a skills audit of municipalities, to introduce more rigorous training for councillors and staff, and to employ more technically competent people to run local government (*Mail & Guardian* 03–09.03.06).

In the event, the ANC surmounted the electoral threat and again routed the opposition in almost every area of the country (except, most notably, in Cape Town). While this once again demonstrated its prowess as an electoral campaigning machine, the result – as Collette Schulz-Herzenberg discusses in her chapter – was more ambiguous than it initially appeared. The ANC won well, but in conditions of a lower overall electoral turnout, patchy performance, the continuing lack of a credible and united opposition, and, as Mcebesi Ndletyana illustrates in his chapter, the failure of social movements and independents to take full advantage of its discomforts. However, the ANC's victory obscured the growing chasm between the party's rank and file and the national leadership, this demonstrated after the election by a series of local revolts against the national leadership's imposition of mayoral nominees in favour of preferred local candidates (*Mail & Guardian* 24–30.03.06). Continuing battles between factions supporting and opposing mayors not approved of by the ANC provincial hierarchies mean that, in practice, some municipalities are today virtually ungoverned, as officials struggle to do what they can from day to day without council mandates. However, as Karima Brown has argued (*Business Day* 21.02.06), more serious for the ANC is that such local discontent is an expression not just of the resistance of vested local elites to Mbeki's modernising project, but also of a highly divisive struggle for the succession which has thrust the organisation into the worst crisis since it was founded in 1912.

The succession struggle and the erosion of political capacity

Political capacity refers to what makes for an effective structure of governance. From this perspective, Mbeki's modernising project – his bid to strengthen the state's implementational capacity by crafting a more centrally-driven yet locally-responsive structure of 'co-operative governance' – is critical if central government policies are to be realised and delivery enhanced. However, the prospects of such realisation are threatened by the contemporary battle for the political succession, which has exposed fault lines within the government, the ANC and its alliance partners.

The succession struggle is analysed by Anthony Butler in detail in his chapter. Suffice it to say here that it has come to loom so large politically because, whereas previously in South Africa no limits were imposed upon the tenure of the presidency, a limitation of two five-year terms was imposed upon incumbents by the Constitutions of 1994 and 1996. Mbeki's capture of the deputy presidency in 1996, at the expense notably of Cyril Ramaphosa, had provided him with the platform to secure the presidency unchallenged in 1999 when Nelson Mandela chose to step down. This was in conformity with ANC tradition whereby – with open campaigning inhibited by the politics of exile and the assumption that destiny not personal ambition should dictate the choice – presidents of the party had been selected by party elites and endorsed by the mass organs. Even so, in 1999, Mbeki sought to protect his political pre-eminence by plucking Jacob Zuma, previously a minister in the provincial government of KwaZulu-Natal, from relative obscurity. In so doing, he elevated him to the role of president-in-waiting because of the precedent that his own succession had set.

Zuma's rise was dramatic in that, although he was a powerful figure within the party by virtue of his having been head of intelligence during the days of exile and having played a major role in reconciling the ANC and the Inkatha Freedom Party (IFP) in KwaZulu-Natal during the lead-up to the 1994 elections, he had had no formal education, and thus seemed an inherently unlikely candidate to run a modernising state as complex as South Africa. Yet Zuma's strength lay in his personal qualities, notably his capacity for promoting reconciliation amongst conflicting parties through a combination of charm, arm-twisting and appeal to 'African values'. More to the point, however, was his garnering of support among significant elements of the ANC and tripartite alliance who were becoming alienated by the style and substance of the Mbeki presidency, which especially among the trade unions and the poor was seen as distant, dictatorial, unduly favourable to established large-scale capital and, perhaps most damning, representative of an emergent wealthy, political and empowered black elite. Zuma, in short, although lacking serious leftist credentials, managed to position himself as the candidate of the dispossessed who would recapture the ANC for the people. However, Zuma's bid for the presidency was to fall badly awry as a result of his becoming implicated in corruption by evidence offered in the 2005 trial of Shabir Shaik.

In November 1998, government announced the preferred suppliers of new aircraft, helicopters, corvettes and submarines, and in December 1999, Defence Minister Mosiuoa Lekota signed off on a multi-billion rand arms package. However, by this time concerns had already been raised about corruption in the allocation of contracts, and in September 2000 the Auditor-General recommended a forensic audit. Subsequently, in January 2001, the *Mail & Guardian* revealed that Durban businessman Schabir Shaik – who was brother to Chippy Shaik, a government arms procurer – was a director of Nkobi Holdings, a company that had won a R400 million tender in the arms deal. Mbeki thereafter ordered a probe of the deal by the Auditor-General, the National Prosecuting Authority (the 'Scorpions') and the Public Protector, and on the basis of evidence they produced, Schabir Shaik – who described himself as an economic advisor to Zuma – was arrested in November 2001. There was no evidence, declared the three investigative bodies, of improper or unlawful conduct by the government as a whole, but their findings led to the suspension (and later resignation) of Chippy Shaik on grounds of his having been involved in a conflict of interest over Schabir's involvement. Meanwhile, there were concerns that the extent of official corruption went far deeper than the government was prepared to admit, this, *inter alia*, leading to the resignation of opposition MP Gavin Woods as head of Scopa in protest at what he alleged was ANC interference into the committee's own investigations.[3]

Subsequently, after the Pretoria high court had ordered the Auditor-General to hand over documents relating to the failed bid of the Cape Town-based CCII Systems to win a contract to supply combat technology which had gone to Nkobi Holdings, Schabir Shaik was officially charged with corruption. However, although Zuma was named in those corruption charges, the National Director of Public Prosecutions, Bulelani Ngcuka, announced in August 2003 that even though there was '*prima facie*' evidence linking the deputy president to the corruption, a case would not be brought against him because it was not winnable.

Zuma immediately claimed that he was victim of a conspiracy designed to sully his reputation. The unstated accusation was that Mbeki was orchestrating a campaign to knock him out of the race for the succession, and he accordingly mobilised his extensive support base to fight back.[4] One outcome was publication of an accusation in September 2003 that Bulelani Ncguka had been an apartheid spy upon the ANC, this resulting in Mbeki's appointment of Judge Joos Hefer to test the allegations. Hefer reported in January 2004 that Ngcuka was 'probably never' an apartheid spy, but in the meantime the Public Protector, Lawrence Mushwana, was launching a probe into allegations by Zuma that Ngcuka had abused his office during the course of his investigations. Mushwana reported in May 2004 that Ngcuka's August 2003 statement about Zuma was 'unfair and improper', a finding which although rejected by Ngcuka led to his resignation in July 2004. Shaik's trial commenced in October 2004, and in June 2005 he was found guilty on two charges of corruption and one of fraud. Politically, however, the real dynamite was that Judge Hilary Squires found that Shaik had made payments amounting to R1.2 million to Zuma with the express intent of ensuring that the latter use the influence of his name and office to further his business interests. Furthermore, he found Shaik guilty of attempts to solicit a R1 million bribe over two years from French arms dealer Thomson (later renamed Thint) on Zuma's behalf with a view to the latter promoting Thomson's interests. Zuma, who had been portrayed by evidence led by the state as a deeply indebted man unable to manage his personal financial affairs (and hence by implication to oversee the fiscal affairs of South Africa), was found by Squires to be in a 'generally corrupt' relationship with the convicted Shaik, who was later sentenced to 15 years' imprisonment and fined R3.9 million.

The political fallout was huge. Zuma and his supporters claimed that it was Shaik who had been convicted, and not Zuma himself, that his guilt could not be assumed, and that he deserved his day in court to argue his innocence. Further, Zuma effectively challenged Mbeki by declining to voluntarily resign from his position as deputy president. The upshot was that on 14 June 2005 Mbeki informed Parliament and a riveted nation that, without making any presumption of his guilt, he had chosen to 'release' Zuma from his duties. Mbeki's brave move was swiftly followed by two further dramatic developments. The first was the announcement by the National Prosecuting Authority that it was formally charging Zuma with corruption. The second was Mbeki's controversial decision to replace Zuma as deputy president with Phumzile Mlambo-Ncguka, who although highly esteemed, was the wife of Bulelani Ncguka, and hence viewed by Zuma's supporters as party to their champion's downfall. She was also someone who further enquiry might reveal as having been implicated in 'Oilgate'.

Mbeki's firing of Zuma was widely hailed as an act of statesmanship. However, his decision provoked an immediate crisis within the ANC and the tripartite alliance, revealing them as split down the middle. Mbeki was forced to dispatch senior party leaders around the country to quell a mounting rebellion in favour of Zuma, who continued to serve as deputy president of the ANC. The NEC sought to resolve the dilemma this posed by deciding that Zuma should be 'allowed' to stand back from active party duties whilst nominally retaining the post of deputy president, but Mbeki was soon to be humiliated by delegates to the party's National General Council overturning that decision on the grounds that a person was presumed innocent until proved guilty. Zuma's supporters thereafter launched a Friends of Jacob Zuma Trust in the lead-up to his to being formally charged in court on 11 October 2005, and thereafter the crisis saw, in broad terms, the ANC Youth League, the Congress of South African Trade Unions (Cosatu), the South African Communist Party (SACP) and the National Student Council taking up cudgels on Zuma's behalf, the thrust of their campaign being that the Mbeki camp was conspiring to use the machinery of state against him. Such was the division that the NEC, fearing that fragmentation of the party would threaten its performance in the forthcoming local elections, compelled Mbeki and Zuma to issue a joint statement which formally committed them to taking a united stand against factionalism. While clipping Mbeki's wings, this move simultaneously sought to require Zuma to discipline his supporters. However, it was a bargain that Zuma failed to keep, as his supporters continued to rally noisily behind him as he hit the local government campaign trail. Ostensibly he was campaigning on behalf of the party, but the political effect was to keep his own presidential ambitions alive, raising the spectre that if he were to be found innocent of corruption he would be propelled to the presidency on the back of mass-based support. Zuma's star only began to wane when, following dramatic accusations made by the 31-year-old daughter of a long-term family friend, he was charged with rape and subsequently brought to court for trial in February 2006. In the event, he was to be found not guilty, and subsequently his triumphant supporters rallied around him as once again he resumed his position as deputy president of the party in full standing. Once again, it seemed (if the noise generated by his backers was anything to go by) his campaign for the presidency was back on track. Yet this was to overlook the fact that the disquieting revelations about his sexually irresponsible behaviour revealed during the rape case had not only convinced liberal and business elites of his lack of fitness for high office, but had also severely undermined his standing amongst socially conservative members of the ANC.[5] However, with Zuma now set to vigorously contest his prosecution for corruption, the struggle for the presidency was leaving major political uncertainties in its wake.

There is an extensive critique of the ANC, which argues that it has used its political dominance to subordinate supposedly independent institutions to its authority. Although the ANC has always vigorously repudiated this argument, its claim to be protecting the distinction between the ruling party and the state was to be undermined by successive revelations which indicated how the party's own divisions had penetrated the intelligence services, amongst whom Zuma's former role as ANC intelligence chief had translated into support at senior levels. This had been suggested, initially, by the efforts of Billy Masetlha, the Director-General, together with other members of the security establishment, to incorporate the Scorpions – which had been deeply involved in investigating allegations of Zuma's corrupt involvement in the arms deal – into their own National Intelligence Agency (NIA). Following this, in October 2005, Intelligence Minister Ronnie Kasrils suspended Masetlha and two other senior officials for allegedly illegally placing empowerment icon Saki Macozoma under surveillance. Macozoma, who had moved from politics into business, was known to be an Mbeki ally, was himself deemed a potential contender for the presidency and, indeed, had been accused by Brett Kebble before his death of plotting to deny Zuma the succession (*Mail & Guardian* 21–27.10.05). Meanwhile, ANC Youth League president Fikile Mbalula complained that he himself had been illegally monitored by NIA agents (*Sunday Independent* 23.10.05). By the closing months of the year, it was common cause that the security services were internally divided between the ANC's two factions. Yet worse was to come when, at a meeting of the NEC, Secretary-General Kgalema Motlanthe circulated copies of supposedly intercepted email messages which purported to reveal an attempt by Macozoma, Deputy President Phumzile Mlambo-Ngcuka and Scorpions boss Vusi Pikoli to discredit both Zuma and Motlanthe himself (*Business Day* 24.10.05). Following this, Motlanthe – who by now had been cited as a potential alternative candidate for the left, and as backed by Masetlha – was linked by an investigation into the veracity of the emails as possibly associated with an initiative driven by Muziwendoda Kunene, a Kwazulu-Natal businessman, to hack into the government's communications mainframe, thereby compromising top-level security (*Business Day* 23.12.05). Meanwhile, the situation was further confused by a kite flown by Joel Netshitenzhe which argued that it was not clear that the same person should necessarily fill the offices of state president and president of the party, giving credence to speculation that Mbeki is contemplating remaining a power behind the throne after he stands down as state president in 2009 (*Mail & Guardian* 14–20.10.05).

One influential interpretation of the division within the ANC views Mbeki as representing a historically necessary modernising project: creating a modern state, transforming the ANC into a modern political party, and forging a competitive, modern economy in alliance with both large-scale (white) and emergent (black) capital. From this perspective, Zuma represents backwardness, corruption, old-fashioned 'Big Man' politics, and a potential lurch back into distributive not productive economics. Meanwhile, an alternative interpretation views Mbeki as having constructed an over-powerful presidency, driven by a new political elite of state managers and technocratic ministers and supported by a new generation of empowerment managers and capitalists. This commandist state has negated the ANC's history as an organ of popular power, marginalised the SACP and Cosatu, and alienated ordinary working people and the poor. No wonder, then, that Zuma has claimed the support of the disaffected (*Business Day* 31.11.05).

Both perspectives are overdrawn. The first, which pits modernising 'rationality' against Zuma's 'populist' irrationality, ignores the extent to which the might of the machinery of state, especially at local level, has become increasingly dysfunctional and the extent to which corruption and 'crony capitalism' has billowed under Mbeki's stewardship. In contrast, the alternative view tends to discount many of the real achievements of the Mbeki presidency, while proposing no new strong counter-vision in its place. At issue is decreasing agreement about what sort of country South Africa should be.

The challenge to state legitimacy

Ideational capacity refers to the degree to which the legitimacy of the state is embedded in state institutions, political practices and the ideas of individual members of society. In 1994, there was widespread optimism that a remarkable consensus had been achieved in a previously divided South Africa around a constitution entrenching democratic values of individual freedoms, racial and gender equality, and political accountability. However, the contemporary crisis reminds us that there were (perhaps inevitable) silences. Two of these are particularly germane.

The first silence was about the nature of the ANC, most particularly what was required of it if it was to transform itself from a liberation movement into a modern political party operating within a liberal-democratic framework. As the experience of Zimbabwe demonstrated, this was dangerous, for the rhetoric and political righteousness of liberation politics can too easily translate into the assertion by a nationalist elite that they have an unchallengeable right to rule, whatever their incompetence and abuse of power. There are certainly disturbing echoes of this in the ANC's own behaviour, notably in its determination to leave no outpost of state power unconquered, even if this means overruling the wishes of the voters: as Zwelethu Jolobe outlines in his chapter, if this means the making of cynical overtures to members of smaller parties to cross the floor so as to unseat the fragile coalition which the Democratic Alliance has constructed to rule Cape Town City Council in the aftermath of the local elections, so be it! Yet the broader issue is the failure of the ANC to move away from the commandist political culture of exile, and the triumph of vanguardism over the participatory democratic tradition of the UDF which the party absorbed. One outcome was the party leadership's turning its back on socialist economics and its espousal of capitalism without ever saying so publicly. This paradox has deepened under Mbeki's centralising presidency, for this has combined a reliance upon the deep-seated, historic popularity of the ANC amongst the vast majority of ordinary black people, with the cracking down on dissent within the tripartite alliance and the marginalisation of the left. What has followed has been the increasing domination of the highest organs of the party by a state, technocratic and empowerment elite which, appropriating the badge of racial entitlement, is engaged in a project of blatant accumulation, if divided about which champion to follow. There should be little surprise that its example is followed by ANC apparatchiks at lower levels of the state and party hierarchy.[6]

The second silence concerns the fact that South Africa is a society increasingly divided by class. In overall terms, the economy has prospered under the management of the ANC, having enjoyed the longest period of sustained growth since the 1960s. Large-scale capital has profited enormously from the liberalisation of the economy: an emergent black capitalist class, although still small, has made massive strides through black economic empowerment; the majority of white people are materially better off than they were before 1994; and, of course, there is a burgeoning black middle class, segments of which may well constitute the primary beneficiaries of ANC political hegemony. Yet the class benefits are highly uneven. The working class is increasingly divided into core and non-core elements, subject to the uncertainties of the increasing flexibility of post-apartheid work regimes, a weakened trade union movement, and the constant downward wage pressure of a vast army of the formally unemployed. Meanwhile, the more numerous 'working poor' are condemned to making a tenuous living from the informal economy and/or surviving upon state pensions and handouts. In these circumstances, it is scarcely surprising that the Mbeki camp should have come to be so strongly backed by the beneficiaries of the ANC's economy, whilst Zuma should have appealed to those who have been left behind: not only the poor and the organised left, but also a motley crew of political entrepreneurs and Zulu ethnic dissidents who perceive a 'Xhosa nostra' within the ANC or who are fleeing a dying IFP.

The danger is that the two competing camps could fight themselves to a standstill. This would be to the detriment of South Africa as a whole, for the evidence is clear that there is as yet no alternative to the ANC as the government and as the glue which holds the country together. Nor would an outright victory for either side provide a sustainable way forward; if large-scale capital recognises a Zuma triumph as a threat to the political and economic accommodation attained in 1994, the untrammelled success of the Mbeki camp could lead to a dangerously destabilising alienation of the outsiders. What is required is that the ANC should not only recognise the limits to its dominance, but also reposition itself as a party of genuine political consensus.

Conclusion: dysfunctionality and the developmental state

The analysis here recognises the major economic and social advances which have been made by the ANC in government since 1994, yet argues that the latter's aspirations to transform South Africa into a genuinely 'developmental state' are critically threatened by worryingly dysfunctional aspects of the state. This occurs at different levels. In the present volume, apart from exploration by different authors of delivery deficits by local government, it is suggested that the restructuring of the parastatals has had as much to do with new class formation as it has in rendering them efficient and profitable (Roger Southall); that government lacks the capacity to make appropriate technological choices concerning power generation, yet opts for the preferences of large-scale capital without adequate democratic decision-making (David Fig); that the public health system (Helen Schneider, Peter Barron and Sharon Fonn) and hospital system (Karl von Holdt and Mike Murphy) are in a state of acute degeneration, and staff severely demoralised; and that despite good intentions, the reform of correctional services is running aground upon the rocks of staff interest and corruption (Julia Sloth-Nielsen). All this is not to even mention the state of the Department of Home Affairs, whose notoriety receives ample airing in the media, and not least amongst the hapless victims of its red tape and corruption (such as the Zimbabwean refugees whose desperate experiences are recorded in the chapter by Elinor Sisulu, Bhekinkosi Moyo and Nkosinathi Tshume). It is a not insignificant factor that it is the state's 'outsiders' – the unemployed, the poor, the destitute and the refugees – upon whom the weight of this dysfunctionality of the state falls most heavily. Yet even if much dysfunctionality can be ascribed to implementational and technical deficits, it is nonetheless in the political and ideational spheres that the principal challenges lie.

It was argued previously (Southall 2006) that progress towards a 'developmental state' would require compromises across and between classes, this involving the articulation of a common vision of a mutually caring and socially equitable society. In 1994, many of the elements of such a deal were already in place. Established capital had reached an accommodation with the ANC; a democratic Constitution offered a framework for balancing majority rights and needs against minority rights and fears; the ANC itself constituted a broad church and cross-class agreement which it institutionalised in the tripartite alliance; and Mandela's message of racial reconciliation marked out South Africa as a home for all. The present crisis within the ANC suggests that this achievement now stands in danger of beginning to unravel. On the one hand, Mbeki's centralising and modernising project is challenged by offended local elites and resented for its perceived authoritarian thrust by the left and much of civil society. On the other, social tensions are rising as South Africa moves away from a racially-polarised to an increasingly class-divided society. Clearly, the government is not unaware of the growing threats to peace and political stability, as Thabo Mbeki's constant references to the need for South Africa to bridge the gap between the 'first' and the 'second' economies indicate.

Against this background, the battle for the succession within the ANC constitutes an enigma. For its part, the party denies in public that it is taking place at all and insists that the succession will, in the best traditions of the liberation movement, be decided by consensus behind closed doors. However, in reality, the battle for the presidency is being manifestly fought out in the corridors of government and in the full glare of the media, with bitterly opposed camps competing to install their own candidate.

Mbeki's historic gesture, as the outgoing president, should be to change the rules of the ANC's game, and to open up the contest to succeed him for all to see. The ANC has a right to choose its own leader, by appropriate procedures of its own choosing, yet as the presently unchallengeable ruling party it should go out of its way to canvass opinions from across society. In a liberal democracy, aspiring candidates should be allowed to campaign openly and publicly. By abandoning the habits of a liberation movement and embracing those of a modern political party, the ANC would stand a better chance of resolving its inner divisions and selecting a president capable of appealing to the entire nation, and realising the promise of 1994.

Notes

1 Mbeki has been forthright in appointing a number of women as premiers, yet the lack of popular support that such appointees as Nosimo Balindlela (Premier of the Eastern Cape) enjoy reinforces the view that such 'powerful' women would not be able to survive politically in what is still a very patriarchal society without the president's backing.

2 Kebble's assassination, crookery and political connections have been voluminously covered in the investigative and business media. It is of note that his funeral, held in Cape Town's St. George's Cathedral with khaki-clad ANC marshals forming a guard of honour, was attended by 'a range of senior party and ANC Youth League officials, captains of industry and many of the emerging black businessmen whom Kebble had supported'. Speakers included Andile Nkuhlu of the ANC Youth League, Western Cape Premier Ebrahim Rasool, and former ANC provincial chairman Chris Nissen (*Business Day* 05.09.05). Kebble's murder, headlined the *Financial Mail* (07.10.05), evoked 'The Adoration of the Bent'.

3 The coverage of the Shaik trial in the media has been too extensive to cite here. For a useful summary of events, see *Saturday Star* 04.06.05. For Judge Squires's judgement, see Durban high court, Case No. CC27/04, 31 May 2005.

4 The interpretation of the Mbeki/Zuma struggle is drawn from extensive reading of the media, notably the *Mail & Guardian, Sunday Times, Sunday Independent, Business Day, Star* and *Financial Mail*.

5 A Markinor poll published a few days after the trial, although limited in value by its having been conducted in urban areas only, reported that 64 per cent of South Africans felt that Zuma's behaviour should disqualify him from the presidency (*Sunday Times* 14.05.06).

6 This interpretation draws upon valuable analytical articles in *Business Day* (9.11.05, 25.11.05, 31.11.05, 05.12.05).

References

Auditor-General (2006) *Report on Declarations of Interest by Ministers, Deputy Ministers and Government Employees.* RP 19/2006. Pretoria: Auditor-General.

Chisholm L (2004) Introduction. In L Chisholm (Ed) *Changing class: Education and social change in post-apartheid South Africa.* Cape Town: HSRC Press.

Crawford-Browne T (2004) The arms deal scandal. *Review of African Political Economy* 31(100): 329–42.

Cummings S & Norgaard O (2004) Conceptualising state capacity: Comparing Kazakhstan and Krygystan. *Political Studies* 52(4): 685–708.

Daniel J, Southall R & Lutchman J (2005) Introduction: President Mbeki's second term: Opening the golden door. In J Daniel et al. (Eds) *State of the Nation 2004–2005.* Cape Town: HSRC.

February J (2006) More than a law-making production line? Parliament and its oversight role. In S Buhlungu et al. (Eds) *State of the Nation 2005–2006.* Cape Town: HSRC Press.

Fiske E & Ladd H (2004) *Elusive equity: Education reform in post-apartheid South Africa.* Cape Town: HSRC Press.

Hugo P (1992) Whites in the South African public service: Angst and the future. In P Hugo (Ed) *Redistributive and affirmative action: Working on the South African political economy.* Johannesburg: Southern Book Publishers.

Hyslop J (2005) Political corruption: Before and after apartheid. *Journal of Southern African Studies* 31(4): 773–89.

Lodge T (1999) *Consolidating democracy: South Africa's second popular election.* Johannesburg: Electoral Institute of South Africa, Witswatersrand University Press.

Lodge T (2002) *Politics in South Africa: From Mandela to Mbeki.* Cape Town: David Philip.

Mbeki T (2006) 'State of the Nation' Address by the President of South Africa, Thabo Mbeki to the Joint Sitting of Parliament, Cape Town, 3 February 2006.

Moleke P (2006) The state of labour market deracialisation. In S Buhlungu et al. (Eds) *State of the Nation: South Africa 2005–2006.* Cape Town: HSRC Press.

Naidoo V (2006) Reviewing 'blackness': Race and redress in the South African public service. Unpublished. HSRC.

Nowak M (2005) The first ten years after apartheid: An overview of the South African economy. In M Nowak & L Ricci (Eds) *Post-apartheid South Africa: The first ten years.* Washington: International Monetary Fund.

Orkin M & Jowell R (2006) Ten years into democracy: How South Africans view their world and themselves. In U Pillay, B Roberts & S Rule (Eds) *South African social attitudes: Changing times, diverse voices.* Cape Town: HSRC Press.

Picard L (2005) *The state of the state: Institutional transformation, capacity and political change in South Africa.* Johannesburg: Wits University Press.

Sole S (2005) The state of corruption and accountability. In J Daniel et al. (Eds) *State of the Nation: South Africa 2004–2005*. Cape Town: HSRC Press.

Southall R (2004) Political change and the black middle class in democratic South Africa. *Canadian Journal of African Studies*, 38(3): 521–42.

Southall R (2006) Introduction: Can South Africa be a developmental state? In S Buhlungu et al. (Eds) *State of the Nation: South Africa 2005–2006*. Cape Town: HSRC Press.

Thompson K & Woolard I (2002) Achieving employment equity in the public service: A study of changes between 1995 and 2001. Working Paper No. 02/61. Cape Town: Development Policy Research Unit, University of Cape Town.

UNDP (United Nations Development Programme) (1995) *Human development report 1995*. New York: UNDP.

UNDP (2004) *Human development report 2004*. New York: UNDP.

Part I: Politics

Politics: introduction

Sakhela Buhlungu and Doreen Atkinson

The few years leading up to the 2006 municipal elections have been the most turbulent in post-apartheid South Africa. For a while it appeared that the post-liberation consensus that the African National Congress had succeeded so well in forging within its own ranks and between itself and its allied organisations was beginning to unravel. Signs of unhappiness within the ruling alliance appeared in the early 2000s when a handful of vocal activists expressed unease with aspects of the ANC's political and macroeconomic policies. When these individuals were ejected from the ruling party and when some of them spearheaded the formation of several 'new social movements', there was speculation that the alliance could begin to fragment and lose support to these emerging organisations. But that has not happened as virtually all these social movements have remained small and extremely fragile (Ballard et al. 2006).

The significance of the political events of recent years is not that they are the result of a challenge by a hostile oppositional force but that they are the outcome of serious contradictions within the ruling alliance and inside the structures of governance in the new democratic dispensation, particularly local government. The sources of these tensions are linked as the ANC is the dominant party in all tiers of government. It thus stands to reason that the municipal level should be the point where the tensions erupt. It is the frontline of government not only in the sense of being the interface between the government and citizens, but also in that it is the first port of call for service provision by state institutions. Besides, local government is an important site of patronage by any ruling party and those who fail to access such patronage often resort to local mobilisation to force the hand of party bosses.

Local government therefore provides the largest focus in this section. However, in order that these can be adequately located in context, it is necessary first to provide a basic historical background to local governance in South Africa.

A brief history of local government in South Africa

In the 1996 South African Constitution, local government is described as a 'sphere' of government. South Africa now has three 'spheres' of government – national, provincial and municipal – and each of them has a kind of autonomy of its own. Significantly, local government is not described as a 'tier' of government, for that would denote an unequal hierarchical relationship.

The history of local government in South Africa consists of two interwoven strands: the creation of a strong legacy of municipal administration alongside the painful process of transition from racially-structured institutions to non-racial municipalities.

Much of municipal history is that of 'white local authorities'. These had their roots in the nineteenth century, when local white communities created municipalities to provide basic infrastructural services. The black population was considered to be a second-class society, and consequently saw little improvement in terms of housing and infrastructure. During the apartheid era, this racial demarcation intensified, because many black people lost their rights to residence in 'white South Africa'. Many black people who could not prove long-term residence in 'white South Africa' were deemed to be illegally present in urban areas. Influx control limited the number of black people legally resident in urban areas; and the group areas policy limited black residence to specially designated townships.

In the later years of the apartheid era, these policies began to encounter internal tensions. Increased demand for skilled urban black labour confirmed the inevitability of the presence of a large black working class in urban areas, whose militancy the National Party government sought to contain through the promotion of a black middle class which could take on the functions of local governance. New municipal infrastructure and services had to be provided to black residents, some form of housing title had to be conceded, and some kind of political representation was required.

From the early 1980s, the government experimented with 'community councils' in black residential areas, a political innovation which was doomed to fail given the level of political resistance at the time. But some of the government's other experiments had more long-term significance. The Regional Services Act of 1985 made provision for regional services councils (RSCs) which were the first institutions to allow joint decision making by the local institutions established for the different race groups. The significance of the RSCs lay in their function to redistribute wealth from urban to rural areas, and from white to black communities. Notwithstanding their lack of political legitimacy, the RSCs can be regarded as harbingers of the system of developmental local governance which was to emerge some years later. A notable feature of the 1985 Act was that it provided local authorities with an additional income stream by way of business levies which were specifically earmarked for infrastructure provision in the poorer areas (Craythorne 2003; DBSA 2000).

The reformist momentum, albeit hesitant and emerging against a background of endemic civic unrest, found further expression in the repeal of over 160 discriminatory laws in the period between 1981 and the early 1990s (Binza 2005: 77–78). With its back to the wall, the government released Nelson Mandela in February 1990, thereby precipitating the transition to a new democracy, with concomitant implications for a new local government dispensation.

The country entered into a ferment of negotiation centred around the Convention for a Democratic South Africa (Codesa), which commenced at Kempton Park in 1991. That same year saw the passing of the Interim Measures for Local Government Act which allowed local communities to negotiate from a range of institutional options, from total amalgamation to various forms of resource sharing or the establishment of joint service bodies (Craythorne 2003). This Act prefigured the formation of the Local Government Negotiating Forum (LGNF), an offshoot from the Codesa negotiations. The LGNF was, in effect, a dialogue between a 'statutory' element of local government, dominated by the National Party, and its 'non-statutory' counterpart, namely the recently-unbanned local structures of the ANC. At the LGNF, it was agreed that there would be two stages in local government reform – an interim phase and a final phase.

The Local Government Transition Act of 1993 constituted the basis for the first phase, and laid the groundwork for democratic local government by permitting the establishment of appointed 'transitional councils' which joined black and white areas into single municipalities for the first time. New local structures, such as transitional rural local government councils, were introduced and district councils replaced the RSCs. The purpose of the Local Government Transition Act was to establish a process for change which required hundreds of locally negotiated transitions (Atkinson & Reitzes 1998). The era of participatory developmental local government had dawned.

South Africa's first democratic elections took place in April 1994 and were followed by staggered local government elections beginning in October 1995 and extending through to June 1996 (Craythorne 2003; Reddy et al. 2005). The 'transitional councils' consisted of all race groups, but the white, coloured and Indian components still received protection. At least half the members of the transitional councils were drawn from these groups, so that the black communities received a maximum of 50 per cent of the seats.

The 1996 Constitution of the Republic of South Africa came into effect on 4 February 1997 and established the objectives of local government as:
- Democratic and accountable government;
- The provision of services to communities in a sustainable manner; and
- Facilitating the involvement of communities and associated organisations in local governance.

Chapter 3 of the Constitution recognised local government as a distinct, autonomous sphere of government, while Schedules 4 and 5 provided lists of envisaged competencies. The Constitution also specified the circumstances under which municipalities could be supervised by the provincial and national spheres of government. The relationship between the spheres of government was described as one of 'co-operative governance'. This entailed 'mutual respect for one another's status, institutions, powers and functions' and, significantly, the directive that other levels of government should 'support and strengthen the capacity of municipalities to manage their own affairs and exercise their powers'. The distinction drawn between local municipalities as semi-autonomous 'spheres', as opposed to hierarchically subordinate 'tiers', of government was a novel one, and was regarded as important given the implications which might be inferred from the assertion that the three spheres were 'distinctive, interdependent and interrelated' (DBSA 2000: 17).

The next milestone was the release of the *White Paper on Local Government* in March 1998. This fleshed out the framework provided by the Constitution and placed local government at the centre of driving an ambitious programme designed to address developmental backlogs, the eradication of poverty, the promotion of sustainable development and the provision of safe and secure environments. The process leading up to the White Paper involved extensive consultation in the course of which overarching normative questions were addressed, culminating in the concept of 'developmental local government'. In this comprehensive vision, one may discern the seeds of the enormous expectations which came to be placed upon municipalities.

With the release of the White Paper, the Department of Provincial and Local Government (DPLG) set to work on a series of Acts to provide the legislative framework for the new municipal system. The first was the Municipal Demarcation Act of 1998, which undertook the seismic redemarcation and amalgamation of transitional local and rural councils that preceded the next round of local government elections in December 2000. The number of municipalities nationally was reduced from 843 to 284, and the concomitant redemarcation profoundly altered the electoral landscape. The watershed December 2000 elections formally marked the closure of the final phase of the local government transition period.

The second was the Municipal Structures Act of 1998, which determined three different categories of municipality. Category A municipalities are metropolitan areas, with extensive authority. However, Category B municipalities (local municipalities) operate within the administrative boundary of a district (or Category C) municipality. The intention behind the two-tier system, outside of the metros, was to promote locally responsive governance by means of Category B ('local') municipalities, and district-level planning and co-ordination by means of Category C ('district') municipalities. However, the relationship between local and district municipalities remains a contested issue (Atkinson et al. 2003).

The third significant piece of legislation was the Municipal Systems Act of 2000. This introduced innovations such as ward committees, a code of conduct for councillors, integrated development planning, performance management, development partnerships, and alternative service-delivery mechanisms.

The theme of 'integrated development' became a key dimension of municipal discourse with an intent to overcome divisions between racial groups, between different types of economic function, between rural and urban areas, and between governmental sectors. All municipalities are legally required to draft an integrated development plan (IDP). Its compilation is a legal requirement and goes well beyond promoting the IDP as being a useful planning tool that municipalities might choose to avail themselves of at their discretion. It is now incumbent upon municipalities to participate in the IDP ethos and give effect to it (Craythorne 2003).

Numerous municipalities have buckled under the strains imposed by the amalgamation exercise. Many have not managed to amalgamate their administrative systems successfully. In addition, municipalities are faced with a wide array of new functions, including promoting local economic development, alleviating poverty, addressing the impacts of HIV/AIDS, and undertaking land reform. Even though the twin challenges of democracy and non-racialism have been met, the developmental demands placed on municipalities appear to be growing exponentially. Consequently, the government has launched various DPLG initiatives to strengthen municipalities. DPLG has undertaken programmes to bolster municipal administrative skills, from Project Viability in 2001 to Project Consolidate in 2006. The National Treasury has launched its own capacity-building programme to assist municipalities with their financial management systems, and national government is providing ever greater fiscal resources (the so-called 'equitable share' of government revenue) for municipalities to implement capital projects and to provide free basic municipal services to the poor.

The municipal order in South Africa has experienced a dramatic and exciting decade of transformation. It represents many of the developmental goals espoused by the new democratic government. A new generation of local leaders has emerged, and a vibrant electoral culture has been created. But the rapid transformation has also shown up the inadequacy of administrative skills, financial systems, and popular accountability. 'Developmental local government' will need a great deal more nurturing before it can reach its full potential.

Problems and protests: local government today

Four of the chapters in this section of the volume reflect on the mixed track record of local government to date.

Neva Makgetla considers the developmental implications of local government budgets and seeks to move beyond the simplistic view that puts all failure to deliver basic household infrastructure down to incompetence by municipal officials. In particular, she examines how local government budgeting perpetuates the spatial inequalities created by apartheid. This chapter provides a compelling explanation of why poor municipalities, particularly those in former homeland areas, remain stuck in what Makgetla calls a 'vicious cycle of poverty'.

Doreen Atkinson points to the fragility of the local government system put in place after 1994. This 'paradox of formal success and popular grievances' shows that the process of transformation is not complete. Atkinson attributes the mass protests of the last couple of years to three causes: namely, municipal ineffectiveness; poor responsiveness to popular grievances; and conspicuous consumption and self-enrichment by municipal officials and leaders. However, as the 2006 municipal election results showed, none of the protests reflected deep-seated electoral disenchantment with the ruling ANC. Thus the chapter presents an argument that is also explored by other authors, that is, that electoral behaviour at local level seems not to be based on service delivery and hence elections do not function as mechanisms of 'quality control'.

Mcebisi Ndletyana's chapter explores the theme of mass protests and its relationship to the performance of independent candidates and opposition parties in the 2006 elections. He shows that black voters are highly discerning, and tend to regard their vote for independent candidates as being consistent with their maintaining overall loyalty to the ANC. Ndletyana also discusses the protests triggered by cross-border municipal disputes (Moutse and Khutsong) and how these disputes suggest intra-party contestation over the meaning of democracy (whether it should be representative or direct) at municipal level.

In his chapter, Zwelethu Jolobe focuses on the state of coalition politics, or to be more precise, the present crisis of coalition politics in the Cape Metropolitan Council which centres around the inability of either of the two largest parties (the ANC and the Democratic Alliance) to muster a simple majority, thus necessitating the formation of coalitions with smaller parties. According to Jolobe, coalitions have many advantages, including the potential of fostering inclusiveness and consensus-based politics. However, he also notes that coalitions can be fractious and produce disharmony.

The changing political arena

Collette Schulz-Herzenberg broadens the debate by focusing upon a largely unnoticed, yet inexorable, process of the demographic transformation of the South African electorate between 1994 and 2004 and the implications this has for the support bases of the various political parties. About one-third of the potential voters in 2004 were too young to vote in 1994. This change is related to shifting socio-economic conditions that have an impact on the social composition of the electorate, for example, redistributive and employment equity policies which are resulting in the increase of the black middle class. Schulz-Herzenberg argues that the unchanging social composition of ANC support conceals the growth of a floating and independent electorate, a declining voter turnout and flux and change in the composition of the general electorate. Based on hard research from eight national public opinion surveys, the 'silent revolution' among voters raises fundamental questions that should be at the centre of debates about the trajectory of South African politics.

In his contribution, Anthony Butler considers the future of South African politics by focusing on the state of the ANC whose 'health', the author argues, is 'crucial for the state of the nation'. Butler presents one of the most comprehensive analyses of the ANC in recent years. The chapter attempts to find a delicate balance by highlighting the achievements of the ANC as a liberation movement and as the first ruling party in the new democracy, on the one hand, and by identifying the emerging internal tensions within the ANC and its allies, on the other. Hopefully the ANC itself will find this chapter a worthwhile contribution to the debate about the future of the party and, by extension, the future of the country.

Unity in diversity

Three broad themes emerge from the six chapters in this section. First, all the authors acknowledge the remarkable success of the South African transition where, to use Butler's words, 'a new system of government was created out of the ruins of the apartheid state'. The ANC was crucial to all these processes of change and it deserves credit not only for making sure all the agreements were implemented, but also for having a vision to transform society in a democratic and inclusive manner.

Second, the chapters grapple with the enormous challenges facing the new government. To a large extent the problems arise because of the legacy of apartheid which allocated rights and resources unequally for the different racial groups. As Makgetla shows, the apartheid legacy has proved extremely intractable. But the problems of changing the society have also arisen because of failure, omission and/or commission, by political leaders, principally those of the ruling party, and top officials of the various spheres of government. In this regard we can mention issues of incompetence, self-enrichment and conspicuous consumption, although more important is the context of inexorable social change and class formation as discussed by our authors. There is the distinct impression that the South African government underestimated the enormity of the local government transition, and the huge administrative resources this transition would require.

The third and final theme that is implied in this section is the element of uncertainty about the future. Whether one is talking about succession in the ANC, the future of the tripartite alliance (of the ANC, the South African Communist Party and the Congress of South African Trade Unions), the future of coalition politics, the role of independents and social movements, or the voting behaviour of the younger generation – all of this remains uncertain. For those who are looking for predictability, such uncertainty is unwelcome because history did not prepare them for it. But for those who have lived with a lack of predictability most of their lives, particularly the youth and marginalised sections of society, it is more likely that uncertainty in politics is healthy.

References

Atkinson D & Reitzes M (Eds) (1998) *From a tier to a sphere: Local government in the new South African constitutional order*. Sandton: Heinemann.

Atkinson D, Van der Watt T & Fourie W (2003) Role of district municipalities. In *Hologram: Issues and practice in South African Local Government*. Cape Town: Nolwazi Publishing.

Ballard R, Habib A & Valodia I (Eds) (2006) *Voices of protest: Social movements in post-apartheid South Africa*. Scottsville: University of KwaZulu-Natal Press.

Binza SM (2005) The evolution of South African local governments: The politics of memory. *Journal for Contemporary History*, 30(2): 69–87.

Craythorne DL (2003) *Municipal administration: The handbook* (5th edition). Lansdowne: Juta & Co.

DBSA (Development Bank of Southern Africa) (2000) *Development report: Building developmental local government*. Halfway House: DBSA.

Reddy PS, Naidoo P & Pillay P (2005) Local democracy and developmental local government in South Africa beyond the first decade: Quo vadis? *Africanus*, 35(2): 40–52.

1 The state of the African National Congress

Anthony Butler

The African National Congress (ANC) was the key agent of South Africa's political transition. The liberation movement seems set to be the party of government for the foreseeable future. Its own intellectual frameworks and political processes – rather than the institutions of constitutional democracy – will forge the society's sense of collective purpose and make its key political and policy choices. The health of the ANC is therefore a crucial indicator of the state of the nation.

Despite the centrality of the ANC to South African politics, scholars have struggled to characterise its internal workings.[1] As an elite formation pursuing African political freedom, it dates back almost one hundred years. In the second half of the twentieth century, it became an exile movement, working to liberate South Africans from apartheid rule through military and diplomatic struggle. The ANC played a marginal role in the decisive labour movement and popular domestic struggles of the 1980s. Nevertheless, the ANC embraced labour and civil society allies in the transition period and it was widely acknowledged as the natural party of government. As it became a mass political movement it demonstrated a capacity to reconcile disparate interests and to develop a coherent overall programme of government. Over its first decade of rule, it also became an impressive electoral machine, increasing its majority in national elections from less than 63 per cent in 1994 to 70 per cent in April 2004.

During the past five years, however, the politics of the liberation movement have become increasingly unpredictable. Recently there have been episodes of open rebellion against the leadership. Conflict has come to a head over the desirable character of the movement in the post-liberation era, and in battles for succession to ANC and state presidencies.

The first part of this chapter sets out the central accomplishments of the ANC since 1994. The second section explains how the character and internal processes of the liberation movement have allowed it to bring these achievements about. A third section addresses emerging internal tensions within the ANC, and argues that these have primarily resulted from the movement's techniques for regulating internal and societal conflict. It identifies in addition a significant deterioration in the external environment within which the ANC must now govern. The chapter concludes that presidential successions may bring some resolution to current conflicts. However, it is an open question whether the ANC leadership in fact possesses the political and moral resources to achieve a desirable outcome.

Key accomplishments of the ANC

The ANC has managed very considerable political and economic challenges associated with profound inequality and social division. It has neutralised potential conflicts, defused racial and ethnic tensions, and disciplined potentially anti-democratic leaders. Moreover, it has brought consensus to an active membership of former communists, trade unionists, rural traditionalists, religious leaders, and black business entrepreneurs. Five achievements since 1994 are of special importance:

- The ANC has secured political stability. Political violence has been drastically curtailed, and the territorial conflict that characterised the 1994 elections has been reduced, in particular in KwaZulu-Natal. Electorally successful, this 'dominant party' has mostly avoided the use of non-democratic means to achieve its goals. It has maintained public participation in democratic elections, albeit at decreasing levels,[2] and it has elaborated an integrated programme of government that has helped to contain social conflict and stabilise the democratic settlement. Its carefully constructed programmes have helped to structure citizens' electoral choices, filtered, prioritised and reconciled demands, and neutralised potentially divisive ideological conflict. The ANC has also demonstrated that, under certain conditions at least, the rule of law applies to senior figures in the liberation movement.
- The movement's electoral invulnerability has allowed it to enforce an unpopular but necessary programme of economic stabilisation. The ANC's orthodox or even conservative overall economic policy, the Growth, Employment and Redistribution (GEAR) strategy, has increased the prospects of sustainable economic growth (Maphai & Gottschalk 2003). In this way – although at the political cost of placing the burden of adjustment on the shoulders of the poor – it has made it more likely that democracy will survive in South Africa (Przeworski et al. 2000; Przeworski & Limongi 1997).
- The ANC has created a new system of government out of the ruins of the apartheid state. The scale of this achievement – in incorporating former bantustans (rural areas set aside for particular black groups), creating new municipalities and provinces, reconfiguring the centre of the state, developing an integrated national planning framework, and moving to medium-term financial planning – has gone largely unrecognised (see Picard 2005). The transition from authoritarian rule itself created vulnerability to corruption and criminality. Moreover, the local state, the legal system, and the police were compromised by the history of apartheid. Bantustan bureaucrats brought with them traditions of bribery, money laundering and nepotism. The ANC acted energetically to create an institutional framework for good governance, and legislated widely to limit the abuse of public authority by officials.
- The ANC has shown a considerable capacity to manage citizens' aspirations and to respond to political discontent. It has retained a degree of trust among

the poorest citizens, for whom the first decade of democracy has often brought a deepening of poverty rather than a relief from it (Simkins 2004). The South African electorate has been characterised by its realistic expectations about the pace of change, a realism that has been encouraged by the ANC's ability to rebuild relationships of trust with its constituencies. Recent battles in Khutsong municipality – where trust in ANC leaders has broken down – are a reminder that a coercive state unsupported by legitimate political representation cannot be an effective mechanism of social control. Alternative instruments of mediation – such as electoral campaigning, parliamentary politics, and the criminal justice system – do not yet provide a credible alternative to ANC political processes.

- Finally, the ANC has performed the crucial role of discouraging racial and ethnic conflict. Racial antagonisms are an inevitable product of the country's political and social history. After three centuries of white supremacy, segregation and apartheid, Africans were relocated to bantustans, restricted to unskilled or semi-skilled work, prohibited from property accumulation, and consigned to a life of labour by 'Bantu Education'. Black South Africans more generally were denied the basic social infrastructure required to lead a dignified and productive life. The depth of this economic and political disempowerment necessitates an empowerment strategy that is just as broad and far-reaching (Ramaphosa 2004). Moreover, it demands ongoing political intervention to limit the racialisation of conflict over resources.

Ethnicity is also of enduring significance as a result of colonial tribalist doctrines and the apartheid state's project of 'retribalisation'. The liberation movement has emphasised that tribalism was 'invented' by missionaries and colonial administrators to 'divide and rule', control native populations, and exploit their labour. However, African ethnicity is more than just an imposition. It was also built out of the beliefs, interests, and experiences of Africans themselves (Vail 1989). Ascendant clans created historical 'tribal' justifications for their rule in the colonial period, and African intellectuals willingly took upon themselves the role of interpreters of native tradition. Bantustan political and business elites later used tribalism to justify their power and accumulation of wealth.

Black South Africans combine awareness of the artificiality of tribal division with pride in the diverse history and culture of African peoples. Ethnic tensions are usually subtle and occur as much within as between language groups. However, more substantial tensions with potentially serious political ramifications result from the particularities of Zulu identity and from the historical ascendancy of isiXhosa speakers who have been especially prominent in leadership positions in the liberation movement as well as in professional and intellectual life.

The ANC has controlled racial and ethnic antagonism. As Jones (2000) observes, it is quite appropriate for a government in a heterogeneous society to focus its efforts first and foremost on the resolution of ethnic conflicts and to ensure that disparate groups are provided with the means for political participation and representation. The movement has performed this function with exceptional dedication and success. It has relentlessly promoted non-racialism as an ideology and as a guide to practice. Moreover, it has made ethnicity almost invisible despite a history of ethnic balkanisation and systematic 'retribalisation'. The ANC has regulated internal discussion of ethnicity and it does not allow 'factional' competition for office. Ethnic balance is a cornerstone of ANC party lists and National Executive Committee (NEC) elections. Office-holders, such as the ANC president, deputy president, chair, and secretary-general, come from different language groups. An ethnic balance is maintained in Cabinet appointments. Within the state presidency, the minister, policy co-ordination director, and director-general come from smaller ethnic communities. As we shall see, these efforts represent the management rather than the resolution of ethnic and racial tensions. The ANC's achievement of racial and ethnic accommodation may have been taken too much for granted.

The foundations of ANC success

The effectiveness of the party

These various accomplishments would not have been possible without the movement's transition from a party of exile to a mass movement with a membership of perhaps 400 000 by 2004 (Lodge 2005: 111). The ANC combines the hierarchy and democratic centralism of an exile movement with the mass organisational politics that once characterised domestic anti-apartheid struggle. The rigorous organisation and discipline of exile have proved useful traits for effective electoral competition. Members continue to voice their demands for participation, and committed activists bewail any dilution of the party's ideological character in the pursuit of wider electoral support. As an electoral party, however, the ANC has predictably become 'catch-all' in character, concentrating on 'bread and butter' issues, stressing competence above ideology, and trying to appeal to many sectors of society (Kirchheimer 1966). Moreover, media-driven politics has led, here as elsewhere, to new forms of centralisation (Mair & Katz 1994), and the classic organisational trends associated with size, complexity, professionalisation, and bureaucratic character (Michels 1962) have concentrated information and power in the hands of an elite.

A system of alliances

The diversity of interests and voices that the movement accommodates dictates that both central discipline and wider deliberation are necessary to maintain political unity. A wide activist base remains essential for the ANC to mobilise electors at registration and voting time, and to enhance the legitimacy and understanding of the movement's programme of government. The ANC's system of alliances allows diverse class and ideological interests to be represented. The key relationship is the tripartite alliance with the Congress of South African Trade Unions (Cosatu) and the South African Communist Party (SACP). The SACP is essentially a faction within the liberation movement, although it possesses residual independence and periodically makes symbolic threats to leave the alliance. Cosatu operates in a competitive environment that limits its leaders' ability to strike lasting deals with the ANC. Cosatu activists are generally ANC supporters, however, and often important opinion formers and branch leaders.

The ANC's wider allies include the South African National Civics Organisation, the decayed residual shell of a once important tradition of community level organisation. The ANC is also promiscuous in party political partnerships, engaging in relationships of varying depth and endurance with Africanist and black consciousness competitors, the Inkatha Freedom Party, and the New National Party (which the ANC ultimately digested). It has also fraternised with Western Cape party the Independent Democrats, probably destroying that nascent grouping's future electoral prospects in the process. The ANC adopts similar tactics in civil society, building relationships with non-governmental organisations that refrain from public criticism of the party and government. It expects its partners to represent but also to control – to make representations to the ANC but at the same time to refrain from public denigration of the movement and its representatives in government. The ANC has been ruthless, adroit and successful in using its system of alliances to its own benefit, and to produce widespread consensus around most of government's programmes (but see Butler 2005a).

The ideological basis of consensus

The ANC's ability to maintain unity and to consolidate alliances is sometimes explained in terms of African social conservatism and a preference for consensus over contestation. Nelson Mandela has celebrated the idealised democracy of tribal meetings he observed in his childhood, in which the fundamental equality of men was purportedly expressed through a right and freedom to speak regardless of rank and social position. 'All men,' Mandela claims, 'were free to voice their opinions and were equal in their value as citizens.' Moreover, 'majority rule was a foreign notion. A minority was not to be crushed by a majority' (cited in Nash 1999). In addition, many former exiles and communists idealise a participatory democracy (Suttner 2004). However, the ANC's ability to secure consensus in a complex and class-divided society must be explained by reference to wider intellectual systems and organisational practices.

The ANC explains its own project in terms of a struggle to achieve a more just society through a 'national democratic revolution' (NDR). Communist intellectuals developed this revolutionary conception of democracy in the 1960s when trying to analyse the relationship between the overarching goal of international socialism and the immediate anti-colonial project of national liberation (ANC 1969; Slovo

1988). The SACP was an orthodox pro-Moscow vanguard party that subordinated long-range socialist goals to the immediate struggle for national independence. The party sought political alliances that might bring national liberation without jeopardising a socialist future. NDR has been characterised as 'a process of struggle that seeks the transfer of power to the people', whose 'strategic objectives' in this 'current phase' include the creation of 'a non-racial, non-sexist, democratic and united South Africa where all organs of the state are controlled by the people' (Netshitenzhe 2000). It is based upon a foundation of nation building, anti-tribalism, non-racialism, and anti-colonialism (Cronin 1996). Since 1994, however, its content and interpretation have become controversial.

NDR is unspecific about time frames and about the strategic relationships between avowed immediate (national) and ultimate (international socialist) objectives. This fundamental ambiguity has allowed the discourse to survive in post-apartheid and post-communist conditions and to maintain a commitment to an overarching project – however vaguely defined – that holds the ANC together despite growing divergence of interests (Cronin 2003). NDR's nebulous phases and stages can be manipulated in order to deflect conflict by conflating principles with tactics and immediate goals with ultimate social outcomes (Netshitenzhe 2000).

NDR also provides a language for political argument that accommodates diverse protagonists. The SACP uses NDR to reiterate the ultimately anti-capitalist character of the ANC's historical project; yet the ANC also uses it to isolate and castigate leftists in the trade unions and civil society whose naive pursuit of socialism today is 'voluntarist' and ignores 'profound objective reality' in its fight for 'simplistic and dramatic abolition of the capitalist market' (ANC 2002). Those on the right of the movement, by contrast, conceive NDR as market-oriented at least for the foreseeable future. Josiah Jele and prospective finance minister Jabu Moleketi (2002), for example, influentially argued that the socialist orientation of NDR is a matter for philosophical deliberation and should not be seen as possessing any practical import or policy relevance in current conditions.

The NDR framework has mostly been used quite pragmatically to legitimate necessary compromises between ANC constituencies. One important ANC discussion document (ANC 2000), for example, emphasised that a 'united, non-racial, non-sexist and democratic society' could only be built by addressing the needs and interests of the poor, 'the majority of whom are African and female'. Liberal constitutionalism, competitive elections, and 'independent and representative' opposition parties, unions and community organisations are all defended on essentially pragmatic grounds using Marxist categories (ANC 2000: Sections A4, A6).

Growing internal strains

The ANC's organisational and intellectual character has brought stability in the first decade of democracy, but primarily by circumventing fundamental differences of principle. Profound disagreements – *inter alia* over the market economy, liberal constitutionalism, and the nature and significance of race and ethnicity – have been mediated but not resolved. As we shall see, these differences have resurfaced and gained fresh resonance in changed political conditions, and they have been given expression in the movement's succession struggles.

Generational turnover and careerism

A growing proportion of the ANC's active membership has no direct experience of the struggle for liberation, and no intrinsic respect for conventions of authority in the movement. Many older ANC supporters are uncertain whether their tradition of reconciling diverse interests in the pursuit of NDR will survive generational change and the fading of the morality of the struggle.

Given the ANC's political predominance, activism is often a first step towards public office and potential private gain. ANC Secretary-General Kgalema Motlanthe (2005) used the ANC's National General Council to lament that:

> The central challenge facing the ANC is to address the problems that arise from our cadres' susceptibility to moral decay occasioned by the struggle for the control of and access to resources. All the paralysis in our programmes, all the divisions in our structures, are in one way or another, a consequence of this cancer in our midst.

The liberation movement is struggling to assert control over the activities of its own cadres, but senior office-holders' threats to impose disciplinary action or redeployment lack moral authority. Local and provincial politics involve routine accommodations with questionable power brokers. As Southall observes in the introduction to this volume, the leadership is compromised by its own open pursuit of wealth and its own ethically dubious behaviour. There have even been claims that the ANC's NEC is 'mortgaged to capital' (*City Press* 27.11.05; see also Netshitenzhe 2003).

Cronin (2005) observes that leadership tensions have been managed by 'deploying' cadres into private business. However, he notes that 'the converse of this is that the leading financial and mining conglomerates are increasingly reaching into the state and the upper echelons of the ANC and its Leagues – actively backing (betting on) different factions and personalities, and seeking to influence electoral outcomes and presidential succession'. Economic empowerment vehicles, moreover, can be used to hide patronage and corruption. Shame and public exposure do not seem to be effective instruments for controlling such behaviour in South Africa today. Some leaders of the ANC Youth League, for example, seem to revel in the contradiction between socialistic rhetoric and self-enrichment.

Ethnic and racial politicisation only partially managed

Conspiracy theories popular among supporters of Jacob Zuma have an ethnic dimension. Activists in KwaZulu-Natal, in particular, argue that Zuma's prosecutions for rape and corruption are parts of a plot to prevent the rightful succession of a Zulu. The ANC's ethnic balancing act has been undermined during Thabo Mbeki's second term in office. Nelson Mandela's prophecy – that the succession of a second Xhosa leader would come back to haunt the movement – has proved correct. Mbeki's actions have fuelled suspicion that non-Xhosa leaders are not treated with respect. Soweto-born politicians Tokyo Sexwale and Cyril Ramaphosa, in particular, are widely believed to have been precursors to presidential plotting around Jacob Zuma.

Mbeki's second-term Cabinet reshuffle left 13 Xhosa-speaking Cabinet ministers and 6 deputy ministers, an insensitive tilt away from ethnic balance. Meanwhile, the collapse of the Inkatha Freedom Party in KwaZulu-Natal handed control of the province to the ANC and left a cohort of ethnic activists looking for a new political home. Soon afterwards, the position of Jacob Zuma, perceived guarantor of conservative Zulu interests, was undermined. This combination of circumstances has made it possible for Zuma's supporters to advance the notion that a Xhosa cabal is determined to monopolise the presidency and to deny the office to a rightful Zulu successor. The potential resonance of this position demonstrates how essential it is for perceptions of ethnic favouritism to be consistently countered.

A resurgence of racial antagonism remains possible. Many white people have capitalised on their skills and asset advantage to benefit from higher wages in the knowledge economy and from capital gains in the property market. There is no longer an apartheid state to enforce segregation, but there has been a privatisation of apartheid as a result of new security estates, guarded shopping complexes, private health services, and fortress business parks and leisure centres. White people's denialism about their culpability for apartheid meanwhile reinforces a submerged racial antagonism that may yet be exploited by political entrepreneurs. In an interview with the *Washington Post* in 1990, Nelson Mandela observed that 'the ANC has never been a political party...the ANC is a coalition...Some will support free enterprise, others socialism. Some are conservatives, others are liberals. We are united solely by our determination to oppose racial oppression. That is the only thing that unites us' (*Washington Post* 26.06.90). In circumstances of ANC fragmentation and white arrogance, it may even be ANC leaders who decide to use racial politics in an attempt to sustain liberation movement cohesion.

Constitutional democracy defended but not entrenched

ANC activists often view liberal democratic institutions as western impositions that entrench the privileges of a property-owning white elite. The movement has not successfully inducted such cadres into liberal democratic values. ANC internal politics is meanwhile secretive, hostile to open debate and to the media, and increasingly paranoid in character – one discussion document suggests there are 'forces opposed to transformation' seeking to sabotage change, aggravate social problems, undermine investor confidence and promote 'neo-liberal ideas' (ANC 2000).

Meanwhile, the wider citizenry continues to show limited enthusiasm for liberal institutions (Mattes et al. 2003). Only a third of South Africans consider the procedural components of the political system – majority rule, regular elections, freedom to criticise government, and multiparty competition – as 'essential' to its democratic character (Mattes et al. 2003). Citizens more often consider economic or substantive considerations to be the non-negotiable aspects of a democracy.

South Africa can expect prolonged ANC electoral dominance, the key benefit of which should be stability and predictability. A dominant party can sustain the 'founding pact' of a democracy, using its strength to prevent old hostilities from re-emerging, to promote reconciliation, and to change attitudes towards democracy (Randall & Svasland 2002). However, dominant parties can be undemocratic, intimidating minorities and participating only in elections they are sure they will win. Unlike multiparty politics, dominant party systems lack the regular and routine party competition which facilitates 'horizontal' accountability of the executive to the legislature, and the 'vertical' accountability of government to the electorate. The negative impacts of dominant parties increase the longer they endure. An unbalanced party system endangers effective political opposition and weakens the boundary between state and party. When a genuine electoral challenge finally emerges, the dominant party may pack the electoral commission with loyalists and stifle the editorial independence of the media.

The leadership has encouraged the subordination of the legislature to the executive. As Cachalia (2001) notes, such subordination can be averted only if the ruling party adopts a deliberate counter-strategy to build parliamentary oversight capacity. The ANC caucus code of conduct, however, privileges party over parliamentary policy authority (Lodge 2004). The ANC has also made it increasingly difficult for parliamentarians to perform legislative and oversight functions. While the ANC has shown more respect for the courts, ANC leaders sometimes mobilise behind critics of the bench, and controversial legislation may soon place the administration of the courts in the hands of the executive, and strip the Judicial Services Commission of some of its key powers.

Economic realism not entrenched

The ANC inherited the consequences of late apartheid fiscal recklessness. Any sustainable growth path in the 1990s, moreover, was clearly going to require re-entry to international capital markets and enhanced international competitiveness. As Gelb observes, these inescapable truths forced business into an 'implicit bargain' with the ANC before transition was complete (2005: 369). The liberation movement promised macroeconomic stability and international openness. Business meanwhile acknowledged that white economic predominance was unsustainable and that ownership and management needed to be opened to black citizens.

Businesses sheltered for decades from international competition were rapidly exposed by a removal of direct and indirect import protections. Essential productivity gains resulted in significant job losses. Economic openness has had especially severe consequences for many sectors in which organised labour is strong. Meanwhile, government's economic programme was packaged in the ideologically unpalatable form of GEAR, and imposed upon ANC and alliance structures without the case for stabilisation being made and accepted. In consequence, conflict continues within the tripartite alliance about the fundamental orientation of the economy. For business, this uncertainty inhibits longer investment horizons, and sustains doubt about the sustainability of orthodox economic policy. For activists, the illusion persists that there is some easy alternative route to economic growth and enhanced employment. Abandon 'neo-liberal' GEAR, many believe, and a return to the mythical wonders of the Reconstruction and Development Programme era is possible. Economic illiteracy is widespread across the liberation movement and its alliance partners, and this allows economic populism to be used as an instrument of factional struggle.

State and ANC centralisation

The president is elected by the National Assembly, and appoints a Cabinet that is collectively responsible to Parliament. According to the Constitution, Cabinet governs together with the president. There is a relatively clear allocation of responsibilities to three spheres of government. The Constitution is supreme. Under Thabo Mbeki, however, the system of government has seen growing tension between its constitutional form and the reality of growing centralisation in the state presidency. Power has drifted from society to state, from provincial to national level, from the legislature to the executive, and within the national executive from Cabinet to presidency.

Cabinet cluster support systems and a policy co-ordination unit have moved the role of ultimate adjudication of interdepartmental conflict to the Union Buildings. In early 2004, Mbeki appointed deputy ministers across almost all departments. Meanwhile, the centre of executive power, the management committee of the Forum of South African Directors-General, is co-ordinated by the presidency's Director-General. Senior officials are on contract to the presidency rather than being the servants of Cabinet ministers. A powerful presidency is primarily a genuine response to the challenges of service delivery and policy co-ordination.

However, it can also provide a vehicle for personalised rule (Southall 2003), it can be abused to exercise unaccountable power, and succession problems are likely to arise as factions compete for a prize that no significant political or economic actor dare leave in the hands of others.

Within the ANC, a parallel centralisation has occurred. This process also has two faces. On the one hand, the ANC head office in Luthuli House has controlled factionalism, neutralised ethnic and racial politics, regulated careerism, secured economic orthodoxy, and turned the ANC into a professional mechanism of electoral competition. On the other hand, centralisation has been used to stifle debate, impose favoured candidates, and control competition for office so relentlessly that a backlash on the part of branch activists and provincial structures became inevitable.

Manipulated candidate and leadership choice has especially far-reaching consequences: 'the most vital and hotly contested factional disputes in any party are the struggles that take place over the choice of its candidates; for what is at stake in such a struggle, as the opposing sides well know, is nothing less than control over the core of what the party stands for and does' (Ranney 1981: 103). The ANC does not allow factions representing ethnic or communal groups to organise, and it operates according to a principle of non-racialism. Class factionalism has been partially institutionalised in the tripartite alliance but this does not have any formal role in selection processes. While ANC provincial structures play a key role in candidate selection, moreover, the list process is heavily regulated at the national level.

Elections for the NEC and senior officials have been closely managed, although there have been occasional expressions of branch activism – such as Mosiuoa Lekota's defeat of Mbeki-loyalist Steve Tshwete for the party's chairmanship in 2002. Until the National General Council meeting of 2005, democratic centralism prevented major eruptions of discontent. Many critics have argued that the political habits and ideologies of exile have been the key reason for declining internal democracy. According to Cronin (2002), the 'bureaucratisation', intimidation and centralisation that have bedevilled the movement reflect 'Stalinist party school education' among exiles and in guerrilla camps (see also Suttner 2003).

ANC policy documents confirm a hardening of leadership attitudes. A 1997 discussion document (ANC 1997a) highlighted concern about the ANC's 'top-down and elitist' character, and its lack of 'a climate for free, open and critical debate'. Questioning the legitimacy of GEAR and leadership interventions in provinces, the document reiterated that the ANC is a democratic organisation that subscribes to principles of free speech and free circulation of ideas. A second 1997 discussion document (ANC 1997b) observed that 'it is natural and necessary that there should be contest among individuals and lobbying by their supporters. Our challenge is to ensure healthy and comradely competition.'

In 2001, however, the leadership started to prohibit debate about internal democracy. Steve Tshwete slandered potential leaders Cyril Ramaphosa, Mathews Phosa and Tokyo Sexwale, and Communications Director Smuts Ngonyama attacked SACP Deputy General Secretary Jeremy Cronin for raising the issue of the legitimacy of debate. A National Working Committee dominated by Mbeki loyalists circulated a crudely anti-democratic discussion document (ANC 2001) which stipulated that competition for positions encourages 'the pursuit of selfish interests' and the abuse of elected office for personal gain. Alluding to potential ethnic mobilisation, it alleged that competition can unleash a 'federalism by stealth' that can 'tear the movement apart' (ANC 2001: paras 48–50). The document proposed severe limitations on individual and factional competition, reiterating no less than eight times (ANC 2001: paras 26, 27, 28, 30, 31, 32, 68, 75) that delegates possess only a broad mandate, and are obligated to 'consult widely' and 'seek consensus' at the convention before voting. 'Profound cultural practice' meanwhile prohibits self-promotion or canvassing, a prohibition on lobbying or campaigning that leaves the electoral process open to manipulation by the leadership (ANC 2001: para 63). The National Working Committee even invented a 'tradition' to undermine Cyril Ramaphosa and Mathews Phosa, arguing that 'individuals who target positions of influence and leave when they lose; and then seek to come back only as leaders would have to show how this serves the interests of the movement, and whether they can be relied upon during difficult times' (ANC 2001: para 72). It is in the context of such a tightening of the space for competition and debate that suspicion and resentment about the fortunes of Jacob Zuma's candidacy for the ANC presidency must be understood.

A worsening external environment

While the ANC has been embroiled in internal power struggles, the external environment has decisively worsened in three key respects:

- South Africa is facing a maturing HIV/AIDS epidemic which is beginning to have major economic and political repercussions. More than half a million South Africans who need antiretroviral (ARV) drugs are denied them, while obstacles to sustainable and universal ARV provision remain entrenched (Butler 2005b). There are too few health professionals, and dramatically insufficient capacities for counselling, testing, monitoring, associated infrastructure, and supply chain management. The AIDS crisis will continue to deepen, and the number of citizens needing medication is going to grow dramatically over the next decade.
- The politics of local service delivery is becoming increasingly torrid. Many municipalities exhibit dramatic human resource deficiencies, and most labour under growing debt burdens. It is likely that the intractable nature of the service delivery challenge will result in increasing recourse to protest in local-level politics.

• Despite the ANC's orthodox economic policy, the economy presents
   particular political challenges that demand strenuous management.
   Inequality and poverty remain entrenched, most importantly because of an
   intractable unemployment crisis (Simkins 2004). A more open economy and
   fiscal prudence have done nothing to reduce South Africa's vulnerability to
   capital outflows and foreign exchange crises. These dangers have powerful
   political ramifications, in particular if the recently buoyant global economy
   slows with implications for the domestic economy. Reduced growth would
   necessitate trade-offs between welfare and investment and threaten multiple
   compromises between business, the new middle class, organised labour and
   the rural poor. The black middle class so essential to political stability is
   becoming heavily indebted as it seeks to make up for its deficit of property
   and consumer goods. Meanwhile, the new generation of black economic
   empowerment deals is vulnerable to economic downturn or interest rate
   hikes. Worsening economic conditions would therefore bring rising
   unemployment, a debt crunch for the new middle class, and the collapse of
   empowerment deals that implicate both the black business elite and 'broad-
   based' beneficiaries.

Conclusion: the challenge and opportunity of succession

In the light of this challenging external environment, the significance of the succession process cannot be overemphasised. Many of the differences exposed in the
succession struggle – over economic policy, race and ethnicity, and the nature of
political freedom – demonstrate both the scale and the limitations of the ANC
achievement since 1994. Internal tensions have been exacerbated by a centralisation of the state and the ANC that has been only partly a response to the challenges
of careerism, latent ethnic competition, and an inability to deliver universal public
services.

It is evident that neither Thabo Mbeki nor Jacob Zuma can expect to function
effectively as state president after 2009 – too many antagonisms have been created
and too many bridges burned. Neither does it seem possible, politically or practi-
cally, to imagine a sustainable 'dual leadership' solution, in which Mbeki retains the
ANC presidency in 2007 while a new state president takes over at the Union
Buildings in 2009. The key rationale behind Thabo Mbeki's re-election to the ANC
presidency would be that only he can stop Jacob Zuma. Meanwhile, Zuma's candi-
dature is bolstered as much by antagonism towards Mbeki as by his own particular merits.

At the time of writing,[3] however, it is unclear whether a compromise figure with
appropriately broad-based support can be identified, and whether such a candidate can in fact prevail. One key dimension is the disarray that now affects the
component parts of the alliance. We do not find some parts of the alliance con-

fronting others – rather, all three elements are dramatically divided. Mbeki is widely disliked in Cosatu, and its central committee has in effect supported Zuma as the federation's candidate – primarily, it would seem, in response to his perceived victimisation. Zuma is also one of the very few senior candidates not tarnished in Cosatu's eyes by association with either the 'neo-liberal' policies adopted under Mbeki's rule or the perceived excesses and moral compromises of black empowerment. Nevertheless, Zuma's performance in his rape trial has offended many trade union members, and the lack of any demonstrable substance to his claims to be a leftist or friend of the workers will eventually count against him.

The SACP is similarly divided. Across the party there is a sense that a leftist candidate should rightfully be selected, but there remains no real consensus around Zuma. The head office and the Young Communist League have voiced strong support for his candidacy, but many activists caution that SACP Secretary General Blade Nzimande is in danger of sacrificing the independence of the party to a Zuma-led ANC with at best questionable leftist credentials. The strong anti-Zuma sentiment among some white SACP stalwarts, and clear generational tensions, are together threatening to destroy the organisational and intellectual integrity of the party.

Meanwhile, the ANC itself is split at the level of the NEC, through provincial structures, and down to the branches. Zuma's support has been exceptionally strong in KwaZulu-Natal. While such emphases have been partially neutralised by ANC tradition, it is unfortunate that Zuma has felt obliged to allow his supporters to abuse ethnic mobilisation. Equally noticeable is generational division, with the ANC Youth League consistently backing Zuma most strongly. There is also a class dimension to the succession debate, with many intellectuals and middle-class activists supporting Zuma primarily on tactical grounds – as a foil to Mbeki's personal ambitions or as an insurance policy against the imposition of Mbeki's preferred successor. Ordinary members, meanwhile, are often more deeply committed to Zuma's cause. While the black elite and middle class have been won over to the market economy, organised workers and the poor have had little reason to celebrate the past decade's economic growth and have developed little understanding of the imperatives behind GEAR. Zuma's strength as a candidate is magnified by Mbeki's record of disciplining provincial ANC structures, and imposing premiers and other executive appointees upon them.

Potential compromise candidates can only partly satisfy the competing ideological, ethnic, generational and class demands of different constituencies. Moreover, responsible ANC elders cannot simply ignore the growing uncertainty in business circles around the future of orthodox economic policy or the need for continuity in the policy process and machinery of government created under Mbeki. Centrists with a degree of sympathy on the left, such as Mosiuoa Lekota, Kgalema Motlanthe and Cyril Ramaphosa, seem most likely to secure grudging assent across the wider alliance. Other senior figures currently in business or elsewhere, untarnished by Zuma factionalism, might also be prevailed upon to return to government.

Now is very much not the time for an open and competitive election to the presidency of the ANC. Divisive consequences – including the disastrous scenario of a head-to-head pitched battle between Mbeki and Zuma – would be a distinct possibility.[4] However, given that the electoral system for ANC president decisively influences the outcome of the contest, it would be prudent for the ANC to institute new and more transparent mechanisms for leadership choice to avert a repetition of today's crisis in five or ten years' time.

In the immediate future, however, it is to be hoped that a groundswell of opinion will result in both Mbeki and Zuma standing aside in the interests of unity. While the NEC has been divided to the point of paralysis, there is evidently full awareness within the NEC of the gravity of the crisis facing the movement. Moreover, there are senior figures with little directly to gain from the outcome of the succession that have hitherto held their tongues. Their moral authority may yet be required to win the movement over to a compromise candidate who will inevitably be a second best choice in the eyes of almost all ANC members.

Notes

1   For recent efforts, see Lodge 2004, 2005; Butler 2005c; and Reddy 2005.

2   86 per cent of eligible voters in 1994, 72 per cent in 1999, and 58 per cent in 2004 (Piombo 2004).

3   The chapter was written at the end of May 2006.

4   Still less sensible would be a popular presidential election, an idea floated in recent months by prominent editors Barney Mthombothi of the *Financial Mail*, Ferial Hafferjee of the *Mail & Guardian* and Peter Bruce of *Business Day*. Such an election would secure for the president an unchecked authority independent of party and Parliament, it would open the way to third terms (including for Mbeki), and it would pave the way for political instability in the event of conflicts between president and Parliament.

References

ANC (African National Congress) (1969) *Strategy and Tactics of the ANC*. ANC. Available at <http://www.anc.org.za/ancdocs/history/stratact.html>

ANC (1997a) Organisational democracy and discipline in the Movement. *Umrabulo 3*. Available at <http://www.anc.org.za/ancdocs/discussion/discipline.html>

ANC (1997b) Challenges of the leadership in the current phase. Discussion document for the ANC national conference. *Umrabulo 3*. Available at <http://www.anc.org.za/ancdocs/discussion/leadership.html>

ANC (2000) Tasks of the NDR and the Mobilisation of the Motive Forces. ANC discussion document. *Umrabulo 8*. Available at <http://www.anc.org.za/ancdocs/ngcouncils/docs2000/discuss1.html>

ANC (2001) Through the eye of a needle: Choosing the best cadres to lead transformation. Discussion document of the National Working Committee of the ANC. *Umrabulo 11.* Available at <http://www.anc.org.za/ancdocs/pubs/umrabulo/umrabulolld.html>

ANC (2002) People's power in action: A new preface to The Strategy and Tactics of the ANC (African National Congress). Available at <http://www.anc.org.za/ancdocs/history/conf/conference51/strategy.html>

Butler A (2005a) The negative and positive impacts of HIV/AIDS on democracy in South Africa. *Journal of Contemporary African Studies,* 23(1): 3–26.

Butler A (2005b) South Africa's HIV/AIDS policy, 1994–2004: How can it be explained? *African Affairs,* 104(417): 591–614.

Butler A (2005c) How democratic is the African National Congress? *Journal of Southern African Studies,* 31(4): 719–36.

Cachalia F (2001) Good governance needs an effective Parliament. *Umrabulo 11.* Available at <http://www.anc.org.za/ancdocs/pubs/umrabulo/umrabulo11f.html>

Cronin J (1996) Thinking about the concept 'National Democratic Revolution'. *Umrabulo 1.* Available at <http://www.anc.org.za/ancdocs/pubs/umrabulo/umrabulo1.html>

Cronin J (2002) Interview with Helena Sheehan. Cape Town, 24 January. Available at <http://www.comms.dcu.ie/sheehanh/za/cronin02.htm>

Cronin J (2003) Here comes the sun – Drawing lessons from Joe Slovo's 'No middle road'. *African Communist,* 163. Available at <http://www.sacp.org.za/ac/ac163g.html>

Cronin J (2005) The people shall govern. Archived at the Communist University of Johannesburg, 5 November. Available at <http://www.suntimes.co.za/2005/11/20/cronin.pdf>

Gelb S (2005) An overview of the South African economy. In J Daniel et al. (Eds) *State of the nation: South Africa 2004–2005.* Cape Town: HSRC Press.

Jones A (2000) Political parties and plural politics. *The Round Table,* 357: 557–62.

Kirchheimer O (1966) The transformation of the Western European party system. In J La Palombra & M Weiner (Eds) *Political parties and political development.* Princeton: Princeton University Press.

Lodge T (2004) The ANC and the development of party politics in modern South Africa. *Journal of Modern African Studies,* 42(2): 189–219.

Lodge T (2005) The African National Congress: There is no party like it; Ayikho Efana Nayo. In J Piombo & L Nizjink (Eds) *Electoral politics in South Africa: Assessing the first democratic decade.* New York: Palgrave Macmillan.

Mair P & Katz R (1994) (Eds) *How parties organise.* London: Sage.

Maphai V & Gottschalk K (2003) Parties, politics and the future of democracy. In D Everatt & V Maphai (Eds) *The real state of the nation.* Johannesburg: Interfund.

Mattes R (2002) South Africa: Democracy without the people. *Journal of Democracy,* 13(1): 22–36.

Mattes R, Keulder C, Chikwana A, Africa C & Davids Y (2003) Democratic governance in South Africa: The people's view. *Afrobarometer Working Papers* 24. Available at <http://www.afrobarometer.org/papers/AfropaperNo24.pdf>

Michels R (1962) [1911] *Political parties: A sociological study of the oligarchical tendencies of modern democracy*. New York: Free Press.

Moleketi J & Jele J (2002) Two strategies of the national liberation movement in the struggle for the victory of the National Democratic Revolution. (No publisher named.)

Motlanthe K (2005) *ANC Secretary-General's Organisational Report*. ANC National General Council, June. Johannesburg: ANC. Available at <http://www.anc.org.za/ancdocs/ngcouncils/2005/org_report.html>

Nash A (1999) Mandela's democracy. *Monthly Review,* 50(11). Available at <http://www.monthlyreview.org/498nash.htm>

Netshitenzhe J (2000) The NDR and class struggle: An address to the Executive Committee of Cosatu. *The Shop Steward,* 9(1). Available at <http://www.cosatu.org.za/shop/shop0901/shop0901-06.html>

Netshitenzhe J (2003) The courage to search for the new: Personal reflections on Joe Slovo's 'No middle road'. *African Communist,* 163 (First quarter). Available at <http://www.sacp.org.za/ac/ac163.html>

Picard L (2005) *The state of the state: Institutional transformation, capacity and political change in South Africa*. Johannesburg: Wits University Press.

Piombo J (2004) *The result of the election '04: Looking back, stepping forward*. Centre for Social Science Research Working Paper No. 86. Cape Town: University of Cape Town Centre for Social Science Research.

Przeworski A, Alvarez M, Cheibub J & Limongi F (2000) *Democracy and development: Political institutions and well-being in the world, 1950–1990*. Cambridge: Cambridge University Press.

Przeworski A & Limongi F (1997) Modernization: Theories and facts. *World Politics,* 49: 155–83.

Ramaphosa C (2004) Black empowerment: Myths and realities. In F Sicre (Ed) *South Africa at 10*. Cape Town: Human and Rousseau.

Randall V & Svasland L (2002) Political parties and democratic consolidation in Africa. *Democratization,* 9(3): 30–52.

Ranney A (1981) Candidate selection. In D Butler, H Penniman & A Ranney (Eds) *Democracy at the polls*. Washington DC: American Enterprise Institute.

Reddy T (2005) The Congress Party model: South Africa's African National Congress (ANC) and India's Indian National Congress (INC) as dominant parties. *African and Asian Studies,* 4(3): 271–300.

Simkins C (2004) Employment and unemployment in South Africa. *Journal of Contemporary African Studies,* 22(2): 253–78.

Slovo J (1988) *The South African working class and the National Democratic Revolution.* Umsebenzi Discussion Pamphlet, South African Communist Party. Available at <http://www.sacp.org.za/docs/history/ndr.html>

Southall R (2003) *Democracy in Africa: Moving beyond a difficult legacy*. Cape Town: HSRC Press.

Suttner R (2003) *Review of Saul Dubow, The African National Congress* (H-SAfrica, H-Net Reviews, January). Available at <http://www.h-net.msu.edu/reviews/showrev.cgi?path=297501047652081>

Suttner R (2004) Democratic transition and consolidation in South Africa: The advice of 'the experts'. *Current Sociology,* 52(5): 755–73.

Vail L (1989) (Ed) *The creation of tribalism in Southern Africa*. London: James Currey.

2 *Taking to the streets: has developmental local government failed in South Africa?*

Doreen Atkinson

The transformation of local government in South Africa since 1994 has been nothing short of remarkable. The system of local government has been de-racialised, municipal jurisdictions have been consolidated, a philosophy of developmental local government has been introduced; and the intergovernmental fiscal system has been overhauled to bring far more financial resources down to municipal level.

Yet, in 2005, numerous towns saw mass protests, marches, demonstrations, petitions, and violent confrontations. For a 'Rip van Winkel' who had fallen asleep in 1988 and awoken in 2005, it might appear as if the 'rolling mass action' of the end-of-apartheid period had simply continued into the dawn of democratic government in South Africa. Furthermore, in many cases, government responses to such protests have been as uncompromising and inscrutable as those of the National Party of old. This chapter proposes that there are three main causes for the mass protests of the last two years: municipal ineffectiveness in service delivery, the poor responsiveness of municipalities to citizens' grievances, and the conspicuous consumption entailed by a culture of self-enrichment on the part of municipal councillors and staff.

However, it is also argued that the blame cannot be placed solely at the door of municipalities, for the intergovernmental system has largely failed to support local government adequately. Powers, functions and capacity-building responsibilities remain poorly defined. Even though there has been a rapid roll-out of infrastructure and an increase in governmental grants, much more effective and sustained support is required by sectoral departments.

A compounding factor is that municipalities are facing severe strain in attempting to deal with poverty, unemployment, marginalised communities, urbanisation, and HIV/AIDS. Municipal governments are bearing the brunt of state failure regarding policies that actually have nothing to do with them. Municipal actors are visible, local, and vulnerable; and they may be paying the price for inept policies and programmes at national, provincial and district level.

The reaction of government to local protests has ranged from an honest acceptance of guilt, at the one extreme, to autocratic obstinacy, at the other. To be sure, there are indications that the African National Congress (ANC) government is paying considerable attention to the causes of the protests by, for instance, seeking to speed up infrastructure delivery and municipal technical skills. However, there remains a fundamental ambiguity in the ANC's understanding of local accountability; on the one hand, it attempts to promote accountability by means of ward committees, but on the other, it engages in practices that undermine accountability.

Finally, the municipal election of March 2006 did not unseat the dominant party, even within the municipalities that had experienced widespread protests. It would seem, therefore, that electoral behaviour is not based on service delivery and that elections do not function as 'quality control mechanisms'. This raises the question of the relationship between the street-level protests, delivery and democratic elections.

Towards an understanding of a social phenomenon

This chapter focuses on the social protests – many of them violent – that wracked black and coloured townships during 2005 and 2006. Such mass social phenomena are complex, and it requires a great deal of in-depth investigation to do justice to them. Such investigations have not yet been done. This chapter, therefore, can only attempt a portrayal of these phenomena at a fairly superficial level. It relies primarily on newspaper reports. However, the media are not equipped to do in-depth research and therefore tend to produce anecdotal evidence. Consequently, in this chapter media-based information has been supplemented with observations from surveys, as well as more scholarly articles, even though their findings are also largely speculative.

There is manifestly a major need for detailed and meticulous investigative research to be undertaken. Communities may differ radically from one another in terms of the causes and dynamics of social protest. It is therefore only by undertaking a series of in-depth individual case studies that the build-up of cause and effect, leading to a climax of social protest and an aftermath of political reaction, can be understood fully. In the absence of such in-depth studies an initial survey such as this will of necessity remain somewhat speculative, particularly where causes, reasons and motives for social events are suggested.

The scale of the protests

On 5 July 2004, violent protests erupted in Diepsloot on the periphery of Johannesburg. About 3 000 protesters marched through the streets, demanding that councillors be sacked for the sub-standard services provided. About 16 000 families, or 150 000 people, live in these informal settlements – in backyard shacks, many of them assembled from scrap metal, wood, plastic and cardboard. Many families lack access to basic services such as water, sewage, electricity and rubbish removal (Dlamini 2004).

In the first week of September 2004, South Africa was jolted by violent protests taking place in Harrismith in the eastern Free State province.[1] Residents demanded that the town be withdrawn from Maluti-a-Phofung Municipality. They also called for the resignation of the mayor and five councillors. The unhappy residents raised a host of additional issues: there had been no service delivery in Harrismith, the council was beset with corruption ('cash for houses') and nepotism, councillors failed to respond to demands and written protests, and the municipality and Eskom had failed to provide 'free basic electricity'. One young boy was killed during skirmishes with police.

Soon after the violent protests in Harrismith there were violent protests in the Phumelela Municipality in the northern Free State. Soon afterwards, residents of the townships of Warden, Memel and Vrede expressed anger about the municipal manager, the mayor and the council. As in Harrismith, tyres were burned, buckets of excrement and rubbish were emptied into the streets, and a night-soil truck was overturned at the entrance to the town. Residents accused the local council of poor service delivery, unacceptable living conditions, nepotism, unwarranted salary increases, irregularities in the allocation of tenders and Reconstruction and Development Programme (RDP) houses, and weak management which had resulted in failed development projects. The mayor and councillors were shouted down by young people when they tried to address the crowd. Some councillors were briefly held hostage, and were released only on condition that the Free State Premier, Beatrice Marshoff, would visit the municipality. About 500 residents of Vrede in the Free State handed over a petition to the municipality, complaining about poor service delivery, including dirty tap water, the lack of street lights and sports facilities, the quality of roads, and 'improper' allocation of RDP houses. They also demanded the removal of the municipal manager. They were joined in their protests by the largely white Phumelela Ratepayers' Association.

From September 2004, protests took place all over the country. In Ekurhuleni Metro (East Rand), residents from the Harry Gwala informal settlement took to the streets of Benoni, in protest against the council's poor record of service delivery. On 11 September, two houses were petrol-bombed in Vryburg in North West province, where residents demanded the dismissal of corrupt councillors. In Cape Town, Mitchells Plain residents erected burning barricades in protest against poor workmanship in RDP houses and evictions for non-payment of rent. In Durban, 5 000 people from an informal settlement held the third march of the year, demanding houses and services. In Delmas in Mpumalanga, angry residents demanded the resignation of the municipal manager, following the typhoid outbreak in the area. In 2005, 600 residents of the town were diagnosed with typhoid fever, and at least four residents were reported to have died of the disease (SAIRR 2006: 551). On 22 September 2005, *The Star* reported that the police were firing randomly at residents who had taken to the streets to protest against the outbreak.

The mass action in Harrismith and Vrede was subsequently continued in municipalities elsewhere. On 15 March 2005, people from Emalenhle township took to the streets of Secunda in Mpumalanga, protesting about nepotism and poor service delivery, and demanding the resignation of the councillors of the Govan Mbeki Municipality. In March 2005, residents of Harding in KwaZulu-Natal voiced an unequivocal vote of no confidence in the management of Umuziwabantu Municipality, and threw apples at the mayor as he was preparing to address the marchers.

In Uitenhage in the Eastern Cape, angry residents took to the streets on 23 March 2005 in protest against corrupt councillors and housing officials alleged to have mismanaged various projects in the Nelson Mandela Metropolitan Municipality. Police had to be called in to defuse the situation as the crowd demanded to speak to the mayor, who had failed to turn up. In May 2004, angry residents in Port Elizabeth's townships of New Brighton, Motherwell and Veeplaas protested against widespread corruption and poor administration in the metro, which they held responsible for the fact that the local authority had achieved only half its housing construction target for 2003. Protesters said that they felt abandoned by the metro, and had been tired of the municipality not keeping its promises. On 11 May, residents of informal settlements marched to the City Hall demanding help after their houses had been damaged by floods two months earlier; and on 12 May, protesters from the Matthew Goniwe Hostel in KwaZakhele set tyres ablaze, demanding that the mayor talk to them about houses he had promised but never delivered.

The protests then spread to other areas such as Secunda in Mpumalanga and Ocean View in the Western Cape. In Port Elizabeth, weeks of protest by thousands of people from informal settlements, low-cost housing developments and hostels culminated in a meeting on 25 May with the Eastern Cape premier, the mayor, the provincial housing minister, and national Minister of Housing Lindiwe Sisulu. Sisulu maintained that problems had arisen as a result of inadequate communication between the 'three spheres of government and the affected communities' (*Local Government Briefing* June 2005: 32). Such inadequate communication has been a regular occurrence, with municipalities receiving highly contradictory information about budgetary allocations and spending deadlines.

In May 2005, King William's Town residents barricaded the N2 highway with burning tyres, demanding ownership of their rental homes which they said had been promised to them. A week later, protesters from Kwa Nomzamo near Humansdorp blocked the R330 highway during peak-hour traffic because they were angry over the slow pace of housing in the Kouga municipal area. In Cape Town, residents of Khayelitsha and Gugulethu invaded open city land and protested at the municipality's lack of progress with housing and services (Johnson 2005). In Hopetown (Thembelihle Municipality), protesters blocked the N12 highway for several hours because of their dissatisfaction with municipal service delivery (*IOL* 25.05.05).

In Frankfort in the Free State (Mafube Municipality), violence erupted on 15 August in protest against the ANC's allegedly 'unilateral' appointment of election candidates. Residents complained about the poor treatment of disabled children, about RDP houses built on the wrong erven, maladministration of service fees, nepotism in appointments, and funding for job creation that had not yet been utilised. The protesters burned down the houses of two councillors (*Volksblad* 18.08.05). In Clarens (Dihlabeng Municipality), protests broke out after allegations of nepotism and the concealment of a damning forensic audit. On 23 August 2005, residents in Bothaville (Nala Municipality) rioted over service delivery, disrupting schools and damaging property. Civic leaders called on the premier of the Free State to investigate irregularities in awarding tenders, nepotism, and the allocation of houses in the municipality. In Mathjabeng Municipality (Welkom area), the mayor and the police had to calm the community's anger at residents being evicted from their homes due to their failure to pay back housing loans to developers (*Volksblad* 22.07.05). In Mantsopa Municipality (Ladybrand/Excelsior area), angry residents threatened to 'take back' their municipal management because the municipality was ignoring their grievances – dirty water, frequent electrical outages, illegal suspensions of staff, poor skills levels, faulty street lights and overflowing sanitation mains. The situation in Mantsopa was particularly ironic, as the municipality had won the national VUNA Award in 2004 – an issue that is discussed in more detail later in this chapter.

Soon after, a new type of municipal protest took place in communities affected by redemarcation from one province to another. By November 2002, government had become convinced that the new system of 'cross-border municipalities' – in which a municipality straddles two provinces – was unviable (Goodenough 2004). The first area that witnessed such protests was Bronkhorstspruit in Kungwini Municipality, which straddles Gauteng and Mpumalanga provinces. In several townships, irate youths mounted a week of protests during December 2004 due to a decision by the ANC's National Executive Committee to move Kungwini out of Gauteng. Kungwini residents said that they would burn their ANC cards as an indication of their opposition to the proposal. Their chief concern was that their municipality is the most poverty-stricken in Gauteng, and 'now they want to move us to a poor province' (*Local Government Briefing* January 2005).

Protests about demarcation erupted in two other areas. In September 2005, the Matatiele community in the Eastern Cape took to the streets to demand that the town remain part of KwaZulu-Natal and not be incorporated into the Eastern Cape, as they believed that their interests could be more effectively served this way because 'the Eastern Cape has failed in delivery; officials there are inefficient in everything' (*Local Government Briefing* September 2005: 15). The residents' association demanded a referendum on the matter. The most vigorous and sustained protest took place in Khutsong in Merafong Municipality (Carletonville area on the West Rand). Residents first resorted to written submissions to protest against the planned inclusion of Khutsong into North West province, before violence erupted in November. Angry residents barricaded streets using burning tyres and dismantled public telephone booths. Protesters described the North West as 'very hungry and very poor', and demanded that the Minister of Provincial and Local Government come and listen to their complaints. Their protests continued until a few days before the municipal election on 1 March 2006, and resulted in a near total (approximately 95 per cent) boycott of the election. Anti-demarcation protests also took place in the settlements of Setlhakwane and Roossenekal in Mpumalanga, where residents objected to being included in Limpopo (SAIRR 2006: 553).

Clearly, the protests were widespread. Between 1994 and 2005, at least 50 protests were recorded in various local authority areas. According to the Minister for Provincial and Local Government, Sydney Mufamadi, in 2005 protests were recorded in 90 per cent of the 136 municipalities identified as needing urgent assistance. The estimate by Minister for Safety and Security Charles Nqakula, was higher: in the 2004/05 financial year, there had reportedly been 5 085 legal protests and 881 illegal protests (SAIRR 2006: 551).[2]

Understanding popular protest: where does the shoe pinch?

Ordinary residents' frustrations can be due to a variety of problems: the unavailability of infrastructure, particularly if other communities are seen to have access; poor maintenance of infrastructure; the high price of services (particularly water and electricity); the erratic provision of infrastructure (power and water outages); rudeness and shoddy treatment by front-end municipal staff; patronage networks which seem to benefit particular individuals or communities; and resentment at the sight of the rapid financial privileges enjoyed by councillors and senior officials. Generally, a public protest is the result of a culmination of numerous frustrations, often building up over a long period of time. Every town and every municipality is likely to have its own particular combination of factors leading to public protest. In the case of South African municipalities, these frustrations can be divided into three main categories:

- Municipalities are not providing services or are providing shoddy services (a set of technical issues);
- Decision-making is unresponsive and undemocratic, thereby undermining people's livelihoods and interests;
- Protests are against perceived corruption, sudden enrichment and conspicuous consumption by municipal councillors and staff.

Some intriguing observations can be made in this regard. In fact, these arguments have very different premises and evidence, and lead to some very unexpected conclusions.

Inadequate service delivery

Government acknowledges that everyone has the right to at least a basic minimum level of services, within certain affordability parameters. Municipalities are expected to provide free basic services to indigent households, normally defined as those households earning less than R1 100 per month.

The infrastructure programmes have had very real achievements to date. Almost 18 million of the total poor population of 30 million are currently receiving free basic water (FBW), with the majority of municipalities now providing FBW to at least some of their residents. In a Department of Provincial and Local Government (DPLG) survey in March 2005, 81 per cent of municipalities reported that they are implementing FBW policy, while only 19 per cent are not doing so yet. A total number of 165 municipalities (64 per cent) reported that they currently provide free basic electricity to communities (DPLG 2005a). However, only 44 per cent of municipalities reported that they have implemented free basic sanitation programmes.

The sheer scale of the developmental task needs to be appreciated. These programmes have required ever-increasing funding to be allocated to local government. Over the past ten years, local government has been receiving an increasing percentage of national revenue at an average annual growth rate of 15 per cent (*Local Government Briefing* August 2004: 8). Figure 2.1 shows the dramatic increases in municipal allocations in intergovernmental grants, a trend which is expected to continue.

In the context of such a rapid provision of funding for municipalities, and rapid roll-out of infrastructure, why would there be popular discontent? The most obvious

Figure 2.1 *National transfers to local government*

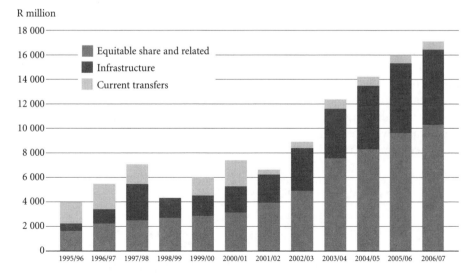

Source: National Treasury (2004)

explanation for the protests is that, despite rapid roll-out of services, at least some South African municipalities are not fulfilling their developmental mandate.

There are at least three possible reasons for this. Firstly, while the statistics show the percentage of municipalities engaged in *provision* of free basic services, they do not reflect the distribution of services, whether to informal neighbourhoods or to remote rural towns. There may well be residential areas within these municipalities which have not yet received services – particularly in the deep rural areas, which are lacking in reticulated services. According to DPLG figures issued in September 2005, many municipalities were having difficulties in providing services: of 284 municipalities, 203 could not provide sanitation to 60 per cent of their residents; 182 were unable to provide refuse removal to 60 per cent of their residents; 155 could not provide water for 60 per cent of properties; 122 could not provide electricity to 60 per cent of homes; 116 were unable to provide housing for 60 per cent of their residents; and 42 were unable to execute 50 per cent of their functions (SAIRR 2006: 551).[3] Secondly, these statistics do not reflect the *technical* aspects of infrastructure, such as maintenance of services, once installed. Thirdly, these statistics do not reflect the *human* aspects of service delivery, such as dealing with bills, complaints and waiting lists. These factors raise the question of the institutional capacity of municipalities.

Organisational difficulties at municipal level

Government capital grants have become increasingly generous, but the maintenance of existing infrastructure has become increasingly compromised. This is largely due to municipalities' inadequate cash flows (caused, in turn, by high salaries and poor levels of payment by the public), so that 'operations and maintenance' (O&M) are seldom adequately budgeted for. In fact, even the paltry O&M budgets are often not spent on infrastructure maintenance as municipalities struggle with poor cash flows and many unforeseen expenditures. The result is that water pipes leak, water-borne sewage mains become blocked, and sewage leaks out into public spaces and flows into natural watercourses. The overview of municipal protests provided in this chapter shows a repeated concern with poor water and sanitation delivery, reaching its nadir with the typhoid outbreak in Delmas and the cholera epidemic in rural KwaZulu-Natal.

In September 2004, President Thabo Mbeki referred to Warden in a speech to the South African Local Government Association:

> Of course, resources are limited and government continues to ensure
> that basic services do reach our people as urgently as possible. But still,
> why would stinking buckets not be collected for two weeks? Why are
> the taps not fixed? Has there been representation to the Department of
> Water Affairs about both the taps and the sewerage? Has the local
> leadership raised the problem with other spheres of government,

and if so, what was the response? Is it true that councillors and officials don't attend meetings, and why? (*Local Government Briefing* October 2004: 14)

His queries reflect the amazement of ministers at the unresponsiveness of some municipalities to people's concerns.

In March 2006, the Minister of Water Affairs and Forestry, Ms Buyelwa Sonjica, noted that '63 per cent of municipalities could not confirm that they met the drinking water quality guidelines...Also, there are serious problems in the management of wastewater (sewage) treatment works' (*Business Day* 13.03.06). Correspondingly, the Water Research Commission has found alarming data regarding municipal treatment of drinking and waste water (*Business Day* 25.09.06).

These problems suggest numerous and deep-seated problems with regard to municipal management. Such problems appear at different points in municipal organisations: stalemates between councils and officials; rivalries between mayors and municipal managers; tensions between senior and junior staff; a loss of morale and an ethic of service delivery amongst staff members; convoluted procedures and red tape; and the appointment of staff with inadequate formal qualifications, expertise and experience. Decision-making by some councils is deadlocked, or based on ignorance or lack of experience, especially in the light of the fact that after the first democratic local government elections in 1995 many councillors were people with very limited experience in modern organisations.

All over the world municipalities depend on the organisational experience and proper conduct of people who are familiar with overseeing large organisations, substantial budgets, complex legal requirements, and sophisticated technical decision-making. By 2005, South African municipal administrations had borne the brunt of rapid transformation. Valuable skills had been lost, institutional memory had dissipated, senior posts had become sinecures for the party faithful and junior posts had been filled by inadequately trained people. In many rural municipalities, senior posts have become monopolised by people from the teaching profession, with little experience in management, infrastructure, or civic affairs. A 2004 survey conducted by the Municipal Demarcation Board (Goodenough 2004) showed that many municipalities have fewer than five years of municipal experience (this applies to 48 per cent of the managers in North West province, 57 per cent of managers in Limpopo, 48 per cent of Free State managers, 34 per cent of Eastern Cape managers, and 33 per cent of Gauteng managers).

Similarly, the South African Institute of Civil Engineers found that 74 of the 231 local councils, and 4 of the 47 district councils, have no civil engineers, technologists or technicians. Those local and district municipalities which did have civil engineers on their staff reported that on average 35 per cent of the existing posts were vacant, in addition to newly created posts not having been filled (*Rapport*

22.01.06). It is no surprise, then, that infrastructure maintenance or construction projects have floundered.

There are various reasons for this poor skills profile. Injudicious affirmative action and the exodus of skills are the obvious explanation, but the matter goes further. Werner Zybrands, a noted local government analyst, has observed from first-hand experience that many black candidates are not appointed, despite their high level of competence and experience, because municipalities make appointments on the basis of political and family ties (*Volksblad* 26.07.05). Furthermore, once an organisational culture of incompetence and nepotism is created, it is likely that skilled and honest officials may decide to bail out and it will become increasingly difficult to entice such skilled people back into public office.

The Local Government Sector Education and Training Authority is currently engaged in a sectoral skills plan review, the preliminary findings of which reveal skills gaps among key municipal professions (*Local Government Briefing* September 2005). There are indications that when specialist posts are filled, inadequately qualified people are placed in these jobs. These posts include senior information technology specialists, senior medical and allied staff, environmental health specialists and occupation and safety specialists, librarians, local economic development specialists, finance managers and personnel, engineers, electricians, meter readers, fire-fighters and emergency services workers. The skills shortage is now so serious that government is contemplating importing skilled people from countries such as India. Furthermore, President Mbeki has called for a search for retired accountants, engineers and project managers (*Business Day* 17.10.05).

At senior levels, municipal salaries have increased exorbitantly over the last ten years, giving rise to much publicity about municipal managers earning more than the South African president or Cabinet ministers. At middle and blue-collar levels, municipal staff have benefited from vigorous trade union lobbying to increase the minimum municipal wage rate. Furthermore, the National Treasury lays down guidelines to indicate the maximum salary bill on a municipal budget (about 35%). The result is that municipalities have increased wages, but kept posts vacant – often with detrimental consequences for service delivery. The large wage bill has also put pressure on capital expenditure, whether for new projects or for infrastructure maintenance (*Business Day* 04.10.05). In Phumelela Municipality, for example, only 2.9 per cent of its budget is set aside for capital expenditure, while Mafube Municipality spent almost half its total budget (47.6%) on salaries, and only 3.6 per cent on capital expenditure. Further, the prescribed salary limit of 35 per cent is easily manipulated by outsourcing core functions to consultants, whose fees are not included in the salaries component. This is also a way in which former municipal professional officials, squeezed out of their jobs by affirmative action, find a more profitable use for their expertise.

The combination of inexperienced, poorly qualified staff, with similarly inexperienced councillors, in a context of substantial financial flows in and out of municipalities, creates fertile ground for irregularities, malpractice and ineffective expenditure. For the 2000/01 financial year, of the 543 audits that had been completed up to 30 September 2002 and for which audit reports had been issued, only 159 (29%) of the audit opinions expressed were not qualified (*Local Government Briefing* September 2003: 20).

Municipalities are complex organisations, and malpractices can surface at various strategic points. The case of Phumelela Municipality, in the Free State, shows how numerous municipal failures become linked to create a crisis of governance. Consumer debts had risen in 2004 to R28 million, an increase of 39 per cent on the previous year – a phenomenon which simultaneously reflects popular alienation and municipal administrative ineffectiveness. The municipality had spent almost 45 per cent of its operating expenditure on salaries – a figure much higher than National Treasury guidelines of 35 per cent. The municipal manager had not entered into a performance agreement with the council, and therefore his appointment was illegal in terms of legislation. The council claimed that the municipal manager was keeping the council in the dark about key issues. The municipal manager was subsequently 'redeployed' to Harrismith, an equally troubled municipality (*Sunday Times* 22.01.06). In the meantime, only 16 per cent of households in Phumelela have access to sanitation, roads are pitted with potholes, many residents have to use a bucket toilet system, and streams of effluent pour into a river feeding the reservoir that supplies the town's water. It would be difficult to pick a single cause for the municipality's woes; the various components of administration, politics, finance and infrastructure are inextricably interlinked.

These difficulties have been partly due to the institutional upheavals caused by the demarcation process. In 2003, the Auditor-General cautioned that the demarcation process had impacted negatively on the external audit function. The extent of auditing had increased as a result of the demarcation, split-offs as well as the creation of new municipalities, especially where none had previously existed. Furthermore, control risk in general increased due to the establishment of new organisational structures and the harmonisation process of different computer and record systems. It seems that the impact of the redemarcation will be felt for years to come.

Responsiveness and communication

The protests have not only been about houses, water, taps and toilets, but also about political process. At municipal level, protesters have regularly complained about the unresponsiveness of officials and councillors. Channels of communication with municipal mayors and councillors are blocked. The Harrismith protests took place after community leaders gave the municipality ten days to respond to their grievances, to no avail. In Frankfort (Mafube Municipality), violence broke out in August 2005 because the council did not respond to a petition (*Volksblad* 23.08.05). In Excelsior in Mantsopa Municipality, a group of angry residents threatened to take the municipality by storm if the municipal manager continued to ignore their grievances (*Volksblad* 31.08.05). In Welkom, a group of protesters claimed that their petitions had been ignored for two years (*Volksblad* 13.07.05). Sometimes municipalities bear the brunt of other government agencies' lack of responsiveness, as happened in Bothaville, where no one from the office of the MEC for local government was available to receive a petition, and the protesters resorted to violence and looting (*Volksblad* 24.08.05).

This raises the question of the client interface, or the point at which the state meets the citizen. For observers such as Steven Friedman, it is evident that the state is not necessarily failing as regards the delivery of infrastructure, but it is often failing as regards the service ethic of its officials (*Business Day* 22.03.06). Municipalities, as well as other government departments, often do not have a track record of good client-oriented service. A study conducted by Afesis-Corplan in the Eastern Cape listed key findings that were relevant to the existing crisis of municipal governance. Firstly, the key decision-making structures of council (that is, mayoral committees or executive committees) are often closed to public scrutiny, and even when they are not formally closed, the public and even some officials regard them as such. Secondly, public attendance at council meetings is poor (Hollands 2005: 8).

There has also been repeated evidence that the government's most important innovation to promote public participation – the ward committees – has not been particularly effective. Ward committees are statutory bodies, introduced in terms of the Municipal Systems Act of 2000. In many municipalities, ward committees have not been established or they have been dominated by political favourites or specific racial groups. The public's lack of knowledge of their right to attend ward committee meetings is a key reason for non-attendance, and even when members of the public do attend, they do not think they have made an impact on decision-making in the municipality (Hollands 2005: 8). Many ward committees remain uncertain of their functions, because municipalities have failed to flesh out the details of their terms of reference and operating procedures. The result is that many ward committees suffer a crisis of credibility in the eyes of the community, and many ward committees have had little involvement with key processes such as integrated development plans (Hollands 2003).

At the heart of the ANC's approach to municipal politics lies a fundamental ambiguity. While the ANC supports the principle of local accountability, the practice of 'deploying' nationally-selected people to serve as mayors weakens local accountability. Critics have argued that the lack of delivery and the rise of corruption at council level, ostensibly the cause of the public protests, are in fact merely the symptoms of a general lack of accountability to the voting public. Participatory democracy has been undermined by the floor-crossing system, the practice of deployment, and the executive mayoral system. Opposition parties are excluded entirely from the decision-making process in an aggressive winner-takes-all approach. Mayoral committees operate in secrecy, closing meetings to the general public, failing to publish agendas or minutes, and presenting important decisions to council meetings as *faits accomplis* for rubber-stamping by the party faithful. Ward committees are loaded with appointees of the dominant party, and portfolio committees lack the authority to call the executive to account. Open debate, the cornerstone of participatory democracy, no longer occurs in any meaningful way at local government level in South Africa (*Business Day* 07.02.06).

The starkest example of non-responsiveness must be the case of Khutsong, a township in the Merafong Municipality in Carletonville, Gauteng province. When the cross-boundary municipalities were abolished, the possibility of the inclusion of Merafong into North West province was mooted. Submissions and petitions to the demarcation board by the residents of Carletonville clearly stated the case that residents wanted to remain part of Gauteng. But despite this, on 15 November 2005 the National Assembly approved the Constitution 12th Amendment Act. It was only by the casting vote of the deputy speaker that the ANC was able to obtain the two-thirds majority necessary for this constitutional amendment.

The Minister for Provincial and Local Government, Sydney Mufamadi, has consistently defended the government's decision. He confused the issue by arguing for the principle of abolishing cross-boundary municipalities – a principle that has not been contested at all. The real difficulty was that towns such as Khutsong and Matatiele objected to the *specific* demarcation decisions. The demarcation board prevaricated, saying that it had no jurisdiction over provincial boundaries – even though the board is the repository of spatial and demarcation-related information. In fact, on balance, the board appeared to prefer to keep Merafong within the West Rand of Gauteng. It was clearly the minister who pushed through the Khutsong decision, for no apparent reason. Even violent resistance before the local election of 1 March 2006 could not sway government's determination to force through its decision. The residents made their sentiments known by a very low turnout in the election, but to no avail. The emperor had spoken.

Government is aware of the growing culture of unresponsiveness. The ANC's secretary-general has warned that the weakness of ANC party branches will prevent local communities from improving their quality of life. Almost 49 per cent of ANC branches have become seasonal – activated a few months before the party's conferences, and disappearing between scheduled major events (*Business Day* 05.07.05).

Just before the March 2006 election, President Mbeki laid down tough requirements that all ANC councillors need to live in the areas that they represent – to end a trend where well-paid councillors abandon the poverty-stricken communities which elected them and move to middle-class suburbs. ANC councillors will now have to sign an oath, subject themselves to a code of conduct, and report back to their wards at least four times a year (*Business Day* 22.02.06). It is not clear yet, however, whether these requirements will actually be enforced, but it seems unlikely that they will address the culture of unresponsiveness.

Corruption, nepotism and self-enrichment

During the last few years, municipal malpractice has become extensive. A vast number of municipalities have been mentioned in the media and government reports, in the context of malpractice and corruption: councillors may become spokespersons for special interests, or may take financial rewards to promote those interests, or they may award themselves special allowances and perks. Officials may be appointed because of their personal and political connections. Party political networks have captured civil-service jobs for patronage (Mamphela Ramphele, cited in SAIRR 2006). Municipal officials may conspire to take bribes or elicit tenders in return for kickbacks. Within municipal administrations, municipal property may be used for private purposes.

Many councils have attempted to deal with malpractice by suspending officials, but such proceedings have commonly degenerated into endless lawsuits between the municipality and the supposed offenders – who continue to draw a full salary while the legal proceedings drag on.

There are numerous ways in which municipalities lend themselves to personal enrichment. Typical problems are the abuse of mayoral funds, unauthorised transfers of municipal money to outsiders, favouritism in procurement processes, the payment of bribes to secure services, the abuse of travel allowances, fictitious tenders, involvement of councillors with companies which then win tenders, non-payment of municipal services by councillors, councillors using municipal facilities for party-political or personal purposes, and irregular performance bonuses.

What this litany of malpractice shows is that councillors need to have a built-in sense of self-control and should be able to derive income from other means (such as employment or private enterprise). In many municipalities, councillors are unemployed people, with little or no previous employment experience, but significant political ambitions. Furthermore, the fact that they have very few employment options *other* than being a councillor, encourages them to score private benefits while they are councillors and to ensure that they remain councillors for as long as possible.

Several senior officials and observers have commented on the acquisitiveness of new municipal office-bearers. KwaZulu-Natal's local government MEC, Mike Mabuyakhulu, has warned municipalities that they should not become a 'milking cow' for people to enrich themselves (*Local Government Briefing* January 2006). In his keynote address to the ANC's national general council in Port Elizabeth in July 2000, President Mbeki warned against the 'opportunists and careerists' who had joined the ANC not because they respected or supported these strategic objectives, but 'with the sole aim of furthering their personal careers and using the access to state power we have as a ruling party, to enrich themselves'. Five years later, Mbeki's admonition that in all instances of corruption, 'it is the masses of the people who get robbed and condemned to perpetual poverty, while a small elite flourishes on the basis of its ill-gotten gains' is as true today as it was then (*Local Government Briefing* April 2005: 1). The Deputy Minister of Provincial and Local Government, Ms Nomatyala Hangana, has warned municipal councillors that corruption and official ignorance are standing in the way of service delivery (*Volksblad* 26.07.05).

Over the last five years, matters have become steadily worse – local government corruption sometimes appears to be so entrenched as to be endemic. The politics of patronage and nepotism continues to blight municipal politics. In a Public Service Accountability Monitor survey of public officials' perceptions and experiences of corruption in the Eastern Cape (Allen et al. 2005), the following data illustrate the pervasive public culture of acquisitiveness:

- 48 per cent of officials believed that it was wrong but understandable to receive gifts in return for something that is part of their job;
- 27 per cent reported witnessing political patronage (awarding jobs or contracts to political allies);
- 33 per cent felt they witnessed nepotism (awarding jobs or contracts to relatives);
- 29 per cent said they had witnessed the theft of public resources;
- 23 per cent said that 'all' or 'most' of their fellow government officials in the province were involved in corruption; and
- 41 per cent expressed the fear that syndicates would intimidate them if they reported corruption.

Similarly, several qualitative case studies conducted between 1999 and 2003 suggest that the most widely perceived instances of municipal corruption are nepotism in the appointment of municipal staff (Hollands 2006: 2). In the Free State, an internal ANC document ('Patronage and criminalisation of the ANC'), written by a municipal mayor, has pointed to the phenomena of personal wealth accumulation: 'Pay your allegiance to the leadership of your patronage and you will easily become a mayor...or municipal manager...Leaders will reward [comrades] by so-called deployment' (*Express* 16.05.05).

Corruption appears to take place on the basis of individual acquisition, or the co-operation of small and informal friendship groups. Impressionistic evidence suggests that local party branches are very prone to capture by small informal networks, which then conspire to capture the key positions in municipalities. The competition for office was intensified after the 2000 municipal restructuring, simply because there were fewer positions to go round. Furthermore, the current decision by DPLG, to double the allowances of mayors and councillors, is likely to intensify the competition for office (*Mail & Guardian* 18–24.03.06).

The causal relationship between the municipal protests and municipal corruption is not clear. Certainly, the issue of corruption is frequently mentioned in public petitions; there is a growing popular concern in South Africa about real or perceived government corruption. In 2005, 24 per cent of respondents in an Institute for Democracy in South Africa survey believed that local governments and local councils are corrupt (Idasa 2005). In the Transparency International *Corruption Perceptions Index*, which lists 91 countries, South Africa dropped from 38th place in 2001 to 46th place in 2005 (Transparency International 2001, 2005).

Residents may also be tempted to take to the streets because of the conspicuous consumption by municipal officials, which may be linked to corruption. This conspicuous consumption is not necessarily the result of corrupt practices; it is also a result of the general upswing in municipal salaries – which is not illegal, although highly inadvisable. According to Kevin Allen and Karen Heese, 'A lack of delivery combined with increased municipal salaries and the perceived fat-cat lifestyle of councillors and officials will increasingly not be tolerated, and will provide fertile ground for protests and civil unrest' (*Business Day* 19.03.05).

There have been official attempts to eradicate corruption in the municipal sector. For example, the DPLG has implemented a Local Government Anti-Corruption Strategy (as of 2003) to deal with what it refers to as 'a very real danger that, unless DPLG produces and champions an anti-corruption strategy, the legitimacy of the new system of local government will remain questionable and unacceptable to the majority of our people' (*Local Government Briefing* April 2005: 4).

Several provinces have taken steps against corrupt councillors and officials. For example, in Gauteng, the DPLG expelled 43 officials in Emfuleni Municipality (Vereeniging) (*Business Day* 17.10.05). In KwaZulu-Natal, councillors are now required to pay back their irregular loans received from municipalities (*Local Government Briefing* January 2006). The Eastern Cape Joint Anti-Corruption Task Team was constituted to deal with the challenges posed by corruption in that province. It incorporates the National Prosecuting Authority, the South African Police Service, the forensic division of the Auditor-General's office, the Special Investigating Unit and the National Intelligence Agency.

Another encouraging development is the passing of the Municipal Finance Management Act (2004). A key element of this piece of legislation is that it has the potential to curb corruption and cronyism among elected officials by bringing local government in line with the Public Finance Management Act and the new state supply-chain management framework. Accordingly, councillors are barred from serving on municipal tender boards and instead the accounting officers of various municipalities are required to take responsibility for financial decisions. In terms of the Municipal Finance Management Act, municipal managers, who are the chief accounting officers at municipal level, are held responsible for wasteful and fruitless expenditure incurred by municipalities under their control.

The jury is still out on the effectiveness of government efforts to curb corruption in the future. But the significant fact, in the context of municipal protests, is that government is all too aware of the dysfunctions caused by rapacious municipal robber barons, and is increasingly responsive to this dimension of popular anger.

The paradox of formal success combined with popular grievances

The analysis offered thus far focuses on the inadequacies of municipal governance. But the issue goes further. What is the responsibility of higher tiers of government as regards service delivery? A remarkable fact is that many of the municipalities that experienced popular protests have recently won VUNA awards – best practice awards sponsored by the Development Bank of South Africa, the DPLG and the National Productivity Institute. These include Mantsopa Municipality (Ladybrand in the Free State), eThekwini Metro (Durban) and Nelson Mandela Metro (Port Elizabeth). In the Free State, several of the troubled municipalities were listed as runners-up in the provincial VUNA awards in 2004: Maluti-a-Phofung (Harrismith), Mafube (Frankfort) and Matjhabeng (Welkom) (HSRC 2004). The Free State municipalities were evaluated according to an extremely long and exhaustive list of indicators, so the selection process appears to have been rigorous.

There are at least three possible reasons for the paradox of ostensibly successful municipalities combined with popular protests:
• The municipalities provided information about themselves, which may have led to a bias in the evidence.
• The methodology for evaluation of municipalities is still poorly developed, and tends to focus on formal office requirements (such as integrated development plans), rather than on more informal political dynamics.
• Municipalities may be making serious efforts to improve performance at head-office level, but these efforts have not yet percolated down to community level (*Volksblad* 17.09.05). If this is the case, then performance successes will become more visible in the future.

Another manifestation of the paradox is the Markinor survey, which found that the provinces where protests occurred (Gauteng, Eastern Cape, Western Cape and Free State) were *not* the provinces where the majority of respondents were most critical of service delivery. In the 2006 Markinor survey, only 11 per cent of respondents in the Free State said that there had been 'no improvement in service delivery'; other figures worth noting are 17 per cent in Gauteng and KwaZulu-Natal, 16 per cent in the Eastern Cape and 13 per cent in the Western Cape. This compares very well with 40 per cent of respondents in the Northern Cape, and 26 per cent in Mpumalanga, who complained that there had been no improvement in service delivery (Markinor 2006).

These findings suggest that there is no neat correlation between popular discontent and government failure. It is not always the most aggrieved citizens who take to the streets. Other important factors are at play, such as the local political culture, leadership, and interpretations of events.

Municipal culpability and intergovernmental relations

It is possible that local protests do not signify only municipal failures, but also failures of government departments. Municipal councillors and officials may be becoming the scapegoats for problems that are way beyond their control.

Municipalities have undergone rapid changes in jurisdiction, administration, and developmental mandate. The original 843 municipalities have been reduced to 284; rural and urban areas have been conjoined in the same jurisdictions; racially-based municipalities have been summarily amalgamated; and many white officials have been replaced by inexperienced officials, sometimes with little more merit than their political affiliation. Municipalities have to implement developmental policies and programmes ranging across at least 15 sectors: housing, health, HIV/AIDS, poverty alleviation, land reform, community-based public works, environmental management, local economic development, water, sanitation, transport, road maintenance, sport and recreation, arts and culture, agriculture and infrastructure provision.

The key question is: if municipalities lack the skills to attend to their infrastructure, whose responsibility is it to assist municipalities to develop this capacity? Government has been less than effective in assisting municipalities to develop viable systems of management, operation, and maintenance of infrastructure. It has done little to assist municipalities to improve their front-end standards of client service, whether on the part of municipal office staff, meter readers, technical maintenance staff, or complaints office staff. In some areas of governance (notably the introduction of integrated development planning and the new municipal accounting system), the government has provided support to municipalities. However, municipalities have been left to figure out their own indigent policies, to work out their own infrastructure maintenance programmes, and to design their own information systems.

Sectoral government departments have barely begun to provide sustained assistance to municipalities. They have paid scant attention to Section 154(1) of the Constitution, which provides for the following: 'The national government and provincial governments, by legislative and other measures, must support and strengthen the capacity of municipalities to manage their own affairs, to exercise their powers and to perform their functions.' Until now, only DPLG, National Treasury and – to a lesser extent – the Department of Water Affairs and Forestry have put some effort into implementing this provision. As a result, municipalities have found themselves at the receiving end of new tasks and functions, with little real support from government departments – typical examples of this creeping decentralisation are land reform, community-based agriculture, local economic development, HIV/AIDS and community-based public works.

The problem is not only due to weak systems of capacity building. It is also caused by unresolved systems of the intergovernmental allocation of powers and functions. As the finance minister has observed, there are widespread questions about the powers and functions of the three spheres of government (*Business Day* 21.09.05). Schedules 4 and 5 of the Constitution, which stipulate the functions of municipalities, fail to mention many of the new functions which municipalities have to perform, with the result that the allocation of powers and functions has depended on very loosely articulated national and provincial departmental ideologies.

The difficulties experienced by municipalities in the housing sector are particularly significant. Housing has repeatedly formed the focus of popular protests. Curiously, housing is not a municipal function and, until now, provincial departments of housing have done little to devolve the housing function to municipalities, yet municipalities have, de facto, been the main implementers of housing schemes – hence their role as the target of popular frustrations. In June 2005, the Department of Housing acknowledged that the protests are aimed at local government's apparent lack of service delivery, but pointed out that the department has no jurisdiction over local government. This is a remarkable statement, partly for its willingness to admit that there is something wrong, but more importantly, it creates the impression of far more municipal autonomy than exists in practice. The housing function has never been formally assigned to municipalities, with the result that a great deal of ambiguity remains regarding who is actually in charge of housing (*Local Government Briefing* June 2005).

Even the Department of Water Affairs has not created sufficient operational systems to assist municipalities to perform their technical maintenance tasks. Evidence has built up over many years to show that municipalities are defaulting on their water, sanitation and solid waste management responsibilities, and there has been insufficient intervention to detect, intercept and remedy these local problems.

In this unclear intergovernmental relations system, it is very difficult for new and inexperienced municipalities to make sense of their powers and functions, and the attendant financial and human resources required to exercise such functions. It is difficult to budget for staff, vehicles and capital expenditure if the terrain is so unclear. It is almost impossible to develop technical competence in new developmental fields if they are not assisted and mentored by national and provincial departments.

The need to assist municipalities is belatedly being recognised. In particular, the Department of Housing has responded to the widespread protests regarding housing by admitting that it needs to do more to build municipal capacity. It is now focusing on the 'accreditation' of municipalities, so that they have the skills and resources to perform the housing function adequately.

These examples of unresolved intergovernmental relations do not absolve municipalities of their misdemeanours as regards management and service delivery. However, they do show that the state architecture is still very uncertain, with unresolved questions regarding powers, functions and capacity-building responsibilities – hardly a conducive environment for effective and sustainable service delivery. Simply put, the demands on municipal services completely outstrip their capacity, and they have been largely left to cope with these demands on their own. The state has simply not comprehended the scale of the task of transforming municipalities into developmental institutions, or that of creating municipalities from scratch, particularly in the rural areas.

The social context of local government: unemployment, poverty and marginalisation

While municipalities are often blamed for poor service delivery, they are also trapped in a vicious cycle of poor rates bases, low levels of payment for services, poor cash flow, poor maintenance, public disaffection, and further deteriorating payment levels. At the heart of the matter lies the fact that municipalities are battling to make ends meet.

Municipalities have to function in a context of widespread unemployment. Indigent households are entitled to free basic services, and most municipalities attempt to provide this. The indigent policy is a huge drain on municipal financial resources. Although it is supported by fiscal grants from national government ('equitable share grants'), this is often insufficient to cover all the hidden administrative costs of the indigent policy. Municipalities have to maintain indigent lists, periodically update these lists, deal with indigents who use more than their allotted water and electricity quotas, and fight a rearguard action to prevent illegal electricity and water connections.

The essence of the problem is the extent and prevalence of poverty and unemployment in many communities. This is exacerbated by rapid urbanisation in many towns and cities. In the Western Cape, for example, it is estimated that the Cape Town area receives an additional 16 000 households per annum, mainly from the Eastern Cape (according to the municipal manager, *Local Government Briefing*

June 2005). Rapid demographic change is taking place as households 'unbundle' – overcrowded households split up and find separate lodgings. This poses difficult challenges to service delivery. In Cape Town, for example, the housing programme has been caught up in lengthy processes of locating sufficient land in a congested urban environment (*Cape Times* 26.05.05). There are high levels of migration as people move in search of jobs. This means that the housing and services backlogs are almost impossible to reduce. At the same time, HIV/AIDS is contributing to household poverty and further demographic changes as households 're-bundle' in the wake of the death of wage-earners.

In several cases, the municipal protests involved young people. Given the frustration of unemployed young people, who have strong material wants and virtually no opportunity of meeting these, this is probably not surprising. According to one school of thought (*Volksblad* 26.03.06), the 'young, unemployed and angry' stratum of society may become a permanent fixture of South African politics. In a postmodern knowledge economy, the children of poor families have great difficulties in securing proper employment, and this will spill over into resentment and frustration.

However, it is not the core function of municipalities to generate employment or enterprise. Despite all the rhetoric about local economic development, municipalities are still by and large oriented towards providing infrastructure. The failure of employment creation lies at a different level altogether – in departments such as labour, trade and industry, agriculture, and minerals and energy. But these institutions are far distant from the burning tyres and smouldering barricades of the townships, while public anger is turned towards the most visible target – municipal councillors and officials. Their all-too-evident personal self-enrichment and management failures become the lightning conductor to draw the ire of the disaffected and alienated 'lost youth' of South Africa.

The issue of poverty explains one of the most significant types of municipal protest that occurred during 2005 – the cross-border demarcation disputes. In the cases of Bronkhorstspruit, Carletonville and Matatiele, communities feared being included in the 'hungry and poor' provinces – usually the North West, Mpumalanga, and the Eastern Cape. These poor communities know that their only chance of improving their fortunes is to be linked to areas where some level of economic growth exists, together with significant government capacity to promote development.

A potentially important hypothesis can be made: that municipalities are bearing the brunt (and paying the price) for policy failures and ineffective programmes in issue-areas which are not of their own making. In the context of ineffective job-creation policies, inadequate HIV/AIDS support programmes, and a virtual absence of urbanisation policies, it is almost impossible for municipalities to promote effective development – even when they are not plagued by their own internal dysfunctions.

The vote as a last resort?

The protests against municipalities took place in the year before municipal elections were held in March 2006. Significantly, the dominant party retained its position in all the municipalities where protests had taken place – with one exception: in Umuziwabantu in KwaZulu-Natal's Harding area, the Inkatha Freedom Party majority was replaced by an ANC majority. In some municipalities, the ANC majority was actually strengthened. ANC support declined in certain wards where protests had been evident, but despite this, the ruling party still swept to victory in these troubled municipalities.

What this signifies about the importance of these protests is not clear. People may be disillusioned by the ANC, but reluctant to vote for an opposition party. Alternatively, voters may doubt that an opposition party can do any better, or believe that a vote for the party that rules at national level provides a more effective chance of services than a vote for an opposition party. These are preliminary hypotheses that need to be empirically investigated.

Clearly, elections are not a form of quality control at local level. Malpractices and inefficiencies do not get punished at the voting stations, as people do not appear to vote according to their views of past performance. Other factors, such as racial and party allegiances, seem to override questions of competence and administrative integrity. Another way of assessing the impact of the protests on the electoral system is to consider voting polls. In some of the areas, such as Harrismith, Kungwini, and Nala, the ANC not only retained its power base, but there was an increased poll. In most other areas, the voting poll declined slightly, but not very significantly (only in Merafong Municipality can a strong message be read into the large decline in voting poll). This suggests that many voters do not use elections to remove ineffective representatives.

The aftermath: how has government responded?

There have been different kinds of responses to the protests from government – ranging from defensiveness to a more honest acknowledgement of problems and a search for solutions. Some government officials dismissed the legitimacy of the protests entirely. For example, the Free State premier referred to 'political opportunists and criminal elements' who hijack the concerns of the community to follow their own agendas (*Volksblad* 01.09.05). In the words of Elroy Africa of the DPLG, many government officials 'found it very difficult to understand why people need to take to the streets, because we have put in place formal structures for people to channel their grievances, their concerns and to work with government in tackling service delivery, corruption and governance challenges' (DPLG 2005: 26). These responses fail to acknowledge the lack of responsiveness of municipal councillors and officials to community grievances.

As regards the redemarcation dispute, the obstinacy of the Minister of Provincial and Local Government, Sydney Mufamadi, in his response to the cross-border protests was remarkable. But there were also more constructive responses. A notable case is that of Matjhabeng Municipality (Welkom and Hennenman in the Free State): some councillors resigned (*Volksblad* 29.09.05) and Mayor Serake Leeuw has promised to restructure the municipality to create more effective developmental departments, and to give more operational capacity to each of the outlying towns (*Volksblad* 15.07.05). In certain cases, the ANC decided not to nominate serving mayors because they were implicated in corruption, or because of unrest over poor service delivery. In Delmas, Secunda, Rustenburg, and Bloemfontein, political notables were passed over when nomination lists were drafted (*Mail & Guardian* 22–27.01.06). In Welkom, northern Free State has recently expelled ANC councillors who do not hold community meetings or establish ward committees (*Volksblad* 09.06.06). These are important attempts to improve the local political culture of accountability, but it remains to be seen whether this will be successful on a large scale.

Another response to the protests has been to speed up the delivery of infrastructure. In Gauteng, for example, Premier Mbhazima Shilowa promised to spend R3 billion on upgrading township infrastructure, in a bid to improve the living conditions of residents (*Business Day* 14.02.06). Another important intervention is the decision by government to actively recruit skilled people for the municipal sector. The Development Bank of Southern Africa has initiated the first phase of 'Operation Siyenza Manzi' ('we do it now'). By March 2006, the first group of skilled staff (32 technical and financial specialists) had been recruited. This programme is being run in partnership with DPLG, National Treasury and the South African Local Government Association.

For the present, government is placing its faith primarily in 'Project Consolidate', a programme which has identified 136 municipalities as particularly fragile. Service-delivery facilitators have been appointed to visit these municipalities and offer hands-on support. The project is the beginning of a new attempt by national and provincial governments to address the challenges facing local government. It remains to be seen whether the facilitators will be able to effectively address the intractable political and administrative problems within these municipalities.

Conclusion

In the wake of the various protests throughout the country, the fragility of the municipal system has been revealed. There is an incipient autocratic governmental style, at municipal and national level, which is unresponsive to the deep frustration and anger experienced by communities.

This chapter has shown the enormous costs of institutional transformation. Given the loss of key skills, the rapid changes in institutional structure, and the loss of institutional memory, the decline of many municipalities into a morass of venality and dysfunction is hardly surprising. This points to the crucial need for other spheres of government – notably sectoral departments at national and provincial level – to prioritise municipal capacity building. Technical assistance, mentoring, policy-making guidance and management inputs are now more urgently required than ever. Surprisingly, this component of the Constitution has hardly been implemented. Whereas government has made progress with the roll-out of infrastructure, free basic services and intergovernmental grants, the actual management of municipalities has been left to the paltry skills of new and inexperienced municipal councillors and officials. Government has now introduced 'Project Consolidate', a two-year programme, to address these difficulties in specific municipalities.

For the time being, the status quo remains. With rare exceptions, the municipal election of 2006 did not unseat the majority party. Clearly, municipal elections are not about quality control; they are about other symbolic issues unrelated to actual service delivery. The pressure of the populace will have to be felt at the barricades, not at the ballot box. It remains to be seen whether government departments will respond to this pressure by beefing up their hesitant support for municipalities, and whether municipalities will become the developmental agencies they were intended to be.

Notes

1   Much of the empirical information in this section was drawn from several editions of the *Local Government Briefing*, a monthly email magazine service provided by Clive Keegan of Cape Town (available from keegan@iafrica.com) and funded by the Development Bank of South Africa.

2   This information was based on information from *Financial Mail* 09.09.05; *The Star* 23.09.05; and *The Citizen* 13.10.05.

3   These figures are based on *Financial Mail* 09.09.05, and *The Star* 23.09.05.

References

Allen C, Mattes R & Millie U (2005) *Government corruption seen from the inside: A survey of public officials' perceptions of corruption in the Eastern Cape*. Rhodes University: Public Service Accountability Monitor (PSAM).

Bryant C (1991) Sustainability revisited: States, institutions and economic performance. Paper presented at the Annual Meeting of the American Society for Public Administration, Washington DC, March 23–27.

Dlamini N (2004) *The race to house Diepsloot*. Available at <http://www.joburg.org.za/2004/july/July27_diepsloot.stm>

DPLG (Department of Provincial and Local Government) (2005a) *Study to determine progress with, and challenges faced by municipalities in the provision of free basic services: Final Study Report.* Available at <http://www.dplg.gov.za/documents/annualreport/FBS_Study_2005_Final report.doc>

DPLG (2005b) *Service Delivery Review,* 4(1).

Goodenough C (2004) *Shaping South Africa: Reflections on the first term of the Municipal Demarcation Board.* Pretoria: Municipal Demarcation Board.

Hollands G (2003) The performance of ward committees. In *The best of hologram 2001–3: Issues and practice in South African local government.* Cape Town: Nolwazi.

Hollands G (2005) Predicting breakdowns in municipal governance, *Local Government Transformer,* 11(5): 8.

Holands G (2006) Beating the corruption drum, *Local Government Transformer,* 12(1): 2.

HSRC (Human Sciences Research Council) (2004) The best practice report on the performance of municipalities short-listed for the Free State Provincial VUNA Awards. Unpublished report for DPLG Free State province, Bloemfontein.

Idasa (Institute for Democracy in South Africa) (2005) *AfroBarometer,* 10 March 2005. Available at <http://www.idasa.org.za>

Johnson T (2005) Mass protests against housing shortages in South Africa. Summary provided on the Centre for Civil Society, University of KwaZulu-Natal website. Available at <http://www.ukzn.ac.za/ccs/default.asp?3,28,10,2080>

Markinor (2006) *Perceptions of government responsibility and delivery.* Available at <http://www.markinor.co.za/press_31.html>

National Treasury (2004) *Trends in intergovernmental finances.* Pretoria: National Treasury.

SAIRR (South African Institute of Race Relations) (2006) *2005/5 Survey.* Johannesburg: SAIRR.

Transparency International (2001) *Corruption perceptions index.* Available at <http://www.transparency.org/layout/set/print/policy_research/surveys_indices/cpi.2001>

Transparency International (2005) *Corruption perceptions index.* Available at <http://www.transparency.org/policy_research/surveys_indices/cpi/2005>

UNDP (United Nations Development Programme), HSRC & DBSA (2005) Synthesis report of the 2005 development report: Overcoming underdevelopment in South Africa's second economy. Available at <http://www.hsrc.ac.za/media/2005/6/20050630Synthesis.pdf>

3 'Things fall apart, can the centre hold?' The state of coalition politics in the Cape Metropolitan Council

Zwelethu Jolobe

In this chapter I analyse the politics of coalition governance in the City of Cape Town in the period between 2000 and 2006. I argue that the Cape Metro's first term in the new system of local government was characterised by a crisis of governance and institutional instability. This was the consequence of the inability of the major political actors to establish an effective and sustainable governance coalition in the aftermath of the 2000 local government elections. The result was a prolonged period of political turbulence and institutional instability that saw government turnovers and the inauguration of three mayors in a space of three years. The effects of the executive instability, and consequent high turnover of senior management, have led to the decline of morale within the city's civil service.

The politics of coalition governance in the City of Cape Town thus raises important questions about the relationship between types of political coalitions and political stability. I will illustrate the political implications of this crisis of coalition governance through a discussion of three interrelated political processes that have dominated the political landscape of the City of Cape Town between 2000 and 2006: the formation of the Democratic Alliance (DA) in June 2000; the political scandal which dominated much of Cape Metro politics in 2001 leading to the fragmentation of the DA; and the formation of the African National Congress (ANC)–New National Party (NNP) alliance following the passing of floor-crossing legislation in June 2002. The chapter will also discuss the emerging coalition politics in the aftermath of the 2006 local elections.

The chapter is divided into three sections. The first section very briefly discusses the concept of political coalition and coalition governance. The second provides a discussion on the politics of coalitions in the City of Cape Town, and the third discusses the political developments that immediately followed the outcome of the 2006 local elections in the City of Cape Town.

The dynamics of political coalitions

A political coalition is a temporary alliance of political groups formed in order to achieve a common purpose or to engage in some joint activity. The building of coalitions thus involves a process in which different parties come together to form a partnership collectively in pursuit of a common objective. This process can include the mobilisation of resources in pursuit of the common goal, the formation of binding decisions and commitments concerning the common objective, and agreements on the distribution of political resources and patronage that may emerge from the realisation of the objective.

Political coalitions can thus take a variety of forms, and can operate in different political and legal or constitutional environments. There are three general and broad types of political coalition that have existed in the post-apartheid South African context: Cabinet or executive coalitions, legislative coalitions, and electoral coalitions.

Cabinet/executive coalitions

A Cabinet or executive coalition usually refers to a Cabinet in a parliamentary government in which several parties come together and co-operate (Karume 2003). The reasons for the co-operation vary, but one of them could be that no party on its own has a majority in the legislature. Where there is no clear legislative majority – where the winning party after an election only achieves plurality, so producing a hung Parliament or municipal council – parties could be forced to come together in order to form a collective majority in the legislature and consequently a majority government. A recent example of such a coalition is the DA-led governing alliance that formed in the City of Cape Town after the 2006 local elections produced a hung council. In order to elect a new mayor, deputy mayor and a speaker, and thus form an executive, seven parties comprising the DA, the African Christian Democratic Party (ACDP), the Freedom Front Plus (FF Plus), the African Muslim Party (AMP), the United Democratic Movement (UDM), the United Independent Front (UIF), and the Universal Party (UP) entered into a political coalition in the council and, from that, formed a coalition executive led by the DA.

Majority coalition Cabinets, that is, Cabinets based on coalitions that form an absolute majority in a legislature (50 per cent plus one), ideally are more stable and long-lived than minority coalition Cabinets, that is, Cabinets formed by the leading party that has simply won plurality but not a majority of seats in the legislature. While a majority coalition is prone to internal party-political struggles – both intra- and inter-party battles inside the coalition – they are less prone to votes of no confidence from opposition party blocs than minority coalitions. A minority government thus tends to be more unstable than a majority government.

Another reason for co-operation is in response to times of crisis such as a war or other major political crises. In this regard, parties may form a 'grand coalition', which is in essence a coalition government where those political parties that represent substantial constituencies in the legislature (and collectively a vast majority) unite in a coalition. The term usually refers to a situation where large political parties with divergent political orientations overcome their differences in the interests of political stability. Good international examples of a grand coalition are the national governments of the UK during World War 1, between the two world wars and during World War 2. Parties may also form national unity governments, which are broad coalition governments that include all parties (or all major parties) in the legislature. Israel has had several national unity governments in which the political rivals, the Israeli Labour Party and Likud, formed a ruling governing coalition.

Following from the above, Cabinet coalitions can be constitutionally enshrined and consist of only the major parties that gain the most number of seats in the legislature. South Africa's Interim Constitution of 1993, for instance, provided for a power-sharing Government of National Unity (GNU) that essentially worked on the basis of consensus and was made up of the three most powerful parties in South Africa at the time – the ANC, National Party, and the Inkatha Freedom Party (IFP). According to the GNU, every party with at least 80 seats (20%) in the National Assembly could delegate from among the members of Parliament an executive deputy president, and Cabinet positions were given to these major parties in proportion to their seats in the National Assembly. And finally, Cabinet coalitions can also form as a response to co-operation agreements between parties inside or outside Parliament. The ANC–NNP alliance in 2002 was an example of such a co-operation agreement forged outside the legislature but that eventually produced a Cabinet coalition.

Legislative coalitions

Legislative coalitions are political alliances that do not share executive or Cabinet functions but rather support parties represented in Cabinet during the parliamentary or legislative processes of voting and debates. They are therefore more policy alliances involving co-operation agreements between parties with similar interests. The most recent example is the support the ANC receives from the Minority Front (MF) in the legislature (Karume 2003). The MF, in particular, 'believes that co-operative arrangements with a party that claims some degree of an electoral majority automatically gives a smaller party such as theirs a leverage of negotiation on certain issues' (Karume 2003: 8). Such coalitions can therefore broaden the policy base of governance and help secure the vital interest of minority parties.

Such coalitions, however, need not necessarily include the same parties on all issues as parties may shift political alliances depending on the issue at hand and the principles they hold on such issues. Such agreements, therefore, are not as comprehensive and binding as Cabinet coalitions, and consequently do not pose a threat to political stability if and when they collapse.

Electoral coalitions

Electoral coalitions are political alliances between different parties in the process of engaging in competitive multiparty elections. The objective of such coalitions is to 'pool votes', that is, to mobilise and collect votes across different constituencies so as to gain an electoral majority (Horowitz 1991). These can be highly effective means of gaining electoral majorities, particularly if political entrepreneurs are able to play on common themes, grievances and issues. However, their main challenge concerns their ability to consolidate and maintain political power after an electoral success.

Recent political instability in Kenya under the National Rainbow Coalition (NARC), for instance, is an example of the inability of an effective electoral coalition, between the National Alliance Party of Kenya and the Liberal Democratic Party, to consolidate the gains of a historic landslide victory over the Kenyan African National Union (KANU) in December 2002. Unable to effectively fill the power vacuum after KANU's exit, NARC has been bedevilled by infighting involving serious allegations of corruption between political leaders, and serious issues concerning the amendment of Kenya's Constitution. This culminated in President Mwai Kibaki firing and reconstituting his entire Cabinet in November 2005. Similarly, as we shall see in the case of South Africa, the exit of the NNP faction from the DA in 2002, signalling the end of a DA-led Cape Town administration, was also indicative of the inability to consolidate the gains made at the polls.

Thus, the major disadvantage of electoral coalitions is that they are in essence pre-election alliances between parties with, at times, very different ideological orientations and political cultures, but at the same time, formed with the sole purpose of winning an electoral majority (Karume 2003). Such alliances can reach crises, especially when the policy co-ordination mechanisms and internal management structures of the different parties in the pre-election phase are ill-defined. Such was the case with the DA, for instance, where the lack of an effective co-ordinative mechanism for policy development and the lack of effective internal disciplinary structures created a structural basis for the NNP to exit from the alliance.

Coalition governance

It follows then that the ability of parties to effectively maintain political coalitions depends, to a large extent, on whether coalition partners are able to construct effective internal structures, procedures and mechanisms to manage internal coalition issues, resolve internal conflict and discipline coalition members. Such internal structures and mechanisms include consensus-seeking procedures aimed at achieving consensus in decision-making, dispute resolution committees to adjudicate disputes among coalition members, and joint task teams and working committees that manage the day-to-day functioning of the coalition (Karume 2003). All these formal and informal institutions need to be enshrined in the initial coalition agreement, binding all the relevant members.

Coalition agreements can thus be seen as policy co-ordination devices that effectively co-ordinate the different ideas, cultures and functioning of the different parties. Given that coalition governments are bound to face many challenges because of the inevitable diversity of coalition partners, such structures and mech-anisms are an essential ingredient of any coalition as they enable the different part-ners to deal effectively with political differences that will inevitably arise in the day-to-day workings of politics (Karume 2003). More importantly, these struc-tures become relevant for parties that decide to join together and forge electoral and governance coalitions under a single political entity, such as the DA in South Africa and NARC in Kenya. Sustainable political coalitions therefore need effective internal structures and mechanisms in order to resolve internal conflicts and co-ordinate the different policies of coalition partners.

The crisis of coalition governance in the Cape Metro

The political dynamics of the Cape Metro provide a good illustration of the polit-ical consequences of the lack of effective internal management structures in coali-tion governance. This was one of the main reasons for the collapse of the DA administration and the consequent crisis of governance and political turbulence in the Metro. However, the politics of the Metro also provide a good illustration of the stabilising role an effective and comprehensive coalition agreement can play in coalition governance. The National Co-operation Agreement (NCA) that gave birth to the ANC–NNP alliance on 20 June 2002, and the Developmental Local Government Framework that emerged from that, stabilised Cape Metro politics, despite the Blackman Ngoro racism incident[1] and the Big Bay debacle that plagued the Cape Metro administration under the third mayor, Nomaindia Mfeketo.[2] The NCA and Developmental Local Government Framework, however, seem also to have been the policy vehicles used to integrate the NNP into the ANC, resulting in the dissolution of the NNP. Political stability in the ANC–NNP coalition therefore seems to be the result of a possible merger in the future, that is, there was political will to maintain coalition and institutional stability.

In the period between 2000 and 2006 political developments in the Cape Metro were dominated by the politics of two coalitions: the DA (formed by the Democratic Party (DP)–NNP coalition); and the ANC–NNP coalition.

The formation of the DA

The DA was formed in June 2000 and involved the coming together into an alliance of the DP, the NNP and the Federal Alliance (FA).[3] The idea was essentially an elec-toral coalition for the December 2000 local government election which was intend-ed to pave the way for a merger of parties at provincial and national levels. Due to the then anti-defection clause in the Constitution, before the passing of the floor-crossing legislation in 2002 parties could not legally merge between elections, and as such, the DA negotiations were pushed through in order for the DP and NNP to contest the local elections as one organisation (Faull 2004). Given the emergence of a dominant party system in South Africa, the DA's goal was to provide a strong and effective challenge to the disadvantages that such a system entails in general and to the ANC's electoral strength in particular. More specifically in the Western Cape, it was formed to prevent the ANC from obtaining a strong political position. Therefore, while the DA was committed to growing and acting as an effective and efficient opposition party, in the Western Cape and in Cape Town in particular, it sought to gain an effective electoral majority and worked tirelessly toward achieving this objective. After its formation in June 2000, its main objective was the mobilisation of the DP, NNP and FA constituencies under the DA banner for victory in the 2000 municipal elections.

The DA electoral coalition was a highly effective mobilisation outfit whose performance in the local government elections of December 2000 was better than expected. According to Faull, this was largely due to an effective campaign that 'focused on local issues in the particular areas that the DA campaigned in, and the ability of the DA to get its voters to the polls in proportionally higher numbers than competing parties' (2004: 2). In contrast to the DA's targeted campaign, 'the ANC had focused on issues of local government in the abstract and failed to produce elections materials specific to the areas they campaigned' (Faull 2004: 2). Consequently, there was a very high voter turnout in white suburbia where the majority of voters support the DA, and the ANC was not able to mobilise sufficient turnout in black neighbourhoods (Faull 2006). The DA's voter turnout proved to be the decisive factor – in Cape Town, 375 000 voters turned out to vote for the DA, while 270 000 voters turned out to vote for the main rival the ANC (Seekings 2005: 8).

Therefore, in the final analysis, the overall result reflected more the success of the DA in mobilising its supporters in white areas relative to the ANC's success in black townships (Lodge 2002; Seekings 2005). Apart from electoral victories in Stellenbosch, Swellendam and other high-profile Western Cape municipalities, the DA consequently won the important and rich city of Cape Town, receiving 53 per cent of the votes, translating into an electoral majority of 107 of 200 councillors, while the ANC received 38 per cent of the votes (Seekings 2005). Peter Marais was subsequently inaugurated as DA mayor of the Cape Metro.

Despite the fact that the DA was now a majority political party at the local level, controlling a key and strategic metropolitan government, the DP and NNP remained separate political entities in a legislative coalition at provincial and national level – sitting separately in the legislatures, receiving separate allocations of public money – but operated as one entity – caucusing together, voting as one and so on. Only through floor-crossing legislation could the respective members embrace their new identity and constitute themselves as one party in these two spheres, a matter that the DA argued in favour of initially, but one that came to haunt them eventually as the NNP leadership took advantage of the new political game of musical chairs and jumped ship to the ANC.

However, despite the DA's successes in mobilising different constituents in their electoral victory, the alliance had not been established on a solid enough political foundation – in essence, the main objective in the Western Cape, and Cape Town in particular, was to keep the ANC out of power and less attention was paid to the consolidation of political power. Thus, once that objective had been achieved, cracks began to appear in the political coalition. At the heart of the difference between the two major alliance partners were not only broad ideological and cultural orientations, but also what each party wanted out of the coalition. The objective of the DP was to build an alternative base of power in South Africa's emerging dominant party system by uniting the political opposition in South Africa in general. In this regard, a fragmented opposition was seen as a contributing factor to the continued electoral dominance of a single party, namely, the ANC. The overall objective of the strategic move of forming the DA was the creation of a two-party system in South Africa in which the DA would be an integral part. DA leader Tony Leon clearly articulated this overall objective in a statement in the run-up to South Africa's milestone 2004 general election, marking the ten-year anniversary of South Africa's democracy:

> We are going to give our democracy the best 10th birthday present it
> could hope for: we are going to create a genuine two-party system. We
> are going to give people a real choice, and we are going to give
> government a real run for its money. (Leon 2004)

By contrast, the NNP's decision to enter the political alliance was more of a survival mechanism and had to do with its inability to adapt to a new political environment that was hostile to, and negated, everything the party had stood for. The end of apartheid and the party's exit from the GNU in 1996 saw a decline in the NNP's fortunes as the dominant and largest white party under apartheid, as the multiparty system emerged with new alternatives that capitalised on the disillusionment of its constituency. From gaining over 20 per cent of the vote in the 1994 election, and down to 6.87 per cent in the 1999 election, the NNP leadership saw the DA alliance as a way out, a lifeline that gave it the opportunity to gradually and smoothly integrate into a new post-apartheid political entity that showed much promise, and in which they could continue to exercise power but from a different base. The essence, however, was political survival, and it is this factor that explains the ease with which they integrated into the ANC in 2002, a mere two years after the formation of the DA.

Why these differences between the DP and NNP became fatal was largely due to the lack of effective management structures and procedures necessary to deal with the challenges that would arise from such differences. As a result, when the DA was faced with its very first challenge at local government level, the street-naming scandal, conflicting parties and resultant political factions coalesced around the DP and NNP entities, as the internal procedures of the DA were largely ineffective.

The street-naming scandal

The street-naming scandal demonstrates the damaging effect of the lack of internal conflict resolution structures in political coalitions. In April 2001, the mayor, Peter Marais, designed a proposal to change the street names of Adderley and Wale Streets in the Cape Town central business district to Mandela and De Klerk Avenue respectively. This initiative was seen as part of a reconciliation programme in the racially fragmented city. The problem arose when opposition to the idea emerged in May, and this was expressed by the public in the media. At a Cape Town Press Club meeting on 24 May, the mayor nonetheless announced that there was overwhelming support for his street-naming plan, and he initiated a petition that, he argued, proved the extent of support in favour of the street-naming process (Cameron 2003).

The scandal broke in the *Mail & Guardian* newspaper on 8 June 2001 where it was revealed that there were several lists of alleged forged signatures in favour of the mayor's plan contained in the petition (Cameron 2003). The newspaper had even commissioned a handwriting expert, Gert Burger, who confirmed the vote-rigging exercise (*IOL* 08.06.01). This was further corroborated by the affidavit of a whistle-blower, senior Cape Town legal advisor Victoria Johnson,[4] in which serious allegations of fraud and misconduct were made against two senior officials who were administering the process. The affidavit implicated Marais's right-hand man and mayoral spokesperson, Johan Smit, and the city's legal advisor, Ben Kieser, who allegedly rigged 300 votes in favour of Marais's initiative when it became clear that the 'no' vote would win by about that margin (*IOL* 01.08.01).

Subsequently, a meeting of the top DA leadership (DP leader Tony Leon, NNP leader Marthinus Van Schalkwyk, NNP Provincial Premier Gerald Morkel, NNP MEC for Local Government Pierre Uys, and Mayor Peter Marais) agreed that under Section 106 of the Municipal Systems Act, Judge Willem Heath should set up a commission of inquiry to investigate the allegations, that the mayor ask the city manager to put the two senior officials, Smit and Kieser, under immediate suspension, and that the mayor withdraw the proposed street-naming initiative (*Business Day* 26.07.01; Cameron 2003; *Cape Argus* 26.07.01; *Cape Times* 26.07.01).

The Heath Inquiry turned into what some observers considered to be a Cape Town spectacle of high drama and glamour. Writing in the *Cape Argus* on 11 August 2001, Murray Williams explained:

> Like a scene from a John Grisham court drama, the Wale Street
> chamber was brimming with characters: the beautiful blonde star
> witness Victoria Johnson, flanked by her Harrison Ford-lookalike
> husband David; the national corruption-busting superhero presiding;
> some of the country's best lawyers leading argument; a Porsche-driving
> official in the dock and the DA's warring leaders, charismatic Marais
> and an earnest-looking [Deputy Mayor Belinda] Walker looking on.

In late August 2001, the Heath Report was submitted to the MEC for Local Government, Pierre Uys. Judge Heath found that 'Marais had misinformed the media [and] was also misinforming the public to whom he is accountable'. He also found that 'he had not performed the functions of his office in good faith, honesty and in a transparent manner [and was] not acting at all times in the best interest of the municipality' (Heath Special Consultants 2001: 71–82). Heath found evidence of fraud on the part of the two DA councillors in respect of the fraudulent filing of the petitions and they were subsequently found guilty of maladministration, with the recommendation that the issue be forwarded to law enforcement (Heath Special Consultants 2001).

After numerous attempts to further investigate whether Marais had breached the code of conduct for councillors (including the formation of a special committee headed by Judge King and a multiparty rules committee established by the council which eventually cleared Marais), the DA formed a three-person, dispute resolution committee, which included party veteran Colin Eglin, to investigate whether the mayor had broken party rules (*Sunday Argus* 07.10.01). This DA committee, however, was overtaken by another party-political process. When Leon had 'unsuccessfully attempted to get Van Schalkwyk to fire Marais', Leon bypassed the workings of this committee and 'sent a letter to Marais calling on him to resign and saying that a motion to this effect would be put to the DA's National Management Committee [NMC]' on the following Friday (Cameron 2003: 130). The grounds for dismissal included the fact that Marais had 'caused division in the executive and caucus; that under his stewardship, the DA's public image had hampered its ability to mobilise political support; and that he had failed to establish a sound working relationship with the province' (cited in Cameron 2003: 130).

Events took a sudden turn on 12 October 2001 when the DA deputy leader Van Schalkwyk publicly opposed Leon. This public defiance of Leon set in motion a process to force Van Schalkwyk and his key lieutenant, NNP National Executive Director Renier Schoeman, out of the party (*Sunday Times* 04.11.01). In support of Marais, Van Schalkwyk publicly accused Leon of being unprincipled, unfair, not following due process and holding a 'kangaroo court' to get rid of Marais (*Saturday Argus* 13.10.01; *Sunday Independent* 14.10.01). He was unanimously supported by the NNP's highest decision-making body, which adopted a motion on 15 October that Marais should not go (*Dispatch Online* 15.10.01). This in turn resulted in a counter-attack, with Leon accusing his deputy of 'wilful misrepresentation', harbouring desires to be provincial premier and threatening the alliance (*SABCNews.com* 19.10.01).

However, the show of support from the NNP leadership did not stop the DA's NMC from stripping Marais of his mayoral chain. Despite protests that the meeting should in fact have been a disciplinary hearing, the DP majority ruled that sacking Marais was purely a political decision, which was Leon's right as DA leader after losing faith in Marais's ability to lead the city (Cameron 2003; *Weekend Argus*

20.10.01). Leon then turned his sights on Van Schalkwyk and attempted to rein him in and take disciplinary action at a routine party meeting the following Monday (*Cape Times* 22.10.01). The public slanging match between Leon and Van Schalkwyk, however, had resulted in a complete breakdown of trust in the relationship between the two leaders. Thus, once Marais was removed, and faced with the potential destruction of their political base in the DA, Van Schalkwyk and senior NNP leaders decided to pull out of the alliance and engage in a series of secret talks with the ANC's national chairman, Mosiuoa Lekota, around the building of a new political coalition between the ANC and NNP.

The reasons for the break up of the coalition seem to be the lack of internal mechanisms to deal effectively with the 'Peter Marais issue', and in particular, the kinds of mechanisms that would prevent the issue from developing into a competition between NNP and DP factions. The structures that the DA instituted proved to be ineffective in dealing with the two factions. For instance, the dispute between the party leadership over the handling of the Marais issue remained unresolved by the three-person committee designed for this purpose – Marais did not undergo an internal party disciplinary hearing and process. The implication is that the competing factions did not sufficiently resolve the issue through DA internal procedures. When Marais challenged the NMC decision to fire him as mayor and expel him from the DA in the Cape high court, 'the judge questioned the fact that the DA's three-person commission, which was supposed to investigate the matter, had apparently been dispensed with when the matter had been referred to the NMC' (Cameron 2003: 131). The court also ruled that only the relevant municipality could remove a mayor from office, and therefore, that the NMC's decision to fire the mayor was beyond their power. The judge also said that 'it was difficult to avoid the conclusion that the NMC had devised a scheme to yield a pre-determined outcome' and ultimately ruled that 'the decision of the NMC to fire Peter Marais as mayor be set aside with immediate effect' (Cameron 2003: 131). The mayor subsequently returned to his chambers and later resigned.

On the NNP front, Premier Gerald Morkel had rebelled against the NNP leadership on 31 October for the decision to enter into a coalition with the ANC (*Cape Argus* 01.11.01). On 8 November, Morkel faced a 'palace revolution' for his actions and was subsequently suspended from the NNP. Marais was then elected leader of the Western Cape NNP (*Dispatch Online* 10.11.01). Morkel eventually resigned as premier and decided to stay with the DA (*Sunday Times* 11.11.01).

The NNP exit from the DA led to a change of power and a reversal of roles at both the provincial and local level respectively. As a result of the new ANC–NNP alliance, Peter Marais became the new premier of the Western Cape. At the local level, however, because the floor-crossing legislation had yet to be enacted, NNP councillors stayed within the DA and subsequently the former premier of the province, Gerald Morkel, became DA mayor in Cape Town (Cameron 2003). The premier and mayor had thus reversed roles.

It is clear that the electoral coalition of the DA (the DP and the NNP) fell prey to the disadvantages of such a type of coalition – it encouraged a pre-election alliance between parties with very different political orientations but failed to provide adequate structural measures to hold the centre and maintain and consolidate political power. The main purpose of the coalition was to secure an electoral majority against the ANC, and once that objective was achieved cracks began to appear. The lack of effective internal policy co-ordinating structures made the collapse of such a coalition, when facing a political crisis, imminent. The street-naming scandal, the very first challenge faced by the DA once in power, revealed the political implications of this weakness.

The ANC–NNP alliance

What emerged out of the ashes of the failed NNP–DP coalition was an unlikely political marriage between the ANC and NNP. This was in essence a legislative and Cabinet coalition, later solidified through floor-crossing legislation, and designed, *inter alia*, to propel the ANC into the driving seat of Cape Metro politics. For the NNP leadership this was a convenient strategy to maintain some access to political power and thus save face following the damaging fallout with the DP. The ANC–NNP coalition was the outcome of the NCA between the two parties established in June 2002, and the partnership operated at all levels of government (local, provincial and national). The NCA can be seen as a good example of the stabilising role internal governance mechanisms can play in effectively instituting and maintaining a political coalition. Furthermore, the significance of the NCA was that it began a process that eventually led to the integration of the NNP into the ANC, and the eventual disintegration of the party that had dominated white (and South African) politics for more than 40 years.

However, it is important to note that it is precisely because this political coalition was specifically concerned with governance – and the maintenance of political power at the local level in particular – that it was able to develop the necessary structures for the sustenance of a partnership between ideologically and historically divergent political parties. In addition this factor created a more than adequate structural basis for the absorption, of the NNP into the ANC. This is in contrast to the DP–NNP coalition, which placed greater emphasis on mobilising constituents to ensure an ANC electoral defeat and less on governance and the maintenance of power. The DA alliance structures created around coalition governance proved too fluid and unable to withstand the challenges that lay ahead.

It is important to identify key issues in the agreement that allude to the success of the ANC–NNP alliance. The preamble of the Developmental Local Government Framework of the two parties, the policy framework for the NCA, identified the main reason for political co-operation as the 'institutional instability experienced at local level'.[5] The agreement between the parties was founded on three main principles:

- That all political positions in local government be distributed between the parties to achieve a partnership based on fair representation;
- That the cause of the governance crisis at local government was institutional instability and as a solution, the contract emphasised the need to promote stability;
- That a joint task team be established as the institutional mechanism to ensure consensus seeking in decision-making.

The parties also established a dispute resolution committee and agreed that the agreement would be in place well beyond the 2004 election. The NCA and the Developmental Local Government Framework can therefore be seen as the policy instruments used to integrate the NNP into the ANC.

The new ANC–NNP coalition wrested power from the DA in the City of Cape Town during the window period for floor-crossing in October 2002. The new coalition lobbied Provincial and Local Government Minister Sydney Mufamadi to fast track an amendment to the Municipal Structures Act, changing Cape Town's mayoral election system to make it consistent with all ANC-controlled metropolitan governments, so as to secure Nomaindia Mfeketo as the executive mayor (*Cape Times* 16.10.02). Subsequently, the DA lost all its seats on the city's executive committee. The DA lost power in the metropolitan government when 27 of its councillors defected to the NNP, enabling the NNP to establish a city government with the ANC. This began a political process that ultimately saw NNP councillors using the floor-crossing window period in 2004 to cross to the ANC, and the final dissolution of the NNP in the 2006 local elections.

For the NNP's senior leadership, the political lifeline thrown by the ANC was secured through the distribution of political patronage. In June 2002, Marthinus Van Schalkwyk was appointed premier of the Western Cape after Peter Marais could not survive the political impact of a sexual harassment charge. Van Schalkwyk was subsequently appointed Minister for Environmental Affairs and Tourism in President Thabo Mbeki's Cabinet after the 2004 general elections. In November 2002, Renier Schoeman was appointed as the national Deputy Minister for Health and former Western Cape Environmental Minister David Malatsi was appointed Deputy Minister for Social Development, and NNP member Francois Beukman was elected as chairperson of Parliament's 'influential' watchdog committee on public accounts, the Standing Committee on Public Accounts.

In a statement issued at the time, President Thabo Mbeki confirmed that the appointment of Schoeman and Malatsi as deputy ministers had been made in consultation with government's partners at the time – the IFP and the Azanian People's Organisation. The president stressed that: 'The appointments *reflect the broadening of co-operation among various political formations, at national and local level*' (GCIS 2002, emphasis added). Thus it can be seen that the distribution of government and political positions was an outcome of the new co-operation agreement between the ANC and the NNP.

Into the future: post-2006 Cape Metro politics

As discussed in other contributions in this volume (see Ndletyana, Herzenberg, Makgetla and Atkinson), there were interesting and important developments during the 2006 local elections, especially with regard to coalition politics. Cape Metro politics has witnessed some important continuities and discontinuities from the post-2000 local elections era, but it is important to understand these within the context of the broader political dynamics within the Western Cape province.

Political dynamics in the Western Cape after the 2006 local elections

The 2006 local elections produced no clear majority in all but four Western Cape municipalities: the ANC and the DA won controlling majorities in Hessequa and Bitou (ANC), and Swartland and Overstrand (DA). The trend was that the ANC attained plurality overall, with the DA coming a close second. The significant factor, however, was that the ANC did not achieve controlling majorities in most of these municipalities. The implication is that the multiparty political system in the Western Cape has become more competitive and, as a consequence, both the support bases in the province of the ANC and the DA have either remained static or have been in decline. Despite this, these two parties are still the main political players and the political struggle between the two in the province as a whole is as fierce as ever.

The main factor explaining the emerging competitive multiparty system in the province is the floor-crossing legislation introduced into the South African political system in 2002. This factor alone added new dimensions in provincial politics between 2000 and 2006. Firstly, it created the mechanism for the NNP walkout from the DA into alliance with the ANC, and at the same time gave elected representatives serious political leverage over party leaderships. Secondly, it facilitated the formation of a new political player in the Western Cape, the Independent Democrats (ID), that not only grew in stature but also began to compete in both the ANC's and DA's constituencies.

The impact of the ID was considerable: in its first local election, the party won 289 360 votes and 10.54 per cent of overall support. This effectively made the ID the third largest party in the province, after the DA and the ANC, and consequently led observers to argue that the party held a balance of power with high expectations of a possible 'kingmaker' role in provincial politics. As the local elections produced no clear winner in the Western Cape, the majority of municipal councils were 'hung', forcing the formation of political coalitions in order to make up the

51 per cent threshold needed to form stable majority executives. Consequently, the Western Cape has seen the proliferation of very interesting coalitions between the major political players. However, the important difference from the 2000 local elections is that there have not been any electoral coalitions, but rather executive and legislative coalitions forged as a result of hung councils.

The political scenario in the Cape Metro after the 2006 local elections

The competitive nature of the provincial-wide post-election political dynamics was replicated in Cape Town. The city's council consists of 210 seats. Therefore, for a single party to assume executive power and form a government, they would need to win 106 or more seats. However, in the final analysis, following the provincial trend, no single party won a controlling majority in the council. The DA attained plurality – 90 seats which translated into 42.86 per cent of council seats. This meant that their support had decreased by 10.64 per cent since the 2000 election. This was largely due to the coalition break up with the NNP and the inroads made by the ID. The ANC won 81 seats, or 38.57 per cent of council seats. The new 'kid on the block', the ID, made significant inroads into the city vote in their debut local election, taking 23 seats and 10.95 per cent of council seats.

The DA maintained its majority support amongst voters, but lacked the controlling majority it had enjoyed in 2000. The City of Cape Town's council was therefore hung, necessitating a scramble for the formation of a ruling coalition. In the immediate aftermath of the election, political researcher, Jonathan Faull (2006) of the Institute for Democracy in South Africa (Idasa), suggested a number of possible coalitions. These were, firstly, that the ANC and DA could form a unity government with a cumulative total of 171 seats. This would require that the ANC and DA resolve their political differences at all levels of government, especially with regard to the politics of race and race relations. Secondly, the DA could lead a coalition with either the ID, taking the total seat allocation to 113, or the totality of the smaller parties, which together with the DA's allocation would verge on the 106 threshold. This was the coalition which eventually materialised and is discussed further below. A third scenario was that the DA run the council through a combination of the ID and some of the smaller parties. Faull fourthly suggested that the ANC could assemble a coalition with the ID – 104 seats – and with the support of one or two of the smaller parties could reach the 106 threshold. Finally, there was the option of the ID sticking to their pre-election stated intention of remaining completely independent, forcing the need for a consensus multiparty democracy on every key issue (*Cape Times* 08.03.06).

After a week of high drama and behind-the-scenes deal-making, the post-election shenanigans culminated in a showdown at the first sitting of the new council on 15 March. The session involved the election of the new mayor, deputy mayor and speaker. The outcome was a version of scenario 2 above with the DA linking up with six opposition parties – the ACDP, the FF Plus, the AMP, the UDM, the UIF, and the UP – and thereby consigning the ANC and ID to the opposition benches. The DA's Helen Zille was elected mayor by 106 to 103 votes. The ACDP's Andrew Arnolds was elected deputy mayor and the FF Plus's Dirk Smit was elected speaker, both by 105 to 104 votes.

What some had predicted, and no doubt de Lille wished for, namely the ID's 'kingmaker' role, did not come about. Reflecting on this, Faull argued that the ID 'had put itself in a difficult position with its voters after backing the unpopular Mfeketo against Zille'. He argued that 'the party hoped to secure the deputy mayor's post for ID mayoral candidate Simon Grindrod in exchange for its backing of Mfeketo'. However, Grindrod lost to the ACDP's Arnolds by a narrow margin of one vote (*Business Day* 16.03.06).

As for the ANC, crucial questions were raised over its inability to secure the support of both the largely 'black African' groupings of the PAC and UDM, parties traditionally closer to it than the DA (*Business Day* 16.03.06). Reflecting on the vote, the ANC's provincial chairperson, Ngculu, said that the ANC 'need[s] to sit down and analyse what went wrong' (*Business Day* 16.03.06). However, as the dust from the shoot-out was settling, party politics in Cape Town took a sudden turn when Zille announced that her new administration would immediately conduct a forensic audit of all tenders, contracts and other financial dealings concluded during Mfeketo's tenure. Of particular importance was the contract of City Manager Wallace Mgoqi, which Zille argued had been illegally and fraudulently extended by Mfeketo to pre-empt a possible DA victory at the polls. In the run-up to the local elections, Zille had accused Mgoqi of campaigning for the ANC, thereby signalling that his future in the administration was in doubt, and this has led to the breakdown in trust between the two. Mgoqi was subsequently axed by the DA-led council and lost a Cape high court appeal in May 2006. The Zille vs. Mgoqi showdown sharpened the differences between the DA and the ANC, with the latter coming out strongly in support of Mgoqi, to the point of showing public support in his court appearances.

Conclusion

Six years of Metro politics in Cape Town has seen the emergence of a competitive multiparty system accompanied by an emergent political culture of coalition building and coalition governance. Coalition politics in multiparty systems has advantages. They can lead to more consensus-based politics in the sense of a government or legislative coalition comprised of different parties (at times based on different ideologies) having to seek common ground and work together on policy matters. This inclusive feature can serve the purpose of uniting different constituents in a polity, especially if the electorate is fragmented. Furthermore, and following from this, political coalitions also normally better reflect the views and opinions of the electorate, particularly in a fragmented electorate such as Cape Town clearly is currently.

A major disadvantage, however, and one that has plagued Cape Town politics, is that coalitions do have a tendency to be fractious and are prone to disharmony, especially in challenging times. This is especially the case with coalitions comprising parties with different political and ideological orientations. At times, and especially, in hung legislatures, election results are such that coalitions that are mathematically most probable are ideologically unfeasible, creating 'unholy alliances' between very different political entities. Another disadvantage is that coalitions can hold themselves hostage to partisan commitments, paralysing governance through catering to narrow and marginal principles for the sake of coalition survival.

The next major challenge to Cape Town's emerging competitive multiparty system, with two competing coalition blocs, will be the next floor-crossing window period. This is scheduled for September 2007, unless the provision is scrapped prior to that date. This seems unlikely, although possible. The 'musical chairs' of the previous floor-crossing periods has wreaked havoc with both politics at the regional level in the Western Cape, as well as with the politics of the capital. The real test next year will be whether the two competing power blocs in the current Cape Metro Council will consolidate in the floor-crossing period, or whether it will be reconfigured, leading to another round of political instability. Whatever the outcome, six years of Metro governance in the Cape has shown the vibrancy, energy and excitement of a competitive multiparty system in South African politics.

Notes

1   For the full text of Blackman Ngoro's editorial, see <http://www.iol.co.za/index.php? set_id=1&click_id=&art_id=vn20050725064508261C103893> (*Cape Times* 25.07.05).

2   Roderick 'Blackman' Ngoro was Nomaindia Mfeketo's media spin doctor. Ngoro had said in an essay on his website that coloured people were culturally inferior to black people, whom he termed 'Africans'. He said coloured people would die a 'drunken death' if they did not go through a process of ideological transformation. The Big Bay debacle involved the perception that the ANC administration had hand-picked half the list of companies that were to be offered beachfront plots at heavily discounted prices. These companies included those with links to the ANC Youth League, a national minister's husband, the city manager Wallace Mgoqi's wife, etc. (*Cape Argus* 03.08.05).

3   The Federal Alliance was founded in 1998 by Louis Luyt, a former president of the South African Rugby Football Union (SARFU). The FA views itself as a Christian democratic party whose mission is to fulfil the objectives of federalism in South Africa. Luyt gained notoriety when, in 1998, the SARFU he headed forced then President Nelson Mandela to appear in court to justify his decision to order a probe into rugby.

4   Victoria Johnson was in charge of the public participation process initiated after Marais's proposal.

5   See ANC–NNP Agreement (2002: 1). The text of the full agreement is available on <http://www.anc.org.za/ancdocs/misc/agreement.html>

References

Cameron R (2003) Local government in South Africa: Political decentralisation, party centralisation, corruption and maladministration. In A Hadenius (Ed) *Decentralisation and democratic governance: Experiences from India, Bolivia and South Africa*. Stockholm: Almqvist and Wiksell International.

Faull J (2004) Floor-crossing. Paper presented at the Democracy Development Programme Workshop, Royal Hotel, Durban, 13 October.

Faull J (2006) Local government elections 2006: The race for the City of Cape Town. *ePoliticsSA – Edition 01*. Cape Town: Idasa.

GCIS (Government Communication and Information Systems) (2002) Statement on the appointment of Deputy Ministers by President Thabo Mbeki, November 4. Available at <http://www.dfa.gov.za/docs/2002/depmin1104.ht>

Heath Special Consultants (2001) *Investigation in terms of Section 106 of the Provincial Government. Municipal Systems Act, 32 of 2000. Proposed Renaming of Adderley and Wale Street*. Available at <http://www.capegateway.gov.za/Text/2003/heath_report.pdf>

Horowitz D (1991) *A democratic South Africa? Constitutional engineering in a divided society*. Berkeley: University of California Press.

Karume S (2003) Conceptual understanding of political coalitions in South Africa: An integration of concepts and practices. Paper presented at an Electoral Institute of Southern Africa round table on Strengthening Democracy through Party Coalition Building. Vineyard Hotel, Claremont, Cape Town, 19 June.

Leon T (2004) South Africa deserves better. Statement issued by Tony Leon, Leader of the Official Opposition, 4 February.

Lodge T (2002) *Politics in South Africa: From Mandela to Mbeki*. Cape Town: David Philip.

Seekings J (2005) *Partisan re-alignment in Cape Town, 1994–2004*. Centre for Social Science Research, Working Paper No.111, University of Cape Town.

4 Municipal elections 2006: protests, independent candidates and cross-border municipalities

Mcebisi Ndletyana

The 2006 local government elections took place in a context different from that of earlier post-1994 national polls. In the months prior to the poll a number of communities around the country experienced sometimes violent protests directed at their democratically-elected councillors, drawn largely from the ruling African National Congress (ANC). In other cases, local leaders turned on national figures, while in a few cases one-time allies broke ranks and challenged each other at the polls.

What initially seemed a routine electoral exercise akin to the 1995/96 and 2000 local elections developed some unusual scenarios that highlighted contradictions within the ruling ANC, as well as between the ANC and its South African Communist Party (SACP) ally. The results of the 2006 elections therefore afford us an opportunity to examine changes and continuities in the political behaviour and culture of the electorate. Likewise, and probably for the first time, the results provide an insight into the viability of alternative political actors – in the form of independent and social movement candidatures – taking on the political establishment, so to speak, in the form of the ANC.

This chapter seeks to do two things. First, it examines the 2006 elections with a view to establishing the electoral fate of those one-time ANC figures who left the party to follow an alternative or independent political route and to ascertain whether such candidates resonated at all with particularly black voters. Second, using the turbulent Moutse and Khutsong townships as focal points, it seeks to analyse the intra-party dynamics within the ruling ANC and the SACP. The chapter argues that there are contending notions of democracy within the ruling party between those who insist on direct democracy, on the one hand, and representative democracy, on the other, and that the Moutse case in particular highlights the existing tensions between the ANC and the SACP, and suggests how the ongoing debate within the SACP on whether or not to break away from the alliance with the ANC is likely to be settled.

The 2006 election results: overview and implications

Analysis of the results of the March 2006 contest suggests a strengthening of the ruling party and consequent weakening of opposition parties. Electoral support for the ANC rose from 59 per cent (in 2000) to 66 per cent (in 2006). Similarly, of a total of 238 councils nationwide, the ANC won control of 179, an increase of 17 over the result in 2000 – including winning 5 of the country's 6 metropolitan councils. It is therefore clear that the opposition lost ground overall, none more so than the regionally-based United Democratic Movement (UDM) and the Inkatha Freedom Party (IFP). The number of IFP-controlled councils in KwaZulu-Natal dropped from 33 to 23, whilst the UDM lost the Sabatha Dalindyebo Municipality, the only municipality it controlled in the Eastern Cape. Although the Democratic Alliance (DA) garnered the largest number of votes in the Cape Town Metro (42%), the number of councils it won throughout the country dropped from 12 (in 2000) to 8 (in 2006). Overall, the DA received 15 per cent of the votes cast. The gulf, it would seem, between the ruling party and the opposition is widening nationally.

This chapter focuses on independent candidates and those drawn from the social movement strata. Of 690 independents who contested the 2000 elections, only 17 were elected to wards (independents are obviously not eligible for seats on the proportional representation ballot). Though the number of independent candidates dropped slightly to 667 in the 2006 elections, the number of seats won by independents doubled to 34, just more than 2 per cent of the total ward seats. While an increase, this is still a relatively negligible number. As for the social movement candidates, they performed even more poorly (as will be shown in this chapter). This was something of a surprise given that a number of these movements had been at the centre of community protests in the last five years or so, and many of their leading figures had become well-known names. There had been some expectation that these candidates would capitalise on these factors in the election.

In the following section we examine two cases – an independent candidate and a social movement leader. Though conclusions drawn from the two case studies may not be generalisable, they nonetheless give us some insight into what makes for a successful independent candidate and why social movements have thus far failed to convert their successful community campaigns into electoral gains.

Independent candidates: contrasting paths, a similar fate

In this section we compare the political fortunes of two former ANC leaders who stood in the 2006 municipal elections: Japhta Moswang Lekgetho, an independent, and Trevor Ngwane, leader of the newly formed political party Operation Khanyisa Movement (OKM), a political extension of several social movements. Both men are based in Soweto and joined the ANC after its unbanning in 1990 – Lekgetho through community activism, and Ngwane via the trade union movement.

Lekgetho: a community activist

Lekgetho first attained prominence in the late 1970s as a community activist. Based in Dobsonville, Soweto, Lekgetho earned much local admiration when he resigned his teaching post at Morris Isaacson High, a school at the centre of the 1976 student revolt that followed the police shooting of black students in Soweto who were protesting against the use of Afrikaans as a medium of instruction at their schools. Lekgetho resigned in solidarity with the students, motivated by a refusal to continue being part of a racist educational syllabus that the students had themselves denounced (interview 23.03.06).

It was his social activism, however, that was to make Lekgetho a household name beyond his locale of Dobsonville. Soon after the 1976 uprising, he founded the National Environmental Awareness Campaign (NEAP) to promote environmental awareness throughout Soweto. The success of this campaign soon earned him the nickname 'Mr Clean'. It began modestly as a clean-up campaign, as Soweto had become filthy due to the collapse of local authorities in the aftermath of the uprising. This posed a health hazard, as Lekgetho put it: 'When the rubbish starts to rot, the air is filled with bad smells that spread diseases. Many township babies have died because of the diseases that are carried in the air' (*Learn and Teach* n.d.: 47). Residents, also cognisant of the danger, responded positively to the call to clean up their townships.

The campaign soon evolved to the greening of the community, with rubbish dumps converted into parks throughout Soweto. In the 13 years of the NEAP's active existence, Lekgetho estimates that the group created some 10 to 14 parks. This was accompanied by annual tree-planting campaigns held in September and October. Schools were particularly pivotal in the campaign (interview 23.03.06). After its unbanning in 1990, the ANC designated Lekgetho as its national spokesperson on the environment. Lekgetho seemed set to play a key role in a post-apartheid ANC government (Lawson 1991).

Ngwane: a working-class intellectual

Trevor Ngwane first made a name for himself as a fiercely independent and left-wing intellectual within the labour movement. In the late 1980s, he was a junior lecturer at the University of the Witwatersrand (Wits) where he completed an honours degree in sociology. It was his teaching that introduced him to workers' issues. Ngwane invited workers to his classes to narrate their real-life experiences on the shop floor. Through this, Ngwane came to understand the depth of illiteracy among workers. Together with his students, he began literacy classes for workers. This later mushroomed into the Wits Workers Literacy Project in which Ngwane became a full-time teacher.

In the early 1990s, Ngwane took up the position of education officer within the Transport Workers' Union (Ngwane 2003). His position did not prevent him from airing criticism of the trade union leadership whenever he saw fit. In 1993 he penned a critique of the Congress of South African Trade Unions' (Cosatu) endorsement of co-determination policies, which earned him an expulsion. But Ngwane's popularity among workers saw him reinstated following a protest (Ngwane 2003).

Ngwane had a different orientation and base to Lekgetho. He was located in working-class politics and was uncompromisingly leftist and vocal where he felt those principles were betrayed. Lekgetho was a community activist, with his politics essentially issue-based, not ideologically-driven. His constituency thus cut across class lines, whereas Ngwane had an unflinching bias toward the working class. Inevitably their constituencies and predisposition towards an ANC government differed, and this was to prefigure their political fortunes once they left the ANC.

Their departure from the ANC in 1999, though a surprise, was nonetheless under-standable. Ngwane refused to retract comments in which he criticised a privatisa-tion programme that the national government had begun to implement. His criticism was a direct response to President Thabo Mbeki's repeated assertion that 'the people had spoken', which implied that by voting ANC the electorate had given the ANC government a mandate to privatise. Ngwane was promptly suspended from all official positions for two years. His suspension extended to his position as councillor of Pimville, Soweto, to which he had been elected in 1995. Attempts to have him withdraw his comments failed (interview 18.03.06).

If Ngwane's departure was precipitated by ideological differences, Lekgetho's departure appears to have been as a result of his feeling unappreciated by the party hierarchy. He had been passed over for nomination to official positions three times: in 1994 (for Parliament), in 1995 (for local government) and in 1999 (for Parliament once again). Each time Lekgetho had been nominated by his branches, but, as he put it, his 'name always disappeared between Dobsonville and the ANC's national office' (interview 23.03.06). Lekgetho felt he deserved an official place-ment and, at the age of 60, he was not getting any younger and was unemployed. He had resigned his job as a statement of opposition to apartheid education 20 years before and since then he had immersed himself in community development. When the party hierarchy did not reciprocate, Lekgetho felt unwanted:

> Sometimes you say you have contributed a lot, why then if there's a
> vacancy nationally or provincially you're not considered. I'm not going
> to be bitter about this. It's political I know, perhaps there's something
> I lack politically, which does not qualify me for higher office...Perhaps
> there are people who are harbouring hatred against me. I realised that
> I can work alone, then I decided to continue my way in a small way.
> (Interview 23.03.06)

Both Ngwane and Lekgetho were expelled from the ANC after announcing their intention to stand as independent candidates in the 2000 local elections. They were among a group of more than 80 local leaders who left the ANC. The party's

Secretary General, Kgalema Motlanthe, subsequently admitted that the breakaways were partly of the party's own making due to improper handling of the electoral list (*Sunday Independent* 25.11.2000).

Independent politics: no easy walk

For independent candidates to prevail in current circumstances in South Africa they need to develop a reputation that would give them a support base beyond and independent of the organisation. For that candidates need an independent track record within the community upon which to anchor their candidacy. The latter point is particularly crucial for their campaigns since they lack resources and have limited visibility and media coverage, while ANC candidates have all these factors in their favour. Their success also depends on the electorate being open to voting for alternative candidates outside of the ruling party. This requires that voters evaluate candidates on their individual merit – what they have done in the past and what they are capable of doing in the future.

In post-apartheid South Africa, few independent candidates have enjoyed political success in elections. In the 2000 local government elections in KwaZulu-Natal, for example, 100 independents contested ward seats with only 4 being successful. Of these, 2 later crossed the floor to established parties in the 2002 'floor-crossing' period. In the most recent election in KwaZulu-Natal, 109 independents ran for office with only 2 being successful. The Lekgetho case is, in some respects then, the 'exception that proves the rule.

Both Ngwane and Lekgetho ran as independents in the 2000 elections but lost – Ngwane lost in Ward 22 in Pimville, while Lekgetho's debut in electoral politics failed in Dobsonville. However, luck favoured Lekgetho. The incumbent in his ward, Mokone Sebolai, passed away and a by-election was held on 15 May 2002. Eight candidates contested the ward and Lekgetho won by 182 votes. With a low voter turnout – only 2 957 of the 14 673 registered voters – the ANC could have been disadvantaged. If this was a result of complacency – feeling confident that they would be returned to office and thus insufficient effort employed to mobilise their support base – the 2006 elections presented the ANC with an opportunity to rectify the situation. The results of the 2006 elections, therefore, would be an indicator of whether Lekgetho's 2002 victory was a chance factor or whether he had won on the strength of his candidacy. He was re-elected by 2 840 votes compared to 2 497 for his rival from the ANC. In other words, he more than doubled his majority. Deputy secretary of the ANC in Gauteng, Mandla Nkomfe, could only concede, with a tinge of awe: 'We don't seem able to figure that guy out' (interview 17.03.06).

As for Ngwane, after his defeat in 2000 he changed paths. He opted out of independent politics and pioneered the formation of the Anti-Privatisation Forum (APF), one of many social movements that emerged around 2000 to challenge the government's neo-liberal policies (Habib 2003). Ngwane became the prominent face of the APF both nationally and internationally. He was even the subject of an international television documentary entitled 'The Two Trevors Go To Washington' that documented his anti-globalisation activities. Ngwane became the most recognisable face of all APF leaders. While this owed initially to the publicity generated by his expulsion from the ANC in 1999, he subsequently endeared himself to the media with his eloquence and charm.

Of the leftist intellectuals of the early 1990, Ngwane is one of the few who remain engaged in grassroots activism. In 2000 he spearheaded Operation Khanyisa (literally, 'switch on the lights'), a campaign against electricity cut-offs to households in arrears. According to Ngwane, within 6 months they had reconnected about 3 000 households. Sisi Mtungwa, also a leader in the movement, explains the procedure: 'If they cut off someone, you report to our offices at OKM, explain your plight and that you have no money. OKM comes and reconnects them' (interview 18.03.06). OKM has a number of 'connectors' (individuals that connect electricity), and can reconnect as many as 12 households on any given day. They also remove pre-paid meters, which allows residents to use water without being billed – and these households are often headed by old people and the unemployed.

In June 2001, Operation Khanyisa made even bigger headlines by disconnecting power at the house of Johannesburg mayor, Amos Masondo. According to Ngwane, this was simply intended 'to remind [the mayor] that he had promised to give us free water and electricity the next day', as during the 2000 election campaign the ANC had promised that the city council would start rolling out free basic electricity and water in July 2001 (interview 18.03.06). The protesters forced their way into the mayoral premises, including the swimming pool, threw litter all around, and cut off the electricity supply to the house. The march ended in mayhem. Eighty-seven people were arrested and charged, but acquitted in March 2003 (Ngwane 2003).

The plight of poor residents who could not pay for services gained tremendous publicity through Operation Khanyisa. Even though councils throughout the country had begun to provide a certain quota of free basic water and electricity, some residents had already accumulated so much in arrears that they could not pay, while others could not pay for electricity and water they consumed above and beyond the free supply. In May 2003, the government was eventually moved to write off R1.4 billion owed by residents to Eskom, the state-owned supplier. Even though the Soweto Electricity Crisis Committee (SECC) and the APF were not invited to the talks that yielded this partial cancellation of arrears, their campaign had played a key role in that decision (*Mail & Guardian* 13.05.03).

When leaders of Operation Khanyisa formed a political party, Operation Khanyisa Movement, in January 2006 to contest the upcoming local government elections, they were hoping to capitalise on the publicity and gains of Khanyisa. Their electoral campaign, for instance, called for the free provision of basic services – that is, water, electricity and affordable housing for the homeless. Soweto, where the OKM was to contest the elections, had been declared a hotspot area in the City of Johannesburg Metro Municipality, with several protests taking place in townships including Phiri and Kliptown. The protest in Kliptown, on 27 July 2005, was organised to coincide with the celebration of the ANC's historical document, the Freedom Charter, which had set out a vision of a post-apartheid South Africa under an ANC government. The protest sought to highlight symbolically that some of the promises contained in the Charter, such as decent and affordable housing and free education, had not materialised. In a memorandum handed to the Minister of Social Development, Zola Skweyiya, the protesters demanded: 'Decent housing, schools, libraries, clinics, jobs and an end to the bucket system...They stressed that their lifestyle of poverty in the shack land around the memorial was unacceptable ten years into democracy'.

The protests in Soweto mirrored a phenomenon that was widespread. Minister of Safety and Security Sydney Mufamadi put the number of protests at 881 in the year leading up to October 2005 (*New York Times* 25.12.05). Cabinet was taken aback by their frequency and the violent nature of some of the protests, and reportedly ascribed their eruption to the work of 'a third force'. This statement implied that the protests were not spontaneous and genuine, but were consciously instigated by individuals bent on undermining the government. Following an uproar, including from members of the ruling party outside government, Cabinet recanted on the conspiracy theory. It now conceded that the protests were understandable, taking place as they were in communities in which municipalities had been targeted for immediate hands-on intervention due to the severity of the problems afflicting them (*The Star* 10.06.05).

Municipalities throughout the country were generally in a less than satisfactory condition. The government's own audit in 2004 revealed that of the total of 284 municipalities:

- 203 could not provide sanitation to 60 per cent of their residents;
- 182 were unable to remove refuse from 60 per cent of the households;
- 155 could not provide water to 60 per cent of the properties within their jurisdiction;
- 122 could not provide electricity to 60 per cent of the households;
- 116 were unable to provide housing to 60 per cent of their residents; and
- 42 per cent were generally incapable of performing 50 per cent of their functions. (*Independent On Saturday* 01.10.05)

Insufficient funds and lack of capacity to manage the provision of services were at the core of municipal woes. Most were stifled by enormous financial debt, with one estimate putting it at around R40 billion countrywide (*Business Day* 08.09.05) – up from R24.3 billion in 2003, and R22 billion at the end of 2001 (*Business Day* 05.03.03). In some Free State municipalities, for instance, debt soared even after they had improved measures for credit control and revenue collection. This meant that a significant portion of their funds had to be diverted towards servicing debt. As a result, as one government official put it: 'Other important issues such as essential repairs and maintenance, the upgrading of service delivery and the filling of critical key vacancies are not attended to' (*Cape Times* 18.09.05). For other municipalities insufficient funds meant they could not even 'pay for audit fees to get audited by the auditor-general' (*Cape Times* 18.09.05). Thus problems that could have been uncovered by an audit, and possibly remedied in time, went undiagnosed.

Residents were left not knowing why the delivery of social services was not happening or whether it would happen at all. Ward committees, the supposed mechanism of accountability and interaction between councillors and their electors, had simply collapsed in most communities. Councillors were hardly seen in their own wards. After they had been elected, some simply relocated their residence to other neighbourhoods and scarcely visited their constituencies. A survey undertaken among Gauteng residents, for instance, showed that only 10 per cent felt that their councillors are in touch with their constituents (*Business Day* 20.09.05).

The prominence of social delivery and associated problems even limited the options of the ruling party's choice of an electoral strategy in the 2006 elections. Their message could not be overly positive as it had been in the 2000 elections ('Let's Speed Up Delivery'). This had enabled the ANC to tout its record and hope that voters, notwithstanding existing backlogs, would be convinced that it was capable of achieving even more. This time round, however, the campaign was defensive, acknowledging the problems that had dominated the headlines in the months before the election. The best the ANC campaign could offer was: 'A Plan to Make Local Government Work Better.' In their election manifesto of 2006, a number of remedies were proposed, ranging from providing technical capacity to municipalities to forcing candidates to take an oath committing them to holding ward meetings, to residing within their ward constituency and to not engaging in corrupt practices.

OKM leaders, through their affiliation to the APF and the SECC, were central in the protests. However, this did not translate into significant political capital at the 2006 local polls. Of the 109 wards contested, the OKM won none. Only 883 votes of a total of 481 893 were cast for their ward candidates. The OKM was able to secure only one seat on the Johannesburg Metro Council by way of the proportional representation formula.

Ngwane downplayed the OKM's poor showing. The movement, he argued, 'was a political statement, rather than a serious attempt to win votes. We didn't intend to take over council…We just wanted to demonstrate to the working class that we can do something' (interview 18.03.06). It is difficult to believe, however, that the OKM did not wish for a better electoral showing because their primary objective is to revive civic participation. As Ngwane put it:

Social activists should not celebrate when voters stay off the polls as a sign that voters don't want the ANC and thus take this as some kind of a victory for them. This indicates more than just loss of 'hope in the ANC' and 'in the power of the vote to change things for the better'. But it also indicates that people may have lost hope in politics, they lost hope in organisation, they lost hope in political parties. In fact, they lost hope in a better future, they lost hope in their own power to change things. Our job is to restore the confidence of the masses in their own power – to provide a platform for them to bring out their frustrations, to remember what happened in the past and be inspired to change their plight. (Interview 18.03.06)

The premium OKM places on the instrumentality of political power in attaining their political objective makes it even more difficult to believe that the movement did not wish for a better electoral performance. Seizure of political power is central if they are to change the existing socio-economic structure, as Ngwane explains:

The objective of the OKM is not reforms, but revolution…the campaigns are more or less keeping things where they are…The Treatment Action Campaign got antiretrovirals, that is why it is the most successful social movement in the world. But, what use are the antiretrovirals without water, without food, without even a proper health system…There is a contradiction here between reform and revolution or fundamental change. The ANC defeated apartheid, but left the economic structure intact. This is what you can call defeat in victory…Clear class politics is necessary and not simply more militancy. (Interview 18.03.06)

Ngwane attributed OKM's poor electoral showing to a myriad of reasons ranging from candidates registering in wrong wards, poor campaigning, voters not recognising OKM candidates on the ballot paper, to him not standing in the elections. OKM candidates were ordinary township folks, 'including grannies'. His non-participation, Ngwane argues, 'cost us a few votes, perhaps a thousand or two…But I don't think I would have won, perhaps I could come out third or got half of the votes' (interview 18.03.06). He explained that his reason for not running:

was a political decision…We can't say we are against the politics of the Messiah, the big man, then do exactly that. You can't say the most important people are the grannies, the ordinary people in Soweto. Then come elections, it's you standing. Our stand is that the candidate is not important, it's the constituency that is important. Trevor alone cannot change much, but it's the constituency that changes things. (Interview 18.03.06)

Political independents: what makes for electoral success?

The contrasting political fortunes of Ngwane and Lekgetho provide a telling insight into the political culture and behaviour of South African voters, particularly black voters. It is also a useful indicator of the responsiveness of the state to the needs of the citizenry as well of its effectiveness in addressing those needs.

Some scholars ascribe the ANC's dominance of South Africa's electoral politics to its historic role as a liberation movement. It has liberation credentials and history unmatched by any other party, and produced heroes and heroines that shaped defining moments of South Africa's history. It is inevitable, the argument goes, that the populous African community who were victims of apartheid would develop a natural affinity towards the party that liberated them from oppression. That allegiance, the argument continues, leads to a situation where black people blindly vote for the ANC, regardless of its performance in office. Voters are, therefore, neither critical nor do they consider the merit of the candidates or party, but are simply directed by sentiment towards the ANC (Lodge 1999).

Lekgetho's success in Dobsonville, however, challenges this theory. His political success owes more to his personal reputation and record, and less to his erstwhile affiliation to the ANC. He was a community activist with a strong track record, long before joining the ANC in 1990, and thus did not need party legitimacy or association to be a credible candidate. Dobsonville voters, who are traditionally predominantly ANC supporters, made an independent political judgement. They evaluated all candidates on merit and Lekgetho's candidacy, given his record in the township, prevailed.

However, Lekgetho's re-election does not necessarily signal voter rejection of the ANC. Lekgetho himself is emphatic that he is not in opposition to the ANC:

> We don't have strong political parties, we have opposition parties. Sometimes you even oppose progress. With me I'm not there to oppose, I'm there to work, to secure services and other things for my constituency. I work well with colleagues, all of them. I'm not adversarial or anything. The problem is this constant opposition, now you can't even work with your colleagues. Anyway my loyalty will always be with the ANC as an organisation. (Interview 23.03.06)

Lekgetho's electoral campaign focused on community issues. Despite the fact that the ANC made Lekgetho the target of their campaign, he explains: 'I was not against them. My focus was on service delivery, which is the policy of the government, the government that I support. So whilst they were talking about me, I was talking about service delivery' (interview 23.03.06). While the ANC received extensive airtime and distributed posters widely, Lekgetho's media campaign was limited and did not even attract the attention of the local media. The news editor of the local radio station, Soweto Community Radio, had not heard of him until I enquired, while an Internet search revealed less than 20 stories about Lekgetho. Instead, he utilised community networks, door-to-door visits and public meetings.

Conversely, the OKM received wide media attention, even featuring on the popular TV programme *Special Assignment* the night before the election. But this publicity did not yield results for the party, nor did its anti-government stance or socialist rhetoric appeal to voters. Ngwane, however, does not construe OKM's poor showing as a failure of its leftist politics to find resonance with the working class. Rather, he attributes it to workers' short-term economistic orientation, which, in turn, hinders them from developing long-term revolutionary aspirations. As Ngwane puts it:

> People vote for the ANC, despite their discontent with the party. This reflects the contradictions within the workers. They may be unhappy with the system, but are somewhat attached to it. They don't see it as the source of the problem, but want to improve their plight within. They want better wages and better working conditions, but not to overhaul the entire system. Workers lack a revolutionary consciousness. (Interview 18.03.06)

Perhaps Ngwane was unreasonably optimistic to expect voters to shun the ANC and opt for his party instead. It may well be that, as Ferial Haffajee, editor of the weekly newspaper *Mail & Guardian* noted, Ngwane believed his own rhetoric that social conditions have deteriorated so much in the new South Africa that things were even better during the apartheid years. It was this penchant for exaggeration, Haffajee continued, that led to authors like David McDonald and John Pape announcing that they had uncovered 'that 10 million people had had their electricity cut off and 10 million more had their water pipes staunched' (Haffajee 2004: 6). These figures turned out to be exaggerated, as Mark Orkin, then chief executive officer of the Human Sciences Research Council (HSRC), explained: 'The HSRC has clarified that the figure is an extrapolation by an independent, external researcher in an HSRC survey of three months duration, and considerably overestimates the phenomenon' (cited in Haffajee 2004: 6).

The fact is that capitalism in South Africa has not yielded a level of misery that sows mass discontent. Admittedly, approximately 30 per cent of the economically active population is out of work and suffers all the unpleasantness that comes with poverty. But this is assuaged by the welfare services that the state provides. These include grants to senior citizens, the disabled and children with single parents, free quotas of water and electricity to households, subsidies for affordable housing, and free health care for pregnant women and children under the age of six, as well as providing food at some public schools. It is not surprising, therefore, that a survey by the HSRC in October 2005 found that 56 per cent of South Africans felt that their lives 'have improved over the last five years' (HSRC 2006: 5). This partly explains why a survey conducted in December 2005 by Cosatu revealed that 65 per cent of Cosatu-affiliated workers indicated that they would vote the ANC in the 2006 local elections (*Mail & Guardian* online 27.02.06).

The cross-boundary municipality controversy: an insight into intra-party dynamics

The disputes in 2005/06 over cross-boundary municipalities (CBMs) signify two crucial dynamics within the ruling ANC. First, they reflect different contentions over the form of democracy South Africa should assume – whether it should be representative or direct. Second, they provide the first tangible indication of how the ongoing debate within the SACP, on whether it should break away or retain its alliance with the ruling party, is likely to develop.

The Moutse and Khutsong communities were 2 of the 16 CBMs that were set to be eliminated by legislation passed in December 2005 (the Twelfth Amendment Bill and the Cross Boundaries Municipalities Laws Repeal and Related Matters Bill of 2005). CBMs straddled provincial boundaries and fell under different provincial jurisdictions. According to national government, this presented administrative complications with decision-making being unduly long as CBMs had to consult and get approval from two provincial administrations. In some cases, they would have to administer the same function differently in each province due to varying legal systems, health systems and traffic systems.

Moutse and Khutsong residents put up fierce and sustained resistance to being relocated from one province to another. Moutse, formerly part of the Sekhukhune District Municipality in Mpumalanga, was to be relocated to Limpopo, and Khutsong, which formed part of the Merafong Municipality, was to be moved from Gauteng to North West. Residents objected that the provinces to which they were being relocated were poorly resourced and less developed, and that the quality of services available would be poorer and more difficult to access.

A public hearing held jointly by the North West and Gauteng legislatures in November 2005, for instance, heard that applications for identity documents in North West were processed once a week, whereas in Gauteng they were processed every working day. Another objection highlighted the inadequacy of the health and emergency services in the North West. Kokosi township, it was cited, only had two clinics catering for its residents and 'the clinics are normally without medicines and the staff services are not available after normal working hours', whereas Gauteng hospitals and clinics are within reach as compared to those of North West province, and 'the provision of primary health services in Gauteng is reported to be more efficient and effective' (Gauteng Legislature 2005a: 5). The advanced economic development of Gauteng alone, it was stated, is a compelling reason to have Merafong Municipality incorporated into Gauteng. The diversity and size of the

Gauteng economy would be able to absorb the labour force that is likely to become redundant as the mines in the North West, which are already ailing, shut down. The North West would not be able to offset this because its local economy is much smaller and mostly agricultural (Gauteng Legislature 2005a).

In light of the uneven development among the provinces, these objections were not entirely unexpected. The tenor of the protests and the identity of their leaders, however, were a surprise. Both are predominantly ANC areas, and the protests that began in November 2005 were led by ANC local leaders. Protests in Khutsong were marked by violent scenes. Houses belonging to ANC councillors were set alight and 14 representatives fled the neighbourhood for the safety of a nearby mine compound. Municipal offices, the local library and some shops were also torched. The damage caused by the blaze was estimated at R20 million. The Minister of Defence and a popular ANC figure, Mosiuoa 'Terror' Lekota, was dispatched to quell the situation, but his attempts to hold three public meetings failed. The meetings were all poorly attended. As one of the placards hoisted up by a resident read, 'Lekota, *jy vat 'n kans* [Lekota, you're taking a chance]' (*Mail & Guardian* 17–23.02.06).

Khutsong's violent scenes were not the only distinct feature of the protest. Unlike in Moutse, the Khutsong leadership (the Anti-North West Committee) called for a boycott of the local government election. They even made an application to the Constitutional Court, arguing that the poll would not be free and fair due to the prevalence of violence. The court ruled against the application. Ultimately, though, little voting took place on election day – of the 29 540 registered voters, only 232 voters turned up to vote, and 12 of those ballots were spoilt (*City Press* 05.03.06).

The Khutsong case provides an insight into competing notions of democracy within the ruling party, particularly between local leadership and membership, on the one hand, and the national leadership, on the other. Following a government promise in 2005 that local wishes would be heeded, Khutsong residents thought the government would grant their wish to have the Merafong Municipality incorporated into Gauteng province. Indeed, the portfolio committees for Local Government of both Gauteng and North West legislatures, after a jointly-held public hearing, concluded that: 'An overwhelming majority of people attending the public hearing were opposed to the proposal to incorporate Merafong City Local Municipality into the North West province, due to the fact that they were not provided with substantive and compelling reasons' (Gauteng Legislature 2005b: 9).

It was on the basis of this majority opinion that Gauteng's portfolio committee resolved to support the Merafong community:

> In light of the outcome, impact assessment and analysis of the public hearing submissions, [the portfolio committee on Local Government]

agrees with the inclusion of the geographical area of Merafong Municipality into the West Rand District Municipality in the Gauteng province.
(Gauteng Legislature 2005a: 9)

On 30 November 2005, the committee recommended to the Gauteng provincial
legislature that its delegation to the National Council of Provinces (NCOP)
should argue in favour of providing 'for the inclusion of the municipal area of
Merafong into the municipal area of the West Rand District Municipality of the
Gauteng province', and in support of the constitutional amendment 'on condition
that the municipal area of Merafong is included in the municipal area of the West
Rand District Municipality of the Gauteng province' (Gauteng Legislature 2005a:
10).

A few days later, however, upon the return of its delegation from the NCOP, the
portfolio committee reversed its decision. It now mandated its NCOP delegation
to withdraw its support for the Merafong Municipality to be incorporated into
Gauteng province. The views of Merafong residents, the portfolio committee had
now decided, in concurrence with the technical reasoning offered by the ministry,
were secondary to the government's view that sound municipal administration
with a viable and sustainable revenue base was a more important consideration.

The Khutsong case reflects the ascendancy of the notion of representative democracy over that of direct democracy. Cabinet and parliamentary representatives are
of the view that decision-making rests solely with them, a prerogative they believe
derives from them having being elected to Parliament to represent the will of the
electorate. They construe this not only as a mandate, but as one that lasts throughout the entire parliamentary term to represent the electorate as they see fit on any
issue, and, as the case of Khutsong illustrates, without considering the input of
local communities. The implicit assumption is that the elected representative not
only knows better, but also knows what is in the interests of the electorate. Policy
analyst Steven Friedman ascribes this to the government reducing democracy to
service delivery (*Business Day* 22.03.06). The roles of the state and the citizenry are
supposedly neatly delineated – the former 'rolls out goods and services', whilst the
latter simply receives. The emphasis, Friedman continues, is misplaced on delivery,
as opposed to service. Prioritising delivery 'virtually removes people from the
equation turning government and those who work for it into a machine', whereas
stressing delivery entails that government listens, respects and does what the citizenry asks of it. The citizens of Khutsong, as evidenced by their vociferous protests,
share Friedman's conclusion that 'democracy works best when the most important
thing delivered is the messages [citizens] sent to those who serve [them]' (*Business
Day* 22.03.06).

Top-down decision-making is not a rarity in the South African governance system.
It is in fact typical of how the system functions. South Africa's elected representatives, for instance, seem to have abrogated the function of initiating legislation

entirely to the executive. Of the legislation passed between 1994 and 2003, the bulk was initiated by the executive. The role of parliamentary representatives has largely been confined to deliberating and voting on the Bills. Little consideration is given to strengthening the impact of public input into the legislative-making process. No system exists, for instance, to ensure a systematic review of public submissions, nor is crucial and relevant information guaranteed to be culled off any submissions and fed to the committees for consideration (Habib & Schulz-Herzenberg 2005).

Parliamentary functioning seems to have borrowed heavily from the leadership style within the ruling party. However, this phenomenon has not gone entirely unchallenged by the lower layer of leadership. At the National General Council of the party held in June–July 2005, delegates reversed a decision taken by the party's National Working Committee (NWC) to suspend its deputy president, Jacob Zuma, from his official positions within the party. Zuma had recently been charged with corruption. Delegates contended that, as a non-elected body, the NWC lacked powers to suspend an elected official. Only the membership that elected Zuma had the prerogative to decide his fate and they had him reinstated (*Business Day* 04.07.06).

Similarly, the Khutsong ANC leadership was insisting on determining a decision that affected them, as opposed to them receiving instruction from above. This, they believed, is how decision-making should proceed within the party. However, the fact that the top leadership insisted on the opposite did not turn Khutsong ANC leaders against the party. They did not resign their positions within the party, nor turn independent. They remained within the ANC, but simply refused to vote as a protest – theirs is not a rejection of the party and government, but a contestation of who has the prerogative to decide on matters that affect them.

If Khutsong reflects contestation within the ruling party, the situation in Moutse illustrates the rising of tensions within the alliance between the ruling party and its SACP ally, and gives the first indication of how that tension might eventually pan out. Moutse township was formerly located in Mpumalanga province but was relocated into Limpopo province following the redetermination of provincial boundaries. Moutse had been part of the Sekhukhune Municipality that straddled the provincial boundary shared by Mpumalanga and Limpopo provinces. Residents of Moutse opposed the incorporation of their municipality into Limpopo, insisting on staying within Mpumalanga instead. The demarcation board agreed and recommended to the Minister of Local Government that Moutse be retained within Mpumalanga, but under a reconstituted municipality. Their request ignored, the residents launched a series of protests within the six-month period leading up to the elections. The protests were led mainly by local SACP officials, who were also office-bearers of the party in the District of Moutse. Their demand unheeded, the protests eventually saw SACP leaders contesting the elections as independents. This was a historic moment in the post-apartheid era as they were essentially defying the national SACP leadership, which had taken a decision that they would again support the ANC and its electoral campaign. It also meant that, as independents, they essentially stood in opposition to their ruling party ally, whilst retaining their positions within the SACP. The (SACP) independents had chosen not to stand on an SACP platform because the latter had resolved not to contest the elections independently of the ANC. Notwithstanding the strength of local feelings, the dissidents failed to win a seat on the council.

On one level, this rebellion could be interpreted as a minor act on the part of a few undisciplined SACP leaders. However, in my view it reflects the very strong feelings of a section of the SACP leadership about whether or not the SACP should become independent of the ANC. A final decision on the matter will be taken at the party's congress in 2007.

In contributing to the debate, the SACP Central Committee (CC) issued a discussion paper entitled 'Should the Party Contest Elections in its own Right?' (SACP 2005). The discussion paper argues for the party remaining within the alliance, at least for the moment, citing the fact that an independent SACP might not be able to sustain itself due to a lack of financial resources. This might even hinder the party from contesting elections effectively due to the exorbitant expense involved. Even if it were able to make some electoral gains, the CC cautions that it would gain very little political authority. Electoral power does not translate into real power, as the CC points out with regard to neighbouring Zimbabwe, where the opposition controls the mayoral positions in most towns but is constrained by the legal and political framework within which it operates.

Rather, the CC counsels, the party should maintain its current focus on strengthening the working class and the party's power and influence in all 'sites of power' without focusing narrowly on electoral politics. The question that should preoccupy the party instead is how it can increase its influence and impact throughout society. The CC believes that this strategy has already begun to pay dividends, as evidenced by newly introduced measures within the financial sector to extend banking services to the unemployed and low-income earners, as well as home loans to the latter. Going alone, the CC concludes, will not necessarily yield more gains from those that have already been achieved by operating within the alliance (SACP 2005).

Vishwas Satgar, provincial secretary of the SACP in Gauteng province – and an advocate of an independent SACP – counters that the pro-alliance viewpoint reflects naivety as it assumes that it can achieve 'socialism through the ANC'. For, within the ANC, the SACP has effectively 'operated as a collective opportunist waiting for concessions from the ANC and a social watchdog that makes a lot of noise when upset' (Satgar 2005: 41). Satgar further asserts that it is pointless building a mass-based movement without harnessing it to seize state power and, in the absence of the latter, the party will not be able to attain its socialist objective. As a mere organ of civil society outside of the state, the party, Satgar adds, reduces itself to 'a lobbyist for reforms or a pressure group' (Satgar 2005: 42). Satgar is optimistic that the SACP not only has enough support to make a decent electoral showing, but can also raise enough financial resources from its membership to compete effectively.

The position of the (SACP) independents in Moutse should, therefore, be understood in the context of this debate. The candidates actually wanted to contest elections on the SACP platform, but were dissuaded by the national leadership and hence they opted to contest as independents. However, one senior official of the Young Communist League contends that even though the party was officially opposed to its members standing on an independent platform, it nonetheless discreetly supported their candidacy 'to test the waters' (interview 15.03.06). Nor will the party, according to Moutse's district organiser, Seun Mokgotsi, take a hard-line stance towards them, as the ANC has done with independents within its ranks. Mokgotsi maintains that they were reassured by the national leadership that they would not be expelled (interview 04.04.06). In an interview with a senior SACP official, Nkosipendule Kholisile, he reaffirmed that the party was unlikely to expel the Moutse leadership (interview 23.03.06).

Conclusion

The lenient manner in which the SACP leadership appears to be dealing with its members who defied instructions and contested the election as independents suggests an openness within the party towards an independent route. It is not certain that it will eventually turn out that way, as there is an equally strong opposing view within the party against taking this direction. What is most likely to sway the debate is the relationship with, and the ideological orientation of, the ruling party. If the SACP feels less excluded from the decision-making process and sees a shift more towards the left in government policies, this may strengthen the argument that the party can achieve more from within than outside the alliance. If the ANC takes the opposite route, it will strengthen the argument for an independent party.

Lekgetho's re-election in 2006 suggests that the black electorate is open to political choices from outside of the ruling party. Lekgetho won because he had a history of community activism, a strong local base and his campaign was anchored on specific local issues relevant to the lives of the voters. And, though the SACP shares a similar ideological leaning with the OKM, it does not mean it will suffer a similar fate if it were to contest elections independently. Unlike the OKM, the SACP has formidable political credentials owing to its long history of involvement in liberation politics. The party also has long-standing ties to the trade union movement, which may secure it a much more favourable response from workers than the OKM was able to. A left-leaning party, therefore, with a profile and a history such as the one enjoyed by the SACP, may still perform far better than the OKM at the polls.

But, that the SACP is considering a split from the ANC reflects more than just mere ideological differences. It also stems from discontentment with what they have experienced, despite frequent references to collective leadership, as a unilateral style of leadership, particularly by the ANC presidency. And the local protests led by ANC leaders over the redrawing of municipal boundaries, and the subsequent boycotting of the 2006 poll in Khutsong, show that the SACP is not just being singled out for exclusion by the ANC leadership. This experience extends even to the local membership and leadership of the organisation. It is thus a reflection of the top-down leadership style that is pervasive not only within the alliance, but also within the organisation itself and in Parliament. However, the local protests and the overturning of the leadership's decision to suspend Jacob Zuma as deputy president, at the ANC 2005 National General Council, illustrate that the membership is seeking to reverse the concentration of power away from the leadership back to its membership. And, given that a different leadership style has now been advanced as a prerequisite in whoever is elected to succeed President Mbeki, the ANC membership may just succeed in redefining leadership within the organisation.

Note

1   Available at <http://www.newsnet/upload research>. Accessed on 27 July 2005.

References

Gauteng Legislature (2005a) *Portfolio Committee on Local Government, negotiating mandate on Constitution Twelfth Amendment Bill [B33b-2005]*. Johannesburg: Gauteng Legislature.

Gauteng Legislature (2005b) *Portfolio Committee on Local Government, final voting mandate on Constitution Twelfth Amendment Bill [B33b-2005]*. Johannesburg: Gauteng Legislature.

Habib A (2003) State-civil society relations in post-apartheid South Africa. Paper delivered at the Anthropology and Development Studies Seminar, University of Natal, 10 October.

Habib A & Schulz-Herzenberg C (2005) Accountability and democracy: Is the ruling elite responsive to the citizenry. In R Calland & P Graham *Democracy in the time of Mbeki*. Cape Town: Institute for Democracy South Africa.

Haffajee F (2004) The state of the media ten years into democracy. Paper delivered at the Harold Wolpe Lecture Series, Centre For Civil Society, University of Natal, 27 May.

HSRC (Human Sciences Research Council) (2006) *Survey on South African voter participation. A study commissioned by the Independent Electoral Commission*. Available at <http://www.elections.org.za/papers/237/ 2006%20HSRC%20Final%20Report%20Summary%20on%20Voter%20Participation.doc>

Lawson L (1991) The ghetto and the greenbelt. In J Cock & E Koch (Eds) *Going green: People, politics and the environment in South Africa*. Cape Town: Oxford University Press.

Learn and Teach (n.d.) *For our children's children: NEAC Project Nature.* Johannesburg: Learn and Teach.

Lodge T (1999) *South African politics since 1994.* Cape Town: David Phillip.

Ngwane T (2003) Sparks in the township. *New Left Review,* 22: 37–56.

SACP (South African Communist Party) (2005) Should the Party Contest Elections in own Right? *The African Communist,* 168: 31–33.

Satgar V (2005) Has the ANC failed? The South African Communist Party and the struggle for socialist democracy in South Africa. *The African Communist,* 168: 38–46.

Interviews

Nkosipendule Kholisile, senior SACP official, Gauteng, 23.03.06.

Japhta Moswang Lekgetho, independent candidate, Soweto, 23.03.06

Seun Mokgotsi, Moutse's district organiser, 04.04.06.

Sisi Mtungwa, from leadership of Operation Khanyisa Movement, Soweto, 18.03.06

Trevor Ngwane, leader of Operation Khanyisa Movement, Soweto, 18.03.06

Mandla Nkomfe, Deputy Secretary of the ANC in Gauteng, Soweto,17.03.06.

Senior official of the Young Communist League, Gauteng, 15.03.06.

5 A silent revolution: South African voters, 1994–2006

Collette Schulz-Herzenberg

Since the onset of democracy in 1994, South Africa's elections have returned similar levels of support for the major political parties. The static nature of electoral outcomes has arisen out of the politicisation of numerically imbalanced, stable social cleavages. This has 'racialised' the nature of voting results and resulted in the continued electoral dominance of the African National Congress (ANC) over weak and fragmented opposition parties, raising concerns that genuine multiparty competition is limited and that potential for the alternation of power through the ballot box is substantially diminished. However, aggregate electoral stability does not necessarily shed light on the complexities that affect party support and voting intentions, nor does it tell us much about the increasing impact of socio-economic change on long-standing cleavages or electoral behaviours. Although party loyalties seldom shift abruptly, it would seem that partisanship in South Africa has fluctuated considerably more than is usually acknowledged.

Changes to partisan support and voter motivations are signals of electoral fluidity in the party system that may have gone undetected because of the focus on aggregate electoral results. Alternatively, it may be that South Africa is on the cusp of an increasingly fluid party system. Either way, a 'silent revolution' among voters impacts on the quality and consolidation of South African democracy.

De-alignment, or weakening partisan ties, holds contrary implications for democracy. Firstly, the stabilising influence of partisanship on party alignments is diminished. This should benefit South Africa, which requires greater electoral volatility to ensure a more competitive democracy, by freeing more voters to shift their party support to other contenders. Volatility also increases the unpredictability of elections and uncertainty of their outcomes, which, in turn, encourages parties and candidates to be more responsive to voter interests. Against this, the weakening of party bonds can have negative consequences for the political process in the form of stagnation among voters, this typified by an increasing number declining to cast their ballots for any party whatsoever. Larger percentages of the vote for a governing party, from a decreasing number of voters as turnout decreases, indicate a decline in the quality of democracy.

This chapter looks at trends and patterns in partisanship over time.[1] Data from eight national public opinion surveys spanning 1994–2004 explore changes to the demographic support bases of parties and the motivations of South African voters.[2] Finally, the results of the 2006 municipal elections are compared to overall trends in party support.

An electorate in transformation

Voter behaviour is shaped by social and economic conditions. Rapid socio-economic and political transformation can therefore alter long-standing or 'frozen' cleavage structures that often guide electoral behaviour.

The South African electorate has been subject to enormous change. First, the demographics of the electorate are vastly different to that of 1994. Generational change has dramatically altered the age composition of the population with an increasing proportion of youth voters aged between 18 and 30. Approximately one-third of the potential electorate in 2004 had been too young to vote in 1994 (Seekings 2005a: 24). Demographic population shifts and growth have also altered the regional and racial composition of the electorate, with the urban and African share rising.

Second, socio-economic patterns have shifted. The emergence of a new black middle class due, in part, to redistributive policies and anti-discrimination measures, has begun to address income inequality between race groups. In 1995, 73 per cent of the individuals in the top decile (the richest 10 per cent) were white, but by 2000 there were as many African households in the top income quintile (20%) as there were white households (Seekings 2005a: 24). Long-term trends point to a substantial growth in the distribution of national income accruing to Africans, with its share increasing from 19.8 per cent in 1970 to 35.7 per cent in 1996 (Southall 2004: 531). Southall also observes that by 2004 around 27 per cent of formally employed Africans can be broadly defined as 'middle class'.

In contrast, stubborn structural constraints on job-creating economic growth, persistent and high levels of unemployment, poverty and inequality, plus the inaccessibility of the formal economy for particularly the unskilled combine to widen the inequality gap between the rich and the poor, as well as between workers within the formal sector of the economy and those who struggle to make a living outside it. The country's Gini co-efficient rose from 0.73 per cent in 1995 to 0.80 in 1998 (Southall 2004: 531). While interracial inequality has declined, intra-racial inequality is on the increase – among Africans the Gini co-efficient rose from 0.70 to 0.81 between 1995 and 1998 (Southall 2004: 531). Changing material conditions have encouraged a shift from race to class as the basis of inequality, and led to a shift in self-defined social identities away from race towards class and occupations (Lombard 2003).

A fundamental shift in social delivery and budgetary spending ensures social spending is heavily focused on the poor. Nonetheless, despite the extension of social welfare and redistribution, the post-apartheid state has shown limited capacity to rapidly address poverty and inequality . The rise of social movements connected to delivery issues is also indicative of an emerging class consciousness among the poor (Ballard et al. 2006). Moreover, other societal developments – such as the HIV/AIDS pandemic, increasing educational opportunities and access to media and information – have made a major impact on many people's lives.

After what is now over a decade of democracy, the focus of politics in South Africa has shifted from the realisation of 'liberation' towards urgent concerns such as social redress and nation building facing a post-apartheid society. South African citizens confront and debate issues that represent a more 'normalised' political terrain, such as housing, education and budgetary matters, and directly experience the outcomes of policy choices, and the political successes and failures of an ANC-led government.

By 2004 the electorate differed substantially from the one that had participated in the 1994 elections in terms of generational experiences and expectations, historical memory, class mobility, poverty levels, education, and political information. Such rapid social transformation might be expected to hold consequences for voting patterns by reshaping the static cleavage structures inherited from apartheid, yet dramatic socio-economic changes do not seem to have impacted heavily on the social composition of the ANC's support base. Instead, the strongest suggestion of electoral volatility lies in diminishing party loyalties for all parties and the corresponding growth of a 'floating' or an independent electorate.

Looking beneath aggregate electoral outcomes

At first glance, voting patterns in South Africa appear fairly stable at the macro level. Table 5.1 presents aggregate election results over three national elections, showing similar outcomes with consistent proportions of votes obtained by the governing party and opposition parties respectively.

However, when turnout figures and the percentage of all eligible voters supporting the ANC across the three national elections since the 1994 elections are considered,

Table 5.1 *Aggregate electoral results, 1994–2004*

	1994 (%)	1999 (%)	2004 (%)
ANC	63.12	66.35	69.69
Opposition parties*	36.88	33.65	30.31
Total	100.00	100.00	100.00

Source: Compiled from IEC data, available at <http://www.election.org.za>
Note: * The principal opposition parties during these elections were: the National Party (to become the New National Party and was not an opposition party at the time of the 1994 election as it constituted part of the Government of National Unity); the Democratic Party (to become the Democratic Alliance); the Inkatha Freedom Party; the Freedom Front Plus; the Pan Africanist Congress; the United Democratic Movement (from 1999 election onwards) and a number of smaller parties.

Table **5.2** *Registration, turnout and percentage of voting age population voting for governing party and opposition*

	1994*	1999	2004
VAP	22 709 152	22 589 369	27 865 537
Number of registered voters	No registration	18 172 751	20 674 926
VAP registered (%)	No registration	80.4	75.4
Overall turnout/total votes cast	19 533 498	15 977 142	15 612 671
Turnout of registered voters (%)	No registration	89.3	76.7
Turnout of VAP (%)	86	71.8	57.8
% of VAP vote for ANC**	53.8	46.9	39
% of VAP vote for opposition parties	32.1	23.7	16.9
% of VAP abstaining	14	29.4	43.9

Sources: Reynolds 1999; Piombo & Nijzink 2005; IEC election data, available at <http://www.election.org.za>
Notes: * In 1994 there was no formal registration and hence no voters' roll. To vote in the 1994 elections citizens simply had to present their identity document.
** Calculated using total votes for ANC/total VAP

they suggest that several major changes have occurred in the last ten years, particularly in terms of the size of the active ANC electorate (see Table 5.2).

South Africa has witnessed a general decline in electoral participation in terms of both registration and voter turnout. First, whilst the eligible voting age population (VAP) has increased (due to population growth) by approximately five million over ten years, the number of registered voters has not increased at the same rate. Between 1999 and 2004 the Independent Electoral Commission increased the voters' roll by 2.5 million to 20.6 million voters. Yet, according to VAP figures, 7 million potential voters were not recorded (Kabemba 2005: 95). Second, the number of votes cast (or overall turnout) has actually decreased by roughly 3.9 million since 1994 *despite* growth in VAP and increases in registration.

Third, despite increasing electoral margins for the ANC from 63 per cent to 69 per cent, the percentage of the VAP voting for the governing party has not increased or even remained static in proportion to population growth. In fact, its percentage of actual support has *decreased* from 53 to 39 per cent of South Africa's eligible voting population. By calculating the proportion of the VAP who voted for the ANC (calculated using total votes for ANC/total VAP), we can see that the ANC has retained 72 per cent of its original 1994 vote share but lost approximately 28 per cent. Significant decreases in turnout and a reduced share of the vote qualify the nature of the ANC's victory in the 2004 national election. In a corresponding fashion, the opposition has lost one-half of its vote share among the eligible voter population. If the magnitude of the ANC's latest 2004 election victory shrinks under scrutiny, so do the gains of the opposition.

Data show increasing percentages of potential voters, and an increase in the number of registered voters since 1999, but the number casting a vote has declined.

Apparent aggregate electoral stability can conceal significant individual-level flux and disguise significant changes to internal party coalitions. Yet, it is harder to predict who the abstainers are, and whether they are government or opposition supporters. Moreover, aggregate data do not shed light on whether there is any significant voter realignment between parties, nor can it tell us about the intensity of commitment towards a party and the motivations or reasons for support.

Aggregate distributions of party identification

Using survey questions that measure the concept of party identification, this section taps macropartisan movements in the population over time. Party identification (PID) is widely used as an indicator of partisan loyalty and measures the extent to which voters 'identify with' or 'feel close to' political parties in much the same way that they identify with social groups. Partisanship questions are designed to measure the basis of party support among the mass electorate.

US and European studies show that PID is analytically separate from actual vote choice but often guides it (Campbell et al. 1960; Green et al. 2002). Despite criticisms that the concept's explanatory powers as a measurement variable are limited, particularly outside the US, recent studies show that the concept remains a significant methodological variable in electoral studies (Green et al. 2002). PID can still provide a common explanatory framework and be usefully applied across different political settings and therefore provides an appropriate starting point for any analysis of a partisan political preference. Consequently, numerous international surveys use the indicator to tap long-term commitment to parties with the concept applied successfully in post-Communist, Asian, African, and Brazilian studies. If the same holds true in South Africa then we should also be able to use the PID concept to assess the overall extent of partisan stability, volatility and de-alignment among voters.[3]

Levels of partisanship: partisans vs. non-partisans

After initially high levels of partisanship after the historic 1994 'liberation' election, the proportion of partisans in the electorate declines significantly thereafter, fluctuating between 64 per cent and 45 per cent over the following ten years (see Figure 5.1). Since 1995 no more than 64 per cent of the population have ever stated that they feel close to a political party. Decreases in partisanship are accompanied by corresponding increases in the proportion of non-partisans or 'independents'. By the end of 2004 the percentages of partisans and independents were almost equal in number, with partisans at only 53 per cent. Ten years into democracy almost half the electorate were not overly loyal to one particular political party, nor guided at elections by long-standing partisan ties when deciding which party to support, suggesting that short-term forces are potential influences on party support.

Figure 5.1 *Partisans vs. non partisans among South African voters, 1994–2004*

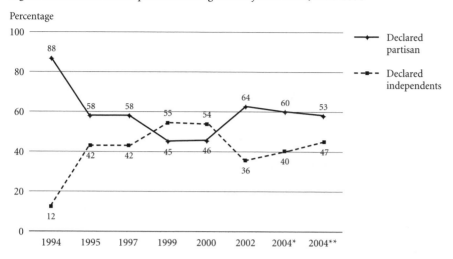

Source: * Figures from Afrobarometer 2004 survey. ** Figures from CNEP 2004 survey. For more information see the appendix to this chapter.

South Africa matches European figures more closely than other emerging democracies. In most western European countries, 60–70 per cent of voters identify at least somewhat with a party, though this figure has declined in recent decades. In Latin America party identification was 67.1 per cent in Uruguay, 37.6 per cent in Argentina, 35.9 per cent in Chile, 33.3 per cent in Venezuela, and 32.5 per cent in Brazil (Mainwaring 1999: 30). Only 22 per cent of the Russian electorate identifies with a party, while 40 per cent does so in the Czech Republic, 30 per cent in Slovakia, 20 per cent in Hungary and only 15 per cent in Poland (White et al. 1997: 135).

Direction of partisanship: ANC vs. independents vs. opposition

Self-declared partisans can be further divided into those who support the ANC and those who support opposition parties. Figure 5.2 shows the ratios of ANC supporters, opposition supporters (includes all opposition parties) and independents across the electorate over time. Although the vast majority of declared partisans are ANC supporters there are several developments.

First, PID seems to be weakening for all parties. Both the ANC and opposition parties have leaked partisans to the independents category, which has increased dramatically over time. Yet independents are disproportionately coming from the opposition parties, which have experienced a much higher rate of decline than the ANC. This development can be best described as 'asymmetrical partisan de-alignment', as people move away from feeling close to a particular party but more so from the opposition. Unable to maintain their proportional share of partisans, opposition parties have been the biggest losers. That opposition parties have proliferated and fragmented since 1994, together with the fact that they share an increasingly smaller portion of partisans, suggests that they have to work harder to convince voters to support them at elections.

Second, non-partisans now make up a remarkable proportion of the eligible electorate (defined here as surveyed citizens who are eligible to vote), fluctuating between 36 per cent and 56 per cent. The high number of floating voters whose support is in doubt at the beginning of an election suggests that there is a higher than expected potential for electoral competition or movement in support across political parties.

Figure 5.2 *Direction of partisanship among South African voters, 1994–2004*

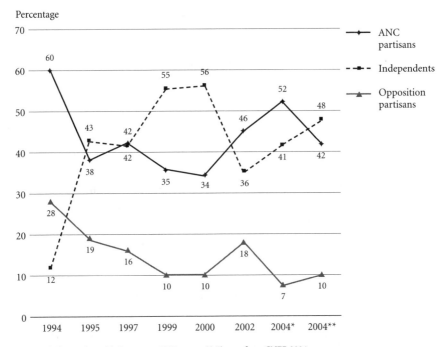

Sources: * Figures from Afrobarometer 2004 survey. ** Figures from CNEP 2004 survey.
Note: For more information see the appendix to this chapter.

Lastly, on average less than half the electorate are ANC partisans. In 1994, 60 per cent of the electorate were ANC partisans, but this figure has since fluctuated between 34 and 52 per cent of the total electorate.

The partisan responses of social groups

Despite general consensus that the African population continues to identify with the ANC while minority groups identify more with opposition parties, limited empirical knowledge exists about the demographics of supporters and non-voters. I analyse the partisan responses of key demographic groups to detect changes in the social composition of party support bases. The strength of partisanship among social groups also informs us as to whether today's ANC partisans are as loyal as they once were.

Race groups

Black African voters are consistently more likely to identify with a party than are minority race groups (see Figure 5.3).[4] Yet on average only 65 per cent of black voters are close to a particular party, whereas up to 49 per cent have declared themselves to be independents in some years. Subtle changes to the strength of support given to the ANC by black Africans are also noticeable. The proportion of party identifiers who are 'very close' to the party has increased while those who feel 'somewhat' or 'not very close' have steadily decreased. This makes sense when one considers that de-alignment is most likely to occur first among the weakest partisans. Black voters are not an enthusiastic, unquestionably loyal electorate, as is often assumed. Levels of ANC partisanship among black South Africans have fluctuated between 62 per cent and 42 per cent, decreasing steadily since 1994, but have not been counterbalanced by shifts to opposition parties. Instead there is a significant increase in independents among this racial group, suggesting that core ANC support is smaller than initially supposed and many voters support this party, not because they are loyal partisans, but because they do not regard opposition parties as feasible alternatives.

Levels of partisanship among white South Africans have fluctuated between 16 per cent and 41 per cent, decreasing dramatically since 1994. Correspondingly, the increase in independents is significant. Support for the governing party remains negligible. Among coloured South Africans we see a mixed trend emerging. Support for opposition parties has declined steadily over time, due possibly to the demise of the New National Party (the formerly ruling party which merged itself into the ANC in 2005), offset somewhat by the growth in support for the Democratic Alliance (DA) among this racial group, while support for the ANC has also increased. Overall, there are more independents than partisans among coloured people since 1995. Indians reflect similar trends to that of other minority racial groups although de-alignment has been remarkably rapid. Support for both the ANC and opposition parties is consistently low. The proportion of independents among Indians is the highest out of all racial groups and fluctuates between 57 per cent and 96 per cent.

While racial minority voters may still participate at elections the data imply that opposition parties have to actively campaign to mobilise the support of these voters compared to the ANC, which still attracts a relatively higher proportion of partisans among black South Africans (see Figure 5.3). While higher ratios of inde-

Figure 5.3 *Partisans by racial group*

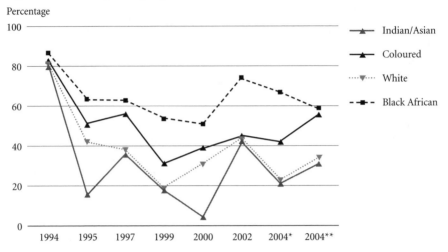

Sources: * Figures from Afrobarometer 2004 survey. ** Figures from CNEP 2004 survey.
Note: For more information see the appendix to this chapter.

pendents exist among smaller racial groups, a smaller proportion of independents among black Africans can still amount to more independents numerically compared to the total of independents coming from minority groups. Given the demographic composition of South Africa, continuing increases in non-partisans among the black electorate hold the key to future electoral realignments.

Figure 5.4 *Partisanship by urban vs. rural voters*

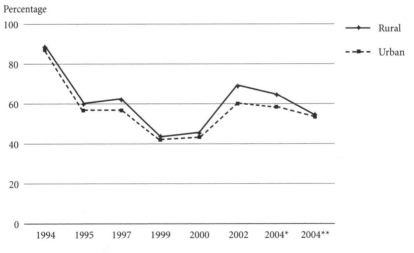

Sources: * Figures from Afrobarometer 2004 survey. ** Figures from CNEP 2004 survey.
Note: For more information see the appendix to this chapter.

Urban vs. rural residents

Trends in data confirm the overall decline in PID among urban and rural voters.[5] However, data also indicate that there are consistently fewer partisans and more independents among urban residents. In some years independents make up a majority of the urban electorate. In contrast, rural areas consistently have more partisans. Yet by the end of 2004 the level of rural partisanship had dropped to urban levels (53%) (see Figure 5.4).

There is a consistently higher ratio of ANC supporters among rural compared to urban partisans and, when testing for strength of party identification, there are consistently more strong ANC partisans among rural residents than urban residents. Overall, rural areas offer more loyal ANC identifiers compared to their urban counterparts. Opposition partisans among urban and rural residents are in steady decline over the years, with only a slightly higher proportion in urban areas. Opposition party identifiers are mainly urban dwellers.

Age cohorts

Four age cohorts were designed to loosely reflect or capture four different political generations and to provide a simple way to measure whether different age groups

Figure 5.5 *Partisanship among South African voters by age group*

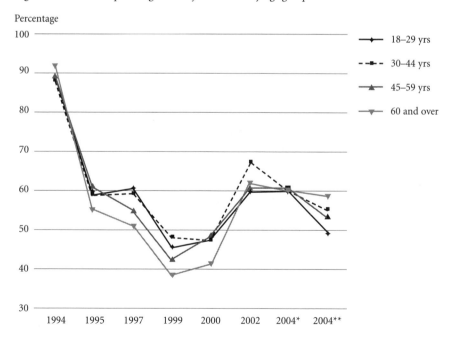

Sources: * Figures from Afrobarometer 2004 survey. ** Figures from CNEP 2004 survey.
Note: For more information see the appendix to this chapter.

or generations affect partisanship (see Figure 5.5). In 1994, the 18–29-year-olds had reached the age of 16 years between 1981 and 1992 and are the 1980s' generation. The 30–44-year-old cohort in 1994 had reached the age of 16 between 1966 and 1980; they therefore comprised the cohort that experienced the 1976 youth uprisings. The 45–59-year-old cohort in 1994 had reached the age of 16 years between 1951 and 1965 and constituted the pre-Soweto generation that witnessed the rise and incarceration of Nelson Mandela. Anyone aged 60 or over in 1994 had turned 16 in or before 1950. Finally, a post-apartheid generation who have little direct early-adult experience of apartheid enters the electorate around the year 2000.

While a sharper decline in partisanship among younger cohorts might have been expected, data show little variation between cohorts with no remarkable patterns or trends. Trends among ANC partisans also show little variation. It appears that the growth in independents and the corresponding decline in ANC partisanship have little to do with voters' age groups. In fact, the youngest cohorts have the highest proportion of ANC partisans. Yet, rapid population growth among the youngest cohort also suggests that this group will have a higher *number* of independents compared to older groups. The impact of the post-apartheid generation is only likely to be detected after 2000, which is somewhat confirmed by the decline in partisanship among the 18–29-year-olds, and in 2004, when older cohorts also show the highest number of loyal partisans who feel 'very close' to a party. Does this reflect the beginning of a new post-apartheid age cohort entering the electorate with less partisan attachments? This can only be confirmed in time. Young voters also show less support for opposition parties compared to their older counterparts, a possible indicator of the increasing stagnation of opposition parties if they are unable to mobilise the pool of growing young 'independents' in coming years.

Class

While few surveys have a variable measuring class specifically, they all tap class through questions that ask respondents about their occupation and working status.[6] Defining the notion of class in an industrialising and post-colonial setting such as South Africa is problematic (Southall 2004). In particular, when one uses occupational categories to determine class categories, results must be interpreted cautiously. Nevertheless, for parsimonious reasons and because these questions, and not items tapping income, appear in every survey, responses were divided into four main categories using occupational and employment data (see Figure 5.6). The owner/employer category includes people who own businesses or employ people, the self-employed, managing directors and commercial farmers. This constitutes what Dalton (1998) has called the 'old middle class', or in Marxist terms, those who own the means of production. The professional/supervisory category includes office supervisors, industrial foremen, and professionals (lawyers, engineers, doctors). According to Dalton this constitutes the 'new middle class' since these people live middle-class lifestyles but do not own the means of production. The worker

Figure 5.6 *Partisanship among South African voters by class group*

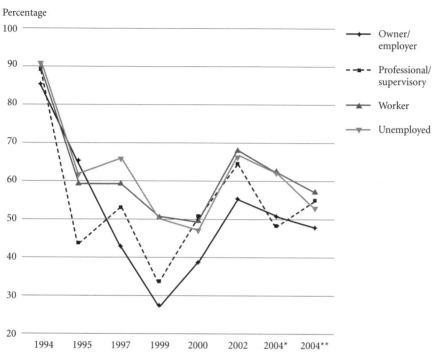

Sources: * Figures from Afrobarometer 2004 survey. ** Figures from CNEP 2004 survey.
Note: For more information see the appendix to this chapter.

category includes non-manual and manual, skilled and unskilled workers, soldiers, police, other security workers and subsistence farmers. The final category includes those who are unemployed, never had a job or have not worked long enough to consider themselves as workers. Housewives, students and the disabled are excluded from the above categories as it is unclear into which economic class they fit (especially when cross-tabulated with secondary variables such as income).

Middle-class respondents within the 'old' and 'new' middle classes evinced a steady decline in partisans until 1999 and a steady rise thereafter. Similarly, respondents from the working class and those who were unemployed also showed an overall decline in partisanship but there are consistently more partisans in the latter categories. By 2002 partisanship among all class groups had stabilised, rising slightly and clustered between 55 per cent and 68 per cent. By 2004, the working class had the highest level of partisans, replacing the unemployed who began to show slight signs of decline by 2004. Subtle changes may present the beginnings of a newly emerging pattern among classes, where the unemployed slowly withdraw support from parties in general, while the wealthier middle classes increase their partisanship.

After 1994, ANC partisanship droped dramatically among the owner/employer category whilst the proportion of independents increased steadily. Opposition partisans showed slight decreases until 2002 after which they decreased sharply. By 1999, however, the number of ANC partisans in the owner/employer category began to rise steadily, overtaking opposition partisans by 2002, while independents began to stabilise. The data may reflect the emergence of the new black African middle class, whose support for the ANC began to dominate this social category by the year 2000. Where control over the means of production lay firmly with middle-class white people in the early years after the end of apartheid, by 2000 the African middle-class share had increased, thereby changing the proportion of ANC partisans in this category. ANC partisans slowly came to supplant the older white middle class, whose partisanship had steadily declined since 1995.

The direction of partisanship in the professional/supervisory category was reversed by the end of 2004. Whereas opposition partisans made up 70 per cent of this category in 1994, while the ANC only enjoyed 21 per cent support, by 2004, 34 per cent of partisans were ANC supporters while only 19 per cent were opposition supporters. Again, this is reflective of the rise of a new professional black middle class whose aspirations have been met and, as a social class, they respond with higher levels of party support for the ANC. A dramatic decline in opposition partisans is reflected in a steady rise of independents in this category. By the end of 2004, 47 per cent are independents.

Changes to the middle-class categories do not exemplify a situation of changing partisan minds but rather of changing partisan groups. In other words, middle-class voters have not necessarily changed their partisan opinions – instead, fluctuations are more likely due to the introduction of a new set of partisan minds as the overall racial composition of this social group readjusts.

Among workers, ANC partisans remain steadfast over time, but never constitute more than half the electorate in any year (see Figure 5.7). Opposition partisans among workers are low and decline from 28 per cent in 1994 to 10 per cent in 2004. Independents rise steadily over the years, only declining slightly between 2000 and 2002, but rising again thereafter. In the unemployed category, the pattern is largely the same. If we look at ANC partisans across social groups, ANC partisans are highest among the unemployed and then workers, whose trends largely mirror each other. Yet these two categories show decreases in support over time. In contrast, the two middle-class categories show clear increases in support for the ANC, especially among owner/employers at the end of the time span. Variations may also be reflective of emerging tensions between black capitalists and the civil petty bourgeoisie versus the working class and unemployed as former groups become less inclined to remain their traditional political allies (Southall 2004).

Data permitting, it may be interesting to look more closely at variations to partisanship *within* the (new) black middle class. As Southall (2004) states, various factions of the black middle class have shared the benefits of economic growth and transformation differentially. In particular, the relative economic advantage of 'state managers', corporate factions of the black middle class, along with the more

Figure 5.7 *ANC partisans among South African voters across class groups*

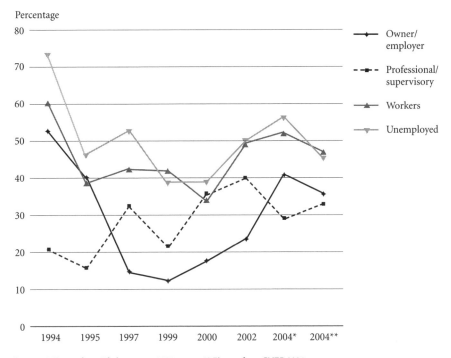

Sources: * Figures from Afrobarometer 2004 survey. ** Figures from CNEP 2004 survey.
Note: For more information see the appendix to this chapter.

advantaged sections of the civil petty bourgeoisie, suggests the possibility that partisanship is stronger among these groups compared to the black trading petty-bourgeoisie or 'traders', although a dependence of the latter upon procurement might mean that they are even more strongly partisan.

The impact of class on voting has been more regionalised and more pronounced among minority groups. In the Western Cape, working-class coloured voters tended to support the New national party (NNP) (before its demise) and the DA, whilst middle-class coloured voters were divided, with many supporting the ANC (Seekings 2005b). Habib and Naidu (1999) also concluded that class played a role in Indian areas in KwaZulu-Natal.

So far, analyses focus on fluctuations and variations in levels and direction of party identification within social groups. However, an important part of this exercise is to investigate which social groups have the highest proportions of ANC or opposition identifiers and independents (see Tables 5.3 and 5.4). After comparing the median averages of all social groups, the social or demographic groups with the most ANC partisans are black Africans, the unemployed, rural dwellers, and workers.

Table 5.3 *ANC identifiers in each social group, by percentage*

Social group	Percentage
Whites	1
Indians	11
Coloureds	24
Professional/ supervisory	29
Owner/employer	30
60+ years	36
Urban residents	39
45–59-year-olds	41
30–44-year-olds	44
18–29-year-olds	46
Workers	46
Rural residents	50
Unemployed	50
Black African	56

Table 5.4 *Opposition identifiers in each social group, by percentage*

Social group	Percentage
Black African	9
Unemployed	10
18–29-year-olds	12
Rural residents	12
30–44-year-olds	15
Workers	15
Urban residents	17
45–59-year-olds	18
Indians	19
60+ years	20
Owner/employer	21
Professional/supervisory	25
Coloureds	26
Whites	37

The most likely social groups to provide opposition partisans are white and coloured people, middle-class and older voters. However, by looking at Tables 5.3 and 5.4 it is clear that the highest averages among opposition identifiers are much smaller compared to averages of ANC partisans found in other social groups. Opposition partisans only make up an average of 26 per cent in the white racial group, the group with the most opposition partisans, compared to 56 per cent of ANC identifiers among black Africans. Racial groups always hold the most partisans.

Table 5.5 *Independents in each social group, by percentage*

Social group	Percentage
Black African	36
Rural residents	38
Unemployed	40
Workers	40
30–44-year-olds	41
45–59-year-olds	42
18–29-year-olds	43
60+ years	44
Urban residents	44
Professional/supervisory	47
Owner/employer	49
Coloureds	50
Whites	62
Indians	70

Black Africans have the least independents of all social groups followed by rural dwellers, the unemployed and workers (see Table 5.5). Minority racial groups have the most independents, followed by middle-class urban voters.

Overall, the data show that the number of voters who feel close to a particular party has declined significantly since 1994. Less than half the electorate are ANC partisans while, on average, almost half are not guided by long-standing party ties at elections. While both the ANC and opposition parties have experienced losses to their long-standing support bases, the latter have lost more. PID has also fallen relatively evenly across social groups, with the greatest losses experienced among minority racial groups. The relatively even pattern of de-alignment across all social groups meant that the key cleavage structures that defined party support in 1994 were much the same in 2004.

Perhaps the most interesting finding is that there is little if no shift of allegiance across party lines by racial and other social groups. Rather than voters moving their support to another political party, partisanship has simply declined. Yet partisan de-alignment, coupled with a higher potential for inter-party movement, also suggests that static cleavage structures inherited from 1994 do not determine voting behaviour. Instead, voters appear to make reasoned judgements when choosing which party to support.

The micro-motivations of voters

People generally choose political parties in response to a number of factors. Scholars argue that although party identification may be learned through early family socialisation, it is also a running tally of current party assessment or a 'standing decision' that is constantly updated through evolving evaluations of government performance, party images, and cognitive skills (Achen 1992; Fiorina 1979; Inglehart 1977; Popkin 1991). Recent analyses confirm that long-standing party loyalties do not prevent partisans from updating their evaluations in light of new information (Green et al. 2002). Short-term changes to PID can and do occur. If this is also true in South Africa, then we can expect to see similar short-term factors influencing PID. Accelerated socio-economic transformation has changed the social structure of South African society, potentially affecting factors that shape political behaviour. If a person's position in the social structure is changing, the kinds of partisan cues that emanate from social positioning may be changing. Besides, people's value systems are not simply robotic reflections of the social structure; as people acquire new information and skills their experiences and evaluations also matter. Adjustments therefore involve changes to the way people evaluate economic and political governance, levels of cognitive skills, and the type of information available.

Evaluations of government performance

The literature suggests voters judge which party is best suited to govern by looking at evaluations of their past performance and future promises (Downs 1957; Fiorina 1979). Voters then use economic and political performance evaluations to reward or punish government for their material improvements or economic decline.

Taking into account increasing unemployment, job losses, HIV/AIDS and poor service delivery, one might expect a significant decline in ANC support. While there is a decline in PID and turnout for the ANC, the party continues to attract majority support at elections. Why? Firstly, as shown earlier, votes for opposition parties have fallen faster than votes for the ANC. However, support for the ANC can be accounted for by the positive ratings of its performance in government. As voters evaluate the ANC government, they do so by also looking at the massive relative improvements in their lives. Government's redistribution policies have offset much of the negative economic development of the past decade and partly account for high levels of electoral support. The majority of voters also perceive that their future socio-economic interests can be best achieved by an ANC government.

Data from the Opinion '99 survey (see the appendix to this chapter) show that South African voters do not automatically form opinions about the national economy from their personal conditions. Second, voters make distinctions between overall government performance and performance within specific issues areas (Mattes & Piombo 2001). Voters praise government on areas where they have experienced profound social change such as the provision of essential services, housing and education. Correspondingly, they criticise government on the very issues that they see as the country's most pressing problems such as crime and unemployment, as seen in the downward trend in public opinion on these issues since 1994 (Mattes 2005). Yet, when asked for an overall assessment of government performance, voters give generally positive remarks. Overall positive evaluations are therefore informed by a balanced assessment of specific policy areas. When Mattes, Taylor and Africa (1999) tested the influence of attitudinal evaluations of government performance and political parties, whilst deliberately excluding race and other sociological variables, they found that a very large majority of partisan choices can be correctly predicted.

While these voters do not make up their minds anew at every election, the data do suggest that new information about political and economic developments combines with partisan loyalties. So although voters take their socio-economic positions into account, the electoral consequences of poverty and unemployment are offset by successful redistributive social policies. The poor do not seem to hold government directly responsible for their financial situations and partisan loyalties are able to withstand short-term disappointments. For those whose loyalties are shifting through poor evaluations of economic performance, the data suggest that they simply move into the non-electorate. Table 5.6 compares the evaluations of identifiers with non-partisans among black Africans, a social group who were generally pro-ANC during 2000. Black African identifiers consistently have higher proportions of positive evaluations of government performance than their non-partisan counterparts.

Cognitive mobilisation

There is convincing evidence from post-world war western Europe and the United States to suggest that voter evaluations of political parties depend largely on access to and the use of political information (Dalton 1988; Inglehart 1977). As socio-economic development occurs, the expansion of education produces a more sophisticated public by increasing voters' political skills, while the availability of

Table 5.6 *Government performance evaluations: identifiers vs. non-identifiers among black Africans by percentage, 2000*

Economic evaluations	Identifiers	Non-partisans
Are you satisfied or dissatisfied with economic conditions in SA?		
Dissatisfied/very dissatisfied	60	69
Satisfied/very satisfied	19	14
How do economic conditions compare to one year ago?		
Much worse/worse	49	59
Better/much better	19	16
Overall direction of the country?		
Going in the right direction	49	34
Gong in the wrong direction	42	55

political information broadens resources and reduces the cost of acquiring political information. Access to formal education and electronic news media, or 'cognitive mobilisation', has steadily reduced the effects of sociological factors such as class and religion on party identification. Voting is influenced by what people know as well as by who they are. Voters use available information to reason about political parties, candidates, and issues and connect information to government performance.

In South Africa it is reasonable to expect that the developmental changes described earlier do play a role in shaping the partisanship of different groups. Yet despite the relatively high levels of media use and formal education compared to other African countries, there is little evidence to suggest that access to news has increased since 1994 (Mattes 2005).

The use of news media and the level of formal education are indications of the amount of political information to which voters are exposed and the cognitive skills required to make use of that information. Yet they do not tell us whether citizens are more or less politically aware or engaged in the political process. Idasa and Afrobarometer surveys asked people about their interest in politics and the frequency with which they engage in political discussion (see appendix to this chapter). Since 1994, no more than one-twentieth frequently engages in discussion with family or friends and more than one-third stated that they never do. Only one-tenth frequently follows public affairs (Mattes 2005). Levels of political cognitive engagement are low among the South African electorate and a large percentage of voters remain relatively unengaged and uninformed about politics and policy issues.

Yet variations in the level of cognitive awareness among voters do play an indirect role in party identification. Depending on whether a voter is evaluating the governing party or opposition parties, cognitive awareness shapes voter evaluations differently. Voters with limited access to news media and education can still acquire information about the governing ANC party by assessing national performance from their personal situations. However, assessing opposition-party performance is a little more difficult due to a lack of performance track records. Voters do not possess sufficient performance-based information and therefore need to rely on alternative information sources to inform themselves about opposition parties. Party imagery or the racial credentials of political parties then become important influences on voters' views of how well parties represent them. However, different levels of cognitive skills moderate the influence of these racial or ethnic images. Voters with limited access to information and/or limited cognitive skills make greater use of information short cuts or identity cues such as race.

The influence of party images

When voters have little information they rely on 'information short cuts', often in the form of clues supplied by a candidate's dress, race and accent, which provide information as to the potential attitudes and performance of that party in government. Party images therefore act as an alternative source of voter information and are cues that help voters complete their assessments (Popkin 1991). They take on either positive or negative connotations for voters as people use them to judge, among other things, whether parties are exclusive or inclusive. Inclusivity shapes the credibility and trustworthiness of a party and reveals important information about whether it is representative of the voter's interests.

The role of race in South African elections is linked to the way voters perceive whose group interests particular parties represent. Afrobarometer data show that people generally see their own parties as inclusive of all South Africans. Voters are not overly preoccupied with affirming their racial identities through political parties at election time. Yet, significant numbers of voters are unsure about whether other opposition parties are inclusive or exclusive of them, or simply perceive opposition parties to be solely exclusive. The 1994 Idasa survey and its companion survey in 1999 asked a series of questions about the exclusivity of different parties, such as: 'Do you think that (Party X) looks after the interests of all in South Africa or after the interests of one group only?' Fewer than 5 per cent of black Africans viewed the ANC as an exclusive party, whereas white, coloured and Indian people largely saw it as representing only one group. Data also show that while non-partisan black African voters do not support the ANC, they often hold more negative views of opposition parties. As for the Democratic Party (the predecessor to the DA),[7] while white people did not see it as exclusive, black Africans did, particularly in 1999, and they generally identified the nature of the exclusion as racial.

Voters use the logic of exclusion rather than representation to judge where their interests lie: voters judge a party by who is excluded from it, not who is represented by it. The racial credentials of parties and evaluations of party images therefore appear to affect voting behaviour.

The influence of sociological factors

Voting is as much conditioned by who one is as by what one believes and, as seen above, the sociological context can act as an information source to inform voters about which party is likely to reflect their interests best.

Using Opinion '99 data, Mattes and Piombo (2001) show that voters from different race groups form different evaluations of the same criteria – leading them to conclude that race tends to shape what voters think, not the way they think about issues. Race therefore takes on an indirect or moderating effect on the voting decision by providing an important information cue about government performance and party images.

This has come about as a result of radical differences in living conditions across racial lines, which has led to relative homogeneity of economic and political interests within racial groups. Overlapping class and racial identities partly account for continuing racial polarisation of party politics. The resilience of race, and not class, in electoral politics is also aided by political rhetoric, transformatory legislation, redistributive policies, and patronage. While these are justifiable and necessary facets of a post-apartheid South Africa, they continue to affect voter perceptions by sending out racial cues that reinforce the belief that group and individual prospects correlate. The irony of the transition process lies in the extent to which apartheid identities are relied upon in efforts to bring about positive transformation. These cues act as useful directives to voters by helping them make a connection between their interests and electoral options.

Despite signs of a growing class salience these identities are not yet affecting electoral politics. The ANC has proved itself adept at building a cross-class support base thus disallowing class to eclipse race as the basis for political identities. The ANC's 'double class compromise', where business, the working classes and the poor have benefited in different ways, has paid electoral dividends (Seekings 2005a).

Afrobarometer data do not show any major divergences of opinion across racial groups about policy areas and also show that most South Africans are in agreement about the key challenges facing the country. Moreover, there are no substantial divergences on salient political and economic policy between political parties, which could account for racial explanations. Major parties do not necessarily offer the electorate a choice of contrasting ideological positions, with most manifestos in recent elections essentially calling for the strengthening of the formal economy through increased investment, improved delivery to the people in the form of jobs and a widening of the social security net. There may be differences between parties on how to realise various policies or on distributional issues but where differences do exist, they are subtle and to be found in the technical details, and it remains difficult to grasp how their impacts would differ across different groups.

After testing data, Seekings (2005b) found race to be a more powerful factor in explaining voting behaviour than other sociological or attitudinal variables on their own. But it was no more powerful than partisan identification or a combination of other sociological or attitudinal variables. As Seekings concluded, 'the most complete explanation of voting behaviour needs to include some of these other variables alongside race' (2005b: 18).

Towards an integrated model of voter behaviour

South African voters do not make up their minds anew at each election – to a large extent partisanship guides electoral outcomes. Yet survey data show that multiple factors drive PID as new information about political and economic developments combines with assessments of party images and cognitive skills.

Race is clearly an important factor in South African elections yet data show little evidence for theories that characterise voting as a racial census. If voting is an expression of racial identity, then voters should connect the party they are supporting with their identity group. However, data show that South Africans are not overwhelmingly preoccupied with affirming their racial identities through political parties at election time. The high number of independents across racial groups and the influence of evaluations on partisanship also suggest that voters do not use elections merely to register their communal ties or racial identities.

If this is true, how does one explain the appearance of racially aligned voting outcomes? Scientists are quick to remind us that correlation does not equal causation. As Christopher Achen explains, 'correlation between demographic factors and the vote do not explain the vote – they themselves need to be explained' (1992: 198). So how does race help our understanding of voting behaviour? The intersection of individual and group interests means that a group identity, like race, can act as an indirect information short cut for South African voters. Voter calculations aim for maximising electoral pay-offs, whilst reducing inherent costs that go with obtaining information to inform themselves about politics, by turning to available information sources that are sociological by nature. 'Race is not important because of the passions it inspires or tradition it embodies but because of the information it conveys' (Posner 2005: 104).

South African voters are not unlike voters found elsewhere. Green et al. (2002) found that partisanship in the United States is also guided by a sense of who belongs to various social and economic groups and voters' relationship to them. Voters compare their self-image to what they perceive as the social bases of parties and then conduct a matching process to find an appropriate fit between the two.

It seems likely that racial groups will remain important cues or information short cuts for partisan identities among South African voters for as long as these group stereotypes persist as salient identities in politics.

The 2006 municipal elections

Following a year of nationwide protests over poor service delivery, analysts expected the 2006 local elections to provide some indication of voter dissatisfaction with ANC incumbents at the local level where municipalities deliver basic services. Events over the previous year had clearly indicated that the electorate was willing to express its discontent at the slow pace of service delivery in some localities. Many citizens also believe that municipalities perform worse than national and provincial government. The results from the 2005 Human Sciences Research Council/IEC survey also indicated that the local sphere of government was viewed less favourably than were the provincial and national spheres of government (wa Kivilu et al. 2005). The election offered voters an opportunity to punish incumbents for delivery failures at local level. The potential for realignment was also deemed to be higher than usual. Voters were offered new political choices with a wider array of localised parties and grassroots organisations, such as the Operation Khanyisa Movement. The number of self-declared floating voters or independents prior to the elections was also significant. A Markinor survey done on 15 February 2006 recorded that 30 per cent of voters were undecided on the eve of the election – a potentially significant 'swing vote'.

Despite these uncertainties, the ANC marched to victory once again, increasing their percentage of the vote share in many municipalities. Opposition witnessed further fragmentation with the associated rise of smaller, localised parties in some areas. So how does one explain the increased dominance of the ANC at local level, and the concomitant stagnation of opposition party fortunes despite the indicated discontent over service delivery? Election results show continuity with earlier analyses. Asymmetrical de-alignment continues while changes in demographics and turnout continue to affect overall trends. Results also reaffirm that voter evaluations of government performance affect party support while party images continue to affect the way in which voters align themselves to parties.

Trends in turnout

Trends show consistently higher turnout at national and provincial elections than at municipal elections, which averages 48 per cent across all three municipal elections (see Table 5.7).

Table 5.7 *Comparison of turnout as percentage of registered voters*

Local elections	1995	2000	2006
	48.5	48.1	48.4
National elections	1994	1999	2004
	No registration	89.3	76.7

The national elections also have a turnout rate much higher than that of the local elections in the provinces and at local level. For example, provincial turnout at the 2006 local election in the Western Cape was 51 per cent versus 73 per cent in the 2004 national election. Whereas the City of Cape Town metropole achieved 86 per cent in 1999 and 73 per cent in the 2004 national elections, the turnout for the 2006 metropole was only 52 per cent. Turnout figures are consistent with many other democratic countries where the electorate seems to favour national and provincial elections over municipal or local elections (Wa Kivilu & Langtry 2005).

While turnout averaged 48 per cent of registered voters in 2006, when turnout is calculated using figures for all eligible voters (VAP), it is clear that a growing proportion and increasing numbers of voters chose not to vote. As Steven Friedman remarked, about a quarter of all eligible voters are not registered, which meant

Table 5.8 *Provincial turnout at local elections as percentage of registered voters*

Province	1995	2000	2006
Eastern Cape	55	56	57
Free State	53	49	47
Gauteng	49	43	42
KwaZulu-Natal	46	47	51
Limpopo	46	42	45
Mpumalanga	53	45	46
North West	45	45	46
Northern Cape	65	58	54
Western Cape	60	58	52

Source: IEC 2006

that, at best, only 50 per cent of three-quarters of all eligible voters went to the polls (or only two-fifths of the population voted) (*Business Day* 08.03.06).

Evaluations of government performance

Turnout figures are instructive when it is considered that they may represent an indirect method of lodging dissatisfaction with government performance. Many voters punished incumbents (and challengers) by not voting at all. Abstentions do not necessarily signal voter apathy, since citizens also withdraw their temporary support from politics to show their discontent over the lack of service delivery.

Local protests also suggest that voters are inclined to hold government to account between elections, not just at elections. Moreover, while voters may feel strongly that government has failed them on specific areas of delivery, many believe that the ANC has done a good job overall. Positive national performance ratings almost certainly worked favourably for the ANC's local government election campaign strategy, which emphasised government's success at the national level, through the use of billboards promoting its achievements in positive economic growth, the 'feel-good factor' in the country and the use of President Mbeki as the focal point. Mbeki also elevated developmental issues in his 'State of the Nation' speech in a local election year while offering honest appraisal of failures at local level with the campaign slogan 'Make Local Government Work Better'. Delivery failures were openly acknowledged and then sidelined. The campaign also pointed to the massive relative improvements in people's lives, reinforcing the perception that an ANC government can best achieve the majority's socio-economic interests.

Party images

Party images still resonate in voter evaluations and present the other half of the story. Further fracturing of the opposition bloc shows some inter-party movement between opposition parties. However, there is little evidence that opposition voters moved their support to the ANC or vice versa. Low turnout coupled with a lack of realignment was partly attributable to the limited appeal of opposition parties which failed to encroach into the ANC support base.

Several smaller parties managed to undermine both DA and ANC power bases in the Western and Northern Cape, where they look set to dominate future coalition agreements. Their successes suggest voters are prepared to realign themselves politically. In particular, the DA suffered at the hands of the newcomers to local elections, the Independent Democrats (ID), who gained a crucial portion of the opposition vote across the Western Cape, effectively denying the DA its outright majority in the Cape Town Metropolitan Council and smaller local councils. The ID attracted increased support, partly because its more 'inclusive image' allowed for voting support from across the traditional political spectrum, but also because it represents a new political home for coloured voters in these provinces, many of whom may have formerly voted for the NNP. In contrast to older parties which opted for more inclusive campaigns but failed to convince voters (such as the NNP during the 2004 election), the ID may stand a chance to appeal across old divides and build a broad multiracial support base. It lacks the history that tainted older 'apartheid generation' parties such as the NNP.

The DA's campaign strategy, particularly in the Western Cape, starkly reflected its ongoing dilemma – its increasing need for a performance track record in governance coupled with the need to remedy its negative party image among black voters.

We know that voters use party images as secondary information sources when no performance track record is available. In South Africa, most opposition parties face this dilemma. The DA embarked on the most likely strategy to win Cape Town, thereby earning the chance to obtain a performance track record, at the expense of making short-term gains among the black African electorate. The decisive factor for the political fate of Cape Town metropole was the relative turnout of the different partisan groups. In 2000 the DA mobilised its supporters in higher numbers than the ANC, thus giving it control of the Unicity, only to lose it shortly thereafter to the ANC in the floor-crossing period. The DA knew that a 2006 victory relied on ensuring high turnout among white and coloured voters, particularly former NNP voters. While African and white citizens constitute approximately 50 per cent of potential voters in Cape Town, the other half consists of the politically fragmented coloured community. Especially crucial was the need to ensure that the bloc opposition vote was not fragmented any further by smaller opposition parties, which would have the effect of nullifying higher turnout for the DA.

These demographic calculations informed DA strategy – that a reactionary campaign message would be most successful in attracting its target partisan groups. 'Take our city back' and 'Stop ANC racism' both served the purpose of 'racially grouping' the scramble for resources in the city and show a clear attempt to mobilise the vital coloured portion of the vote.

Having secured the mayoral position in the City of Cape Town metropole by a slim coalition-led majority, the DA will be set on achieving an outstanding performance track record which black African voters can turn to to evaluate the party, *before* they turn to using the DA's traditionally negative party image. The irony lies in the party's choice to utilise negative and limiting messages and imagery to secure power which may, in turn, help it to mobilise a wider political audience in the future.

The highly contested multiparty environment in Cape Town also reconfirmed the fallacy of the uniformity of the so-called 'coloured vote' and the inadequacies of the 'racial census' argument. Results again show that the coloured sections of the electorate are not politically homogenous or predisposed to a particular party, dividing their support between the ANC, DA and ID. Electoral trends since 1994 in the Western Cape support the general interpretation that voting is also contingent on short-term factors such as campaign and circumstances (Seekings 2005b). Yet the electoral volatility witnessed in Cape Town over the past ten years may lessen as in-migration of Africans expands the ANC's support base, thereby changing the proportional sizes of precariously balanced partisan groups.

Conclusion

The argument of this chapter is that a silent revolution is under way among South Africa's voters. Its characteristics may be found in the increasing numbers of 'floating voters' who are not overtly loyal to one particular political party, nor guided by long-standing partisan ties when deciding which party to support at elections. Where party identification was crystallised and reinforced in 1994 by historical factors, a dozen years later there are fewer voters predisposed towards any party. The fact that the extent of mobile voting or electoral availability is significant offers the potential to reshape future electoral outcomes.

Levels of partisanship have generally fallen across all social groups. Black African voters are consistently more likely to be party identifiers than other race groups but, on average, only 65 per cent of black voters are close to a particular party. Rural voters are more likely to support a party than their urban counterparts, middle-class voters are slowly becoming more partisan, while workers and the unemployed show signs of partisan decline. The silent revolution may have its biggest hold among the youngest voters who are becoming less aligned and the new middle classes who show signs of growth in partisanship.

The ANC still holds mass appeal across key demographic groups. Yet several factors signal that the ANC's support may become less broad-based as the party becomes increasingly reliant on specific segments of the public for its electoral support. Its vote share has decreased significantly. Second, its percentage of identi-fiers has declined with less than half the electorate declaring themselves to be ANC partisans. The degree of loyalty felt towards the party has also diminished. Finally, while its strongest partisans are found among black Africans, the unemployed, rural dwellers and working-class voters respectively, this looks set to change if emerging trends stabilise, such as the increase in support from middle-class and older voters, and the decline among workers and the unemployed.

Moreover, individual voters are not dominated by long-term socialised party attachments but also inform their party identification using evaluations of gov-ernment performance and make logical deductions about their information sources when making a choice of which party to support.

Nonetheless, changes in electoral trends or patterns should not be mistaken for changes in the behaviour of individual voters. As the South African population undergoes further demographic and socio-economic changes, it is likely that the sizes and distribution of different social groups will alter and affect voting results. For example, changes over time to the age, race or class status composition of the population can produce different results in certain areas.

Moreover, in situations where partisan groups are relatively equal in size differen-tial, turnout can cause swings and shifts entirely unrelated to changes in individ-ual voter behaviour. Major power shifts in Cape Town are not necessarily voter realignments but due rather to demographic change as migration into the city boosts the ANC's share of traditional voters (Seekings 2005b). In KwaZulu-Natal, the Inkatha Freedom Party's support base has also been eroded as demographic processes, such as integration into the urban economy, proceed (Friedman 2005).

For the moment demographics will also dictate the degree of electoral competi-tion. Areas, such as Cape Town, that have several relatively evenly-sized demo-graphic groups, particularly racial, are likely to experience higher levels of electoral contestation and volatility.

Of concern is the de-alignment trend displayed in the data. As PID declines the majority of voters do not realign themselves politically. Instead, they become non-partisan in attitude, become harder to mobilise and generally abstain. Electoral change has not yet had visible electoral consequences for the percentages of sup-port for the governing party but instead has subtle implications for active political engagement and partisanship. Electoral stagnation may have negative effects on the quality of South Africa's democracy. De-alignment should free more voters to shift their party support. Yet new political contenders are slow to emerge and gar-ner a serious portion of the national vote. The lack of realignment also decreases the chances for electoral uncertainty, thereby discouraging incumbent responsive-ness to voter interests. Where the outcome of an election is not in doubt, incum-bents have less incentive to be responsive and accountable to the citizenry. Declining support for the opposition has also served to strengthen relative support for the ANC. In the face of continued one-party dominance, the greatest challenge for democracy in the next decade will be maintaining high levels of incumbent responsiveness towards citizens.

Social groups remain important cues or information short cuts for South African voters and while electoral politics continues to pivot around fixed identities, such as race, weakening party bonds will simply continue to provide the governing party with larger majorities from increasingly smaller electorates. In the medium term, electoral outcomes will continue to mirror the racial cleavages of the past.

The findings here also hold implications for the conduct of party politics. The problems of de-alignment do not lie with voters as such. Instead, the limited appeal of many opposition parties is a primary factor. To seriously contest future elections, these parties need to be more attentive and responsive to subtle shifts in political identities. Parties wanting to build multi-ethnic and racial coalitions will need to address the way in which they are perceived in terms of racial exclusivity. Those that struggle to present genuinely inclusive racial and ethnic imagery will not attract widespread support. Finally, any chance of increased political competition still seems to pivot around intra-ANC contestation. Demographic changes to the party's core support base may force new shifts in policy positions, which could deepen the ideological rift with the tripartite alliance and alter its party profile.

Notes

1   I would like to give thanks to Associate Professor Robert Mattes and Professor Jeremy Seekings of the Centre for Social Science of the University of Cape Town for their comments and advice. I would also like to acknowledge my debt to the SABC National News Research, the Independent Electoral Commission, the Afrobarometer team, the National Research Foundation, and the Mellon Foundation.

2   Refer to the appendix for survey and methodological information.

3   The measures of partisan identification were gauged by the following questions in all eight surveys: 'Do you usually think of yourself as close to any particular party?' (If yes) 'Which party is that?' The dependent variable was dichotomised into identification with a party or as a non-partisan (independent) and this measures the extent of PID. Later, the dependent variable was further divided into three-way identification with the ANC governing party, the opposition or non-partisan to measure the direction of PID. Lastly, ANC party identifiers were isolated from the entire survey sample and tested using the strength of PID variable, 'Do you feel very close, somewhat close, or not very close (to the ANC)?' The wording of the PID question differs slightly in the 1994 survey. Thereafter the question wording follows the international standard using the 'party closeness scale', which was developed for use outside of the US and particularly in multiparty systems.

4   Whilst race is not recognised as a scientific category, for historical reasons socially-constructed racial identities continue to be relevant in South Africa.

5   Surveys from 2002 onwards use the urban–rural definition adopted by Statistics South Africa. Surveys prior to 2002 use the definition adopted by Markinor and the All Media Products Survey (AMPS).

6   The class status variable was constructed using survey questions that ask respondents to choose among several occupational categories and an item that asks about status of (un)employment.

7   The Democratic Party changed its name to the Democratic Alliance (DA) after a merger with the New National Party (NNP) took place in 2000. The DA retained its name when the NNP left the alliance in 2001.

Appendix: Methodology

This chapter is based on ongoing doctoral research which consists of an analysis of change over time in the aggregate patterns of party support among social groups and the motivations of voter behaviour by comparing different electorates over 12 years using data from a series of cross-sectional surveys. To test for changes the study operationalised sets of independent variables or competing theoretical models of voting behaviour. Findings are based on a range of statistical analyses such as cross-tabulations of structural and demographic variables and multivariate data analyses (logistic regression).

Most of the national public opinion surveys were fielded around the time of national, provincial and local elections in South Africa and were designed precisely for electoral research purposes. Moreover, the designs reflect well-established traditions of electoral research, originating at the University of Michigan, which have been used extensively in similar survey-based research projects worldwide. Consequently, the surveys used here employ indicators which have been tested rigorously in other country studies. In particular, the Afrobarometer series is based on the international Barometer surveys (Eurobarometer, Latino-barometer, and so on). In line with these regional survey instruments, Afrobarometer's design takes into consideration South Africa's peculiarities and contextual constraints, whilst still employing international best practice and experience in its choice of variables and overall design.

Although the data are sourced over time from cross-sectional surveys, each consisting of individual samples, the sampling frame, method of sampling and sample size are all sufficiently similar to make comparisons over time valid. Each sample is representative of the wider South African population, using probability sampling methods such as stratified and multi-stage cluster sampling. Sample quality was also improved by applying statistical weighting adjustments during the analysis stage to minimise sample biases. Large sample sizes ensure that the surveys have a sampling error between 3 and 2 per cent allowing for 95 per cent confidence levels.

Idasa post-election study (1994)

This survey focused on the 1994 general election and specifically on voting intention, attitudes towards democracy, economic evaluations and various other political issues. Personal interviews were conducted with 2 517 eligible voters. The type of instrument used was a semi-structured survey personal interview recorded on questionnaires. The final results were weighted to reflect an electorate estimated at 24 million voters.

Idasa local government election study (1995)

The Idasa local election study provides the first systematic evidence about individual attitudes toward the legitimacy of the new local government system. This study consisted of a sample that is nationally representative, drawn using a multi-stage, clustered random probability sample disproportionately stratified by province, population group and community size (metro, city, large town, small town, village and rural). Interviews were conducted with 2 674 people. The type of instrument used was a semi-structured survey personal interview recorded on questionnaires. The final results were weighted to reflect an electorate estimated at 24.3 million voters.

Political culture study (1997)

This study focused on people's attitudes toward identity, diversity, citizenship, democracy, and democratic institutions. The study consisted of a sample, which was nationally representative, drawn using a multi-stage, clustered random probability sample disproportionately stratified by province, population group and community size. Structured personal interviews were conducted with 3 500 respondents and final results were weighted to reflect an electorate estimated at over 24 million voters.

Opinion '99 (1999)

Opinion '99 was a series of opinion polls conducted prior to the 1999 election by Idasa, Markinor and the South African Broadcasting Corporation, and the Electoral Institute of South Africa. They provide information about South Africans' views of the political, social and economic developments in the country since 1994. The polls covered key issues related to the conduct of free and fair elections, voter participation, and other economic, political and partisan trends. In each round between 2 200 and 3 493 interviews were conducted. The samples for Opinion '99 were drawn using a multi-stage, area stratified probability sampling methodology, stratified by province, population group and community size. All three samples were representative of the population from which they were selected. The type of instrument used was a semi-structured survey personal interview recorded on questionnaires.

Afrobarometer Rounds 1; 2; 2.5 (2000, 2002, 2004)

The Afrobarometer survey series of South Africa is designed to assess attitudes about democracy, markets, and civil society in South Africa and to track the evolution of such attitudes over time. The samples are drawn using multi-stage, stratified, area cluster probability samples. Each survey carries out at least 2 200 personal interviews.

Comparative National Elections Project (CNEP) (2004)

The CNEP is a multinational project that studies political communication and social structure within the context of election campaigns. The CNEP survey was carried out nationally across South Africa in 2004 and covers aspects of the third democratic election that took place during that year. The sample was drawn using multi-stage, stratified, area cluster probability samples. During the survey at least 1 200 personal interviews were carried out.

References

Achen C (1992) Social psychology, demographic variables, and linear regression: Breaking the iron triangle in voting research. *Political Behaviour,* 14(30): 195–211.

Ballard R, Habib A & Valodia I (2006) Social movements in South Africa: Crisis or creating stability? In V Padayachee (Ed) *The development decade? Economic and social change in South Africa, 1994–2004.* Cape Town: HSRC Press.

Campbell A, Converse P, Miller W & Stokes D (1960) *The American voter.* New York: John Wiley & Sons.

Dalton R (1988) *Citizen politics in Western democracies: Public opinion and political parties in the United States, Great Britain, Germany and France.* New Jersey: Chatham House Publishers.

Dalton R (1998) *Citizen politics: Public opinion and political parties in advanced democracies* (2nd edition). New Jersey: Chatham House Publishers.

Downs A (1957) *An economic theory of democracy.* New York: Harper Collins.

Fiorina M (1979) *Retrospective Voting in American Presidential Elections.* New Haven: Yale University Press.

Friedman S (2005) A voice for some: South Africa's ten years of democracy. In J Piombo & L Nijzink (Eds) *Electoral politics in South Africa: Assessing the first democratic decade.* New York: Palgrave Macmillan.

Green D, Palmquist B & Schickler E (2002) *Partisan hearts and minds: Political parties and the social identities of voters.* New Haven: Yale University Press.

Habib A & Naidu S (1999) Election '99: Was there a 'coloured' and 'Indian' vote? *Politikon* 26(2): 189–200.

IEC (Independent Electoral Commission) (2006) Municipal elections results. Report presented at IEC's National Results Centre, Pretoria, 3 March.

Inglehart R (1977) *The silent revolution: Changing values and political styles among Western publics.* New Jersey: Princeton University Press.

Kabemba C (2005) Electoral administration: Achievements and continuing challenges. In J Piombo & L Nijzink (Eds) *Electoral politics in South Africa: Assessing the first democratic decade.* New York: Palgrave Macmillan.

Lombard K (2003) *The SA reconciliation barometer, prospects for reconciliation: Race and class.* Cape Town: Institute for Justice and Reconciliation Survey Report, University of Cape Town.

Mainwaring S (1999) *Rethinking party systems in the third wave of democratization: The case of Brazil.* California: Stanford University Press.

Mattes R (2005) Voter information, government evaluations and party images in the first democratic decade. In J Piombo & L Nijzink (Eds) *Electoral politics in South Africa: Assessing the first democratic decade.* New York: Palgrave Macmillan.

Mattes R & Piombo J (2001) Opposition parties and the voters in South Africa's general election of 1999. *Democratization,* 8(3): 101–28.

Mattes R, Taylor H & Africa C (1999) Judgement and choice in the 1999 South African election. *Politikon,* 26(2): 235–47.

Piombo J & Nijzink L (Eds) (2005) *Electoral politics in South Africa: Assessing the first democratic decade.* New York: Palgrave Macmillan.

Popkin S (1991) *The reasoning voter.* Chicago: University of Chicago Press.

Posner D (2005) *Institutions and ethnic politics in Africa.* New York: Cambridge University Press.

Reynolds A (1999) *Elections '99 South Africa: From Mandela to Mbeki.* Cape Town: David Philip.

Seekings J (2005a) The electoral implications of social and economic change since 1994. In J Piombo & L Nijzink (Eds) *Electoral politics in South Africa: Assessing the first democratic decade.* New York: Palgrave Macmillan.

Seeking J (2005b) *Partisan realignment in Cape Town, 1994–2004.* The Centre for Social Science Research Working Paper No. 111, University of Cape Town.

Southall R (2004) Political change and the black middle class in democratic South Africa. *Canadian Journal of African Studies,* 38(3): 521–42.

wa Kivilu M, Davids Y, Langa Z, Maphunye K, Mncwango B, Sedumedi S & Struwig J (2005) *Survey on South African voter participation in elections.* Prepared by the Socio-Economic Surveys Unit of the Knowledge System Group, HSRC for the IEC. Available at <www.elections.org.za/papers/237/2006%20HSRC%20Final%20Report%20Summary%20on%20Voter%20Participation.doc>

wa Kivilu M & Langtry S (2005) *Identity documents and registration to vote.* Prepared by the Socio-Economic Surveys Unit of the Knowledge System Group, HSRC for the IEC. Available at <http://www.elections.org.za/papers/206/2005%20REGII_HSRC%20Report.pdf>

White S, Rose R & McAllister I (1997) *How Russia votes.* New York: Chatham House.

6 Local government budgets and development: a tale of two towns

Neva Seidman Makgetla

Makhuduthamaga in the former Lebowa homeland was the poorest municipality in South Africa in 2004, spending just R50 on each of its 250 000 inhabitants every year.[1] If you lived in Makhuduthamaga, you would likely be desperately poor, unemployed, and dependent on social grants and remittances. You would almost certainly carry in your water and have a pit toilet. In 2001, only 11 per cent of households in the municipality had piped water on site, while just 2 per cent had flush toilets and 16 per cent had no toilets at all. In 2004, just under half the population living in this municipality went hungry at least sometimes.

Life was much more pleasant in South Africa's richest municipality, Overstrand, in the Western Cape. It spent an average of R4 000 apiece for its 56 000 residents. Most of its citizens had a job, running water and electricity. Hunger was still a problem – one person in seven went hungry at least sometimes – but, in contrast to Makhuduthamaga, this was not the norm. Since the town is about three-quarters white and coloured, it enjoyed substantial investment in infrastructure even under apartheid. In 2001, nine out of ten households had flush toilets and water on site.

As these two extremes illustrate, 12 years after the transition to democracy the spatial inequalities built up under apartheid largely persist. Almost half of all Africans still live in the former homeland areas (the impoverished rural areas where Africans were legally citizens under apartheid) where a lack of basic infrastructure reinforces high unemployment, underemployment and mass poverty.

In the local government campaigns of 2006, all parties seemed to agree that shortcomings in the delivery of basic household infrastructure – water, electricity, rubbish removal and so on – arose largely out of incompetence at the municipal level. This argument, however, ignores the economic realities.

Before the transition to democracy in 1994, apartheid shaped poverty spatially, with the homeland areas left without industry, viable agriculture or adequate infrastructure. Yet even after 1994, local governments were expected to raise the bulk of their funds from rates and taxes, with only a limited national subsidy. As a result, the former homeland areas remained in a vicious cycle of poverty, unable to provide infrastructure because low household incomes still translated into inadequate government revenues. Without more funds, however, local governments could not provide the basic services needed to address mass poverty and underemployment.

Underlying the fiscal shortcomings was a more basic challenge. More than a decade after liberation, the future of the homelands remained highly uncertain. Overcoming apartheid inequalities would require a far more substantial redistribution of resources to the poorest municipalities. Without a spatial vision for the economy and employment, however, that investment could be wasted as people migrated to the more prosperous cities.

This chapter explores in greater depth the role of municipalities and district councils in addressing backlogs in household infrastructure. The next section quantifies the impact of apartheid on access to basic services. The second section reviews the role of local governments in overcoming these problems. A spatial analysis of local government budgets demonstrates that they have tended to reinforce, rather than diminish, the spatial inequalities left by apartheid. The final section outlines current policy responses to address these problems. It suggests that sustainable policies require fundamental decisions about the spatial allocation of investment – and by extension settlements – in the future.

The apartheid legacy in infrastructure

A central pillar of apartheid was the maintenance of high standards for government services in white and, to a lesser extent, Indian and coloured communities, paid for in large part by depriving African areas. This system left enormous backlogs and inequalities in access to water, sanitation, electricity and other municipal services.

In 1996, as Figures 6.1 and 6.2 show, virtually all white and coloured households had running water and flush toilets on site, as well as electricity. In contrast, less than half of African households had these amenities. By 2004, half of African households had water on site and three-quarters used electricity for lighting. For most services, the share of African households in total recipients had risen to two-thirds, up from about half eight years earlier. Still, African communities continued to lag substantially behind.

Progress in terms of the share of households accessing basic infrastructure was slowed by a rapid fall in household size after 1994. This phenomenon apparently reflected both rural–urban migration and the large-scale provision of small so-called Reconstruction and Development Programme houses. According to the *Labour Force Survey* (Stats SA 2004a), the number of formal houses with less than three rooms grew by over 1.5 million between 1994 and 2004. Meanwhile, between 1996 and 2004, the average household declined from five members to four. African households shrank even faster, from almost six members in 1996 to under four in 2004 (calculated from Stats SA 1996, 2004b).

This shift meant that the number of households rose far faster than the population. For instance, suppose the same number of African households received water on site as in 2004, but the number of households rose only 1.5 per cent per year (about the same rate as the population) between 1996 and 2004, then some 80 per cent of

Figure 6.1 *Access to basic water and sanitation by race, 1996 and 2004*

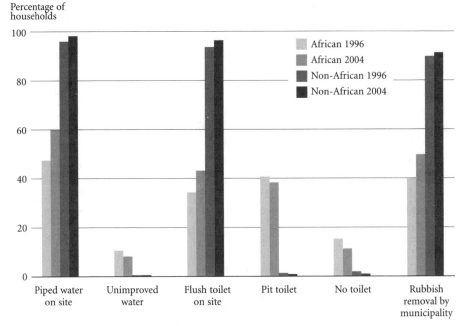

Source: Calculated from Stats SA (1996, 2004b)

Figure 6.2 *Access to basic electricity for cooking and lighting by race, 1996 and 2004*

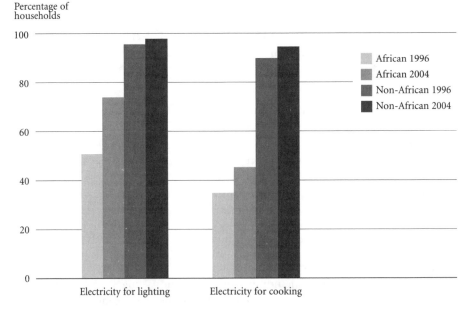

Source: Calculated from Stats SA (1996, 2004b)

Figure 6.3 *Households with access to basic services in predominantly homeland and other areas, 1996 and 2004*

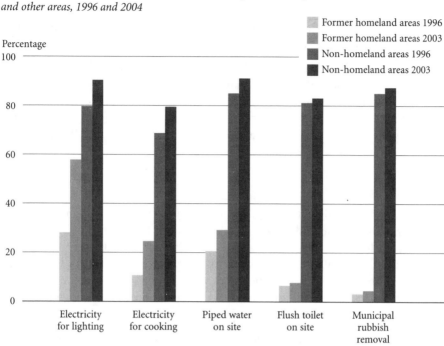

Source: Calculated from Stats SA (1996, 2004b)

Note: The areas included as predominantly homeland areas are the rural regions of KwaZulu-Natal, Limpopo, the Eastern Cape, the North West and Mpumalanga. They therefore include some historically white-owned farming areas.

African households would have water on site by 2004, as opposed to the current 60 per cent.

The former homeland regions lagged far behind the rest of the country in terms of access to services. Between 1996 and 2004, the share of households in these areas remained fairly stable at 35 per cent, although the share of the population declined. As Figure 6.3 shows, however, they did not come close to catching up with the rest of the country.

The backlogs left from apartheid meant that South Africa remained noticeably behind comparable economies in providing basic infrastructure – according to United Nations Development Program (UNDP) data, in the early 2000s South Africa ranked 49th in the world on gross domestic product (GDP) per capita, but only around 75th on access to improved sanitation and water.[2]

Local government and the infrastructure backlogs

Both the Constitution and the 1998 *White Paper on Local Government* located local government at the centre of the effort to increase access to basic infrastructure.

This strategy represented a major change from the period before 1994, when local governments in African areas were weak and largely rejected by residents. Moreover, the demarcation of municipalities sought, for the first time, to set up a unified fiscal and political basis for neighbouring black and white communities.

Despite the fundamental changes in local government structures, the poorest areas in the former homelands remained far too impoverished to make much independent progress. Yet national government grants were still higher for the richer municipalities. In the following section I first analyse municipal budgets and the reasons why the poorest regions cannot raise more funds, before looking at the implications for service delivery.

Local government budgets

In 2005, for the first time, the Treasury published the budgets of all municipalities on a common format, making it possible to analyse the extent of redistribution through local-government budgets. To do this, the municipalities are divided into quintiles of the population based on expenditure per person; that is, the municipalities are split into fifths by population, with the ones that spend the least per person in the lowest quintile and the ones that spend the most in the top quintile (see the appendix to this chapter).

In the top quintile of municipalities, the average expenditure per person came to R3 637. This quintile includes Overstrand, as well as Cape Town and Johannesburg. Municipalities in the poorest quintile spent on average R146 per person. Most of the municipalities in this quintile are predominantly rural and located in the former homeland regions.

Table 6.1 *Average expenditure per person per year by quintile of municipalities, 2004*

Quintile	Average expenditure (rand)
Quintile 1	3 637
Quintile 2	2 630
Quintile 3	1 488
Quintile 4	504
Quintile 5	146
Total	1 699

Source: Calculated from National Treasury (2005)

Low levels of local-government expenditure still align closely with apartheid spatial planning. This emerges from the composition of the population in the different quintiles. As Table 6.2 shows, the 2001 Census shows a close correlation between the size of the white population and the level of the budget. In the poorest municipalities, virtually the entire population was African.

Table 6.2 *Racial composition of population by municipality income quintile, 2001*

Quintile	Black (%)	White (%)
Quintile 1	81.0	19.0
Quintile 2	86.0	14.0
Quintile 3	88.0	12.0
Quintile 4	97.0	3.0
Quintile 5	99.7	0.3
Total	90.0	10.0

Source: Calculated from Stats SA (2001)

The poorest 20 per cent of municipalities received almost no income from payment for services (electricity, water and so on) or rates,[3] which constitute most of the income of richer municipalities. As a result, they depend almost entirely on transfers from the national Budget.

By definition, each quintile must provide for around a fifth of the national population. But as Figure 6.4 shows, municipalities in the poorest quintile reported virtually no income from residents in the form of rates or service payments. Meanwhile, the top quintile received close to half the income derived by all municipalities from services, rates and other income other than subsidies.

Figure 6.4 *Shares in total municipal revenue by quintile, 2004*

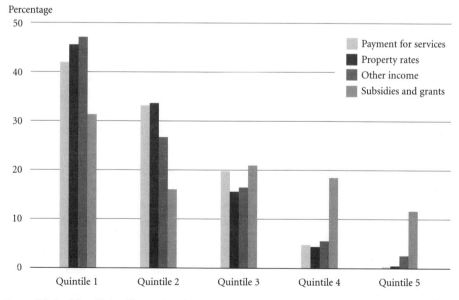

Source: Calculated from National Treasury (2005)

The reason the poorest municipalities did not get much in the way of rates and service payments was simple: these areas remained so poor that residents could not afford to pay rates, and most either got no municipal services or did not pay for them. Poverty indicators for the municipalities are discussed in greater detail later in the chapter. If the national transfers that constitute the bulk of subsidies and grants in the municipal budgets were transferred on a completely equitable basis to the municipalities, each quintile would get 20 per cent. In fact, the poorer quintiles receive less than their fair share, while the richer ones receive more.

As Figure 6.4 shows, in 2004 the poorest quintile received only 12 per cent of all subsidies and grants to local municipalities, while the richest quintile enjoyed almost half. The average subsidy for a resident in a municipality in the poorest quintile was R115, compared to R287 in the richest quintile.

This situation apparently reflects the tie between the subsidy and existing infra-structure. To a large extent, national government grants were linked to mainte-nance and current costs of historic capital expenditure. This system inherently disadvantaged municipalities in the former homeland regions that suffered from extremely low public investment under apartheid.

Despite the continued inequality in local-government funding, national subsidies made up the bulk of municipal budgets in the poorest quintile. As Figure 6.5 shows, in 2004 two-thirds of total revenues in the poorest quintile came from grants and subsidies, compared to under one-tenth in the richest quintile.

Most of the revenue received for rates and services was used on the cost of provi-sion. Still, the higher revenue in richer municipalities translated into much higher service levels, including some cross-subsidisation for poorer neighbourhoods. The fall-off in revenues to the poorest quintile emerged most sharply with electricity, presumably because Eskom provided electricity directly to consumers in most of these municipalities. In contrast, the decline in revenues from water, refuse removal and other services was less pronounced. From electricity alone, the rich-est municipalities received the equivalent of around R1 000 per resident – largely from industry – while the poorest quintile got virtually nothing.

In expenditure terms, the poorer municipalities tended to spend more on salaries and less on bulk services – which they did not provide – and interest. The relatively high share of salaries in the budgets of poorer municipalities did not reflect higher pay or staffing levels, but rather low overall expenditure. In fact, the available evi-dence suggests that the poorer municipalities were generally understaffed. Local gov-ernments in richer communities apparently had well over twice as many employees per resident, although they spent a smaller share of their budgets on personnel.

The published data provide local-government employment only by province, not by municipality or district council. Still, as Table 6.3 shows, five provinces – Limpopo, the Eastern Cape, North West, Mpumalanga and KwaZulu-Natal (KZN)

Figure 6.5 *Sources of municipal revenue by quintile, 2004*

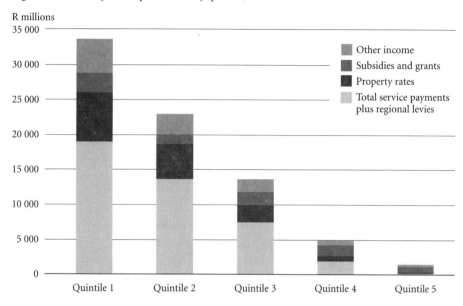

Source: Calculated from National Treasury (2005)

– contain all the municipalities in the poorest quintile. In these provinces, local governments in 2003 had on average 2.8 employees per resident, compared to 6.7 employees per resident in the four richer provinces of Gauteng, the Western and Northern Cape, and the Free State.

Using provincial averages reduces the apparent discrepancies, because every province has some richer municipalities. Only around a third of the population of the poorer five provinces lived in the poorest quintile of municipalities.

Municipal employment by function did not differ greatly between the two groups of provinces. The provinces with poorer municipalities had a smaller share of local-government employees providing health services (historically mostly a metro

Table 6.3 *Municipal employment by groups of province, 2003*

	Gauteng, Northern and Western Cape, Free State	Limpopo, KZN, North West, Mpumalanga, Eastern Cape
Percentage of population living in poorest quintile of municipalities	0%	31%
Municipal employees	116 000	78 000
Population (2001 Census)	17 million	28 million
No. of municipal employees/100 000 residents	6.9	2.8

Source: Employment data from Stats SA (2001, 2003)

Figure 6.6 *Municipal revenue from services by quintile, 2004*

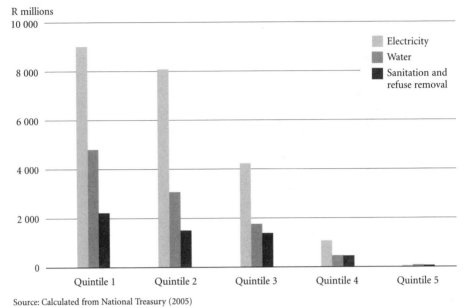

Source: Calculated from National Treasury (2005)

Figure 6.7 *Municipal expenditure by quintile, 2004*

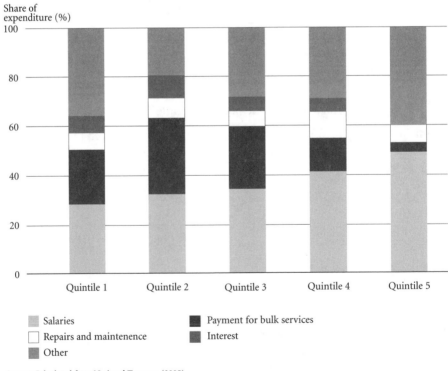

Source: Calculated from National Treasury (2005)

function), recreational facilities and sanitation, and a larger share working on housing, roads and electricity (calculated from Stats SA 2005 Table 1).

The perception that top managers in smaller towns effectively loot the local budget was rather widespread in the mid-2000s (see, for example, *Mail & Guardian* 10.10.05). In the event, however, according to municipal reports to National Treasury, senior managers in the poorest municipalities typically served larger numbers on a lower salary. In 2004 in the poorest quintile, the average chief executive officer (CEO) was paid just under R500 000 a year to manage a municipality with 170 000 inhabitants. She/he had around three other senior managers, earning an average of R33 000 a month. In contrast, the richer municipalities generally paid more and had more senior managers. But the pay of senior managers took up a smaller share of their budgets because their revenues were so much larger.

In 2006, in an effort to improve the quality of municipal management, the national state set new guidelines for salaries for senior local politicians and managers. The new guidelines would essentially double the pay for these officials in all municipalities. The government promised to set aside R600 million in order to help the poorest towns pay for their new personnel (*Mail & Guardian* 24.03.06). The new salary costs would come to about 2 per cent of all transfers to local government, and would presumably increase expenditure on senior managers in the poorest municipalities to over 10 per cent of the total. While the measure aligned with the belief in government that higher pay would attract better managers to the public sector, the cost certainly seemed high.

In sum, as of 2004 local-government budgets did little to support redistribution to overcome the backlogs left by apartheid. In the poorest regions of the country, municipalities depended almost exclusively on transfers from the national Budget. But these transfers were not nearly enough to ensure equitable expenditure, and vast discrepancies persisted.

Table 6.4 *The cost of senior municipal management, 2004*

	Average population per senior manager	Average senior manager pay (excluding CEO)	Average CEO pay	Senior management as % of municipal budget
Quintile 1	114 000	615 000	746 000	0.17
Quintile 2	87 000	544 000	667 000	0.29
Quintile 3	31 000	384 000	506 000	1.11
Quintile 4	39 000	346 000	429 000	2.75
Quintile 5	68 000	330 000	431 000	5.91

Source: Calculated from National Treasury (2005)

The implications for service delivery

The poorest local governments could not raise funds locally because their populations mostly remained in poverty. But the lack of municipal resources made it harder to provide basic infrastructure that would both raise living standards and open up economic opportunities.

The 2001 Census (Stats SA 2001) gives some idea of the backlogs faced by the poorest municipalities. As Table 6.5 shows, only 5 per cent of residents in the poorest quintile of municipalities had flush toilets, and only 20 per cent had piped water on site.

Table 6.5 *Access to water and sanitation by percentage within quintiles of municipalities, 2001*

Quintile	Flush toilet (%)	Piped water on site (%)
Quintile 1	80	83
Quintile 2	67	75
Quintile 3	56	72
Quintile 4	20	42
Quintile 5	5	20

Source: Calculated from Stats SA (2001)

The *Labour Force Survey* (Stats SA 2004a) provides more recent data than the Census and through comparison with the *October Household Survey* (Stats SA 1996) can provide longer-term trends. Unfortunately, it does not provide municipal-level data. It does, however, give figures for the next highest administrative level of the district councils, each of which includes between three and ten municipalities.

As with municipalities, the district councils are here divided into quintiles by expenditure per person in order to assess how levels of income and access to infrastructure have changed in different areas. Inequalities between municipalities would be greater than between district councils, since most district councils contain municipalities spread across two or three quintiles.

Figure 6.8 shows the number of households gaining access to services between 1996 and 2004. As the figure shows, the bulk of new infrastructure was built in the richer district-council areas. In contrast, the poorest quintile saw virtually no growth in infrastructure other than pit latrines and electricity. In part, this reflected the national government's policy of providing only so-called ventilated pit latrines in rural areas. Only electrification was more or less equitably spread across municipalities and households.

It is noteworthy that of the services analysed in Figure 6.8, only social grants had a redistributive effect. They were, however, not a local-government function. Rather, they were provided by the national government based on some rather crude indicators of need – primarily age and poverty.

Figure 6.8 *Share of district-council quintiles in new infrastructure and expansion in social grants, 1996 to 2004*

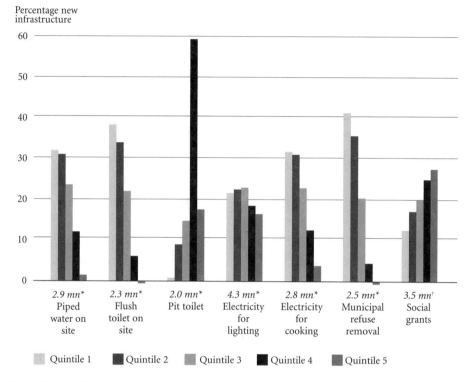

Source: Calculated from Stats SA (1996, 2004b)
Notes: The figure for social grants in 1996 relates to social grants and state pensions;
the figure for social grants in 2004 relates to all social grants.
* This figure reflects the increase in total households with access to the service.
† This figure reflects the increase in total households getting at least one social grant.

As Table 6.6 shows, the result of this pattern of expenditure was – not surprisingly – that there was little or no improvement in the share of households with access to most services in the poorest district-council areas. In terms of infrastructure, only use of pit toilets and electricity for lighting improved substantially. Access to social grants increased from 17 per cent to 63 per cent, suggesting that these grants must have a real impact on both poverty and local economies.

As has been noted already, the very rapid growth in the number of households meant that the expansion in proportional terms was limited in all quintiles, despite increased access for millions of households. In each case, the number of households gaining access increased by between two and four million, as Figure 6.8 indicates.

The data on service delivery demonstrate that local-government funding did not support the redistribution needed to overcome the spatial poverty gap created

Table 6.6 *Percentage of households with access to selected services by district-council quintile, 1996 and 2004*

Service	Quintile 1		Quintile 2		Quintile 3		Quintile 4		Quintile 5	
	1996	2004	1996	2004	1996	2004	1996	2004	1996	2004
Piped water on site	84	88	84	87	68	76	43	47	30	27
Only unimproved water	0.2	0.0	2	0	7	2	18	11	31	31
Flush toilet on site	82	85	81	82	53	59	33	31	17	13
Pit toilet	12	8	11	13	23	28	40	50	48	56
Bucket/nothing	4	3	5	3	21	11	19	16	28	29
Electricity for lighting	85	88	80	86	62	82	51	71	32	61
Electricity for cooking	77	82	75	80	48	59	36	41	19	21
Municipal refuse removal	80	89	82	85	58	62	36	31	16	13
Social grants*	9	25	10	29	15	38	16	51	17	63

Source: Calculated from Stats SA (1996, 2004b)
Note: * The figure for social grants in 1996 relates to social grants and state pensions; the figure for social grants in 2004 relates to all social grants.

under apartheid. Instead, the poorest regions tended to slip further behind, while poor communities in richer municipalities saw substantial improvements in services.

The economic context

The failure to improve services in the poorest municipalities undermined living standards directly. It also made it more difficult for households there to engage productively with the economy. But the converse also held true: mass poverty in the poorest municipalities meant that the local governments had inadequate funding, and therefore could not do much to support expansion in infrastructure.

As Table 6.7 indicates, in 2004 households in the poorest quintile of district councils were much more likely to be economically inactive, virtually destitute and dependent on social grants or remittances for their income. If they were employed, they probably worked in the informal sector and earned very little. Close to half went hungry at least sometimes, and only a third got most of their income from wages or salaries.

Household destitution meant that municipalities in the poorest districts ended up providing a greater share of basic services free. But the main reason their revenues from these sources were low was that most households did not get the services at all.

Table 6.8 shows that the share of free water and electricity was higher for the poorest district-council quintiles. It shows that households in the poorest areas had much lower access to basic services, with fewer municipalities providing free basic

Table 6.7 *Incomes, employment and household expenditure by district-council quintile, 2004*

	Quintile 1	Quintile 2	Quintile 3	Quintile 4	Quintile 5
Average per capita revenue of municipalities (rand)	3 633	2 676	1 561	930	497
% of those aged 15 to 65:					
Employed	49	44	39	31	24
Not economically active	36	42	47	57	66
% of employees:					
Individual income: R0–R500 per month	4	8	16	31	45
Informal	14	14	18	31	45
% of households:					
Gaining most income from wages	74	67	60	45	31
Gaining most income from grants and remittances	18	21	32	47	60
Goes hungry always or sometimes	17	16	29	41	41

Source: Calculated from Stats SA (2004a)

Table 6.8 *Access to free basic services by district-council quintile, 2003*

	Quintile 1	Quintile 2	Quintile 3	Quintile 4	Quintile 5
Electricity					
% of households using electricity	90	78	52	32	20
Average KwH used per person per month	3 024	2 910	1 321	511	163
% of users covered by free basic services	35	21	26	30	34
% of total KwH provided free	1	1	3	2	3
Water					
% of households getting municipal water	85	71	68	61	37
Average litres used per person per month	7 303	3 975	3 751	1 986	563
% of users covered by free basic services	63	89	83	68	73
% of water provided free	10	10	16	15	17

Source: Calculated from Stats SA (2003)
Note: The definition of households used by municipalities differs from that in the *Labour Force Survey* (Stats SA 2004a), so the data are not compatible.

services. Even so, a larger share of their supplies of water and electricity went for free services than in richer districts.

The spatial dimensions of poverty ultimately caused massive differentials in local-government budgets. At the same time, the inequalities in municipal spending deepened poverty and undermined economic development in poorer areas.

Policy responses

The government effectively adopted three different policy responses to the failure of local governments to bring about greater spatial equality: it focused on improving capacity in the poorest municipalities; it committed to larger and more targeted subsidies; and it argued that the artificial homeland settlements set up under apartheid should be allowed to disappear through rural–urban migration. Clearly, these responses were potentially contradictory.

Two national strategies – the Integrated Sustainable Rural Development Programme (ISRDP), initiated in the early 2000s, and Project Consolidate from 2005 – sought to increase the management capacity of poor municipalities. The ISRDP identified 13 rural development nodes, including 8 of the 11 local governments in the poorest quintile of municipalities, 2 in the second poorest quintile, and 1 in the third quintile. Project Consolidate also focused initially on the neediest areas, but ultimately expanded to cover a much greater number, including some metro areas.

These programmes were notable for their commitment to avoiding additional resource flows to the municipalities concerned (see Everatt et al. 2004). Instead, they argued that local governments could not deliver because of a lack of capacity and co-ordination, both within the municipality and with other spheres of government. They therefore prioritised support for capacity building for local people and the importation of outside experts. While improving capacity always helps, improved co-ordination and capacity building alone seemed unlikely to make a dent on the structural economic problems facing the poorest rural municipalities.

A second response to the ongoing inequalities between local governments was an effort by National Treasury to increase its transfers to municipalities and target them more toward poorer regions. This new strategy reflected a significant, although not explicitly acknowledged, shift in fiscal policy.

In the late 1990s, the government cut national spending by around 1 per cent a year. In this context, the share of the national Budget going to local governments dropped, from a high of 3.7 per cent in 1997 to a low of 2 per cent in 1998, and remained under 3 per cent until 2002. As a result, the national subsidy to municipalities fell almost 50 per cent in real terms, and until 2002 remained lower than in 1997.

Because richer local governments could raise their own funds, despite the cut in transfers, local-government spending as a whole rose by almost 1 per cent a year between 1997 and 2002, or about half the rate of population growth (calculated from National Treasury 2004: Table B21; expenditure figures deflated using March consumer price index). Given the dependence of the poorest municipalities on national transfers, however, they presumably saw real spending cuts in this period.

Between 2002 and 2006, as the Budget became more expansionary, the Treasury at least implicitly reversed its initial assumption that local governments should fund almost all their own spending. This shift arose in part because the systematisation of municipal budgets made it possible to analyse the extent of poor communities' dependence on national subsidies (National Treasury 2004).

The 2006 Budget in particular foresaw very substantial growth in the share of national revenue going to local governments. The Treasury expected the subsidy for operating expenses – the 'equitable share' for local government provided under the Constitution – to grow by 14 per cent in real terms, and infrastructure grants by 15 per cent. Thereafter the transfers would continue to grow faster than the national Budget and far above inflation, at about 7 per cent a year for operating expenditure and over 20 per cent a year for infrastructure. As a result of this vigorous expansion, the Treasury predicted that subsidies to local government would increase from 3.3 percent of the national Budget in 2002 to 5.9 per cent in 2006 and 6.5 per cent in 2009.

At the same time, to ensure that the poorest municipalities benefited most from the equitable share, the government introduced a new formula, which is to be implemented in full in 2007. The new formula seemed unlikely to redistribute grants substantially toward the poorest municipalities, however, because it focused resources on households with access to municipal services. Essentially, it expected the central state to meet the cost of free services for these families. It therefore provided around three times as much for each indigent but connected household as it did for each unconnected household. As noted in Table 6.8, however, the poorest quintile of municipalities had much lower connection rates than richer areas, as well as higher indigency rates. They could therefore end up with substantially lower subsidies per household. A failure to redistribute through operating expenses could be offset through grants for infrastructure, which in 2006 came to around a quarter of total national transfers to local government. Judging by the first decade of democracy, however, ensuring that infrastructure spending targeted low-income communities would prove a major challenge.

A third policy response to spatial inequalities argued that homeland settlements were artificial creations of apartheid, which had no economic base and should not survive. This view was explicitly endorsed by the National Spatial Development Perspective (NSDP), developed by the presidency and endorsed by Cabinet in 2003 (The Presidency 2003) but tabled neither at the National Economic Development and Labour Council nor in Parliament.

The NSDP argued that:

> Efforts to address past and current social inequalities should focus on people not places. In localities where there are both high levels of poverty and development potential, this could include fixed capital investment beyond basic services to exploit the potential of those

localities. In localities with low development potential, government spending, beyond basic services, should focus on providing social transfers, human resource development and labour market intelligence. This will enable people to become more mobile and migrate, if they choose to, to localities that are more likely to provide sustainable employment or other economic opportunities.

In order to overcome the spatial distortions of apartheid, future settlement and economic development opportunities should be channelled into activity corridors and nodes that are adjacent to or link the main growth centres (The Presidency 2003).

The NSDP responded to the difficulty of maintaining state services where there is no economic base. In the poorest municipalities, the majority of the population in 2004 lived off social grants and remittances from family members, a situation that cannot provide a foundation for local economic development (see also Hindson & Vicente-Hindson 2005). But risks are never fully avoidable. The NSDP essentially accepted that continued impoverishment in the former homeland regions would cause their near depopulation – an approach that seemed certain to cause far-reaching political debates and, in some areas, discontent. It also meant that the richer areas would continue to face ever-growing demand for employment and infrastructure, demands they struggled (and in some cases failed) to meet in the first decade of democracy.

In any case, from at least 2006 the NSDP vision was contradicted by the commitment to increase capacity, funding and infrastructure, particularly in poor regions. Still, the growth in central government transfers was not linked to a robust rural development strategy that could over the long run establish an economic basis for the poorest municipalities. By itself, then, the increase in subsidies seemed unlikely to establish sustainable communities.

Conclusion

Analysis of local-government budgets indicates that in the first 12 years after democracy the fiscus did little to overcome the inequalities left by apartheid. The poorest districts continued to fall behind in terms of access to basic infrastructure. In these circumstances, there was little hope of stimulating local economies and raising incomes. The result was ongoing destitution and migration to the metro areas, particularly to Gauteng.

Government's responses did little to challenge the economic roots of the problem. They focused on building capacity and increasing subsidies for infrastructure, without a strategy to stimulate local economies and employment in the former homeland areas. While greater subsidies for basic services would certainly help alleviate poverty, they seemed unlikely, however, to build sustainable communities in the longer run.

An effective economic solution would require both substantially more funds from the national government and a real agrarian reform – a type of radical approach that did not form part of the policy discussion as of the mid-2000s. The alternative, however, was to let economic forces radically restructure the municipalities, as apartheid settlements in depressed rural areas translated into mushrooming informal settlements around the metro areas.

Notes

1   Information on budgets in Makhuduthamaga and Overstrand is calculated from National Treasury 2005, using population data from the 2001 Census (Stats SA 2001); on access to water and sanitation, from the 2001 Census (Stats SA 2001); and on hunger, the data relate to the district municipalities containing the municipalities, drawn from *October Household Survey* (Stats SA 2004).

2   The number of countries in the GDP sample was 163; for water and sanitation, the number of countries in the sample was 148 and 153 respectively. Calculated from UNDP (2004: Table 7).

3   That is, local government property taxes.

Appendix

Municipalities by quintile of population in terms of budget per resident.

The names of some municipalities vary between official documents.
The names used here are those used in the Treasury's local-government budget database.

Quintile 1

WC032	Overstrand
	City of Cape Town
	City of Johannesburg Metro
WC047	Plettenberg Bay
WC048	Knysna
Pretoria	City of Tshwane Metro
WC014	Saldanha Bay
EC000	Nelson Mandela

Quinile 2

WC043	Mossel Bay
GT422	Midvaal
East Rand	Ekurhuleni Metro
WC024	Stellenbosch
Durban	Ethekwini
WC044	George
NC083	‖Khara Hais
NC01B1	Gamagara
WC023	Drakenstein
NC061	Richtersveld
NW402	Potchefstroom
MP313	Middelburg
WC033	Cape Agulhas
NC091	Sol Plaatje
FS172	Mangaung
KZ282	uMhlathuze
KZ225	Msunduzi
KZ5a3	Matatiele
FS184	Matjhabeng

Quintile 3

FS204	Metsimaholo
EC108	Kouga
GT421	Emfuleni
WC015	Swartland
GT411	Mogale City
WC042	Langeberg
MP307	Highveld East
EC125	Buffalo City

GT423	Lesedi
NW373	Rustenburg
WC026	Breede River/Winelands
NC074	Kareeberg
CBLC2	Kungwini
MP312	Emalahleni
NW403	Klerksdorp
WC051	Laingsburg
WC022	Witzenberg
WC025	Breede Valley
GT412	Randfontein
KZ222	uMngeni
NC073	Emthanjeni
EC105	Ndlambe
WC045	Oudtshoorn
WC034	Swellendam
KZ292	KwaDukuza
NW392	Naledi
NC081	Mier
KZ234	Umtshezi
WC053	Beaufort West
FS192	Dihlabeng
WC031	Theewaterskloof
EC102	Blue Crane Route
KZ241	Endumeni
KZ5a4	Greater Kokstad
FS201	Moqhaka
EC131	Inxuba Yethemba
WC013	Bergrivier
CBLC8	Merafong City
EC104	Makana
MP321	Thaba Chweu
NC093	Magareng
WC012	Cederberg
NC066	Karoo Hoogland
MP323	Umjindi
NC077	Siyathemba
MP305	Lekwa
NC062	Nama Khoi
KZ252	Newcastle

NC065	Hantam		EC128	Nxuba
NP334	Ba-Phalaborwa		KZ223	Mooi Mpofana
WC041	Kannaland		NC076	Thembelihle
MP311	Delmas		NC078	Siyancuma
NW396	Lekwa-Teemane		MP304	Seme
NP354	Polokwane		NP365	Modimolle
NP361	Thabazimbi		FS171	Naledi
FS203	Ngwathe		FS185	Nala
WC011	Matzikama		EC107	Baviaans
NC072	Umsombomvu		FS163	Mohokare
MP306	Dipaleseng		FS161	Letsemeng
MP302	Msukaligwa		NC082	Kai !Garib
NP366	Bela-Bela		FS183	Tswelopele
EC101	Camdeboo		EC134	Lukanji
NP364	Mookgopong		FS194	Maluti a Phofung
NC071	Ubuntu		KZ212	Umdoni
NC064	Kamiesberg		EC106	Sunday's River Valley
KZ216	Hibiscus Coast		NC092	Dikgatlong
EC143	Maletswai		NW393	Mamusa
NC085	Tsantsabane		EC109	Kou-Kamma
NW372	Madibeng		NC067	Khâi-Ma
FS193	Nketoana		FS195	Phumelela
FS181	Masilonyana		NW384	Ditsobotla
NW374	Kgetlengrivier		NP333	Greater Tzaneen
EC144	Gariep		FS182	Tokologo
NC075	Renosterberg		EC133	Inkwanca
MP314	Highlands		NW383	Mafikeng
FS173	Mantsopa		KZ263	Abaqulusi
FS191	Setsoto		MP303	Mkhondo
FS205	Mafube		NP367	Mogalakwena
NW401	Ventersdorp		EC127	Nkonkobe
GT02b1	Nokeng tsa Taemane		NC084	!Kheis
NP341	Musina		KZ5a2	Kwa Sani
KZ232	Emnambithi/Ladysmith		EC123	Great Kei
			EC157	King Sabata Dalindyebo
			KZ275	Mtubatuba
Quintile 4			KZ245	Umvoti
WC052	Prince Albert		NW395	Molopo
NC086	Kgatelopele		EC124	Amahlathi
EC103	Ikwezi		EC132	Tsolwana
NW404	Maquassi Hills		KZ253	Utrecht
CBLC1	Ga-Segonyana		NP344	Makhado
CBLC7	Phokwane		NW382	Tswaing
FS162	Kopanong		EC138	Sakhisizwe
MP322	Mbombela		EC122	Mnquma
GT414	Westonaria		EC126	Ngqushwa
NP362	Lephalale			

NW375	Moses Kotane		MP316	Dr JS Moroka
MP301	Albert Luthuli		NW391	Kagisano
NW385	Zeerust		NP04A1	Maruleng
MP324	Nkomazi		EC152	Ntabankulu
CBLC3	Greater Marble Hall		EC137	Engcobo
KZ261	eDumbe		KZ271	Umhlabuyalingana
KZ285	Mthonjaneni		KZ242	Nqutu
KZ262	uPhongolo		NW371	Moretele
KZ291	eNdondakusuka		EC153	Qaukeni
KZ266	Ulundi		KZ221	uMshwathi
KZ273	The Big 5 False Bay		EC121	Mbhashe
EC142	Senqu		EC05b2	Umzimvubu
KZ214	uMuziwabantu		KZ211	Vulamehlo
KZ284	uMlalazi		MP315	Thembisile
KZ227	Richmond		KZ254	Dannhauser
CBLC4	Greater Groblersdal		KZ224	Impendle
NP342	Mutale		CBLC5	Greater Tubatse
EC136	Emalahleni		NP03A3	Fetakgomo
KZ5a5	Ubuhlebezwe		KZ233	Indaka
NP355	Lepele-Nkumpi		NW381	Setla-Kgobi
NW1a1	Moshaweng (Segonyana)		NP351	Blouberg
CBLC6	Bushbuckridge		KZ244	Msinga
			EC155	Nyandeni
Quintile 5			KZ265	Nongoma
EC156	Mhlontlo		KZ281	Mbonambi
EC151	Mbizana		KZ272	Jozini
NP332	Greater Letaba		NP352	Aganang
NW394	Greater Taung		KZ286	Nkandla
EC141	Elundini		KZ293	Ndwedwe
EC154	Port St Johns		KZ235	Okhahlamba
KZ215	Ezingoleni		KZ294	Maphumulo
EC135	Intsika Yethu		KZ283	Ntambanana
NP343	Thulamela		KZ5a1	Ingwe
NP331	Greater Giyani		KZ236	Imbabazane
KZ226	Mkhambathini		KZ274	Hlabisa
EC05b1	Umzimkhulu		KZ213	Umzumbe
NP353	Molemole		NP03A2	Makhuduthamaga

References

Everatt D, Dube N & Ntsime M (2004) Integrated Sustainable Rural Development Programme, Phase I evaluation: Nodal Review. Johannesburg: Independent Development Trust. Available at <http://www.sarpn.org.za/documents/ d0000920/P1016-ISRDP_Phase1_June2004_t.pdf>

Hindson D & Vicente-Hindson V (2005) Whither LED in South Africa? A commentary on the policy guidelines for implementing local economic development in South Africa, March 2005. Hindson Consulting. Available at <www.selda.org.za/newsletters/whither_led.htm>

National Treasury (2004) *Intergovernmental fiscal review 2004*. Pretoria: National Treasury.

National Treasury (2005) *2004/05 Local government capital and operating expenditure budgets*. Pretoria: National Treasury.

National Treasury (2006) *Budget review 2006*. Pretoria: National Treasury.

Stats SA (Statistics South Africa) (1996) *October household survey 1996*. Pretoria: Stats SA.

Stats SA (2001) *Census 2001*. Pretoria: Stats SA.

Stats SA (2003) *Non-financial census of municipalities for the year ended 30 June 2003*. Available at <http://222.statssa.gov.za>

Stats SA (2004a) *Labour force survey September 2004*. Pretoria: Stats SA.

Stats SA (2004b) *October household survey*. Pretoria: Stats SA.

Stats SA (2005) *Non-financial census of municipalities for the year ended 2004*. Pretoria: Stats SA.

The Presidency (2003) *National Spatial Development Perspective (NSDP)*. Pretoria: Policy Co-ordination and Advisory Services. Available at <http://www.idp.org.za/content_CSIR/news/News_NSDP.html>

UNDP (United Nations Development Programme) (2004) *Human development report 2004*. Available at <http://hwww.undp.org>

Part II: Economy

Economy: introduction

John Daniel

> For all the government's good intentions on growth, not all of its
> parts are in synch…In South Africa's current 'season of hope', the
> government's main question is whether it can achieve 6 per cent
> economic growth. However, that begs a more basic question at the
> very heart of its growth drive: can South Africa keep the lights on?
> (John Reed, *Financial Times*' Special Report: South Africa, 06.06.06.)

There is a widespread consensus that the South African economy is doing not just
well but better than at any time since 1994. In a recent review, the *Economist* commented approvingly on the fact that the economy has grown 'for an impressive 87
straight months' (08.04.06) and observed that 'the government should be basking
in the glow of an outstanding economic performance over the past decade'. Two
months later, the *Financial Times* (06.06.06) adopted a similar line in a special
report on South Africa, noting the buoyant sentiment of the private sector generated by such factors as high commodity prices, increased inward investment, low
interest rates and the sustained record of solid growth.

Both reports, however, cast a shade on their optimism by noting a range of caveats
that produce a blurring of the glowing picture. These include, among others, an
uneven record of delivery, persisting high unemployment, skills shortages compounded by the legendary incompetence – willful and unintended – of the
Department of Home Affairs, electricity-supply problems and, inevitably, corruption. In reference to the 2010 World Soccer Cup and the government's ambitious
plans to build five new stadiums and refurbish five others, develop new road and
rail links and the like, the *Economist* noted that 'as likely as not, the project will get
caught up in the twin bottlenecks that have already caused so much trouble in the
new South Africa; a severe skills shortage and a failure to deliver services at the
local level' (08.04.04: 3).

What the sentiments in these two paragraphs, as well as in the quote at the head of
the chapter, reflect is the 'developmental but dysfunctional' theme articulated by
Roger Southall in the overall introduction to this volume. The seven chapters
included in this section of the volume reflect the unevenness of the growth or
developmental process on the part of this now not-so-young democracy which,
like most adolescents, is doing well in some areas and poorly in others.

The section begins with Nicoli Nattrass's discussion of what many regard as one of
the success stories of the new South Africa, namely, its emerging welfare system

which Nattrass describes, using Jeremy Seekings's words, as 'exceptional among middle-income and developing countries' (2005: 1). However, as Nattrass argues in this fascinating study, the very success of the emerging welfare net as a means of tackling South Africa's chronic poverty may also be having the unintended effect of undermining another of government's development objectives – that of improving the health of the poor and, in particular, of confronting the HIV/AIDS pandemic.

Each month some ten million social grants of one kind or another are dispensed to several million South Africans. These include old-age pensions, child-support grants and so-called disability grants. According to Nattrass, the take-up of the disability grant has been extraordinary with the number of recipients rising between 2000 and 2004 from 600 000 to some 1.3 million. This is due largely to the fact that those on the ground charged with administering the grant have interpreted its eligibility criteria liberally, treating it more as a poverty-relief programme than one dealing with only some form of disablement; thus, for example, HIV-positive status is treated as a disability, as is tuberculosis. The unanticipated consequence of this, as Nattrass shows, is that illness is now conceived by the very poor as 'an important source of income' and that this in turn is creating 'incentives for people to become or to remain ill'. Could there be a more stark testimony to the desperation of those who occupy the margins of what President Mbeki calls the 'second economy'?

Nattrass then goes on to examine a number of possible ways of plugging what she calls 'this hole' in the welfare net. These involve a managerial approach with stricter and more restrictive eligibility criteria. These would, however, cut the number of grantees, would be politically unpopular and would 'do nothing to address the perverse incentives associated with the disability grant'. A second option would be to introduce an unemployment grant which would, she believes, be administratively complicated and bureaucratically burdensome. Her alternative, and the option she favours, is the basic income grant or BIG which would have the advantages of universal cover while being easier to administer. This, in her view, would be a way of addressing the root cause of the problem in the welfare system, namely South Africa's dire levels of poverty. But, she concludes, government's resolute opposition is a major obstacle.

In his chapter, Roger Southall builds on his important analysis of the black economic empowerment process (BEE) published in last year's volume. Here he focuses on a sector of the economy targeted as a key element of the development-state strategy, namely, the parastatals or state-owned enterprises (SOEs). Capture of the state, he suggests, has provided the African National Congress (ANC) with the means to use parastatals as instruments for both promoting BEE-related goals (like extending black control over the economy and increasing opportunities for an expanding black middle class), as well as pumping vast amounts of capital into the economy to build infrastructure, create jobs and the like. There is no doubt that this leverage has strongly influenced its economic strategy, for although veering towards liberalisation under the Growth Employment and Reconstruction strategy, the outcome of the initial partial sale of Telkom pressed home the dangers that unregulated privatisation could mean sale of the 'family silver' to foreign capital without any effective transfer of economic resources to black people. It is highly significant that subsequently, with the partial exception of Telkom (in which government has continued to retain a significant 40 per cent stake), there has been no major transfer of assets to private hands, and that privatisations have otherwise been, and in the foreseeable future are likely to be, restricted to 'non-core' assets which are relatively affordable for black investors.

Southall argues that government's economic thinking has of late been shaped by its recognition of the fact that South Africa's core parastatals occupy strategic sites in the economy. The decline of both mining and manufacturing and the associated rise of finance and services which is taking place during the present era suggest that the minerals–energy complex (MEC) is no longer as central to the economy as it once was. Nonetheless, it is significant that the mining, fuels and telecommunications sectors have – along with finance – been the principal targets of the government's empowerment strategy. It is no coincidence that Patrice Motsepe's African Rainbow Minerals and Tokyo Sexwale's Mvelaphanda Holdings are amongst the largest empowerment groups and that BEE charters for the fuels and mining industries were amongst the earliest to be developed. Furthermore, as Daniel and Lutchman (2005) have demonstrated, the government attaches the highest importance to securing South Africa's mineral and energy assets by promoting South African public and private investment in these sectors throughout the wider continent. Within this context, present strategy towards the parastatals appears to remain what it always was – designed principally to service the needs of the MEC.

A significant critique of current government policy argues that it is returning to the essentials of the disastrous industrial strategy previously pursued by the National Party (NP): that it has privatised before liberalising the market (for example, Telkom); it has done nothing to break the power of privatised monopolies (notably Iscor and Sasol) which are squeezing key manufacturing sectors such as polymers and chemicals; and it is unduly protecting public monopolies such as South African Airways. From this perspective, the government's declared intent of restructuring the parastatals to reduce the cost of business in South Africa is suspect: publicly-owned arms industries are likely to turn out to be little more than money-guzzling machines, and while reforms may render state monsters like Transnet more profitable and efficient in the short term, such gains will be difficult to sustain over the longer term. The way forward, therefore, must be via the formation of public–private partnerships.

In response, Southall suggests that though such arguments are often both ideological and put forward by private capital, it does not mean they lack power, especially in a context where the ANC is manifestly using the parastatals as instruments of empowerment and class mobilisation. Under the NP, the parastatals became notorious for inefficiency and corruption. The challenge for the ANC, if its own project of a 'developmental state' is to succeed, Southall concludes, is for the SOEs to avoid a similar fate.

In a critical and provocative chapter, environmental specialist David Fig interrogates aspects of South Africa's development path and particularly the commitment to the so-called 'modernisation approach', which he suggests elevates growth above all other considerations, particularly environmental concerns. He argues that far from delivering growth and jobs, it will, as elsewhere in the developing world, deepen poverty. Fig suggests that to avoid this some of the key concepts of the 'sustainable development' model, particularly those relating to ecological limits, inter- and intra-generational equity, and popular empowerment, need to be taken seriously and applied to the policy framework. Though some of these notions have been written into the Constitution's Bill of Rights (Article 24), Fig argues that they have not been integrated into the thinking of government's macroeconomic strategists and that government's key statement of industrial policy ignores them altogether.

Fig demonstrates his argument by reference to three case studies where the decision to support and utilise specific technologies in the case of the pebble-bed nuclear reactor, the proposed development of further aluminium smelters at Coega and Richards Bay, and the development of a genetically-modified agricultural sector will, he argues, be 'unsustainable in terms of equity, empowerment and environmental protection'. He goes on further to assert that the use of these technologies will 'commit South Africa to a development path which favours greater centralisation of power, the enclosure of the commons, and the dangers of a security state'.

In speculating why government appears to be so committed to these technologies, Fig suggests that the answer lies in part in the deeply-embedded view in mainstream macroeconomic thinking that 'growth is the panacea for development' and, lip service notwithstanding, a belief that small- and medium-scale technologies are less effective in growth/development terms than large-scale hi-tech infrastructural projects. Finally, he suggests too, a whiff of 'technological nationalism' based on a notion that sees high technology as an indicator of a nation's global status.

Fig's contribution is an important one in that it not only challenges key orthodoxies that have informed government's thinking since 1994 but, in effect, rubbishes them. We hope that this chapter will generate comment and debate.

Bezuidenhout and Buhlungu's chapter moves us from issues of industrial strategy to the arena of industrial relations through a fascinating case study of how one of South Africa's most politically significant unions, the National Union of Mineworkers (NUM), is adapting to changes in the industrial structure of mining, as well as to changes in work organisation and employment practices which are posing fundamental challenges to worker power. Basing their observations upon a survey conducted among unionised mineworkers, they note that the historically important NUM is the single largest union in South Africa with some 470 000 members. However, today the number of workers employed in mining is declining, so this membership now also accounts for workers in the construction and electricity-generating industries, requiring the union to respond creatively to the issue of greater diversity. Yet there are also many other major changes with which the NUM is having to grapple. First, the mining compound is no longer the sole centre of union activity today. Whereas the union's solidarity was in the past premised upon the fact that the overwhelming majority of its members were migrants who lived in mining compounds, today many of them now live in informal settlements or in townships with their families or friends. Furthermore, many are now informally or casually employed, a factor related to an increase in the industry's growing practice of subcontracting the hiring of workers to labour-brokers. Second, competition for jobs and better-paid positions in the mining labour market is resulting in workers competing with one another along ethnic and national lines. Third, improved opportunities for upward occupational mobility – with shop stewards commonly moving on to supervisory or managerial positions – are having a negative effect upon union organisational capacity and solidarity. Fourth, changes within the industrial landscape are resulting in the erosion of union democracy and a decline in the practice of leaders consulting with members. Finally, the NUM is finding difficulty in adapting to a key change in its social composition, namely, the increasing number of women amongst its membership. Generally young, on lower wages, single and living at home, the NUM's female members are demanding equality of pay and opportunity, but complain that the union is failing them. In short, whilst Bezuidenhout and Buhlungu argue that the achievements of the NUM mirror those of the most advanced sectors of the union movement in the post-apartheid sector, they highlight key challenges to which it needs to respond if it is to retain its prominence and ability to defend the interests of its members.

Heather Hughes's chapter focuses on one of the more successful areas of post-apartheid policy planning, namely heritage and cultural tourism. In a rich and fascinating discussion of the concept of heritage Hughes illustrates how the heritage debate has been a contested one both globally and in the democratic era in South Africa and that in the process, it has emerged as a multifaceted and nuanced notion. Hughes illustrates how the effort to build a new post-apartheid heritage has been vigorous, fraught and energetic, an argument waged in academic circles, in galleries, in museums old and new, at prehistoric archeaological sites, at new so-called 'struggle' sites (Soweto) and sites weighed down by the apartheid past (such as the Voortrekker and South African War Museums).

The overall effect, in Hughes's view, has been positive both in a nation-building sense as well as in the promotion of tourism with its attendant economic spin-offs.

In regard to the latter, Hughes notes that heritage and cultural tourism has emerged as 'amongst the fastest growing of the so-called "new" forms of tourism' (as opposed to the traditional sun, sea, sand and sex varieties) and that South Africa, with its now seven sites accorded World Heritage status, has been part of this boom, attracting increasing numbers of both domestic and foreign (largely from Europe) visitors to these and other local sites. Hughes is realistic enough not to overplay this realm, however, noting that the heritage tourist is still a minority within the flock of pleasure seekers and cross-border shoppers but it is nonetheless a growth area with potential.

In regard to the harnessing of heritage in the service of nation building, Hughes shows how the passage from the Mandela to the Mbeki presidencies has seen the dominant discourse shift from notions of the 'rainbow nation' to those of the 'African Renaissance'. The latter, she notes, 'has tended to privilege different kinds of heritage, such as hominid origins and ancient black African cultures'. Hence the successful campaigns to gain World Heritage status for the Cradle of Humankind caves at Sterkfontein and the ancient palace ruins at Mapungubwe, as well as the restoration of the ancient history archives at Timbuktu – an Mbeki presidential lead project.

The African Renaissance project is not all about antiquity, Hughes notes. Its main modern expression is the Freedom Park project, which has been deliberately located on a site opposite that principal monument to Afrikaner nationalism, the Voortrekker Monument. Its intent is to convey a 'message from Africa and South Africa to the world, of suffering and the triumph of the human spirit'. While Hughes's view of Freedom Park is a positive one, she is less comfortable with another of the current manifestations of heritage in the form of cultural villages, numerous examples of which have sprung up all over the country. Representing, in her view, a cynical use of ethnicity in the vein of apartheid, Hughes sees a key aspect of this phenomenon, namely, the stress on ethnic uniqueness, as running contrary to the 'one South Africa' nation-building effort so central to the Mbeki presidency – just one more contradiction in the complex tapestry of the emerging South Africa.

By contrast with the upbeat tone of Hughes's chapter, this section is completed by two studies of what is perhaps the least successful and most fraught of the service-delivery sectors of the economy, namely, the public health arena. The first, by prominent health academics Helen Schneider, Peter Barron and Sharon Fonn, takes a broad macro-view of developments in the national health system since 1994 while the second, by Karl von Holdt and Mike Murphy, is more micro, being a case study of the public hospital system based on five years of research focused on eight hospitals, including the mother of them all, so to speak, Chris Hani Baragwanath (CHB). Despite their different foci, the conclusions of both are remarkably similar and overall non-optimistic. As Schneider et al. put it, 'despite numerous initiatives to transform the South African health system, the reality is that, in WHO's summary terms of good health, equity and responsiveness, this system is as problematic as it was 12 years ago'. B plus for effort and D for delivery might be the way a teacher would put it.

Schneider at al. begin their study by outlining the health legacy of the apartheid system, which they summarise as one of fragmentation and inequity in regard to governance and finance, human-resource provision and the skills levels thereof, physical infrastructure and so on. They then move to analysing the many initiatives post-1994 to address these inequities and acknowledge some successes, particularly in regard to the physical restructuring of the system from 14 separate but racially unequal departments down to one central ministry and nine provincial departments. They also note better regulatory oversight of the private health-care sector and overall a net growth in public health expenditure. But they go on to argue that the cumulative effect of this decade or so of policy formulation and implementation has been 'disappointing' and, in regard to the public hospitals, 'things appear to have worsened. Demoralised and demotivated are now commonplace descriptors of health-care providers and many are making use of opportunities to leave the public health system'. Von Holdt and Murphy would not disagree, nor would they dispute the fact that beyond the policy failures and frustrations lies the crushing impact on the health system of the HIV/AIDS pandemic which is literally draining the life out of the system and those charged with working in it.

Nonetheless, Schneider et al. argue that it would be an oversimplification to characterise the system as being in 'a state of collapse' and, in fact, point to some positive signals. These include the promulgation of the 2005 National Health Act which they suggest offers a real chance to co-ordinate all role players – public and private – in one common framework and in a policy context of widespread recognition that much more needs to be done to address the human resource crisis and the burden of HIV treatment. The key question now for our authors is whether the national ministry has the legitimacy and the will to reinvent itself as a 'strong steward of the health system'. Watch this space.

Von Holdt and Murphy conclude from their study that South Africa's hospitals are 'stressed', a term which refers to a plethora of ills – management incapacity, staff enduring excessive workloads and poor labour relations, and outcomes which include inadequate patient care, to cite but a few. They note too a continuance of a number of apartheid differentials; for example, a formerly black hospital like CHB enjoys a significantly lower resource allocation than a formerly white hospital located in an upmarket Johannesburg suburb.

Contributory factors to these ills are numerous but include a changing health environment consequent to the rapid rate of urbanisation in recent decades and the dramatic rise in numbers requiring medical care. However, above all, von Holdt and Murphy target the inertia and incompetence of management at the national and provincial levels, which has had the effect of producing paralysis and disempowerment at the actual hospital level.

Amongst the recommendations proposed by the authors and picked up by their principal sponsor, the National Labour and Ecomomic Development Institute, is that 'full management authority should be devolved to hospitals while provincial head offices should concentrate on auditing hospital performance in relation to clinical patient care and financial targets…' and so on. In a dramatic policy shift in July 2006, the new health MEC in Gauteng announced the adoption of this proposal, and stated that, beginning with CHB, there would be a full delegation of authority to hospital managers.

So, just as Schneider et al. detected signs of hope in regard to health-care policy, so perhaps there is optimism to be derived from this initial government response to the recommendations emanating from the work of von Holdt and Murphy. Beyond that, what these two chapters illustrate is that the provision of adequate health care to its citizenry is an enormous and complex task, which taxes the ingenuity and resources of even the wealthiest of states. The problems besetting Britain's National Health Service – regarded by many as amongst the most effective health-care systems in the world – have burdened successive British governments for the past two to three decades. The fact is that what we have today is a curious paradox, namely, that as the people of the modern world grow taller and stronger, eat better and live longer, it is becoming harder and harder and certainly more expensive to keep them healthy.

References

Daniel J & Lutchman J (2005) South Africa in Africa: Scrambling for energy. In S Buhlungu et al. (Eds) *The State of the Nation: South Africa 2005–2006*. Cape Town: HSRC Press.

Seekings J (2005) *Prospects for basic income in developing countries: A comparative analysis of welfare regimes in the South*. Cape Town: Centre for Social Science Research Working Paper, No. 104. Available at <http://www.csr.uct.ac.za>

7 Disability and welfare in South Africa's era of unemployment and AIDS

Nicoli Nattrass

South Africa's welfare system is exceptional among middle-income and developing countries (Seekings 2005a). It provides contextually generous means-tested non-contributory old-age pensions for the elderly, disability grants for those too ill or incapacitated to work, and child-support grants for the caregivers of children. Approximately ten million social grants are paid out each month, amounting to about 3 per cent of the gross domestic product (GDP). Nonetheless, despite this relatively generous level of social assistance, pressure on the welfare system continues to grow – most notably on disability grants which rose from about 600 000 in 2000 to almost 1.3 million in 2004 (Nattrass 2006).

This is in part a consequence of the AIDS epidemic. As can be seen in Figure 7.1, South Africa has one of the highest rates of HIV infection in the world. According to the Actuarial Society of South Africa 2003 demographic model, by 2004, half a million new AIDS-sick cases were occurring each year.[1] Many of these people were able to access disability grants. A recent analysis of a sample of disability grant files reported that the number of disability grants for people suffering from 'retroviral disease' or who were 'immuno-compromised' rose from 27 per cent in 2001 to 41 per cent in 2003 (CASE 2005: 63).

However, AIDS is not the only reason for the rapid take-up in disability grants. The increase was facilitated by institutional changes to the disability grant system that enabled local decision-makers to respond to growing pressure from citizens to use the disability grant in part as a form of poverty relief. This pressure, in turn, is a consequence of South Africa's high rate of unemployment (see Figures 7.1 and 7.2) and the absence of any social security for the unemployed.[2] Unemployment is now the major driver of poverty and inequality (Seekings & Nattrass 2005) – a situation exacerbated for many by the AIDS epidemic (Nattrass 2004a). Given that the disability grant is the only social grant available to adults of working age, it is unsurprising that South Africa's dual crisis of unemployment and AIDS (see Figure 7.1) is resulting in a sharp increase in the number of disability grants allocated.

This poses a major challenge for South Africa's welfare system: should it continue to be based on the manifestly incorrect premise that all able-bodied adults can support themselves through work, or should it be redesigned to address the large hole in the welfare net through which so many unemployed people are currently falling? This chapter argues that in light of the perverse incentives generated by the current

Figure 7.1 *A comparative perspective on AIDS and unemployment*

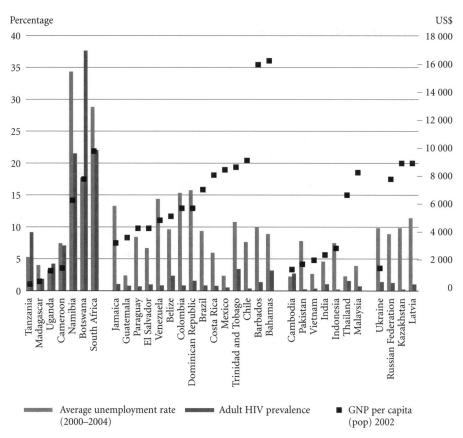

Sources: Ilo <http://www.laboursta.ilo.org>; World Bank Development Indicators <http://www.worldbank.org>;
UNAIDS/WHO <http://www.who.int/globalatlas/default.asp>.

system (which leaves many people choosing between income and health), wide-ranging changes are needed to the welfare system. Building on earlier work (Nattrass 2006), the chapter argues that there is growing evidence that current disability policy is creating incentives for people to become and/or remain ill – and that this could be exacerbating the AIDS epidemic and undermining the anti-retroviral treatment roll-out.

There is also evidence of an emerging recognition on the part of local decision-makers of the legitimacy of claims by poor people to improved levels of social security – especially for the unemployed. Recent changes wrought by the national government to tighten up access to the disability grant thus fly in the face of this emerging discourse of citizens' rights. They are therefore likely to be unpopular and will probably continue to be subverted by local decision-makers wherever possible. Rather than attempting to restrict access to social grants, a case is made for broadening access to the unemployed either by introducing an employment guarantee scheme (to provide jobs directly) or a basic-income grant (to provide a minimum, unconditional income to all citizens).

The disability grant system

As specified in the Social Assistance Act (Act 59 of 1992/Act 13 of 2004), individuals are eligible for a disability grant if they pass a means test and if, as a result of mental or physical disability, they are unable to provide for themselves through employment or professional activity. The grant is designed for working-aged adults[3] under the clear expectation that those who are in principle capable of working should not be eligible. According to regulations issued by the national Minister of Social Development, a person is only eligible if the degree of his or her disability makes him or her incapable of entering a labour market. The applicant must not refuse to accept employment which is within his or her capabilities, or to receive treatment which may improve his or her condition. In other words, the grant is not designed to compensate people for their disabilities per se, but rather to compensate them for the impact of their disability on earning potential – that people may be able and desire to work, but unable to find it, is irrelevant to the legislation. But it appears not to have been irrelevant for all of those awarding disability grants between 2001 and 2004.

There is evidence that the rapid take-up of disability grants between 2001 and 2004 was facilitated by institutional changes to the grant awarding process and by sympathy on the part of at least some decision-makers towards using the grant to provide poverty relief for applicants. The 2001 amendment (effective from December 2001) to the Social Assistance Act empowered provinces to disestablish the role of the Pension Medical Officer (PMO), who previously had evaluated and adjudicated disability grant recommendations made by medical officers (MOs), thereby ensuring a degree of oversight and standardisation to the system. The amendment gave provinces the choice of continuing with the old system, or replacing it with assessment panels (APs), whose members did not necessarily have to be medical doctors, or with a mixture of APs and MOs (see the appendix to this chapter for a summary of the different approaches adopted by the provinces). This move in the direction of 'community-based' targeting was consistent with the growing recognition internationally that, given the complexity and high cost of disability targeting, the community may be in a better position than bureaucrats to determine eligibility.[4] However, it enabled 'social' factors to be introduced into what the legislation envisaged should be a purely 'medical' decision.

In 2004, the National Treasury commissioned a group of researchers from the Community Agency for Social Enquiry (CASE) to determine the reasons behind the sharp increase in disability grants. As part of this project, researchers visited

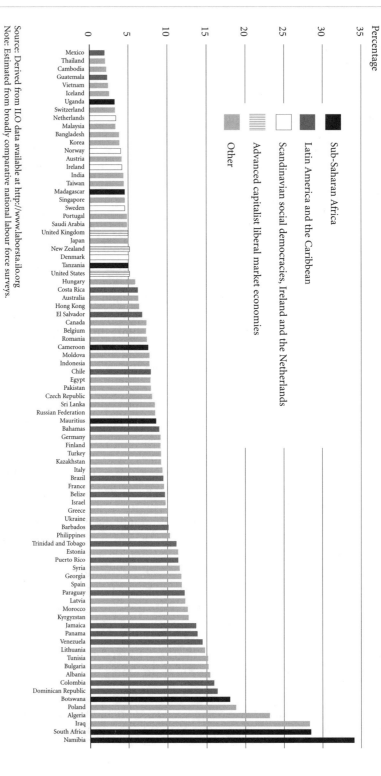

Figure 7.2 *National strict unemployment rates, 2000–2004*

Percentage

Sub-Saharan Africa

Latin America and the Caribbean

Scandinavian social democracies, Ireland and the Netherlands

Advanced capitalist liberal market economies

Other

Source: Derived from ILO data available at http://www.laborsta.ilo.org
Note: Estimated from broadly comparative national labour force surveys.

selected sites in all provinces and spoke to a range of officials involved in the assessment and award of disability grants. They reported that poverty and unemployment were the most commonly cited reasons for the increase in the number of grants:

> The perception that the disability grant is viewed as a form of poverty alleviation by both applicants and some involved in the assessment and approval process was almost universal, although interviewees differed in whether they were sympathetic to this interpretation or not. (CASE 2005: 92)

The research report includes a set of perceptive quotes and observations on this issue. For example, at Ongoye in KwaZulu-Natal, the clerks argued that poverty is rife in the area and that the disability grant is viewed as '*igrant yokuhlupheka*' or 'the grant for the poor people', both by the general public and some involved in the assessment process. A provincial verification official from Xhariep in the Free State is reported as saying that: 'The problem is that people seem to think that if I do not have a job, then I can apply for the disability grant so that I can get some money to feed my family' (CASE 2005: 92). Officials told researchers that APs in KwaZulu-Natal and the North West province were sympathetic to the social plight of people and awarded grants to help them 'maintain themselves'.

This growth in the number of disability grant recipients was not always seen as a problem by officials. A senior official in the Xhariep District Office described the introduction of APs as 'effective in that many people came into the system and that is an improvement that one would say the department has achieved in terms of bringing services to the people'. He did observe, however, that the department 'did not have enough funds' for this (quoted in CASE 2005: 93). A similar note was struck by an official from KwaZulu-Natal:

> The disability grant, as the name indicates, should be based only on disablement [sic]. But somehow it becomes a bit difficult to ignore the socio-economic part...because people who are living in rural areas may not be working or do not necessarily have opportunities to work. But we don't necessarily want to change the disability to be a basic income [grant]. (Quoted in CASE 2005: 94)

The above quotes point to the ambiguity experienced by officials involved in the disability grant system at local levels: they see the need for greater social security, yet appreciate that the disability grant may not be the appropriate vehicle for it. At the same time, they appear to recognise (and appreciate) an emerging discourse of access to social grants as a right of citizens and an obligation of the state. According to the CASE report:

> Interviewees also noted that in the context of high unemployment many people feel that the government has a responsibility to provide

them with social assistance and that they are entitled to these grants. In some provinces this was blamed on the government's 'marketing' of the social grants, which leads the public to believe that if they have no income they will be entitled to access assistance from the government. A senior verification official at the Bloemfontein provincial office remarked: 'Is it not that people think [they can get the disability grant] because the government is saying that every person has the right to social security?'(CASE 2005: 95)

This emerging interpretation of the rights of citizens to social assistance seems to have been assisted by the expansion of the number of Department of Social Development service points and by various awareness campaigns. As an official from the Northern Cape put it:

There are many people who are more aware of their rights. If you look at places like the old homeland states, those people never knew what a grant was. They only knew the old age grant. So as freedom came with education and the bill of rights and the necessary campaigns and *imbizos* of government, [that] made people to knock on government doors. (Quoted in CASE 2005: 95)

In order to stop the disability grant from becoming a form of poverty alleviation, the CASE report recommended a narrow set of managerial solutions including the adoption of standardised assessment tools and clear uniform eligibility criteria, the simplification of the means test and its enforcement for every applicant, and better education of frontline staff about the rules of disability grant management (CASE 2005). Such recommendations were consistent with the letter and spirit of many reforms that had already taken place in 2004 to reduce the growth in disability grants. These included the scrapping of APs and/or the sharp curtailment of the discretionary powers of local officials (see the appendix for more detail).

The problem with this policy response is twofold. Firstly, it does nothing to address the social roots of the growth in disability grants – that is, unemployment, poverty and AIDS. Secondly, it is blind to the complex reasons why many local-level MOs and/or APs, responding to local conditions, awarded large numbers of disability grants as soon as the system provided the flexibility to allow it. Although this resulted in policy variation within the country (something which neither the CASE researchers nor the National Treasury approved of), it had the advantage of being responsive to local conditions and social attitudes. The new measures are thus likely to lack legitimacy and will probably continue to be subverted by sympathetic MOs and other local officials.

A possible response to this would be to tighten the rules yet further and introduce another layer of bureaucrats to check local officials. This, however, could raise costs substantially. For example, in the USA, where successful applicants have to survive a rigorous 'five-step disability test', disability payments comprise only 15 per cent of total social security benefit payments, yet account for 45 per cent of the administrative costs (Mitra 2005). Reducing the number of beneficiaries in this way will thus come at the (deadweight) cost of a more bloated bureaucracy whilst doing nothing to address the underlying problem of inadequate social assistance for the unemployed. Furthermore, it will do nothing to address the perverse incentives created by the system for people to become and remain ill/disabled.

Perverse incentives to become and remain ill or disabled

Given South Africa's high unemployment rates and relatively generous disability grants, illness has itself become an important source of income (Nattrass 2006). This reality is reflected in the following quote from a MO in a tuberculosis (TB) clinic in the Western Cape:

> In my experience, the majority of the patients are really coming mainly because they are unemployed and not so much because of illness. It seems sometimes to me that developing TB is a kind of a blessing for some of them, that they now stand a chance of getting a grant.
> (Quoted in CASE 2005: 93)

The problem with this, of course, is that if illness is a much desired ticket to a grant, then this may well undermine adherence to the treatment required to cure (or manage) the illness. A MO from the Northern Cape complained of precisely this with regard to TB patients: 'People won't take their tablets...because they want to stay on the system. Poverty is in such a proportion that people will do things that could kill them to get the grant' (quoted in CASE 2005: 93).

The same problem is evident with regard to AIDS. There are reports that people may be attempting to become HIV-positive in order to get the disability grant (Leclerc-Madlala 2005; Nattrass 2006). The fact that until late 2004, the North West province allocated disability grants to people simply on the basis of being HIV-positive may have contributed to this problem. Since then, provincial policy towards AIDS-related disability grants has been standardising around a medical model which restricts disability grants to those who are AIDS-sick (that is, in the final stages of the illness – usually understood to occur when a patient's CD4 cell count drops below 200 cells per millilitre of blood).[5] This means that being HIV-positive is not enough; people must be deemed to be suffering from AIDS. This, in turn, has created incentives for people to become ill. In this regard, a representative of the National Association of People with Aids, has been quoted as saying that HIV-positive people who had not yet become 'sick enough' to qualify for the disability grant start 'neglecting themselves' in order to 'qualify for government grants to put bread on the table'.[6] He went on to argue for job creation for HIV-positive people. This highlights, once again, the growing desperation amongst adults of working age who cannot access social assistance – and the enormous pressure that this is placing on the disability grant as a consequence.

As discussed in Nattrass (2006), this problem is also potentially serious with regard to the antiretroviral (ARV) treatment roll-out. ARV treatment has the effect of restoring a person's immune system, thereby facilitating a rebound in their CD4 cell counts. As their health improves, they therefore no longer qualify for the disability grant. This is entirely consistent with the underlying premise of South Africa's welfare system – that only those too sick to work should be provided with social assistance. As the ARV roll-out progresses through the country, more and more people will lose their disability grants. It has been estimated that by 2010, more people will be losing their disability grants through restored health than will be gaining access to them (Nattrass 2006).

This is likely to cause severe economic hardship to households that had previously relied on the grant (Nattrass 2006) as well as undermine the food security and health of people on ARV therapy. According to Dr Khumalo of Rob Ferreira Hospital in Mpumalanga:

> It does not help that the government takes away the grant once a person becomes better on treatment. Personally, I don't approve because most people on antiretrovirals are poor and they need the grant to survive. With the grant they are able to buy basic food that is necessary to complement antiretroviral treatment. After the 12-month deadline of the grant expires, patients start to become depressed and they start developing side effects to their treatment since most of them have to take their medication on an empty stomach. Without the grant you find that the patient's CD4 counts drop and they start becoming very ill again. (Quoted in *Equal Treatment* December 2005: 11)

Anecdotal evidence from patients and doctors suggests that some individuals may opt to stop adhering to their ARV therapy in order to increase their viral loads and reduce their CD4 cell counts in order to re-qualify for the disability grant (Leclerc-Madlala 2005; Nattrass 2006). A recent AIDS Consortium meeting of representatives of close to 100 organisations dealing with HIV/AIDS from Limpopo and Gauteng highlighted the poverty-alleviating aspect of the disability grant and reported that people were indeed refusing to adhere to ARV therapy 'because they are scared that their CD4 count will improve and they will lose the grant' (AIDS Consortium Press Release 15.08.05). The press release noted that some people would 'rather die of AIDS than lose the disability grant'.

That people are considering trading off their health in order to obtain access to a disability grant is an act of terrible desperation. It reflects the enormous problem of poverty and unemployment in a context where the only form of social assistance for able-bodied adults is the disability grant. No wonder, then, that many APs and MOs between 2001 (when greater discretion was facilitated by institutional changes) and late 2004 (when greater controls were imposed in all provinces) felt compelled to consider the socio-economic environment facing disability grant applicants when making their recommendations for disability grants. This was not simply a matter of them adopting a rival 'social' model of disability over the managerially neater (and fiscally cheaper) 'medical' model. It almost certainly also reflects the fact that medical approaches to illness could not be isolated from the social context. Discussion of policy options needs to be cognisant of this reality.

Towards policy reform

All welfare systems are predicated to some extent on the duty of individuals to work, the idea being that welfare should function as a safety net rather than as an alternative to work. However, welfare systems differ in terms of the level of welfare support and in terms of the policing mechanisms they put in place to ensure that the so-called 'undeserving' do not access social assistance.

In developed economy welfare systems people of working age are either assisted to find employment, or have access to social security in the form of income support for the unemployed (or if they are disabled, in the form of disability grants). The underlying assumption is that adults of working age should be productively engaged, and where possible should contribute to social insurance schemes to provide for their own retirement, disability, and periods of unemployment. Social assistance from the state is targeted specifically at those who have been unable to contribute to social insurance schemes or whose benefits from such schemes have proved inadequate (for example, for long periods of unemployment). Social assistance is typically means-tested and in many countries is increasingly dependent on participation in labour-market programmes designed to improve the employability of grant recipients and to assist them in finding work. This approach has been made easier by buoyant economic conditions in the advanced capitalist countries and by specific labour-market reforms to boost employment.

By contrast, most developing countries do not have such comprehensive welfare nets. Instead, they rely on people being able to earn an income through employment (whether in the formal or informal economy, or in the agrarian sector) and being supported by their kin (Seekings 2005b). Over the past two decades, urbanisation, de-agrarianisation and a declining capacity to absorb new labour-market entrants into formal employment have posed challenges for many developing country welfare regimes. Some, like Mexico, opted to boost employment through labour-demanding growth strategies (including flexible labour-market policies) and by supporting the incomes of the poor through a set of targeted programmes (Mitra 2005; Whitworth et al. 2005). Others have opted to introduce more 'workfare' oriented policies. Such countries include India, which expanded the Employment Guarantee Scheme (previously limited to Maharashtra) to the entire country (Bagchee 2005; Seekings 2005b); Ethiopia, where social assistance in the form of food aid is conditional on participation in public works programmes, and only those too sick to work are allocated free food aid (Quisumbing & Yohannes

2005); and Argentina and South Korea, which introduced massive public works programmes to cope with economic crisis (Seekings 2005b).

In neither the developed nor developing economy welfare regimes do the disabled have an incentive to become or remain disabled. In developed economy welfare regimes people are provided with support if they are poor, unemployed and want to work, or are too disabled to work (see Figure 7.3). There is no hole in the welfare net. Most developing countries target the poor in general (rather than the disabled in particular) and place great importance on promoting income-earning opportunities. There is thus no incentive built into these welfare systems for the poor to become disabled, or to prevent themselves from becoming cured of their disabilities. South Africa is one of only a few developing countries that provide a disability grant[7] – but it has done so in a context in which there is little or no support for the unemployed, thus resulting in a set of perverse incentives to become or remain disabled.

One option is for South Africa to scrap the disability grant system altogether. However, this would be unethical and unpopular as public opinion in South Africa seems to be supportive of the disability grant (Seekings 2005c). Another option would be to provide special labour-market programmes for those losing their disability grants as a result of restored health (that is, providing support for a rightward shift in Figure 7.3). The state could, for example, introduce specially targeted job creation schemes or provide tax incentives for firms to provide preferential employment for such individuals. The problem with this option is twofold: it is expensive and administratively complex, and it is unfair. Other unemployed people could justifiably ask why those who had previously benefited from a disability grant are given preferential treatment. Such a situation could exacerbate the existing perverse incentive to become disabled.

Alternatively, the state could improve the leftward shift options outlined in Figure 7.3, and provide social support for the previously disabled unemployed. This could, perhaps, take the form of a reduced disability grant for those whose health has improved, but who cannot find a job. In the case of AIDS patients, this could perhaps be called a 'treatment-support grant', which although lower in value to the disability grant, would serve to provide some poverty relief. But, like the preferential or targeted labour-market support, such policies may be perceived as unfair by those who never had access to the disability grant in the first place. And, once it became known that people with AIDS were able to access a disability grant when they were ill, and then a 'treatment-support grant' once they were on treatment (and had their health restored), this could exacerbate the perverse incentive to become HIV-positive.

In short, there are compelling reasons for the government to reconsider the structure of the entire welfare system if it is to address the problems currently posed by the disability grant. Crucially, it needs to address the incentive problems posed by the mismatch between the premise of full employment and the reality on the ground.

Figure 7.3 *Labour market participation and the disabled adult*

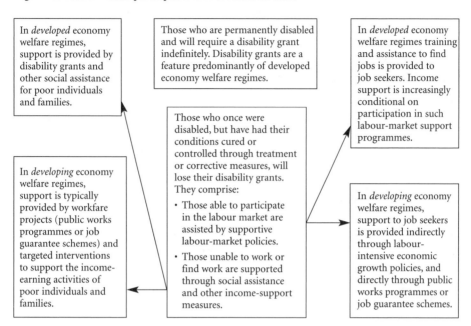

The most obvious policy response is to boost the rate of job creation. This, however, will not be easy. Despite relatively rapid economic growth since 2000 (the economy is growing at 4.5 per cent, its fastest rate since the boom years of the 1960s), unemployment rates have barely changed since 2000.[8] Although there has been some improvement in the rate of job creation since 1995, much of this is a statistical artefact (resulting from measurement changes) or driven by the expansion of low-earning, low-productivity informal sector activities (Casale et al. 2004). The fact that the expansion in formal jobs has been so sluggish in response to rapid economic growth indicates that South Africa's long-standing employment problem is likely to remain intractable in the short to medium term. This is in part a consequence of South Africa's economic structure, and in part a consequence of resistance on the part of South Africa's trade unions to labour-market reforms (Nattrass 2004b; Seekings & Nattrass 2005).

Employment guarantee scheme

Another possible response is for the government to deliver jobs directly through an employment guarantee scheme (EGS) such as that in the Indian state of Maharashtra, now recently expanded to the whole of India (Bagchee 2005; Pellissary 2005). Although the South African government supports the idea of 'massive' public works programmes as its preferred policy response to unemployment, this has been more of a rhetorical commitment than a reality. The Community-Based Public Works Programme of 2002/03 was able to provide only 1 per cent of the number of work days demanded by South Africa's unemployed, and the Expanded Public Works Programme (initiated in April 2004 to improve the labour intensity of infrastructure provision) is unlikely to do any better (see McCord 2003; McCord & Van Seventer 2004).

In short, if public works programmes are to succeed in making a significant dent in unemployment, a major increase in managerial and financial resources is required.[9] However, as is the case with promoting labour-demanding economic growth, this task will remain hampered by wage-setting institutions. Mean wages paid by the Gundu Lashu infrastructural project in the Limpopo province of South Africa are five times higher than that available on the Indian EGS and double the earnings in South African subsistence agriculture (McCord 2004; Seekings 2005c). This has resulted in some disruption of local labour markets (8 per cent of workers on the scheme reported giving up or reducing alternative work) and in poor targeting (as only 1 per cent of job opportunities went to previously unemployed individuals). If wages continue to be set at (or close to) industrial sector minima, the number of employment opportunities created will be constrained and poorly targeted at those who need them.

Such institutional constraints on the implementation of an extensive pro-poor public works programme suggest that South Africa may have to address the problem of unemployment and poverty by plugging the hole in the welfare net by other means. This could be done through the introduction of targeted social assistance for the unemployed (a 'dole'). The downside of this proposal is that additional financial and human resources would need to be deployed to manage such a new means-tested grant and to prevent fraudulent claims. This task would be made all the more difficult by the fact that unlike the disability grant (which requires documented assessment of disability) or the old-age pension (which is linked to age as well as income), the labour-market status of people describing themselves as unemployed will be difficult to prove and monitor over time.

A possible solution to this problem would be to go down the route of Indian 'workfare', where the state guarantees each household 100 days of low-wage employment, and if in the unusual event of there being insufficient work opportunities, the state is required to pay the wage as a grant. In the Maharashtra EGS, the grant was never paid but rather its potential claim by villagers petitioning the state for employment to be provided in their area was sufficient to embarrass the state into providing the necessary jobs (Bagchee 2005). As Bagchee points out, the system was successful precisely because it was politicised at every level, with villagers expressing their voices through village structures which were subsequently successfully channelled to those responsible for providing employment projects on demand.[10] Given South Africa's massive unemployment problem and the major challenges entailed in improving local government structures and providing work opportunities for all, the introduction of an EGS in South Africa would, at least in the short term, almost certainly result in the payment of a substantial number of grants. This would inevitably result in poor targeting because it is only once low-wage employment comes on line that only the very poor – those prepared to work for low wages – become self-targeted.

What would this cost? As of March 2005, there were 4.3 million unemployed people actively seeking work. The number of unemployed rises to 8.1 million if we include in the definition of the unemployed those who say they want work but are not actively seeking it. Let us assume that the government introduces a low-wage EGS paying R20 a day (a wage which is over three times that paid on Indian job guarantee schemes) for a maximum of 100 days a year and that 75 per cent of the active job seekers queue up to demand this work. The total wage bill will amount to R6.45 billion. If we assume that the administrative and managerial costs double the costs of the programme, then the government would have to find an extra total of R12.9 billion a year to fund a job guarantee scheme; if 75 per cent of the broadly defined unemployed demand work, then the costs would rise to R24.3 billion a year. In other words, depending on take-up, the cost of a low-wage job guarantee scheme would cost between 1.1 per cent and 1.8 per cent of GDP, and would require an increase in the tax-take of between 3–7 per cent. Note, however, that if labour-market and economic policy reforms were implemented to encourage the growth of labour-intensive employment, then the numbers of unemployed would fall, and the number of taxpayers would rise, thereby reducing and spreading the tax burden associated with an EGS. And, if the value of existing welfare grants were reduced, this would also reduce the pressure on the fiscus.

A basic-income grant

The alternative to such a 'workfare' or targeted welfare policy interventions for the unemployed is to opt for a universal, non-conditional basic income grant (BIG) that is paid to all citizens.[11] This idea was proposed by the government's Taylor Committee (2002), supported by academics,[12] and promoted by a wide range of civil society organisations (the BIG coalition). A BIG has the advantage of being administratively efficient as no means test nor test of employment status needs to be administered (as would be the case with the introduction of a unemployment-linked social assistance), and neither would additional government resources need to be mobilised to provide employment opportunities for the poor (as would be the case with an EGS). As Seekings points out, as the state:

> already delivers 10 million grants every month, increasingly making use of computerised banking technologies, introducing a basic income grant would double the welfare budget and entail between four and five times as many payments per month, but this challenge would be minor compared to that of implementing massive public works programmes. (2005b: 22)

The downside of a BIG is that the government is opposed to it and public opinion seems to favour the allocation of social assistance to the 'deserving' poor more than it favours universal grants, which are seen as being paid to the (undeserving) rich and poor alike (Seekings 2005c).[13] Of course the introduction of a BIG can be highly targeted and redistributive if linked to a simultaneous increase in value-added tax (VAT) – but this is a complex argument to put across to the average citizen. Le Roux (2003) has shown that a BIG of R100 a month to all citizens would cost R54 billion a year – but that most of this could be 'clawed back' if VAT was increased by seven percentage points, resulting in a net additional cost of R15 billion a year. His calculations suggest that people who spend less than R1 000 a month will be net beneficiaries of the BIG, and all those rich enough to spend more than R1 000 a month will pay more in VAT than they benefit from the BIG. Such a tax-financed BIG would thus be highly redistributive, but would require that VAT rises to the levels found in Kenya and Tanzania. It is also likely to be resisted by those groups (including most unionised workers) whose monthly expenditures exceed R1 000 a month (Matisonn & Seekings 2003).

Managing disability in the context of an employment guarantee scheme or a basic-income grant

Whether South Africa opts for targeted social assistance for the unemployed, an EGS or a BIG, there is a strong case for addressing the large hole in South Africa's welfare net – not only will it address the problem of poverty experienced by many unemployed people, but it will help reduce the perverse incentive built into the current system for people to become or remain ill/disabled. However, if the income gap between the disability grant and these new forms of support for the unemployed remains large, then the incentive problem may not disappear altogether.

Table 7.1 explores the impact of the loss of a disability grant on a hypothetical grant-dependent household. In the current policy context, the loss of a disability grant results in a 100 per cent drop in income for the disability grant recipient, and a 40 per cent decrease in household income. If the loss of the disability grant occurred in the context of an EGS offering R20 a day for 100 days per year to the unemployed (that is, an average monthly income of R167), then not only would the household be better off to start with, but the drop in personal income for the disability grant recipient would be smaller (R613 as opposed to R780) and household income would fall by only 27.2 per cent. A similar cushioning effect is evident if the loss of the disability grant takes place in the context of a BIG.

In other words, if additional forms of social assistance were available to other members of the household (for example, a BIG or an EGS), then the loss of disability grant income is less severe for total household income – and there will thus be less pressure on people to undermine their health in order to access disability

Table 7.1 *The negative impact on household income of the cancellation of a disability grant in rands, different scenarios*

	Current package of social assistance (R)	With an EGS* (R)	With a BIG (R)	With an EGS* and 10% lower-value grants (R)
Disability grant recipient	780	780	780	702
Unemployed adult 1	0	167	100	167
Unemployed adult 2	0	167	100	167
Non-labour force participant	0	0	100	0
Child of qualifying age for the child-support grant 1	180	180	180	162
Child of qualifying age for the child-support grant 2	180	180	180	162
Child not of qualifying age for the child-support grant	0	0	100	0
Old-age pensioner	780	780	780	702
Total household income	1 920	2 254	2 320	2 062
Total household income minus disability grant	1 140	1 474	1 540	1 360
New income source for previously disabled individual	0	167	100	167
Total household income following the loss of the disability grant	1 140	1 641	1 640	1 527
Absolute drop in household income as a result of the loss of a disability grant	780	613	680	535
Drop in household income (%)	40.6	27.2	29.3	25.9

Note: * If a person works 100 days at R20 a day, this amounts to R2 000 a year – an average of R167 a month.

grant income. However, the fall in personal income as a consequence of the cancellation of the disability grant is still substantial. This is a consequence of the relatively generous levels of social grants in South Africa.

As South Africa already allocates a much greater share of GDP to social grants than any other middle-income or developing country, consideration should probably be given to reducing the value of existing grants when expanding coverage to repair the hole in the welfare net. Although reducing the value of grants will not be popular because existing grants comprise such an important share of household income for the poor, if this is accompanied by the introduction of new grants or income opportunities which more than make up for the loss in value of existing grants, then the measure will be easier to sell politically. The final column of Table 7.1 shows the impact of the loss of a disability grant in the context of an EGS and a 10 per cent reduction in the value of existing social grants. In this scenario, household income falls by 26 per cent as a consequence of the loss of disability grant income, and the disability grant recipient experiences a decline of R535 rather than the R780 which is currently the case. Reducing the value of existing social grants thus has the benefit of freeing up 0.3 per cent of GDP (which could finance between 17 per cent and 27 per cent of the resources needed for an EGS)[14] as well as substantially reducing the trade-off between income and health.

The discussion so far has sought to address the problem of perverse incentives to become or remain disabled by discussing policies designed to narrow the income differential between disabled and non-disabled adults. An alternative approach is to address the problem by changing the way that disability grants are administered – especially those for people with long-term chronic conditions which could be managed successfully with treatment.

It would be possible, for example, to address the problem of people choosing not to comply with their medication by requiring proof of compliance with treatment regimens. This appears to be the emerging policy stance in the Eastern Cape and the North West provinces (see appendix). However, short of the kind of 'directly observed therapy' policy whereby patients have to take their medication in the presence of a witness, treatment adherence is impossible to monitor in any fooproof manner. Pill counts can be subverted and clinical markers (such as falling CD4 counts in the case of patients with AIDS) are not always indicative of non-compliance. For example, CD4 counts may fall because the patient stopped taking his or her medication, or they could fall because of emerging drug resistance, thus indicating that the patient needs to change drug regimens. Certainly in the case of ARV treatment, attempts to enforce adherence through coercive measures are likely to be resource-intensive and unlikely to succeed. Addressing the root of the problem – the need for income on the part of the person on treatment – is almost certainly preferable.

In the scenario sketched in Table 7.1, a person becoming well enough to work (and hence no longer eligible for the disability grant) at least has the prospects of earning an average of R167 per month through the EGS. Officials managing the EGS should be sensitive to the needs and capacities of people living on ARV treatment (they have to attend clinics regularly and may not be able to perform heavy manual labour) and be required to offer appropriate jobs to people on ARV therapy. If no appropriate jobs are available, then (as would be the case in any job centre which cannot provide work to those demanding it), the applicant for the EGS should be awarded a cash grant equivalent to the average monthly earnings on the programme (R167 in Table 7.1) until appropriate work can be found.

Conclusion

In sum, there are two ways to address the problems facing South Africa's disability grant system. The first is to adopt a managerial solution by developing stricter guidelines for eligibility. This will probably restrict the numbers of people accessing disability grants (although local officials will no doubt continue to impose local interpretations of the rules). More importantly, it will put a lid on the number of grants (at the cost of considerable hardship for many poor households) and will do nothing to address the perverse incentives associated with the disability grant. This could well undermine the success of the ARV treatment programme and undermine other disease management programmes, such as that for TB.

The second option is to address the root cause of the problem by repairing the hole in South Africa's welfare net. This could be done through the introduction of a grant for the unemployed (a 'dole'), or an EGS, or a BIG. The biggest problem with a grant for the unemployed is that it is administratively difficult to determine which individuals are really unemployed – that is, would be prepared to work if offered a job. An EGS has the advantage of self-targeting the poor unemployed (only those prepared to work at low wages will take advantage of the job opportunities). For this to work, however, wages would need to be low, and there may well be opposition from organised labour to this. Another challenge for the EGS is developing the institutional capacity at local level to provide jobs on demand. A BIG has the advantage of providing universal cover, and is administratively easier. However, the government's opposition to a BIG remains an important obstacle.

Notes

1   The ASSA model can be downloaded from the ASSA website at <http://www.assa.org.za>.

2   There is some social insurance for the unemployed. The Unemployment Insurance Fund (UIF) provides income support for up to 36 weeks for those who have contributed to the fund who subsequently become unemployed. However, typically fewer than 5 per cent of unemployed people receive UIF payments.

3   Disabled individuals below the age of 18 are eligible for child-support grants (through their caregivers), and those who have reached pensionable age (60 for women, 65 for men) receive the old-age pension rather than the disability grant.

4   See Mitra (2005) on international recognition of the complexities and expense of disability targeting, and the advantages that community targeting may bring to the system. Responsibility for disability grants has been devolved to provincial/state level in Canada, and to municipal level in Sweden precisely to ensure that it is tailored to local conditions (Whitworth et al. 2005).

5   Leclerc-Madlala reports that a Durban hospital has decided to support applications for disability grants only for those patients whose CD4 counts are below 50 in order to 'stem the rising tide of patients seeking grant certificates' (2005: 6).

6   Quoted in HIV/AIDS News no.126, 15/7/05, available at <http://www.learnscapes.co.za>.

7   Others include for example Namibia, Mauritius, Argentina, Barbados, the Bahamas, Brazil, Costa Rica and Bermuda (Mitra 2005).

8   In September 2000 and March 2005, the percentage of the workforce actively seeking employment was 25.4 per cent and 26.5 per cent respectively.

9   Non-wage costs of public works programmes are likely to be at least 27 per cent of total expenditure, as has historically been the case in the Maharashtra EGS (Dev 1995), and possibly as high as 48 per cent, which was the average non-wage cost of the South African public works programme implemented between 1992–98 (McCord 2003: 18).

10 Pellissery (2005), however, cautions that the political mobilisation was not always in the best interests of the poor as there was potential for political elites to control access to jobs, and to direct the creation of productive assets through the programme to private interests.

11 As such, it would need to be paid only to those with valid identity documents. Introducing a BIG would thus require that all administrative backlogs with regard to issuing of identity documents be addressed.

12 See articles in the edited collection by Standing and Samson (2003).

13 For example, a representative survey of Cape Town found that over 80 per cent of respondents agreed that the government should do more to help the unemployed, but smaller majorities (less than 60 per cent) supported the introduction of a BIG (Seekings 2005d: 12).

14 The estimate is based on the assumption that South Africa currently spends 3 per cent of its GDP on social grants. A 10 per cent reduction in the value of social grants will thus free up 0.3 per cent of GDP. As estimated earlier, an EGS will probably absorb between 1.1 per cent and 1.8 per cent of GDP depending on take-up rates. Thus, 0.3 per cent of GDP will pay for between 27.3 and 16.7 per cent of the resources needed to introduce an EGS.

Appendix: *Provincial differences in disability grant policy and trends*

Province (percentage of total disability grants as of August 2005)	Percentage of grants awarded by APs (2003)*	Other institutional changes
Eastern Cape (18.7)	0	PMOs stopped in 2001. APs not introduced. Decisions made by MOs alone until April 2004 when a medical assessment unit was introduced and district medical officers appointed. Guidelines introduced in August 2004 (person must be significantly impaired and if treatment is available, provide documentary evidence of treatment compliance).
Free State (8.6)	7	PMOs stopped in 2001. Continued using MOs with APs (until Sept. 2004), now MOs only. No guidelines for HIV/AIDS until late 2004.
Gauteng (12.9)	0	PMOs stopped in 2002. Continued using MOs (no APs introduced). Guidelines updated in 2003 to include specific reference to HIV/AIDS (criteria of not being able to work introduced).
KwaZulu-Natal (25.7)	21	PMOs stopped in 2001. Parallel use of APs and MOs until 2004 (now MOs only). As of August 2004, MOs have to sign that they are complying with eligibility regulations.
Limpopo (7.6)	78	PMOs stopped. As of 2002, a MO does the assessment, the AP (based in hospitals) makes the recommendation, and the head of social security makes the final decision. A person must not be able to compete in the open labour market. People with chronic illness usually given temporary disability grants and reviewed after 12 months.
Mpumalanga (5.4)	92	APs work with MOs. Final decision made by PMO or district head. No clear guidelines.
Northern Cape (3.2)	0	MOs do the assessment, PMOs make the final decision (as in the past). APs introduced briefly (as part of a pilot) and scrapped.
North West (7.5)	95	MOs used for assessment, APs make the recommendation and the provincial office makes the final decision. Up to October 2004, just being HIV+ was sufficient for a grant. Now recipients have to be in clinical Stage 3 or 4. People with chronic illness are supposed to be awarded temporary disability grants, to take medication, and be reviewed after 12 months.
Western Cape (10.4)	0	PMOs stopped. Eligibility determined by a MO who decides whether a person is able to work or not. HIV+ people must be in clinical stage 3 or 4. Policy reinforced in several circulars. No APs introduced.
Total (100)	47.4	

Sources: CASE, 2005: 19–24, 29, 42, 61–4; Simkins 2005.
Note: * Calculated from sample of disability grant records (CASE 2005: 61–64).

As summarised in the table above, the provinces adopted different approaches, with only two retaining the services of a PMO (the Northern Cape maintained the old system, and Mpumalanga required that either a PMO or an official from the Department of Social Security make the final decision). The other provinces left the award decision to the discretion of MOs or APs. The Eastern Cape, the Western Cape and Gauteng chose not to introduce APs. Others introduced a mixture of APs and MOs (KwaZulu-Natal, Mpumalanga, Free State, Limpopo), but to varying extents. The Free State and Northern Cape piloted the AP system, but discarded it soon thereafter. KwaZulu-Natal introduced the AP system widely, but suspended all the APs in August 2004. In Limpopo, APs were located in hospitals and made up of health professionals, in the North West province and Mpumalanga, they were linked to social security offices. In KwaZulu-Natal, which experienced the most rapid growth in the number of disability grants, it appears that APs included a wider variety of community involvement.

The provinces adopted different approaches to HIV/AIDS-related disability. Up until October 2004, the North West province allocated disability grants simply on the basis of being HIV-positive but now requires that people have to be in clinical Stage 3 or 4, that they (like other people with chronic illness) be expected to go for treatment, and that they should only be allocated temporary disability grants that get reviewed after 12 months. Gauteng (from April 2003) and Limpopo require that HIV-positive people are too sick to work to qualify – as does the Western Cape (which also requires that people be in clinical stage 3 or 4). The Northern Cape and Mpumalanga have not produced any guidelines on this matter, leaving it up to the relevant MO. Initially, the Eastern Cape left it to the discretion of MOs, but since August 2004 has produced guidelines requiring that people with chronic illness be significantly impaired and provide documented evidence of treatment compliance (where treatment is available). KwaZulu-Natal introduced similar guidelines in August 2004.

References

Bagchee A (2005) Political and administrative realities of Employment Guarantee Scheme. *Economic and Political Weekly,* 40(2) 15.10.05.

Casale D, Muller C & Posel D (2004) 'Two million net new jobs': A reconsideration of the rise in employment in South Africa. 1995–2003, *South African Journal of Economics,* 72(5): 34–58.

CASE (Community Agency for Social Enquiry) (2005) *Investigation into the increase in uptake of disability and care dependency grants since December 2001.* Johannesburg: CASE.

Dev S (1995) India's (Maharashtra) Employment Guarantee Scheme: Lessons from long experience. In J von Braun (Ed) *Employment for poverty reduction and food security.* Washington DC: International Food Policy Research Institute.

Leclerc-Madlala S (2005) Juggling AIDS, grants and treatment in South Africa: Predicaments of second phase HIV/AIDS. Paper presented at the 2005 Anthropology Southern Africa Conference: 'Continuity, Change and Transformation: Anthropology in the 21st Century', University of KwaZulu-Natal, 22–24 September.

Le Roux P (2003) Financing a universal income grant in South Africa. *Social Dynamics,* 28(2): 98–121.

Matisonn H & Seekings J (2003) The politics of the Basic Income Grant in South Africa, 1996–2002. In G Standing & M Samson (Eds) *A Basic Income Grant for South Africa.* Cape Town: University of Cape Town Press.

McCord A (2003) *An overview of the performance and potential of public works programmes in South Africa*. Centre for Social Science Research, Working Paper No 49, University of Cape Town. Available at <http://www.cssr.uct.ac.za>

McCord A (2004) *Public works: Policy expectations and programme reality*. Centre for Social Science Research, Working Paper No 79. Available at <http://www.cssr.uct.ac.za>

McCord A & van Seventer D (2004) *The economy-wide impacts of the labour intensification of infrastructure expenditure in South Africa*. Centre for Social Science Research, Working Paper No 93. Available at <http://www.cssr.uct.ac.za>

Mitra S (2005) *Disability and social safety nets in developing countries*. Social Protection Discussion Paper Series, No 0509, May, Social Protection Unit, Human Development Network, World Bank.

Nattrass N (2004a) *The moral economy of AIDS in South Africa*. Cambridge: Cambridge University Press.

Nattrass N (2004b) Unemployment and AIDS: The social-democratic challenge for South Africa. *Development Southern Africa*, 21(1): 87–108.

Nattrass N (2006) Trading off income and health: AIDS and the disability grant in South Africa. *Journal of Social Policy*, 35(1): 3–19.

Pellissery S (2005) *Process deficits or political constraints? Bottom-up evaluation of non-contributory social protection policy for rural labourers in India*. CPRC Working Paper No 54, Chronic Poverty Research Centre, University of Oxford.

Quisumbing A & Yohannes Y (2005) *How fair is Workfare? Gender, public works and employment in rural Ethiopia*. Policy Research Working Paper, No 3492, World Bank, Washington.

Schneider M, Claassens M, Kimmie Z, Morgan R, Naiker S, Roberts A & McLaren P (1999) *The extent of moderate and severe reported disability and the nature of the disability experience in South Africa*. Johannesburg: Community Agency for Social Enquiry.

Seekings J (2005a) *Prospects for basic income in developing countries: A comparative analysis of welfare regimes in the South*. Centre for Social Science Research, Working Paper No 104, University of Cape Town. Available at <http://www.cssr.uct.ac.za>

Seekings J (2005b) Employment guarantee or minimum income? Workfare and welfare in developing countries. Unpublished paper.

Seekings J (2005c) *The colour of desert: Race, class and distributive justice in post-apartheid South Africa*. Centre for Social Science Research, Working Paper No 126. Available at <http://www.cssr.uct.ac.za>

Seekings J (2005d) *The mutability of distributive justice attitudes in South Africa*. Centre for Science Research, Working Paper No 125. University of Cape Town. Available at <http://www.cssr.uct.ac.za>

Seekings J & Nattrass N (2005) *Class, race and inequality in South Africa*. New Haven: Yale University Press.

Simchowitz B (2004) *Social security and HIV/AIDS: Assessing 'disability' in the context of ARV treatment*. Centre for Social Science Research, Working Paper No 99. Available at <http://www.cssr.uct.ac.za>

Simkins C (2005) Disability grants: Evidence from SOCPEN and the 2004 General Household Survey. Discussion Paper for the Treasury, September.

Standing G & Samson M (Eds) (2003) *The Basic Income Grant in South Africa*. Cape Town: University of Cape Town Press.

Taylor Committee (2002) *Transforming the present: Protecting the future*. Report of the Committee of Inquiry into a Comprehensive System of Social Security for South Africa, RP/53/2002. Pretoria: Government Printer.

Whitworth A, Wright G & Noble M (2005) *A review of income transfers to disabled and long term sick people in seven case study countries and implications for South Africa*. Oxford: The Centre for the Analysis of South African Social Policy, University of Oxford.

8 The ANC, black economic empowerment and state-owned enterprises: a recycling of history?

Roger Southall

The changing position of the post-1994 government towards South Africa's parastatals or state-owned enterprises (SOEs) is usually situated within the context of its macroeconomic policy. That is, having abandoned the Freedom Charter's commitments to nationalisation during the political transition, the leadership of the African National Congress (ANC) espoused privatisation of state-owned industries as a key plank of its Growth, Employment and Reconstruction (GEAR) strategy. Adopted in 1996, this registered a top-down shift away from the more collectivist Reconstruction and Development Programme (RDP). Subsequently, so the conventional treatment continues, the fervour of the government's conversion to privatisation has waned to a more pragmatic approach which views retention of state control of key industries whilst disposing of 'non-core' assets as central to its economic strategy. This has come about, it is said, for three broad reasons: first, the early privatisation exercise faltered in the face of financial and logistical obstacles; second, privatisation has encountered strong resistance from the Congress of South African Trade Unions (Cosatu); and third, given the failure of GEAR to promote envisaged inflows of foreign capital, job creation and growth, the ANC has moved away from brazenly pro-market policies towards the pursuit of a 'developmental state' (Gumede 2005; Southall 2006).

This reading of policy is not inaccurate, yet it is only a partial interpretation, for the government's stance towards parastatals needs rather to be located within a much broader framework. Central to the latter are two propositions. First, South Africa's parastatals were initially developed to service what Fine and Rustomjee (1996) term the 'minerals–energy complex' (MEC), and remain central to it. Historically, the state sector has enjoyed a symbiotic relationship with private capital, and the present government is correspondingly reluctant to cede ownership of strategic assets to forces which might prove beyond its control. Second, the parastatals have always been central to class and ethnic mobilisation, and just as the National Party (NP) used them to promote the development of Afrikaner capital, so the ANC today views them as key instruments for black economic empowerment (BEE). This chapter will therefore argue that while the government's shifting stance on the parastatals has to be considered against the drive for satisfactory fiscal performance and growth and so on, it is predicated upon the use of the state to promote black ownership and control of the economy.[1]

The origins and development of the state sector

Fine and Rustomjee (1996) argue that the MEC has historically been the core site of accumulation in the South African economy. More than 90 per cent of South Africa's electricity is generated from coal with the balance sourced from hydro-electric and nuclear stations; iron ore, coal and electricity constitute the major inputs to the steel industry; and one-third of manufacturing exports consists of processed minerals, steel and chemicals. A MEC can therefore be identified which is composed of coal, gold, diamond and other mining sectors; electricity; non-metallic mineral products; iron and steel basic industries; non-ferrous metals basic industries; and fertilisers, pesticides, synthetic resins, plastics, chemicals and petro-leum. These industrial sectors exhibit strong linkages between each other and weaker linkages with other sectors. Furthermore, they are also linked together through the highly concentrated pattern of ownership which, at the time Fine and Rustomjee were writing, had culminated in the domination of the MEC core by six major conglomerates (SA Mutual, Sanlam, Anglo-American, Liberty/Standard, Rembrandt/Volksas and Anglovaal), each of which had varying interests in mining, manufacturing and finance. Within this context, state sector investment had been of two major sorts. First, it had been concentrated in specific large-scale MEC core industries such as steel, chemicals, processed minerals and energy; and second, it had provided indirect support to the MEC through its provision of railway, harbour, fuel pipeline and telecommunications facilities.

The origins of the parastatals lie in the era of the Pact Government of 1924 which brought the Labour Party (representative of English-speaking white workers) into junior partnership with the early NP (representative of Afrikaner farmers and workers). The dominant narrative – whether presented from a liberal or a Marxist perspective – argues that the Pact Government pursued policies which were costly to mining capital (notably, state aid to white farmers and 'poor whites') and an industrialisation policy which was favourable to 'civilised labour' and developing 'national capital' (Davies et al. 1976; Lipton 1985). By imposing high tariffs on imported goods, and creating the Iron and Steel Corporation (Iscor) in 1928, the Pact Government aroused the wrath of the mining industry (imperial capital) and commerce, but enjoyed the support of the white unions, white agriculture and the small manufacturing class. After that, the fears of the mine owners were to be realised, for steel prices were higher than international levels for some decades thereafter (Lipton 1985).

Fine and Rustomjee (1996: 121–146) contest the view that the inter-war period is one in which imperial capital lost its hegemony to national capital. Instead, they see it as one of both conflict and compromise between 'imperial', (English or for-eign) and 'national', (Afrikaner or domestic) capitals, different elements of which benefited, or otherwise, from the industrial policies which were adopted. Hence, for instance, the foundation of the Electricity Supply Commission (Escom) in

1922, which was progressively to take over the supply of electricity from private concerns (culminating in the industry's nationalisation in 1948), provided what Christie (1984) has termed an 'electric start' for the entire economy, even if it was disproportionately advantageous to mining. Similarly, although Iscor was created by the NP, its foundation had been laid by Smuts's lobbying of the mining houses to support the creation of an iron and steel industry which would absorb many of their products. Again, although highly capital-intensive industries were to be developed behind the tariff walls that the NP erected, most – such as those in the fertiliser, chemicals and explosives sectors – had originated within the mining sector, and retained strong linkages with it. Nonetheless, they concede, the disjuncture between Afrikaner political and English/imperial economic power was such as to impede the development of industrial diversification beyond the MEC. In contrast, the postwar period was to witness the erosion of this disjuncture, and by the 1970s was to allow the state to adopt co-ordinated industrial policies for the first time.

Following the capture of power by Malan's reformed NP from Smuts's United Party in 1948, the state sector underwent a major expansion. Under the auspices of the Industrial Development Corporation (IDC), new parastatals were established such as the Phosphate Development Corporation (Foskor) in 1952, the South African Coal, Oil and Gas Corporation (Sasol) (for the production of oil from coal) in 1954, and the Southern Oil Exploration Corporation (Soekor) (1965), and existing ones such as South African Railways & Harbours (SAr&h) and Escom were extended. As a result, the public sector's share in South Africa's gross fixed investment rose from 6.2 per cent to 11.5 per cent between 1946 and 1973 (O'Meara 1996: 79), while its share of capital stock increased from 3 per cent in 1946 to 13 per cent in 1979 (Nattrass 1981: 83). Subsequently, the state sector underwent further expansion through the development of a state-led armaments industry in response to the threat of sanctions and armed struggle by the ANC with the creation from the 1960s of bodies like Armscor, Atlas Aircraft Corporation, the Atomic Energy Board and Ucor (the Uranium Enrichment Corporation) (Lipton 1985). Overall, these interventions served to expand the MEC core.

The extension of the state sector was accompanied by the appointment of Afrikaner businessmen to key positions on state economic boards, just as Afrikaners were favoured for the public service and senior and middle-management positions within the parastatals. (By 1976, some 60 per cent of the white labour force in the public service and parastatals were Afrikaners [Giliomee 1979: 165].) Furthermore, financial assistance to Afrikaner companies via such entities as the IDC, the switching of government accounts and the allocation of government contracts to Afrikaner-run banks and businesses, alongside the expansion of the parastatals, all served to ensure the integration of Afrikaner capital on favourable terms into emerging corporate capitalism. Indeed, in many ways, 'this class force was the major beneficiary of NP rule' (O'Meara 1996: 80). In 1948 there were very few Afrikaner business undertakings of any significance, but by 1970 the Afrikaner finance company Sanlam was second only to the Anglo-American Corporation (AAC) as the largest concentration of non-state economic power in the country, whilst two other Afrikaner undertakings, Rembrandt and Volkskas, had joined the small group of conglomerates which dominated the economy. 'Afrikaner control of private industry rose from 6 per cent in 1948 to 21 per cent in 1975. If the state corporations are included, industrial output under "control" of Afrikaans-speakers was calculated to have risen to 45 per cent of the total by 1975' (O'Meara 1996: 80). Meanwhile, public investment was central to the government's industrial decentralisation policy and its pursuit of separate development.

This expansion of the public sector may have provoked considerable resentment within English-dominated business circles, yet as O'Meara (1996) remarks, Anglophone businessmen seemed able to overcome their scruples concerning NP racial policy. Even if NP policy was constructed around Afrikaner 'ethnic mobilisation' (Adam & Giliomee 1979), its interventions in the economy, including those to contain black wages, created conditions for the accumulation of capital in all sectors. As Fine and Rustomjee (1996) observe, while the 1950s saw Afrikaner capital consolidate its position within finance and gain footholds in the coal-mining and fuels-chemical sectors, the 1960s saw a much wider Afrikaner penetration of the economy, a development which was considerably facilitated by the collapse of the stock market following Sharpeville (which allowed institutions like Sanlam to buy up shares at rock-bottom prices). By the late 1970s, relations between the NP government and English-speaking and mining capital had considerably improved. The mines were by now largely domestically owned and had diversified into other sectors (and hence were less hostile to the government's industrialisation policy). Furthermore, encouraged by the AAC (which hoped for easier relations with government), Afrikaner capital had acquired a significant stake in mining, and by the 1980s the economy was dominated by just five 'axes of capital' (AAC, Sanlam, Rembrandt, Anglovaal and Thomas Barlow/SA Mutual), which straddled the mining, manufacturing and financial sectors (Liberty/Standard having yet to branch out beyond finance). Within this context, the policies adopted by the parastatals and investment agencies such as the IDC were overwhelmingly complementary with, for instance, Sasol being partially privatised in 1981 in order to raise capital for a third oil-from-coal plant, a venture which was vital for boosting the country's capacity to withstand UN oil sanctions imposed in 1978 (Davies et al. 1984).

Fine and Rustomjee (1996) stress that this symbiosis between state and capital provided for the greater co-ordination of industrial development. Yet the crises of apartheid – growing industrial unrest, political turbulence and international isolation – were to foreclose the possibilities of a cohesive industrial strategy. The government's move, after 1979, towards the incorporation of emergent black trade unions into state-regulated industrial relations increased divisions between verkrampte (conservative) and verligte (enlightened) Afrikaners, a divide which overlapped that between Afrikaner workers and small-scale capital on the one hand, and large-scale Afrikaner business on the other. Uncertainty also encouraged speculative rather than productive investment, and hugely increased the illegal export of capital. Ironically, too, the very success of NP policy led to increasing complaints about the growth of the state sector and the dangers of 'creeping social-ism' (Wassenaar 1977). However, more important was the growth of antagonism to state ownership as majority rule loomed, a stance which drew sustenance from the growing influence of neo-liberal ideas and the need to curb soaring public debt.

The government's position during the 1960s was that it limited its intervention to establishing utilities and basic industries and services where the private sector was unwilling to invest (RSA 1967). However, between 1970 and 1985, more than 64 per cent of all net fixed investment was made by public services or state corpora-tions, and by the late 1980s, the government was proclaiming that its direct engage-ment in the economy had gone too far and therefore a 'drastic decrease' in the state's economic involvements had become 'imperative' (SAIRR 1988).

This new approach was embodied in President Botha's announcement in February 1988 that large state undertakings such as the South African Transport Service (Sats – the successor to SAr&h), telecommunications services, and Eskom (succes-sor to Escom) would be reorganised to become profit making, while some major road networks and state enterprises such as Iscor, Foskor and the Mossel Bay gas project would be privatised (SAIRR 1988). Subsequently, the first major privatisa-tion was accomplished with the sale of shares in Iscor in October 1989. While the state retained a significant minority interest through shares bought by the IDC, the bulk were purchased by institutional investors (SAIRR 1990).

Meanwhile, initiatives were put in place to commercialise other entities in order to prepare them for later privatisation. The major move was the incorporation of Sats into a new state company called Transnet, which was placed in charge of five sub-sidiaries, namely, Petronet (pipelines), Autonet (roads), Railnet (later Spoornet – railways), Portnet (harbours) and South African Airways (SAA). By this time, how-ever, the government's privatisation ambitions were running into trouble. Although it managed to divest itself of its interest in the production of sorghum beer to various black consortia (which were financially backed by Volkskas) in 1989, thereafter it ran up against a mix of practical difficulties: privatisation of the post office's telecommunications network was impeded because its profits cross-subsidised losses made by the postal service, while most sectors of industry opposed the privatisation of Eskom as they feared it would lead to increased tar-iffs. Yet more influential was the marked hostility of the democratic movement, notably the ANC and its allied trade unions. The latter argued that privatisations would lead to both higher costs of service delivery to black workers and wide-rang-ing job losses. Indeed, an anti-privatisation campaign undertaken by Cosatu in 1990 was hugely reinforced by Sats's dismissal of 23 000 workers in November

1989, a move which unions claimed had been designed to avoid the payment of retrenchment benefits (SAIRR 1990: 585). Such experiences were to confirm Cosatu's distrust of 'rationalisation' and privatisation over the longer term. However, the ANC's position was to change.

The ANC and the parastatals: from left, to right, to centre

The ANC inherited a public sector of uncertain size in 1994, but SOEs probably exceeded 300 in number and employed around 300 000 people. They ranged from primarily financial bodies like the IDC, the Public Investment Commission (which served as fund manager for different public service pension schemes) and the Development Bank of Southern Africa (whose particular role had been to fund industrial decentralisation projects in the homelands), through a number of significant industrial undertakings to a variety of utility companies ranging through full to partial state ownership. Overall, however, the public sector was dominated by the 'big four' SOEs – Transnet, Denel, Telkom and Eskom. In 1999, they comprised approximately 91 per cent of estimated total assets of the top 30 SOEs (R130.8 billion), provided 86 per cent of their turnover (R76.9 billion) and 94 per cent of their net income (R7.9 billion), and employed 77 per cent of their employees (*Financial Mail* 26.06.99).

The conventional narrative focuses upon three phases through which ANC policy towards the state sector has passed since the early 1990s.

The first phase, a relatively short one, began with the pronouncement by Nelson Mandela upon his release in 1990 that the ANC remained committed to extensive nationalisation as highlighted by the Freedom Charter of 1956. Gumede (2005) has indicated how a mix of influences was influential in bringing about the rethinking of this strategy. Mandela was to maintain for a year that nationalisation was the only way of addressing the inequalities of apartheid, but meanwhile the business community and, importantly, Thabo Mbeki and others had got to work. ANC President Oliver Tambo had long been convinced that South Africa should avoid repeating the mistakes of African countries whose statist policies had led them into economic crisis and debt. Since the mid-1980s, therefore, he had supported Mbeki – who had been positively underwhelmed by his experiences of communist economics in Eastern Europe – in quietly talking to white business, seeking to convince them that the ANC was not the devil incarnate. After the fall of the Berlin Wall, developments conspired to turn events in his favour, as leading sectors of capital, backed by the World Bank and the International Monetary Fund, stepped up their lobbying of the ANC. In this atmosphere, Mandela's continued backing of nationalisation caused a massive crisis of business confidence, so much so that Mandela soon found himself persuaded to change his tune, and by early 1992 he was singing the praises of private investment. Significantly, his conversion was brought about not just by vigorous wooing by business, but also by leaders of both western social democratic parties, who explained that their promotion of a public sector had taken place in a less globalised era, and by leaders of communist China and Vietnam, who explained that the collapse of the Soviet Union had forced them to embrace private enterprise. Thereafter, Mandela worked closely with Mbeki to reform ANC policy.

Mbeki and Mandela ran into strong opposition from within the ANC and Cosatu. Nonetheless, by late 1992 they managed to secure the adoption of a compromise proposal, embodied in the ANC's *Ready to Govern* (ANC 1992), which called for public sector involvement to be expanded or reduced on a case-by-case basis. Within a year, they had succeeded in having nationalisation virtually expunged from all the movement's policy documents, having acted ruthlessly to wrest control of economic policy within the tripartite alliance from Cosatu and the South African Communist Party and to propel centrists (such as Trevor Manuel) into key economic positions. Subsequently, the shift to a second, more rightward phase in policy was quietly confirmed by the RDP with which the ANC fought the 1994 election, for although this paid homage to the 'enabling role of the state', it spoke also of the need for a 'thriving private sector' and made only a low-key reference to nationalisation: while there might be a 'significant role for public sector investment' in complementing the private sector, it might also be necessary to reduce the public sector in certain areas to 'enhance efficiency' (ANC 1994: 80). Mbeki's subsequent luring of Alec Erwin, Cosatu's leading economist, into the Cabinet, completed the rout of the left and cleared the way for the later adoption of GEAR.

Thereafter, the government adopted a more assertive posture in favour of privatisation, although the preferred terminology was that of 'restructuring' so as to avoid antagonising unions and other elements of its constituency. Nonetheless, the shift in favour of privatisation became apparent as early as August 1995 during debates occasioned by a discussion paper on the restructuring of state assets produced by the Department of Public Enterprises (DPE 1995). Despite earlier warnings by Cosatu that unions would engage in mass action against privatisation of SOEs, Mbeki announced recommendations in December 1995 whereby government would seek strategic equity partners for public corporations, beginning with the Airports Company of South Africa (Acsa), SAA and Telkom; sell off enterprises which were not considered to be strategic, including Autonet, Sun Air and Transkei Airways; and internally restructure other enterprises to render them more competitive. Meanwhile, the Cabinet had also decided to sell Mossgas and to phase out subsidies to Sasol by 1999.

Trade unions immediately announced their opposition, with Cosatu threatening a work stoppage in December to be followed by a one-day anti-privatisation strike in January 1996. This resulted in talks, whose outcome was a National Framework Agreement whereby the government agreed to negotiate any restructuring of state assets with the unions, while the latter conceded they would support restructuring if jobs could be guaranteed and quality, affordable services could be delivered (SAIRR 1996). Although the anti-privatisation strike was scrapped, the government's subsequent adoption of GEAR reaffirmed its commitment to 'restructuring' as necessary to promote economic growth, attract international investment, create wider ownership of the economy, mobilise private capital, render SOEs more competitive, and reduce government debt (Gumede 2005).

Despite the racier talk, the pace of privatisation was slow. Apart from having to fend off opposition from the unions, the government faced bureaucratic constraints and the need to tackle SOEs' debts. Yet it was also engaged in a balancing act. On the one hand, if it undertook unrestricted privatisations, then the likelihood was that it would end up selling SOEs only to established or foreign capital. On the other hand, because there were very few black individuals or ventures with the capacity to purchase SOEs, the transfer of state assets to promote black empowerment ran into the immediate difficulty of financing. Although this difficulty was to be partially resolved by the creation of the National Empowerment Fund (NEF) – with the objective of buying of shares in SOEs being privatised from government at a discount for resale to the 'historically disadvantaged' – the amounts of capital required to facilitate such deals remained formidable. The outcome of the government's early privatisation initiatives was therefore limited and distinctly mixed:

- In 1997 several SABC radio stations were sold to private buyers for R510 million. Telkom was also partially privatised. Ten per cent of its shares were set aside for black investors, but when the deal was complete, 30 per cent of what had been a wholly South African-owned asset had been sold to an American company (SBC) and Telkom Malaysia for R5.6 billion. Sun Air, a small airline, was sold to the Rethabile Consortium and British Airways' Comair for R97 million, only to collapse in August 1999 amidst complaints about having been deliberately undermined by SAA.
- In 1998, when the state put Acsa up for sale, the empowerment stake was set at 10 per cent of the shares. However, due to the high prices offered by foreign bidders and a shortage of black finance, the outcome was the sale of a 20 per cent stake to Aeroporti di Roma for R819 million, with only a 4.9 per cent shareholding having been sold to black empowerment groups for R201 million. Against this, a 30 per cent stake of Transnet's fleet management company, Viamex Fleet Solutions, was sold to a black consortium for R12 million.
- In 1999, 20 per cent of SAA was sold to Swissair for R1.4 billion; Connex Travel, a Transnet subsidiary, was sold to a consortium of Rennies Travel and El Shaddai Equity Investments for R13.5 million; and an Alexkor (diamond mining) management contract was awarded to the Nabera consortium. Against this, the attempted sale of 75 per cent of the state-owned Aventura Resorts to Kopano ke Matla, a union investment company, for R93 million fell through when the latter failed to raise the funds, and eventually a management contract with Protea Hotels was negotiated instead. Meanwhile,

the Post Office entered into a strategic management partnership
with New Zealand Post International (SAIRR 2000: 483, 2001: 396;
Southall 2004a).

This chequered record led to an early reassessment of the restructuring process fol-
lowing the 1999 election and to a third phase in policy. A new Minister of Public
Enterprise, Jeff Radebe, announced a determined initiative to tackle the problems
of the big four while maintaining a parallel process for the smaller and non-core
enterprises (Radebe 1999). The outcome was a document entitled *An Accelerated
Agenda Towards the Restructuring of State Owned Enterprises* (Ministry of Public
Enterprises 2000) published in August 2000. This argued that the establishment of
SOEs under apartheid had skewed development paths, and that since 1994 many
state corporations were struggling to overcome unsustainable debt burdens,
underinvestment, and unmanageable corporate structures. Furthermore, public
ownership of some SOEs – due to their enormous debt – was all but nominal, with
effective power lying with international financiers. Nonetheless, SOEs represented
massive financial, investment, labour and technology resources and dominated
sub-Saharan Africa's transport, communication, power and defence-related technology sectors. The restructuring of SOEs therefore had to be far more than a simplistic process of privatisation. Although the promotion of competition should
remain an integral aspect of any policy, the state had the responsibility to play a
developmental role in addressing the legacies of apartheid.

Restructuring should involve a variety of options including full and partial privatisation to access additional capital, markets or technology, and involving joint
ventures, employee participation schemes and community participation where
appropriate. Any equity sales should maximise returns to the national fiscus, yet
should not be at the expense of the poor and their access to services. Finally, the
document also put forward major plans for the restructuring of the big four which,
inter alia, included proposals for extensive corporatisation, the commercialisation
of many entities as a step towards their outright sale or entry into equity partnerships, the concessioning of others, the making available of some enterprises,
including SAA, for an initial public offering, and the outright sale of various non-
core units (Ministry of Public Enterprises 2000). Radebe added that the privatisation of state assets would be completed by 2004 with a large portion of the sale
revenue of about R40 billion consisting of direct foreign investment (SAIRR 2001:
396).

These targets were only to be partially met. According to Gumede (2005: 108), the
government privatised some 18 enterprises between 1997 and 2004, raising about
R28.7 billion, of which some R12 billion was used to pay off the national debt,
while it has been otherwise suggested that about R35.5 billion was realised, of
which R22.5 billion was absorbed by the National Revenue Fund between 1997 and
2003. The specificity of the figures matters rather less than the reality that privatisation was in practice severely constrained not just by opposition from the unions

but also by the sheer difficulties of turning the major state corporations around. Thus it was that this third phase of policy drifted almost seamlessly into the government's espousal of the 'developmental state'.

The ANC's commitment to the 'developmental state' grew from the beginning of Mbeki's second presidential term. Seeking to borrow lessons from successful examples of postwar developmentalism (notably the fast-growing Asian economies), this new thinking argued that the state should become more active in correcting market failures (Southall 2006). In particular, it envisaged a more active role for the parastatals, the latter's importance reflected in the appointment of one of the government's most vigorous ministers, Alec Erwin, to head the Ministry of Public Enterprises following the general election of 2004. Hitherto, Erwin declared, the performance of the SOEs had been anything but satisfactory. However, together they represented hugely strategic resources with a turnover of R83.7 billion in 2004, combined assets of R175 billion and employing 136 000 people; if properly restructured they could be transformed into 'drivers of growth and development' (*ANC Today* 5[15], 15–21.04.05). Reflecting growing government disillusion with the capacity of the private sector to bridge the alarming gap between South Africa's 'two economies', the shift indicated aspirations towards a much stronger, more interventionist state. Yet it also reflected the dual agenda of combining a commitment to 'restructuring' with 'transformation'. This can be put into perspective with particular reference to the big four.

The SOEs and 'transformation'

Its capture of the state in 1994 enabled the ANC to focus upon the public service and the parastatals as 'sites of transformation'. This had two closely related aspects. On the one hand, democratisation required that the policies and machinery of the former apartheid state had to be turned around to pursue the ANC's agenda. On the other, while adhering to constraints imposed by the 'sunset clauses' of the Interim Constitution (which guaranteed white public servants their jobs for a minimum of five years, or equivalent financial recompense), the ANC put in place top officials and managers it felt it could trust, and overhauled public sector staffing policies in terms of interrelated strategies of 'affirmative action', 'employment equity', 'black empowerment' and the achieving of 'demographic representivity'. As the NP had used the state since 1948 to promote the welfare and upward mobility of Afrikaners, so now would the ANC use it in favour of its own constituency.

The 'transformation' of the SOEs was central to this strategy, and had two prongs: staffing and procurement. These entailed that there would be winners and losers, and implied that there would be struggles and controversies which would be disruptive to the smooth running of what were all highly complex organisations. These can be illustrated by reference to the early experience of Transnet, the largest of the parastatals.

Transnet

After its formation in 1989, Transnet had embarked upon a programme of commercialisation. This had seen its workforce slashed by around 100 000 between 1982 and 1990, following which a further 50 000 retrenchments were effected by 1992 to reduce the workforce to around 116 000. Despite these cutbacks, Transnet only recorded its first profit in 1994, and that was a desperately slim one of R200 million on a turnover of R15 billion and assets of R40 billion. Although some individual subsidiaries had become profitable, Transnet as a whole was weighed down by an accumulated deficit in its pension fund. After handing over its investment portfolio to private sector investment companies, this had been reduced from R10 billion in 1990 to R4.6 billion in 1994 (partly through a scaling down of benefits), but it continued to soak up operating profits. Nonetheless, the progress made was sufficient to convince commentators that Transnet was becoming 'ripe for privatisation' (*The Star* 08.12.94). Yet within a very short time, Transnet was back in the red. In broad terms, it had proved unable to combine 'transformation' with commercialisation.

Transnet's first four black executive directors were installed in early 1996. Appointed for five years to join Managing Director Anton Moolman, they included Saki Macozoma (who stepped down as an ANC Member of Parliament to become deputy managing director) and Mafika Mkwanazi, the chief executive of Metrorail, who was placed in charge of Spoornet. Macozoma was immediately viewed as heir apparent to Moolman and as leading a drive for 'transformation'. They were soon followed by further black appointments: a third of the 60 new senior managers who had been appointed by late 1996 were black, and despite assurances that the restructuring process would be consultative ('everybody' from cleaners upward would be involved), there was immediate concern amongst the mostly white management that they would be replaced by inexperienced black appointees. It was not long before tensions between an old guard and new black management broke out into the open, with fears surfacing in the press that political correctness was running counter to 'sound market principles'. The increasing priority given to procurement from black companies was cited as compromising profitability, black managers were presented as unwilling to stand up to trade unions, and there was complaint about the awarding of 'massive' salaries to senior management. These developments were accompanied by the departure of a considerable number of white technical staff, and by a flurry of resignations by senior white staff. Moolman himself retired in mid-1996 to be immediately replaced by Macozoma (*Business Day* 08.07.96).

Macozoma conceded that low morale was partially responsible for Transnet's relapse into the red (a R253 million loss in the year ending March 1996) (*Business Day* 08.07.96; *Mail & Guardian* 12–19.07.96). He admitted a lack of skill amongst black professionals, but urged the necessity of appointing black employees to senior appointments and then sending them on management courses. Too many employees had hitherto been 'cocooned in an Afrikaans white world', rendering the culture of the organisation unacceptable to black people. There were assurances that the white community and 'other minorities' would be treated fairly, but these latter were given little comfort by the dismissal of a senior Indian executive who, in approving the grant of a procurement deal between Portnet and a black supply company in apparent ignorance that it had been especially set up for the purpose, was deemed to have fallen foul of a power struggle. A newspaper headline soon spoke of a 'race war' at Transnet, while allegations of credit card fraud made against a senior black executive were portrayed by the South African Railway and Harbour Workers' Union as a 'witch-hunt' conducted by his white predecessors (*Sunday Tribune* 03.11.96). Notwithstanding union support, the black director was found guilty and fired, followed swiftly by the dismissal of another of the original seven black directors for 'gross misconduct'. The 'big bang' approach to transformation, declared *Business Day* (23.10.96), badly needed to be rethought.

Central to Transnet's empowerment drive had been its aggressive shift of procurement contracts to black-controlled companies. While this had come about, in part, in response to direct prompting from the Department of Public Enterprises, it also reflected Macozoma's explicit commitment to the 'national democratic revolution'. Under his auspices, Transnet had adopted the goal of setting aside 50 per cent of its procurement expenditure for black companies. Black businesses acquired only R800 million worth of procurement deals from Transnet in 1995–96, but by the end of 2000–01, this had increased to R2.2 billion, and by a year later to R3.45 billion (*Star* 29.06.01, 22.10.02). Subsequently, Transnet awarded a single R2.4 billion tender to a consortium of seven empowerment companies to supply Transnet and all its subsidiaries with 60 per cent of its fuel needs over the next 36 months (*Business Day* 24.04.03). Some displaced suppliers argued that Transnet unfairly awarded contracts to black companies that lacked competence, experience and financial viability, whilst black companies themselves objected that preferential procurement was being awarded to white companies using BEE fronts. Despite such travails, Transnet stuck to its guns. By 2002, BEE managers had been appointed in all the company's 34 divisions and subsidiaries, with BEE and small business growth being proclaimed a strategic tool to increase market share, sustain capitalism and eliminate poverty (*Star* 22.10.02).

Transnet's procurement drive was matched by continued 'rightsizing' and affirmative action. Some 23 000 people had 'voluntarily' left the company and 200 had been retrenched between 1996 and 2001. By this time, some 63 per cent of Transnet's then total of 76 272 workers were from 'historically disadvantaged groups'. By 2002, the proportion of black staff in senior management had risen to 51 per cent and in middle management to 41 per cent, with targets for increasing these numbers being established for subsequent years (*Star* 13.06.02). Although executives worried that this left a 'cappuccino' problem whereby white employees continued to be overrepresented at senior and middle levels (*Star* 11.09.01), the worst of the racial tension seems to have been overcome.

The problems and achievements of Transnet have been repeated elsewhere. Overall, Eskom, Denel and Transnet deployed a combined BEE procurement budget of R9 billion in 2001–02 (*Enterprise* 31.07.02). Meanwhile, the rapid transformation of personnel has been uniform, as have been the tensions which have gone with it. By 2005, for instance, 69 per cent of Eskom's 30 000 staff were black, as were 58 per cent of its managers, whilst the company reported that its preferential procurement spending had amounted to R28.9 billion over six years (*Business Report* 22.07.05). Similar changes at Denel were accompanied by the rapid exit of skilled staff, mostly middle-aged white men, and extensive reports about demoralisation (*Star* 16.04.05).

Even a brief review suggests that 'transformation' of the SOEs has been achieved with remarkable speed and ease. Yet this has not been without cost. White staff may have opted to go without a struggle, yet in so doing they may have quietly conceded to a new racial segmentation of society wherein the public sector is increasingly viewed as exclusively black 'territory'. Retrenchment packages offered to white employees set up a drain of scarce skills, at artisanal as well as at managerial levels, often leaving SOEs severely (if hopefully temporarily) incapacitated. And there can be little doubt that rapid transformation added to the challenges of rendering the parastatal sector efficient and profitable.

Restructuring and the limits to privatisation

When Transnet returned to the black (a profit of R278 million) in 1997–98, it was widely assumed that Macozoma would continue to oversee its restructuring. However, Macozoma departed Transnet for the private sector in 1999, and was succeeded by his deputy, Mafika Mkwanazi. He was left with the old problem that Transnet's subsidiaries were starved of new capital by the pension fund deficit, with the consequence that their returns on operating assets were far below private sector norms. Any plans for privatisation of subsidiaries therefore appeared to depend upon government taking over or radically restructuring the debt. For its part, however, the Treasury was reluctant to assume an unacceptably heavy burden. A compromise was therefore in the offing whereby Transnet's pension fund would be separated from the company by a special purpose vehicle (SPV) which would take on its financial obligations. In turn, Transnet's subsidiaries would then become a more attractive proposition for privatisation. But in compensation, Transnet – rather than as at present being tax exempt – would have to become a taxpaying entity, with this tax being largely earmarked for supporting the SPV (*Financial Mail* 06.11.98). However, Transnet's various restructuring plans were thrown into disarray by major problems, notably at SAA.

SAA's spiral drive

SAA had long been seen as a strong candidate for privatisation and, as noted, a 20 per cent stake in the airline had been sold to Swissair for R1.4 billion in 1999. But thereafter matters went awry. When Swissair itself collapsed in 2001, its shares reverted to Transnet. If this was attributable to bad luck, SAA was manifestly more culpable regarding three successive corporate scandals. The first involved the collapse of the privatised Sun Air in August 1999 amidst complaints that the cut-price airline had been deliberately undermined by unfair competition by SAA. Although an official inquiry later revealed that Sun Air had been seriously undercapitalised, claims that SAA had abused its dominant position in the local industry were sustained. It was fined R45 million by the competition board and subsequently reached an out-of-court settlement whereby it paid a mere R14.25 million to the liquidators of an airline which had once been valued at R200 million (*Business Day* 29.07.45). The second scandal concerned the hiring and firing of an American high-flier, Coleman Andrews, as chief executive officer (CEO). Brought in to revitalise SAA, Andrews instead signed up for a R4 billion Boeing B737 deal which the airline could not afford and brought it to the edge of crisis. This led to his contract being terminated early, but at the cost of his receiving the richest golden handshake (R232 million) in local corporate history.[2] Thirdly, management then proceeded to gamble on the then declining value of the rand by converting its hedge funds into dollars, only for the unforeseen rise in the rand's value to result in a massive R8.77 billion loss and a whopping R15 billion trading deficit in 2003–04 (*ThisDay* 16.09.04). Had SAA not been financially backed by the state, it would have been bankrupted, although the lack of definitive statements of assets provided by four successive annual reports from 1999 meant that its insolvency was never accurately quantified. However, by continuing to allow SAA to trade whilst insolvent the airline was in breach of the rules of the International Air Transport Association whilst its senior management was criminally liable under the Companies Act.

Paradoxes of empowerment and privatisation

Under GEAR, the privatisation of state assets was viewed as an important tool for reducing national debt. Furthermore, while invigorating local industry and attracting foreign investment, it was also seen as an instrument for promoting black empowerment. However, the difficulties of combining these objectives had already been demonstrated by the partial privatisation of Telkom in 1997 when, as previously noted, attempts to steer a third of the 30 per cent up for sale into black hands had failed. Therefore, when in 2003 government pursued a similar partial privatisation of Eskom it took stronger steps to secure a more 'broadly-based' empowerment – yet only to meet with further difficulties.

Accompanied by Telkom's listing on the Johannesburg and New York Stock Exchanges, the partial privatisation was intended to secure major institutional investment by offering a further 30 per cent stake in the company for sale, while reserving a further 10 per cent for black investors via the so-called 'Khulisa' offer. This attracted more than 127 000 small investors drawn, *inter alia*, from *stokvels*, other saving societies and church groups, yet although it was consequently hailed by government as a triumph, along the way it had occasioned major controversy. First, the government had chosen to back down when challenged by Solidarity, a white trade union, that its targeting of 'historically disadvantaged individuals' for discounted shares was discriminatory and unconstitutional – thereby arousing the ire of black business, which objected to the substitution of 'income level' for 'race' as the main criterion for eligibility (*Business Day* 30.01.03). Second, it ran into strong protests by Cosatu, which complained that partial privatisation had not only led to 20 000 retrenchments since 1997, but that the raising of domestic phone tariffs had been at the expense of poor communities, with only 667 000 of the 2.67 million recently installed new lines remaining in service (*Business Day* 26.01.03). Third, Cosatu and black business argued that Telkom shares had been sold during a downturn in the global telecommunications market. This had led to a slash in the valuation of Telkom from R19 billion in 1997 to R15.6 billion in 2003, one outcome of which was the acute embarrassment of existing black investors, notably Ucingo Investments, an empowerment group which, having bought when share prices were higher, was now having to radically restructure its debt to avoid foreclosure (*Business Day* 18.03.03).

These lessons led to a postponement of further privatisation plans for Eskom, despite its remaining the flagship amongst the parastatals. Apart from meeting ambitious equity employment and procurement targets, Eskom had consistently recorded profits and had mapped out ambitious plans for expansion domestically and throughout the wider continent. Between 1994–2000, Eskom played the major role in increasing the proportion of electrified homes from 36 to 70 per cent, and had committed itself to targets which focused upon the greatly extended provision of electricity to rural households (only 41 per cent of which had been connected by 2001). By early 2005, it had secured approval from Cabinet for a five-year R93 billion expansion, to be funded initially by its own cash flow but gradually augmented from the local and foreign capital markets, which would add 5 000 megawatts (MW) to its existing installed capacity of 42 000 MW. Facilitated by the revival of three previously mothballed power stations (Camden, Grootvlei and Komati), this would also entail the establishment of a pump storage scheme in the Free State and two open-cycle gas turbines (at Atlantis and Mossel Bay), with additional power to come from seven other gas turbines in terms of a R1.8 billion deal concluded with Siemens in July 2005. Beyond that, Eskom was considering the establishment of a new coal-fired power station in Limpopo, increasing hydropower from Inga in the Democratic Republic of Congo, and possibly developing nuclear power from a fleet of pebble bed reactors (Daniel & Lutchman 2006).

This developing scenario had seen the announcement by Minister Radebe in 2002 that Eskom was ripe for further privatisation, and that the disposal of a 10 per cent stake in the company to empowerment concerns would be accompanied by the sale of a further 20 per cent on the open market (SAIRR 2003: 431). However, despite assurances of interest by major black concerns, these plans were thereafter placed on the back-burner. It was not just that Eskom continued to face constant battles in the collection of payments and arrears (especially from poor communities) and against numerous illegal connections. It was also that it took a large knock when a subsidiary, Eskom Enterprises, established amidst much fanfare in 1999 to drive into Africa, had to be re-absorbed into the holding company in 2005 after a R719 million loss in 2003 had signalled an overexpansion (*Business Day* 27.06.05). More significantly, there were also criticisms that the cost of Eskom's expansion plans was hugely inflated, ignored renewable energy options which would be cheaper and generate more jobs than fossil fuel-based sources, and that repayment of expansion costs would be met only by virtue of the company misusing its monopoly powers. 'Public utility managers', commented an industry observer, 'are notoriously bad at making appropriate investment decisions in the face of the economic risks of long-life, power-sector investments' (*Financial Mail* 12.11.04), a judgement reinforced by widespread power failures throughout the Western Cape in early 2006 which caused huge damage to the provincial economy. There were fears, in other words, that Eskom's pretensions were rather too grand, and major concerns about how even its partial sale could be rendered broad-based (*Financial Mail* 31.03.06).

Yet Eskom's worries were small compared to those of the state's arms manufacturer. Founded in 1973 as a strategic asset to supply the apartheid war machine, Denel had prospered as a result of the state's need to contain the security situation. However, after separation from Armscor (the sales arm) in 1992, Denel was to be crippled by both post-apartheid cuts in defence spending and the legacy of its own peculiarly unfortunate culture (which was notoriously conservative if not racist). Meanwhile, commercial successes in developing internationally sought-after G5 and G6 artillery systems had been undermined by the expensive flop of the Rooivalk attack helicopter (bought minimally only by the South African air force), and successive retrenchments meant that by 2005 Denel's staff complement had been reduced to 10 700, about a sixth of its wartime high.

Denel had been earmarked for early privatisation, but this fell through after government had failed to secure agreement with British Aerospace. It was, after all, an unattractive proposition. It consistently recorded heavy losses; there were numerous allegations that, despite checks imposed by the democratic government, its products regularly found their way to war zones as diverse as Colombia, Rwanda and Kashmir; and – like Armscor itself – its operations seemed to be unduly corrupt even by the notoriously lax standards of the international arms industry. Yet central to its problems were those of 'transformation' which culminated in debacle under the tenure of former Umkhonto we Sizwe veteran, Victor Moche, as CEO in May 2003. Arriving after a successful stint at Telkom, Moche sought to combine a far-reaching cost-cutting exercise with an aggressive empowerment campaign through unorthodox means, launching an unprecedented series of disciplinary actions for a variety of infringements (fraud, sexual harassment, corruption and financial misconduct), which the mainly white middle-aged staff affected interpreted as designed to find them guilty and thus to avoid payment of retrenchment expenses. Whatever the validity of the disciplinary charges, they resulted in a major exodus of skilled technical and managerial staff that left the company facing a collapse of global confidence in its products and ability to provide after-sales service. This cost Moche his job and, ironically, he was replaced in mid-2005 with a white male, Shaun Liebenberg, recruited from technology group Grintek. Although he centred his revival strategy around partnerships with international arms companies and partial sale of its business units, it was inevitable that it would require major recapitalisation and increased funding from government. Liebenberg promised a move away from a 'subsidy mindset', but after he touted an expected loss of R1.6 billion for 2004–05, government stumped up loan guarantees of R1 billion to keep creditors at bay, and subsequently announced a contribution of R2 billion towards a R5 billion recapitalisation over the next five years. In short, Denel remained as dependent upon government handouts as ever.

A new strategic direction?

Despite bold talk by Minister Alec Erwin after the 2004 election that the SOEs were ready to undertake a 'major investment and efficiency programme' (*ANC Today* 15–21.04.05), it was manifestly clear that they continued to be beset by problems. While the government could claim that the SOEs had undergone a major demographic transformation and had provided a significant boost to black empowerment via preferential procurement, its privatisation forays had enjoyed limited success, corruption remained a major concern, and vitally, parastatals registered only erratic profitability and were the constant butt of complaints about poor performance. Hence, whilst the government's embrace of the 'development state' reflected disillusionment with the ability of GEAR to attract foreign investment, its renewed emphasis upon parastatal restructuring also suggested its preparedness to make a virtue out of necessity.

The strategic shift was most overtly indicated by appointments of new, 'no-nonsense' CEOs to head some of the leading SOEs, with emphatic instructions to devise plans for corporate renewal. The most high profile of these appointments was the transfer to head Transnet in early 2004 of Maria Ramos from the Treasury, where she had served as a director-general, earning a reputation for ruthless competence. Together with the later appointment of Liebenberg to Denel, Ramos's arrival dispatched a message that commitment to efficiency was more important than colour, and that she had high political backing to take on vested interests, even if that necessitated stamping hard on important black toes.

Ramos's task was unenviable. Figures provided by Transnet's annual report for 2004 provided some alarming figures: revenue had grown 5.7 per cent from R41.3 billion to R43.6 billion during 2003–04, but this was far less than the 14 per cent growth of the previous three years; operating profit had fallen from R5.1 billion to R187 million; asset impairment charges were R4.2 million, up from R493 million the previous year, whilst its gearing (the ratio of debt to equity) was an excessive 83 per cent; return on equity was a negative 7 per cent; total debt had risen since 2000 from R40 billion to R63.7 billion; SAA had cost it R11 billion over the previous two years; and pension liabilities had increased to R7.6 billion (*Mail & Guardian* 03–09.09.04). These figures did little to dispute the judgement of the *Financial Mail* (03.09.04) that previous attempts to restructure had amounted to little more than 'corporate bungling'.

Backed by Erwin's appointment of new boards at Transnet and SAA, Ramos launched 'perhaps the biggest corporate turnaround ever undertaken in South Africa' (*Business Report* 20.01.05). Transnet would henceforth focus upon three key businesses (Portnet, Spoornet and Petronet), whilst SAA (which would be refinanced by a R6 billion share issue) would be transferred out of Transnet to be housed elsewhere in government; Metrorail would be ceded to the Department of Transport; and non-core subsidiaries would be concessioned or privatised, these including the road passenger division Autopax and the telecommunications subsidiary, Transtel. Service contracts for the transport of iron ore would be renegotiated and particular attention paid to the mining industry's frustration at Spoornet's inability to transport ore, minerals and metals to harbours at a time when the Chinese economy was crying out for them. Meanwhile, alongside extensive financial re-engineering (inclusive of the pension fund), Ramos tackled management issues head-on. She created a new executive committee made up of the chiefs of the main divisions, and brought in a swathe of new executives. It was soon an open secret that she clashed with some of the most senior existing staff and precipitated their rapid exodus. Amongst these was Dolly Mokgatle, who had only been appointed to head Spoornet in June 2003 and who, although widely praised, had herself had a turbulent relationship with her senior managers but who now accused Ramos of treading on her turf. Ramos also announced plans to cut the bloated head office in Johannesburg from 600 to 50, while also cracking down hard upon corruption. Several senior managers were suspended, and in particular she braved unpopularity by banning Transnet employees from serving on the boards of companies which secured tenders from their employer. (The practice was not in conflict with the Companies Act so long as directors disclosed their interest and recused themselves from meetings at which the relevant tenders were awarded, but Ramos nonetheless condemned it as leading to corruption.) It was not long before she was facing accusations of undermining black talent and singling out black executives, but she replied by referring to her empowerment record at the Treasury and her demand for competence (*Financial Mail* 27.08.04, 03.09.04, 21.01.05).

Ramos's efforts reaped early, impressive results. For 2003–04 she announced a profit of R6.8 billion (based in part upon renegotiation of the service contract with Kumba and other exporters, but otherwise ascribed to improved operational efficiencies). Transnet had paid off SAA's R6 billion hedging loss and returned the airline to profitability, with plans in place for it to be transformed into a separate entity operating under the Department of Public Enterprises.[3] There would be a R40 million recapitalisation over the next five years (the bulk to be spent upon the refurbishment of Spoornet's ageing infrastructure, locomotives and wagons), half of which would be funded from Transnet's own resources rather than from the market. Around R8 billion of this internal investment would come from the privatisation of eight non-core companies over the next 18 months, this providing the transformation of Transnet into a focused state-owned freight transport company (*Business Report* 11.07.05).

Accusations by four concerned unions that the streamlining would negatively affect the conditions and security of 30 000 workers led to a clash, with the unions conducting a rolling strike around the country in February 2006, their complaint being that Transnet was implementing its plans unilaterally, without adequate negotiation and was ignoring their preferred option that the non-core assets should be sold off to worker co-operatives or union investment companies rather than to private companies (*Mail & Guardian* 03–09.03.06). Ramos, directly backed by Erwin, remained firm on the essentials, but in the face of a threatened four-day national strike by Cosatu, agreed to postpone the transfer of Metrorail out of Transnet to allow further time for negotiations with the unions, while Erwin proposed that his department, rather than Transnet, should handle the disposal of Autopax, Transnet's long-distance bus service (*Mail & Guardian* 17–23.03.06). The financial press widely regarded this as a victory for the unions, and worried that the latter were challenging management's right to manage, but Ramos insisted that the broad thrust of the restructuring would go ahead with the sale of assets in excess of R7.7 billion to firms with appropriate black empowerment credentials (*Business Report* 20&23.03.06).

Despite these difficulties, Transnet's improving performance was presented as validating Erwin's broader restructuring plans, which he pronounced in his 2004/05 budget speech as based around four pillars: the hiring of performance-driven CEOs; the rationalisation of conglomerates to create focused businesses; the elaboration of the R165 billion investment programme to address chronic backlogs; and the harmonisation of strategies (including co-ordination of SOEs' ventures across the wider continent). The SOEs were to become 'centres of excellence' operating to the same standards as the private sector, which would be invited to participate in strategic partnerships to bring in capital and know-how. Overall, some 26 non-core assets would be sold off. 'Staggering turnarounds' were held to be already happening, and at last the parastatals were moving in the right direction (*Business Report* 17.04.05).

SAA was hailed as one of the enterprises jetting into a brave new future. Now headed by Khaya Ngqula, who had formerly presided over the IDC and was styled as one of the brightest of Erwin's dynamic new managers, the airline broke back into the black in 2004 with a R966 million profit from a loss of R8.6 billion. This was attributed to strict cost containment, increased route networks, and improved efficiencies, and the new CEO pronounced SAA as poised to achieve sustainable profitability (although this was clearly based upon South Africa's taking a hard mercantilist line in international air services negotiations, Erwin insisting that that liberalisation of the local skies to open competition would swiftly lead to SAA's demise). But the shine was taken off SAA's performance by controversies which soon surrounded Ngqula's leadership: allegations that he was using disciplinary procedures to purge dissent amongst senior management; indulging in short-term cost cutting at the expense of long-term strategy; using private helicopters rather than using SAA's own regular flights; and, not least, sailing close to the wind on corporate governance issues (*inter alia*, it was revealed that he had taken a holiday in the Indian resort of Goa courtesy of Jet Airlines chairperson Naresh Goyal shortly before awarding the latter the lease of three airbuses, despite a bid by a rival airline that was worth R110 million more).[4] Rumours of low morale under his tenure were subsequently confirmed by the largest strike ever to hit SAA in July 2005, which threatened to undo the airline's financial progress, a R250 million interim loss being reported in March 2006 (*Mail & Guardian* 08–14.07.05, 29.07–04.08.05). Finally, although SAA triumphantly announced its joining of Star Alliance, a global network of airlines allowing it to expand its wings without using its own aircraft, there remained deep-seated concerns that its high costs rendered it unfit to compete with no-frills airlines. Further gloom was occasioned by permission granted by the competition board to allow Nationwide Airlines to commence a R200 million complaint against the national carrier (*Business Report* 10.01.05).

There were also concerns about corporate governance. It is true that the government had proclaimed its intent to deal strongly with corruption. For instance, Spoornet CEO Zandile Jakavula had been dismissed in 2002 after being found guilty of illegally acquiring a government-owned house at a price far below market value, despite his being credited with having returned the enterprise to profit. Yet the scope for questionable practices seemed deeply embedded in the culture of the parastatals, as illustrated in the following examples:

- A lack of transparency accompanied Transnet's sale of its 18 per cent stake at R13.90 a share in MTN to Newshelf 664 in 2002. The latter was a company whose ordinary shares were held by a trust of which the beneficiaries were supposed to be MTN employees, but there were strong rumours that government and Transnet employees also benefited.

- Parastatal tendering seemed to encourage cronyism. Ramos had clamped down on board members holding shares in firms securing contracts from Transnet, but elsewhere the practice was rife: Tommy Oliphants, chairman of Acsa, had a 25 per cent stake in Partners International, which bid for the latter's R80 million contract to supply new passenger loading bridges. Likewise, Nomazizi Mtshotshisa, chairman of Telkom, also served on the board of Admiral Industries which supplied Telkom with work wear. Tihalefang Sekano, executive chairman of the Communication Workers Investment Company, represented employees on Telkom's board, but he was also a director of Telesafe Security, which was paid R39.9 million for security services by the former in the year to 2004. Subsequently, CEO Monhla Hlaha of Acsa admitted to having considerable shareholding in two companies that were service providers to Acsa, but claimed that because the value of her shareholding was only 'a few hundred thousand rand', it was too small to constitute a conflict of interest. These were just instances of a much wider practice (*Business Report* 18.04.05; *Mail & Guardian* 22–28.07.05).
- Parastatal requirements that tendering firms meet empowerment credentials were not matched by sufficiently regulatory procedures. Eskom was the only parastatal which had a definition of fronting.
- Ramos was much praised for taking home a considerably lower salary (around R2 million) compared to her predecessor Mhwanazi (R6 million), but there was wide concern about the high salaries awarded to CEOs and high-level officials of various state agencies and about the high cost of golden handshakes provided to those whose contracts were terminated early for poor performance.

There were, to be fair, indications that government was seeking to get on top of such problems. Yet much of its good work was undone by 'Oilgate', a party funding scandal which seemed to indicate that the government was prepared to put the interests of the ANC well ahead of those of corporate governance.

Revealed after extensive investigation by the *Mail & Guardian* (24–30.06.05, 15–21.07.05, 22–28.07.05), the scandal centred around Imvume – an empowerment company owned by Sandi Majali, an economic advisor to ANC Secretary-General Kgalema Motlanthe – being awarded a lucrative tender to supply Mossgas with oil condensate. Imvume was given a R15 million advance by PetroSA (formed as a merger between Mossgas, Soekor and other assets in October 2002) to pay for the condensate. However, after receiving the money, Imvume donated R11 million to the ANC prior to the 2004 election. This left Imvume with inadequate resources to pay for the condensate, prompting PetroSA to release another R15 million and pay it directly to the Swiss-based supplier. Meanwhile, Imvume was also alleged to have paid R40 000 to a company owned by Bonga Mlambo, the brother of Phumzile Mlambo-Ngcuka, who prior to being appointed deputy president in mid-2005 was Minister of Minerals and Energy Resources and hence politically responsible for

PetroSA. It was also suggested that prior to Imvume's donation to the ANC, both Mlambo-Ngcuka and Motlanthe had written letters in support of a trip by Majali to Saddam Hussein's Iraq, where he had managed to procure oil by agreeing to pay bribes demanded by Iraqi officials, something that other South African firms also bidding (including Tokyo Sexwale's Mvelaphanda) refused to do.

In the wake of the story, legal writs were issued by Majali and Motlanthe against the *Mail & Guardian*. It was joined by a host of other voices in deploring a report on the affair by the Public Protector Lawrence Mushwana, which was widely condemned as a whitewash as he claimed his mandate did not allow him to investigate what happened to public money once it was in the hands of a private entity. Subsequently, PetroSA officials conceded to Parliament's Standing Committee on Public Accounts (Scopa) that there may have been procedural lapses, but insisted that they had no knowledge that Imvume had channelled money to the ANC. While the Minerals and Energy Portfolio Committee endorsed Mushwana's findings, Scopa found the loan to have been improperly made (*Business Day* 30.03.06). Subsequently, although President Mbeki appointed a commission to investigate the allegation of kickbacks made to Majali and ANC heavyweights (*Sunday Times* 21.02.06), 'Oilgate' appeared to demonstrate an incestuous relationship between the ANC, parastatals and empowerment which was potentially undermining of both corporate governance and the 'developmental state'.

Conclusion: a recycling of history?

Capture of the state has provided the ANC with the use of parastatals as instruments for extending black control over the economy, increasing opportunities for an expanding black middle class, and for promoting black empowerment. There is no doubt that this leverage has strongly influenced its economic strategy, for although veering towards liberalisation under GEAR, the outcome of the initial partial sale of Telkom pressed home the dangers that unregulated privatisation could mean sale of the 'family silver' to foreign capital without any effective transfer of economic resources to black people taking place. It is highly significant that subsequently, with the partial exception of Telkom (in which government has continued to retain a significant 40 per cent stake), there has been no major transfer of assets to private hands, and that privatisations have otherwise been, and in the foreseeable future are likely to be, restricted to 'non-core' assets which are relatively affordable for black investors, albeit often in direct or indirect association with established companies, often backed by state-controlled finance deployed by institutions like the Public Investment Corporation and NEF.

Government policy has also been shaped by its recognition of the core parastatals as occupying strategic sites in the economy. The decline of both mining and manufacturing, and the associated rise of finance and services which is taking place during the present era, suggest that the MEC is no longer as central to the economy as it was. Nonetheless, it is significant that the mining, fuels and telecommunications sectors have – along with finance – been the principal targets of the government's empowerment strategy. It is no coincidence that Patrice Motsepe's Africa Rainbow Minerals and Tokyo Sexwale's Mvelaphanda Holdings are amongst the largest empowerment groups and that BEE charters for the fuels and mining industries were amongst the earliest to be developed. Furthermore, as Daniel and Lutchman (2006) have demonstrated, the government attaches the highest importance to securing South Africa's mineral and energy assets by promoting South African public and private investment in these sectors throughout the wider continent. Within this context, present strategy towards the parastatals appears to remain what it always was – designed principally to service the needs of the MEC.

A significant critique of government policy argues that it is returning to the essentials of the disastrous industrial strategy previously pursued by the NP: that it has privatised before liberalising the market (for example, Telkom), it has done nothing to break the power of privatised monopolies (notably Iscor and Sasol) which are squeezing key manufacturing sectors such as polymers and chemicals, and it is unduly protecting public monopolies such as SAA. From this perspective, the government's declared intent of restructuring the parastatals to reduce the cost of business in South Africa is suspect: publicly-owned arms industries are likely to turn out to be little more than money-guzzling machines, and while reforms may render state monsters like Transnet more profitable and efficient in the short term, such gains will be difficult to sustain over the longer term. The way forward, therefore, must be via the formation of public–private partnerships.

That such arguments are often both ideological and put forward by private capital does not mean they lack power, especially in a context where the ANC is manifestly using the parastatals as instruments of empowerment and class mobilisation. Under the NP, the parastatals became notorious for inefficiency and corruption. The challenge for the ANC – if its own project of a 'developmental state' is to succeed – is for the SOEs to avoid a similar fate.

Notes

1   This chapter was completed under the auspices of a HSRC project on 'Race and Redress in South Africa' financed by the EU's Conflict and Governance Facility.

2   SAA has subsequently announced that it will bring charges against Andrews and his six-member executive team for alleged abuse of the staff payroll system and irregular expenditure under the Public Finance Management Act (*Business Day* 26.06.05).

3   Some observers argued that the glitter should be taken off this performance for two reasons. First, because Treasury would have approved SAA's notorious hedging exercise Ramos should take some responsibility for the airline's huge hedging loss. Second, Transnet's losses the previous year may have been exaggerated (*Financial Mail* 15.07.05; *Mail & Guardian* 17–22.09.04).

4   SAA claimed that Ngqula's helicopter flights had saved valuable time, and that price had
     not been the only consideration in the Jet airbus deal (*Business Report* 23.06.05). While at
     the IDC, Ngqula had been suspended over a delivery of furniture to his house he had not
     paid for, and there was controversy over generous loan terms offered to Worldwide, an
     investment corporation in which he held a large stake. There were also major ructions
     concerning his attempts to cut a lucrative deal between the Mozal aluminium plant in
     Mozambique and Glencore (with which he was rumoured to have a relationship) at the
     expense of BHP-Billiton (the largest shareholder in Mozal). After he accused senior IDC
     managers of colluding with BHP-Billiton, the Department of Trade and Industry was
     brought in to investigate, and exonerated them (*Mail & Guardian* 08–14.07.05).

References

Adam H & Giliomee H (1979) *The rise and crisis of Afrikaner power.* Cape Town: David Philip.

ANC (African National Congress) (1992) *ANC, ready to govern: ANC Policy Guidelines for a Democratic South Africa.* Johannesburg: ANC Policy Unit.

ANC (1994) *The reconstruction and development programme.* Johannesburg: African National Congress.

Christie R (1984) *Electricity, industry and class in South Africa.* Albany: State University of New York.

Daniel J & Lutchman J (2006) South Africa in Africa: Scrambling for energy. In S Buhlungu et al. (Eds) *State of the Nation: South Africa 2005–2006.* Cape Town: HSRC Press.

Davies R, Kaplan D, Morris M & O'Meara D (1976) Class struggle and the periodisation of the state in South Africa. *Review of African Political Economy,* 7: 4–30.

Davies R, O'Meara D & Dlamini S (1984) *The struggle for South Africa: A reference guide to movements, organizations and institutions.* London: Zed Books.

DPE (Department of Public Enterprises) (1995) *Discussion document on the consultative and implementation framework for the restructuring of state enterprises.* Pretoria: DPE.

Fine B & Rustomjee Z (1996) *The political economy of South Africa: From minerals-energy complex to industrialisation.* London: Hurst and Company.

Giliomee H (1979) The Afrikaner economic advance. In H Adam & H Giliomee (Eds) *The rise and crisis of Afrikaner power.* Cape Town: David Philip.

Gumede W (2005) *Thabo Mbeki and the battle for the soul of the ANC.* Cape Town: Zebra Press.

Lipton M (1985) *Capitalism and apartheid: South Africa 1910–1986.* Aldershot: Wildwood House.

Ministry of Public Enterprises (2000) *An accelerated agenda towards the restructuring of state owned enterprises.* Pretoria: Ministry of Public Enterprises.

Nattrass J (1981) *The South African economy: Its growth and change.* Cape Town: Oxford University Press.

O'Meara D (1996) *Forty lost years: The apartheid state and the politics of the National Party, 1948–1994*. Johannesburg: Ravan Press.

Radebe J (1999) Press briefing by the Minister of Public Enterprises, Jeff Radebe, on the Strategic IMCC Lekgotla on the Restructuring of State Assets, Union Buildings, Pretoria, 7 December.

RSA (Republic of South Africa) (1967) *State of South Africa: Economic, financial and statistical year book for the Republic of South Africa*. Johannesburg: Da Gama Publications.

SAIRR (South African Institute of Race Relations) (1988) *Race Relations Survey 1987–88*. Braamfontein: SAIRR.

SAIRR (1990) *Race Relations Survey 1989–90*. Braamfontein: SAIRR.

SAIRR (1996) *Race Relations Survey 1995–96*. Braamfontein: SAIRR.

SAIRR (2000) *Race Relations Survey 1999–2000*. Braamfontein: SAIRR.

SAIRR (2001) *Race Relations Survey 2000–2001*. Braamfontein: SAIRR.

SAIRR (2003) *Race Relations Survey 2002–2003*. Braamfontein: SAIRR.

Southall R (2004a) The ANC and black capitalism in South Africa. *Review of African Political Economy*, 31: 313–28.

Southall R (2004b) Black empowerment and corporate capital. In J Daniel et al. (Eds) *State of the Nation: South Africa 2004–2005*. Cape Town: HSRC Press.

Southall R (2006) Can South Africa be a 'developmental state'? In S Buhlungu et al. (Eds) *State of the Nation: South Africa 2005–2006*. Cape Town: HSRC Press.

Wassenaar A (1977) *The assault on private enterprise*. Cape Town: Tafelberg.

9 Technological choices in South Africa: ecology, democracy and development

David Fig

In the context of South Africa's emergent economy, are our technological choices appropriate? Will they enhance our development or retard it? Will they contribute to the consolidation of a democratic future or impinge on our hard-won constitutional rights? These questions imply that technologies are not neutral, but that their adoption has specific political, social and also environmental consequences. In raising these questions, we are interrogating our development path, our industrial strategy and raising the issue of democratic oversight over our technological choices. This will be done, not just with reference to principle, but also through the examination of some national choices to adopt or support particular technologies.

In raising these questions, the intention is not to provide a comprehensive analysis of South Africa's science and technology policy. This has been done in various ways elsewhere, particularly focusing on the development of a national science and technology system (IDRC 1993; Marais 2000). Instead, the aim is to raise questions about particular technological choices in the context of debates about South Africa's development path.

This chapter will first examine some conceptions about growth and development, and then raise some observations about how 'modernisation', an approach which elevates growth above all else, has deepened poverty in Africa. If our development is not to imitate the pitfalls of the modernisation approach, some of the notions associated with the concept of 'sustainable development' will have to be taken seriously, particularly those of ecological limits, inter- and intra-generational equity, and popular empowerment. Some of these notions have been imported into South African legislation, including the Bill of Rights in the Constitution. Yet the case studies in this chapter reveal that these commitments are not being respected. The case studies attempt to analyse government material and ideological support for specific technologies such as pebble bed nuclear reactors, aluminium smelters and genetically modified agricultural crops. Not only are these technologies unsustainable in terms of equity, empowerment and environmental protection, but they commit South Africa to a development path which favours greater centralisation of power, the enclosure of the commons, and the dangers of a security state. It is hoped that the questions raised in this chapter will spur further empirical research on technological choices that meet our development needs.

Growth and development

South Africa's political transition to democracy has been accompanied by an economic transition to a more liberalised form of capitalism. Under the exigencies of globalisation, local capital is no longer given the extent of state protection enjoyed during the apartheid years. Competition is no longer restricted to a protected local market, but needs to be more robust and innovative on a global scale.

The recent revival in South Africa of the push for economic growth, particularly in the form of the Accelerated and Shared Growth Initiative for South Africa (ASGISA), raises questions about how development is conceptualised. The equation of growth with development has permeated macroeconomic thinking and strategy over the past half-century. One of the clearest statements of this position is by Beckerman who believes that 'a failure to maintain economic growth means continued poverty, deprivation, disease, squalor, degradation and slavery to soul-destroying toil for countless millions of the world's population' (1974: 9).

In the new century there are few alternative development models, and states have become less effective in delivering their citizens out of poverty. While the growth mantra persists, there are some caveats that need to be tabled.

The first and most obvious is how the fruits of that growth are distributed. In South Africa we have seen a number of years of jobless growth, where economic expansion has been capital- rather than labour-intensive. Unemployment is rising – as is the gap between rich and poor. Our leaders have conceptualised a 'second' economy in which the semi-proletarianised are regarded as being almost permanently excluded from formal employment. Even the 'developmentalist' state (Southall 2006) displays difficulties delivering on services and poverty relief, and eschews a basic-income grant to the unemployed proposed by unions, faith-based groups and the social movements.

In the formal sector, business is baulking at what it considers to be an elevated level of labour standards. A package of labour rights, which includes provisions for fair labour practices and employment equity, was introduced in the latter half of the 1990s to remedy an elaborate legacy of exploitation during and prior to apartheid. Business argues for more 'flexibility' to downsize, outsource, casualise and subcontract labour, in order to evade the primary responsibility entailed in being the employer. Commercial farmers are unhappy to pay the monthly minimum farm wage, which is set between R885 and R994 (DoL 2006; *Farmers' Weekly* 21.04.06) and is well below poverty levels.

While some provinces struggle to spend the social development parts of their budgets, and the fiscus claims unprecedented tax collection rates, the question arises as to whether we need to set targets of huge additional growth when we should rather be paying attention to more effective redistribution strategies.

A further problem with growth is its environmental impact. The extensive growth in the Chinese economy in recent years has led to major environmental degradation, with specific reference to air and water quality and to the disposal of waste. This has produced a huge cost to human health, compounding poverty (Flavin & Gardner 2006). Even the Chinese authorities are no longer happy to externalise these costs, and are beginning a process of setting higher environmental standards for steel production and other highly polluting industries.

One of the key objections to using gross domestic product as a measurement of growth is that, when internalised, the costs of pollution are included as part of production costs. Therefore higher pollution costs are reflected as higher growth.

Some writers have argued for achieving 'zero growth'. Neo-Malthusians have warned of the limits to growth. The resource difficulties of the 1970s, especially with oil, pointed to the global over-reliance on finite resources, and limits to the earth's ability to absorb pollution without fatally disturbing the ecosystems on which all life depends (Meadows 1972).

In promoting his idea of a 'steady-state' economy, Herman Daly (1996) argues for governments and institutions to aim for sufficient wealth for the maximum number of people within the constraints of the earth's capacity over time. Unlike the neo-liberal economic theorists, Daly feels that states should in the first instance promote local production for local markets, only resorting to global trade to satisfy unresolved needs.

The modernisation paradigm

The notion that growth is imperative for development is the kernel of modernisation theory. This holds – in its Rostovian version (Rostow 1960) – that, with sufficient capital, technology, skills and bureaucratic organisation, societies will progress from the traditional to the modern with teleological inevitability. At a certain point in the accumulation process, there will be sufficient dynamism for development to 'take off' and for the fruits of accumulation to be diffused from rich to poor in a 'trickle-down' process. This all depends on the obstacles to accumulation being removed. Amongst these are numbered traditional and indigenous value systems.

Modernisation placed great store on industrialisation, which relied on the application of advanced technology and resulted in important social transformation. Many of the processes of industrialisation in the Third World relied on foreign direct investment.

The modernisation project dominated thinking about African development from the 1950s. It was broadly implemented from the time of independence in the 1960s to the present time. As the dominant approach to African development, we need to ask whether it was at all suitable for Africa's needs. The reality today is that the model has failed us. According to all statistics, African development has been reversed since the 1960s. Investment, production, exports, livelihoods and lifespans have all fallen, whilst poverty, insecurity and disease have grown. This is due to a complex network of factors including corruption, state failure, the removal of rights, economic mismanagement, conflict, drainage of skills, contrary terms of trade, misguided donor aid strategies, and notions of national prestige.

Critics have thrown up numerous alternatives, but the modernisation path was the one historically most treaded. Even state–socialist experiments were a variant of the modernisation model, substituting the state for private accumulation. The state's provision of investment, jobs, social services and production systems was expected to lead to greater equity and respect for the commons. Yet in practice the state-driven models created unanticipated hierarchies and proved ultimately unsustainable in economic, social, political and ecological terms. The challenge for socialist theorists is for a re-evaluation and re-crafting of a vision for a more equitable society which also takes ecological considerations more seriously.

Modernisation as a model seeks growth at all costs. This means a minimum of restraints on industry and markets, a justified depletion of natural and human capital, and an enclosure of the commons. It favours jobs that are less protected, dirtier, lower paid and, in more recent times, more 'flexible' (informal, outsourced, dependent on street or home production, impermanent, unlinked to benefits, often only rewarded for piecework, discouraged from unionising, and so on).

There are at least three variants of this model. In the capitalist variant of modernisation, investment entirely depends on the confidence and whims of the owners of capital, who expect private profit from production. Intensified under conditions of globalisation, particularly in the last quarter of the twentieth century, there has been a veritable 'race to the bottom' in which the developing country offers the outside investor the lowest wage levels, environmental standards, and company taxation.

A second variant, which ultimately failed to deliver, includes a number of state-led industrialisation projects, including import substitution, state-socialism and even versions of African socialism (*ujamaa*) in which the state played the roles of the investor and sometimes also the organiser of production, employer and provider of social services. This variant was also not immune to the development of social hierarchies, massive pollution, resource depletion, inefficiency of production and, in some cases, authoritarian workplace regimes.

A third variant of the model is called 'ecological modernisation', which largely follows the neo-liberal recipe for development, but requires that environmental services be recognised and internalised in the cost of production; in other words, it calls for the marketisation of ecology. We are seeing this occurring in numerous ways, one of the most recent being the carbon trading system.

Apartheid and industrialisation

Historically the South African economy may be periodised into roughly four phases of accumulation. The first is an agrarian phase, during which settler and indigenous economies revolved around the production of crops and animals with some artisanal activities in the towns. Wars of conquest resulted in a loss of land for African people, while the settlers produced not only for the domestic market but also engaged in limited exports of wool, wheat, wine, hides and fruit. The second phase was centred on the mineral revolution initiated in the last third of the nineteenth century and which required the application of large amounts of private capital, cheap labour, water and energy. A third phase saw the growth of manufacturing, at first to support the mining industry, but after the mid-twentieth century it came into its own largely in terms of servicing growing domestic demand. A fourth phase coincides with more intensive globalisation and liberalisation measures from the 1990s, seeing enhanced production in low-cost countries, a potential oil shortage which has led a renewed boom in many resources, a stress on the service economy, and a greater application of information technologies.

With the onset of apartheid, industrial policy was characterised by a number of elements. These included aspects of import-substitution industrialisation, which had initially emerged during the two world wars when South Africa was isolated from its major trading partners, but became more widespread as tariffs were imposed on imports, and local manufacturing benefited from protectionism.

The state played an important interventionist role in the economy, particularly its establishment of parastatal corporations related to infrastructural provision in cases where private capital saw no investment advantage. This intervention was aimed not only at servicing private capital more broadly, but also at driving large-scale industrialisation. The state created monopolies in electricity provision, railways, postal services, telephony, broadcasting, iron and steel, air transport, harbours and an oil-from-coal company. In addition, it became a significant player in arms manufacturing and procurement. Some of these industries clearly served to preserve apartheid through combating sanctions or through the direct application of coercion against resistance both locally and in the wider region.

Another leg of apartheid industrialisation was the establishment of 'border' industries, an attempt to foster industrial activity on the fringes of the so-called 'homelands' or bantustans. These industries largely attracted fly-by-night investors, many from Israel and Taiwan, who were drawn by high labour subsidies, low wage levels and tax holidays. When apartheid ended, so did the subsidies, and most of the investment subsequently dried up.

More broadly, apartheid repressed labour and the political movements which articulated resistance to apartheid. Workers had few rights in the urban areas, and their low wages were justified in terms of rural areas (particularly women located in homelands) absorbing the costs of reproduction of labour. The absence of rights and facilities forced most black workers into urban poverty and squalor, whilst in contrast white workers were granted rights and many of the provisions of a welfare state.

Apartheid industrialisation took place with little concern for the environment, and left a legacy of massive degradation (Durning 1994). The burden fell most sharply on black workers, subjected to dirty and unsafe working conditions, and whose segregated residential areas were often placed close to and downwind of heavy industry. In some cases, like Merewent in South Durban, communities found themselves encircled by a complex of petroleum refineries, paper mills and other dirty industries. There were few penalties for companies causing pollution, and victims of mercury recycling or asbestos mining had to sue the perpetrators in other jurisdictions.

Sanctions, state protectionism and capital immobility meant that local industry had little incentive to innovate or renew technology, except in the case of the military-industrial complex. As a result, by the end of the apartheid era, many manufacturers were left with outdated, dirty and inefficient equipment.

Current industrial policy

South Africa's transition to democracy was simultaneously accompanied by a stronger transition to a liberalised economy under conditions of extensive globalisation. The accession to office of President Nelson Mandela and the inauguration of the World Trade Organization occurred in the same year – 1994.

Trade liberalisation took place without insulating local industry from the shock of global competition. As a result, sectors such as clothing and textiles could not compete with cheaper imports, and large numbers of jobs were shed as the sector began to collapse. Dismantling of the agricultural commodity boards, which under apartheid had played the role of controlling prices, led to sharp increases in food prices, dealing a blow to household food security.

An early focus of government industrial strategy was to support a number of spatial development initiatives, which attempted to focus investment and create public–private partnerships in particular geographical areas or corridors. This was coupled with the promotion of certain development nodes as export development zones, aimed at the establishment of customs- and tariff-free areas alongside ports, devoted to the processing of exports.

The focus on export-led growth indicated a clear break from the import-substitution industrialisation path which had characterised the South African economy since the 1920s. This shift reflected the impact of globalisation on production whereby numerous commodity chains no longer occur within specific national boundaries. Instead, production has been diffused across borders with various production lines in different localities participating in the value chain (Bezuidenhout 2002).

The Industrial Strategy Project (ISP), initially commissioned by the Congress of South African Trade Unions, drew a number of academic economists into an analysis of various of South Africa's manufacturing sectors, with a view to recommending a new industrial development path for the post-apartheid democracy. The detailed sectoral studies diagnosed the uncompetitive nature of South Africa's overprotected manufacturing sector, which had fallen behind in terms of technology and efficiency. It was argued that there was a need to move to an export-led strategy, which could capitalise on the country's resource base by, for example, the increased beneficiation of minerals. Upgrading of skills and technology was a further strong recommendation aimed at offsetting the lags experienced under apartheid (Joffe et al. 1995).

Other economists pointed to the centrality in the economy of the minerals–energy complex (Fine & Rustomjee 1996). Dominant minerals monopolies had directed investments towards manufacturing during apartheid because of the difficulties placed on exporting their capital. Resource exports remained the engine of growth, and the switch to a focus on manufacturing would require considerable investment in infrastructure. Their recommendation was that the emphasis of South Africa's industrialisation strategy should rather be to capitalise on the strong resources base.

Much of this thinking influenced the Department of Trade and Industry (DTI), as contributors to the ISP like Zav Rustomjee, Dave Kaplan and Dave Lewis took various DTI-related offices. At various times since 1994, the DTI drafted documents attempting to outline a policy approach. By 2000, pressure increased on the department to develop a comprehensive approach to its interventions on questions of enhancing different sectors of manufacturing, competition, small business development and black economic empowerment (BEE). Further pressure was placed on President Mbeki to do so by James Wolfensohn, head of the World Bank, at their meeting in November 2000. By May 2001, the DTI had released a discussion document which stressed the importance both of skills enhancement and the need to move towards a knowledge-based, globally competitive economy if the export orientation was to succeed. Manufacturing was seen as the key engine of growth (DTI 2001).

Despite sector summits, the growth and development summit and other multistakeholder processes, there has been enormous concern that industrial growth has not been accompanied by an expansion of employment.

Five years later the DTI is again responding to renewed pressures to produce a more coherent industrial policy, but this time in a context in which there is increased stress on growth of the economy. New leadership of the DTI has emerged, with changes of minister and the appointment of two deputy ministers and a new director-general. By April 2006, the DTI was said to be in the final stages of preparing a broad strategic framework document outlining an industrial policy for South Africa (Davies 2006). The new emphases will most likely be on the state's role in infrastructural development – R370 billion budgeted under the Medium Term Economic Framework – as well as on customisation of conditional incentives for different industrial sectors, stronger support for small-scale business (the 'second' economy), and broad-based BEE. The industrial policy will be a pillar of ASGISA, the thrust for increased growth (Davies 2006).

Sustainable development

Although a highly contested concept (Bond & Guliwe 2003), sustainable development has for around two decades been a key principle on which the United Nations system bases its simultaneous concerns for social, environmental and economic development. The idea was first mooted in a World Conservation Union report in 1980, was given further impetus when defined by the 1987 report of the Brundtland Commission, and was finally enshrined in the set of multilateral agreements forged at the Earth Summit in Rio de Janeiro in 1992.

The hagiographic Brundtland definition of sustainable development is 'development that meets the needs of the present without compromising the ability of future generations to meet their own needs' (World Commission on Environment and Development 1987: 4). It stresses intergenerational equity and implies the eradication of poverty, within the carrying capacity of the planet's natural systems. It has gained a place within recent development discourse, without providing strict theoretical rigour. As such it has been adopted globally, for example in the 1992 Rio Declaration, but increasingly appropriated by governments and private enterprise to mean the process of attaching economic values to the environment.

South African law has also enshrined the concept, firstly in the Constitution (Act 108 of 1996) where Article 24 of the Bill of Rights states that:

> Everyone has the right – (a) to an environment that is not harmful to their health or well-being; and (b) to have the environment protected, for the benefit of present and future generations, through reasonable legislative and other measures that – (i) prevent pollution and ecological degradation; (ii) promote conservation; and (iii) secure ecologically sustainable development and use of natural resources while promoting justifiable economic and social development.

In the framework National Environmental Management Act (107 of 1998), a commitment to sustainable development is evident in Section 2 where it states that 'sustainable development means the integration of social, economic and environmental factors into planning, implementation and decision-making so as to ensure that development serves present and future generations'.

In 2002, South Africa played host to the World Summit on Sustainable Development. The commitments arising from this summit included the

Johannesburg Plan of Implementation (JPOI), which contained 37 important targets for reaching sustainable development goals.

More recently, South Africa has been obliged by its commitment to paragraph 162 of the JPOI to formulate a National Strategy for Sustainable Development (NSSD) which includes bold, goal-oriented policy frameworks and strategies to meet the Millennium Development Goals. Although this was supposed to be lodged with the UN by the end of 2005, the strategy was still in the making at that time, and the difficulties of gaining buy-in across government departments has reduced its status to a 'framework' rather than a strategy. The document outlining the NSSD accepts the broad vision of ASGISA. Yet it also calls on the government to 'decouple growth from natural resource consumption and continued degradation of ecosystems' (DEAT 2006: 38). While this is a healthy departure from the mantra of 'growth *über alles*', the document is not explicit about how decoupling might occur. It attempts to outline a strategy for sustaining natural ecosystems, investing in sustainable infrastructure, creating sustainable communities, enhancing systems for integrated planning, and building human resources for sustainable development. It is to date the most explicit statement for the integration of sustainability criteria into national policy. However, there is a hiatus on the question of industrial and trade policy, and how sustainability criteria could be used to shape these.

The NSSD may provide glimmers of inspiration, but it walks a tightrope between conformity with other parts of government policy (like ASGISA) and the impulse to propose a more radical development path.

Significantly, the culture of sustainable development has not been integrated into the thinking of key macroeconomic strategists. Unlike most other portfolios, the organogram for the Office of the President contains no environmental desk. The key statement of industrial policy ignores the principles of sustainable development, instead arguing for continued exploitation of its natural resources, including 'cheap electricity' (DTI 2005: 18). Even the ISP, which originally excluded sustainability criteria from its remit, was obliged – through pressure from progressive environmental non-governmental organisations and donors – to remedy this omission (Bethlehem & Goldblatt 1995).

The most recent exposition of South Africa's macroeconomic policy formulation since 1994 (Hirsch 2005) makes no mention of environmental criteria, and only uses the term 'sustainability' in relation to growth.

The only acknowledgement of the need to promote sustainable development by the National Treasury has been the announcement that a number of 'green' fiscal measures will be applied in the near future. Such measures, for example, include the removal of value-added tax exemption from pesticides (*Business Day* 24.04.06).

Technological choices

Nowhere is the disjuncture between the growth strategy and sustainability criteria more explicit than in the state's promotion of certain technologies. The most glaring examples of this are to be found in the following three case studies.

Aluminium smelting

South Africa is not a producer of bauxite ore (the raw material from which aluminium is derived). We consume 253 kilotons per year yet we have the capacity to produce three times this per year[1] from smelters at Richards Bay owned by BHP Billiton, one of the world's largest mining companies. What is the reason for our involvement in this industry? Aluminium smelting and production are very energy intensive, and we have one of the cheapest electricity rates in the world, further discounted for bulk users by Eskom. Eskom was able to offer the smelting companies these rates at a time when electricity was plentiful and the utility wished to encourage demand.

The cost of our electricity is relatively cheap by world standards because we are not including the 'externalities' in the price – that is, the costs to our health and to our environment (Van Horen 1997). Our coal is extremely low quality, resulting pollution is high, and the rates of respiratory disease in South Africa are very high. Because of our burning of coal, we account for between 1 and 2 per cent of the contribution to global warming. Under the provisions of the Kyoto Protocol, South Africa has no obligation to reduce its emissions of greenhouse gases during the current commitment period which lasts until 2012. Thereafter it is likely that global negotiations will impose some explicit targets for reduction.

If the NSSD has any meaning, the industrial trend should be to move away from industries which are energy intensive, at least until we are substantial producers of renewable energy. Objectively, we are not so much exporting aluminium as exporting cheap electricity, and the health and environmental costs are being borne not by Eskom or BHP Billiton, but by our communities, our health bills and our pollution clean-up bills.

What are the impacts of the industry for the country? Firstly, the bulk supply of cheap electricity purely for export is never raised as a contributory factor to the current electricity 'shortage', which is being used to justify the reinstatement of previously mothballed thermal (coal) power stations as well as further nuclear capacity (discussed further in the section on nuclear reactors). Secondly, we need to note that whilst BHP Billiton and other bulk users have their electricity charges subsidised, such subsidies are not granted at the same levels to those who need them most: new users, generally in townships, informal settlements and rural areas. New users pay higher charges per unit of electricity used than more traditional users, because their charges include the capital costs involved in extending the infrastructure. The new users find it more difficult to afford the high charges and as a result face debts, cut-offs, and may resort to illegal connections – often with dangerous consequences.

Currently government is seeking to install yet another aluminium smelter, this time located outside Port Elizabeth at the Coega site. The state is trying desperately to promote Coega as an alternative deep-level port, with the smelter forming the basis of the entire development (the 'anchor' tenant). Leaving aside the fact that we do not need an extra deep-level port, that Port Elizabeth is already depressed, that the plans for Coega compromise our environment (especially plans to expand the Addo National Park into a malaria-free 'big five' reserve), that there will only be limited numbers of jobs for local people, and that there is a glut of aluminium on world markets, the Coega project was originally mooted as part of the 'offset' of the arms deal set up by former Defence Minister Joe Modise, his advisor Chippy Shaik, and others. The offset deal failed, and so apparently has the possibility that Pechiney of France would step in (having been purchased by Alcan of Canada which has continually expressed very little interest in the investment). A third possibility might be SUAL of Russia, through the intervention of its director, Brian Gilbertson, formerly head of BHP Billiton (which has the investment in smelters at Richard's Bay). Recent responses to power outages in the Western Cape have discouraged investors in a Coega smelter, and cast doubts on the project as a whole.

The entire Coega development is a potential white elephant. Since its basis is the export of our cheap (and increasingly 'scarce') electricity, it is questionable whether the project has anything to do with a sustainable approach to jobs and development (Bond & Hoskin 2002; Haines & Hoskin 2005).

Nuclear reactors

A sustainable energy policy would seek solutions that minimise carbon emissions, decentralise control over generation and distribution, and enhance job creation. Despite claims by the nuclear industry, nuclear energy is not carbon-friendly, especially when one takes the entire life cycle of this source into account. Mining, milling, conversion, enrichment, fuel fabrication, construction, transport, waste disposal, reprocessing, decontamination, decommissioning – together they are said to add around 40 grams of carbon dioxide equivalent per kilowatt generated. This is quite apart from other concerns about the industry: added problems of massive costs, additional radiation risks, transportation dangers, the insoluble problem of waste disposal, the risks of proliferation of weapons of mass destruction, the skills deficit in South Africa and the difficulties faced in regulating the industry (Fig 2005).

These risk factors place a much higher social, political and environmental burden on future generations, since high-level nuclear waste must be isolated from the environment for up to ten times the half-life of plutonium (10 x 24 400 = 244 000 years). If not a technically impossible task, this is certainly a timescale fraught with unpredictable elements. We therefore cannot be certain that future generations will be insulated from this risk. We cannot know that future political life will be stable and that no leaders will appear wanting to make use of nuclear material for weapons purposes. Having painstakingly sacrificed and won a democratic political dispensation, South Africans are now being expected to opt for a technology that requires high levels (and long duration) of secrecy, policing, and the reviving of a culture of heavily extended security procedures.

Nuclear energy also requires a high degree of centralisation of the energy industry, whereas renewables allow for decentralisation and local control. The over-central-isation due to investment in nuclear was amply demonstrated in the power outages in the Western Cape over the summer of 2005–06. In the 1980s, the apartheid state built two nuclear reactors at the Koeberg site, 24 kilometres north of Cape Town. It took some years before these plants were to reach full efficiency, but they ended up being responsible for providing 80 per cent of the Western Cape province's electricity. A series of small incidents in the last months of 2005, including a fire under-neath a pylon, caused one of the two units to trip, leading to a number of unplanned power outages. The problem was compounded when it was discovered, on Christmas Day 2005, that a misplaced bolt in one of the unit's generating sets had caused considerable damage to its rotor. The plant had to be shut down while a global search for a replacement rotor took place. It took until early April 2006 to source and ship the part from France. The closure of this unit created a situation of random power outages, sometimes lasting days, and devastating production.

The economy of the Western Cape suffered major losses, estimated at R6 billion by a regional chamber of commerce survey (*Cape Times* 30.03.06). Harvests of wine and fruit had to be destroyed, while the failure of electric sewage pumps caused damage to wetlands and other fragile ecosystems which will take at least a decade to rehabilitate. All systems relying on information technology were disrupted, and the region's important service industries, including tourism, have suffered blows to operations and to their reputations.

The second unit at Koeberg underwent routine fuel replacement in 2006, forcing it to shut between April and July, creating the risk of further major power cuts should the first unit not be fully functional for any reason.

By way of contrast, replacing nuclear with renewable energy sources removes the problem of over-centralisation. Multiple and localised energy sources, easily repaired at local level, would create considerable jobs spread over many communi-ties, instead of requiring small numbers of highly skilled nuclear engineers and reactor operators. It has been estimated, for example, that if South Africa were to generate 15 per cent of total electricity from renewable sources by the year 2020, this would create 36 400 direct jobs at no additional cost to the economy (Agama Energy 2003). Increasingly scholarship on renewable energy in South Africa is showing how it has the potential to replace our consumption of fossil fuels (Banks & Schäffler 2006). Yet renewable energy, despite the issuing of a White Paper on the subject, remains, according to one analyst, 'peripheral to actual policy' (Hallowes 2006: 36).

Instead of exploring these options more rigorously, the state prefers to devote taxpayers' money to the unsustainable development of the pebble bed modular reactor (PBMR). This amounts to R1.5 billion to date – including recently an extra amount of R500 million agreed to by the Minister of Finance – and is envisaged to total R15.9 billion for the pilot plant, which is planned for the Koeberg site, as well as a fuel fabrication plant at Pelindaba and some costs of commercialisation. By way of contrast, the amount of money devoted to the promotion and development of renewable energy sources has been derisory.

The pebble bed technology is one which uses fuel in the form of billiard-ball size spheres of enriched uranium coated in a layer of graphite. The technology uses helium as a coolant, and each reactor will generate 165 megawatts of electricity (MWe) (compared to each unit at Koeberg which generates around 900 MWe). The units are capable of being placed alongside key industries or in residential areas. Waste will be stored on site for most of the life of the reactors. There have been extensive lags in development of the technology, with major design changes, prompting an entirely new environmental impact assessment (EIA). The final design has not yet been disclosed to the Regulator, nor has the EIA been completed. Yet contracts have already been awarded for the manufacture of some of the PBMR's components.

Since 2002 Eskom's board has been expressing reluctance to adopt the technology, and the publication of key studies on the viability of the PBMR has been suppressed. Despite its misgivings, Eskom has been obliged to place on record its intention to order the PBMRs. Although the intention was to generate exports of the reactors, no orders have yet been received, and competition with a similar Chinese-built reactor will be keen.

Just as it succeeded in doing under apartheid, the nuclear industry is seeking special privileges from the state. The PBMR project is clearly too risky to attract much private investment, although the Toshiba company recently purchased 15 per cent of the PBMR company when it assumed the obligations of a close-to-bankrupt British Nuclear Fuels Ltd. The remaining 85 per cent is bankrolled by the South African taxpayer.

The original EIA process for the demonstration model of the pebble bed reactor was so flawed that even our courts pronounced it unfair in November 2004 when challenged by Earthlife Africa, a civil society watchdog organisation. In April 2005 the organisation attracted presidential ire for blowing the whistle on an unsafe-guarded former calibration site close to Pelindaba. In response to this the then Minister of Minerals and Energy Phumzile Mlambo-Ngcuka (now deputy president) went so far as to propose legislation to curb 'scaremongering', despite confirmation by the National Nuclear Regulator that Earthlife's Geiger readings at the site were accurate.

The state response to critics is nothing new, since by its nature the nuclear industry requires a climate of secrecy, high security, and guarantees that there will be no proliferation of weapons of mass destruction. During apartheid, the industry (along with Armscor) manufactured such weapons. Although they were dismantled on the eve of democracy, our thousand or so bomb-makers were never brought before the Truth and Reconciliation Commission. Some were subsequently recruited by the Pakistani nuclear trafficking ring under AQ Khan, using South Africa as a conduit to provide Pakistan and Libya with dual-use equipment aimed at proliferation.

The industry requires that we revert to becoming the national security state that we were during the apartheid years. Do we want that kind of future for our fragile new democracy? Or do we want a set of technologies that promotes more equity in society?

Genetically modified crops

Genetic modification (GM) is another controversial and unsustainable technology which presents high risks and potentially negative impacts on society. The technology is able to splice the genes of one living organism into another of a different species. Principally the technology has been used to add bacteria with insecticidal properties to food and fibre crops. The risks include potential danger to human and animal health, to biodiversity (the spread of the GM pollen could contaminate indigenous varieties of crops, important to food security), and to the livelihoods especially of small-scale peasant farmers. A highly unacceptable element is the emergence of large biotechnology companies which have increasingly monopolised control over seed and agriculture. Instead of protecting farmers from dependence on large corporations, GM crops require increased dependence on these transnational companies.

The intellectual property laws and international trade regimes allow for these companies to patent their 'inventions' – the first time in history that patents have been allowed over life forms. When farmers buy GM seed, they have to sign contracts agreeing not to swap or sell or re-utilise the GM seed after the growing season. This flies in the face of practice over the centuries, when small farmers traditionally would exchange seed with their neighbours, or replant from seed collected during the harvest, in order to find the best variety. With GM, this element of strengthening food security has been eliminated, since the farmer has to return to the company each time she wants to plant a crop. This places huge power over our food chain in the hands of the large biotechnology companies.

Africa has also become a dumping ground for GM food in the form of food aid, provided by the agencies of the US government through UN food schemes. The US subsidises its farmers who plant GM crops, and further purchases from them the surpluses that they generate over and above the needs of the marketplace. The excess food is stored. When the UN appeals for surplus food from countries to support drought-ravaged regions, the US insists that the recipient countries must accept its GM surplus. During the droughts of 2002 in southern Africa, it was discovered that the UN World Food Program had been distributing GM food aid without informing governments. It announced that countries of the region would starve unless this aid was accepted. Most countries in the region succumbed to this rhetoric – though some with the proviso that the GM maize should be milled into flour so that farmers would not be tempted to plant the seed (the US was unwilling to bear the costs of such milling). One country stood out against these offers: Zambia refused to accept the GM food aid, returned the stocks of GM aid that the World Food Program had introduced, sourced non-GM supplies from other countries in the region and revived the use of non-maize staple foods like cassava, of which there was an excess inside the country. Zambia argued that because of the potential risks of GM crops, these should not be introduced until there was a fully-fledged and capacitated regulatory system and a set of laws to protect citizens and the environment from the risks of GM. Zambia sent a scientific fact-finding mission around the world to report on the risks. Their findings confirmed to the president that the precautionary principle was the soundest scientific option for Zambia. The decision not to accept GM products until there is an appropriate bio-safety policy and suitable risk-averse legislation is one that stands as an example to the rest of Africa, challenging the attempts of larger powers to use Africa as a dumping ground for a questionable technology. By choosing to honour the organic path to agriculture, Zambia is also continuing to secure its market for fresh vegetables in the European Union countries, whose consumers have resisted GM products.

South Africa adopted the opposite course, succumbing to pressures from the biotechnology transnationals in its eagerness to introduce and promote GM crops. In the past five years, hundreds of thousands of hectares have been turned over to the planting of GM crops, making South Africa the sixth largest producer of GM plants in the world. Our regulatory system is skewed in favour of the GM companies and our authorities have bent over backwards to support the new technology. Small farmers have been supported to plant GM cotton (especially in the Makhatini flats), but are increasingly finding difficulties with debt, low cotton prices, withdrawn extension services and a lack of irrigation.

Requests for access to information from the Regulator have been stalled and refused, resulting in legal action by the non-governmental organisation Biowatch South Africa, which recently won the right to such information. The secrecy with which the Regulator has been giving blanket permission to biotech companies to spread GM seed also flies in the face of the development of our democratic rights-based culture.

The problem also resides in the fact that the Regulator resides within the Department of Agriculture, which at the same time is promoting the technology. It poses problems for good governance when the referee sides with one of the opposing teams on the playing field instead of being neutral and objective, and recognising its duties to protect the public and the environment. Important also to note is the fact that the Genetically Modified Organisms Act in South Africa was passed in 1997 without a great deal of public scrutiny, and is out of line with international commitments which South Africa has made in terms of the Convention on Biological Diversity and the Cartagena Protocol on Biosafety. At present the state is considering amendments to the Act, but these are so weak and tentative that they will preserve the status quo if they are accepted as drafted. Little has been done to inform decision-makers and legislators about the risks attached to the technology. Most of all, the technology is not in line with support for sustainable agricultural systems, something to which South Africa's Department of Agriculture is committed on paper through its Land Care Programme.

Going beyond growth

Why is there such strong government commitment to technologies which are patently unsustainable? Part of the answer rests in the deeply-held view, embedded within mainstream macroeconomic analysis, that growth is the panacea for development. Secondly, there is a strong adherence to spending on large-scale infrastructure, and dismissing small- and medium-scale technologies which would be in greater harmony with the proliferation of small businesses in our communities. A third strand of the bias is related to a technological nationalism, which sees high technology as an important indicator of the nation's global status. Technological advancement is seen as a ticket to global respect and a South African leadership role in Africa, and potentially in the UN Security Council. Nuclear technology, in particular, is strongly associated with these symbolic claims to prestige and a guarantor of sovereignty.

These values need to be reversed. It would create far greater prestige, and a larger development dividend, if South Africa could become a leader in, for example, renewable energy technologies or successful low-input agriculture.

Yet the case studies reveal that some key technological choices made in the name of South Africans reflect contrary values, and promote an unsustainable development path. This points to the fact that, despite legal and constitutional provisions, notions of sustainability have yet to be integrated into our macroeconomic and industrial policy thinking. If the NSSD is to succeed, it will need to ensure that such consciousness becomes embedded in the minds of our policy-makers, including parliamentarians and a range of government departments, especially the presidency. Recent announcements by the National Treasury that it will begin to implement a series of green taxes provide a useful beginning.

The US Congress has an Office for Technological Assessment which is independent of government departments and political parties. Although the model might not fit South African conditions precisely, there is a case for arguing that the adoption of key technologies be subjected to greater public debate and scrutiny, with alternatives being researched thoroughly and transparently. With regard to Latin America, for instance, Bastos and Cooper (1995) argue for the state's need to forge good links with society to enhance accountability and transparency in the interests of forging better technology policies. The NSSD is also proposing a multi-stakeholder Commission for Sustainable Development, as well as a sustainability cluster equivalent to the other clusters at Cabinet level, and a Parliamentary Portfolio Committee on Sustainability (DEAT 2006).

A clearer case will need to be made for sustainable development as an alternative model to patterns of modernisation which elevate growth at all costs. There is a strong need for decision-makers to internalise the analysis so cogently offered by Hallowes and Butler (2003). It would be far smarter, as the *Jo'burg Memo* pointed out, for countries of the global south to end the fixation on the historically obsolete development model of the north, and leapfrog into the solar age. 'A solar economy,' it argues, 'holds the prospect for including people and saving resources' (Sachs 2002: 23).

Note

1   Our annual production in 2002 was 707kt (DME 2003: 65–8).

References

Agama Energy (Pty) Ltd (2003) *Employment potential of renewable energy in South Africa*. Johannesburg: Sustainable Energy and Climate Change Project of Earthlife Africa.

Banks D & Schäffler J (2006) *The potential contribution of renewable energy in South Africa* (updated edition). Johannesburg: Sustainable Energy and Climate Change Project of Earthlife Africa.

Bastos MI & Cooper C (Eds) (1995) *The politics of technology in Latin America*. London: Routledge.

Beckerman W (1974) *In defence of economic growth*. London: Jonathan Cape.

Bethlehem L & Goldblatt M (Eds) (1995) *The bottom line: Industry and the environment in South Africa*. Cape Town: UCT Press.

Bezuidenhout A (2002) An evaluation of industrial policy perspectives in the South African context. *South African Labour Bulletin*, 26(3): 12–15.

Bond P & Guliwe T (2003) Contesting 'sustainable development': South African civil society critiques and advocacy. In G Mhone & O Edigheji (Eds) *Governance in the new South Africa: The challenges of globalisation*. Cape Town: University of Cape Town Press.

Bond P & Hoskin S (2002) The development of underdevelopment in Mandela Metropole: Coega's economic, social and environmental subsidies. In P Bond (Ed) *Unsustainable South Africa*. Pietermaritzburg: University of Natal Press.

Buhlungu S, Daniel J, Southall R & Lutchman J (Eds) *State of the Nation: South Africa 2005–2006*. Cape Town: HSRC Press.

Daly H (1996) *Beyond growth: The economics of sustainable development*. Boston: Beacon.

Davies R (2006) Budget vote speech by Deputy Minister of Trade and Industry, Dr Rob Davies, 30 March. Pretoria: Department of Trade and Industry.

DEAT (Department of Environmental Affairs and Tourism) (2006) South Africa's National Strategy for Sustainable Development. Draft Integrated Strategy for review. 21 April.

DME (Department of Minerals and Energy) (2003) *South Africa's mineral industry, 2002/3*. Pretoria: DME.

DoL (Department of Labour) (2006) Sectoral determination for farm workers (number 13). *Government Gazette* 28518, 17 February.

DTI (Department of Trade and Industry) (2001) Driving competitiveness: Towards a new integrated industrial strategy for sustainable employment and growth. Discussion document.

DTI (2005) A national industrial policy – draft. Internal discussion document. 18 September.

Durning A (1994) *Apartheid's environmental legacy*. Washington: WorldWatch.

Fig D (2005) *Uranium road: questioning South Africa's nuclear direction*. Johannesburg: Jacana.

Fine B & Rustomjee Z (1996) *The political economy of South Africa: From minerals–energy complex to industrialisation*. London: Hurst.

Flavin C & Gardner G (2006) China, India and the new world order. In *Worldwatch Institute State of the world 2006: Special focus on China and India*. New York: WW Norton & Co.

Haines R & Hoskin S (2005) A bridge too far? The arms deal, the Coega IDZ and economic development in the Eastern Cape. *Society in Transition*, 36(1): 1–23.

Hallowes D (2006) *Sustainable energy? Towards a civil society review of South African energy policy and implementation*. Johannesburg: Sustainable Energy and Climate Change Project of Earthlife Africa.

Hallowes D & Butler M (2003) *Forging the future: Industrial strategy and the making of environmental justice: The groundWork report 2003*. Pietermarizburg: groundWork.

Hirsch A (2005) *Season of hope: Economic reform under Mandela and Mbeki*. Pietermaritzburg: University of KwaZulu-Natal Press.

IDRC (International Development Research Centre) (1993) *Towards a science and technology policy for a democratic South Africa: Mission report*. Ottawa: IDRC.

IUCN, UNEP & WWF(1980) *World conservation strategy: Living resource conservation for sustainable development*. Gland, Switzerland: IUCN, UNEP & WWF.

Joffe A, Kaplan D, Kaplinsky R & Lewis D (Eds) (1995) *Improving manufacturing performance in South Africa: The report of the Industrial Strategy Project*. Cape Town: UCT Press.

Marais HC (2000) *Perspectives on science policy in South Africa*. Pretoria: Network.

Meadows DH (1972) *The limits to growth*. Washington DC: Earth Island.

Redclift M (1994) Development and the environment: Managing the contradictions. In L Sklair (Ed) *Capitalism and development*. London: Routledge.

Rostow W (1960) *The stages of growth*. Cambridge: Cambridge University Press.

Sachs W (Ed) (2002) *The Jo'burg Memo – Fairness in a fragile world: Memorandum for the World Summit on Sustainable Development*. Berlin: Heinrich Boell Foundation.

Southall R (2006) Can South Africa be a developmental state? In S Buhlungu et al. (Eds) *State of the Nation: South Africa 2005–2006*. Cape Town: HSRC Press.

Van Horen C (1997) Cheap energy – At what cost? Externalities in South Africa's energy sector. In L Bethlehem & M Goldblatt (Eds) *The bottom line: Industry and the environment in South Africa*. Cape Town: UCT Press.

World Commission on Environment and Development (1987) *Our common future*. Oxford: Oxford University Press.

10 Old victories, new struggles: the state of the National Union of Mineworkers

Andries Bezuidenhout and Sakhela Buhlungu

In 1946, mineworkers led by the African Mineworkers' Union (AMWU) staged a spectacular strike to protest their working conditions. They were forced to go back to the rock face at gunpoint, and the union and the process of mobilisation that had brought it about ended in defeat (Allen 1992). Two years after the strike, the National Party came to power and built its apartheid regime on the foundations created by the mining industry's migrant labour system. Mineworkers sporadically resisted racial abuse, the hostel system, and pass laws, but it was only in 1982 that black mineworkers succeeded in organising a union that could collectively challenge the employment practices of the mining industry. They formed the National Union of Mineworkers (NUM), which was in 1985 to become part of a new labour federation, the Congress of South African Trade Unions (Cosatu) (Allen 2003a, 2003b; Moodie 1994).

The labour movement has played, and continues to play, a key role in the democratic transformation of South Africa. Although many acknowledge this role, the focus is often on national federations and union engagement at national level and as a result little is known about the industrial unions that make up those federations. Yet it is at the level of industrial unions that ordinary workers experience day-to-day trade unionism with all its victories, setbacks and defeats. This chapter is based on a research project which investigated whether or not members of the NUM are satisfied with the services they get from the union.[1] Is the union dealing successfully with the legacy of racial despotism in the industry? Does the leadership of the union consult the membership before taking decisions? What about the living conditions and the compound system? To what extent is the social composition of the mining workforce, and the union's membership, changing? In this chapter we examine some of these issues and illustrate the key issues facing trade unions today, not only in relation to how unions have shaped the transition, but also the ways in which they in turn have been impacted upon by the democratic transition and by globalisation.

The NUM is the largest single trade union in the history of South Africa,[2] and its success in pushing back the frontier of despotic control in the mining industry, with all its private police forces and prison-like compounds, is a monument to the struggles of thousands of black mineworkers and a powerful illustration of the multifaceted nature of the South African transition[3] (Crush et al. 1991; James 1992; Jeeves 1985; Moodie 1994; Wilson 1972). The NUM's history has been intimately linked to the struggle for social transformation both at the workplace and in the social and political arenas. Ironically, the hostel system that was used as a form of near-totalitarian labour control became the organisational fulcrum of many of the union's activities. Its strategic location in the mining industry gave it considerable bargaining power in the workplace and the economy as a whole.

But this union's significance as an agent of social change goes further than its role at the point of production. The NUM did not only successfully improve the wages and working conditions of hundreds of thousands of mineworkers, it also produced some of the most prominent political and business leaders of contemporary South Africa. These include Cyril Ramaphosa, a key negotiator during the early phases of the transition and past secretary general of the African National Congress (ANC), now a business leader, as well as Kgalema Motlanthe, the current secretary general of the ANC. Both are past general secretaries of the NUM. Other business leaders include James Motlatsi, past president of the NUM, who is now a significant player in the mining industry on the other side of the negotiating table,[4] as well as Marcel Golding, who used the NUM's investment company to launch his own career as a new South African capitalist along with Johnny Copelyn, previously from Cosatu's textile union.[5]

In addition, scores of black miners, many of them unskilled or semi-skilled, rose through the ranks to become important leaders of the union and in the period since 1994 many NUM shaft stewards and full-time officials have moved on to play leading roles in the workplace as foremen and managers, as well as in their communities as local government councillors and even mayors (Macun & Buhlungu 1996).

While recognising its historical role in bringing about and shaping South Africa's transition, the NUM can be seen as a union of the past that organises workers in a sunset industry. By nature mines close down at some point, and hence the mining industry is seen as a waning part of the economy. However, while consistently shedding jobs since the decline of the gold price in the 1980s, it has become clear that the industry remains a key part of the South African economy. Three factors contribute to this continued relevance.

The first is the re-appreciation of the gold price in the context of global instability following the attacks on New York and the subsequent invasions of Afghanistan and Iraq by the US and its allies. The second is the economic growth of China, and its need for resources – especially steel and platinum. Indeed, the mining of platinum has given the South African mining industry a new lease on life. The third is the fact that South African mining capital, after a process of 'depatriation' (moving primary listings to the stock exchanges of London and New York) and mergers, now plays a leading role in the mining industry globally. While technically no longer South African corporations, many of their operations are still located in South Africa.[6]

Hence, while the government consistently ignores the role of the mining industry in its attempts to construct an industrial policy, it remains a key part of the South African economy.[7]

Given that, and the fact that this industry still has the highest level of union density in the country, how has the union movement engaged with the transition? In addition, it needs to be noted that the NUM does not organise only mineworkers. Significant numbers of its members are drawn from the construction and electricity-generation and distribution sectors. How does the union cope with the high numbers of contract and casual workers in the construction industry? How does it deal with the restructuring of Eskom and the introduction of regional electricity distributors?

The flip side of this discussion is, how has the transition impacted on the NUM? We argue that democracy has not only brought opportunities to entrench gains made during the liberation struggle, but it also presents the labour movement with a paradox. Those measures that are put in place to promote transformation and redress also tend to weaken union capacity to bring those changes about (Buhlungu 1999, 2001, 2002; Von Holdt 2002, 2003).

Turning despised subjects into dignified citizens

Black labour has been the backbone of the mining industry since its early days in the nineteenth century. But these workers did not join the industry voluntarily nor did they enjoy rights like their white counterparts; they entered the industry under duress and were forced to become part of a pool of cheap labour that did not enjoy citizenship rights as workers and as members of society. Managerial control was exercised though a range of measures including the pass system, prison-like single-sex compounds and the generalised use of violence to enforce compliance with mine regulations. For over a century black mineworkers were despised subjects in the mining industry. In addition, many in the black community also looked down upon these workers (Johnstone 1976; Wilson 1972). Mineworkers were sometimes derided as *AmaJoyini* ('Joiners') or *AmaGoduka* (those who have to go home). People regarded mine work as a lowly and dangerous job, and also saw contract miners as people with little or no formal education. Many communities saw factory work as a more dignified or respectable form of work. Factory workers were seen as more urban and in touch with new trends in the urban centres such as music and fashion. In contrast, mineworkers were seen to be rural, unsophisticated, and they listened to *mbaqanga* and *maskandi* music.

Attempts to organise black mineworkers and mobilise against their dreadful wages and working conditions were always met with violent responses by employers and the state. White miners were also threatened by the prospects of black unionisation and always fought to maintain the job colour bar in the industry. However, black mineworkers engaged in numerous struggles to improve their wages and conditions and made several efforts to establish trade unions. Prior to 1982, the formation of AMWU in the early 1940s was the most successful attempt. But the AMWU was short-lived as it collapsed following the defeat of the 1946 strike (Allen 1992).

It is against this background that the history and struggles of the NUM from 1982 to the present are significant. The successful formation of the union broke the cycle of failure that black mineworker unionisation had gone through before. Indeed, the success of the union in negotiating agreements with employers, thereby regulating wages and working conditions for workers, helped turn these workers into industrial citizens with rights and dignity. Previously there was no pension fund for black mineworkers. The Mineworkers Provident Fund, which was founded by the NUM in 1989, is now worth more than R10 billion, thus providing for some security for retired and retrenched mineworkers. The NUM also found common cause with other unions and political movements in the struggle for democracy in the country. At Cosatu's historic second national congress in 1987, the NUM was one of the main sponsors of a resolution to adopt the Freedom Charter (Allen 2003b).[8]

Within its own structures, the union created opportunities for mineworkers to exercise democratic rights as members by participating in decision-making at various levels. Through the provision of education and training for members, not only were mineworkers given opportunities to shape their union, they were also able to shape the future of the workplace and the country. With its motto 'Only the Best for the Mineworker!', the NUM helped turn black mineworkers into dignified citizens who were able to play a meaningful role in the democratic transformation of South Africa.

Several factors made it possible for the NUM to achieve these and other gains. First, the union benefited from the labour-law reforms of the late 1970s which made it possible for black workers to belong to registered unions. Although things were not smooth for the union, its leadership was successful in combining worker mobilisation and use of labour law to build the union.[9]

Second, the union has a militant membership which is ready to stand up to employers and the state. An example of this is the historic 1987 strike which demonstrated the willingness of thousands of miners to risk their jobs and even their lives in the struggle for improved wages and working conditions in the industry.

Third, the union managed to develop an impressive layer of organic worker leadership who were deployed at various levels of the organisation, including shaft stewards, health and safety committee members, branch, regional and national executive committee members and full-time officials. Indeed, the NUM prides itself on its success in recruiting its full-time officials from within the ranks rather than from outside the union. For the union, this is one of the measures of success of worker control and worker empowerment.

Fourth, the union was particularly successful at using the single-sex compounds as recruiting bases. The compounds provided ample opportunities for union mobilisation with their large concentrations of workers, sports facilities suitable for meetings, and intercom systems as a mode of communication.

Fifth, the union has built up a significant resource base since it was formed. Some of this is from membership subscriptions (over R100 million per annum), but high levels of unionisation also mean the union benefits from agency fees paid by non-union members who stand to benefit when the union negotiates wage increases. Unlike other unions, NUM can make enormous savings from free office space at each shaft, free meeting places such as halls and stadiums, sometimes free transport and education and training activities paid for from agency fees.

Finally, the fact that NUM is affiliated to Cosatu, a union federation known for its militancy and strong track record in fighting for transformation of workplace relations and for democracy in society, has made it possible for the union to advance some of its organisational and political gains.

In addition, the union has been active in looking after the welfare and dignity of its members in other ways. These include access to the union's scholarship scheme for mineworkers and their dependants, a programme funded by the profits from the union's investment wing, the Mineworkers Investment Company. The union also owns property in the form of its impressive head-office building in Johannesburg,[10] several regional offices, and the Elijah Barayi training centre, which is available for use by the union and rental by other organisations. The union's campaigns over the years have also produced significant rights under a new mining health and safety dispensation. In recent years, the union has been centrally involved in initiatives to negotiate a charter to transform ownership, control of and participation in the mining industry, including opening up access for women to work in this male-dominated industry. Campaigns against single-sex hostels have reshaped the landscape of mining towns, with many converted into family units, and mines increasingly offer their employees a living-out allowance as an alternative. This gives workers the option to explore various other forms of accommodation, including township living or informal settlements as an alternative to a life of constant migration.

While also organising workers in the energy sector (primarily Eskom), and now also the construction sector, the bulk of the NUM's membership is still located in the mining industry. In 2004, of its almost 260 000 members, nearly 220 000 were located in various parts of the mining industry (see Table 10.1). It is important to note that the largest single region is now Rustenburg, showing the increased importance of platinum. Members in gold mines are predominantly concentrated in three areas – Klerksdorp, Carletonville, and the Free State (mainly around Welkom). In addition, 30 000 members were located in the construction sector, and 10 000 in energy. Since 2004, the union has significantly increased its membership in the construction sector, taking the overall membership to 269 000 in 2006. The overwhelming majority of members are men. Indeed, only 5 per cent of our sample was female, with the overall proportion of women as members of the union even lower than this.

Table 10.1 *NUM membership data by region and sector, 2004*

	Mining	Construction	Energy
Carletonville	30 143	166	
Eastern Cape	59	7 274	
Free State	38 668	269	
Highveld	21 023	1 807	
Kimberley	5 995	553	
Klerksdorp	25 410	744	
Natal	2 197	1 099	
North Eastern Transvaal	12 932	2 141	
PWV**	24 940	8 877	
Rustenburg	55 352	1 624	
Western Cape	4 199	3 356	
Sector total	220 918	27 910	10 979*

Source: NUM 2004
Note: * Regional breakdowns for the energy sector were not available.
** This refers to the Pretoria–Witwatersrand–Vereeniging region.

Gains made by the union have, however, also brought about new contradictions, many of which threaten to fragment the solidarity forged during the period before 1994. Our study of union members' attitudes towards the union and the services it provides highlighted some of these contradictions.

Occupational mobility: a double-edged sword

The organisational achievements of the NUM, the gains it has won for its members and the shift from apartheid to democracy have meant that the NUM's member-ship base has become more diverse in occupational terms. Moreover, a combina-tion of gradual deracialisation, the education and training of existing workers and recruitment of better-educated workers has made it possible for black workers in general, and NUM members in particular, to move rapidly up the occupational ladder, into artisanal and other skilled positions as well as supervisory and mana-gerial positions. In an industry where these positions had been the preserve of white workers, occupational mobility for black mineworkers has been a positive development.

However, this upward mobility has introduced serious tensions and new dynamics in the union. In particular, it has put the position of the shaft steward under the spotlight because this layer of union leadership is a popular recruiting ground for management in the industry. The occupational mobility of shaft stewards and leading activists has the potential to impact negatively on the servicing of union members because it removes skilled shop-floor leaders from the union and leaves a leadership vacuum. The NUM has two kinds of arrangements for shaft stewards. Some are part time, which means that they perform their union duties while they remain in their jobs on the mines, power stations and construction sites. These officials do not receive any payment over and above their regular wages. On the other hand, the union has an arrangement for some shaft stewards to become full time in their union positions. They do not stay in their jobs but become full-time union operatives working from an office within the premises, or from the union's regional offices. In virtually all cases, full-time shaft stewards receive higher remuneration and benefits and often do not ever return to their shop-floor positions. A mineworker who gets elected to the position of full-time shaft steward can triple his monthly salary, as the norm is to remunerate these positions at the level of a personnel officer. This raises the stakes, and where shaft stewards were often victimised in the past, the position has now become a ticket to advancement. The other problem is that, as we shall see, not all members feel that they can advance. Indeed, many still argue that racial discrimination holds them down. This often leads to serious tensions between members and some shaft stewards.

The NUM members we surveyed did a vast array of jobs. The majority (62%) worked underground. A growing number of women are joining the ranks of the mining workforce and many are members of the NUM. Women members tended to work on the surface, although 26 per cent of them worked underground.

Members' wages ranged from a minimum of R300 per month (pm),[11] with the highest paid member, an engineer, at R19 400 per month. This shows the diversity of the membership base of the NUM. The overall average wage was R3 287 pm. Men on average earned more than women – R3 306 per month as opposed to the R2 898 monthly average for women. Another source of difference regarding wages was the three broad sectors organised by the union. Members in the construction sector earned much less money than those in mining and energy. Indeed, the average monthly wage for construction workers in our sample was R2 334 pm. In mining, members received an average of R3 207 pm, and in energy, a much higher average monthly salary of R6 216.

Our study found that the occupational mobility of shaft stewards had a negative impact on solidarity in union branches. Many union members generally felt that full-time shaft stewards, in particular, were becoming removed from the membership base and this led to high levels of distrust. Competition for these positions was also destructive and sometimes took on the form of violent conflict.

At Kumba Resources in Thabazimbi a member expressed the feeling that the mine 'promotes shop stewards so they can forget about the union'. A recent incident at Impala Platinum in North West province highlighted the impact of the mobility of shaft stewards on solidarity in the branch. According to the members, there were three bargaining units at this company. Bargaining units are different categories of employees, based on their skills and their position in the grading system. For example, people at managerial level constitute a discrete bargaining unit, as distinct from general workers in skilled and unskilled positions. In this case, the NUM is recognised for the bargaining unit of workers in grades 1 to 6. The problem arose when shaft stewards were appointed into jobs outside the NUM's bargaining unit, but held on to their union positions. The matter came to a head during a strike, which meant that, because they were outside the bargaining unit, they could not strike legally alongside the membership. To resolve this contradiction, some took sick leave during a strike. A member remarked bitterly: 'With all the perks they receive, shop stewards are like nobles in the old class structure. Members are just peasants.'

Another related theme that emerged – in the context of perceived racial barriers to upward mobility and the positions of power of shaft stewards – was allegations of corruption and the selling of jobs by shaft stewards. At Karee mine, members alleged that promotions were monopolised by shaft stewards. In addition, the perception at this branch was that shaft stewards demanded bribes (*intshontsho*) in order to facilitate the appointment of new employees. A member said that the price of a job was R1 500, half of which went to the shaft steward and the other half went to the person in the human resources department of the company. At President Steyn mine, a member also made allegations about the buying of jobs: 'You have to buy your way into promotion by paying bribes.' (At this mine it also seemed that the inheritance of jobs when old workers retire was still taking place.) Another member raised the issue of ethnicity: 'When there are promotions in the branch, some people are favoured on the basis of ethnicity.' This implies that at some mines shaft stewards are beginning to play the role of recruitment agents and gatekeepers in making new appointments and promoting workers.

We now turn to a discussion of three aspects related to occupational mobility, namely, the legacy of racial discrimination, the rise of subcontracting, and the increased employment of women in the industry.

The stubborn legacy of racial discrimination

Since its formation in 1982, the NUM has been a leading force in the struggle against racism and racial discrimination in the mining industry, particularly in relation to wages, occupations and the general treatment of black workers. There is little doubt that the union has had an enormous impact in this regard and some of the gains in terms of opportunities for occupational mobility are a result of its efforts. However, the legacy of racial discrimination has remained extremely intractable. At several of the mines visited during our study, NUM members felt that the apartheid workplace regime was still partially in place and that white employees were still using informal mechanisms to exclude black employees. Members often felt that there was a lack of capacity at union branch level to enforce the implementation of laws such as the Employment Equity Act and the Skills Development Act. At Richards Bay Minerals a NUM member remarked angrily: 'There are no promotions for us. Only the *impimpis* [spies or sell-outs] get promotion.' At workplaces such as Karee mine, union members argued that the education provided in terms of Mineworkers' Qualification Authority and the Skills Development Act was not useful because there were no avenues for promotion. Similar complaints were received from members at almost all the workplaces we studied. A President Steyn worker was expressing a generally-held view when he said:

> You only go somewhere if you know someone. Whites still use race for promotion possibilities. When you seek out a promotion they say: 'Go paint yourself white.' Whether or not you have experience is not an issue – apartheid is still very rife. The union tries very hard to fight, but it is difficult to change.

It is important to note that members were often positive about black economic empowerment (BEE) and felt that new ownership structures could impact positively in the workplace by removing discrimination from white managers. For example, Transhex workers from the Western Cape felt that there have been many changes since Tokyo Sexwale became Transhex's BEE partner. In the words of one worker: 'Certain changes have taken place since Tokyo came in. Living is mixed [and] we have now black/coloured managers. Training is now happening, although it is slow.' The same attitude was expressed about Patrice Motsepe at Harmony-ARM in Klerksdorp. However, many NUM members felt that the treatment of black workers by black managers was still in the authoritarian mould of the old order, or as one member remarked: 'Black shift bosses still get pressure from white managers.'

Notwithstanding the above, NUM members remain extremely loyal to the union. One of the reasons for this loyalty derives from the continued efforts of the union to confront and eliminate the legacy of racism and discrimination. Many union members have a clear sense of how far they have come with the union and have no illusion about how long it will take to remove racial discrimination in their workplaces.

Authoritarian restoration through subcontracting

Recent studies of the post-apartheid workplace have identified attempts at some firms to return to an authoritarian past – a strategy termed 'authoritarian restoration' (Von Holdt 2003; Webster & Von Holdt 2005). One method used was subcontracting. It is not a new phenomenon in the sectors that the NUM organises. However, since the mid-1990s, mining houses have increasingly subcontracted actual 'core' mining operations. Subcontractors in the industry range from large registered companies to 'fly-by-nights' – often retrenched white miners acting as labour brokers. Non-core functions that are traditionally subcontracted include shaft sinking, wire meshing and underground construction. Employment by 'outside contractors' in mining increased from 46 355 in January 2000 to 90 231 in November 2003. Gold mining accounted for 27 717 of these workers and platinum for 31 833. Mining and quarrying employed a total of 438 000 formal sector employees in December 2003, so subcontracting accounted for roughly 20 per cent of all employment in the sector.[12] This increase is taking place despite a range of agreements between the NUM and the Chamber of Mines. A part of the problem is that the chamber consistently refuses NUM's attempts to set up a body for contractors to register with. Another problem is that many mines do not fall under the chamber's agreements.

As in the case of the mining industry, non-standard employment has also increased in the construction sector – especially the employment of workers through labour brokers (Bezuidenhout et al. 2004). While the NUM has succeeded in expanding its membership base in this industry, aggressive employment of workers through intermediaries or on limited duration contracts undermines these gains. Even before the integration of the Construction and Allied Workers' Union into the NUM, a number of the bargaining councils[13] in the industry collapsed because in many cases non-standard employees actually outnumbered permanent workers.

Regarding the energy sector (largely Eskom), the NUM is also confronted with subcontracting and outsourcing that goes along with the commercialisation of electricity utilities. Reopening mothballed power stations, Eskom has refused to re-employ previous employees. Instead, they have used labour brokers to hire workers. There is also a general trend in the company to outsource so-called non-core functions such as security, cleaning, and so on. A new development in the last five years is the use of subcontractors in maintenance work.

The NUM has recognised that this continued trend towards subcontracting of labour is undermining its gains, as the union's Secretariat report of 2004 points out:

> Outsourcing and contracting out continues to be the biggest enemy of the working people. It is central to a capital accumulation strategy. It is based on super exploitation, intense utilisation of labour and profit maximisation. It is a strategy that will not disappear in the short term. Hence the need for a short-term programme and long-term strategy. (Cited in Bezuidenhout et al. 2005: 30–1)

The union's approach to this issue includes defending existing jobs and organising the vulnerable workers into the NUM. However, the NUM report points out that very few regions have taken campaigns against outsourcing seriously. It commended the Free State region for its active campaigns in this regard, specifically the branches of President Steyn and Target, where campaigns led to contract workers being employed directly by the mine. Also, the PWV[14] region succeeded in limiting the use of labour brokers at ERPM mine. Nevertheless, most regions were criticised for seeing outsourcing as 'God-given'.

The report points to some of the contradictions:

> Many of our campaigns focused on using these vulnerable workers as the first victims in case of retrenchment. They are used as an 'avoidance measure'. This is dangerous in that it does not, of necessity, save jobs. It gives our branches short-term satisfaction, because in most cases permanent workers get retrenched. (Cited in Bezuidenhout et al. 2005: 30–1)

It is then acknowledged that, in the case of the above, union structures 'end up helping management in victimising the vulnerable section of the workforce'. Indeed, argues the report, '[t]his must change decisively'. The report proposes that:

> Regions must be more hands on. The rule that no retrenchment agreement should be signed without the region's approval has been systematically put aside by many of our branches. Only the regions themselves can recapture this space. It is dangerous for the structures of the union to have so serious a suspicion and lack of trust, that they will hide what they are doing from each other and seek a second opinion from another structure. (Cited in Bezuidenhout et al. 2005: 30–1)

Our study found that subcontracting remains a serious issue and that it is one of the major reasons why members think that the NUM has lost some of its power. Most members in our survey (93%) were employed on permanent contracts. A further 6 per cent were employed on fixed-term (temporary) contracts. More men (94%) were employed in permanent contracts than women (86%). Despite the growth of subcontracting in mining, only 10 per cent of NUM's members are employed by subcontractors, which seems to suggest that the union is not making much headway organising subcontracted or labour-broker workers. Another indication of future trouble for the union is the fact that 61 per cent of subcontractor or labour-broker workers work underground. Further investigation showed that these workers tend to do exactly the same tasks as those performed by permanent workers employed by the mines. In addition, there is a growing trend for retired or dismissed permanent workers to be replaced by subcontractor workers. Interestingly, women in our sample tended to be employed by mines directly, rather than through contractors or labour brokers.

The growth of these categories of workers is creating tensions within the workforce and threatening the solidarity that helped unite mineworkers to confront injustices in mining. A union member at Richards Bay Minerals expressed his frustrations with these workers:

> Contract workers take our jobs, they are not registered, they have no say and no benefits. They are not under the union. They are not

allowed to join a union! They work the same jobs as permanents. If two permanent workers leave, their jobs are taken by two contract workers. Management doesn't say anything to inform us about these contract workers. The union doesn't have power to fight management on contract workers. If it was up to us we would throw out contract workers and put permanents in their place!

Another worker at Harmony-ARM in Klerksdorp voiced his serious concern about subcontracting:

Contractors are a major issue. There were several injuries, but not compensation…Contractors tend to work more in dangerous places. Permanents and contractors get exactly the same jobs, and don't even work in separate gangs! The only distinction is overalls.

At Eskom in Lephalale there has been some subcontracting. These subcontractors were doing work that had previously been done by Eskom employees, such as electrical work, cleaning and fire extinguishing. One member made another point about this situation: 'Air conditioning used to be done by eight people, now it is done by two after it was subcontracted.' At Eskom in Welkom, subcontractors do cleaning and are not allowed to join the union because they have their own union. As one member said: 'They are only here for a limited time.'

Subcontracting is also an issue in the construction industry. Members in the Natal region pointed out that companies take on contractors who work when they go on strike. Some contractors do the same jobs as permanent workers, while others are employed in specific areas of work. They also mentioned that there were young people who were hired on fixed-term contracts for three months, and then discharged. As a shop steward in the Western Cape pointed out: 'We can talk until tomorrow on subcontracting because it is a big issue in the construction industry. Big companies give work to subcontractors, then subcontractors give work to sub-subcontractors who also subcontract what they have been given.'

Subcontracting is probably the single most serious threat to worker solidarity and worker power in post-apartheid South Africa. It exposes union vulnerability and pits worker against worker. Asked why the union was not drawing workers employed by subcontractors into the union, the Western Cape construction shop-stewards spoke of the difficulties of organising these workers:

When these workers indicate willingness to be part of a union, they are dismissed instantly. These subcontractors know that there are thousands standing next to robots, ready to fill the vacancies of those dismissed. Organising subcontracted workers is like pouring water in a drum with a hole. You recruit today and your members are shown the door without being given a blue card so as to claim unemployment insurance. As a union we want to organise them but it is difficult.

'How do you do first aid on a woman?' Women in a man's world

As can be expected in an industry such as the mining industry, the majority of NUM members (95%) surveyed were men. Women comprised only 5 per cent of the sample. They were mostly employed on platinum mines, followed by gold mines and some in Eskom. The women were generally younger than men, received lower wages, tended not to work underground, were single, and lived in family homes.

The picture that emerged from our study is that women do a range of jobs in the different sectors organised by the NUM. As a union member at Richards Bay Minerals put it: 'Women workers do everything – even construction.' Their arrival in traditionally male workplaces, such as the mines, has created difficulties for NUM and its predominantly male membership. Prejudices against women miners emerge most starkly when working underground is discussed. A union member at St Helena Mine, Welkom, suggested the following reasons why employing women can create tensions:

> Women are working underground. They can do some jobs, but not
> others. Men and women are not the same – they are different, but now
> there is equality. So they can work wherever…But we feel that they
> can't do the job well. They don't have the strength, but they do work
> there. The union places them in levels where they can work better.

Similar reservations about the capabilities of women emerged in discussions with NUM members in construction subsectors such as civil engineering and building construction. A shop steward at Concor in Modderspruit in the Western Cape argued that:

> Women can never survive in the construction industry. They won't last
> more than three months. Do you have a picture of a woman carpenter?
> Such a woman will never be able to lift her toolbox.

A similar sentiment was expressed by workers at Harmony-ARM in Klerksdorp who argued that women should have their own teams underground. A male mine worker suggested that the arrival of women workers placed men in a predicament: 'It is difficult to work with women underground! How do you do first aid?'

However, a shop steward from Cape Concrete disagreed with this sentiment: 'There is a lot of work that women in the construction industry can do. It's just that employers do not want women in the industry.'

However, the truth seems to be that the union and its members have not come to grips with the implications of women joining the workforce in these traditionally male industries. A union official admitted that although the NUM is in the forefront of getting women into these industries:

> The union does not fully appreciate conditions under which women
> members will feel acceptable in the mining industry. As a union we've

demanded two-piece overalls when we realised that women were not comfortable in men's overalls. We also demanded separate toilet facilities underground. But this is not enough. We need to find what is it that will make women members fully integrated in the work environment underground.

At Harmony-ARM in Klerksdorp we conducted a focus group with women mineworkers to explore this issue from their point of view. They were the first group to be employed underground at this mine. They had not undergone formal training, so they did not have certificates. They had taken up the issue, but there was no action by either management or the union. They are generally used as a pool of labour that is moved around. They were dissatisfied about this, and wanted specific job titles. They said that no job was too hard for them. 'We can do everything, but they pay us less money,' one woman pointed out. Another expanded on this: 'We started on R1 600 a month, but other workers get R3 000 plus.' This is in spite of the fact that they are permanent workers and NUM members. 'The issue of certificates is used to discriminate against us', said one, 'they say we are still "learning".' Recently their wages were raised to just above R2 000 per month, but this is still less than the men's wages. The matter is still being handled by the NUM. However, one of the women pointed out, 'some men in NUM are supporting the fact that we get lower wages'. Some of the women who work at this mine live in a section of a hostel converted into family units.[15] They complain that sexual harassment is a problem. They reported this to the union, but the union said they should 'forgive those who put them under pressure'. Some men are happy with them working there, but feel women should have special accommodation to protect them from harassment. The NUM shaft stewards advised them to visit their office frequently. They did this to raise their issues with the shaft stewards, but no action was taken.

At Matimba Power Station four members of a seven-person focus group were women. They were younger than the men in the group. This representation of women was also reflected at a general meeting held at Eskom's Western Cape regional office in Bellville. Half of the participants were women and they participated fully at the meeting, most of the times leading issues from the floor.

Generally members knew that it was union policy to campaign for the employment of more women. However, when we probed further, stereotypical thinking emerged. To be sure, one of the implications of a growing female membership in NUM is that the union should consciously revisit its current organisational culture which is male, patriarchal and sometimes sexist. In the meantime, there is no doubt that management is using gender differences and entrenched notions of patriarchy to exploit women workers. An issue of concern is management paying these workers less and hiring them on less secure terms.

Solidarity and divisions in the union

Despite a sense of the union losing some of its power, members remain very loyal to the organisation. A majority are also loyal supporters of the ANC. In terms of political culture, NUM members 'sing one song, that of the ANC', as a worker in Klerksdorp remarked. The union clearly still has remarkably high levels of unity and solidarity. However, the transition introduces new dynamics that threaten these levels of solidarity. We have already shown how careerism leads to severe division and disillusionment with the union in certain branches. When lobbying for positions becomes more about career opportunities, and less about the traditions of solidarity that brought about the transition, non-class identities are often mobilised. We found numerous instances where ethnic and, in fewer cases, racial divisions were threatening to tear branches apart – especially at times running up to union elections (see Bezuidenhout et al. 2005).

A further threat to union solidarity and members' support of the union is the visible presence of legal insurance companies at the mines. NUM members often use membership of these organisations as a fallback for when the union fails them. These include Scorpions,[16] Legal Wise, as well as a legal advice firm that workers claim belongs to Matthews Phosa, the former premier of Mpumalanga province. The latter even has shaft stewards acting as its agents at some of the branches. The popularity of legal insurance among NUM members should be seen against the background of a perception amongst members that the union is not always able to win their cases.

At Karee mine, for example, members said that they were members of Scorpions because 'we are not happy with the NUM'. They related a story about a member who went to the Transkei. When he came back, the NUM did not want to represent him, saying that he had 'absconded'. He went to Scorpions and got his job back. He is still a member of the NUM, and he is a significant member, because he was one of the founding members of the branch. This example was used to show how Scorpions were able to win cases where the NUM could not. At the time of our research in 2005 there were huge tents right outside the gate of this mine that belonged to Scorpions and Legal Wise. A union member remarked: 'The thing with NUM is that it is not functional. If you are a member [of Scorpions], you have a card to show. But NUM does not have a card that you can carry to show that you are a union member.' At De Beers in Kleinsee, one worker stated, 'I don't trust the branch leaders, that's why I chose Legal Wise to represent me.'

But other members disagreed that they were joining legal insurance schemes because of a lack of faith in NUM. As one member put it: 'The union is for workplace problems and Scorpions and Legal Wise are for when furniture shops take you to court and when you have other problems outside of the working environment.' At another mine a member remarked: 'NUM told workers that Scorpions is like insurance. NUM works hard for workers, but it ends in the workplace.'

Conclusion: NUM and the changing landscape of union organisation

A typical NUM member in the past was a migrant worker from the Eastern Cape or Lesotho, who lived in a single-sex hostel and worked in a gold mine. Mine employment was relatively stable and the union used the concentration of large numbers of workers in hostels as an organisational base. Initially, mineworkers were mostly employed as contract labour. The union succeeded spectacularly in mobilising these vulnerable workers to improve their employment status and to campaign for better health and safety laws and regulations. The union also limited the ability of mines to use the racial order of apartheid to enforce discipline. This was the source of the NUM's strength – very high levels of solidarity in response to racist white managers and a racist state, and the ability to bring mining production to a complete standstill with strikes, or at least to disrupt production.

With the transition to democracy, many of the gains that the union achieved in the 1980s were formalised. The NUM developed more sophisticated strategies and is now a well-resourced union with a significant infrastructure. However, certain changes in the industrial structure of the mining industry, as well as changes in work organisation and employment practices, are posing fundamental challenges to the union's main sources of power.

In addition, democratisation, deracialisation and work restructuring have introduced several other changes to the union organising landscape, particularly for the mining industry. First, the mining compound is no longer the sole centre of union activity today. Many workers have moved out of the compounds and now live in informal settlements or in townships with their families or friends. As a result, the task of mobilising workers is no longer a simple matter of getting every worker out of their dormitory to the stadium to listen to speeches and participate in singing. The compound dormitories house a diminishing number of mineworkers. The NUM has discovered that it has to cater for the needs of workers in converted family units, those in informal settlements, those living in townships and those in single-sex compounds.

Second, competition for jobs and better-paid positions in the mining labour market has resulted in workers competing with one another along ethnic and national lines.[17] One example is the unhappiness among Nguni-speaking workers about what they perceive to be the preferential employment of only Tswana-speaking women on the platinum mines of the North West province. Another is the frequent explosion of conflict between South African and foreign workers such as Mozambicans, which on the surface would appear to be over trivial conflicts, but is in reality about competition over scarce jobs and other resources.

Third, in this chapter we have discussed the implications of occupational mobility for union organisation. But occupational mobility is part of a bigger process of social change in the form of upward social mobility. Upward mobility is an aspect of class formation and it affects all sections of the NUM's membership and leadership. An example of how it affects the union is the case of a full-time shaft steward and regional leader we interviewed for our study. Following his election to the full-time position, this leader's wage was adjusted to the same level as that of a personnel officer. In addition, the union's agreement with management stated that a full-time shaft steward who was not re-elected could not become worse off in earning terms. Effectively it meant that the person would not be demoted and therefore would not go back to the shop floor as an ordinary worker. To prepare for this eventuality, the mine and the union agreed to take their full-time shaft stewards to leadership development courses at several university business schools. When we met this full-time shaft steward, he was doing a short business development course at the University of the Witwatersrand's business school. At that time his monthly wage was at least four times the average wage for a mineworker!

Hundreds of other shaft stewards and leaders of the union have followed a similar course and over time become increasingly alienated from their membership base. It has happened often that the election of a worker to the position of full-time shaft steward has become a stepping stone out of the rock face and, ultimately, out of the union and into politics and business. This is the path followed by many former leaders of the union such as former president James Motlatsi (now deputy chairman of AngloGold) and former national treasurer Paul Nkuna (now chief executive officer of the Mineworkers Investment Company).

Fourth, the change in the union organising landscape has resulted in the erosion of democratic practices within union structures. The alienation of the leadership from the rank and file has been accompanied by a decline in the practice of consultation with members and participation of members in decision-making. Although it is sometimes valid to say that some issues require speedy discussion between the union and the state and employers, this often results in a smaller group taking most of the decisions in the name of the union. In the past this resulted in misunderstandings leading to the formation of splinter groups such as Mouthpiece, and to tragic incidents such as the killing in 1999 of regional chairman, Selby Mayise, by the union's own members.

Finally, the changing union organising landscape is shaped by broader processes of economic restructuring and globalisation. We have already discussed the impact of subcontracting on NUM. To this we can add the continued decline of employment in the sectors organised by NUM, particularly mining.

This chapter illustrates the enormity of the new challenges and struggles that have arisen for the NUM. Unfortunately none of the union's gains and victories from the anti-apartheid struggle days make it immune to these new pressures. In addition, many of the strategies and tactics that helped the union achieve the spectacular successes of the 1980s and early 1990s are not necessarily appropriate to these new circumstances. Thus one of the key conclusions of our study was that the union has to search for new solutions to a new set of problems. The NUM is certainly not unaware of these challenges. Indeed, it has developed a series of ten-year plans in order to strategise around issues of organisational renewal (see Majadibodu 2001; NUM 2003), and has been commissioning research to track whether these interventions are successful (see Bezuidenhout et al. 1998, 2005). The union has also taken decisive steps towards combating corruption, and its leadership has acted whenever these issues are brought to its attention.

Finally, we should point out that the NUM's roots in the black consciousness movement enabled it to play a leading role in sensitising the more 'workerist'-oriented unions to issues of racial oppression, and thus the centrality of national liberation for black workers in Cosatu. Ironically, Cosatu's affiliate that came from a black consciousness tradition was the first union officially to adopt the Freedom Charter – in 1987 – and later that year it sponsored a similar motion at the federation's second national congress in opposition to some of the manufacturing unions. It is no wonder then that two of the unbanned ANC's general secretaries (1991 to the present) have come from the NUM.[18] Indeed, what is remarkable about the NUM is the way in which it has been able to accommodate and incorporate various political traditions – black consciousness, the Charterist movement expressed in the politics of the ANC and the South African Communist Party, as well as the United Democratic Front in the mid-1980s, and even far-left intellectuals.

In part this can be explained by the fact that mineworkers themselves are drawn from various parts of the southern African region, and in addition to the worst forms of racial oppression and abuse, their union has always had to deal with issues of internal diversity and contestation. In other words, the NUM's vantage point for its struggles has been informed not only by the class position of its members, but also by issues of race, ethnicity and nationality. Its blind spot, however, is gender. To be sure, the different political traditions of liberation are as complex in the labour movement as they are in the 'broad church' of the ANC itself.

The NUM mirrors all the achievements, setbacks and problems facing the other unions from the militant tradition of unionism that is represented in Cosatu. That tradition of unionism is now a permanent feature of our country's industrial relations and politics and no narrative thereof is complete without reference to unions such as the NUM.

Notes

1   For the perspective presented in this chapter, we draw on a survey of 724 members of NUM, supplemented by 44 focus group interviews, as well as 15 interviews with regional and national office-bearers and officials. The research was conducted in the Free State, Natal, North East, Klerksdorp, Rustenburg and Western Cape regions of the NUM. These interviews were conducted in 2005 as part of a study commissioned by the NUM to consider the quality of its services rendered to members. Because of the absence of a sampling frame (which ruled out random sampling) a quota sample was used to reflect

the proportions of members in the sectors and regions included in the study. Members were selected with the assistance of branch committees. Branches were selected for focus group interviews based on the findings of the survey – particularly taking into consideration different levels of servicing reported by members (see Bezuidenhout et al. 2005). We would like to thank the NUM for allowing us to draw on this research for this chapter. We would also like to thank Gwede Mantashe and Frans Baleni for commenting on earlier drafts of the chapter. We take full responsibility for the analysis and interpretation of data, which does not necessarily reflect the views of the NUM.

2   According to the NUM's general secretary, the union had 269 000 members in 2006.

3   The role of the labour movement is often not adequately recognised in popular renditions of the liberation struggle – such as the Apartheid Museum in Johannesburg, which almost completely ignores the labour movement's contribution. The legacy of organised labour in the South African struggle has been neglected in new initiatives to create memorials and heritage sites.

4   James Motlatsi is the deputy chairman of AngloGold and the CEO and owner of TEBA Ltd. TEBA is the remnant of the old migrant-labour recruiting agency of the mining industry. Incidentally, Motlatsi came to South Africa as a migrant worker recruited by TEBA from Lesotho in the 1970s.

5   Hosken Consolidated Investments, Golding and Copelyn's company, owns e-tv, and recently became a majority shareholder in Johnnic, the owner of the *Sunday Times*. It should be noted that Golding and Copelyn used their association with the labour movement to launch their careers as capitalists, and did not get any personal financial backing from their unions. Golding was part of the planning of the Mineworkers' Investment Company, and served on its board, but did not receive any material benefits from it. We would like to thank Gwede Mantashe for pointing this out to us.

6   Here we refer to corporations such as BHP-Billiton and AngloGold-Ashanti, both results of foreign listings coupled with mergers.

7   Of course, lip service is paid to 'beneficiation' by attempts to support the emergence of a jewellery manufacturing industry that links to the mining of gold and diamonds.

8   This is significant, because the NUM was rooted in black consciousness and was initially affiliated to the Council of Unions of South Africa, a black consciousness federation.

9   Indeed, Cyril Ramaphosa, the first general secretary, was a trained lawyer and later distinguished himself as a skilled negotiator during the democratic transition.

10   In fact, the union owns the whole block, and counts Johannesburg Water among its tenants.

11   This extremely low wage is clearly not in line with the NUM's wage agreements with the Chamber of Mines and mining houses that fall outside the scope of these central agreements. Indeed, the worker who earned only R300 pm was employed through a subcontractor, illustrating the dire circumstances many of these workers have to contend with.

12 Data from the Department of Minerals and Energy.

13 A bargaining council is an industrial forum where organised business and labour negotiate wages and conditions. Certain minimum standards are set for entire industries based on agreements reached by these forums. In the construction industry, bargaining councils covered certain geographical regions – the Durban Bargaining Council was the first to collapse, followed by Gauteng and a number of others.

14 This refers to the NUM's Pretoria–Witwatersrand–Vereeniging region. The union's regional demarcations do not necessarily follow the new provincial boundaries.

15 This section is called 'Gwede Mantashe'.

16 Scorpions here should not be confused with the office of the National Prosecuting Authority, which is also known as the Scorpions. We refer to a legal insurance firm with the same name. The similarity in names could potentially create confusion, which most probably works in favour of the insurance firm.

17 We refer here to competition between South African citizens and foreign migrant workers from, especially, Lesotho and Mozambique.

18 We refer here to Cyril Ramaphosa (1991–97) and Kgalema Motlanthe (1997 to present).

References

Allen V (1992) *The history of black mineworkers in South Africa: The techniques of resistance 1871–1948* (Volume I). Keighley: The Moor Press.

Allen V (2003a) *The history of black mineworkers in South Africa: Dissent and repression in the compounds 1948–1982* (Volume II). Keighley: The Moor Press.

Allen V (2003b) *The history of black mineworkers in South Africa: The rise and struggles of the National Union of Mineworkers 1982–1994* (Volume III). Keighley: The Moor Press.

Bezuidenhout A, Buhlungu S, Hlela H, Modisha MG & Sikwebu D (2005) *Members first: A research report on the state of servicing in the National Union of Mineworkers*. Johannesburg: Sociology of Work Unit, University of the Witwatersrand.

Bezuidenhout A, Godfrey S, Theron J & Modisha MG (2004) Non-standard employment and its policy implications. Report submitted to the Department of Labour. Johannesburg: Sociology of Work Unit, University of the Witwatersrand.

Bezuidenhout A, Kenny B, Masha G & Tshikalange H (1998) *A strong branch is a strong union: Servicing the National Union of Mineworkers*. Johannesburg: Sociology of Work Unit, University of the Witwatersrand and National Union of Mineworkers.

Buhlungu S (1999) Generational change in union employment: The organisational implications of staff turnover in Cosatu unions. *Transformation*, 39: 47–71.

Buhlungu S (2001) The paradox of victory: South Africa's union movement in crisis. *New Labor Forum*, 8: 67–76.

Buhlungu S (2002) *Comrades, entrepreneurs and career unionists: Organisational modernisation and new cleavages among Cosatu union officials*. Occasional Paper 17. Johannesburg: Friedrich Ebert Stiftung.

Crush J, Jeeves A & Yudelman D (1991) *South Africa's labor empire: A history of black migrancy to the gold mines.* Cape Town: David Philip.

James WG (1992) *Our precious metal: African labour in South Africa's gold industry, 1970–1990.* Cape Town: David Philip.

Jeeves AH (1985) *Migrant labour in South Africa's mining economy: The struggle for the gold mines' labour supply, 1890–1920.* Johannesburg: Witwatersrand University Press.

Johnstone FA (1976) *Class, race and gold: A study of class relations and racial discrimination in South Africa.* London: Routledge & Kegan Paul.

Macun I & Buhlungu S (1996) 'When the rain comes, it rains for everybody': Interview with Gwede Mantashe. *South African Labour Bulletin*, 20(1): 24–31.

Majadibodu E (2001) *Implementing the ten dimensions for quality service to Members.* Johannesburg: NUM internal report.

Moodie TD (1994) *Going for gold: Men, mines and migration.* Johannesburg: Witwatersrand University Press.

NUM (National Union of Mineworkers) (2003) Ten year plan, second edition. Johannesburg: NUM internal report.

NUM (2004). *Secretariat report.* Johannesburg: NUM.

Von Holdt K (2002) Social movement unionism: The case of South Africa. *Work Employment and Society,* 16(2): 283–304.

Von Holdt K (2003) *Transition from below: Forging trade unionism and workplace change in South Africa.* Durban: University of Natal Press.

Webster E & von Holdt K (2005) *Beyond the apartheid workplace: Studies in transition.* Pietermaritzburg: University of KwaZulu-Natal Press.

Wilson F (1972) *Labour in the South African gold mines, 1911–1969.* Cambridge: Cambridge University Press.

11 Rainbow, renaissance, tribes and townships: tourism and heritage in South Africa since 1994

Heather Hughes

This chapter explores the ways in which the creation of heritage and the growth of tourism have converged since 1994.[1] It suggests that the deliberate act of display, and therefore the need for an audience, that is implicit in heritage has meant that tourism has been an important arena for debates about the ways in which the past has been reinterpreted. The often contradictory demands of social justice and profitability, which have characterised many development agendas in South Africa, have produced a number of disparate representations of heritage. The state has actively promoted an official version of heritage which is markedly different to the pre-1994 canon, yet this version has itself undergone shifts as a result of changing leadership priorities. Along a rather different trajectory, manifestations of heritage outside state control have produced surprising continuities with and resurrections from a pre-democratic past. Before exploring these trends in South African heritage, I first attempt a definition of heritage more generally, and an explanation of the element of display that is increasingly part of cultural production and reception.

Heritage, nature and culture

At its most basic, 'heritage' is about invoking a sense of the past, if not glorious then at least heroic, in order to satisfy present needs, whether these be allaying fears of uncertainty, compensating for some felt loss, or establishing political or material claims. Heritage is frequently taken to refer to cultural – that is, human-produced – artefacts and practices, and its most enduring expression is in the preservation of built environments. The passion for preservation is a phenomenon associated very largely with modernity and its voracious urban and industrial expansion (Graham et al. 2000); voluntary groups were its first main champions, joined later by government organisations. Yet heritage is increasingly treated as referring to the natural environment as well. Simon Schama has argued that our ideas about nature and what constitutes natural beauty are as much cultural productions as any craft item or monument: 'it is our shaping perception that makes the difference between raw matter and landscape' (1996: 10). Increasingly, in organisations whose task is the custodianship of heritage sites, and in line with the current dominance of holistic approaches to sustainable development, the distinction between 'cultural' and 'natural' is becoming blurred. The United Nations World Heritage Commission has created a new category of 'World Heritage site' that is both cultural and natu- ral, to reflect this change. In similar vein, many sites that previously considered themselves either natural or cultural are now emphasising their dual significance; an example is the high profile now given to cultural/archaeological sites in the Kruger National Park. For all these reasons, the discussion of heritage here includes natural environments and cultural sites, and the ways in which both are inscribed with meaning.

Heritage also includes small-scale, popular recreations of tradition (bearing in mind that tradition is subject to its own laws of change over time). There is an extensive literature on 'ethnic tourism' that tends to give the impression that it is qualitatively distinct from 'heritage tourism' – local, naïve and timeless, as opposed to large-scale, sophisticated and historic. Recent studies have begun to refer to small-scale cultural stock, such as oral narratives, indigenous knowledge and inherited ritual, as 'intangible heritage' (Deacon et al. 2004). All these forms call on the past for legitimacy (of which 'authenticity' can be treated as a variant), and are therefore joined by a common set of concerns about how heritage is understood and reproduced.

Since 1994, there have been vigorous efforts to build a post-apartheid heritage in South Africa, across a wide front. Local museums have mushroomed and national ones been overhauled, and new heritage trails have been mapped onto the land- scape. Seven sites in the country have been inscribed with World Heritage status and many others officially recognised for the first time. In a recent study, Coombes (2004) captures the enormous energy and fraught debates that have gone into the process – in galleries, prehistoric sites, struggle sites, even sites still weighed down by apartheid baggage. She barely mentions tourism as an imperative in all this. This is a useful corrective to the temptation – as is so often the case – to treat all heritage initiatives as somehow designed for tourists: the experience of transfor- mation has meant that heritage has been about far more than 'an industry' to please tourists. Yet it is also the case that heritage sites are nothing if they are not visited. The very notions of display and exhibition imply an audience.

'Visitable history'

Heritage sites today are caught up in a more general culture of display. As Bella Dicks explains:

> When we visit places we expect them to present us with readable
> views and vistas capturing the qualities promised by postcards and
> brochures. And, furnished with this exhibitionary imagery, everyone
> becomes a tourist, mentally logging the environment they move
> through into signs and symbols. It is, therefore, unsurprising that
> public environments of all kinds are being constructed to respond to
> this imagery. (2003: 17)

On this basis, Dicks defines heritage as 'visitable history' (2003: 119). Immediately, in the very terms she uses, she moves beyond the well-worn grooves of the history–heritage debate. Those who initiated it in the late 1980s – including Hewison (1987), who coined the term 'the heritage industry', and Lowenthal (1985, 1998) – argued forcibly that although history and heritage were perpetually intertwined, they nevertheless operated by different rules, had different purposes and ultimately were at odds with one another. Whereas heritage induced a nostalgic somnolence and shrank from awkward questions in its quest to sanitise the past and turn it into an object of entertainment, history kept its integrity through rigorous method, disdain for the marketplace and distance from present-day concerns. As Lowenthal put it:

> Heritage is not history at all; while it borrows from, and enlivens historical study, heritage is not an enquiry into the past but a celebration of it, not an effort to know what actually happened but a profession of faith in a past tailored to present-day purposes'. (1998: x; see Guy 1998 for a South African application)

One of the results of such an argument was to mask the considerable role of historians in shaping heritage, and to underestimate vastly the way in which present needs shape history as well as heritage. It also underestimates the extent to which heritage and history, within and outside the academy, have been caught up in global currents, propelling them towards 'market forces'.

It is frequently noted that contemporary heritage possesses both economic and political dimensions. It is a resource that can be used to promote economic regeneration, and it is an expression of relations of power and subordination. In the economic sense, objects and places associated with the past are revitalised to enjoy 'a second life as display' (Dicks 2003: 136): thus, a disused warehouse can become a gallery, or a jail can be transformed into a museum. The same may be said for newly built markers of historic sites, such as battlefields or streets of struggle, since they transform an original, lived significance into a retrospective spectacle to be consumed. In either case, visitors are obliged or encouraged to treat sites and landscapes as commodities to be purchased, thereby contributing to economic development.

Apart from its supposed economic advantages, heritage is also a political resource: it 'helps to define the meanings of culture and power...[in consequence] it is accompanied by an often bewildering array of identifications and potential conflicts' (Graham et al. 2000: 17). Heritage sites can be a particularly important element in the construction of national identity, in that a legitimising ideology can be presented through selected sites for both domestic and foreign visitors, who are thereby exhorted to extol and embrace national aspirations (Pretes 2003). A number of recent studies have shown how citizens have been urged out onto the road to see their country, and directed to specific sites, as a means of realising their identity. In the United States, 'tourism not only reshaped and redefined the built and natural environment [from the 1880s]…but also influenced the way people defined and identified themselves as Americans' (Shaffer 2001: 6). Identity and display therefore become two sides of the same political process.

There are elements of a similar process at work in South Africa, where billboards along motorways urge passers-by to 'Grow Tourism' and proclaim that 'There's a tourist in everyone'. Television programmes such as *Going nowhere slowly* and *Sho't left* have used local idiom to portray the attractions of taking to the open road. When Valli Moosa was Minister of Environmental Affairs and Tourism, he made the connection between heritage, tourism and nation building explicit: referring to the country's newly-proclaimed World Heritage sites in 1998, he asserted that: 'We cannot say that our campaign to market South Africa to potential British tourists can be separated from nation building' (cited in Marschall 2004: 97). The message is that leisure mobility – of the newly enriched black middle class as much as of foreign visitors – is a way of demonstrating support for the government's chosen strategy of economic development through tourism. However, an examination of the profile of tourists reveals that there is something of a gap between the government's exhortations and tourists' preferences.

As catalysts for material well-being and pride in national belonging, heritage sites are subject to much discussion and debate about the ways in which they are sacralised – set apart from their surroundings and elevated into attractions (MacCannell 1999). Heritage objects and sites do not speak for themselves, especially if they are being harnessed to some greater purpose; they must be interpreted. This applies not only to the display of the historical fabric and the design of physical surroundings such as car parks, amenities and shops, but also to the textual/oral/aural interpretation that is attached to a site, such as signage, labels, audio-tours and film orientations (see Kirshenblatt-Gimblett [1998] for a discussion on textualising objects). And choices concerning interpretation have implications for the level and type of commodification, an inevitable consequence of a second life of display. Commodification throws up its own contradictions, such as focusing on the special and unique, yet according to a standardised, marketised format, and the temptation to promote purist or essentialist forms of culture in an increasingly multicultural, cosmopolitan environment (Dicks 2003). These issues are explored below, in relation to key South African sites.

Tourism and heritage

Not all kinds of tourism, of course, can be harnessed to heritage. Yet internationally, heritage and cultural tourism are among the fastest growing of the so-called 'new' forms of tourism: alternatives to mass sun, sea and sand tourism, focusing on increasing value (receipts) rather than volume (arrivals). The distinction between 'new' and 'mass' forms is in reality not as clearly drawn, since most destinations aim to attract ever-increasing numbers, in addition to finding ways of encouraging higher tourist spend. The attractions of culture and heritage, from a tourist point of view, reflect a growing preoccupation with lifestyle and the accumulation of cultural capital in the swelling middle classes, those most likely to embark on ever longer-haul expeditions from the major generating regions of Western Europe, North America and Northeast Asia. There is, then, a supposedly receptive audience for heritage attractions.

The number of foreign visitors to South Africa has increased vastly since 1994; the latest figures put the number at just over 6.8 million (World Tourism Organisation 2005: 9). Figure 11.1 records South Africa's rapid growth as an international destination.

Figure 11.1 *Foreign tourist arrivals to South Africa, 1965–2004*

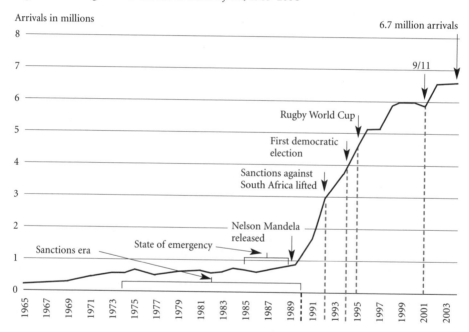

Source: Rivett Carnac 2006

The number of domestic visitors has likewise increased. In 2001, South Africans took 33.5 million overnight trips and 57 million day trips annually (WTTC 2002: 18); by 2003 overnight stays had increased to 49.3 million (SA Tourism/KPMG 2006).

What role has heritage played in achieving this growth? It is difficult to estimate, but the available data are suggestive. According to one source, in the late 1990s heritage/culture accounted for over half of foreign tourists' motivations to visit South Africa (Koch cited in Schutte 2003: 476). This is more likely, however, to be over half of *overseas* visitors, mainly from Europe: these are the high-spending visitors that government and industry have in mind when promoting international tourism growth. Yet over the past decade and more, they have constituted around only one-quarter of international visitors. In line with global trends for intraregional travel, three-quarters of South Africa's international tourists come from other parts of Africa, particularly other parts of southern Africa. Their purpose would seem to be largely for urban retail experiences.

The proportion of domestic visitors motivated by the desire to accumulate cultural capital is small. South African Tourism calculates that 60 per cent of domestic trips are for purposes of visiting friends and relatives while only 16 per cent are for leisure/holidays. Moreover, 61 per cent of domestic tourists remain within their provinces of residence, and KwaZulu-Natal and the Western Cape dominate in the holiday market (SA Tourism/KPMG 2006). Clearly if South Africans are to realise their national identity through travel, and foreign tourists are to be motivated to share in the South African nation-building project, a more concerted strategy will be needed to promote local and foreign leisure tourism. These figures do not undermine the connection between heritage and tourism – the 16 per cent of South Africans who take leisure breaks retain the greatest spending power (Koch & Massyn 2001: 146) and are most likely to be in pursuit of cultural capital; this also applies to the 24 per cent of foreign visitors from outside of Africa. Moreover, many sites and routes are very busy. Yet such statistics do point to some of the difficulties in realising heritage goals when the intentions and ambitions of the 'supply side' are not matched by demand.

A further difficulty has been that the connections between identity and display have been fiercely contested, for a number of reasons: the nature of political transformation, the effects of a global process that has caused states to shrink and market forces to strengthen, and the intentions and actions of the South African government itself.

The politics of heritage in South Africa: a brief overview of the period before 1994

In anti-apartheid discourse from the 1970s, heritage was highly politicised and closely intertwined with academic history. The first of what evolved into 'township tours' were initiated by radical social historians in collectives such as the History Workshop at the University of the Witwatersrand. Tours to neglected 'people's sites' – crumbling migrant workers' hostels, far-flung townships, unmarked sites of struggle – were organised as part of conference gatherings from the late 1970s; they were a deliberate challenge to received heritage wisdom. Many of the people active in such initiatives then are today influential figures in tourism provision and heritage hierarchies.

It was rare to find such challenges from within public institutions before 1994, because of the threat of withdrawal of state funding. Yet there were cases. In Durban, where the local state was politically at odds with central government, a new museum was launched: KwaMuhle, dedicated to the history of ordinary

African people in the city. The first of its kind to examine the lives of the popular classes, it was a direct attempt to present the concerns of radical history in a 'visitable' way – showing, for example, how Africans had paid for their own oppression in the early twentieth century through the 'Durban System', the municipal monopoly on the sale of beer, profits from which paid for the administration of African areas of the city (La Hausse 1992).

There were other instances, as the apartheid state lost its hegemonic grip on cultural institutions from the late 1980s. In South Africa's premier heritage institution, the South African Museum in Cape Town, staff introduced a series of new practices, encouraged by academics who had previously disdained involvement in museum politics. One was a series of 'dilemma labels', whose purpose was 'to highlight problems of interpretation and omission in the ethnographic displays' (Davison 1998: 152), thereby undermining the sense of confidence and completeness in the museum's collection. Another was to superimpose sharply contrasting images over very traditional exhibits as a means of disrupting expectations:

> Images of San men in the South African Defence Force were placed over exhibits of hunter-gatherer material culture, the dress of African female executives was contrasted with traditional clothing, western religious ceremonial attire juxtaposed with the African equivalent. (Davison 1998: 153)

The main negotiating parties to the political settlement recognised that the dangerously febrile atmosphere of the dying years of apartheid needed to be replaced by a far less charged one if the transition to majority rule were to be manageable. Further, as has been well recognised, the very nature of the negotiated settlement meant that both the apartheid state and the liberation movements had to accept compromises of position and principle. In heritage terms, the uneasy consequences were revealed, often sharply, in the responses of many sites associated with the apartheid order. At the National Military Museum in Johannesburg, long the ultimate symbol of white rule with its comprehensive displays of heavy weaponry and strongly ideological narrative of 'anti-terrorist warfare', the historic role of black soldiers in South African military service was finally recognised, and a number of new displays were added, recounting the history of the guerrilla campaigns waged by the African National Congress (ANC) and Pan Africanist Congress. The museum managed to achieve this without significantly dismantling the old symbolism of white power, engaging in a programme of extension rather than revision – in Coombes's (2004) terms, a superficial rather than a structural sense of retooling. A means of coping with compromise, its message about continuities in the theme of masculine militarism was nevertheless deeply unsettling. A further, and controversial, aspect of this incomplete transition was that of the 24 sites (mostly museums and galleries) that the Department of Arts, Culture, Science and Technology named in 1998 as 'Declared Cultural Institutions' and which were thus to be fully state-funded, all but one were carried over from the apartheid era.

Nevertheless, from the transitionary period in the early 1990s, every cultural and educational organisation in the country eligible for state grants actively engaged in the search for appropriate responses to, and presentations of, a new identity, and how the distorted bequest of the past might be dealt with. At every level, down to the smallest municipality, officials initiated new projects – workshops, trails, exhibits and events – that attempted to harmonise local understandings with the nation-building project. A celebrated example is the District Six Museum in Cape Town, whose exhibits set out to reoccupy, physically and symbolically, an area of Cape Town that had been devastated by the forced removal of its inhabitants in the 1950s (Coombes 2004; McEachern 2001).

The nation-building project has been about inculcating a sense of citizenship that includes all South Africans in a common framework of rights and responsibilities, and that offers the promise of belonging to a qualitatively better 'imagined community'. Unifying cultural and political symbols such as the distinctive new flag, the 'rainbow nation' idea introduced to South Africa by Archbishop Tutu and taken up by Nelson Mandela in his inauguration as president, and the person of Mandela himself were enormously important in promoting this new kind of belonging. In short, nation building has encompassed far more than heritage, as understood here, although heritage has been accorded a key role in its transmission. Critics have charged that the process has had an uneven appeal, addressing the needs of the growing black middle class and ethnic/racial minorities, rather than answering those of poor, marginalised, and especially rural communities. The analysis in the following section would tend to support such an argument.

Frameworks for heritage and tourism

Much of this activity had been under way well before the state published three key White Papers, on tourism development, on arts, culture and heritage, and on the environment, in 1996. Taken together, these documents have formed the framework for the development of relationships – particularly in the public sector – between heritage and tourism.

The *White Paper on the Development and Promotion of Tourism* (DEAT 1996) identified tourism as a priority for national economic development and a major stimulus of the government's Growth, Employment and Redistribution strategy. Three basic principles were spelled out: that tourism should be government-led, in the sense that the state should articulate efficient policies and allocate appropriate funding to the sector; that it would be driven by the private sector, primarily directed by the principles of demand and supply; and that it should be community-based. What actually constituted 'community-based tourism' was not clearly defined; a range of possibilities, from participation to ownership, was mentioned. The precise roles of state and private sector were not well defined either. Any meaningful community tourism, given the enormous structural disadvantages with which it would have to contend, would clearly not happen if left solely to the market.

The tourism White Paper also outlined the new public institutional arrangements for tourism development at national and provincial levels. Tourism in the new South Africa was to be a 'dual power', shared by central and provincial governments, and funding would be allocated accordingly. Thus, the central Department of Environmental Affairs and Tourism (DEAT) would set the parameters of national policy, and each of the nine provinces would have a tourism portfolio, to be exercised in accordance with national policy. The structure would be paralleled in the reorganisation of the tourism authorities charged with marketing as well as research and development: a central South African Tourism Authority to function internationally, and nine separate provincial authorities to raise their tourism profiles domestically.

The lack of clarity on what was meant by 'state-led' and 'private-sector driven' resulted in a number of attempts to firm up a series of working principles for tourism development. A Tourism Business Council was created to represent sectoral interests, and the National Economic Development and Labour Council launched a 'tourism collaborative action initiative'. Working together, several government departments and business interests identified a number of local geographic clusters in order to promote an integrated and rapid approach to tourism development. Yet there were difficulties in achieving take-off, not least because of the far slower rise in high-spending foreign visitors than had been predicted (WTTC 2002).

The *White Paper on Arts, Culture and Heritage* (DACST 1996) defined heritage resources as any place or object of cultural significance, including oral histories and living heritage traditions associated with them. This White Paper led directly to the formation of the institutional centrepiece for the development of heritage, the South African Heritage Resources Agency (SAHRA), constituted in terms of the National Heritage Resources Act (Act 25 of 1999). Its members, who include leading historians, have responsibility for the day-to-day management of the national estate, such as the maintenance of a national register, establishment of criteria for consideration of new heritage sites and providing funding for existing and new sites.

Two immediate changes in the definition of the national estate were that all monuments created by previous white-minority governments were downgraded to provincial status unless a case could be made for designating them of national importance, and a wider definition of 'war graves' was provided so as to include those who died in the freedom struggle, inside and outside South Africa. A National Heritage Council appointed by the Minister of Arts and Culture oversees the work of the SAHRA, advises on overall policy and allocates funding. There is also a Heritage Council in each province, with the intention that devolved powers will enable a far greater degree of community participation in the identification and custodianship of new sites.

The province of KwaZulu-Natal is alone in having enacted its own legislation concerning heritage. In 1997, the provincial council passed the KwaZulu-Natal Heritage Act, in terms of which a statutory body, Amafa, was established 'to administer heritage conservation' (KwaZulu-Natal Heritage Act: 94). Amafa is in effect the Heritage Council in the province. To some extent this was an attempt to assert a position independent of the central state, reflecting political tensions between the ANC and the Inkatha Freedom Party (IFP). Amafa was largely steered into being by conservationists who had long been associated with the ethnic nationalism of the IFP; it was presented as a more effective means of preserving heritage than unfolding central government policy. It therefore represents a strong continuity between old-style thinking and new majority rule, and has contributed to an ethos in which ethnic interpretations of the past predominate.

These have also provided a ready brand for the provincial tourism authority. Tourism KwaZulu-Natal has for some years marketed its region as 'The Kingdom of the Zulu'. In the early days of its campaign, it displayed Henry Cele in full battle regalia on marketing materials, and more recently has accorded the Zulu king a central role in the marketing strategy. Its choice of such an essentialist notion of ethnic culture has been contested (Bass 2002). The Bhaca, for example, who live in the southern parts of the province and strenuously resisted incorporation into the Zulu polity for decades through the nineteenth century, now find themselves labelled as belonging to it in the new South Africa. To show their distinctiveness, they planned to build a cultural village (Julian Ferreira, interview 07.2000). Similarly, there were those among the Indian minority in the region who felt that there was another tradition and identity to offer the 'rainbow nation', of pacifism and non-violent resistance, symbolised by one-time resident Mahatma Gandhi (see for example the guide to Gandhian sites by Tichmann [2000], which was largely written out of this 'Zulu' marketing drive).

In 1996, the DEAT announced a process of consultation about a new national environmental strategy, which resulted in the promulgation of the National Environmental Management Act in 1998. It is explicitly based on the concept of sustainability, and a commitment to ensuring that negative impacts of economic activity are either reduced or eliminated. Tourism as a specific activity is not mentioned, but the interim White Paper (DEAT 1997) did acknowledge that this sector, more than virtually any other, depended on a high-quality natural environment for its development.[2]

The three White Papers discussed have formed the basis for much that has occurred since 1996, particularly but not exclusively in the public sector. They also facilitated a certain amount of interdepartmental co-operation; for example, the DEAT assumed responsibility for World Heritage recognition for Robben Island and six other sites in the country, which required close co-operation with the then Department of Arts, Culture, Science and Technology. For its part, the latter initiated a programme to link cultural activity to tourism strategies (Koch & Massyn 2001).

State-sponsored initiatives provide the clearest evidence of the kinds of meanings intended as the new official heritage canon. Those that have been most closely associated with nation building have, of course, tended to be large-scale projects, as befits the new nation, though heritage activity at the level of regional and local government is instructive too. Alongside public heritage – but not always in tune with it – has been the considerable space created by the market, in which other forms of heritage have begun to appear. Again, these extend from large, nationally important sites to small, local ones. At the local end of the scale, they encompass a great deal of community tourism activity, by encouraging the marginalised to enter the mainstream by deploying the one resource they supposedly possess aplenty: their culture/indigenous knowledge. These largely public and largely private variants of heritage production will be examined separately.

Heritage and the state: 'rainbow nation' to 'African Renaissance'

The freedom struggle itself, cast as the triumph of hope and courage over adversity and despair, was the ANC government's first priority in efforts to establish an official heritage in the service of nation building, social justice and economic advancement. Closely associated with the figure of Nelson Mandela and the then dominant rainbow-nation idealism, there was little doubt that Robben Island would become the icon of the new South Africa. It was declared a national monument in 1997 and a World Heritage site in 1999, and the main attraction became the Robben Island Museum. There were fierce debates about the role that ex-prisoners would play in this development, about how public and private interests would be accommodated, and about how much of its varied history should be included for public consumption (Deacon 1998; Smith 1997). As it prepared to receive its first visitors in early 1997, there were also heated discussions about what version of the liberation struggle would be told. This was partially resolved by the employment of ex-prisoners as guides, which allowed different narratives to be told about the struggle and its goals, depending on which of the once-outlawed political organisations the guide belonged to.

Robben Island Museum has proved to be one of the country's most popular attractions. By 2004 it was receiving close to 400 000 visitors annually, about a third of them South African.[3] The way in which displays have been mounted in the museum – notably the 'Cell Stories' exhibition, for which each ex-inmate donated an item that had been of special significance to him while incarcerated – has met with general critical acclaim (Coombes 2004). The museum also possesses explicitly educational and research functions, being responsible for the main archival collection of the liberation struggle. It has also hosted a number of widely publicised and nationally symbolic spectacles, such as the announcement of Cape

Town's bid for the Olympic Games and the hosting of South Africa's premier millennium party, attended by Nelson Mandela and other luminaries. Over the past six years, it has, among other uses, been the site of numerous mass marriages. According to a Home Affairs spokesperson, 'the marriage fest is becoming a "gala event"' (*Cape Argus* 13.02.06).

That it has played all these parts has led some critics to wonder about its future emphasis: as a shrine (Mandela's cell continues to be the highlight of nearly every visitor's experience), a museum, or a theme park, as echoed in the title of Shackley's (2001) article on the subject (see also Shearing & Kempa 2004), each 'future' entailing a different level of commodification. Compounding and contributing to a seeming lack of clarity of direction have been management problems on the site, serious enough for Unesco to send a mission to investigate in early 2004. Composed of representatives of the International Union for the Conservation of Nature, the International Centre for the Study of the Preservation and Restoration of Cultural Property and the International Council on Monuments and Sites, it identified a number of threats to the integrity of the site: the lack of a director for a two-year period; underfunding of repairs and maintenance; inability to plan for growing visitor numbers; and the presence of invader animal species, reducing numbers of indigenous species (*Cape Argus* 15.07.04).

After extensive consultation, the Department of Arts and Culture unveiled its Legacy Project in 1996. An ambitious programme of large memorial construction, its purpose was to commemorate leaders, cultures and historic places that had been neglected in the past. These included memorials to particular individuals, such as Albert Luthuli, Samora Machel and Nelson Mandela; to events such as Blood/Ncome River (where there was already an Afrikaner monument, but where the Zulu side of the battle was to be represented) and the South African War; to places such as the Old Fort; and to significant groups such as women. One entirely new site, Freedom Park, was also planned.

The projects in the portfolio have had mixed histories. Some, like the Machel monument, have been completed but are in a state of neglect, while others, such as Freedom Park and the Luthuli memorial, remain under construction. Although the museum to Zulu culture has been completed, the symbolic bridge across the Ncome River linking the Zulu and Afrikaner sites has never been built (Flynn & King 2006). Several of these sites are remote and very unlikely to attract the hoped-for visitors; even some centrally located sites are struggling. The Old Fort Museum, part of the Constitution Hill complex, is now closed for much of each weekend, and the retail outlet there has experienced drastically falling demand (site visit, March 2006). While this may be due to the lack of visitor-management expertise, it also reflects a contradiction in state developmental processes. It wishes to present a particular vision of the new nation – or at least to create the (misleading) impression that the suffering experienced in former gaols like the Old Fort and Robben Island is a thing of the past – through an array of new attractions, and to 'grow tourism' in order to support them. Yet it has succeeded in building a number of very expensive displays that serve neither purpose very adequately.

As political leadership passed from Mandela to Mbeki, so the discourse of the rainbow nation, celebrated in Robben Island and much of the Legacy Project, gave way to the more assertive one of 'African Renaissance', reflecting a stronger Africanist tendency in the ruling party. As Lodge points out, since Mbeki referred to it in a speech in 1997, 'the idea of an "African renaissance" has increasingly assumed almost liturgical status' (2002: 227). Lodge distinguishes two strands in Mbeki's African Renaissance thought: it is about asserting African capabilities of handling modernity, in that it urges Africa's governing elites to seize the benefits of economic and technical globalisation. It is simultaneously about the unique legacy to humanity bequeathed by Africans through *ubuntu*, a communal sense of belonging together, found, he alleges, the continent over. The concept bears strong resemblance to negritude, African socialism and African humanism, the founding ideals of the first generation of independence leaders, such as Senghor, Nyerere and Kaunda. Yet it is specific to current circumstances too, representing an attempt on the part of the South African regime to re-engage with the rest of the continent after years of isolation. It also has an edgier class dimension, with its stress on black economic empowerment.

African Renaissance thinking has tended to privilege different kinds of heritage, such as hominid origins and ancient black African cultures, both located geographically to the interior, coincidentally closer to the main base of the new political class in Gauteng province; Robben Island is therefore increasingly remote in this sense too. The Cradle of Humankind complex and Mapungubwe, both World Heritage sites, are presented as testimony to the antiquity of the earth itself and its human inhabitants, which in turn allows the familiar nationalist myth-creation of continuous occupation, belonging and custodianship of this land that has finally been returned to its rightful owners. It enables the South African nation state to assert a more impressive lineage than most – millennia of prehistory, rather than centuries of history, a scale of time far greater than any of its European counterparts has been able to claim. And it legitimises this nation's right to a revered position in the company of all other nation states, given that its origins are simultaneously the origins of all humanity. Connected to this notion is the argument about ownership of artefacts: there has been a heated debate between scientists and politicians about the return of hominid artefacts to 'local communities': as Themba Wakashe, the deputy director-general of the Department of Arts and Culture expressed it, '[these objects] should not be the preserve of intellectual research and scholarship; they are our source of pride and identity' (*Mail & Guardian* 08–14.07.05).

The main heritage expression of the African Renaissance, however, is not the landscape of antiquity, but something quite new: Freedom Park. Now in the process of construction on a site deliberately proximate and challenging to the Voortrekker

Monument, Freedom Park was envisioned in the original Legacy Project document as 'a message from Africa and South Africa to the world, of suffering and the triumph of the human spirit' (Legacy Project 1998: 36). Robben Island set out with a similar message, but Robben Island is indelibly associated with Mandela. Freedom Park is Mbeki's project; it 'will portray a vision of the future embedded in the African Renaissance'.[4] It will eventually consist of a garden of remembrance, a museum to narrate South Africa's history from the time of the earliest life forms from a 'holistic, Afro-centric perspective', and a memorial to all those who have been victims of human rights abuses, from the earliest days of slavery at the Cape to the ending of apartheid (Freedom Park Trust 2002: 5–6). There has been a strong spiritual dimension in the creation of the park, with various religious groups participating in cleansing and healing ceremonies around the country, in a gesture of symbolic reparation.

Freedom Park's director, Mongane Wally Serote, has asserted that the park was not specifically designed as a tourist attraction 'but will undoubtedly become one' (*Sawubona* 04.2004: 45). It is difficult to know what its purpose might be if not to be visited; indeed, it seems already to have declared itself something of a theme park: 'an envisaged one-stop heritage precinct' that will 'tell one coherent story of the struggle of humanity in South Africa'.[5] Although parts of the park are complete, the site is not open at weekends (site visit, September 2005).

Heritage and the market: apartheid, tribalism and townships

The private sector by its nature is more driven to make attractions pay, and this has had several interesting consequences in terms of heritage portrayal, from large-scale sites requiring substantial investment to small-scale recreations of 'tradition'. The Apartheid Museum and Voortrekker Monument are emblematic of the former; cultural villages and township tours of the latter.

The Apartheid Museum, costing R80 million, opened in 2001, and has received much praise for its presentation of the experience of apartheid, particularly in terms of the security apparatus that bore down on resistance – displays include a police surveillance video playing inside an armoured vehicle, and 121 nooses to represent each of those hanged for political offences. However, many felt that there was a deeply disturbing element in the lack of state support: the museum was part of a casino development, the winning consortium's offer to 'give something back to the community' (*The Guardian* [UK] 12.12.01). Both museum and casino adjoin Johannesburg's Gold Reef City theme park, already owned by the same consortium. Seemingly, the association with commercial pleasure pursuits was the only way in which the museum could be funded (*Mail & Guardian* 05.12.01).

A case that serves to underline the central role of tourism consumption in maintaining the viability of a heritage site outside of the state sector is that of the Voortrekker Monument. This monument seemed so inextricably linked to the exercise of Afrikaner power and apartheid indoctrination that its custodians, deeply anxious about what the new government would do with it, effectively privatised it. Then notable black leaders began to declare publicly that there were other ways of reading the site. The gates, for example, are adorned with Zulu spears, which in Afrikaner mythology represented savage barbarism; an alternative interpretation had them as the spears of Umkhonto we Sizwe, bringing an end to barbarism (Coombes 2004). The monument continues to receive a small state grant, but its considerable operating costs and upkeep have been met by some filming contracts and international visitors: tourism has effectively saved it (Grundlingh 2001).

Two main kinds of community tourism have emerged over the past decade: cultural villages in the countryside, and township tours in urban areas. Being largely private initiatives, both instances are more explicitly geared to the tourist market than some of the official sites discussed above. While some domestic tourists do go on township tours and visit cultural villages, as part of a supposed learning experience about their own culture or about how other South Africans live, the real demand for such products has been from foreign visitors, especially on all-inclusive tours (Koch & Massyn 2001).

Many observers have pointed out that the notion of 'community' is a difficult one. As de Kok notes, 'the competition for representativeness, and the responsibilities of policy-making, are certain to sharpen the divisions that naturally exist in any existing or reinvented community' (1999: 66). The sites discussed further in this chapter serve as examples of how these fault lines operate.

Typically, a cultural village is a custom-built attraction sited on or near to an established tourist route through a rural area, consisting of a homestead to show living arrangements, an arena for dance, music, storytelling and other live cultural displays, a restaurant and, of course, a craft/souvenir outlet. There might be add-on features, such as a game enclosure, museum display, historical video, or a visit to a 'real' homestead nearby. Some portray a purist vision of a single culture; most display a number of different cultures, such as Lesedi cultural village north of Johannesburg (site visit, March 2006). There are now around 40 villages operating across the country. They are all built on the conviction of ethnic uniqueness, and consider that they are providing knowledge of both tangible and intangible indigenous heritage.

The goal of apartheid was of course to foster ethnic identity in pursuit of the 'separate but equal' fiction. It was a cynical use of ethnicity, though: before 1994, less than 1 per cent of some 4 000 monuments focused on the pre-colonial period and indigenous culture of the region (Deacon cited in Davison 1998: 150). Yet in the dramatically altered political climate, ethnic identity, certainly for tourist consumption, has found new life. President Mbeki might wish for a vision of South African culture that avoids 'the notion of an Africa slowly condemned to remain a curiosity' (quoted in Witz et al. 2001: 277), but the message from below loudly proclaims an enthusiasm for ethnic curiosity. Ethnic cultures, or more accurately their brokers, continue to define themselves in competition with other ethnic cultures, through a stress on uniqueness, rather than the features they share in common or their historic interdependence. Wood has pointed out that '"Ethnic entrepreneurs" are entrepreneurs in a literal sense here, bringing ethnicity to the market and seldom having to mask their ethnic agendas in the way that ethnic entrepreneurs in the political arena may have to' (1998: 6).

Research into cultural villages has tended to focus on the extent to which they represent fictionalised, romanticised versions of ethnic purism (Schutte 2003) or new patterns of ownership and employment opportunities in deprived areas (Jansen Van Veuren 2004). On this second issue, the picture that emerges is that while a few have been initiated by small business people and are yielding modest returns, most have required levels of investment far beyond the reach of local communities, giving the lie to ideals of small, micro or medium-size (SMME) opportunity. For example, a white ex-nightclub owner established PheZulu Safari Park near Durban. In the late 1980s he 'bought a Zulu dance outfit in a small cultural village', later adding a crocodile farm, snake park, curio shop and restaurant, and built PheZulu into 'the place to take foreigners'. The latest improvement, in partnership with a local chief, is a safari park, in which, apart from the animals, are situated several homesteads and a shanty town. The occupants helped to prepare the land, act as guides and welcome visitors into their homes. The owner's view is that 'this is what tourists want to see – Zulu life as it is' (*Sunday Tribune* 12.08.01). A multi-million rand hotel complex is planned for the future.

Perhaps the pre-eminent cultural village in KwaZulu-Natal, the land of cultural villages, is Shakaland. Of all the pre-colonial leaders, the first Zulu king Shaka's name has most resonance in the minds of an international audience, not least because of the mythology that grew up around his state-building conquests and of the Zulu as a 'proud, warlike' nation. Shakaland is housed in one of the sets especially built for the television series *Shaka Zulu*, starring Henry Cele. The idea of business partners who regard themselves as 'white Zulus', Barry Leitch and Kingsley Holgate, and later taken over by a large hotel chain, Shakaland offers visitors an insight into Zulu cultural practices in a way 'that was more concentrated than the real thing, it was also more perfect' (Hamilton 1998: 197). Meticulously researched and scripted, it nevertheless eschewed politics and violence, thus lending to the experience an eerie unreality, since the destructive violence dominating provincial politics through much of the 1980s and 1990s was over the very issue of Zulu identity. Leitch has recently engaged in the Zulu theming of a new casino development in the region.

There are further factors that help to explain the cultural village phenomenon. In rural areas across South Africa, chiefly power continues uncomfortably alongside the notion of democratically elected representatives. Such power perpetuates strongly patriarchal relations between leaders and people, inhibiting the emergence of a real sense of citizenship and presenting culture brokers with an opportunity to negotiate at 'the top' – not least about leasing communal land – regardless of the views of local people (Hughes & Vaughan 2000). Again, there is the mindset of established tour operators, whose cultural co-ordinates for years have tended to be ethnic ones, and whose tried and tested products continue to feature in their itineraries. In apartheid days (and far fewer international visitors) there was always a stop at an ethnically-specific souvenir market on the 'grand tour' of South Africa.

There have been some dissenting voices against the cultural village model. The ¡Kung and ¡Khwe clans reportedly rejected the notion of a Khoisan cultural village (which would be historically odd in any case), arguing that their culture was constantly adapting to new circumstances. They preferred to talk, they claimed, of an *oorkruisingskultuur* (crossover culture) rather than a static set of traditions (Koch & Massyn 2001). While this does sound like the sort of response some heritage analysts cry out for, and does articulate a fresh approach to the representation of culture, it is no more likely to be the view of 'the community' than in the other cases discussed. In any event, other Khoisan groups have embraced the cultural village idea, their group identity having been strengthened as a result of land restitution claims (Witz et al. 2001).

In a cultural village it is possible to find sensitive portrayals by professional historians, architects and anthropologists, alongside complaints by employees that they have to behave like 'professional tribes' in elaborate reconstructions of homesteads, while not earning enough to move out of the mud and zinc shacks in which they live (Koch & Massyn 2001). Yet the point here is not to debate the degree of authenticity in presentation and performance in cultural villages, but to argue that an essentialist notion of ethnicity has been mobilised as one of the main 'popular' culture/heritage tourist attractions of the new South Africa – and that what has to an extent permitted its re-emergence is that vast area vacated by the state, the market.

A consequence of the growth in cultural villages and the ethnic culture they celebrate is the return of 'tribal' thinking. 'Tribe', it should be noted, is a term that has long been used unproblematically in tourism literature (as in 'tribal tourism' or 'the hill tribes of Thailand'). As is now well established, the term began conceptual life as a means for missionaries, colonial administrators and anthropologists variously to create compact units for administrative purposes, to delineate languages for proselytisation, and to study and protect exotic cultures. All of them were looking for certain boundaries of belonging and exclusion, timelessness and simplicity (see Vail 1989 for the southern African case). From the 1970s, social scientists and many in political movements vigorously disputed the use of the term 'tribe', precisely because of the connotations of a sense of backwardness, stasis, primitiveness and fixity of membership. Their preferred term became 'chiefdom', signifying dynamism and change. Divested of their ideological awkwardness, 'tribes' and 'tribalism' now seem to have been sanitised and reincorporated into the political and social lexicon; tourism is largely responsible. Skalnik's comment that 'what is peculiar about the term "tribe" is that, irrespective of serious criticism, it reappears again and again…' seems aptly prescient (Skalnik 1988: 78).

Despite the criticisms that have been levelled at them, such as that they 'ghettoise' townships and perpetuate the sense of spatial division so central to old apartheid, township tours in many ways subvert the pastoral paradigm of cultural villages. They do not, of course, operate in the same sort of custom-built tourism environments. Most also explicitly stress hybridity and ethnic diversity. Like their rural counterparts, they are now ubiquitous in South African towns and cities. A township tour typically includes a visit to a shebeen, a cultural display, notable heritage/struggle sites, a crèche or welfare facility where visitors may make donations, and possibly a visit to someone's home. It therefore takes place in a somewhat less mediated environment than the cultural village.

The choice of stops on township tours provides an interesting insight into how heritage and culture are being redefined on the ground. One operator who offers a tour to Umlazi in Durban takes visitors past the home of slain anti-apartheid activists Griffiths and Victoria Mxenge, the first church built in Umlazi, the original mission hospital, schools of note and a traditional healer. Tours in cities like Cape Town and Johannesburg provide close parallels.

Some township tours are offered by established operators in partnership with local guides, but emerging operators offering such tours are arguably the most developed form of community tourism in South Africa to date. A few started out as small enterprises and have grown into large-scale ventures, such as Jimmy Ntintili's Face2Face Tours in Soweto. The overwhelming majority, however, remain fledgling micro-companies struggling to raise the capital to make their businesses sustainable. Many operators already had a base in the taxi industry, and have diversified into airport shuttle work and township tours as and when there has been demand. For one of the difficulties with township tours is that supply has been rather greater than demand: one of the most frequent complaints of emergent operators has been that while they have responded with alacrity to the calls for community tourism initiatives, they have lacked the custom to stay afloat (Hughes & Vaughan 2000).

There are a number of reasons for their precariousness. Unlike the cultural villages with their outside financial backers, these are operators who represent a far greater degree of direct local involvement in tourism, offering a potentially more challenging view of cultural borrowing, dynamism, and shared experience. They often lack a secure physical base, possess few promotional materials, must hire vehicles from others, and very rarely have access to electronic communication. Banks have long refused to make loans to such small operations. Notoriously, the only way they were able to raise capital was in the microlending sector, with its prohibitive interest rates (Trevor Enniker, interview 07.2000).

Many feel that the established operators, through industry bodies such as the South African Tourism Services Association, are using 'standards' and high membership fees as a form of closure. Some within such bodies respond that new operators have an 'entitlement mentality' which is unhelpful when 'the industry is already flooded' (Magardie 2001: 44). This attitude would seem to confirm the accusation being made against the established sector – and those few new operators who have managed to comply, who are often the most vigilant gatekeepers. Other complaints include that large venues, such as the big city hotels or the International Convention Centre (ICC) in Durban, actively deny access to potential custom. Hotels do not allow emerging operators to display promotional material, and the ICC prefers to deal with established operators that can handle large client bases. Finally, there is the problem of promotional lead time: many small operators despair that the period between offering a new product and finding it featured in the main promotional sources for international visitors is too long a wait for business to be sustainable.

Only recently have emerging operators begun to define an organisational milieu for themselves; a significant development is the formation of community tourism bodies. Probably the most successful is the Soweto Tourism Association, the model for others around the country. In 2000, a number of emerging operators in the Durban area formed the Black Emerging Tour Operators' Association. They received assistance from the regional tourism authority, though they have experienced difficulties, such as what they consider to be forms of closure, from more established tourism businesses. In 2005, the Umsunduzi Tourism Association was launched in Pietermaritzburg, again composed of SMME hospitality businesses and tour operators in the region, who had felt left out of the established sector (*Mercury* 06.09.05).

Some operators present their tours as far more than a matter of economic survival or memorialisation of local sites: they make explicit links to the political needs of the new South Africa, claiming that those who use their services help to 'build a nation' (*The Observer* [London] 14.03.04). In the end, what is eventually incorporated into a canon of popular culture and heritage in many urban areas may well depend on which of these operators survive to tell the stories of the past.

Conclusion

Heritage since 1994 has variously attempted to satisfy demands for social justice, pursue an explicit nation-building agenda and expand the supply of marketable attractions. In pursuit of these sometimes contradictory purposes, a wide array of new heritage sites and practices has been marked out, and older ones adjusted to new realities. Heritage precepts associated with the apartheid regime, most notably ethnic essentialism, whether applied to Afrikaners or to supposed distinct African groups, have found new life in the process, even as the ideology of an African Renaissance asserts itself. Or as Davison observes, with some understatement, 'accommodating ethnic difference without resorting to essentialist notions of race and culture remains a challenge' (1998: 151).

Tourism will continue to play a part in this process, sometimes a constructive one, as in the case of 'overcoming amnesia about a slave past' in the Western Cape (Ward & Worden 1999: 217) and sometimes a divisive one, as in the case of contested Zulu identities. But it cannot be escaped. It will influence what culture and heritage should be remembered and celebrated, and what is likely to be forgotten, especially at the popular level. This is still a time of transition and fluidity, even if some of the parameters are now clear. It is certain, however, that contests about what happens when (visitable) 'history is rammed against commerce' (Murray 2002: xii) and about whose versions of heritage are worthy of display and visitation, will continue to be expressed in very public ways.

Notes

1   This chapter benefited very greatly from the comments and suggestions made by State of the Nation workshop participants in March 2006, as well as the anonymous reviewer. Thanks to all.

2   See <http://www.environment.gov.za/PolLeg/WhitePapers/EnvMgmt.htm>.

3   See <http://www.robben-island.org.za/news/view.asp>.

4   See 'Values and themes' at <http://www.freedompark.org.za/overview.html>.

5   See <http://www.freedompark.co.za/aboutus.php>.

References

Bass O (2002) Adventure, paradise, indigenous culture: 'The Kingdom of the Zulu' campaign. *Current writing,* 14(1): 82–105.

Coombes AE (2004) *History after apartheid. Visual culture and public memory in a democratic South Africa.* Johannesburg: Wits University Press.

DACST (Department of Arts, Culture, Science and Technology) (1996) *White paper on arts, culture and heritage.* Pretoria: DACST.

Davison P (1998) Museums and the reshaping of memory. In S Nuttall & C Coetzee (Eds) *Negotiating the past. The making of memory in South Africa.* Cape Town: Oxford University Press.

Deacon H (1998) Remembering tragedy, constructing modernity: Robben Island as a national monument. In S Nuttall & C Coetzee (Eds) *Negotiating the past. The making of memory in South Africa.* Cape Town: Oxford University Press.

Deacon H, Prosalendis S, Dondolo L & Mrabulal M(2004) *The subtle power of intangible heritage*. Cape Town: HSRC Press.

DEAT (Department of Environmental Affairs and Tourism) (1996) *White paper on the development and promotion of tourism*. Pretoria: DEAT.

DEAT (1997) *White paper on environmental management policy*. Pretoria: DEAT.

De Kok I (1999) Cracked heirlooms: Memory on exhibition. In S Nuttall & C Coetzee (Eds) *Negotiating the past. The making of memory in South Africa*. Cape Town: Oxford University Press.

Dicks B (2003) *Culture on display. The production of contemporary visitability*. Maidenhead: Open University Press.

Flynn MK & King T (2006) Renovating the public past: Nation-building, symbolic reparation and the politics of heritage in post-apartheid South Africa. In C Norton (Ed) *Nationalism, historiography and the (re)construction of the past*. London: New Academic Press.

Freedom Park Trust (2002) *Annual Report*. Pretoria: Freedom Park Trust.

Graham B, Ashworth G & Tunbridge JE (2000) *A geography of heritage*. London: Arnold.

Grundlingh A (2001) A cultural conundrum? Old monuments and new regimes: The Voortrekker Monument as symbol of Afrikaner power in post-apartheid South Africa. *Radical History Review*, 81: 94–112.

Guy J (1998) Battling with banality. *Journal of Natal and Zulu history*, 18: 156–93.

Hamilton C (1998) *Terrific majesty. The powers of Shaka Zulu and the limits of historical invention*. Cape Town: David Philip.

Hewison R (1987) *The heritage industry. Britain in a climate of decline*. London: Methuen.

Hughes H & Vaughan A (2000) The incorporation of historically disadvantaged communities into tourism initiatives in the new South Africa: Case studies from KwaZulu-Natal. In M Robinson et al. (Eds) *Reflections on international tourism. Management, marketing and the political economy of travel and tourism*. Sunderland: University of Northumbria, Sheffield Hallam University and Business Education Publishers.

Jansen Van Veuren E (2004) Cultural village tourism in South Africa: Capitalising on indigenous culture. In C Rogerson & G Visser (Eds) *Tourism and development issues in contemporary South Africa*. Pretoria: Africa Institute of South Africa.

Kirshenblatt-Gimblett B (1998) *Destination culture. Tourism, museums and heritage*. Berkeley: University of California Press.

Koch E & Massyn P (2001) South Africa's domestic tourism sector: Promises and problems. In K Ghimire (Ed) *The native tourist. Mass tourism within developing countries*. London: Earthscan.

La Hausse P (1992) Drink and cultural innovation in Durban: The origins of the beerhall in South Africa 1902–1916. In C Ambler & J Crush (Eds) *Liquor and labour in southern Africa*. Pietermaritzburg: University of Natal Press.

Legacy Project (1998) Portfolio of legacy projects. Discussion document.

Lodge T (2002) *Politics in South Africa from Mandela to Mbeki*. Cape Town and Oxford: David Philip and James Currey.

Lowenthal D (1985) *The past is a foreign country*. Cambridge: Cambridge University Press.

Lowenthal D (1998) *The heritage crusade and the spoils of history*. Cambridge: Cambridge University Press.

MacCannell D (1999) *The tourist. A new theory of the leisure class*. (2nd edition). Berkeley: University of California Press.

Magardie K (2001) Taking on the old boys' club. *Siyaya!* (Monthly journal of the Institute for Democratic Alternatives in South Africa) 7: 42–5.

Marschall S (2004) Commodifying heritage: Post-apartheid monuments and cultural tourism in South Africa. In CM Hall & H Tucker (Eds) *Tourism and postcolonialism. Contested discourses, identities and representations*. London: Routledge.

McEachern C (2001) Mapping the memories: Politics, place and identity in the District Six Museum, Cape Town. In A Zegeye (Ed) *Social identities in the new South Africa*. Cape Town: Kwela Books and SA History Online.

Murray S-A (2002) Ideas en route: Texts, travel, tourism. *Current Writing*, 14(1): i–xx.

Pretes M (2003) Tourism and nationalism. *Annals of tourism research*, 30(1): 125–42.

Rivett Carnac K (2006) Tourism investment opportunities: South Africa. Department of Trade and Industry presentation. Available at <http://www.southafrica.ch/cgi-bin/20020609-Presentation%20Ms%20Rivett%20-%20Tourism%20Investment%20Opportunities.pdf>.

SA Tourism/KPMG (2006) *South Africa: Domestic tourism growth strategy. Final report – revised value*. Available at <http://www.southafrica.net/satourism/research/>.

Schama S (1996) *Landscape and memory*. London: Fontana.

Schutte G (2003) Tourists and tribes in the new South Africa. *Ethnohistory*, 50(3): 473–87.

Shackley M (2001) Potential futures for Robben Island: Shrine, museum, or theme park? *International Journal of Heritage Studies*, 7(4): 355–63.

Shaffer MS (2001) *See America first. Tourism and national identity, 1880–1940*. Washington: Smithsonian Institution.

Shearing C & Kempa M (2004) A museum of hope: A story of Robben Island. *Annals of the American Academy of Politicial and Social Sciences*, 592: 62–78.

Skalnik P (1988) Tribe as colonial category. In E Boonzaier & J Sharp (Eds.) *South African keywords*. Cape Town: David Philip.

Smith C (1997) *Robben Island*. Cape Town: Struik.

Tichmann P (2000) *Gandhi sites in Durban*. Durban: The Local History Museum.

Vail L (Ed) (1989) *The creation of tribalism in southern Africa*. London: James Currey.

Ward K & Worden N (1999) Commemorating, suppressing and invoking Cape slavery. In S Nuttall & C Coetzee (Eds.) *Negotiating the past. The making of memory in South Africa*. Oxford: Oxford University Press.

Witz L, Rassool C & Minkley G (2001) Repackaging the past for South African tourism. *Daedalus*, 130(1): 277–96.

Wood RE (1998) Touristic ethnicity: A brief itinerary. *Ethnic and Racial Studies,* 21(2): 218–42.

World Tourism Organisation (2005) *Tourism highlights*. Madrid: WTO.

WTTC (World Travel and Tourism Council) (2002) *South Africa: the impact of travel and tourism on jobs and the economy*. London: WTTC.

Interviews

Trevor Enniker, Black Emerging Tour Operator's Association, Durban, July 2000.

Julian Ferreira, Agricultural Extension Officer, KwaZulu-Natal, July 2000.

12 The promise and the practice of transformation in South Africa's health system

Helen Schneider, Peter Barron and Sharon Fonn

This chapter provides an overview of developments in South Africa's health system over the last 12 years. Such an undertaking is not straightforward as health systems are by nature complex institutions with a multiplicity of organisational forms, actors and interests. Possible targets for reform are numerous and an analysis that seeks to represent the problems facing, and initiatives targeting, the South African health sector is bound to be incomplete and interpretive. We nevertheless highlight what we understand as the major legacies and fault lines of this sector and the attempts to address them over the last 12 years.

We draw on the World Health Organization's (WHO 2000) framework for assessing health systems. This framework, summarised in Figure 12.1, proposes a set of health system objectives and underlying functions required to meet these objectives. While an obvious role is to produce good health,[1] health systems do have broader social goals, represented in WHO's framework as responsiveness to citizens and the promotion of fairness or equity.

In order to achieve its objectives a health system must perform a number of functions:
- Provide accessible services of good quality that address health needs. This entails, on the one hand, defining needs and citizen entitlements in relation to the health system (what) and, on the other, managing the organisational aspects (for example, hospitals, clinics) through which these entitlements will be delivered (how);
- Ensure adequate financing of the health system as well as a fair distribution of financing burdens;
- Generate resources required for system functioning. This includes training of health professionals, creating the physical infrastructure, manufacturing or procuring the necessary drugs, supplies and laboratory services, and institutional intelligence (through research and information) to improve system performance;
- Ensure appropriate 'stewardship' of the health system, the overall oversight function which includes establishing coherent governance and legislative frameworks for the health system and defining and managing processes of reform.

Figure 12.1 *Framework for the performance of health systems*

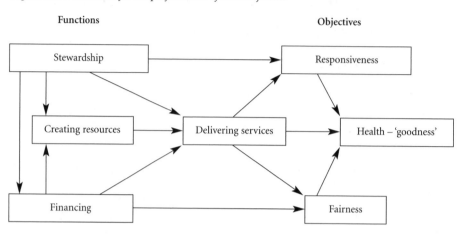

Source: Adapted from WHO 2000: 25

The ANC government in 1994 inherited a plural health system divided into two parallel sectors – a public sector financed through general taxation for the majority and a private sector funded mainly through medical aids for a largely white minority. Governance of the health system was chaotic and fragmented and the processes of resource generation poorly managed. The net result was a highly inequitable, expensive (relative to other middle-income countries) and inefficient system.

The chapter begins with a description of this apartheid legacy and the attempts to reconfigure the health system in the post-apartheid era. We then discuss the rapidly changing epidemiological profile (HIV in particular) confronting the health system and disease-specific (or 'programmatic') interventions since 1994. These responses reflect, on the one hand, efforts to visibly align entitlements with broader democratic goals (for example, the right to termination of pregnancy), or to respond to popular pressure to expand services available through the public system (for example, access to antiretrovirals [ARVs] for HIV). On the other hand, they reflect a growing international focus on a few diseases, most specifically HIV/AIDS, malaria and tuberculosis.

Despite numerous initiatives to transform the South African health system, the reality is that – in WHO's summary terms of good health, equity and responsiveness – this system is as problematic as it was 12 years ago. In a league table of health system performance (WHO 2000), South Africa was ranked 175th out of 191 member states. We discuss explanations for the gap between the promise of transformation[2] and its practice, pointing to the economic (for example, the Growth, Employment and Reconstruction strategy [GEAR]) and political (for example, weak local government) contexts, of the health system, as well as specific health system factors (for example, the overwhelming nature of HIV/AIDS and the difficulties of stewardship).

We conclude by outlining what we see as important emerging opportunities for strengthening the public health system. These are the promulgation of the National Health Act (finally establishing clear legal parameters for the structure of the public health system), a widespread perception of crisis, specifically in relation to human resources and HIV/AIDS, and the recognition that additional resources are required for the health system in order to address the impacts of HIV/AIDS.

Fragmentation and inequity: the apartheid legacy

Governance and financing

The public health system in 1994 was racially fragmented into 14 different operating authorities. These consisted of ten bantustan health departments, three 'own affairs' health departments and the national Department of Health (DoH) that were in line with the ethnic and population divisions of the apartheid state. The public health sector in 'white' South Africa was also vertically fragmented between the national, four provincial and a multitude of local government health departments all rendering aspects of health care, sometimes in parallel with each other. The system was skewed towards urban tertiary hospital care. In 1992/93, 44 per cent of total public health-care expenditure was concentrated in a handful of tertiary and academic hospitals while only 11 per cent of expenditure was spent on primary health care (McIntyre et al. 1995).

In addition to the divisions within the public sector, there was also a large gap between the resources available to the public and private health-care sectors. In 1992/93, 58 per cent of total national health expenditure was occurring in the private sector care, servicing mostly the 23 per cent of people in the country with access to medical aids (McIntyre et al. 1995). The impact of an expensive private sector was such that in 1992/93, South Africa spent 8.5 per cent of its gross domestic product on health, considered very high for a middle-income country (McIntyre et al. 1995). The private health-care sector was most developed in the large urban areas of the Central Witwatersrand, Cape Town and Durban. When pooled with the public academic/tertiary hospitals clustered in these centres, the resources of the private sector produced vast geographical health-care inequities between urban and rural areas of the country.

In 1977, the apartheid government passed the Health Act (replacing the outdated Public Health Act of 1919) in an attempt to develop greater health system coherence, at least in 'white' South Africa. It also instituted a comprehensive review of the health sector through the Commission of Inquiry into Health Services (the Browne Commission) in 1980. When it finally reported in 1986, the Browne Commission highlighted the overall problems of excessive fragmentation of control over health services and a lack of policy direction, resulting in misallocation of resources, duplication of services and poor communication between administrative tiers (van Rensburg & Harrison 1995). In the face of growing political balkanisation, the commission was, however, unable to make substantial proposals to address these problems. Significantly, it recommended the privatisation of non-core public health sector functions and deregulation of the private health sector (van Rensburg 2004a).

In the late 1980s, the rules of cross-subsidy that had historically existed within the medical scheme environment were lifted. This allowed medical schemes to 'cream skim' healthier and younger membership, charging unaffordable premiums for the remainder. The deregulation of approval processes for private hospitals also led to an 87 per cent increase in private-for-profit hospital bed availability between 1988 and 1993 (McIntyre et al. 1995). This combination of factors – over-servicing, declining affordability and perverse incentives in the fee-for-service reimbursement system – entrenched an excessively inflationary trend in the private sector, thus concentrating an increasingly higher proportion of national resources for an increasingly smaller pool of people.

Human resources

One of the historical strengths of South Africa's health system has been the production of skilled personnel. Between 1950 and 1990, the number of registered medical doctors rose from 5 703 to 22 260, increasing the doctor–population ratio from 45 per 100 000 to 74 per 100 000 (van Rensburg 2004b). Similarly, between 1960 and 1994, the number of registered professional and enrolled nurses increased nearly fourfold, from 27 000 to just over 100 000 (van Rensburg 2004b). While medical training was almost exclusively a white preserve,[3] training of black nurses was a high priority of the apartheid government, and by 1990 well over half the country's nurses were black.[4]

However, as with financial resources, the distribution of human resources in the apartheid health system was highly skewed. Table 12.1 illustrates the scale of this inequity by comparing the availability of public sector personnel between a rural (Mpumalanga) and an urban province (Western Cape). In 1994, relative to population size, Mpumalanga inherited one-third of the registered nurses and less than one-quarter of the doctors available to the Western Cape.

The gap between the public and private sectors was even more extreme. In 1992/93, over 85 per cent of dentists and pharmacists, and over 60 per cent of all doctors, psychologists, physiotherapists and other allied health professionals were working in the private sector. Only in the nursing profession was there an appropriate balance between sectors with an estimated 21 per cent of nurses working in the private sector (McIntyre et al. 1995).

Table 12.1 *Public sector personnel in Mpumalanga and Western Cape per 100 000 population, 1994*

	Mpumalanga	Western Cape
Registered nurses	67.6	200.5
Generalist doctors	6.5	30.6
Medical specialists	0.5	23.7

Source: Pick (1995)

In addition to the problems of distribution, the major issues relating to human resources in 1994 included the following (Pick 1995):

- The absence of an overall, coherent framework to guide the provision of human resources throughout the health system in South Africa;
- The need to redress the racial and gender imbalances in the composition of health workers and, in particular, in the managerial layers of the health system;
- The need to re-orient the education and training system of health professionals towards the new goals of the health system and the society;
- Ensuring that health workers provide more compassionate, caring and dignified care to South Africans;
- Improving the management of health workers, addressing authoritarian management styles and poor teamwork between health professionals.

Physical infrastructure

The public health sector asset base in 1994 included 419 hospitals and 3 141 fixed and 1 053 mobile clinics (McIntyre et al. 1995). There were a further 172 private hospitals (Heunis 2004). By international norms for access to primary health care, the country had an estimated shortfall of 600–1 000 clinics (McIntyre et al. 1995). Hospital bed availability (an overall ratio of 4 beds per 1 000 and 2.75 in the public sector) was considered reasonable by international standards although the distribution of hospital beds was skewed towards tertiary/academic facilities. A government-commissioned facilities audit conducted soon after 1994, however, found that many facilities were in a poor condition, with one-third requiring complete replacement or major repair (Boulle et al. 2000).

Drug supply and manufacturing

The pharmaceutical sector in South Africa in 1994 was characterised by the presence of a significant and powerful domestic manufacturing industry that catered for both the public health system (through a state-tender system that allowed for significant volume discounts) and a lucrative private sector. The quality, safety and efficacy of pharmaceutical products used in South Africa were reasonably well controlled through the Medicines Control Council, in existence since 1965. The major problems in this sector included irrational drug use in the public sector, with a drug list that exceeded 3 600 items; excess capacity in manufacturing; unquantified transfer pricing of products and raw materials imported from elsewhere; poor price controls and high mark-ups at the levels of both wholesalers and retailers; as well as uncontrolled buying and selling of pharmaceuticals within the private sector by, amongst others, dispensing doctors (Folb et al. 1995).

Information and research

Health information systems suffered the same fragmentation as that of the system as a whole. A review in 1994 found that the multiple information systems in existence in the public health sector were incompatible with each other and would need to be substantially restructured and re-standardised before any national picture could be established (Bradshaw & Mbobo 1995). In addition, most systems did not provide sufficient information to make coherent planning decisions. They were oriented to budgeting and personnel management purposes and did not provide information related to health status, and health care delivered to the population.

During the apartheid era South Africa developed a significant, and at times prestigious, health research base in tertiary institutions and the statutory Medical Research Council. This research, however, was mainly basic and clinical in orientation with very little public health and even less health systems content. The pharmaceutical industry had also developed a significant (and largely unquantified in 1994) research presence to test new drugs in the country (Jeenah et al. 1997).

In sum, the new government inherited a reasonably well-resourced health system, able to offer quality services to segments of the population. However, it was also deeply inequitable, disorganised and inefficient, with powerful private sector interests and limited institutional intelligence in the form of knowledge and information to plan restructuring.

The situation 12 years later

Governance

Health care is enshrined as a right in the 1996 South African Constitution, which requires government to take reasonable legislative and other measures to ensure that every citizen has access to health-care services. The Constitution also establishes health as a concurrent function of the three spheres of government and therefore the subject of co-operative governance.

As part of general government restructuring, among the first measures implemented by the new government was the creation of a unified public health system. In 1994 and 1995, the 14 departments of health were integrated into a single central ministry and nine provincial departments of health. In the process, the historical dominance of health system administration by white male doctors changed fundamentally.

In 1997, the national DoH published the *White Paper for the Transformation of the Health System in South Africa* (DoH 1997). The White Paper makes central reference to the overarching government framework of the time, the Reconstruction and Development Programme (RDP). It proposed a national health system based on:

- The primary health care (PHC) approach;
- A unified national health system (integrating public and private sectors);
- The development of a district health system;
- The reducion of inequities and expanding access to essential health care.

While undertaking a massive reorganisation of the provincial bureaucracies immediately post-1994, the new government attempted to give expression to the focus on PHC in a number of ways. These included:

- Instituting a PHC facilities building and upgrading programme in which 1 345 new clinics were built and 263 upgraded;
- Removing user fees for public PHC and all fees (including at hospitals) for pregnant women and children under the age of 6 years;
- The formulation of an essential 'PHC package' which set norms for the provision of comprehensive PHC.

In 1995, following a wide consultative process, the DoH also published a draft policy on the district health system (Owen 1995). The district health system (DHS) is intended as the most decentralised structure of health sector governance and management. Its purpose is to ensure co-ordinated provision of PHC and first-level hospital services for geographically coherent populations. It is also supposed to be the focus of intersectoral co-ordination (or 'horizontal government') and local participation in health. Logically, therefore, responsibility for the DHS in South Africa lies with local government,[5] a fact well recognised in policy documents since 1994.

Following the drafting of the DHS policy, the first districts were demarcated along the then still 'soft' local government boundaries. However, DHS structures, teams and processes could not be properly established until local government boundaries were finalised in 2000. A second problem was the reluctance of key players, notably Treasury and the Department of Provincial and Local Government, to saddle the already weak local sphere of government with the additional mandate of the DHS. DHS and PHC have become defined as provincial responsibilities in the National Health Act (61 of 2003), promulgated in 2005. In this legislation, the boundaries of the DHS correspond with those of the first tier of local government, namely the district municipality, and provinces can 'delegate' or 'assign' services to local government if they so wish. The reality is that provinces have seen this as an opportunity to centralise power and functions while financially-strapped local governments have interpreted this legal process as an opportunity to shed many of their health functions as an unfunded mandate. Confusion and considerable to-ing and fro-ing on the fate of the DHS has thus inhibited the establishment of the basic building block of the new health system and, with this, the basis for reorganising the health sector as a whole.

Although somewhat belated, the passage of the National Health Act does finally provide the overall legal framework that formally governs the public health system, with three distinct but interdependent spheres of health-care organisation and delivery: the national, provincial and district levels (corresponding to district municipalities).

Apart from the National Health Act, the legislative programme in the health sector has been extensive in scope and intent. It includes the Choice on Termination of Pregnancy Act (1996), the Tobacco Products Control Amendment Act (1999) and a suite of legislation pertaining to regulation of professions, occupational health and safety, and the private sector.

Private sector

In 2000, government appointed a new and more robust Council for Medical Schemes, facilitating better regulatory oversight of private health financing. This followed the passage of the Medical Schemes Act in 1998 which also re-established cross-subsidy ('community rating') within medical schemes and introduced pre-scribed minimum benefits. However, despite the acknowledged effectiveness of the new regulatory body in ensuring the financial soundness of the medical-scheme environment over the last five years, it has proved difficult to contain costs in this sector.[6] The gap in per capita expenditure in the private sector relative to the public sector has risen from 4.5 in 1997/98 to 7.1 in 2002/03, while the population covered by medical schemes has remained static at around seven million beneficiaries (CMS 2005). As the overall population has grown, the percentage of the population belonging to private medical schemes has declined to 16 per cent, although this much reduced proportion still consumes 59 per cent of the total national health 'pie' (Blecher & Thomas 2004).

Soon after 1994, government initiated discussions on social health insurance (SHI), which remains the main anticipated policy response to public–private inequities in South Africa (Leon & Mabope 2005). SHI would make membership of schemes compulsory for all those in formal employment – thus adding several million beneficiaries into the private financing environment. Theoretically, this would free the public sector to distribute its resources amongst fewer people and to compete as preferred providers in a new generation of low-cost schemes. Steps towards the implementation of SHI being considered include a risk equalisation fund as a mechanism of cross-subsidy between schemes and a mandatory Government Employee Medical Scheme. The implementation of SHI has been mired in numerous delays and several generations of proposals have been produced which increasingly limit the extent of redistribution and cross-subsidy through the SHI mechanism (McIntyre et al. 2003, 2006).

In 2005, the DoH, in collaboration with private sector stakeholders, published a *Draft Charter of the Private and Public Health Sectors of the Republic of South Africa* (DoH 2005a). This charter currently constitutes the formal point of discussion between the DoH and the private health sector as a whole. Whilst recognising the vast inequities between public and private sectors, the charter departs from previous policy statements in having as its first goal to bring ownership of the private health sector into the realm of black economic empowerment (BEE) processes. The emergence of health sector BEE may signal a new policy era in which private sector interests are defended rather than controlled or regulated.

Public sector financing

Over the last 12 years there has been a net real growth in public health expenditure. In provincial health structures this amounts to a 30 per cent growth in health spending (from R30 billion in 1995/96 to nearly R39 billion in 2005/06 in 2003 constant rand) (Blecher & Thomas 2004). This has been accompanied by an increase in the proportion of expenditure on primary health care (Doherty et al. 2003). Overall, however, expenditure has not kept pace with the increase in the population and per capita expenditure remains below a peak established in 1996/97. The increases have also not addressed the additional cost burdens imposed by HIV/AIDS, estimated to be around R6 billion per annum (Blecher & Thomas 2004), and geographical inequities continue to be a significant feature of public health sector spending (McIntyre et al. 2006).

Importantly, this growth in spending has not been even since 1994. An initial period of increased expenditure (1995/96 to 1997/98) was followed by several years of stagnation (1998/99 to 2000/01) in the wake of the new macroeconomic GEAR strategy and the policy of fiscal restraint. Public health spending again increased after 2001, as economic growth picked up and as the state started to make large conditional grants for HIV/AIDS and the revitalisation of public hospitals. Despite a recent relaxation in public health spending, GEAR and its operational presence in the Public Finance Management Act have had an enduring impact on health services, establishing cost-containment as the de facto driver of everyday practice in the health system (Penn-Kekana et al. 2004). Staying within budget became and remains the key preoccupation of managers, implicitly relegating equity and other dimensions of institutional change to secondary goals.

Human resources

In 1999, the DoH appointed a task team to review and propose a strategy for the human resource situation (Pick et al. 2001). In 2005, it published a strategic framework (DoH 2005b), followed by a strategic plan (DoH 2006a) for developing human resources in the health sector. These are long overdue and important steps in comprehensively addressing the production, recruitment and retention of health personnel in the public sector. To date, policy responses to human resources have been piecemeal, focusing on individual strategies such as the recruitment of Cuban doctors in the immediate post-1994 period, compulsory community service for recent graduates and scarce skills and rural allowances.

The poor availability of health personnel, particularly in the geographical areas of greatest disadvantage, has emerged as one of the most significant constraints to improving access to health care in South Africa. The South African health system is facing a growing crisis in this regard. For example, between 1996 and 2003, the availability of doctors and professional nurses in South African provincial health structures declined by 24 per cent and 16 per cent respectively (Table 12.2). By 2005, there was a shortage of nearly 46 000 trained personnel in the health system, representing a 27.1 per cent vacancy rate (Day & Gray 2005).

Table 12.2 *Supply of health professionals working in provincial health services and percentage decline, 1996–2003*

Category	1996	2003	% decrease
Doctors *	36.6	27.8	−24
Professional nurses *	128.2	108.2	−16

Source: Segall & Brijlal (2003)
Note: * Figures are per 100 000 non-insured population

The negative growth in the supply of health personnel is due to a number of factors, some avoidable, others not. Between 1995 and 2005, the population dependent on the public sector grew by seven million while production of certain categories, such as nurses, declined. Decreased production of professional nurses was caused largely by attempts to rationalise nursing colleges in the late 1990s.

It can be argued that the public sector in South Africa is largely dependent on the technical skills of nurses, of whom the professional nurse (that is the fully qualified nurse) is the most important. In primary care, well over 90 per cent of all patients have professional nurses as their main caregiver. In the situation of increased demand placed on the public health system through rising population numbers, as well as the extraordinary additional disease burden created by the HIV pandemic, it would have been logical to expect an increased production in professional nurses since 1994.

The actual situation, paradoxically, has been the opposite. In Table 12.3 the production of nurses at universities and nursing colleges in South Africa from 1996 to

2004 is shown; the table highlights the steadily declining numbers produced on an annual basis. The reasons for this decline in production are complex but include the lack of a human resource plan with human resource norms and corresponding forecasting of production; the rationalisation of existing nursing colleges (as part of cost-containment drives) done on a piecemeal basis at provincial level without consideration of inadvertent consequences; and a lack of co-ordination between the education and health sectors. Overall, the problem is one of poor stewardship of the system at the highest level.

Table 12.3 *Training of professional nurses in nursing colleges and universities for a four-year comprehensive course, 1996–2004*

	1996	1997	1998	1999	2000	2001	2002	2003	2004	Total
No. of nurses trained	2 629	2 682	2 371	2 262	2 494	2 041	1 652	1 553	1 716	19 400

Source: South African Nursing Council Register cited in Subedar (2005)

In recent years, the globalisation of markets of health-care providers has accelerated the exodus of health-care professionals from South Africa, primarily to the United Kingdom and the Middle East. This is to a large extent beyond the control of the Health Ministry and could not have been anticipated in 1994.

One of the key problems facing the health system is the morale of its providers. In one recent survey of nurses working in maternal health services in three provinces surveyed by Penn-Kekana et al. (2005), 60 per cent reported feeling demotivated and 51 per cent agreed with the statement: 'I could see myself working overseas in the future.' Poor motivation was associated with perceptions of poor pay or promotion prospects, feeling unsupported by management and workplace conflict. Managerial capacity across the health system is weak and efforts at strengthening management are poorly developed. A few training programmes have been introduced, although they are undermined by a lack of co-ordination, and the content is often disconnected from local realities and the practical challenges facing local health districts.

There has been a range of policies aimed at improving the interactions between health-care workers and patients, including the *Batho Pele* Strategy, a Patients' Rights Charter, and micro-interventions such as complaints boxes and client-satisfaction surveys. However, the evidence is that little has changed in the culture of service provision in which the apartheid frameworks of patients as subjects to be disciplined, rather than rights-bearing citizens, still dominate. Public sector health workers in South Africa are frequently described as harsh, unsympathetic and as readily breaching patient confidentiality (see for example Modiba et al. 2001).

Information systems

South Africa now has a Health and Management Information System (HMIS) comprising a number of interlinked components. These include information on demography and socio-economic status, health status, finance and personnel. Significant strides have been made in introducing a bottom-up approach to collecting and collating service-related data in the public sector. This district health information system, which is part of the overall HMIS, collects data on a range of indicators in the primary care facilities and hospitals and has the potential to provide managers at all levels with valuable decision-making information, including indicators related to utilisation, equity, outputs and outcomes of service delivery.

However, major challenges to the information system remain:
- The quality of data is still a problem – incomplete, inconsistent and incorrect data returns are common;
- Feedback mechanisms across the national, provincial and local levels are generally erratic;
- There is weak capacity in collating and interpreting information for decision-making;
- The culture of utilising data for planning, implementation, monitoring and evaluation is also weak.

Drug policy

A comprehensive national drug policy was launched in 1996. An early success of this policy was the rapid implementation of an essential drugs list (EDL) in the public sector, which dramatically reduced the number of drugs available at each level of the system. It provided for much more rational drug prescribing and the introduction of generic prescribing throughout the health system. The EDL for PHC is now into its second edition and is accompanied by standard treatment guidelines which ensure quality and efficiency in the use of medicines. In general, public sector availability of drugs is good.

Attempts to regulate private players through the Medicines and Related Substances Control Amendment Act (1997) have, however, encountered stiff resistance. These players include the multinational pharmaceutical industry, dispensing private medical practitioners and, more recently, retail pharmacies. Changes to the procurement, price and dispensing of drugs in the private sector have been the subject of long and acrimonious public debates and litigation, dragging the DoH into court action on a number of fronts. Although the regulatory initiatives taken by the state have been entirely in line with international norms,[7] and the outcomes mostly favourable, the fallout in the public image of the DoH as a capable regulator has been considerable.

Diseases and programmatic initiatives

Priority disease burdens

Prior to the advent of HIV/AIDS, South Africa was on a path of demographic transition involving declining fertility and mortality rates and rising life expectancy. Such shifts are accompanied by (and partly the consequence of) changes in the nature of disease – typically from communicable diseases (such as childhood diarrhoea and pneumonia) to chronic non-communicable diseases (such as diabetes and hypertension) and violence and injury. Changing epidemiologies, combined with an explosive HIV/AIDS epidemic, have produced what is known as the 'quadruple burden of disease' in South Africa (Bradshaw et al. 2004), consisting of:

1. HIV/AIDS (and the associated epidemic of tuberculosis);
2. Cardiovascular diseases (such as stroke and heart disease) associated with 'lifestyle' factors such as smoking, diet, stress and lack of exercise;
3. Violence and injury;
4. Established infectious diseases.

These four groups of diseases constitute the major causes of mortality in South Africa, with HIV/AIDS now by far the largest single cause of death (see Figure 12.2).

Figure 12.2 *Top 20 causes of death in South Africa by percentage, 2000*

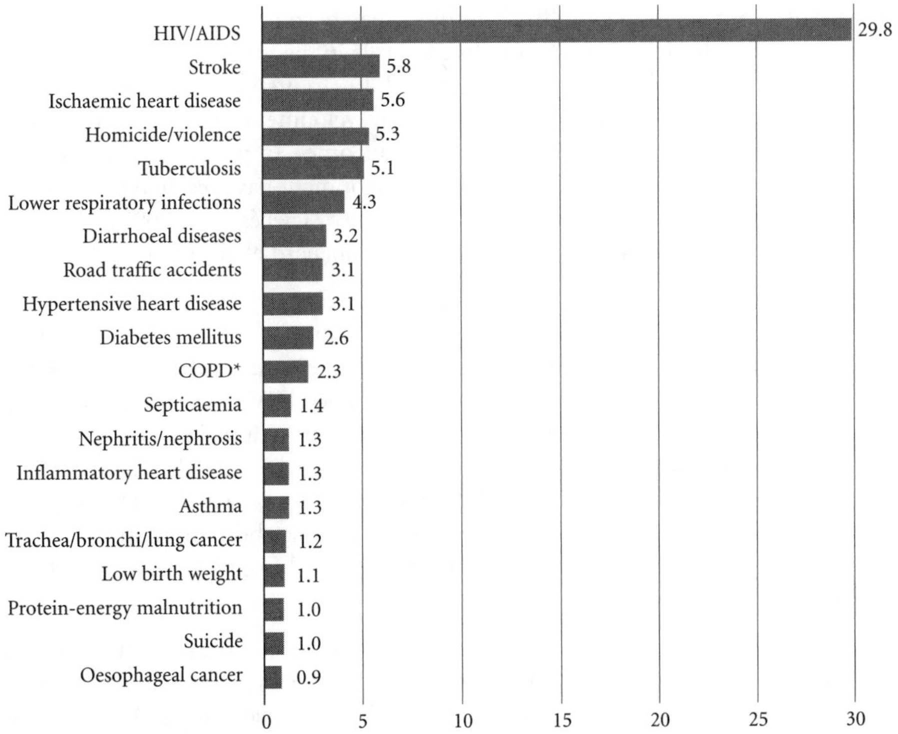

Source: Bradshaw et al. (2004: 24)
Note: * Chronic obstructive pulmonary disease.

Although the HIV epidemic in southern Africa has its origins in the massive social disruptions of apartheid, its impact has been felt principally in the post-apartheid era, precipitating not only a social and demographic crisis, but also a crisis of health sector governance. It has overshadowed other health and health system concerns at all levels. For example, illnesses related to HIV/AIDS now account for between 30 and 60 per cent of hospital bed occupancy in paediatric and adult medical services (Schneider et al. 2005; Shisana et al. 2003). This is a major source of burnout and one of the push factors driving health workers out of the public health system. Unfortunately, the HIV epidemic shows little real sign of abating and it is not clear that the large investments in prevention to date are achieving more than marginal changes in behaviour (DoH 2005c; Shisana et al. 2003).

Programmatic initiatives

In addition to the more generic health system functions already discussed, there have been numerous initiatives targeting specific priority diseases or populations at risk over the last 12 years, some of which are listed in Table 12.4. These are referred to as public health or PHC 'programme' interventions.

The needs of women and children have been a particular priority of the DoH since 1994. Although maternal–child health has long been a focus of public health, the cervical screening programmes, pro-choice legislation and sexual assault services all represent a concern for the health needs of women beyond their role as mothers. In this regard, South Africa played an influential role in the formulation of the rights-based Programme of Action on Sexual and Reproductive Health at the 1994 International Conference on Population and Development in Cairo. Many interventions targeting women have had positive outcomes. In particular, the abortion legislation and the resultant health services development have resulted in improvements in abortion-related morbidity and mortality (Jewkes et al. 2005), although implementation remains far from satisfactory (Blanchard et al. 2003).

Measures controlling tobacco use have led to significant reductions in tobacco consumption (Malan & Leaver 2003). Another recent success is the control of malaria. While malaria has a localised epidemiology in the northeast of South Africa and is not a major cause of ill-health nationally, it exceeds HIV as the foremost health problem in much of Africa.[8] South Africa has been part of a regional collaboration on malaria control with Swaziland and Mozambique which involves active spraying of households (with DDT), implementation of new malaria treatment regimens and uniform surveillance activities. The impact has been dramatic. In South Africa alone, the number of new malaria cases dropped from 64 622 in 2000 to 13 399 in 2004 (DoH 2006b).

It is the HIV/AIDS interventions, however, that have captured much of the 'transformation attention' of the health system. This is in part due to the intense public controversies[9] that have characterised the response since 1994, as well as

Table 12.4 *Examples of programmatic interventions since 1994*

Disease/target population	Interventions
Women	Free health-care services for pregnant women Choice on termination of pregnancy Confidential enquiry into maternal deaths Cervical cancer screening programme Sexual assault services including post-exposure prophylaxis
Children	Free health care for children < 6 years Primary school nutrition programme Expanding the immunisation programme and mass campaigns Integrated management of childhood illness programme
HIV/AIDS	Public education campaigns Condom distribution Voluntary counselling and testing Treatment and surveillance of sexually transmitted infections Community-based care and support programmes Prevention of mother-to-child transmission of HIV Comprehensive HIV & AIDS Care Management and Treatment Programme (incorporating ARV roll-out)
Tuberculosis	Implementation of the WHO-advocated 'DOTS' [directly observed therapy, short course] policy Improved national surveillance Integration of HIV and TB
Tobacco	Legislation/regulations to control tobacco product advertising, promotion and sponsorship Increasing the price of tobacco products
Malaria control	Regional co-operation as part of the Lubombo Spatial Development Initiative including Mozambique, Swaziland and South Africa, involving household spraying, new artemisinin-based drug regimens and improved surveillance

to the rapid succession of new interventions (accompanied by increasingly large budgetary allocations) instituted around HIV. Initially programming was oriented to prevention – educational campaigns, condom distribution, control of sexually transmitted infections and voluntary counselling and testing [VCT]). Care and support strategies were limited to the treatment of opportunistic infections, home-based care of the dying and community-based strategies for orphans and vulnerable children. However, in the face of growing international and national pressure that involved a Constitutional Court ruling, the government was compelled to consider ARV technologies, first for the prevention of mother-to-child-transmission (PMTCT) in 2001 and then for the treatment of HIV. In November 2003, Cabinet approved the Comprehensive Care, Management and Treatment Programme which aims to make ARV therapy universally accessible in the context of an integrated approach to HIV treatment, prevention and health system strengthening. By December 2005, 88 per cent and 77 per cent of public health facilities offered VCT and PMTCT respectively, and more than 100 000 people had initiated ART through a network of 204 public sector sites, which included at least one site in every district of the country (DoH 2006c).

 A significant outcome of several generations of AIDS interventions has been the emergence of a very large body[10] of volunteer and semi-remunerated lay health workers, functioning as counsellors, treatment supporters, home-based carers and support group facilitators. The regulation of these workers falls under a new National Community Health Worker Policy Framework, which aims to create standards of training and remuneration.

Programmes versus systems

Many of the more visible achievements of the post-apartheid health system have been in the implementation of public health or disease programmes. These, however, are double-edged swords. While they focus on specific remediable problems and may achieve short-term gains (and are therefore favoured by donors) this is often at the cost to the system as a whole.

Both nationally and provincially in South Africa, programmes have tended to operate in specialised, vertical 'silos' with their own budgets, training and reporting procedures that are separate from the lines of authority responsible for management of health facilities. As all ultimately target the same providers, the presence of parallel vertical programmes creates a number of problems.

First, the multiplicity of uncoordinated programme and systems initiatives since 1994 has established an environment of 'transformation fatigue' (McIntyre & Klugman 2003), where before one new practice can be institutionalised focus is diverted to the next. As a consequence, the dominant culture of implementation in the health sector is increasingly one of 'muddling through' (Minogue 1983), responding to short-term organisational and political demands rather than to a long-term vision of the health system. Second, programmes do not as a rule invest in strengthening core health systems functions such as undergraduate training, infrastructure and management of districts and facilities. Yet because universal access to programmes depends on a well-functioning health system, this in turn has undermined their implementation (Blanchard et al. 2003; Varkey et al. 2000). Third, programmes entrench a technocratic perspective of the health system rather than a social one in which new, transformed paradigms of health care and management of the health system are made possible.

Of the programmes implemented to date, by far the most ambitious, is the Comprehensive Care, Management and Treatment of HIV and AIDS. The operational plan for this programme fully recognises that universal access to ARV will not be achieved unless the health system is strengthened. It envisages, for example,

14 000 additional posts of which just over 6 000 would be health professionals (doctors, nurses, dieticians and pharmacists) (DoH 2003). There are signs that under pressure to show progress and meet targets, the early implementation of the programme is almost solely focused on ARV roll-out, rather than on broader system benefits. This may change with time.

Between the promise and the practice of transformation

Post-apartheid health sector transformation has been characterised by far-reaching policy statements that recognise the structural weaknesses of the health system. The White Paper on Health Sector Transformation (DOH 1997) and the more recent National Health Act both outline comprehensive frameworks for health system reorganisation rooted in equity and social justice. These overarching policies have been accompanied by a plethora of interventions to effect change. There are many individual stories of success, some of which have been highlighted in this chapter.

The cumulative impact of all this policy formulation and implementation is, however, disappointing. The amalgamation of numerous fragmented authorities into one national and nine provincial authorities, and changes to the gender, racial and professional profile of the health administration, stand as the most significant achievements of the post-apartheid era. Beyond this, many of the structural problems of the health system remain. The distribution of resources (financial and human) between public and private sectors, and within the public sector, is as unequal as it ever was and the performance of the public health system is highly uneven, both within and across provinces. This is reflective of enduring social inequities. In some respects – the availability of skilled providers and strains on the health system, especially public hospitals – things appear to have worsened. Demoralised and demotivated are now commonplace descriptors of health-care providers and many are making use of opportunities to leave the public health system.

With hindsight, it is clear that the context of health sector reform post-1994 has been an unfavourable one on several fronts. Apart from the constraints imposed by an overwhelming HIV/AIDS epidemic and an emerging human resource crisis, transformation began in the midst of international health systems thinking that was neo-liberal and technocratic in orientation, emphasising, for example, new public management techniques, health-care packages targeting the poor (rather than redistribution), and outsourcing (rather than strengthening) of public sector functions. There was little in the way of technical assistance from bilateral and multilateral donor agencies or international debate oriented to equity and redistribution. The shift from the RDP to GEAR also had a powerful influence, not only in limiting the availability of resources for transformation but also in establishing the overriding imperatives of fiscal restraint and the crowding out of other goals.

Finally, the weaknesses and delays in the finalisation of the local sphere of government inhibited the development of the DHS as the core building block of the health system in the post-apartheid period.

Health sector stewardship

From within the health sector a rather blunt approach to the management of actors and complex interests has been a key problem. It is most obvious in the inability to unite governmental and non-governmental players in the national response to HIV/AIDS (Schneider 2002), but is also evident in difficulties of co-operative governance between spheres of government (Blaauw et al. 2004) in creating strategic alliances to achieve significant financing and pharmaceutical reforms (Gilson et al. 2003; Gray et al. 2002) and in achieving buy-in of frontline providers to the process of change (Walker & Gilson 2004). Over time, many health system actors have positioned themselves as agents of resistance, and the capacity and legitimacy of the national DoH to lead the health system has diminished. Conversely, where successes have been recorded – such as in the successful passage of the termination of pregnancy law and tobacco control – these have been achieved through an understanding of change as a strategic process involving evidence and political management (Malan & Leaver 2003).

The failure to rapidly institutionalise the DHS and a host of related managerial and governance systems has led to a loss of an institutional and organisational focus in the health system more generally. Disease-specific processes have dominated to the detriment of systems functions. There has been inadequate investment in key underlying functions such as financing, information systems, infrastructure, human resource development, planning and managerial capacity, and these remain technically weak at all levels of the health sector.

Despite the presence of policy frameworks, most health sector players lack a clear vision of the system and their position within it. The political and administrative leadership of the health system appears to have all but abandoned its stewardship role of mobilising the majority of health system actors around a coherent vision of the health system. In the absence of such a 'big picture', many interventions have been experienced by those at the coalface of service delivery as a form of disjointed incrementalism, re-evoking a central problem of the apartheid health system, namely that of fragmentation.

Challenges for the future

The health system in South Africa is facing a number of serious crises, although it would be an oversimplification to characterise it as being in a state of collapse. There are also a number of positive signals – the recognition that much more needs to be done to address the human resource crisis, large investments in HIV treatment and the health system more generally, and an incremental (albeit slow) process of regulating the private sector.

The promulgation of the National Health Act in 2005 offers the potential to ensure that all role-players (including the private sector) are co-ordinated under a common framework and to reassert a sense of coherence and an equity orientation in South Africa's health system. It also finally provides the legal mandate for the DHS and the opportunity to focus on organisational and systems development rather than on programmatic interventions.

The DoH's 2004–2009 strategic framework includes a number of systems and governance (as opposed to programmatic) foci in its ten priorities (DoH 2004). They include strengthening of:

- Governance and management of the national health system;
- PHC, emergency medical services and hospital service delivery systems;
- Human resource planning, development and management;
- Planning, budgeting and monitoring and evaluation.

Andrews and Pillay (2005) have identified the following as critical to the implementation of the strategic plan:

- Leadership, and in particular political leaders as well as managers in the health system, must clearly articulate and communicate a vision and a mission that will resonate with frontline health workers;
- A programme of action that is developed with, and that captures the imagination of, those charged with its implementation. This would require greater empowerment of leaders at the local level to drive the change agenda;
- A critical mass of skilled and motivated health managers and health workers at all levels of the health system;
- Mechanisms and structures to facilitate community participation, especially of poor and marginalised groups, and strengthened accountability.

A major question remains whether the national Ministry/Department of Health has sufficient legitimacy and willingness to reinvent itself as a strong steward of the health system. This, in part, depends on the ability to fundamentally alter the management of HIV/AIDS and of the broad range of actors implicated in the health system.

Notes

1   However, it is generally accepted that good health is produced less by traditional health system functions of caring and curing than by social factors such as adequate housing, nutrition, and water and sanitation. It is not hard to see how the causes of and solutions to the two major causes of death and disability in South Africa – HIV/AIDS and violence/injury – lie outside of what health systems generally do.

2   As the official terminology for health sector change in the post-apartheid era, the use of the term 'transformation' to describe these processes in this chapter is deliberate. Transformation is taken to mean the extent to which structural weaknesses, inequities and social injustices of the past have been confronted.

3   In the mid-1970s, 93 per cent of doctors were white (Ebersohn 1978, cited in van Rensburg 2004b). Aspiring black doctors had access to two medical schools – Natal University Medical School from the 1950s and the Medical University of South Africa or MEDUNSA from the 1980s – in contrast to five medical schools for white students.

4   Black nurses, as with teachers, were ascribed a special role by the apartheid state in the 'management' of black bodies and minds (Marks 1994).

5   Ideally with the lowest level of local government, namely the local (as opposed to district) municipality.

6   One of the key reasons for this is the presence of an 'oligopolistic private hospital market' concentrated in three hospital networks (McIntyre et al. 2006)

7   For example, the famous 'Section 15c' of the Medicines and Related Substances Control Amendment Act, the subject of court action by the pharmaceutical industry, allowed for two internationally established legal mechanisms for regulating drug prices and access, namely parallel importation of drugs and the issuing of compulsory licences.

8   Malaria is one of three diseases targeted by the Global Fund for AIDS, TB and Malaria and also features in the Millennium Development Goals.

9   The controversies have been amply reviewed elsewhere (see, for example, Mbali 2003; Schneider 2002) and are not discussed in any detail here.

10 The DoH estimated that there were 60 000 such workers in 2004 (Friedman 2005).

References

Andrews G & Pillay Y (2005) Strategic priorities for the National Health System 2004–2009. In P Ijumba & P Barron (Eds) *South African Health Review 2005*. Durban: Health Systems Trust.

Blaauw D, Gilson L, Modiba P, Erasmus E, Khumalo G & Schneider H (2004) *Governmental relations and HIV service delivery*. Durban: Health Systems Trust.

Blanchard K, Fonn S & Xaba M (2003) Abortion law in South Africa: Passage of a progressive law and challenges for implementation. *Gaceta Medica de Mexico*, 138(1): S109–S114.

Blecher M & Thomas S (2004) Health care financing. In P Ijumba, C Day & A Ntuli (Eds) *South African Health Review 2003/04*. Durban: Health Systems Trust.

Boulle A, Fletcher M & Burn A (2000) Hospital restructuring. In A Ntuli et al. (Eds) *South African Health Review 2000*. Durban: Health Systems Trust.

Bradshaw D & Mbobo L (1995) Informatics support. In D Harrison & M Nielsen (Eds) *South African Health Review 1995*. Durban: Health Systems Trust.

Bradshaw D, Nannan N, Laubscher R, et al. (2004) *South African Burden of Disease Study 2000: Estimates of provincial mortality*. Cape Town: South African Medical Research Council.

CMS (Council for Medical Schemes) (2005) *2004/05 Annual Report*. Pretoria: Council for Medical Schemes. Available at <http://www.medicalschemes.com>.

Day C & Gray A (2005) Health and related indicators. In P Ijumba & P Barron (Eds) *South African Health Review 2005*. Durban: Health Systems Trust.

DoH (Department of Health) (1997) *White Paper for the transformation of the health system in South Africa*. Pretoria: Government Printer. Available at <http://doh.gov.za/196.36.153.56/doh/>.

DoH (2003) *Operational Plan for Comprehensive HIV and AIDS Care, Management and Treatment for South Africa*. Pretoria: DoH. Available at: <http://www.doh.gov.za/>.

DoH (2004) *Strategic priorities for the National Health System 2004–2009*. Pretoria: DoH. Available at <http://www.doh.gov.za/196.36.153.56/doh/>.

DoH (2005a) *Draft charter of the private and public health sectors of the Republic of South Africa*. Pretoria: DoH. Available at <http://196.36.153.56/doh/>.

DoH (2005b) *A strategic framework for human resources for health plan*. Pretoria: DoH. Available at <http://www.doh.gov.za/docs/discussion/hr2005/main.html>.

DoH (2005c) *National HIV and syphilis antenatal sero-prevalence survey in South Africa, 2004*. Pretoria: DoH. Available at <http://196.36.153.56/doh/>.

DoH (2006a) *Human resources for health: A strategic plan*. Pretoria: DoH.

DoH (2006b) *Malaria statistics*. Pretoria: DoH. Available at <http://196.36.153.56/doh/>.

DoH (2006c) *Strategic plan 2006/07–2008/09*. Pretoria: DoH. Available at <http://www.doh.gov.za/>.

Doherty J, Thomas S, Muirhead D & McIntyre D (2003) Health care financing and expenditure. In P Ijumba, A Ntuli & P Barron (Eds) *South African Health Review 2002*. Durban: Health Systems Trust.

Ebersohn D (1978) *Geographiese verspreiding van medici in 1975*. Pretoria: Institute for Manpower Research (HSRC).

Folb P, Valentine N & Eagles P (1995) Drug policy. In D Harrison & M Nielsen (Eds) *South African Health Review 1995*. Durban: Health Systems Trust.

Friedman I (2005) CHWs and community Care-givers: Towards a unified model of practice. In P Ijumba & P Barron (Eds) *South African Health Review 2005*. Durban: Health Systems Trust.

Gilson L, Doherty J, Lake S, McIntyre D, Mwikisa C & Thomas S (2003) The SAZA study: Implementing health financing reform in South Africa and Zambia. *Health Policy and Planning*, 18(1): 31–46.

Gray A, Matsebula T, Blaauw D, Schneider H & Gilson L (2002) *Policy change in a context of transition: Drug policy in South Africa, 1989–1999*. Johannesburg: Centre for Health Policy, University of Witwatersrand.

Heunis JC (2004) Hospitals and hospital reform in South Africa. In HCJ van Rensburg (Ed) *Health and health care in South Africa*. Pretoria: Van Schaik.

Jeenah M, Dada Y, Househam C & Harrison D (1997) *ENHR in South Africa*. Geneva: Council on Health Research for Development (COHRED).

Jewkes R & Rees H (2005). Dramatic decline in abortion mortality due to the Choice on Termination of Pregnancy Act. *South African Medical Journal*, 95(4): 250.

Jewkes R, Rees H, Dickson K, Brown H & Levin J (2005) The impact of age on the epidemiology of incomplete abortions in South Africa after legislative change. *British Journal of Obstetrics and Gynaecology*, 112(3): 355–9.

Leon N & Mabope R (2005) The private health sector. In P Ijumba & P Barron (Eds) *South African Health Review 2005*. Durban: Health Systems Trust.

Malan M & Leaver R (2003) Political change in South Africa: New tobacco control and public health policies. In J de Beyer & L Waverley (Eds) *Tobacco control policy: Strategies, successes and setbacks*. Washington DC: World Bank and Research for International Tobacco Control.

Marks S (1994) *Divided sisterhood: Race, class and gender in the South African nursing profession*. Johannesburg: Witwatersrand University Press.

Mbali M (2003) HIV/AIDS policy-making in post-apartheid South Africa. In J Daniel et al. (Eds) *State of the Nation: South Africa 2003–2004*. Pretoria: HSRC.

McIntyre D, Bloom G, Doherty J & Brijlal P (1995) *Health sector expenditure and finance in South Africa*. Durban: Health Systems Trust and the World Bank.

McIntyre D, Doherty J & Gilson L (2003) A tale of two visions: The changing fortunes of social health insurance in South Africa. *Health Policy and Planning*, 18(1): 47–58.

McIntyre D, Gilson L, Wadee H, Thiede M & Okarafor O (2006) Commercialisation and extreme inequality in health: The policy challenges in South Africa. *Journal for International Development*, (forthcoming).

McIntyre D & Klugman B (2003) The human face of decentralisation and integration of health services: Experience from South Africa. *Reproductive Health Matters*, 11(21): 108–19.

Minogue M (1983) Theory and practice in public policy and administration. *Policy and Politics*, 11: 63–85.

Modiba P, Gilson L & Schneider H (2001) Voices of service users. In A Ntuli (Ed.) *South African Health Review 2001*. Durban: Health Systems Trust.

Owen CP (Ed) (1995) *A policy for the development of a district health system for South Africa*. Pretoria: DoH.

Penn-Kekana L, Blaauw D & Schneider H (2004) 'It makes me want to run away to Saudi Arabia': Management and implementation challenges for public financing reforms from a maternity ward perspective. *Health Policy and Planning*, 19 (Suppl.1): i71–i77.

Penn-Kekana L, Blaauw D, Tint KS & Monareng D (2005) *Nursing staff dynamics and implications for maternal health provision in public health facilities in the context of HIV/AIDS*. Johannesburg: USAID/Population Council.

Pick W (1995) Human resources development. In D Harrison & M Nielsen (Eds) *South African Health Review 1995*. Durban: Health Systems Trust.

Pick WM, Nevhutalu K, Cornwall J & Masuku M (2001) *Human resources for health. A national strategy.* Pretoria: DoH.

Schneider H (2002) On the fault-line: The politics of AIDS policy implementation in contemporary South Africa. *African Studies,* 61(1): 145–67.

Schneider H, Kellerman R, Oyedele S & Dlamini N (2005) *HIV impact surveillance system. Summary report: Design and data collection.* Johannesburg: Wits School of Public Health and Gauteng Department of Health.

Segall M & Brijlal V (2003) *Essential health care for all South Africans: An investigation into the adequacy of public health financing and the equity of provincial health resource distribution.* Pretoria: DoH.

Shisana O, Rehle T, Simbayi LC et al. (2005) *South African national HIV prevalence, HIV incidence, behaviour and communication survey, 2005.* Pretoria: HSRC.

Shisana O, Hall E, Maluleke KR et al. (2003) *The impact of HIV/AIDS on the health sector: National survey of health personnel, ambulatory and hospitalised patients and health facilities, 2002.* Pretoria: HSRC.

Subedar H (2005) Nursing Profession: Production of nurses and proposed scope of practice. In P Ijumba & P Barron (Eds). *South African Health Review 2005.* Durban: Health Systems Trust.

Van Rensburg HCJ (2004a) The history of health care in South Africa. In HCJ van Rensburg (Ed) *Health and health care in South Africa.* Pretoria: Van Schaik Publishers.

Van Rensburg HCJ (2004b) The health professions and human resources for health. In HCJ van Rensburg (Ed) *Health and health care in South Africa.* Pretoria: Van Schaik.

Van Rensburg HCJ & Harrison D (1995) History of health policy. In D Harrison & M Nielsen (Eds) *South African Health Review 1995.* Durban: Health Systems Trust.

Varkey SJ, Fonn S & Ketlhapile M (2000) The role of advocacy in implementing the South African abortion law. *Reproductive Health Matters,* 8(16): 103–11.

Walker L & Gilson L (2004) We are bitter but we are satisfied. *Social Science and Medicine,* 59(6): 1251–61.

WHO (World Health Organization) (2000) *Health systems: Improving performance.* The World Health Report 2000. Geneva: WHO.

13 Public hospitals in South Africa: stressed institutions, disempowered management

Karl von Holdt and Mike Murphy

Most of the doctors and nurses we interviewed in eight South African public hospitals believe that staff shortages and management failures compromise patient care. While professionals are generally reluctant to acknowledge that this entails avoidable patient deaths, clinicians at one hospital were more forthright: 'Everything is done in a rush, and staff are left exhausted. The result is a reduction in the quality of care and avoidable morbidity and mortality.' A nurse in a second hospital commented: 'We do not give quality patient care. Now I am alone in the ward, it means I am unable to prevent certain things happening. The result is complications, wound sepsis, longer hospital stays.' This is one among many similar comments from nurses in these hospitals.

It seems clear, on the basis of the eight hospitals we studied, that many patients at public hospitals in South Africa are not receiving adequate health care. The purpose of this chapter is to explore the nature of management failure in public hospitals, assess the causes of this failure, and discuss the potential for change.[1]

At the core of our research is our experience as transformation advisers at Chris Hani Baragwanath Hospital (CHB), the tertiary academic hospital on the edge of Soweto reputed to be the biggest hospital in the southern hemisphere. In 2000, the National Labour and Economic Development Institute (Naledi) for which we work was approached by the trade unions at CHB to work with them in developing proposals for the transformation of the hospital. By 2003, Naledi had been accepted by CHB management, the Hospital Board and the Gauteng Department of Health (DoH), in addition to the trade unions, as transformation advisers at the institution.

From a research point of view, this study has constituted a five-year process of participant observation (Von Holdt & Maseramule 2005). As part of it, a series of intensive interviews and focus groups was conducted with representatives of all occupational categories and management groupings within CHB in 2002 and 2004 so as to identify problems and develop strategic proposals for transformation. In order to ascertain the extent to which the problems we had observed at CHB were present in other public hospitals, in late 2005 we extended our research to a further tertiary (level 3) and six regional (level 2) hospitals in three provinces.

In this extended phase of our research, we conducted on average four interviews in each institution – with the chief executive officer (CEO), a senior clinician, nursing middle manager/s, and trade union shop stewards. While this provides a somewhat limited assessment of hospital functioning, it does nonetheless provide broad indicators. We used the intensive and in-depth analysis developed in the CHB transformation project to guide our interviewing strategy and interpret the results.

The research methodology we employed was essentially a qualitative methodology, which is somewhat unusual in the field of public health. The reasons for this were that quantitative data on hospital management – such as staff numbers, staff vacancies, bed occupancy rates and so on – and data on clinical outcomes at South African hospitals – such as mortality rates, wound sepsis and bedsore rates, patient recovery rates and so on – are frequently unreliable, difficult to access or non-existent (Burn & Shongwe 2004; our research). Indeed, health department officials acknowledged in 2000 that they did not know how many hospitals they were responsible for, nor how many patients were treated, and in 2006, they did not know what staff vacancy rates were (Heunis 2004: 474). We therefore had to rely on the more qualitative and subjective views of those intimately involved in clinical processes, that is, clinicians and nurses. However, there are advantages to qualitative methodologies. They provide for a more complex analysis of the relationship between cause and effect than quantitative methodologies, as well as permitting the 'experience from below' to be captured and explored, thus contributing new insights.

Before discussing problems in the functioning of public hospitals, we provide a rough overview of where they fit into the public health system.

Structure of the public health sector

Public hospitals are managed by the provincial departments of health. The role of the national DoH is to develop policy and channel funding to the provincial departments. The provision of health services is divided between primary health clinics and level 1 (district), level 2 (regional) and level 3 (central) hospitals. Each level provides for more specialist and intensive clinical care than the level below it. In principle, patients should enter the system at the level of the clinic for an initial examination, and should then be referred upwards to the appropriate level if necessary. In practice both the weaknesses of the referral system and the lack of comprehensive hospital coverage mean that regional and central hospitals often accommodate patients who ought to be treated in hospitals at levels above or below them. This is particularly the case with formerly black hospitals because of the patchy provision of hospitals by the apartheid regime. CHB, for instance, has numerous level 1 and level 2 patients because of the lack of appropriate hospitals in its catchment area. All hospitals report to the head office of their provincial department of health, sometimes via regional offices.

The focus of this study was the bigger, more complex and specialist institutions in the system, the regional and tertiary hospitals. There are 63 regional and 14 tertiary hospitals in South Africa, and a total of some 100 000 hospital beds accounting for 60 per cent of the health budget (Dudley 2006; Heunis 2004: 502). In 1994, the newly elected government inherited a distribution of hospitals and hospital services profoundly structured by apartheid, with a fragmented health administration and a ratio in 1986 of 8.2 hospital beds per thousand white people, and 4.2 beds per thousand black people. These figures mask a further differentiation in the quality of the services set aside for different racial groups. During the late 1980s and 1990s there was a general deterioration in conditions in all public hospitals due to growing budgetary constraints and the expansion of private hospitals. Between 1980 and 1990, against an international minimum norm of 4.2 beds per thousand, the total hospital bed to population ratio in South Africa declined from 5.5 to 3.7 per thousand (Heunis 2004: 465).

The primary focus of the new government was on the redistribution of health services from wealthy urban provinces to more rural provinces, and from high-level hospital care to primary health care through the rapid establishment of clinics (Heunis 2004). While some 700 clinics have been established (*Financial Mail* 14.04.06), the impact on hospitals has been severe. Recently Treasury officials have acknowledged that spending on hospitals has been 'fairly flat' while staffing levels have declined and the effects of medical inflation have been substantial (Bateman 2006). Other researchers comment that there have in fact been real, if small, increases in the funding of hospital budgets, but that these have been spent largely on increased salaries and benefits (Boulle et al. 2000). Hospital beds have been closed in almost all provinces, with Gauteng and Western Cape losing the most – 5 000 between them (Boulle et al. 2000: 233–4). Overall staff numbers in the health sector had declined nationally from 235 000 in 1994 to 213 000 ten years later, increasing again somewhat to 225 000 currently. Again, the decrease has been felt most strongly in Gauteng and Western Cape (Bateman 2006). In the context of increased staffing for clinics, this suggests an even greater decline in hospital staff numbers.

While these policies have produced some convergence between provinces, there continue to be large inequities in hospital spending (R173–R958 per capita), bed availability (1.82–3.54 beds/1 000) and staffing (doctors 0.8–6.5/10 000). The intractability of apartheid patterns of health distribution is reflected in infant mortality rates of 11 per 100 000 for white people and 49 per 100 000 for black people (Dudley 2006). On the other hand, the redistribution of resources away from hospitals in the context of the fiscal discipline of the Growth, Employment and Redistribution strategy years has had a negative impact on the quality of hospital services and the workload of hospital staff, as our research indicates.

Indeed, the rapidity of this restructuring in the health sector may well have had a negative impact on quality at all levels. The state-funded Hospital Strategy Project, whose recommendations on hospital reform have informed government policy since it reported in 1996, warned against a too-hasty reallocation of funding to primary health care, and warned also that district and regional hospitals should be strengthened before attempting to reduce services at central hospital level to avoid undermining 'an already precarious system' (Heunis 2004: 469). These warnings have not been heeded, with consequences for the entire health system. Furthermore, such reallocation of resources presupposes that the strengthening of primary health care will take pressure off high-level hospitals, whereas more effective primary health care may in fact increase the number of hospital referrals as more people gain access to the health system.

Some may argue that a rapid redistribution of resources away from high-level hospitals is a progressive policy as the strengthening of primary health-care institutions would have far broader impacts on illness and disease. However, if the political stewards of public health wish to pursue such a policy, it is incumbent on them to make this clear to the public and shut hospitals or sections of hospitals, rather than force public health employees to work under impossible conditions as well as bear the brunt of public dissatisfaction with failing services.

Public hospitals under stress

In broad outline, our investigation indicates that public hospitals are highly stressed institutions due to staff shortages, unmanageable workloads and management failures – a finding consistent with the results of other investigations into public hospitals (Commission of Inquiry 1999; Landman et al. 2001; Schneider et al. 2005; Skuatu 2003). By 'stressed institution' we mean that institutional functioning is stressed (weak functioning, problems and breakdowns not addressed, dysfunctional management, lack of systems), staff are stressed (high workloads, stressed health, high levels of conflict, poor labour relations), and public health outcomes are poor (inadequate patient care, poor and inconsistent clinical outcomes, increased costs of poorly managed illness). Our assessment of the level of stress in each institution is based on the interviews we conducted.

There is a significant variation in the levels of stress and the way stress is managed from institution to institution. Our assessment of the degree of stress at different institutions must be regarded as tentative, given the limited number of interviews conducted at each institution. Nonetheless, certain patterns emerge. The primary factor in influencing the level of stress appears to be differentials in resource allocation and workload between institutions. A secondary factor is the varying strength of management at different institutions.

Differentials in resource allocation are captured in Table 13.1. It should be noted that tertiary hospitals are expected to be more highly resourced than regional hospitals, as level 3 patients require more intensive and specialist clinical interventions.[2]

Table 13.1 *Resource allocations at public hospitals in Gauteng, KwaZulu-Natal and North West provinces*

Hospital	Beds	Budget (R millions)	Nurses (actual)	Nurses (SE)*	Doctors (SE)	CEO (years) (actual)	Total staff (actual)	Total staff (SE) ('000)	Budget per bed	Nurses per bed	Doctors per bed	Staff per bed	Stress**
Gauteng tertiary													
CHB	2 800	922	1 804	2 388	518	3	4 690	5 400	329 (SE=0.85)	0.64	0.18	1.6 (SE=1.92)	High, crisis
Tertiary Hospital B	1 200	875	1 300	1 310	500	Acting (1)	3 500	3 700	729	1.08	0.41	2.91 (SE=3.08)	Medium
Gauteng regional													
Hospital C	780	240	680		100	10	1 450	1 559	307	0.87	0.12	1.85 (SE=1.9)	High
Hospital D	780	214	600	630	100	4	1 340	1 600	274	0.8	0.12	1.71 (SE=2)	High, crisis?
KwaZulu-Natal regional													
Hospital E	922	454	1 363	1 766	220	Acting (1) (?)	2 660 (?)	3 075	492	1.47	0.23	2.8 (SE=3.3)	Low
Hospital F	350	115	500 (actual)		70 (actual)		850		328	1.4	0.20	2.4	Medium
North West regional													
Hospital G	378	120	372	389	74 (Actual =67)	2.75	817	963	317	0.98	0,195	2.16 (SE=2.5)	High, crisis?
Hospital H	865	325	681	887	116 (Actual =81)	3	1 649	2 070	375 (SE=1.02)	0.78	0,13	1.9 (SE=2.39)	Medium – high

Notes:

*SE refers to staff establishment (official posts available).

**The assessment of stress is not directly inferred from the quantitative measures in this table, but is a qualitative assessment based on interviews and observations at the institutions.

It is noteworthy that the differences in resource allocation between the two tertiary institutions indicate the continuation of apartheid differentials: CHB is a formerly black hospital, while Hospital B is a formerly white institution. All the other hospitals studied were formerly black institutions, or amalgamations of black and white institutions, so we are unable to comment further on the persistence of apartheid inequities in budgeting. It is also noteworthy that the Gauteng hospitals generally have the lowest level of resources. The hospitals in North West province have a slightly greater level of resources, while the KwaZulu-Natal hospitals in our study have access to significantly greater resources than do those of the other two provinces.

The most stressed hospitals are those with the lowest resources per bed (CHB, Hospitals C, D, G and H). The least stressed are those with greater resources per bed, as well as with long traditions as high-quality hospitals which provides them with a kind of 'social capital' (Tertiary Hospital B, Hospital E; it should also be noted that the latter hospital is undergoing a process of bed reduction which has reduced workloads). Hospital F, while relatively well resourced, exhibits medium levels of stress because of increasing numbers of patients and management weaknesses. The North West hospitals, while somewhat better resourced than the Gauteng ones, are nonetheless highly stressed institutions. Of the highly stressed and least-resourced institutions, CHB is in crisis (that is, it is in a process of institutional decline that can only be reversed through sustained and far-reaching intervention), Hospitals D and G are highly stressed and possibly verging on crisis, and Hospital C is highly stressed but showing managerial improvement in some areas.

The differences between hospitals with relatively similar levels of resources can be attributed to the management factor – the varying capacity and depth of management between institutions, as well as the more intangible element of 'social capital' referred to above. Thus Hospitals C and H are somewhat less stressed than Hospitals D and G because of a relatively dynamic and experienced management team. In other words, where there are resource constraints the capacity to manage scarce resources (human and financial) effectively is of critical importance.

Our research indicates that hospital stress is concentrated in its most acute form in the nursing function. Nursing is the foundation of clinical and patient care, and it bears the brunt of increased patient loads, staff shortages and management failures. High levels of stress in nursing undoubtedly impact on clinical outcomes and patient care as well as on staff morale, recruitment and personal health. Indeed, the extremely high levels of stress in nursing across the majority of public hospitals amount to a crisis in this function. It is a crisis both of immediate functioning and of the long-term reproduction of nursing numbers and skills in the public sector.

In the following sections of this chapter, we disaggregate the institutional stress experienced by public hospitals, analysing in more depth the cause and nature of this stress.

Changing health environment

Much of the increasing stress faced by the public hospitals studied here may be attributed to the changing health environment in which they operate. Firstly, rapid processes of urbanisation have dramatically increased the population served by these urban hospitals. Much of the newly arrived population lives in informal settlements subject to the health hazards of poverty – a high incidence of trauma and disease. Apartheid isolated many of these problems in the bantustans. Democracy has exposed the cities to their pressures.

Secondly, the HIV/AIDS pandemic has greatly increased the pressures on hospitals. Greater numbers of patients, higher acuity levels and complications, and slower recovery rates all impact on limited resources. High mortality rates take an emotional toll on doctors and nurses (Schneider et al. 2005). The head of the internal medicine department at one of the hospitals reported an average of 150 HIV/AIDS-associated deaths per month, and commented that doctors are choosing to specialise in other areas as a result: 'No one seems to take it as a disaster. But it is like three buses crashing and wiping out their passengers *every month*. That would be a huge disaster reported in all newspapers.'

Thirdly, respondents in all of the hospitals commented that the system of referrals from primary health-care clinics fails to screen out patients who should not be arriving at level 2 or level 3 hospitals. On the one hand, many patients simply bypass clinics or district hospitals and go directly to higher-level hospitals; on the other, clinics are referring patients who should be diagnosed and treated at the clinics or at level 1 hospitals. These failures contribute directly to the pressures in the hospitals studied here. It is beyond the scope of this chapter to assess the reasons for such failure.

Interface between head offices and hospitals

Hospital management across the three provinces reported extreme frustration at the dysfunctional relationship between hospitals and provincial head offices. The latter in the three provinces (indeed, in all provinces as far as we can ascertain) has centralised control over strategic, operational and detailed issues. At the same time, the interface between hospitals and head offices is blurred and ambiguous, and control is exercised in an authoritarian and bureaucratic manner. Head offices provide little or no induction, support or mentoring for new or struggling CEOs.

Centralised control

Some examples will demonstrate just how limited the powers of hospital managers are. They have no control over staff numbers, profiles and skills mix. The staff establishment for each institution is set by the provincial head office, which lays out in minute detail the number of staff to be employed in each staff category. Management has no power to vary this in response to changing operational requirements or to meet the needs of new organisational strategies. Procedures exist for converting an unfilled post into a new post for a different job, but this is discouraged by the head office, at least in Gauteng. Complex procedures exist for converting several low-grade jobs into one new higher grade job, but this requires head office approval.

Institutional management can appoint disciplinary enquiries and investigating officers, but in Gauteng and North West can only *recommend* dismissal to head office. Lengthy delays and arbitrary decisions from head office undermine disciplinary processes in the institution, with a consequence that supervisors withdraw from attempting to discipline subordinates. In KwaZulu-Natal (and in Western Cape) the authority to dismiss has been delegated to institutions.

With regard to financial delegations, hospitals have next to no financial authority. Hospital management has little influence over budgets, which are drawn up at head office. In Gauteng, hospitals do not have a bank account or a cheque book and cannot make payments; they do not input data into the financial system or conduct transactions; nor do they play any role in procurement, or in deciding on suppliers or products (we were unable to ascertain the situation elsewhere).

Gauteng has centralised financial, human resources (HR) and procurement functions and processes in the Gauteng Shared Services Centre (GSSC), further disempowering hospital management. Hospital managers describe the GSSC as 'a failure'. Procurement often results in inappropriate or poor-quality materials and equipment, which on occasion has to be discarded, as well as lengthy delays and lack of information. HR processes such as advertising, recruitment and overtime payment suffer from innumerable delays, and data are error prone. One HR manager who had himself been deployed to the GSSC and then redeployed to his hospital described the GSSC as 'a nightmare' which requires considerable additional 'paper shuffling' at hospitals in order to accomplish anything, and commented that it is extremely difficult to face employees and explain the mistakes and delays made elsewhere.

Hospital managers' lack of control undermines management accountability. Their experience of disempowerment as a consequence of centralisation is uniform across the three provinces, despite variations of degree in certain aspects, as the following quotes from two CEOs demonstrate:

> Head office doesn't have the necessary competence to do their tasks. They are scared to give any direction. Senior people are insecure, they avoid making decisions. They don't know what's happening on the ground. We battle to retain staff, especially clinicians, who become irritable with procurement procedures and tedious motivations required by head office, and the long delays. There is also much wrong

with the way CEOs are currently selected and appointed. There needs to be a formal orientation programme followed by a mentoring period. Head office should provide an enabling environment for good budgeting but that is not what happens. Here we spend up to nine months drawing up our budget and motivation before presenting it to head office. Then they just reject it and give us what they have decided. Then when the end of the financial year approaches, there's a big rush to spend money. We are punished both ways: if we overspend and if we underspend. I am very ready for devolution. More power is precisely what is required, especially for human resources and finance.

Province just does not manage. I was appointed here as acting CEO. I had no experience, no training, but the next thing I am getting demands for quarterly reports! I complained to other more experienced managers about not getting any help out of head office. They just said, 'Welcome to the club!' I keep getting circulars or notices which are out of date. When we raise problems the district manager just notes it, saying it will be attended to. Nothing happens. Or we are asked to put our problem in writing, and if we do that nothing happens either.

Another CEO commented: 'I want real decision-making powers. Currently I make a decision, it is queried, then denied. We want head office to have confidence in us. Head office should play a supportive role and be visible to us.'

Provincial head offices operate on the assumption that they are able to manage the hospitals under their control as if they were simply administrative wings of their departments. This is quite clearly a mistaken assumption. Hospital managers describe continual management failures on the part of head offices: failure to respond to proposals, failure to make decisions, making decisions and drafting regulations that are disruptive and impose failure on hospitals, convening work-shops and developing strategies that are meaningless to hard-pressed managers. Hospital management's authority to improve operational processes and efficiency is undermined by centralised control over crucial operational systems, by centrally determined rules and by operational interference.

Ambiguous interface

Within the general framework of centralised control, it is extremely unclear where head office control ends and institutional discretion begins. Thus, hospital management claims there is very little delegation of powers, whereas provincial officials claim that there is extensive delegation. If hospital managers complain that they have insufficient delegated powers to run their institutions, they are simply told that they are wrong and that the fault is theirs.

In our experience the web of delegations and regulations creates a vast field of ambiguity where many managers are uncertain what their powers and responsibilities are, and which decisions have been made by province or by other managers in the institution. Incompetent managers make use of this ambiguity to conceal their own incompetence. As a result, the prevailing culture is to assume that most decisions have been made by provincial head offices and that it is best to accept the status quo rather than innovate.

At the same time, head office bombards management with demands for information and meetings, and for management to implement new guidelines and systems. This drains management time and energy, especially when there is very little in the way of functional support systems in any discipline at operational level. On the other hand, communications from head office are often slow and impose difficult deadlines on management, contributing to the culture of firefighting rather than focusing on longer-term strategic issues.

Autocratic control, managerial subservience

There is a tendency for provincial officials to adopt an autocratic attitude towards senior managers in the hospital and to treat them as junior employees. The lack of any insulation between hospital and head office means that hospital managements are dependent on provincial officials for the development of their careers. Hospital managers therefore fear to rock the boat, innovate and take risks, or contradict provincial officials. The consequence is that provincial officials and political heads get to hear what hospital managers believe they want to hear, rather than a frank account of what is happening in the institution and on the ground. This contributes to the failure to understand and solve delivery breakdowns, as the following example from Gauteng illustrates.

Head office in Gauteng controls the staff establishment of hospitals in detail, preventing the flexible management of recruitment, employment and promotions in order to deal with locally specific problems and needs. For example, in December 2004 a new staff establishment was introduced across Gauteng. This had a negative impact at CHB, as the new establishment assumed 1 500 beds (the projected number for the new CHB after the migration of beds to two new district hospitals still to be built) rather than the current 2 800 beds. As of the beginning of 2005, management was expected to run a 2 800-bed institution with a staff establishment appropriate for a 1 500-bed institution. Management immediately submitted an interim staff establishment in order to bridge the gap until the institution is downsized. By mid-year head office had acknowledged its error and requested a redrafted interim establishment, which again was submitted as a matter of urgency. By March 2006 there had still been no response to this, and the hospital continues to run with grossly inadequate staffing levels. The disjunction between those with authority to make decisions and those tasked with running the institution undermines accountability for decisions (or failure to make decisions).

The net effect of these dysfunctionalities is that there is no clear locus of power and decision-making authority. Hospital managers are disempowered and cannot take full accountability for the successes and failures of their institution. The structural relationship between province and institution is a disincentive for managerial innovation and responsibility, and rewards subservience, oversensitivity to rules and a lack of focus on problem solving. It is also clear that even if it were desirable for head offices to exercise this degree of control, in many cases they lack the capacity or competency to do so. The sorry saga of the new staff establishment at CHB is a case in point. Lengthy delays and poor decisions in turn encourage passivity and lack of initiative on the part of hospital managers.

The dysfunctional interface between provincial departments and hospital management suggests the need for a fundamental rethink of their respective roles and accountabilities.

Dysfunctional management structures

Hospital management structures are dysfunctional and fragmented, preventing the integrated management of operations, paralysing initiative and preventing accountability. The overall effect is pervasive disempowerment of managers and an experience of managerial vacuum on the part of staff.

The silo structure of management

The management structure of all the hospitals in our sample is essentially the same, fragmented into parallel and separate silos of managerial authority. Thus, nurses are managed within a nursing silo, doctors are managed within a silo of clinicians, and support workers are managed by a web of separate silos for cleaners, clerks and porters.

This means that what should be managed as an integrated operational unit (for example, a ward, or a clinical department) is instead managed in a fragmented fashion with no clear accountabilities. In this situation, all actors are disempowered, and oscillate between diplomacy, persuasion, negotiation, angry confrontation, complaint and withdrawal. In the process, few problems are definitively resolved, with adverse implications for patient care.

This kind of disempowerment and lack of accountability was present in most institutions we investigated, although to varying degrees. At all but one institution clinicians and nurses play no significant role in determining budget, or in monitoring and controlling costs (for the exception, see the section headed 'Improvement and Innovation' on page 334). In other words, those with responsibility for using resources have no accountability for the budget which allocates resources, while those responsible for the budget have no accountability for the activities that the budget must support.

This generates structural conflict between professional staff and managers. At CHB, clinical heads of department have no idea what their budgets are and costs are not disaggregated within the institution. At tertiary Hospital B, which is comparatively better resourced, the chief clinician interviewed for this study commented that he has no direct involvement in the budget, that a management information system for tracking expenditure against budget does not exist, that there is always a crisis towards the end of the year as management attempts to cut costs and reduce a budget overrun, and that in any case budgets are unrealistic. At none of the regional hospitals were clinical heads involved in budget processes, beyond motivating for major equipment expenditure.

In the wards themselves, nursing managers complain that, although they have responsibility for effective ward functioning, they have little control over support staff in the wards (cleaners, clerks, porters) as they are supervised by supervisors within separate silos of authority. On the other hand, nurses tend to defend their silo against interference from doctors or managers, as the following quotes illustrate:

> We are blamed for all the non-nursing things that don't get done –
> but we don't have the power to ensure that they do get done. (Nurse)

> The main snag is the other categories – their refrain is, 'I don't fall
> under a nurse.' (Nurse)

> It is very difficult to work with people who are managed from far away.
> I don't know their job. (Nurse)

> Requisitions are done by the sisters. Clerks are not allowed to order
> anything. We could do a lot of requisitions. (Ward clerk)

> The nurses have an attitude, they say you interfere too much. (CEO)

> The bridge between clinicians and nurses has broken down irrevocably.
> (Chief clinician)

Where institutional stress is somewhat lower, and managerial capacity is somewhat higher, there is more space for doctors, nurses, managers and support staff to negotiate and accommodate the fragmentation of work organisation. Where institutional stress is high, the fragmented silo structures generate the fault lines along which high levels of conflict and managerial failure are manifested.

Culture of bureaucracy and incompetence

Since there is no well-structured locus of authority and control within the institution, managers are not accountable for any particular clinical or operational outcomes. The result is that managers in one section of a hospital, for instance HR or nursing management, will make decisions according to their understanding of rules and procedures and the requirements of their own department, and ignore the disruptive impact on other departments. For example, clinicians and other medical professionals often state that HR shows no interest in filling posts, and mentioned several cases where potential employees were lost due to lengthy delays and lack of communication. As one commented, 'It is always us driving and them slowing things down.'

In a second example, nursing management issued several instructions that made it significantly more difficult for nurses to run the wards, all ostensibly with the aim of reducing costs. The actual impact, though, was to increase inefficiency as well as direct costs. Thus, overtime work was prohibited, so increasing the dependency on agency nurses. Agency nurses were only permitted to be called in on an on-the-day basis, making it impossible to plan ahead, and increasing the workload of already overstretched chief professional nurses. New nursing staff could only be recruited at entry level, thus discouraging the appointment of experienced staff and ensuring that the wards were permanently understaffed. A discussion of the impact of cost-cutting with in-charge chief professional nurses (CPNs) illustrates the impact on nurses and health care:

> CPN 1: We are instructed to organise overtime on the same day when we need it. This is very difficult and time consuming. Off-duty nurses are already committed elsewhere by then, and even if we can locate them, we cannot persuade them to rush back to work.

> CPN 2: I start the day looking for extra staff. Every time I need to make a call out of the hospital, I have to phone switchboard. It is very laborious.

> CPN 3: Ward X was out of control on Monday morning. Nurses refused to go into the ward because of the situation there.

> CPN 4: We had a recent case where the shortage caused a patient who needed turning to get bedsores. This led to complications and then the patient's death. That's an example of the consequence as it affects patients. (CHB Transformation Task Team 2004: 9)

At the same time as administrative and managerial departments generate more problems in the wards, real immediate problems in the wards remain unresolved by administrative departments. Thus, nurses complained about the many beds with broken wheels in their wards, and that nothing had happened for several months although they had submitted requests for repairs through the normal procedures. When this problem was eventually investigated by a senior manager, he found that the contractor who had been appointed to repair beds had gone out of business, and no one had seen fit to find a new contractor. Managers and professionals in the wards had no power to solve this problem, while those who did have the power had no accountability for outcomes in the wards.

It is our experience that disempowered and unaccountable management structures give rise to a specific management culture in the public hospitals. The administration of rules and regulations has become more important than managing people and operations or solving problems and ensuring decent service delivery. We have found a culture of 'management by memo'. Managers believe their task has been completed once they have communicated a change of rules or procedures by means of a memorandum. They will express genuine surprise when asked whether they have actually visited the wards or other work sites to discuss with staff the impact of the new rules on their work. As often as not, such decisions are disruptive because the managers concerned have little understanding of the work process.

Clinical processes displaced by bureaucratic processes

The specific disempowerment of clinicians displaces the clinical process from being the central concern in public hospitals, replacing it with bureaucratic, managerial or financial concerns. Clinical outcomes necessarily suffer as a consequence, and there are high levels of demoralisation amongst nurses and clinicians. This, together with the paralysis of management and absence of clear structures of authority and accountability, generates a permanent state of frustration and conflict within occupational categories, between occupational categories, within management, and between staff and management.

A general view that clinicians do not make good managers has come to predominate in the public service. In our experience this generalisation lacks any foundation. We found clinical heads to be extremely concerned about all aspects of health care – including the organisation of nursing, the movement of patients, the organisation of support services, the use of resources and budgets – and to have clear and often innovative ideas about the effective functioning of their departments. It is worth noting that clinical work is itself highly practical in nature, and that clinicians tend to take a practical view of the clinical process.

The clinical work process entails high levels of skill and complexity which it is difficult for non-clinical managers to understand fully and therefore manage effectively. The current fragmented organisational structure disempowers both clinicians and managers, and prevents either from working effectively. Management and clinical processes need to be integrated if hospitals are to be more effectively run both with respect to optimal resource utilisation and optimal clinical results.

Weak management functions

Apart from dysfunctional structures, management functions remain weak simply because they are under-resourced in virtually all institutions.

A clinical head in one of the stressed regional hospitals commented that management was highly motivated, but very understaffed: 'Those in senior positions are obliged to do hands-on work all the time instead of being free to manage.' He himself had no clerical support and was reduced to typing his own minutes, and his office was too small for him to use for meetings. At CHB managers commented that the institution is characterised by 'permanent crisis management', and clinicians commented that managers 'range across the hospital fighting fires and plugging gaps' instead of managing clinical departments and taking accountability for operational effectiveness. At institutions where management is better resourced and levels of stress are lower, management is able to ensure smoother operations and in some cases adopt a more proactive approach to improving effectiveness, although with quite limited results.

The result of weak management functions is that scarce human and financial resources are often managed in a wasteful and ineffective fashion.

Human resources management

The HR function in public hospitals is essentially a personnel function for administering the payroll, leave, recruitment, and so on. It lacks the strategic or proactive capacity to manage human resource development and labour relations, or improve the disciplinary regime. The hospitals have no skills development plans or employment equity plans. The result of these HR failures is far-reaching, affecting morale, discipline and labour relations.

Discipline appears to be a problem at most public hospitals, particularly in relation to support workers, but also amongst nurses and doctors. The fragmentation of authority structures, lack of accountability, intimidation and the disempowering effect of head office control of discipline, all contribute to this problem. Lack of discipline has a generally corrosive effect on the work ethic and morale. In the words of one enrolled nurse auxiliary:

> There are no disciplinary measures from top to bottom. If a nurse
> steals the clothes of a patient there will be no disciplinary action, they
> will give a lecture on how to conduct ourselves. But the culprit is
> known. Are we not supposed to be disciplined? Where is this
> discipline? A known habitual loafer is never disciplined.

Labour relations are also highly conflictual at several of the hospitals that we visited, particularly with the unions representing support workers. Indeed, nurses at two hospitals described the 'disruptive' growth in the power of trade unions as one of the two most significant features of post-apartheid reality in their hospitals (short-staffing was the other).

The primary reason for both of these HR problems is the absence of a strategic HR function with the capacity to establish proactively a new post-apartheid disciplinary regime appropriate for a constitutional democracy. The old apartheid disciplinary regime crumbled in the face of worker militancy and the democratic breakthrough of the early 1990s, and has not been replaced with a mutually embraced new workplace order, particularly for non-professional staff that tend to feel excluded (Von Holdt & Maseramule 2005).

HR failure is also linked to the broader low morale and frustration of staff who feel that they are not valued and have little prospect for improving their skills or advancing their careers (see Schneider et al. 2005).

It appears to us that neither provincial health departments, nor the national DoH, nor the Department of Public Service and Administration, has a progressive concept of HR strategy which focuses on the proactive management of people and relationships. Instead, the sole emphasis appears to be on the administration of centrally-designed procedures and regulations that govern employees. So, for example, the central developed performance management system is administratively complex and relies for implementation on under-capacitated personnel administrators to support overstretched managers. The result is staff demoralisation and disputes rather than enhanced performance. The critical need is to establish enhanced HR capacity at hospital level. The new HR strategic framework developed by the national DoH does not identify or address this need. Until this issue is addressed, human resources will continue to be managed ineffectively.

Financial management

Likewise, financial departments are generally grossly under-resourced and lack the capacity to draw up or monitor budgets, control costs or expenditure, or monitor shrinkage and waste. Budgets bear little relation to operational reality, and there is consensus that budgets are 'meaningless' as they are based on historical allocations rather than operational activity and realities.

In several of the hospitals management is working towards disaggregating costs and allocating them to operational units, most often wards and/or pharmacy. Although this is described as working towards 'cost centres', this is not truly the case since the fragmented management structures prevent the allocation of accountability for controlling costs. Moreover, most managements acknowledge that cost allocation and recording is still weak and partial, particularly because information systems are weak or even non-existent. In most cases, financial systems are manual rather than digital, which makes real-time cost control and financial management impossible.

Only in one hospital had a dynamic manager, who was in addition willing to bully and defy head office officials, managed to establish a working budget and cost centre-based system (see the section on 'Improvement and innovation' on page 334). In another hospital that did manage to devise an activity-based budget, this was rejected by head office and replaced with a lower budget without any negotiation over the implication for budgeted activities.

All of these limitations make cost controls, financial targets, accountability and budgeting close to impossible.

Data and information

Although the situation varies considerably between hospitals and even between clinical departments, in general weak management and systems, fragmentation and lack of capacity mean that data collection of all sorts – financial, clinical, HR – is non-existent or suspect, which, in turn, means that effective management is impossible.

This is especially the case for auditing and managing clinical outcomes, as effective quality auditing requires a combination of different sources of data that are generated in different staff silos: ratios between mortality figures (clinicians and nurses), various morbidity indices such as wound sepsis rates, bedsore rates, complications and incidents (clinicians and nurses), and patient admission numbers and length-of-stay figures (administration departments). In less stressed hospitals, clinicians may collect accurate data on clinical indices such as mortality rates and correlate these with broad administrative data such as admission numbers, but in most cases the capacity and human resources to integrate the data consistently are lacking. In addition, data collection itself is highly suspect, particularly from administration and nursing because of the workloads and stress of these functions, as illustrated in the following example:

> We ask the group of three chief professional nurses whether they are able to keep accurate records. They look at each other carefully. This is an extremely sensitive point for nurses who are legally and professionally obliged to keep good records. Then they burst out: 'Records are not up to date! We do not have time to take vital data, change dressings, keep records of incidents and mortality and morbidity conferences. We know 'what's not written is not done'. We are trying our best, but it is so difficult.'

> At the same hospital a manager worked overtime in casualty. He recalled some 30 patients coming in, but the following day he noticed that nursing records only recorded 10 patients. They had been too busy to record the missing 20. The CEO commented that they put a lot of effort into trying to reconcile data, but when in doubt simply use the data on the IT system, because that is what head office has access to.

Thus, even where *data* are collected, the transformation of this into reliable management *information* does not or cannot take place. This finding is supported by other studies. For instance, Burn and Shongwe (2004) found that in none of the 27 hospitals they surveyed was there a dataset for routine collection and presentation to the management team. They conclude that 'there is little indicator data about the hospital sector…[and] hospital management does not use information extensively' (2004: 38).

Management skills

Lack of management capacity is often conflated in our national discourse with a lack of management skills. In our view this is misleading. While there is undoubtedly a lack of management skills at many hospitals, the primary problem is the disempowerment that arises from incoherent management structures, a lack of any clear locus of managerial authority and a lack of management resources.

Simply improving skills would have no impact on the managerial crisis unless the problem of managerial structure and accountability is also addressed. As a group of hospital CEOs commented at a conference on management skills: 'You can have all the degrees you like, but it will not help you manage without adequate management authority, staff and infrastructure.' Conversely, once the problem of structure, authority and accountability is resolved, an effective programme of upgrading skills can be implemented.

There are a number of talented managers with initiative and good ideas who are currently thwarted by dysfunctional structures and their resulting disempowerment. If given the opportunity to work within functional structures, they would rapidly learn new skills and take the initiative to solve big problems.

Having said this, skills weakness remains an important problem. Several CEOs referred to the lack of induction and support programmes for hospital managers. This is also a problem affecting heads of HR and finance departments.

The problem is exacerbated by the lack of stability at senior management level. In one hospital the CEO has been in an acting position for a year, simultaneously continuing to operate in his permanent job as a head office official. In another, the nursing manager had been acting CEO for a year, simultaneously continuing to run nursing – and continuing to earn the salary of a nursing manager! Even two of the more long-standing regional hospital CEOs complained about delays in formalising their contracts. This kind of situation suggests that provincial head offices do not take the office of CEO that seriously.

Staff shortages

Staff shortages were a factor at all the public hospitals we visited (except possibly for Hospital E, where the number of beds was being substantially reduced). The most hard-hit categories are nursing, pharmacy and other specialist professionals. Nurses consistently complained of stress, exhaustion and low morale as a result of the heavy workload they have to bear. As one chief professional nurse described the situation:

> We always have to rush: we wash, we medicate, we move on. You miss some things. You cannot listen to the patient. You cannot be broad and implement things that would improve health care and staff morale. You cannot apply your knowledge and improve the unit. We also have to do inventory, push patients to other departments, clean floors, take a trolley to fetch food and dish it up, all because there is a shortage of support staff. You have to do it for the patient, nutrition is part of nursing care. We also have to do the doctor's duties while we wait for him. People resign, die, retire, and they cannot be replaced. The pressure leads to absenteeism, as nurses we become demotivated and no longer have empathy. It affects the patients. You cannot have tea, you cannot eat. At the end you suffer. You become sick. It also affects our families, we come home so irritable and so tired, and we earn peanuts!

A Democratic Nurses Organisation of South Africa representative summed up the experience of virtually all the nurses we interviewed: 'The absenteeism profile is high. Nurses are worked out, stressed out, sick.'

The nursing function is the backbone of the public hospital. The unmanageable workload, staff shortages, lack of support workers and management failures combine to place this function in a general crisis. While there is a national shortage of nurses, the crisis situation in hospitals makes it even more difficult to recruit new nursing staff. Turnover and attrition of new recruits is high, and newly trained nurses tend to leave for private hospitals where the workload is more manageable.

The reduction of the state's commitment to training new nurses and the closure and downscaling of many nursing colleges have contributed to the crisis of this function. Not only has this policy contributed to the national shortage of nurses, but it has aggravated the crisis in the wards. The old system whereby nursing colleges were integrated into the functioning of hospitals meant that there was a steady stream of student nurses contributing 'hands' to the everyday nursing of patients. Nurses who recall the old system frequently commented that the closure of colleges has had a 'disastrous' impact in the wards.

Nurses also expressed anxiety about the future of their profession. Their heavy workload and what they see as a general loss of respect by the public and the hospital community for the nursing profession make it difficult to attract a new generation of trainees. Some nurses expressed quite forcefully their view that conditions for their profession have declined with the advent of democracy:

> The biggest change since democracy is a shortage of staff.

> We really wonder – how does the government value the nurses of this country? Nurses are not happy, they are not treated as professionals.

> The way they treat us! We work like slaves, in the future there will be
> no nurses. The young ones are leaving. The government doesn't know
> anything about us and how we are working – it really hurts us.

Staff shortages do not only affect nurses. Shortages of support workers like cleaners, porters, clerks and messengers all undermine the effective functioning of the hospitals. It appears that these less-skilled functions have been regarded as less important by government authorities under pressure to reduce staff numbers and staff costs, and that these posts were significantly reduced in the staff establishment of many hospitals in the late 1990s. In hospitals where the staff establishment does have unfilled support worker posts these are in some cases unfunded, and in other cases seemingly cannot be filled because of the constraints of national collective-bargaining agreements. However, the essential role that support staff play in many hospital activities means that this is a false saving, impacting adversely on the utilisation of scarce and expensive professionals; as one hospital manager commented, the absence of porters leads to the cancellation of operations. At most hospitals it is clear that staff cannot work at full efficiency because more skilled personnel are forced to do routine and unskilled tasks due to these shortages.

For example, the shortage of nurses means that doctors have to assist each other handling patients or doing basic tasks; the shortage of nursing auxiliaries means that professional nurses have to do more routine tasks; the shortage of ward attendants means nurses have to make tea; the shortage of porters means nurses have to collect medicines from the pharmacy; and clerical shortages mean professionals have excessive administrative loads. Managers are continually firefighting and unable to focus on strategic tasks; for example, pharmacy managers find themselves packing shelves instead of managing. As one clinician put it, 'Everyone is doing the work of categories below them,' which is a wasteful use of scarce skills.

Many hospitals also experience a shortage of doctors. This is particularly acute outside the main metropolitan areas. Thus, the hospitals in North West province experience an acute shortage of specialist and experienced clinicians, and even a hospital only 50 kilometres from Johannesburg described similar problems. While we did not interview allied medical professionals at other hospitals, the figures for CHB below may be taken as indicative, as acute shortages exist in these professions.

It is difficult to quantify staff shortages at the different hospitals because little systematic work has been done to establish what a realistic staff establishment should be for each hospital, and the health department has avoided committing itself to specific staff–patient or staff–bed ratios. Thus, one is dependent on old staff establishment figures which can only be taken as broadly indicative as they do not reflect shifts in service loads over time, or on new staff establishment figures which have been arbitrarily arrived at.

For example, according to the historic staff establishment, in 2006 CHB had an overall staff shortage of 32 per cent, with individual categories as follows:

- 36 per cent shortage of nursing staff;
- 73 per cent shortage of pharmacists;
- 45 per cent shortage of allied health professionals;
- 46 per cent shortage of managers/administrators;
- 30 per cent shortage of support staff; and
- The institution is finding it increasingly difficult to recruit junior doctors.

By far the majority of the vacant posts in the staff establishment are unfunded, which means they cannot be filled because they are not funded by the budget drawn up by head office. The extreme pressure and great workloads in turn mean that the institution has found it difficult to fill even the funded vacant posts, because professionals and nursing staff are reluctant to apply for jobs at the institution, and there is a high rate of attrition. The radiology department has felt the impact of declining numbers of radiographers, down from 80 a decade ago to 55 now, when the increasing workload indicates an optimal staff level of 110. Service and morale inevitably suffer. Pharmacists experience the same problem, and estimate a 50 per cent annual turnover (CHB Transformation Task Team 2004: 8–10).

According to the new reduced staff establishment drawn up by head office, however, the staff shortage is only 13 per cent – a typically bureaucratic way of resolving the problem. According to management assessments, nursing in the surgical department is understaffed by 32 per cent, and according to an expert analysis based on a more systematic application of internationally accepted ratios based on patient acuity levels, understaffing may be as high as 42 per cent (Van der Walt 2005).

In the wards, staff have to cope with a daily crisis as staff shortages mean shuffling staff from ward to ward, or calling in agency staff, to ensure that at least a bare minimum of service can be rendered. Increasing patient numbers and increasing acuity levels are exacerbated by the nursing shortage, and the fact that young nurses leave the institution as soon as possible. The impact on their mental and physical health is acute, with consequent effects on absenteeism and sick leave.

At CHB, we found an informal bonus system in operation, as chief professional nurses and matrons paid 'thank you' money from their own pockets to ward attendants and official 'volunteers' to clear heavy bags of waste from the wards because the ward attendants were so understaffed, as well as to cleaners who put in extra effort.

Clinical/patient care outcomes

As noted in the introduction to this chapter, quantitative data on clinical outcomes such as mortality rates, wound sepsis and bedsore rates, patient recovery rates and so on are frequently unreliable, difficult to access or non-existent. We therefore have to rely on the more qualitative and subjective views of those intimately involved in clinical processes, that is, clinicians and nurses.

Nurses and clinicians note that excessive workloads have the following impacts:

- Inexperienced or underqualified staff taking responsibility beyond their scope of practice, for example an enrolled nurse rather than a professional nurse running a ward or monitoring patients on ventilators and therefore missing vital signs of deterioration in the conditions of a patient;
- Increased cases of patient complications, ensuing in more intensive nursing, greater pharmaceutical costs and greater length of stay;
- More re-admissions because patients are discharged before they have fully recovered;
- Greater risk of infection because of poor infection control, sometimes due to workload and sometimes to management failures such as absence of proper procedures or lack of washing liquid, failure to maintain plumbing, electrical and other infrastructure, and so on;
- Poor patient recovery because of lack of essential drug stocks;
- Lengthy delays before treatment, increasing the risk of morbidity and mortality.

The comments of two clinical heads in regional hospitals are instructive. Both were clearly dynamic leaders who had spearheaded improvements in their respective clinical departments. One had been appointed head of department for two years, and commented that 'preventable deaths have been reduced from a period when mortality was a daily matter'. Whereas previously, for example, some 80–90 per cent of diabetes admissions resulted in death, these had now been reduced below the accepted average of 5 per cent. Nonetheless, he rates the health service provided by his department as '60 per cent of what it should be, up from 40 per cent in the 1990s'. The second clinician had only been appointed head of department for a few months, but observed that morbidity and mortality incidents were down from 45–50 per month to 1–3 per month. It can be assumed that many other clinical departments continue to languish with unacceptably poor levels of health care, as did these departments prior to their interventions.

While many staff show outstanding commitment to working under difficult conditions, and there are clearly pockets of high-quality health care, the high levels of stress in most public hospitals cannot but impact on morbidity and mortality outcomes. Health-care failures, such as lost patients or outbreaks of infection and infant deaths due to the breakdown of infection control procedures, will continue to occur under these conditions, as the following quotes from nurses interviewed illustrate:

> We do not give quality patient care...I am alone in the ward...
> With the correct level of staffing we could get a 60 per cent
> improvement in patient care.

We have had cases of wound sepsis because we had nothing to wash our hands with. You get cross-infection, you have to use more anti-biotics, the patient has to stay longer in hospital.

Shortages definitely affect patient care. You have an enrolled nurse in ICU, she does not fully understand, she does not notice ventilator problems until it alarms and the patient is in crisis. You are supposed to be transfusing a patient but you delay because you are receiving another patient from theatre who also needs blood, and so you get complications.

It is little wonder that a recent survey of public opinion of government services found that hospitals were rated the worst of all public services, with only 10 per cent of respondents trusting hospitals (compared to 18 per cent who trust their local police force) and 12 per cent respecting hospitals and their staff (Bateman 2006).

Improvement and innovation

Despite the stressed nature of the institutions we investigated, we did come across several cases of sustained attempts to improve hospital functioning, as well as cases of innovation. It is worth reflecting on the conditions that have made such improvement or innovation possible. We reflect here on four cases: the CHB transformation project; a clinical networking of level 1, level 2 and level 3 hospitals; and two examples of management attempts to improve functioning in regional hospitals.

CHB transformation project

This project aims to pilot integrated management structures, enhanced management capacity and empowerment in the surgical division (700 beds) at the hospital, with the aim of improving clinical care and resource utilisation. This consists of a systematic attempt to reconfigure the head office/institution interface, devolve significant powers to local management, break the silo system and integrate nursing, systems, financial and clinical management under the leadership of the chief clinician, and identify clear chains of accountability and command. It also aims to address staff shortages, improve discipline, establish teamwork and worker participation processes. The project has been under way since early 2005, and is fully supported by management, labour, and head office.

Critical factors for the successful implementation of this innovation, in what is the most highly stressed hospital we have encountered, have been: political support from trade unions and from the MEC for health, and the availability of external resources in terms of high-level expertise in order to supplement low levels of management capacity.

Since this project constitutes a new way of working, it challenges many of the traditional bureaucratic practices and constraints identified in this chapter. These continue to exert an ongoing constraining effect and even threaten to paralyse critical aspects of the project. Nonetheless, important learning is taking place which could have a wide applicability.

Networking of level 1, 2, and 3 beds

The chief clinician who heads one of the clinical departments at the second tertiary institution investigated for the study has put in place an innovative strategy for shifting level 1 and level 2 patients who inevitably (because of failures in the referral systems) end up in tertiary beds by networking with a nearby district hospital and a nearby regional hospital. He allocates part of his budget to expanding the number of (considerably cheaper) level 1 and 2 beds in these institutions, freeing up level 3 beds at his own institution. Clinicians from his department are involved in clinical work and clinical supervision in the other two institutions. They also work closely with the nurses and clinicians in the two institutions, empowering them to make important decisions concerning levels of health care and referral. This project entails an efficient use of scarce human and financial resources, and allows for a much more effective management of health-care needs of different levels of patients.

This has been possible because of good relations between an innovative clinician and a hospital CEO who had been given a mandate to innovate and who was prepared to 'bend the rules and regulations' to make things happen. The existence of considerable 'social capital' assets at the institution has also been a help. Co-ordination across the three institutions depends on the ability of the chief clinician to conduct multiple negotiations with three different CEOs. The logical next step would be to put in place a co-ordinated management structure for the three institutions, but this would require innovation at the level of the provincial bureaucracy.

Unfortunately, frustration at the constraints of centralisation (as detailed in this chapter) eventually led to the resignation of the CEO.

Two cases of sustained management improvement in regional hospitals

In two of the regional hospitals we investigated, we encountered CEOs who had managed to implement sustained improvements in hospital functioning. In both cases, the CEOs had improved financial management and were able to move towards internal budgeting processes. They had also improved the relationship between managers and clinicians by improving the ability of managers to respond to the needs of the clinicians. In the second of these two hospitals, real cost accounting had been introduced into the wards, and the unit manager we interviewed was impressive in describing how she takes responsibility for managing the budget, planning expenditure and monitoring costs. The clinical head of department interviewed at this institution had greater knowledge and awareness of his budget and costs, but did not directly manage the budget.

In both cases, the CEOs were innovative and had managed to establish strong management teams. The first CEO had been in place for ten years, the second for three years. The latter was a strong leader with wide government experience and networks, and he had no qualms in confronting provincial officials and breaking the rules where necessary; as he put it, 'Rules are not more important than delivery'. Thus, he installed his own financial software and found the expertise locally to make it work, rather than relying on provincial officials. He also described a method for increasing his decision-making ability and circumventing head office constraints: he would write a letter to the relevant official, outlining the reasons for his decision and stating that he assumed he could go ahead and implement unless he was instructed otherwise within two weeks. Invariably there would be no response and he went ahead.

In these two hospitals strong, confident and innovative managers were able to improve functioning. Nonetheless, institutional stress remains high because of staff shortages and because of the ongoing frustration and disempowerment caused by centralisation. These indicate the limits of improvement within the current functioning of provincial departments. Improvement relies on exceptional managers who have had to engage in protracted battles to carve out areas of discretion and control. Neither constitutes an example of systematic restructuring of relations and redistribution of power, which is the goal at CHB.

Conclusion

In all the cases discussed, innovation and improvement were dependent either on informally bending and breaking the regulations that govern the functioning of public hospitals, or on agreement to waive the application of these regulations. This informal approach is not a viable way forward as it relies on exceptional individuals and can easily be reversed. The future of innovation and improvement in public hospitals depends on a substantial change to the regulatory framework and its details.

The high level of institutional stress in public hospitals is the product of two distinct pressures coming from opposite directions. On the one hand, there is the managerial paralysis and disempowerment that follows from the lack of a clear locus of managerial authority and accountability at all levels, which is in turn the outcome of excessive centralisation, dysfunctional management structures and understaffed managerial functions. On the other hand, there is the pressure of work overload, physical and psychological stress, inefficiency and clinical failure caused by understaffing. When managerial paralysis and inefficiency is combined with the daily operational crisis of excessive workload, the result is ongoing institutional stress and compromised health-care outcomes. If this situation is allowed to continue, a long-term erosion of the public service ethos and consequent decline of the public health sector is likely, as the older generation of public service professionals retire, or give up, in despair, and the younger generation is so overwhelmed by workloads that they opt for the private sector.

Recent comments by government officials suggest a belated recognition that underfunding and staff shortages are eroding the functioning of public hospitals. A Treasury official stated that in the current expansionary fiscal climate 'all provincial budgets should be increasing in real per capita terms, a major change from past practice' when better-off provinces were subjected to cuts (Bateman 2006: 168). The director-general of health has announced that the department plans to employ 30 000 additional staff (Mseleku 2006), and hospital managers in Gauteng have been told that the province will be employing 8 000 additional staff over the next three years.

These measures have the potential to improve public hospital functioning. However, deep-seated management failure in the public hospitals suggests that the structural determinants of managerial paralysis and disempowerment will need to be addressed if sustained improvement is to take place. The evidence suggests that neither tinkering with regulations nor establishing new training programmes for hospital managers, will improve the functioning of our public hospitals. Substantial structural reform is necessary if the long-term decline of public hospitals is to be avoided.

Current government policy, in the form of the Hospital Revitalisation Programme, focuses not on these problems, but on a multimillion bricks-and-mortar programme to renovate, re-equip and rebuild hospitals, as well as build new hospitals. Important as this is, the problems of organisation, personnel and systems lie at the root of current dysfunctionality and addressing these issues is crucial for improving hospital performance.

Reversing the decline of public hospitals and improving health-care outcomes requires a far-reaching restructuring of the relationship between provincial head offices and public hospitals, and a substantial empowering of institutional management and enhancement of their capacity, as well as innovative strategies to improve staffing levels. In an environment of scarce financial and human resources, it is all the more important to focus on a sustained investment in management capability so that these resources are managed in as effective a way as possible.

It is not as if government is unaware of these issues. Indeed, decentralisation and the modernisation of management structures was a key recommendation of the Hospital Strategy Project in 1996 and became a central plank of government health policy (DoH 2000; Heunis 2004). Why then has it not been implemented? Health department officials undoubtedly fear that hospital managers lack the capacity to take on additional responsibilities (Heunis 2004). The adoption of crisis measures to contain spending reinforced departmental anxiety to retain centralised control (Boulle et al. 2000).

But there are deeper reasons, embedded in the structure and nature of government departments. Bureaucratic inertia, incompetence, the fear of disruption and the loss of control, and insufficient political will have probably all played a role in preventing the implementation of a decentralisation policy. A similar finding has been made in relation to the failure to decentralise authority for district health care from provincial departments to local government: 'translating policy statements into decentralised practices within the health sector has been hard because the environment has been characterised by uncertainty, opposition and rigidity' (Local Government and Health Consortium 2004: 9). Bureaucratic inertia caused by the fragmentation and dispersion of decision-making and accountability structures and the pervasive constraint of complex and drawn-out rules and procedures, as well as the sheer scale of many state institutions such as the departments of health, may make them relatively impervious to new policies and attempts to introduce change. The accumulated weight of existing practices and procedures, together with embedded hierarchies that institutionalise a specific distribution of power and privilege, tend to overwhelm processes of rational policy debate and the implementation of new policy. Over the past few years we have witnessed much resistance of this sort in the CHB transformation project.

In 2005, Naledi was commissioned to draft a report and recommendations based on the research described in this chapter, for the Department of Public Service and Administration, to be forwarded to the January Cabinet *lekgotla*.[4] Key recommendations, the first two of which are almost exact replicas of the Hospital Strategy Project recommendations, included that:

- Full management authority should be devolved to hospitals, while provincial head offices should concentrate on auditing hospital performance in relation to clinical, patient care and financial targets and indicators, as well as developing broad strategy and policy;
- Management should have the autonomy to manage their hospitals without interference from provincial head offices, according to the budget and business plan and performance targets agreed between head office and institution, and should be fully accountable for this;
- Given the national shortage of professional nurses, a new staffing model should be developed which requires a smaller number of professional nurses to supervise the tasks of less skilled nurses (enrolled nurses and enrolled nursing assistants), as well as expanding the numbers and responsibilities of support workers in order to relieve nurses of unnecessary clerical, routine and cleaning functions;

- The programme to reopen nursing colleges should be accelerated, and they should be reintegrated with hospitals so as to simultaneously provide training and meet the needs for additional nurses in the wards.

These recommendations were accepted by Cabinet, and in his 'State of the Nation' address to Parliament, President Mbeki (2006) stated that the devolution of management authority to hospitals would take place.

What are the prospects for implementation this time around? Factors such as bureaucratic inertia that have prevented the implementation of these policies previously, are still in play. Nor should the scale of the task be underestimated. Breaking up the massive and dysfunctional bureaucracy, and redistributing powers, functions and capabilities from the centre to the hospitals, while at the same time establishing new functions and capacities both at the centre and within hospitals, will constitute a gargantuan task.

In this context it is probably only through the construction of a powerful constellation of decision-makers and interests in a new 'policy juggernaut'[3] that the restructuring of health departments to facilitate the relative autonomy of hospitals is likely to become a reality. It remains to be seen whether a sufficiently powerful policy juggernaut can be assembled to undertake the massive task of restructuring the public health sector bureaucracy. This would require the backing of powerful agents within the state and probably also involve agents outside the state. A key question would be what role Treasury would play since restructuring certainly has financial implications. Trade unions, the vast majority of citizens who depend on the public health system, community organisations, health sector policy and advocacy groups, and forces within the private health-care sector, all have a stake in the outcome. Whether these different forces adopt a passive or active stance on hospital reform, and whether their actions contribute to the formation of a new policy juggernaut or its paralysis, will affect whether the latest policy statement remains a paper tiger or has some prospect of being implemented.

Afterword

As this volume was going to press, the newly appointed MEC for Health in Gauteng, Brian Hlongwa, announced that Gauteng was taking up President Mbeki's call for the delegation of responsibilities to the managers of hospitals, starting with CHB. As of mid-July, the CEO would have the powers to hire and fire staff, control his own budget and manage the procurement of goods and services (*Business Day* 11.07.06). Perhaps the policy juggernaut is beginning to emerge.

Notes

1   We would like to thank Prof. Martin Smith, Head of the Surgical Division at Chris Hani
    Baragwanath Hospital, and Naledi team members, Dr Colin Eisenstein, Bethuel
    Maseramule, and Sandi Baker for their contributions to this chapter, to the research
    process on which it is based, and to the conceptual framework that underpins it.
    We also thank Prof. Helen Schneider for comments and help with sources. Interviews were
    conducted on the basis of confidentiality, so neither our interviewees nor the hospitals
    they work in can be identified.

2   Cost per patient per day was calculated at R984 at regional hospitals and R1 637 at tertiary
    hospitals in 2003/04 <www.hst.org.za>.

3   This term, defined as ' a dense cluster of institutional, personal and economic interests
    which coalesces around a particular policy decision or set of decisions', was first used to
    describe government's privatisation strategy for Spoornet, the state-owned rail freight
    company (Von Holdt 2005).

4   *Lekgotla* (Sotho): meeting of clan or tribal elders presided over by the chief; in modern
    usage refers to a strategic retreat.

References

Bateman C (2006) Lack of capacity devitalising SA's hospitals. *SA Medical Journal*, 96(3):
    168–70.

Boulle A, Blecher M & Burn A (2000) Hospital restructuring. In A Ntuli (Ed) *SA Health
    Review 2000*. Durban: Health Systems Trust.

Burn A & Shongwe G (2004) Development and use of indicators in hospital service
    management. In P Ijumba, C Day & A Ntuli (Eds) *SA Health Review 2003/4*. Durban:
    Health Systems Trust.

CHB Transformation Task Team (2004) *Chris Hani Baragwanath Hospital: Situation analysis*.
    Johannesburg: Chris Hani Baragwanath Hospital.

Commission of Inquiry (1999) *Report by the Commission of Inquiry into Hospital Care
    Practices*. Available at <http://www.polity.org.za/html/govdocs/
    commissions/1999/hospital-care-sep99a.pdf>.

DoH (Department of Health) (2000) *Health sector strategic framework 2000–2004: Accelerating
    quality health service delivery*. Pretoria: DoH.

Dudley L (2006) Address to the NEHAWU Public Service Delivery Summit, 21–22 April,
    Johannesburg.

Heunis JC (2004) Hospitals and hospital reform in South Africa. In HCJ van Rensburg (Ed)
    Health and healthcare in South Africa. Pretoria: Van Schaik Publishers.

Landman WA, Mouton J & Nevhutalu KH (2001) *Chris Hani Baragwanath Hospital ethics
    audit*. Research Report No. 2. Pretoria: Ethics Institute of South Africa.

Local Government and Health Consortium (2004) *Decentralising health services in South
    Africa: constraints and opportunities: a summary*. Durban: Health Systems Trust.

Mbeki T (2006) State of the Nation Address of the President of South Africa, Thabo Mbeki. Joint Sitting of Parliament, 3 February.

Mseleku T (2006) Address to the NEHAWU Public Sector Service Delivery Summit, 21–22 April, Johannesburg.

Schneider H, Oyedele S & Dlamini N (2005) HIV impact surveillance system: Burnout and associated factors in health professionals in four hospitals. Unpublished paper. Wits School of Public Health/Gauteng Department of Health.

Skuatu (2003) Public Health and Welfare Sectoral Bargaining Council – Climate survey management of HIV/AIDS and labour relations in the public health and welfare sector. Unpublished report submitted to the Public Health and Welfare Sectoral Bargaining Council.

Van der Walt (2005) Chris Hani Baragwanath Hospital: Situational analysis of the nursing division. Consultant's report.

Von Holdt K (2005) Saving government from itself: Trade union engagement with the restructuring of Spoornet. In E Webster & K von Holdt (Eds) *Beyond the apartheid workplace: Studies in transition*. Scottsville: University of KwaZulu-Natal Press.

Von Holdt K & Maseramule B (2005) After apartheid: Decay or reconstruction in a public hospital? In E Webster & K von Holdt (Eds) *Beyond the apartheid workplace: Studies in transition*. Scottsville: University of KwaZulu-Natal Press.

Part III: Society

Society: introduction

Jessica Lutchman

The six chapters in this volume's society section focus on issues currently in the public domain – the integration into civilian life of apartheid-era combatants, the state of South Africa's prisons as well as of its churches, the vexed question of transforming the racial profile of our rugby, the epidemic of violence directed against South African women, and finally, the complicated issue of assessing the achievements of our schoolgoing learners. Each of these issues serves as a yardstick for assessing where South African society is going – forwards in terms of social upliftment or backwards in terms of societal degeneration, or both or somewhere in-between? The factor of 'crisis' characterised a majority of the chapters in the society section in last year's volume. This year again four of the chapters contain overtones of crisis while two point to positive forward-moving development. So, here again in this section we find the mix of development and dysfunctionality discussed by Roger Southall in the overall introduction to this volume.

Once considered by many as heroic figures, some of South Africa's former anti-apartheid combatants now exist on the margins of post-apartheid society. The reintegration of these one-time guerilla fighters into civilian society is the focus of Lephophotho 'Pops' Mashike's chapter. He focuses on the state's multi-pronged demobilisation programme and the extent to which it succeeded in its reintegration objective. Unsurprisingly, the picture he paints is a mixed one. A 2003 survey of some 400 plus ex-Umkhonto we Sizwe (MK) and Azanian People's Liberation Army combatants found nearly 60 per cent without work due to such factors as a lack of education and skills, no personal contacts with influential individuals, and scarce job opportunities. On the other hand, Mashike tells us of a number of ex-guerilla success stories from the worlds of business (Tokyo Sexwale, Mzi Khumalo and Papi Kubu, to name only three), politics and diplomacy.

On a darker level, Mashike discusses cases where the one-time fighters have drawn on their combat skills to pursue lives of crime and banditry. The case of Collin Chauke and his cash-in-transit robbers is cited in this regard. While referring to instances of protest action by ex-combatants, Mashike argues that for the present the loyalty of ex-MK operatives towards the ANC government is largely undiminished. Overall, Mashike concludes that the only partial reintegration of former fighters into society is not due solely to some of the programmes failing; there are also contributory factors stemming from the combatants themselves, such as a culture of dependency on the part of some, often combined with a sense of entitlement to such things as employment and housing.

By contrast to Mashike's mixed picture, Professor Julia Sloth-Nielsen's chapter on the state of South Africa's prisons presents a picture of disarray, a patient that is 'critically if not terminally ill'. At the core of the many ills besetting the Department of Correctional Services (DCS) is that of 'overcrowding'. According to Sloth-Nielsen, South Africa's per capita incarceration rate is the highest in Africa, a situation which only compounds the irony in the fact that as South Africa has democratised since 1994, its prison population has risen dramatically.

Sloth-Nielsen also highlights the changes to South Africa's prisoner profile since 1994, the most significant of which is the fact that a rising proportion of prisoners are now incarcerated for violent offences in contrast to the situation under apartheid, where they were serving sentences for such economic offences as shoplifting, theft and burglary. There are also now more long-term prisoners seeing out sentences of ten years or more. These factors, the author suggests, stem from society's backlash to the wave of post-apartheid violent crime, Parliament's laying down of minimum sentences for certain offences and the imposition by magistrates of unreasonable bail conditions. The result is that fully a quarter of all those being held in South Africa's prisons are awaiting trial for periods of time which probably amount to a violation of their constitutional rights. Overcrowding, Sloth-Nielsen argues, also affects negatively the constitutional rights of prisoners in a range of other ways, including their access to health care (and particularly antiretroviral treatment), as well as their rights to dignity, and educational and rehabilitative services. The challenge of overcrowding is further compounded by inadequate training of staff personnel, instability and inefficiency at the management level, and corruption.

In all this doom and gloom, Sloth-Nielsen discerns a glimmer of light in the form of the 2005 *White Paper on Corrections* which, she suggests, succeeds in 'setting the new parameters of a new vision'. It shifts the dominant DCS view of the 1990s from facilities and architecture to human resources and people-centred development. Secondly, it sets rehabilitation as the central objective of imprisonment. Yet many have expressed scepticism about this new vision, suggesting that 'the language and the philosophy…could be dismissed as mere window dressing, a desperate attempt by leadership to dispel the widely held notion that Correctional Services is rotten to the core'.

As a follow-up to our sports focus in last year's volume (see the chapter by Merryman Kunene on soccer), Ashwin Desai and Zayn Nabbi undertake an intriguing analysis of the transformation issue in South African rugby. Making clever use of the 'truck and trailer' analogy, they suggest that within the world of South African rugby 'all is not well'. In rugby, 'for a truck and trailer to be effective…the entire loose maul must be in tandem, must be connected and bound to each other'. But, in its present state, they argue that there is a great disjuncture between rugby at the national and domestic levels and that the issue of race has become far more pronounced in the game since 1994. They reach this conclusion by surveying representation at the national level and by evaluating the effectiveness of rugby administrations in carrying out development programmes for black players. These points are then illustrated by a case study of the Jaguars, a predominantly black rugby club in Sydenham, which was once a coloured group area in Durban.

According to the authors, the introduction of the quota system has been a mixed blessing. While it has undoubtedly created opportunities for black players, it has also made it difficult for them to establish themselves as worthy national representatives. Instead, it tends to challenge their credibility and capability as rugby players. This is not to say that there have not been successful and worthy black players in the national team. Chester Williams, Breyton Paulse and Brian Habana – all wings – are or have been world-class players. But too many other black players who have made the national team find themselves increasingly typecast as 'quota players' or 'speedsters out on the wing'.

Perhaps more pertinent in terms of the growth of the game amongst black South Africans is the tendency of provincial selectors to raid or 'poach' the playing personnel of any black club that comes to the fore. This has certainly been the case for the Jaguars in KwaZulu-Natal where it has in recent seasons yielded the bulk of black players to meet the quota allocations of not only the senior provincial team, the Sharks, but also of the reserve Wildebeeste team, and the age-group teams like the under-21s. The consequence is that week after week the Jaguars field sub-par teams in club contests which blunts their challenge for championship trophies. In short, the authors argue, the quota system can hurt the very teams it was designed to help.

Part of the responsibility for this less than satisfactory situation the authors attribute to the black administrators, too many of whom they suggest simply fit into the system and lack the courage to bring about effective transformation. Moreover, rugby and government officials have found themselves embroiled in a game of 'pass the buck'. As the authors put it, 'the rugby officials pass the ball to the politicians, they in turn look to the private sector, who look to the disadvantaged areas and see no market for their goods. And so the intricate patterns are weaved across the field but there is no one taking the ball beyond the gain line into disadvantaged areas'. Essentially, the authors argue, a lack of support from government and national rugby institutions could spell a halt to the development of 'what is left of amateur club rugby in black areas'.

Gender equality is another issue that has secured an important space in each of the previous *State of the Nation* publications. These chapters have examined the political and social successes and challenges facing women in the advancement of gender equality. In this volume, Lisa Vetten examines the effectiveness of enabling frameworks 'put in place by the state to address the issue of violence against women'. Taking into account the president's 2006 'State of the Nation' speech and reviewing Jacob Zuma's rape trial, the author argues that some commentators on gender equality view the post-apartheid state as contradictory: 'a woman-friendly state with its vision and plans for the achievement of gender equality – including a constitutional commitment to such equality and some of the highest numbers in the world of women holding office – yet marked by intractable persistence of violence against women.' The author argues that this state of affairs represents not so much a contradiction as an illustration of the contingent, conditional, and contested nature of gender equality in South Africa.

Vetten demonstrates that state responses to violence have been primarily confined to the criminal justice system and the Department of Social Development, thus framing violence against women as a problem of crime and welfare. Such systems are concerned with the consequences of violence and ignore its root causes. Using the example of the Domestic Violence Act (DVA), Vetten shows how factors like negative attitudes towards complainants, unreliable, outdated or non-existant data on domestic violence, under-resourcing of courts and police stations, and the under-prioritisation of the DVA in the police budget all undermine the implementation of this framework. Vetten uses two prominent scenarios – the anti-rape Charlize Theron advertisement run some years back in the media, and the Charlene Smith–President Mbeki controversy over rape statistics – to highlight an important fact, namely, that the history of sexual violence has culminated in a 'long and ugly relationship between rape and race'. More often than not, public outrage towards rape has been underpinned by racism. The author argues that these debates should make us mindful that in order to eradicate rape, we need to 'begin exploring the complex interactions…between race, gender and economic marginalisation in individual men's and women's lives' instead of treating them as 'separate, compartmentalised discriminations'. Vetten also uses the Zuma trial to drive home the point that despite positive state interventions regarding gender equality, sections of the populace remain resistant 'to discourse and practices intended to promote women's rights'. If anything, 'legal reasoning in this matter has reinstated a host of anti-women sentiments'.

On a more positive note, Anthony Egan assesses the attempts of South Africa's churches since apartheid to adapt to 'a new, more secular, yet ultimately more equal and just democratic political culture'. He focuses on three main areas – the overall demographic state of the churches after 1994; their responses to the challenges of reconciliation, HIV/AIDS and poverty; and (using brief case studies) three religious forms of response to politics and church–state relations in general: withdrawal, opposition and critical co-operative engagement – to illustrate the transition of churches into the new democracy.

In terms of demographics (utilising statistics from Census 1996 and Census 2001), Egan notes that religion is not 'dying' in the new South Africa and that Christianity in particular is not in decline. If anything, there seem to be religious realignments amongst Christians. He notes that the relatively new so-called African Initiated Churches (AICs) are now the single largest category of churches in South Africa (32.6 per cent of the population in 2001) and, even more significantly, the AICs combined with the so-called 'Pentecostal/Charismatic' and 'Other Churches' now constitute the 'mainline' churches in contemporary South Africa, and not the established Anglican, Methodist and Catholic church groupings. In short, what Egan is saying is that most Christians in South Africa are now black and they belong to black and comparatively young churches and not to the old mainline churches with their roots deep in South Africa's colonial past and to whom most white South African Christians belong.

Egan goes on to argue that the post-apartheid church in South Africa has had the support of the public in its confronting of issues such as reconciliation, HIV/AIDS and poverty. He suggests that churches in general played an important role in the Truth and Reconciliation Commission process by helping victims and perpetrators come to terms with the horrors of the past. Many churches have also been instrumental in supporting grassroots movements and lobbying government on issues related to poverty and socio-economic equality. On the issue of HIV/AIDS, while many churches have played a role in challenging prejudices against those facing the dreaded disease, there are, Egan suggests, still some churches which find the issue problematic. He argues that instead of engaging in dialogue with new values the churches tend to hold fast to traditional sexual morality.

In terms of church–state relations and the political arena in general, Egan suggests that the post-apartheid church has displayed a range of behaviours including patterns of withdrawal, critical co-operation and outright opposition. Some of the newer churches, he argues, have eschewed politics to focus on worship, material gain, personal ethics, and healing. The archetype here is the Rhema Church, a hi-tech group that refrains from engaging with the state and rather concentrates on a socially conservative commitment to 'biblical values'.

Egan cites the case of the African Christian Democratic Party to illustrate politico-religious opposition to the new social order. It is, however, a marginal political force having grown from 0.5 per cent of the vote in 1994 to only 1.6 per cent in 2004. While this is not enough to threaten the government, Egan nonetheless suggests that it illustrates the fact that there is a small portion of the Christian population in favour of a 'constitutional state that promotes Christian moral values and rejects the concept of South Africa as a secular state'.

In the overall introduction to the volume, Roger Southall points out that 'while the government has made strides towards the allocation of educational resources on far more equitable terms, the output in terms of improved learner outcomes remains extremely poor'. Anil Kanjee's chapter on learner achievement in schools demonstrates this assertion. In his view, South Africa is extremely 'data rich' but very 'information poor' on issues affecting learner achievement. He argues that 'the provision of relevant and timeous information to policy-makers and other educational role-players, especially teachers, to effect appropriate change has been a long and slow process'.

By reviewing national assessments such as the Monitoring Learning Achievement (1999), the Grade 3 Systemic Evaluation (2001) and the Grade 6 Systemic Evaluation (2004), the author notes a number of shortcomings related to methodology and design as well as the impact on policy and practice. To a certain extent, information from national assessments has assisted in identifying how learning occurs and understanding what learners know and can do. But too much emphasis has been placed on quantitative data and valid qualitative data has not as yet become a feature of these assessments. To Kanjee, 'qualitative information is vital to obtain a detailed understanding of the specific nuances that define how role-players function within the complex structures and process of the education system'. The chapter points out that no analysis is undertaken on issues such as poverty, race, the capabilities of teachers to undertake their tasks, or the contributions of schools to learner education. These are factors that impact tremendously on learner education and urgently need to be analysed.

Kanjee also acknowledges that 'tenuous links exist between research and practice'. He argues for a 'coherent, strategic and unambiguous national policy on the use of information from national assessment studies'. More often than not, information gathered from these studies is never relayed to the critical institutions like schools so that they can affect change. Kanjee argues for a central database to house the various national assessments that could be made available to important stakeholders. National assessment in South Africa is a fairly 'new phenomenon', but it is imperative that co-ordinated efforts are made to make results relevant to policy in order to effect change in the education sector.

Each of the chapters in this section gives meaning to Mahatma Gandhi's dictum that 'the measure of society is the way in which it treats its lowest member'. Given the plight of some ex-combatants and most if not all prison detainees and the inequalities of race and gender illustrated in the relevant chapters, it could be argued that for many South Africans upward social transformation is proving to be elusive. South African society is vocal on issues of race and gender inequality, yet in practice society tends still to reinforce these very inequalities. There are positive signs as expressed in the chapter on churches but it will take more than the churches to deliver a more just and cohesive society in South Africa.

14 'Some of us know nothing except military skills': South Africa's former guerrilla combatants

Lephophotho Mashike

Throughout Africa, the military has been a major obstacle to achieving democracy and development. In some countries, even when there have been formal cease-fires following armed conflict, peace has often been short-lived and democracy ever elusive. Any transition to peace and democracy depends in part on a process of demilitarisation. The successful and effective demobilisation, disarmament and reintegration into civilian society of former combatants are important components of this process – 'demobilisation' being a shorthand term for the multistaged process of converting a soldier into a civilian. This encompasses the voluntary departure or discharge of soldiers from a statutory force or guerrilla group and their reintegration into civilian society (Mashike 2005). Reintegration is defined as 'the process of facilitating the ex-soldiers' transition to civilian life' (Clark 1995: 50). This chapter focuses on the reintegration of former guerrilla combatants belonging to the Azanian People's Liberation Army (Apla) and Umkhonto we Sizwe (MK) – the armed movements of the Pan Africanist Congress (PAC) and the African National Congress (ANC) respectively – into civilian society during South Africa's transition to democracy.

There were some irregular groups that took part in the armed struggle on the side of the South African government such as the 32 Battalion. The battalion was a counter-insurgency unit of the South African Defence Force (SADF) comprised mainly of former FNLA (*Frente Nacional de Libertação de Angola* or National Front for the Liberation of Angola) and other anti-communist fighters from Angola who had sworn allegiance to the South African government. According to its proponents, 'these troops forged a formidable battalion that became known as one of the best operational units of the SADF – if not in the world'.[1]

However, the concern of this chapter is with former guerrilla combatants belonging to the forces of the liberation movements for three reasons. First, whether or not those who joined Apla or MK did so out of political circumstance or political commitment, they all sacrificed their education and opportunities to earn a living and enjoy normal family life for several years in order to liberate their country and improve the prospects of their compatriots. As South Africa celebrates 12 years of democracy it is therefore appropriate to examine the extent to which they have been able to reintegrate into civilian society.

Second, experiences from neighbouring post-conflict societies such as Mozambique, Namibia and Zimbabwe indicate that even when guerrilla combatants possess skills, reintegration is made difficult by other factors. Former combatants tend to have little or no experience in the labour market, having taken up arms at an early age. They also tend to have an imperfect understanding of the state of the economy. Consequently, former combatants often have unrealistic assumptions about civilian life and require a period of adjustment to assess their personal situation and opportunities. These characteristics are particularly relevant for former foot soldiers, whose opportunities for educational and personal advancement were more limited than those of the officer corps (Ball 1997).

Third, former guerrilla combatants remain in coherent groups for years, with the ability to mobilise around a set of grievances. This has been indicated most dramatically in Zimbabwe, where in September 1997 the War Veterans' Association forced their way into the presidential palace and forced Robert Mugabe to concede a once-off gratuity of Z$50 000 and a tax-free monthly pension of Z$2 000 (later Z$5 000), a move which is judged to have precipitated the government's forced seizure of white farms and the country's subsequent economic meltdown (Moore 2001: 262–3). In general, it is the lack of adequate assistance enabling them to reintegrate into society that is the main source of combatants' grievances. Furthermore, in 'the medium and long term, incomplete or ineffective reintegration of former combatants into civil society may lead to armed criminality by those former soldiers who have no other means of earning a living' (UN 2000: 16).

Effective reintegration refers to the implementation of a programme that meets the immediate and basic needs of former combatants and empowers the recipients to become self-sufficient in the long term. In this sense, a reintegration package is adequate only if it ensures sustained self-sufficiency. For example, in 1980 demobilised soldiers in Zimbabwe received different forms of assistance. However, by 1988, it was estimated that between 15 000 and 25 000 of some 35 709 demobilised Zimbabwe African National Liberation Army and the Zimbabwe People's Revolutionary Army guerrillas were without employment (Mazarire & Rupiya 2000). As Robert Mugabe was consequently to find out, the failure of efforts to reintegrate former combatants into society can well have dangerous repercussions.

The main argument of this chapter is that in South Africa there was never an effective reintegration process in the sense of a systematic and coherent attempt to facilitate the transition of former guerrilla combatants into their communities with access to sources of livelihood and supportive social networks. Consequently, the move of former guerrilla combatants into civilian life has produced sharp inequalities among former comrades. To be sure, there were those who started their own businesses or found jobs in the private and public sector, including in the South African National Defence Force (SANDF), the successor force into which the former SADF, Apla and MK were combined, along with the former homeland armies and various other forces. However, others remained unemployed for many years after the suspension of the armed struggle, and some within this category chose to earn a living through criminal activities.

The fact that in 2006 some former combatants still feel it necessary to organise protest marches to highlight their grievances indicates that they have not been able to successfully resume their life in civilian society. However, it is not the intention of this chapter to present former guerrilla combatants as a threat. The point is rather to examine their socio-economic conditions and to consider the potential social and political consequences.

Defining a 'combatant'

There is no universally accepted definition of a 'combatant' among former guerrillas in South Africa. A former MK commander argued that within MK there was never an effort to define the concept:

> Who is MK? Where do you classify someone who has never been prepared for conflict, someone who has been under a certain ANC structure, but was never military hard core? How do you define a guerrilla, at least in theory? These things were never done. We never did our homework; we never defined a guerrilla. (Binda, interview 26.09.00)

Another former MK soldier observed that a combatant was loosely defined, to the extent that it included anyone who could strip and assemble an AK 47 assault rifle (Tsepe Motumi, interview 18.04.00). The problem of defining a combatant is not unique to MK. For example, a former Apla commander, then a colonel in the SANDF, Lucas Sigela similarly complained about the lack of a clear definition of 'combatant' within Apla:

> Who is a combatant? Do you mean a person who dug up trenches in Lusaka, Dar es Salaam, Cambodia, India, Lebanon, China or Russia, or do we mean somebody who was defending the country against colonialism, inside the country, throwing stones? Those are the people who really felt the heat. They are also combatants, they also qualified from that particular position. The Codesa[2] agreements were a disaster themselves because they did not decide exactly about the self-protection units [SPUs], the individuals who were harbouring the terrorists [the interviewee's usage], the individuals who were harbouring the self-defence units [SDUs] and SPUs. Now that concept [combatant] has got to be redefined. There has to be a reconcep-tualised position, an African position in South Africa, not in terms of Zimbabwe or whatever. We have no doubt that a number of people were excluded because the concepts were not clearly defined. (Sigela, interview 12.08.00)

Experiences from elsewhere indicate that defining a combatant is not an easy task. In 2000, 20 years after independence, Zimbabweans were still struggling with a definition.[3]

Cock (1993) identifies four different categories of MK combatants:
*   Those who left the country, were trained externally for long periods of time and remained in the camps while waiting for deployment in military operations inside South Africa;
*   Those who trained internally for shorter periods (which may have included one or two weeks' training in Swaziland or Botswana);
*   Those who assisted and provided support for MK (in the form of safe houses, courier work and reconnaissance); and
*   Those who undertook non-military tasks such as building underground structures.

A not dissimilar categorisation has been provided by MK combatants themselves: the first group consists of those who were trained (and in some cases spent long periods) outside the borders of South Africa. Those who fell into this category regarded themselves as the 'proper' MK soldiers, since they endured hardships in military camps away from their loved ones. The second group consists of those who were trained inside the country, usually for periods between two weeks and three months. However, this category excludes former members of the SDUs who were trained by returning MK combatants after the suspension of the armed struggle in the early 1990s. The last category consists of former MK members who were detained on Robben Island for a number of years. Interestingly, however, former MK soldiers who spent most of their lives in exile regarded the 'Islanders' as the least important category of MK soldiers, because of a perception that they had an easy time on the island (Mashike 2005).

Apla was divided into two groups, one consisting of members of the guerrilla army proper and another consisting of the task force, 'the PAC's version of a people's militia, whose role was to defend the organisation's members from political thugs' (Mphahlele 2002: 163). The PAC armed the task force better than Apla, and there were even times when Apla had to borrow money from the task force (Mphahlele 2002). However, for the purposes of integration to form the SANDF there was no distinction between the two groups. Similarly, when the time was reached for MK to join with other guerrilla forces and homeland armies in combining with the SADF to form the new SANDF, it chose to include members of its SDUs as amongst its own membership in order to counter being grossly outnumbered by the established military.

The flexibility of the notion of who qualifies as a former combatant inevitably poses difficulties for research. Indeed, not least of the difficulties is that, given an absence of official roll-calls, the study of former combatants relies upon informal networks. The main weakness of this is that former MK combatants (although not, interestingly, former Apla combatants) who served outside the country tend to exclude former members of SDUs. However, in this chapter, the term 'former guerrilla combatants' refers to the more inclusive categories of who can be regarded as having belonged to either Apla or MK.

The demobilisation of former guerrilla combatants

The process to form the SANDF involved integrating seven different armed groups: the SADF, the armies of the four nominally independent homelands (Transkei, Bophuthatswana, Venda and Ciskei), Apla and MK. However, amongst Apla and MK members who entered the assembly camps for integration were the sick, the aged and those without the required educational qualifications. Accordingly, on 21 August 1995 the Minister of Defence announced that former Apla and MK members who did not meet the criteria for integration were being demobilised (Motumi & McKenzie 1998). These included those who were not eligible for integration on the basis of age, education level or health; those who were eligible but who chose not to join the SANDF; and those who were not satisfied with their rank or package after placement (Batchelor et al. 2000). However, demobilisation was subsequently to be implemented without adequate evaluation of the likely capacity of individuals to successfully reintegrate into society, without sufficient provisions for demobilised guerrillas' continuing support and without proper assessment of their potential employment opportunities. This is indicated by the limited scope of the official demobilisation programme which applied only to former Apla and MK combatants who did not meet the criteria for integration (the release of members of the SANDF following integration being known as 'rationalisation').

Those who were demobilised qualified for a reintegration package consisting of three elements: a cash gratuity, a voluntary two-week counselling programme, and an opportunity to join the Service Corps for a maximum period of 18 months.

Demobilisation gratuities and special pensions

The demobilisation gratuities took the form of lump-sum payments to former combatants. The amount awarded was dependent upon the length of time served in either Apla or MK, and ranged from R12 734 to R42 058 (schedule of the Demobilisation Act No. 99 of 1996). The advantage of a lump-sum payment is that it provides an immediately available sum for combatants who want compensation (World Bank 1993). 'The principal benefit of a lump-sum payment is that it is administratively easier to distribute because it is only done once. A single distribution can be done while the combatants are still in one place' (Clark 1996: 15).

However, the disadvantage of demobilisation gratuities in South Africa was that they were not accompanied by training in financial management and investment skills. This was a major omission, for both ordinary combatants and senior figures within MK agreed that, while in exile, the ANC had provided for all the needs of individual guerrillas, who as a consequence had never had the need or opportunity to manage their personal finances (Mashike & Mokalobe 2003). The South African demobilisation process therefore replicated similar experiences elsewhere in which former combatants have enjoyed limited success in investing their lump-sum payments in productive activities because of their limited financial background (World Bank 1993).

Overall, the Department of Defence (DoD) paid out a total of 9 809 demobilisation gratuities, including 677 gratuities paid to dependants of deceased former Apla and MK combatants, between August 1995 and December 2002 (the process officially ended in December 2002). In total the DoD spent R242 million in respect of demobilisation grants (DoD 2004), although there is no clear breakdown of how this sum was paid out. The schedule of the Demobilisation Act (No. 99 of 1996) only provided guidelines and thus amounts were not fixed. For example, during the Centre for Conflict Resolution study (CCR 2003) some individuals stated that they had received R48 000 as a demobilisation gratuity while others stated that they had received R120 000. Furthermore, according to Motumi and McKenzie (1998: 195), the Ministry of Defence noted that by 1997 a total of 5 390 former Apla and MK combatants had been demobilised and that the DoD had spent R117 071 403. However, the figures apart, the main weakness of the demobilisation gratuities was that they were not based on any survey of the needs or the socio-economic context into which those affected were integrating.

Apart from demobilisation gratuities, some former guerrilla combatants also benefited from the special pension open to those who participated in the liberation of South Africa. Section 189(1) of the Interim Constitution (Act No. 200 of 1993) placed an obligation on the state to provide pensions for persons who had made sacrifices or who had served the public interest in the establishment of a democratic constitutional order. The passing of the Special Pension Act (No. 69 of 1996) gave effect to this provision. The special pensions were intended for people who were prevented from providing for a pension because, for a total or combined period of at least five years prior to 2 February 1990, one or more of the following circumstances applied:

> That person was engaged full-time in the service of a political
> organisation; that person was prevented from leaving a particular place
> or area within the Republic, or from being at a particular place or in a
> particular area within the Republic, as a result of an order issued in
> terms of a law…that person was imprisoned or detained in terms of
> any law or for any crime…or that person was imprisoned for any
> offence committed with a political objective. (Section 1[b] of the
> Special Pension Act [No. 69 of 1996])

The pensions ranged from annual amounts of R24 000 to R84 000. In terms of Subsection A of Section 1 of the Special Pension Act, only those who were 35 years or older on the commencement date of the Act were entitled to apply for a special pension. As explained by Muleleki George, Deputy Minister of Defence, on the SABC's TV programme *The Big Question* (12.06.05), this was based on the assumption that former combatants younger than 35 years could still find employment. Despite this somewhat dubious assumption, there was no attempt to assess the skills levels of those excluded from the SANDF as a way of determining the skills shortage and where and how former combatants could fit into the economy.

The Service Corps

The Service Corps was instituted in September 1995 to manage the vocational training of former combatants and other volunteers and liaise with other institutions that would be able to supplement its training capabilities (Mashike 2005). It was anticipated that the Service Corps would train close to 22 000 former soldiers between 1995 and 2001. However, in September 2000 it was revealed that according to an independent audit, the Service Corps used up more than R30 million between 1995 and 2000, but trained a total of just 604 former Apla and MK combatants. The 'success rate [had] been so low that the audit [noted] the corps could have trained each of its recruits to PhD level for the money it has cost to provide basic literacy' (*Mail & Guardian* 08–15.09.00).

It is difficult to obtain official statistics from the Service Corps. However, insiders estimate that the corps trained a national total of 4 600 demobilised Apla and MK combatants during the period 1995 to 2004. The figure should be treated with caution because it probably includes all the people who enrolled, and not necessarily those who completed training. Although they could not give exact figures, the Service Corps officers noted that, in the period 1995 to 1997, the dropout rate was high due to the fact that the corps was still in a learning phase.

There appear to be eight principal reasons why the corps managed to train so few former Apla and MK combatants. The first and principal reason was that at the beginning of the demobilisation process, the Service Corps was not operational:

> There were different offices for engineers, army, navy, infantry and so on, but no office for the Service Corps…it was at that time that we needed the Service Corps the most. It had to be there to look at the needs of these people. (Mokonoto, interview 26.09.00)

As a result many demobilised combatants took their demobilisation gratuities and left the assembly camps instead of waiting for vocational training to commence.

Secondly, when the Service Corps became operational, it offered all its recruits a R600 monthly living allowance, over and above their demobilisation gratuities.

However, whilst this was welcome to the unemployed, it did not take into account the individual circumstances of former combatants who had already managed to obtain either temporary or permanent employment, and for whom the allowance would represent a drop in income (Mashike 2005).

Thirdly, there were (an uncertain number of) former combatants who could not join the Service Corps or left in the middle of training due to illness and disabilities. The fourth reason was that some former combatants were too angry to consider joining the corps following their demobilisation. For example, a former combatant from the Northern Cape said, 'I did not attend the Service Corps training because I was demoralised. I was not expecting to be demobilised (former MK soldier, interview 22.02.02).

The fact that the corps was conceptualised as part of the military is the fifth reason to explain its disappointing performance. Initially, the corps had no facilities of its own and thus all its trainees were housed within army engineer units. It was conceded in retrospect that this was a mistake – as one officer observed: 'You cannot provide skills to someone who is migrating to civilian society inside the military environment' (Ramasodi, interview 26.09.00). Tensions between those who had been retained within the defence force and those who had been selected for demobilisation ran so high that some recruits left the corps before completing their training.

Linked to this was the fact that some former Apla and MK soldiers resented the prospect of learning under the instruction of 'a former enemy'. This was because during military negotiations, the agreement had been arrived at that former SADF instructors would be used to train former Apla and MK combatants during bridging training for the SANDF. Some of these instructors were seconded to the Service Corps.

The seventh factor underlying the limited impact of the Service Corps was somewhat anomalous in that its purpose when it was established was restricted to the training of former combatants who had been demobilised from Apla and MK directly. Ironically, this meant that the corps excluded former Apla and MK combatants who had initially been absorbed into the SANDF, but who later found themselves out of a job when their contracts were not renewed. Nor were any of those – from other backgrounds – who were either dismissed or resigned from the SANDF admitted to the corps, these exclusions holding even though the latter's intake of demobilised combatants was so small. As a result, instructors were wastefully and woefully underemployed. As one instructor at the Centre for Advanced Training (CAT) remarked: 'Look at all these machines; other institutions would like to own this type of training equipment. We have the best training equipment but no one to train' (CAT training instructor, interview 01.12.00).

The final reason for why so few former combatants completed training was the fact that few of those who had done so could be reliably identified as having profited from it despite the rationale of the corps to prepare trainees for their return to civilian life and to provide them with skills to enter the economy. No adequate mechanism was established to evaluate the rate of employment and unemployment among former Service Corps trainees (Painter, interview 12.02.04) and the impression became widespread that few former trainees subsequently moved on to a successful career or profitable employment. Inevitably, this served as a discouragement to potential recruits. As opined by one disillusioned former combatant, 'The Service Corps does not help. People who attended Service Corps training are still unemployed. They are sitting in the township with me and doing nothing' (former Apla soldier, interview 07.11.01).

Despite this chequered record, the main strength of the Service Corps lies in its ability to access funds and the full support of the DoD. This is evident in that, while the institution has come under severe public criticism (such as when an e.tv documentary contrasted its handsome funding against its poor performance), the department has never even suggested closing it down. Indeed, the Service Corps has been retained, and on 1 June 2005 it had an intake of 105 trainees. They were the first group to be trained through the CAT under the Military Veterans' Project with a budget of R39 million (Mashike 2005: 281–2).

The Military Veterans' Project was developed from a pilot project aimed at assisting the reintegration of former combatants and soldiers into society. In 2002, the DoD requested financial assistance from the United States Department of Labour (USDoL) for the implementation of a pilot project to assist in the reintegration of military veterans through access to jobs, self-employment, or higher education. The pilot project was known as Tswelopele and was implemented by the University of South Africa, Florida Campus, with assistance from the Centre for the Study of Violence and Reconciliation. The first pilot of Tswelopele Project (referred to as Tswelopele 1) comprised 40 ex-combatants from two military groups (20 former Apla and 20 former MK soldiers), and ran from October to December 2002. The second pilot (Tswelopele 2) ran from October 2003 to June 2004, and comprised 40 ex-combatants from four military groups (10 former Apla, 10 former Azanla, 10 former MK and 10 former SADF soldiers). Differences between Tswelopele 1 and 2 included: increased duration from three months to eight months; fewer and more expert staff; a new life skills and psychosocial support course; courses on vocational planning and professional development; a focus on referral and on veteran advocacy and networking (Tswelopele Pilot Project 2004). In total, USDoL spent U$1 149 678 on the South African Veterans' Employment Project (Hurst et al. 2004).

The final evaluation report of the Tswelopele pilot noted that the project had developed valuable training and counselling tools, curricula, modules, resources, and materials that can be used for future veterans' employment endeavours (Hurst et al. 2004). Hence, the DoD decided to use the training model developed through Tswelopele 1 and 2 to train former members of the SANDF (irrespective of their former military affiliation before joining the SANDF) through the Service Corps.

Former guerrilla veterans' associations

Above and beyond the various state initiatives, former guerrilla combatants belong to both Apla and MK veterans' associations to address the needs of former combatants. However, neither of the bodies that has been formed, the Apla Military Veterans' Association (APLAMVA) and the Umkhonto We Sizwe Military Veterans' Association (MKMVA), has met with much success.

At the time that the research for this chapter was undertaken, it became manifestly evident that APLAMVA was almost non-existent. Despite the election of six members of the National Executive Committee (the chairperson, deputy chairperson, general secretary, deputy secretary, treasurer and national co-ordinator), the organisation was almost wholly ineffective. There were no provincial structures and, according to the then chairperson, some dedicated Apla veterans operated APLAMVA from their own houses without resources or infrastructure. Due to the lack of resources and energy, the APLAMVA office remained inactive and no one knew the actual number of the organisation's members.

The MKMVA was similarly non-functional. MKMVA was launched in December 1996 to facilitate the economic reintegration of former MK soldiers into society. A number of activities were identified. These included the extension of assistance to veterans of MK who were unable to fend for themselves due to old age and disability; the creation and development of community-based income-generating projects which would involve veterans; the channelling of former combatants into appropriate vocational training and educational opportunities; the provision of assistance for dependants of veterans who fell during the struggle for a non-racial South Africa; the promotion and defence of the rights and dignity of all MK veterans; and the preservation and promotion of the history and heritage of MK (MKMVA n.d.).

Despite these noble ideas, the total number of former MK combatants is unknown and different MKMVA sources provide figures which range from 30 000 to 60 000 (Mashike 2005: 291). This is because MK, like many other guerrilla groups elsewhere, has been unable to compile a comprehensive database of its members. Furthermore, during the process of military integration, some people without any previous links to MK, who now opportunistically claimed to have been members of the organisation and assumed fraudulent combat names, had managed to join the SANDF (Mashike 2005).

As noted, one of the aims of MKMVA was to facilitate the economic reintegration of former MK combatants into society. To this end, around 1998 the ANC donated a farm in Doornkuil, south of Johannesburg, with the aim of setting up a number of small businesses in an industrial park. British Aerospace (BAe), through the Airborne Trust, donated R5 million to the project. BAe's flush of generosity was undoubtedly related to the ANC government's agreement to purchase BAe Hawk and Saab fighters in 1998, the company being awarded the contract in September 1999 (*Mail & Guardian* 02–08.03.01). While BAe's representatives denied this link, one MKMVA document confirmed the speculation:

> Through the establishment of an Industrial and Agri-Business Park under the auspices of a separate company, MKMVA together with the Airborne Trust and other black enterprises will directly contribute to the BAe bid by setting up a set of small enterprises in the Industrial Park that will supply inputs for BAe and its partners in South Africa. (MKMVA n.d.)

According to the document, MKMVA planned to build the Industrial and Agri-Business Park and an associated vocational training centre on the farm. It was estimated that when completed the centre would provide a resource centre for at least 20 000 former liberation movement combatants and retrenched members of the SANDF. According to a BAe press release on 25 March 1998, 'Veterans will become self-sufficient, deriving income through job creation, training and the marketing and sale of products. The long-term benefits will be the provision of housing and support for veterans from disadvantaged groups'. However, by March 2001 no projects on the farm had begun, leading to allegations that the R5 million had been embezzled (*Mail & Guardian* 02–08.03.01). These reports were denied by both BAe and MKMVA, with the MKMVA Treasurer-General Dumisane Khoza declaring that: 'Only R84 894 had been used on services such as surveying of the land in Doornkuil…The bulk of the funds [were] lying in the bank' (*Sowetan* 08.03.01).

The main obstacle to progress was internal divisions within the organisation. In June 2003, members marched on the headquarters of the ANC to demand the removal of Deacon Mathe (National Chairperson) and Dumisane Khoza (Treasurer-General) from their positions in MKMVA (*Business Report* 07.08.2005). The two were accused of fraudulently using the name of MKMVA to enrich themselves. In July 2005 some MKMVA members held a national general council in which they purported to have ousted Mathe and Khoza from their positions. Among the newly elected office-bearers were Nombeko Daniels as chairperson and Reuben Matlagare as secretary. However, Mathe and Khoza argued that 'their' MKMVA was the only one that was recognised by the ANC (*Business Report* 21.08.05). Subsequently it was reported that Daniels and Matlagare were planning to take Mathe and Khoza to court, accusing them of holding office illegitimately because they had been dismissed by an MKMVA general council in July 2005 (*Business Report* 20.11.05). Despite the fact that MKMVA offices were located in the ANC's offices and that the ANC was funding most of the organisation's activities, there was no indication that the ANC was prepared to take decisive action on the matter.

Former guerrilla combatants in post-apartheid society

Long-term reintegration consists of three components: economic, social and political. Economic reintegration is the process through which former combatants build up their livelihoods through production and/or other forms of gainful employment. The lack of economic reintegration often affects former combatants' chances of social reintegration – the process though which former combatants are made to feel part of and accepted by the community. The last component, political reintegration, refers to a process through which former combatants learn to participate fully in the political life of their communities. Political reintegration includes participation in structures such as local councils, schools and local security committees (Kingma 1998, 2000).

Economic reintegration

The only comprehensive study of the socio-economic conditions of former guerrilla combatants since demobilisation has been conducted by the Centre for Conflict Resolution (CCR 2003). Determining a representative sample of Apla and MK combatants posed a major challenge because the total number of former guerrilla combatants was and remains unknown. A total of 42 020 names of former Apla (9 864) and MK (32 156) guerrillas were submitted to the DoD between April 1994 and 11 October 1996 for the purposes of integration. From this total, 21 212 (6 421 Apla and 14 791 MK) combatants were integrated into the SANDF, while 9 809 were demobilised (Mashike 2005: 214).[4] This means that 10 999 former combatants included on Apla and MK lists remain unaccounted for. In November 2001, Apla and MK submitted the additional names of 4 033 (1 419 and 2 614 respectively) former combatants. However, since the final date for submitting names was 11 October 1996, these latter could neither be integrated into the SANDF nor receive demobilisation benefits (Mashike 2005).

The CCR study employed two non-probability sampling strategies, namely purposive and snowball sampling.[5] In the absence of any complete list of Apla and MK combatants which could be provided by the veterans' associations, and taking into acccount the deficiencies of the SANDF's list of Apla and MK combatants who had been demobilised, the study relied on approaching officials of MKMVA and APLAMVA, as well as other influential individuals within the former combatant community, to assist in framing the study as well as in determining an appropriate sample of former combatants. Even though it proved impossible to determine a sample size, 410 former combatants (83% MK and 17% APLA respondents) were eventually interviewed in all nine South African provinces.

The survey revealed that 60 per cent of respondents were unemployed, 9 per cent were directly dependent on some form of pension or government grant, and 3 per cent were supported by family or friends. Only 16 per cent indicated that they were involved in income-generating projects such as waged/salaried employment or as entrepreneurs. In total only 7.5 per cent stated that they were in waged or salaried employment in the formal sector. Thus, ten years into democracy former guerrilla combatants complained that they were 'still faced with unemployment, non-payment of pensions and housing subsidy problems' (*SABC News* 11.06.05). A very small minority indicated they were engaged in volunteer work or enrolled as students.

Former combatants gave various reasons for their inability to secure employment, with the most common being a lack of education and skills, insufficient employment experience, a lack of personal contact with influential individuals who should facilitate access to employment, and the lack of job opportunities in the public and private sectors. In the public sector, the lack of job opportunities was blamed on the privatisation of parastatals. There was a perception among 40 per cent of respondents that former combatants were discriminated against in the job market. To avoid possible discrimination from potential employers, many former combatants reported that they did not mention their military background when applying for employment. Some said they kept two sets of curriculum vitae, one with their military background and the other without (CCR 2003).

Nearly half (46%) of respondents indicated that they had made efforts to start their own businesses, while 48 per cent indicated that they had not considered the entrepreneurial option because of their limited skills and access to resources. Of those who had made efforts to establish their own businesses, very few had succeeded in converting them into successful ventures. This was mainly due to a lack of business skills, funds and profitability. Nine per cent of respondents indicated that they were running their own businesses, with a relatively even split of location within the formal and informal sectors. These included catering; construction; transport; selling groceries, liquor and agricultural products; cutting hair; hawking; and providing security services.

The fact that some former guerrilla combatants in the sample had succeeded in developing their own businesses cannot be attributed to any of the government's reintegration programmes. In fact, all successful former guerrilla combatants complained that the reintegration assistance that they had received both in monetary terms and in the form of vocational training was inadequate.

Other former guerrilla combatants (not part of the sample) who became successful in business include, notably, Tokyo Sexwale who began Mvelaphanda Holdings (Pty) Ltd with a capital base of R1 000 in 1998. Today, the company has gross assets exceeding R2.5 billion and has raised a third-party private equity investment fund with committed capital of R500 million to invest in service-based and industrial-based businesses.[6]

Other former MK combatants in business include Deacon Mathe and Dumisane Khoza, the directors of MKMVA Investment Holdings and its investment arm, Mabutho Investment Company. MKMVA Holdings took a 25 per cent shareholding in CommuniTel, which was part of the consortium for the second network operator, a fixed-line competitor to Telkom (*Business Report* 07.08.05).

Another investment of MKMVA Holdings was a 1 per cent stake in Cell C, South Africa's third mobile phone operator (*Business Report* 10.08.05). Mzi Khumalo owns Metallon Gold, five mines in Zimbabwe bought from Lonmin in 2002 for $15.5 million, as well as the Agnes mine in Mpumalanga, bought from Cluff Mining in 2002. During Metallon's last financial year (2004/05), the Zimbabwe assets produced 156 000 oz of gold – 90 per cent of Metallon Gold's total production (*Business Day* 28.02.06). Overall, a measure of Mzi Khumalo's success is the rather dubious indicator that he is in dispute with the South African Reserve Bank over assets worth about $200 million that he holds offshore (*Business Day* 28.02.06).

A final example of former combatants who have succeeded in business is that of an empowerment outfit led by former MK combatant Papi Kubu, which in 2005 'had bought into Varcol Paints, the Pretoria-based manufacturer and supplier of industrial paints…The Veterans' Foundation has acquired a 40 per cent shareholding in Varcol, a supplier to the defence industry, for R35m funded mainly through debt' (*Fin24.co.za* 12.11.05).

Former guerrilla combatants who have enjoyed success of another kind are those former members of MK who have been appointed or risen to senior positions in the SANDF. These include among others, Lieutenant General Sipho Binda, the current SANDF Chief of Joint Operations; General Godfrey Ngwenya, the current Chief of the SANDF; and Lieutenant General Solly Shoke, the current Chief of the South African Army. It is also significant that all of the first three chiefs of the Service Corps, Lieutenant General Lehlohonolo Moloi, Major General Andrew Masondo and General Wilson Nqose, were former MK combatants.

However, while some former guerrilla combatants were able to start their own businesses or find employment in both the private and public sectors, the majority remain unemployed. This was formally acknowledged by the Deputy Minister of Defence, Muleleki, twice in late 2005: first, during the Military Veterans' *imbizo* (national gathering) in Potchefstroom on 11 October 2005 (*SA Soldier* December 2005), and second, during the signing of the Varcol Paints deal (*Fin24.co.za* 12.11.05). This was significant, for it is the absence of opportunities for former combatants to establish new livelihoods and the scarcity of formal sector jobs that may serve as an incentive to engage in criminal activities.

The involvement of former guerrilla combatants in violent crime

Two factors increase the potential for former combatants to engage in criminal activities. First, crime is often a response to immediate economic pressures in a post-conflict setting. Second, the skills that former combatants gained through military training make it easier for them to engage in violent crime than to fight in a full-scale war (Mashike 2004). While it is important not to criminalise former guerrilla combatants, they themselves often threaten to resort to crime to earn a living. This issue is often raised when former guerrilla combatants argue for the need to receive some form of assistance, as the following quotes illustrate:

> The reason is that some of us know nothing except military skills; therefore it is difficult to get employment. The [Special] pension will help some of us survive before we end up being engaged in criminal activities. (former MK soldier, interview 24.04.02)

> We need a special pension irrespective of our age so that we don't think of crime or shoplifting. For us women, stealing clothes is our main crime. (former MK soldier, interview 19.12.01)

Those who threatened to commit crime often cited Collin Chauke as an example. Chauke was a former MK combatant who was identified as a kingpin of a syndicate that engaged in cash-in-transit vehicle robberies. He eluded police for years, escaped from custody after he was captured, and received substantial media attention until he was rearrested, convicted and later died in prison. But as one interviewee said: 'We are not afraid of committing crime. For example, [Collin] Chauke is a hero – he can give birth to other Chaukes (former MK soldier, interview 04.01.02).

While Chauke received huge media attention, he was not the only former combatant engaged in crime. For instance, as a result of a dispute between the Golden Arrow bus company and the minibus taxi associations in the Western Cape in 2000, Bandile Emmanuel Botya, a former MK combatant, was hired by taxi owners to shoot at Golden Arrow buses. In December 2000, he was sentenced to three terms of life imprisonment for killing a bus passenger and two bus drivers. In addition, he was sentenced to 75 years' imprisonment on 36 counts of attempted murder.[7] In another example, a group of criminals linked to Chauke and deemed responsible for more than 20 cash-in-transit robberies were arrested in Botswana while on a mission to steal more than R50 million. 'The notorious gang [had] been dubbed "The Government" because of its military skills, high-level network and ability to bribe powerful individuals' (*Sunday World* 23.02.03).

Social reintegration

Fifty-seven per cent of the respondents in the CCR study indicated that they were received as heroes by their families, 5.3 per cent reported that their families were shocked to see them, 3.4 per cent stated that their families were indifferent about their return, and less than 1 per cent of the respondents were immediately rejected by their families. However, regardless of their initial reception, 10.7 per cent of the respondents reported that after a brief period following their return, relations with their families became negative while a further 3.9 per cent reported that it was not long before their families had completely rejected them. The change was attributed to the former combatants' inability to generate income and contribute to family income (CCR 2003). One former combatant had the following to say:

> I was forced to leave my home to find a place to call my own. This was because when I had money my family was always accommodative and happy for me. However, when I did not have money I had to sleep outside the house. They locked me outside and would always hide away from me. I had to sleep on an empty stomach on many occasions. (former MK soldier, interview 07.11.01)

The most notable case was that of a former combatant who had to rent a room from his parents:

> If I miss one month without paying my rent my family threatens me with eviction, and the threat is often accompanied by the question, 'Where is your ANC?' This explains why sometimes I think of killing myself, but I always feel sorry for my six-month-old boy. (former MK soldier, interview 11.12.01)

The problem of rejection was worse for unmarried female former combatants who had children. For example, one woman complained:

> My family was at first supportive but later started insulting me for bearing 'fatherless children'. They started hiding food from my children and I, until a friend of mine found me a part-time job and I started earning a special pension grant. I decided to look for my own accommodation, which explains why I am renting this room. (former MK soldier, interview 15.01.02)

However, of those former combatants who have been rejected by their families many indicated that they have found their communities, or at least fellow former combatants, to be more accommodating. For example, one of the former guerrillas stated: 'Financially, they [former combatants] are the first to be approached when I need help. I feel more comfortable to approach my comrades for help than anybody else' (former MK soldier, interview 23.01.02).

The majority (75%) of respondents indicated that the way the community had treated them prior to joining the armed struggle had not changed when compared to how they are currently viewed. A small but significant minority (8%) said that they had encountered a change, with some claiming that they are ridiculed or reviled by members of the communities in which they live. Linked to this was the fact that some former guerrilla combatants suffer from serious psychological problems.

Psychological problems

During armed conflict, soldiers are often exposed to trauma that leads to the development of a psychological condition known as post-traumatic stress disorder (PTSD). While a significant number (38.7%) of the respondents in the CCR (2003) study stated that they suffered from psychological problems, they did not use the term PTSD. In Gauteng some former MK combatants referred to the condition as 'hard-nervous' or the 'Angolan syndrome'.

Former combatants suffering from psychological problems can be divided into three categories (Mashike 2005). The first category is men and women who were exposed to traumatic events during their time in either Apla or MK. One of the respondents who falls into this category said:

> When I remember the day I was shot, this brings back bad memories.
> I was in the river and we were surrounded by South African Defence
> Force and Unita soldiers. There were gunshots all over and at the end
> we lost 50 comrades. My comrades thought that I was dead and when
> they put dead bodies into coffins, they also put me in one of the coffins.
> This was the worst experience I have ever had in my life and even today,
> when I see a coffin, it is like I am involved in that incident again. This
> has created serious psychological problems for me to an extent that I
> cannot watch movies with themes of war or military activities. If I
> watch such movies, the events in the movies take me back to my
> involvement in the fight against the SADF and Unita soldiers. I feel like
> I am back at the time. I generally find myself feeling and acting as if I
> was back at the time. (former MK soldier, interview 22.01.02)

The second category consists of women who suffered rape and other forms of sexual abuse while in military camps. One of the women who spoke about camp life said:

> When I remember my first three years in exile, I feel like crying because
> I had sexual intercourse with more than 20 MK commanders. I also
> saw this happening to other young female comrades who joined MK in
> the 1970s and 1980s. The female comrades were used as sex slaves, but
> if a young male comrade was found having an affair with a female
> comrade, he was punished, in some cases killed. The killing would be
> justified by arguing that the comrade was an enemy agent. All these
> affect me now because every time I see those young girls who work in
> offices, they bring back bad memories. I always think that they found
> their jobs by exposing themselves to sexual abuse by those in authority.
> (former MK soldier, interview, 04.01.02)

Another female former combatant shared her memory of camp life in the following way:

> Sometimes I have flashbacks of how comrades killed the father of my
> child in Angola. He was suspected of being a rapist, and I was
> dissatisfied with the comrades because they killed him in front of me.
> They then took my child to Tanzania where he died of malaria. I always
> think about this and cry because after that I was forced to have sexual

intercourse with the men I did not love. When I think about my dead boyfriend I always become depressed. (former MK soldier, interview 15.01.02)

Lastly, some of those who suffer from psychological problems reported that their condition was caused by their role as perpetrators of violence against suspected enemy agents. These were former members of the Apla and MK security departments. One of the MK security agents recalled:

When in Angola I was based at the Quattro camp where we tortured apartheid spies. We also used to kill them and it was not a nice way of killing them; it was the most brutal way of killing a person. Pictures of the events pop into my mind. The events at Quattro camp affect me a lot. Sometimes I dream about what happened and when these dreams come, I scream. I am too afraid to go to the doctor because I can't even explain why I am like this. That is why I have to drink beers if I want to fall asleep. Even today comrades do not trust me in their discussions. (former MK soldier, interview 11.12.01)

These problems were not unique to MK. A former member of the Apla security department said:

When in exile I was deployed in the security division where we used to kill innocent comrades who were suspected of being enemy agents. After we had killed about 80 comrades we discovered that the enemy set us up and we fell into the trap [of killing innocent people]. Sometimes I hear voices of innocent children screaming, I can also hear the sounds of gunshot similar to the one I heard when we killed the innocent comrades. The main thing that distresses me is when families try to enquire about the whereabouts of their children. All these give me bad dreams and frustrate my life. I try to avoid thinking about it but I can't, especially when it starts flashing in my mind. (former Apla soldier, interview 20.02.02)

Despite the exposure to trauma, very few former guerrilla combatants have received counselling (Mashike 2005). Without proper professional treatment these psychological problems might begin to cause problems in the survivor's family and in the community. The case of a former MK combatant serves as a warning:

I was a commander during the Spolilo operation. We were bombarded from 11h00 until 19h00 non-stop and the enemy [South African Air Force] was using ten warplanes. The bombing went on non-stop and I normally have some flashbacks of the event. When we were detained in prison we spent lot of time thinking about how to correct our mistakes. This paid off because we once brought down a military plane in Viana. Hence, every time I see an aeroplane I immediately look at the possibilities of shooting it down. It does not matter whether it is a civilian or military plane, including helicopters; all I see are the many opportunities of shooting it down with ease. This is because all aircrafts remind me of the Spolilo bombing. I think that shooting down a plane is a nice art. (former MK commander, interview 31.01.02)

The persistence of psychological problems among some former guerrilla combatants might hinder their proper social reintegration. This might also affect their prospects for political reintegration and their failure to participate in the power structures of their communities might lead to further marginalisation.

Political reintegration

The number of former guerrilla combatants in government is an indicator of the extent of political reintegration. Former MK combatants presently in government include Ronnie Kasrils, Minister of Intelligence Services; Zola Skweyiya, Minister of Social Development; Nosiviwe Mapisa-Nqakula, Minister of Home Affairs; Charles Nqakula, Minister of Safety and Security; Lindiwe Sisulu, Minister of Housing; Jabu Moleketi, Deputy Minister of Finance; and Thabang Makwetla, Premier of Mpumalanga province.[8]

Furthermore, the CCR (2003) study revealed that an overwhelming majority (83%) of respondents belonged to one or more community or political organisations. A majority of those who said they held membership of various organisations mentioned the ANC as the only or one of the organisations to which they belonged. This is partly because, as stated earlier, more than 80 per cent of all respondents in the sample were former MK combatants. The majority (75%) of all respondents stated that they were actively involved in the activities of these community or political organisations, which ranged from being chairperson of a street committee to being a branch chairperson of the ANC or PAC.

Respondents gave different reasons for belonging to these organisations. Few reported that they had become involved in organisations to keep themselves busy in order to forget about their hardships. The majority (over 60%) of the respondents reported that they belonged to their original political organisations for sentimental reasons. This was because many former guerrilla combatants literally grew up within either the ANC or PAC in exile. They stated that they grew up in a context where their basic needs, and those of their families, were catered for.

At a superficial level, it appears as though former guerrilla combatants have been relatively successful in terms of reintegrating into civilian life. However, a more critical analysis of the interview data indicates that an adequate reintegration of former combatants has not taken place. First, most respondents were primarily involved in the ANC or PAC and/or veterans' organisations. The manner in which they interact with these entities is similar to how they interacted during the liberation struggle. For example, former MK commanders and commissars are still addressed in terms of their former portfolios in MK. The lack of social reintegration is further illustrated by the fact that some former guerrilla combatants are still suspicious of outsiders who want to undertake investigations into the affairs of former combatants.

Due to these suspicions, some former MK combatants were not prepared to be interviewed during the process of the CCR (2003) study without first consulting with ANC/MK structures. Most former Apla and MK combatants were obsessed with secrecy, and were at times reluctant to give away personal information. The main reasoning was that sinister forces could use information about their personal predicaments to discredit the ANC leadership. The fear was that MK military intelligence would be able to identify the source of the information, thus leading to the marginalisation of individuals within ANC structures.

In Limpopo province a former MK combatant remarked: 'Unfortunately in Limpopo province the government is the source of wealth. The problem in our province is that resources are limited and the demand is high. Thus, no one would like to spoil their chances of getting access to resources' (former MK soldier, interview 22.01.02). MK respondents in various provinces also reported that there were rumours that the office of the president of the ANC had commissioned people to interview former MK combatants to investigate their loyalty to the ANC.

The second factor that indicated the lack of proper reintegration was that being a member of a guerrilla group appears to have created a culture of dependency among former combatants. It is particularly relevant in the case of those former combatants who were in exile as the course that their lives took was largely dependent on commanding officers and/or political leaders. There are two indications of this dynamic. First, a number of respondents lack self-motivation to actively seek employment and improve their standard of living. They tend to wait for others to assist them rather than taking the initiative themselves. Similar behaviour was experienced in Namibia when former People's Liberation Army of Namibia combatants turned down jobs, arguing that it might be disloyal to South West African People's Organisation if they simply found work on their own (World Bank 1993). Second, many former combatants feel strongly that the government must provide them with employment, housing and financial support. Since 1994, therefore, former guerrilla combatants have engaged in protest action at various times to demand assistance from the government.

Protest action by former guerrilla combatants

In the introduction to this chapter, I defined demobilisation as a process of converting soldiers to civilians. An indicator of success is when former soldiers stop seeing themselves as a distinct social group that is entitled to special benefits. In today's South Africa, however, there is clear evidence that former guerrilla combatants continue to see themselves as a distinct social group. This increases the potential for former soldiers to organise around a set of grievances.

In 2000, former MK soldiers from Soweto, Orange Farm and the Vaal Triangle (Sharpeville, Sebokeng and Evaton) planned to blockade the Golden Highway along Orange Farm (south of Johannesburg) on 16 June (Youth Day) to demand jobs. However, the blockade never took place, for two reasons. First, some former MK soldiers within the group felt that others would use the opportunity to commit crime:

> Our idea was positive because it was not against the government. It was simply to say: 'Government remember us, we are still hungry.' Others came with negative ideas and said things like, 'What is happening in Zimbabwe [that is, farm invasions] is good; why can't we do it?' If we do what war veterans are doing in Zimbabwe, we will end up pushing ourselves into a situation that we do not like. We realised that some people would use the opportunity [the highway blockade] to rob people of their money. (former MK soldier, interview 15.08.00)

Second, it was alleged that the head office of the ANC was informed of the planned action, and the 'leadership' requested the 'comrades to be patient as their concerns would be addressed' (former MK soldier, interview 15.08.00).

In December 2000, a group of former MK combatants from Soweto, Orange Farm and the Vaal Triangle planned to take a white Gauteng farmer hostage on 4 January 2001, in order to alert President Thabo Mbeki to the plight of former combatants (Mashike 2004). However, the event never materialised, largely because the idea got 'lost' during the excitement of the Christmas season.

In August 2001, former MK combatants marched on the head office of the ANC in Johannesburg to protest at government's 'negligence' towards them (*Sowetan* 23.08.01). Most recently, on 10 February 2006, about 150 former guerrilla combatants marched on the office of the Minister of Finance, Trevor Manuel, to demand the payment of special pension grants to people who did not qualify because they were younger than 35 years old when the Special Pensions Act came into effect (*Pretoria News* 11.02.06).

There in nothing inherently wrong with peaceful protest action. However, the availability of weapons increases the potential for violence. The proliferation of weapons in the region has in part been the product of peace settlements in southern Africa. Ineffective disarmament during the negotiations ending conflicts in Mozambique, Namibia and Zimbabwe led to the proliferation of small arms and light weapons in the region (Cock 1998). In South Africa, MK arms caches were only cleared by the new SANDF early in 1994. This was because, in South Africa as happened during peace negotiations in conflicts in other countries, weapons and equipment were held back for a variety of individual and political purposes, including the desire for an insurance policy if peace negotiations failed, or to maintain a material base for future political bargaining (Cock 1998).

South Africa remains a heavily armed society (Kirsten et al. 2006). South African civilians own 3.7 million firearms, while the police and the army have 567 000 guns between them. South African civilians thus have more than six times as many firearms as those held by the state security forces (Gould & Lamb 2004), which highlights the potential for violent conflict.

Conclusion

This chapter has shown that reintegration is not one general process, but consists of thousands of 'micro-stories', with individual and group efforts, and setbacks and successes (Kingma 1998). As indicated, attainment of reintegration goals does not necessarily depend on state programmes, nor, as the Zimbabwean instance demonstrates, does official assistance guarantee success. Any assistance requires appropriate formulation, which involves investigating the relevance of other programmes and the inclusion of former combatants in the planning process.

It is clear, as the Zimbabwean case also demonstrates, that there is some risk that if former combatants are treated as a distinct group, separate from the rest of society, they will continue to identify themselves as such, demanding special benefits and targeted economic opportunities over the long term (Mashike 2005). Perhaps more importantly, former combatants who perceive themselves as belonging to a group apart from the rest of society may have trouble reintegrating socially and psychologically (International Peace Academy 2002). It is important to note that in post-apartheid South Africa, the needs of communities are many and those of former combatants are only a subset of these needs, as some former combatants are clearly aware:

> Ex-combatants must come together and develop their own income-generating projects. The government could intervene if necessary, because government intervention is not compulsory. We are not special because we fought in foreign countries. MKMVA and APLAMVA can design targeted reintegration programmes, not the government. The government is the government for all South Africans, not for ex-combatants alone. Targeted reintegration programmes would create some hatred between returning ex-combatants and those who stayed in the country while fighting for the same goal. (former MK soldier, interview 04.01.02)

Two of the respondents to the CCR study emphasised equality. According to one: 'We are all South Africans; we should be treated the same' (former MK soldier, interview 02.11.01). The other respondent added, 'We are not more special than people who were left behind inside the country. Thus, I believe we should all be treated equally' (former MK soldier, interview 11.12.01).

It is not my aim to argue that former combatants do not deserve any assistance. As South Africa celebrates 12 years of democracy it is tempting to argue that it is no longer necessary to assist former combatants. However, as the experience of Zimbabwe shows, if reintegration is not properly implemented, it may well come back to haunt those in power. Today, assistance to former combatants in South Africa is still justified because initially there were no effective reintegration programmes. However, in assisting former guerrillas at this stage, efforts should be made to strike a balance between dealing with the specific needs of former combatants and not creating discontent among the rest of their often poor communities. Failure to do this might jeopardise true reintegration by arousing jealousy among members of the communities into which ex-combatants are reintegrating (Kingma & Sayers 1995). The needs of former combatants should therefore be addressed as part of efforts to uplift entire communities (World Bank 1993): 'At the planning level, the reintegration goal is to bring the majority of veterans to a socio-economic level on a par with civilians' (Kazoora 1998: 35).

While I have argued that former soldiers remain in coherent groups for years – with the ability to mobilise around a set of grievances – it is important to note that grievances in themselves do not lead to violent conflict. However, violence may result if ex-combatants perceive a relative decrease in their standard of living compared with other groups, and when they see little chance of their aspirations being addressed under the status quo (Percival & Homer-Dixon 1998). Furthermore, two factors must be present for high levels of grievance to lead to widespread violence. First, groups with strong collective identities must have the capacity to coherently challenge state authority. Second, there must be clearly advantageous opportunities for violent collective action against authority. 'The aggrieved must see themselves as members of groups that can act together, and they must believe that the best opportunities to successfully address their grievances involve violence' (Percival & Homer-Dixon 1998: 280).

If the above conditions are met, then grievances may produce civil strife, such as riots, rebellion, and insurgency. For the moment, the persistence of former MK combatants' loyalty to the ANC reduces the chances of serious social disruption. However, the potential remains for former combatants to engage in criminal activities as a response to economic conditions.

Notes

1   The official website of the 32 Battalion Veterans' Association, available at <http://www.32battalion.net>, accessed on 19.06.06.

2   Codesa was the Convention for a Democratic South Africa, the first established body wherein the the National Party government negotiated the transition with the ANC and other political actors. The SDUs were established by community members in the 1970s and 1980s and were later put under the control of returning MK cadres in the early 1990s. SPUs were associated with the Inkatha Freedom Party and by referring to SDUs and SPUs, Colonel Sigela was confusing the two categories.

3   This was noted by Knox Chitiyo of the University of Zimbabwe during a Demobilisation and Reintegration Round Table held in Johannesburg in August 2000.

4   The figures are based on the total number of names placed on the Certified Personnel Registers between April 1994 and 11 October 1996. Some former Apla and MK members submitted their names for integration long after the process of integration to form the SANDF had begun in 1992; some members of Apla and MK were still outside the country and/or felt that it was not yet safe to emerge from the underground.

5   Purposive or judgemental sampling is when a researcher selects sample units on the basis of his/her own knowledge of the population, its elements and the nature of the research aims (Babbie & Mouton 2001). Purposive sampling is acceptable when a researcher wants to select members of a difficult-to-reach, specialised population (Neuman 2000). Since I had initially worked on a study of 12 former MK combatants, we approached my earlier contacts as well as the offices of the MKMVA and APLAMVA. Our limited knowledge of the members of the ex-combatants' population meant that we had to rely respondents to direct us to more respondents, hence snowball sampling. Snowball sampling involves asking people who have already been interviewed to identify other people they know who fit the selection criteria (Ritchie et al. 2003). In practice this means that the researcher identifies a relevant research subject, who then provides the researcher with information on where other relevant research subjects can be found, and so the process continues. Snowball sampling is 'particularly useful for dispersed and small populations and where the key selection criteria are characteristics which might not be widely disclosed by individuals or which are too sensitive for a screening interview' (Ritchie et al. 2003: 94). The former guerrilla combatants' community fitted this description. While this worked well among former MK soldiers, it was still difficult to access former Apla soldiers. The reason given by former Apla soldiers was that most of them operated in isolation and thus did not know each other. A major weakness of the snowball-sampling strategy was that in areas where former combatants had strong social networks, for example in Gauteng, the number of respondents was high. In contrast, after spending two weeks in Limpopo province where social networks seem to be weaker, I was able to reach only 19 respondents. Consequently, 76 former Apla and MK combatants were interviewed in the Eastern Cape province, 22 in the Free State province, 106 in Gauteng province, 81 in KwaZulu-Natal province, 19 in Limpopo province, 21 in Mpumalanga province, 19 in the

North West province, 32 in the Northern Cape province and 34 in the Western Cape province. Due to time constraints and the fact that no sample size was determined beforehand, researchers had to use their discretion about whether or not to continue with interviews in each province, hence the disparities in numbers. See page 337–8 for a list of interviews conducted. Please note that military ranks are given as they applied at the time of the interviews.

6   Overview of Mvelaphanda Holdings (Pty) Ltd, from the ARCUS GIBB website available at <http://www.gibb.co.za/profile/main_mvela_profile.htm>, accessed on 01.05.06.

7   Taxi hitman sentenced to three life terms, from IOL 12.12.00, available at <http://www.iol.co.za/index.php?set_id=1&click_id=13&art_id=qw976629660332B263>, accessed on 01.05.06.

8   For full profiles of all the government officials listed here visit the Government Communication and Information System's website, available at <http://www.gcis.gov.za/gcis/directory.jsp?dir=4&heading=Profiles#cat21>.

References

Babbie E & Mouton J (2001) *The practice of social research*. Cape Town: Oxford University Press.

Ball N (1997) Demobilizing and reintegrating soldiers: Lessons from Africa. In K Kumar (Ed) *Rebuilding societies after civil war: Critical roles for international assistance*. London: Lynne Rienner.

Batchelor P, Cock J & McKenzie P (2000) *Conversion in South Africa in the 1990s: Defence downsizing and human development challenges*. Bonn: Bonn International Center for Conversion and Group for Environmental Monitoring.

CCR (Centre for Conflict Resolution) (2003) The reintegration into civilian life of demobilised Umkhonto we Sizwe and Azanian People's Liberation Army ex-combatants. Research Report. Cape Town: Centre for Conflict Resolution.

Clark KM (1995) The demobilisation and reintegration of soldiers: Perspectives from USAID. *Africa Today*, 1st & 2nd Quarters.

Clark KM (1996) *Fostering a farewell to arms: Preliminary lessons learned in the demobilisation and reintegration of combatants*. Washington: USAID Research and Reference Services.

Cock J (1993) Towards a common society: The integration of soldiers and armies in a future South Africa. Unpublished research report. Department of Sociology, University of the Witwatersrand.

Cock J (1998) Light weapons proliferation: The link between security and development. In J Cock & P McKenzie (Eds) *From defence to development: Redirecting military resources in South Africa*. Cape Town: David Philip.

DoD (Department of Defence) (2004) Final integration report to the Joint Standing Committee on Defence sitting as the Parliamentary Integration Oversight Committee (PIOC).

Gould C & Lamb G (2004) *Hide and seek: Taking account of small arms in Southern Africa.* Pretoria: Institute for Security Studies, Centre for Conflict Resolution, and Gun-Free South Africa.

Hurst PA, White P & Statman J (2004) South Africa: Veterans Employment Project, Final Evaluation Report. Development Associates, Inc.

International Peace Academy (2002) *A framework for lasting disarmament, demobilisation, and reintegration of former combatants in crisis situations.* New York: International Peace Academy.

Kazoora B (1998) The Ugandan reintegration experience. In G Kiflemariam (Ed) *Converting defence resources to human development.* Proceedings of an international conference, 9–11 November 1997. Bonn: Bonn International Center for Conversion.

Kingma K (1998) Demobilisation and reintegration: An overview. In G Kiflemariam (Ed) *Converting defence resources to human development.* Proceedings of an international conference, 9–11 November 1997. Bonn: Bonn International Center for Conversion.

Kingma K (2000) Assessing demobilisation: Some conceptual issues. In K Kingma (Ed) *Demobilisation in sub-Saharan Africa: The development and security impacts.* London: Macmillan Press in association with Bonn International Center for Conversion.

Kingma K & Sayers V (1995) *Demobilisation in the Horn of Africa.* Proceedings of the IRG Workshop, 4–7 December 1994, Addis Ababa. Bonn: Bonn International Center for Conversion.

Kirsten A, Cock J, Mashike L & Matshediso R (2006) *Islands of safety in a sea of guns: Gun-free zones in South Africa's Fothane, Diepkloof, and Khayelitsha.* A Small Arms Survey Working Paper 3. Geneva: Small Arms Survey.

Mashike L (2004) 'You are a time bomb…' Ex-combatants in post-conflict South Africa. *Society in Transition,* 35(1): 87–104.

Mashike L (2005) Down-sizing and right-sizing: An analysis of the demobilisation process in the South African National Defence Force. PhD thesis, University of the Witwatersrand, Johannesburg.

Mashike L & Mokalobe M (2003) Reintegration into civilian life: The case of former MK and APLA combatants. *Track Two,* 12(1&2): 6–36.

Mazarire G & Rupiya MR (2000) Two wrongs do not make a right: A critical assessment of Zimbabwe's demobilisation and reintegration programmes, 1980–2000. *Journal of Peace, Conflict and Military Studies,* 1(1): 69–80.

MKMVA (Umkhonto we Sizwe Military Veterans' Association) (n.d.) Business plan for national industrial participation. Unpublished document.

Moore D (2001) Is the land the economy and the economy the land? Primitive accumulation in Zimbabwe. *Journal of Contemporary African Studies,* 19(2): 252–66.

Motumi T & McKenzie P (1998) After the war: Demobilisation in South Africa. In J Cock & P McKenzie (Eds) *From defence to development: Redirecting military resources in South Africa.* Cape Town: David Philip.

Mphahlele L (2002) *Child of this soil: My life as a freedom fighter.* Cape Town: Kwela Books.

Neuman WL (2000) *Social research methods: Qualitative and quantitative approaches* (4th edition). London: Allyn and Bacon.

Percival V & Homer-Dixon T (1998) Environmental scarcity and violent conflict: The case of South Africa. *Journal of Peace Research,* 35(3): 279–98.

Ritchie J, Lewis J & Elam G (2003) Designing and selecting samples. In J Ritchie & J Lewis (Eds.) *Qualitative research practice: A guide for social science students and researchers.* London: SAGE Publications.

Tswelopele Pilot Project (2004) Expression of interest for the Tswelopele II Pilot Project.

UN (United Nations) (2000) *Disarmament, demobilisation and reintegration of ex-combatants in a peacekeeping environment: Principles and guidelines.* New York: Department of Peacekeeping Operations.

World Bank (1993) *Demobilisation and reintegration of military personnel in Africa: The evidence from seven country case studies.* Washington DC: World Bank.

Interviews

Former Apla soldier, Botshabelo, 07.11.01

Former Apla soldier, Soweto, 20.02.02

Former MK soldier, Kimberley, 22.02.02

Former MK soldier, Nelspruit, 24.04.02

Former MK soldier, Orange Farm, 04.01.02

Former MK soldier, Orange Farm, 15.08.00

Former MK soldier, Orange Farm, 02.11.01

Former MK soldier, Polokwane, 23.01.02

Former MK commander, Polokwane, 31.01.02

Former MK soldier, Polokwane, 22.01.02

Former MK soldier, Soweto, 19.12.01

Former MK soldier, Soweto, 07.11.01

Former MK soldier, Soweto, 11.12.01

Former MK soldier, Soweto, 15.01.02

Former MK soldier, Soweto, 04.01.02

Former MK soldier, Soweto, 04.01.02

Former MK soldier, Soweto, 22.01.02

CAT training instructor, Pretoria, 01.12.00

Lieutenant General Sipho Binda, former MK commander, Pretoria, 26.09.00

Lieutenant Colonel Mokonoto, former Bophutatswana Defence Force officer, Pretoria, 26.09.00

Tsepe Motumi, former MK soldier, Pretoria,18.04.00

General Quinton Painter, former SADF officer, Pretoria, 12.02.04

Lieutenant Colonel Ramasodi, former MK soldier, Pretoria, 26.09.00

Colonel Lucas Sigela, former Apla commander, Thaba-Tshwane, 12.08.00

15 The state of South Africa's prisons

Julia Sloth-Nielsen

It is often said that the way in which society treats its prison population is indicative of the human rights health status of that nation. Applying this analogy to present-day conditions for South African prisoners would, unfortunately, lead to the conclusion that the patient is critically if not terminally ill. South Africa's per capita incarceration rate is the highest in Africa, and overcrowding of prisons has risen dramatically since the transition to democracy. Despite the relief occasioned by a special remission for sentenced prisoners granted in June 2005, which resulted in the release of nearly 30 000 prisoners, 72 prisons remain in the region of 150 per cent overcrowded, with prisoners sharing beds, sleeping in toilet areas, and being subjected to degrading and inhumane conditions. The 2005/06 Report of the Office of the Inspecting Judge describes this graphically:

> Examples in recent reports are: inmates sleeping on the floor; medium and maximum prisoners being mixed; 44 beds for about 100 inmates; about 74 inmates in cells for 16; a single toilet and shower being used by 59 inmates; foul smells; no exercise; broken light fittings; shortage of clothes and shoes; insufficient nurses; no washing of blankets; locking up at 3pm; sleeping in toilets and showers; two last meals at 12 noon and 2pm; sharing of beds. (Judicial Inspectorate of Prisons 2006: 18)

Overcrowding and its consequences constitute a key challenge for the future of corrections in South Africa. As such, this chapter will explore the key factors that have given rise to this malaise, detail significant recent developments related to policy and legislation, and highlight challenges that will have to be addressed in order to ameliorate the above-mentioned situation.[1]

Key aspects of transformation since 1994

It is trite to say that the transformation of prisons was a key political goal with the advent of democracy in 1994. After all, South Africa's former political prisoners had themselves experienced the worst features of prison life that prevailed under apartheid, notably racial segregation (until 1989) and a harsh militaristic regime (Luyt 2001; Sloth-Nielsen 2003). Prisoners' rights litigation during the 1980s and early 1990s prior to the adoption of the Interim Constitution had sought to challenge the denial of basic amenities to political prisoners (De Vos 2005). It flowed, therefore, that extensive constitutional protection for the basic rights of prisoners was a notable feature of both the 1994 and 1996 Constitutions, and that a transformative agenda within the Department of Correctional Services (DCS) would prevail consequent upon the transition to democracy.[2]

Shortly after the first democratic elections in 1994, the department tabled a *White Paper on Corrections*, which was rather rapidly adopted. As a conceptual strategy for policy development, this document's shortcomings have been widely noted,[3] most recently and succinctly in the 2005 *White Paper on Correctional Services* (DCS 2005), discussed in more detail elsewhere in this chapter, which has replaced it altogether as a policy instrument.

The most significant initial post-apartheid occurrence was the demilitarisation of the department. Uniforms and military-style rank and parades were abolished virtually overnight on 1 April 1996. The move was poorly planned and led to commentators describing the event as a debacle (Giffard 1997; Luyt 2001; Sloth-Nielsen 2003). At the same time, the Department embarked on a massive affirmative action drive to overhaul the racially-skewed profile of the staff corps. Adequate training and development did not accompany this transformation and the result was that staff and prisoners seized the opportunity provided by the uncertainty, with the consequence that ill discipline became endemic.

It has been noted that subsequent to the acceptance of the 1994 White Paper, the policy environment in the period 1994–2002 was determined, first and foremost, by a stand-off that developed between the (African National Congress [ANC]) chairperson of the portfolio committee and the (Inkatha Freedom Party [IFP]) minister. This was one factor that led to a breakdown in collaborative efforts at managing transformation and the multi-sectoral transformation forum established by the then deputy president withered and disappeared (Sloth-Nielsen 2005a). Without clear leadership, it has been noted that policy-making was eclectic and personality driven (Giffard 1997; Sloth-Nielsen 2005a). A string of senior staff changes took place under both the first and second (IFP) ministers after 1994, ministers Mzimela and Skosana. One of the first departures in late 1998 was the infamous Commissioner Sithole, who had made public pronouncements about the desirability of putting prisoners down mineshafts, and who left under a cloud of alleged corruption. A series of acting commissioners followed, and a permanent appointment of the present commissioner was only made in August 2001. There can be no doubt that instability at the management level over a prolonged period, and the isolation of this department within government more generally, contributed significantly to some of the challenges facing correctional policy and practice today.

Such was the extent of the decline that upon revelations of widespread mismanagement and corruption, and even the assassination of the assistant commissioner in KwaZulu-Natal by a fellow staff member, the state president appointed a judicial commission of inquiry in late 2002, led by Judge Thabani Jali. Initially provided with a fairly limited mandate to investigate seven specified prisons, the scope of this commission's work was ultimately broadened considerably as more dirt surfaced, notably after the broadcast on national and international television of the renowned Grootvlei videotapes, which had been secretly recorded by a group of prisoners – allegedly with the permission of the head of the prison – and purported to reveal illicit trade in alcohol and drugs, and children being sold by warders for sex with inmates. The Jali Commission therefore took considerably longer than expected to complete its work, ultimately handing the final 1 500-page report and recommendations to the state president on 15 December 2005. In his 'State of the Nation' address at the opening of Parliament on 3 February 2006, the president signalled the government's intention to implement the recommendations of the commission, although details on how and when this would occur were not provided.[4] Given that in 2005 the department also received yet another qualified audit from the Auditor-General (*Business Report* 01.02.06), who described the department as one of the two worst performers in government in relation to unauthorised expenditure, it can be predicted that cleaning up the administration of correctional services will have to be prioritised in the coming years. This appears to have been confirmed in the 2006/07–2010 Correctional Services Strategic Plan, presented to the parliamentary portfolio committee on 14 March 2006, which details an elaborate range of interventions aimed at improving governance and eliminating corruption.

The present position is that – consequent upon the dissolution of the Government of National Unity which entailed the IFP acquiring the corrections ministry – the political head has for the last five or so years been a member of the ruling ANC. In addition, the formation of Cabinet clusters has begun to result in far more integration of correctional issues within the security and justice sector. Finally, the appointments of a team of heavyweights at senior level in the department have for the time being resulted in a degree of managerial stability.

A profile of South Africa's prisons

South Africa has approximately 240 prisons functioning at any one time (see Table 15.1). They vary enormously in size, age and level of delapidation (some having been built many decades ago), as well as in access to services such as education, psychological services and opportunities for vocational training. The management of the prisons is divided into six regions, with Limpopo, Mpumalanga and the North West provinces combined into one region, and Free State and the Northern Cape provinces constituting another. The other four regions mirror provincial divisions. The highest number of prisons is located in the Free State and Northern Cape because of the policy of successive apartheid governments to locate prisons in these constituencies (prisons are renowned for their capacity to inject cash and create employment in local economies, and the location of prisons can constitute a valuable vote booster). Perhaps of note, the economic hub of South Africa and the province with the largest metropolitan areas, Gauteng, has the lowest number of prisons in the country at 26.

Table 15.1 *Number of prisons in South Africa, 2005*

Type of correctional facility	Number	
Male only	131	
Female only	8	
Male and female sections	87	
Youth development centres		13
Total	239	

Source: Muntingh (2005)

With approved accommodation for approximately 114 000 prisoners and a prison population of almost 160 000, it is evident that overcrowding is a major problem facing the DCS. It was expected that an additional 12 000 beds would be constructed by 2008, as four new 3 000-bed prisons were to have been built. It must be pointed out, though, that the plans for the four new prisons have been in the public domain since 2001, with the date of the expected commissioning of the prisons being shifted back annually. The Portfolio Committee on Correctional Services was briefed on the delay on 1 February 2006, and informed that the Department of Public Works was still awaiting confirmation from the DCS before awarding contracts as the building price had escalated far above the amount originally budgeted for.[5] The original estimates (in 2002) suggested that the so-called 'new generation prisons' (each accommodating 3 000 prisoners) would cost R50 000 per bed, while estimates now have the figure at R200 000 per bed, and a total capital cost of R3.7 billion (Muntingh 2006). The building boom and increased raw material costs have been cited as the reasons why the projection has climbed so rapidly. With the original tenders having lapsed, it is unclear at the time of writing when the construction programme will continue. Plans to build four additional 3 000-bed facilities were referred to in a parliamentary briefing on 1 May 2006, although the question is being asked, in the light of the remissions of 2005, whether new prisons are in fact necessary.[6] This highly contentious issue seems set to continue for a while.

The official average overcrowding figure provided by the DCS estimates that South African prisons are 163 per cent overcrowded, although this figure may well be dated in the light of the 2005 remission of sentences.[7] At December 2005, the most overcrowded prison was Middledrift at 387 per cent.

All prisons do not uniformly experience overcrowding, with the greater problems frequently being experienced by the larger urban prisons as opposed to prisons in small towns or prisons located on farms. As commentators have pointed out, over-crowding seriously affects the constitutional rights of prisoners in a range of ways, including their access to health, dignity, educational and rehabilitative services, and as staff battle to cope, their personal security (Muntingh 2005; Steinburg 2005; van Zyl Smit 2005).

The late 1990s and early 2000s were dominated by debates about prison construc-tion, including the issue of private prisons (Sloth-Nielsen 2005b). An important development in the 1990s was the political decision to commission two private prisons, a development that has been fully canvassed elsewhere (Berg 2001; Sloth-Nielsen 2003, 2005a). The two prisons, operated by separate contractors, have proved to be extremely costly to the DCS, although this is to an extent disputed by the operators themselves. The fact remains, though, that the two prisons will over the next three years consume between 5.1 and 5.4 per cent of the total correction-al services budget (R642 235 million in 2008/09) for facilities housing only 6 000 prisoners (around 3 per cent of the prison population).

After initially announcing a far more extensive programme, only two private pris-ons were ultimately commissioned. These became operational in 2001 and 2002 – with one prison situated in Mangaung and the other near Makhado. Although pos-itive evaluations of the functioning of the private prisons have surfaced (*Financial Mail* 29.04.05; Tapscott 2005; *The Big Issue* March 2005), the department found the costs unaffordable due to the way in which the original contracts were set up. The contracts provide for both capital repayments and daily per prisoner costs, adjust-ed annually for inflation, but based on exceedingly unrealistic 'input specifications', including a limit of two prisoners per cell, and extensive educational and voca-tional training requirements. It was announced that the DCS wished to renegoti-ate the contracts (which are 25 years in duration) due to their financial unsustainability (Sloth-Nielsen 2005a). A further conceptual hurdle is that these expensive services are being provided to long-term maximum security inmates (as was outlined in the contract specifications), rather than providing quality training for minimum or medium security youth prisoners, a point raised again recently in Parliament.[8] At a briefing of the parliamentary portfolio committee on 1 May 2006, the department confirmed that no more privately managed facilities are in the offing at this stage, although the 2005 *White Paper on Corrections* in South Africa does not exclude completely the possibility of whole-facility procurement (DCS 2005).[9]

A recent development to emerge was the outsourcing of food provisioning in sev-eral major prisons (from October 2004). This is a pilot programme that will have to be evaluated in terms of cost and quality before conclusions regarding the con-tinuation of privatised food services can be undertaken. The DCS has said publicly that the reason for this step was the need to comply with the White Paper which mandates the delivery of three meals a day at specified intervals (DCS 2006a). However, it is probable that other factors may have played as weighty a role, such as the need to stem corruption, which has often been linked to the availability of commodities such as food.

The DCS employs a comparatively large workforce, given its mandate to ensure the provision of services on a round-the-clock basis. According to the department's website, the staff complement is estimated at 134 000, but much has been made of the need to eliminate the enormous amounts paid out in overtime to staff working weekends and holidays, and the need to move to a seven-day shift system, which in turn will necessitate an increase of around 8 000 staff members over the next few years. In February 2006, it was reported that an additional 3 000 correctional services officials had been recruited in 2005.[10] The 2006/07 budget reflects that 2 627 new recruits will be appointed, and again for 2007/08. Ultimately, the DCS envisages that considerable cost savings will accrue due to the savings in overtime payments.[11]

A profile of South African prisoners

A signal feature of the period following democracy in 1994 was the rapid escalation in the numbers of prisoners, both sentenced and unsentenced. In this regard it needs to be noted that, unlike in many other countries, South African prisons accommodate awaiting-trial prisoners, a mandate that the DCS feels is outside the scope of its core business, and which it argues should fall to some other department.

Based on the prison population of 186 000 as at November 2004 (Muntingh 2006), South Africa has the highest proportion of its citizens in prison of any country in Africa, and at present has numerically the ninth largest prison population in the world. While prison population growth is not a new phenomenon, a rapid rise in the prisoner population was experienced in the mid-to-late 1990s, with overcrowding reaching crisis proportions (see Figure 15.1).

Thanks to a special remission of sentences implemented in mid-2005, overall prison numbers dropped rapidly from over 185 000 prisoners to around 157 000 at the end of 2005.[12] This has, by some accounts, had a measurable impact on prison conditions in some prisons, as the overcrowding levels have (temporarily) abated. Regarding sentenced prisoners, the prison population in December 2005 was 111 075, below the approved capacity of 114 000 places (DCS 2006b), although the awaiting-trial prisoner population figure must be added to this figure (Judicial Inspectorate of Prisons 2006). Past experience has shown that amnesties, special releases and so-called bursting initiatives are short-term measures, and that the prison population is likely to return to previous levels within a relatively short period of time.

During the 1990s, the unsentenced prison population climbed almost threefold, from 21 540 prisoners on 31 December 1993 to over 68 000 in 2001. However, the

Figure 15.1 *Total prison population in South Africa, 1995–2005*

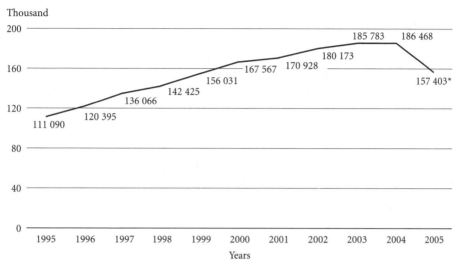

Source: Figures adapted from the Office of the Judicial Inspectorate (2006)
Note: * Numbers dropped substantially in 2005 when a special remission of sentence was granted and 30 000 prisoners were released early.

figure has decreased in more recent times to around 45 000 unsentenced prisoners (DCS 2006b), a trend which fortunately appears to be continuing. Just under half of those in prison awaiting trial have been there for longer than three months (19 277 prisoners out of a total of 46 327 at 31 December 2005). The DCS continues to assert that there is a 'policy gap' in relation to awaiting-trial prisoners, who they maintain should be the responsibility of other departments (a position first articulated in early drafts of the White Paper). The presence of unsentenced and mostly unconvicted inmates (in correctional facilities) who are not eligible for rehabilitative interventions, is regarded as impacting negatively on the department's new strategic direction for rehabilitation. However, it remains to be seen whether provision will be made for alternative lock-ups under the umbrella of another department (possibly safety and security).

As regards sentenced prisoners, a notable trend is the dramatic increase in the length of sentence terms over the last 15 years. This escalation has been attributed to a variety of factors, including an international trend during the 1990s towards the imposition of heavier sentences, public perceptions that sentences (especially for serious and violent crimes) were too lenient, a statutory increase in sentencing competence of the magistracy legislated for in 1998, and the introduction of minimum sentencing laws for certain specified offences (via the Criminal Law Amendment Act 105 of 1997). Most illustrative of the trend towards longer sentences is the growth in the numbers of prisoners serving life sentences, which has resulted in an increase of lifers from 433 in 1995 to 5 432 in 2005, more than a tenfold increase

(Judicial Inspectorate of Prisons 2006; Muntingh 2005; Sloth-Nielsen & Ehlers 2005). Although this cannot yet be authoritatively proven, there is widespread agreement that the single most important driver of the trend toward longer sentences has been the introduction of mandatory minimum sentences.[13] It has been estimated that by August 2006, 62.5 per cent of the prison population will be serving a sentence exceeding seven years in length (Muntingh, personal communication). Prior to the implementation of the minimum sentence legislation, 19 per cent of the prison population was serving sentences in excess of ten years, a figure which has now leapt to 49 per cent of the prison population (*Argus* 04.03.06).

The Judicial Inspectorate recently suggested that the cost per prisoner was R48 000 per year (*Argus* 04.03.05), and that South Africa is spending R890 million a month on prisons. Although these figures are undoubtedly a crude measurement,[14] they nevertheless provide a telling reminder of the fiscal impact of (over)-incarceration and a timely warning for future generations. As the Judicial Inspectorate points out:

> The medium-term expenditure estimate for DCS furthermore indicates that within the next two years (2008/09) we will be spending more than R12 billion per annum on correctional services. Considering that during 1997 we were spending R3.5 billion,[15] the growth rate on expenditure on prisons amounts to 242 per cent over this period of time. This amounts to an increase in expenditure which is much higher that the official inflation rates (between 5 per cent and 8 per cent)[16] and the South African economic growth rates (between 1 per cent and 4 per cent) during the same period of time. (Office of the Judicial Inspectorate 2006)

Furthermore, the unit costs per prisoner will increase with the additional 800 new staff set to join the establishment.

The prison population is predominantly young and male. One study predicts that by 2008 four in every six prisoners (*Cape Times* 03.01.06) will be aged below 25 years. In August 2005, youth aged between 18 and 25 constituted more than one-third of the then prison population.[17] The numbers of female prisoners are low at around 4 000 female prisoners, that is, 2 per cent of the overall prison population.[18] Interestingly, this proportion is very much lower than comparable figures internationally, a phenomenon that is not easily explained. Racially, a disproportionately large percentage of prisoners are coloured males. As Muntingh points out, this group represents only 4.3 per cent of the general population, whilst they constitute 17.7 per cent of the prison population (2005: 33). The rate of imprisonment of coloured males is more than double the rate for black males and ten times the rate for white males (Muntingh 2005). The reasons for this are by and large speculative, and a large-scale study to determine precisely which factors are the principal drivers of this phenomenon is long overdue.[19]

A rising proportion of prisoners are serving sentences for violent offences, by comparison to the situation prior to, and shortly after, the transition to democracy when the greatest proportion of prisoners on any one day were serving sentences for economic crimes. A measurable increase in the category of prisoners serving terms of imprisonment for sexual offences has also been observed. Table 15.2 illustrates these points.

Table 15.2 *Offence profile of sentenced prisoners by number and percentage*

Category	Jan. 1995 No. (%)	May 2002 No. (%)	Dec. 2005 No. (%)
Economic	39 093 (42.2)	39 087 (31.1)	22 320 (20.1)
Aggressive	35 027 (37.8)	59 317 (47.2)	64 666 (58.2)
Sexual	7 825 (8.5)	15 370 (12.2)	18 194 (16.4)
Narcotics	3 875 (4.2)	3 934 (3.1)	2 247 (2.0)
Other	6 761 (7.3)	7 997 (6.4)	3 648 (3.3)
Total	92 581 (100)	125 705 (100)	111 075 (100)

Source: Data supplied to the author by the Judicial Inspectorate

A notable recent phenomenon has been a sharp rise in the numbers of natural deaths of prisoners. The Inspecting Judge of Prisons reported that the figures climbed from 1.65 deaths per 1 000 prisoners in 1995 to 9.2 deaths per 1 000 prisoners in 2005 (Judicial Inspectorate of Prisons 2006). During 2005, a total of 1 554 prisoners died in prisons, 1 507 of which were classified as due to natural causes. The highest death rate was in KwaZulu-Natal, followed by Gauteng and then the Free State province. It is no coincidence that these provinces also exhibit the highest-known HIV/AIDS prevalence rates, and therefore the conclusion is warranted that the sharp rise in deaths of prisoners is directly related to the development of the pandemic (Judicial Inspectorate of Prisons 2006).[20]

It has been recognised that overcrowding compounds the effects of HIV/AIDS in prisons, as it notoriously furthers the spread of associated diseases such as tuberculosis. In a recent judgment of the Supreme Court of Appeal,[21] the court was faced with an appeal against a custodial sentence on the grounds that the prisoner's health status would be extremely compromised if she were to serve the remaining portion of her sentence behind bars (she had served a portion of her sentence in prison, but had since been released on bail pending the finalisation of her appeal). The prisoner had discovered after being sentenced that she had acquired HIV/AIDS and she described how prison conditions had led her immune system to 'crash'. She had contracted tuberculosis, shingles and thrush, and as she faced constant exposure to opportunistic infections, she became sicker. Since her release on bail pending the outcome of her appeal, she had been participating in a government antiretroviral programme that had been effective in improving her health status. She argued (and this was confirmed by her doctors) that a return to prison would impact seriously upon her health and that the lack of proper treatment available to prisoners would lead to her premature death. The head of the prison confirmed that Nevirapine, the antiretroviral drug that is most commonly used in the treatment of HIV/AIDS, was not available in any prison in South Africa. The judgment detailed graphically the results of prison conditions on HIV-positive prisoners, including how the inadequate diet they receive and the lack of necessary vitamins and medical treatment contribute to exacerbating opportunistic infections and accelerating the onset of AIDS.

The Supreme Court of Appeal, whilst noting that the fact of being ill does not necessarily entitle a convicted person to escape imprisonment, nevertheless emphasised that a particular sentence may be rendered more burdensome due to an offender's state of health. However, it was not simply the prisoner's HIV status, but this seen in tandem with actual prison conditions that prevail in South Africa, that was the crucial issue. The court therefore overturned the custodial sentence and substituted her sentence with the time already served pending appeal. The result was that the appellant was not required to undergo any further period of imprisonment.

It has been cogently argued that the DCS is making insufficient use of its power to release terminally-ill prisoners on compassionate grounds, especially in the light of the growth in the numbers of prisoners dying of natural causes. In 2005, only 64 prisoners were granted medical releases, a lower number than in 2004 (76) and 2003 (117). In this regard, policy guidelines about medical releases are required as part of the overall HIV/AIDS strategy of the DCS to guide heads of prisons in making more timeous decisions to release prisoners facing death. The DCS's Strategic Plan for 2006–07 indicates that the development of such a policy is on the cards.

Finally, mention should be made of the current situation as regards children in prison. The period immediately after the transition to democracy was accompanied by sustained legislative intervention to address the detention of children in (adult) prisons, largely focused on the awaiting-trial population. This occurred as a result of damning coverage in the international press during the 1980s, which highlighted the plight of children detained with adults. In the early 1990s, targeted activity by non-governmental organisations called for the release of children and the creation of a new child justice system, which would see any form of detention as a last resort. Hence, one of the first legislative enactments adopted by the new Parliament in 1994 was an amendment to the then Correctional Services Act which effectively contained a prohibition on the pre-trial detention of children aged below 18 years. Instead, they were to be remanded to welfare facilities. However, the latter were not prepared for the influx of delinquent youth, being more used to accommodating children in need of care and protection. In addition, these facilities were soon filled to overflowing and courts were faced with a crisis as there was nowhere to hold awaiting-trial children. Within 12 months, new legislation had been drafted, adopted and promulgated to permit certain children (those over 14 and those accused of more serious offences listed in a schedule) to once more be detained in prison awaiting trial. The data show that some six months after promulgation of the 1996 amendments, which reversed the ban on pre-trial imprisonment of children, approximately 600 children were accommodated on any one day. By 2001, however, this figure had escalated dramatically to nearly 3 000 children detained awaiting trial in prison, occasioning concern from the children's rights sector. Concerted action by government and non-governmental organisations has, however, seen these numbers decrease dramatically in the period 2004–05, and as at December 2005 the daily average of children aged below 18 kept in prison awaiting trial had dropped to below 1 250. Similarly, the number of sentenced children showed a steady decline, with the latest figures (for the average in the third quarter of 2005) being around 1 200 sentenced children, slightly less than the number of children of the same age group detained in the pre-trial phase. However, it is not clear to what extent detention in police custody (which is unlawful after the child's first appearance in court, but is nevertheless known to occur – especially in some of the more rural areas where transporting children over long distances to prisons and alternative facilities poses particular challenges) has become a real substitute for pre-trial detention in prison. Similarly, data on the numbers of children detained in welfare facilities as an alternative to prison are not uniformly available.

The implementation of the new Correctional Services Act and the White Paper on Corrections of 2005

Although passed into law in 1998, the Correctional Services Act was only partially implemented prior to July 2004. Notably, the chapters dealing with the National Council on Correctional Services and the establishment of the Judicial Inspectorate were brought into effect. The Judicial Inspectorate has, especially since the term of office of the second Inspecting Judge of Prisons, become a visible institution with an authoritative voice in the public debates about corrections and allied issues (such as the need for sentencing reform). The Judicial Inspectorate has been considered by external evaluators as having instituted a reasonably effective nationwide system of independent prison visitors drawn from the community, who are tasked with receiving and following up on prisoners' complaints (Gallinetti 2005; Jagwanth 2005).

However, the greater body of the Act, and in particular Chapter 2 providing for the minimum standards for the incarceration of prisoners in accordance with both constitutional standards and international norms to which South Africa has subscribed (the 1955 Standard Minimum Rules for the Treatment of Prisoners, the Convention against Torture, ratified by South Africa in 1998, and various other UN guidelines), almost vanished from public view. However, it was resuscitated somewhat unexpectedly when it was put into operation with effect from the end of July

2004, with the remaining chapter establishing new parole boards that came into effect in October of that year. Several comments about the implementation of the 1998 Act are apposite.

First, little preparation appears to have taken place for the implementation of the Act. Some planning around the composition and establishment of the new parole boards (involving newly appointed civilian members) occurred, but the actual advertisements for posts were placed after promulgation, and the new parole boards only got off the ground in 2005. In other spheres, the only changes that were recorded were the introduction of better-spaced meals (about which the Act is very specific) in some prisons (Law Society of South Africa 2005). Given the general conditions related to overcrowding, the lack of reintegrative services, the poor physical accommodation prevalent in many prisons, the numerous complaints about inadequate health care, all areas in which the Act specifies prescribed norms and standards, it can be concluded that the DCS is facing enormous challenges in working towards compliance with its legislated mandate.

An example in point relates to the specificity of the Act in relation to services that are required to be made available to children. Section 19 of the Act provides that all children who are otherwise subject to compulsory education must attend and have access to educational programmes (referring to a child aged until 15, the age of compulsory school attendance defined in the Schools Act of 1996). This provision is not limited in any respect – for instance to sentenced children only. It therefore applies to all prisons, even those lacking educational facilities, and to both sentenced and unsentenced children falling within the specified age cohort. Furthermore, the section continues to provide that 'where practicable, all children who are prisoners not subject to compulsory education must be allowed access to educational programmes'. This refers to the group of children in prisons aged over 15 but under 18 years. It has been argued that whilst the provision is qualified to the extent that the provision of education to this group of children must be 'practicable', the peremptory use of the word 'must' suggests that extremely good reasons would have to be adduced to justify any lack of access to educational programmes for older children (Sloth-Nielsen 2004). Based on both the wording of the Correctional Services Act and Constitutional Court jurisprudence on children's rights more broadly,[22] it could be inferred that where educational programmes are being considered, established or exist, the access of children to these services should be given priority. Again, the implementation of this right is not confined to those serving longer sentences,[23] or even only to sentenced children, but applies across the board to the children deprived of their liberty in correctional facilities.

The Act is similarly specific concerning accommodation requirements. Section 7 is the primary section in this regard and refers to prisoners being held in accommodation that meets the requirements prescribed by regulation. Regulation 3(e) provides in turn that every prisoner must be provided with a separate bed and bedding that provides adequate warmth for the climatic conditions and complies with hygienic requirements. Regulation 3(d)(i) and (ii) require the provision of hot and cold water for washing purposes, and that in communal accommodation, ablution facilities be partitioned off. There are many instances of prisons in which the accommodation falls short of these requirements.

A project to monitor the implementation of the Act over a three-year period in six (still to be identified) prisons has been launched by the Open Society Initiative of South Africa in conjunction with the DCS, and it is expected that this project will document, at least initially, the extent of the gap between the requirements of the Act and the situation on the ground. As pointed out in the Civil Society Prison Reform Initiative's submission to the parliamentary portfolio committee on 15 March 2006, the costs of implementing the Act have not yet been researched, and there is consequently little in the way of strategic guidance to fulfil the requirement of detention in conditions consistent with human dignity.

A second observation in relation to the implementation of the 1998 Act concerns the fact that even subsequent to its implementation, its contents and the import of the obligations it contains appeared largely unknown, both at grassroots level within the DCS and externally. As far as can be ascertained, the Act has not been simplified, summarised, used as a basis for training, or made accessible in any other way. No academic analyses or commentaries or publications in a like vein seem to have seen the light of day. In short, the Act has not played a central role as one might have expected.[24]

Third, it has been noted that confusion appears to reign regarding the applicability of the Act to prisoners who were already in the system at the time of promulgation. This has been particularly noted in relation to the parole provisions; the legal situation is that parole must be calculated with reference to the law in operation at the time of sentencing, and newly promulgated provisions apply only as at the date of promulgation, not retrospectively. (It is not only parole that is affected, however, as security classifications have also been identified as an area of contest.) The case of *Henry Motsemme v Minister of Correctional Services* and others (Case 04/26569, discussed in Sloth-Nielsen 2005b) bears out this point. Having been admitted to serve an effective sentence of 17 years in 1996, the applicant was initially told that he would be considered for parole after serving one-half of his sentence, once credits earned had been taken into account. However, on appearance before a parole board on or near the designated date, he was told that new policy required that he serve three-quarters of his sentence. A first round of litigation ensured an order setting aside the policy directive that superimposed new mandatory non-parole periods, and requiring a fresh parole hearing. However, the parole board, which sat subsequent to the judgment, postponed the consideration of parole for 12 months, using (again) the serving of three-quarters of the sentence as a criterion. Again the applicant sought relief in the courts. For the second time, the parole board was ordered to re-hear the matter and to take into account the (exceptionally) favourable parole recommendation contained in a report of the Case Management

Committee (CMC) consisting of members of the DCS tasked with reviewing the applicant's progress. However, despite agreeing that the prisoner had been 'fully rehabilitated' and that 'further incarceration would serve no useful purpose', the CMC met again and concluded that the prisoner could not be released on parole, and postponed consideration for two years on account of the length of sentence initially imposed. This procedure was subsequently criticised on review, as it was not only in conflict with the order of the previous judge that the persons conducting the parole hearing should take account of the positive findings of the CMC report, but it was also entirely unclear why the CMC had sat at all after its findings had already been made. A parole board hearing convened a few days after the CMC's second sitting concluded that the board 'was obliged' to follow the CMC recommendation to postpone further consideration of possible release until 2007.

The final round of litigation resulted in an order for the immediate release of the prisoner. The court (Judge Matshipa) found that the parole board had misconstrued its powers, ignored applicable law, and flouted the procedures contained in its own manual. The board was regarded as having been grossly incompetent, the judge going so far as to request an investigation into the board's activities. Although speculative at this stage, it has been rumoured that an unusual number of parole-related challenges are reaching the high courts, which would tend to indicate the uncertainty as to the prevailing legal regime governing the whole issue of parole and the competencies of the newly established parole boards.

Despite its superior status as a binding legal instrument, all indications were that, at the time of promulgation of the main body of the Act in 2004, attention was focused not on preparation for its implementation, but rather on the policy development process that culminated in the White Paper on Corrections released in March 2005 (DCS 2005). Public hearings on an earlier version were held in February 2004, shortly after the release of the initial Green Paper. By the time of its final adoption, the new *lingua franca* espoused in the White Paper was already cascading down to local prison level, and training (or rather, information-sharing and lectures) on the White Paper concepts was well under way. It is arguable that this level of preparation was in sharp contrast to the under-preparedness noted earlier in relation to the promulgation of the Correctional Services Act. [25]

Indeed, insofar as the 'new' Act was actually drafted in the period 1996–97, the argument can be made that the 2005 White Paper represents the key future-oriented policy orientation of the DCS, trumping the more dated legislative enactment. This is reinforced by the weight given to implementation of the White Paper in the recent Budget and Strategic Plan, which appears to envisage initial efforts being aimed at the 36 'centres of excellence' identified in each region. (The 'centres of excellence' programme is another initiative of recent origin, although it is not clear by which criteria the designated centres were chosen, nor how the intended excellence is to be measured and evaluated.)

A definitive independent analysis of the White Paper has not yet emerged in academic or policy quarters at this point. However, based on submissions by such bodies as the Civil Society Prison Reform Initiative and the Centre for the Study of Violence and Reconciliation at the public hearings in Parliament held a year prior to the release of the final product, a few telling points can be adduced. First, parts of the White Paper are regarded as being unusually frank in recognising the baseline problems that will hinder implementation of the ideals and philosophies it contains. These include the challenges occasioned by severe levels of overcrowding currently experienced by the DCS, which has no control over the incoming population, and ever-diminishing control over the duration of any prisoner's stay.[26] Another key stumbling block identified expressly in the White Paper relates to the quality and performance of the existing staff corps, evidenced by such statements as 'the history of the Department shows that correctional officials were not trained in the skills and knowledge critical for a rehabilitation-centered correctional system…as a result the Department faces a major challenge to retrain the members in the new paradigm' (DCS 2005: para. 8.1.3) and 'the past, and in many cases still the existing attitudes regarding the way in which the work should be done as well as the way people are expected to behave cannot be reconciled with an effective rehabilitation-centred strategy' (DCS 2005: para. 8.1.4). The executive summary notes the prevalence of what are described as 'existing human resource inadequacies' (DCS 2005: paras 12, 2.9.9). Reference is also made to the existence of corruption and the broader perception in society that the DCS is riddled with corruption (DCS 2005).[27] The disastrous after-effects of the confusion resulting from the demilitarisation debacle are frankly and succinctly described.

However, the White Paper does succeed in setting the parameters of a new vision in a number of respects. First, as has been pointed out elsewhere, it shifts the focus which dominated prison debates of the 1990s from facilities and architecture (mineshafts, new generation prisons, C max and private procurement), to human resources and a people-centred approach (including both the ideal staff member and the efforts required to be devoted to the eager prisoner) (Sloth-Nielsen 2005a). Building on slogans developed during the course of the White Paper development process, such as 'every member a rehabilitator' and 'every offender a nation builder', the White Paper intentionally aims to revitalise the clearly demoralised staff core,[28] to create a sense of purpose for employees to ascribe to and to steer public perceptions away from the widely held view that prisons are simply warehouses and breeding grounds for further criminality of inmates (and staff!). While the White Paper does not spell out in sufficient detail how retraining, improved professionalism, and securing commitment to service excellence (DCS 2005) are actually going to be achieved, the re-insertion of the human dimension into prisons' discourse was arguably a necessary and timely response.

Second, as is apparent from the above, the White Paper sets rehabilitation at the centre of the objective of imprisonment. The DCS is convinced that rehabilitation and the prevention of repeat offending are best achieved through correction and development, as opposed to punishment and treatment. The department's approach to rehabilitation is based on the conviction that every human being is capable of change and transformation if offered the opportunity and the necessary resources. It is also a tool by means of which the department can contribute to:

- Engendering social responsibility;
- Promoting social justice;
- Bringing about active participation in democratic activities;
- Empowering offenders by equipping them with life and other skills; and
- Making South Africa a better place to live in. (DCS 2005: para.17)

There have been some adverse responses to this vision. Dissel (2004) notes that the danger exists that sentencing officers might begin to believe that it is desirable to impose more prison sentences in view of the rehabilitative benefit and access to psychosocial and other services that may ensue during incarceration. As a century of 'welfarism' in the youth justice field has shown, this raises the spectre not only of disproportionality of outcome in relation to the misdeed committed, imposed under the guise of 'doing good', but also ignores the well-established fact that incarceration is inevitably damaging.

Other experts have been dismissive for other reasons – the standard putting rehabilitation and correction at the centre of the departmental mission is set too high, they argue; the elegant language of 'correcting offending behaviour', 'needs-based correctional sentence plans', and 'rehabilitation and development' are well and good on paper, but simultaneously mask the reality that the DCS cannot even, in present circumstances, deliver on its core constitutional duty to contain prisoners safely and in conditions consistent with human dignity (van Zyl Smit, personal communication). The fact that the lack of human and other resources required to translate this into reality will potentially scuttle the attainment of the stated ideal from the outset has also been pointed out (Dissel 2005).

Then there is the *déjà vu* effect – it is not without some scepticism that the (new round of) terminological alterations have been received (a scepticism with which the present author associates herself). South Africa no longer has prisons, but 'correctional centres', and there was even an attempt to reclassify the inmate population as 'correctional clients', which Cabinet did not approve. Even if these terms are marginally less discriminatory, they are unlikely to be perceived as such by either the public in general or prisoners and warders themselves, and the adage 'old habits die hard' is surely apposite. The new language and philosophy of the White Paper could therefore be dismissed as mere window dressing, a desperate attempt by leadership to dispel the widely held notion that correctional services is rotten to the core.

However, this is, in the opinion of the author, possibly too harsh a judgement. There is undoubtedly a place for a more positive vision for correctional services staff to aspire to purely human containment, and the focus on rehabilitation certainly creates the space for a greater degree of personal and professional fulfilment for correctional officials who take it seriously.[29] The White Paper does appear to have created a new corporate language for corrections, which is now being concretised in strategic plans and medium-term expenditure frameworks. It also establishes a developmental mandate for corrections, much in the same way as the shift from 'welfare' (which gets dispensed to passive recipients) to 'social development' (which seeks to empower and advance active beneficiaries) transformed the ideological underpinnings relating to the delivery of social services in the last decade. Finally, the South African public may be more sympathetic to the difficulties faced by, and lapses that beset, the department if a general belief takes root that, through their rehabilitative efforts, corrections is contributing positively to societal development.

That the above remarks all relate to the medium to long term must, however, not be forgotten. The more immediate challenge is posed by the need to control the size of the burgeoning prison population to alleviate overcrowding, and provide the breathing space for the transformation articulated in the White Paper to commence.

Conclusion

The overcrowding issue, which has come to dominate debates surrounding correctional services in South Africa in this millennium, is both structurally and socio-politically deep-rooted. The courts are not going to send people to prison for shorter periods easily, given the high expectations of the South African public regarding criminal justice reform (meaning bringing more criminals to book more efficiently, in the eyes of most), and given the recently announced increase in systemic capacity to arrest suspects and to process them, and to manage criminal courts more effectively.[30] There is, in a similar vein, no immediate prospect of a dramatic shift (downwards) in sentencing practice, unless initial indications[31] of a shifting stance towards the biannual renewal of the minimum sentencing legislation take root, and the legislation is not extended when it comes up before Parliament again in 2007. However, predictions at this stage are that the minimum sentences legislation will stay until a viable alternative is proposed, in particular one which accommodates the need to ensure a greater degree of sentencing consistency than that which prevailed prior to the Criminal Law Amendment Act (No. 105 of 1997), and one which takes heed of the concern of women's and victims' groups that sexual assault offenders often do not get the severe sentences that they deserve, and that violence against women and children is not dealt with by courts at the same level as other violent crime.

Some contemporary debates proceed from the assumption that the special remissions effected in mid-2005 have sufficiently altered the statistics that overcrowding and prison population growth are, by and large, concerns of the past. However, history teaches us that measures such as bursting and amnesties are of short-term benefit. Against this backdrop, advocates for prison reform assert that South Africa has neither the resources nor would it be strategically appropriate to build its way out of the overcrowding crisis that may shortly again be upon us (Muntingh 2005). There are other compelling and pressing issues (such as improved delivery on socio-economic rights) that are likely in the long term to produce a less crime-ridden society than more prison beds. The primary message has to be that we will not be able to breathe new life into correctional debates until a tourniquet is applied to stem the flow of prisoners – serving ever-longer sentences – into the system. It is worthy of note that this debate will take place alongside a recorded drop in the overall reported crime rate, an ongoing decline in the murder rate, and lower crime rates in key areas of concern (car theft and burglary) (Altbeker 2005). This does raise questions about societal perceptions of crime and punishment as central drivers of incarceration rates in South Africa, and the ability to shift those perceptions over the medium term. However, it is argued that the curative approach needed to stabilise the patient that is corrections today starts with sentencing reforms to lower the imprisonment tariff – albeit that this might be a bitter pill for the undeniably punitive average citizen to swallow.

Notes

1   The summary of policy and other developments from 1994 until 2005 is drawn largely from two earlier publications of the author (Sloth-Nielsen 2003, 2005a).

2   It is with some irony, therefore, that the designation of prisons as heritage sites (Robben Island, the prison on Constitution Hill) that has characterised the post-apartheid era must be noted. The public portrayal of the dreadful conditions that prevailed then seems not to be accompanied by a simultaneous reflection of the awful conditions now. See further Hughes elsewhere in this volume.

3   See, for example, Penal Reform Lobby Group (1995) An Alternative White Paper on Correctional Services, unpublished (copy on file with the author).

4   For a report on the impact of the 2006 'State of the Nation' address on the DCS see <http://www.pmg.org.za/viewminutes.php?id=7255>, accessed on 31.03.06. Muntingh points out that the fact that the contents of the Jali Commission's recommendations were not yet known had the unfortunate consequence that no budgetary provision was made for implementation in the budget presented to Parliament in March 2006 (see CSPRI Newsletter 16 (March 2006). Available at <http://www.communitylawcentre.org/cspri>.

5   See <http://www.pmg.org.za>, accessed on 02.03.06. Even more recently (on 01.05.06) the portfolio committee has been informed that the contracts will be re-advertised shortly.

6   See, for example, CSPRI Submission to the Portfolio Committee on Correctional Services on Budget Vote 20 presented on 15.03.06. Available at <http:// www.communitylawcentre.org.za>

7   See <http://www.dcs.gov.za>, accessed on 22 .02.06. However, as Muntingh points (2005) out, the qualitative impact of overcrowding can be affected by such things as the weather, the amount of time allowed outside of a cell and so forth.

8   See the comments of the chairperson of the portfolio committee at <http://www.pmg.org.za/viewminute.php?id=7255>, accessed on 13.03.06.

9   The image of privatised facilities has undoubtedly further been dented by the unfortunate events of 28 February 2006 at the Makhado facility which resulted from a strike by warders. Several hundred prisoners ran amok and torched part of the prison, damaging accommodation for 800 people. The DCS and the police had to be called in to help prevent the prisoners from running away (*Argus* 04.03.06).

10 See <http://www.news24,com.South_Africa/Politics/0,,2-7-12_1878473,00.html>, accessed on 10.02.06.

11 See DCS (2006b: 44) Recently Treasury reported that it had allocated R40 million in 2005/06 for the implementation of the nutritional programme, and that R50 million and R70 million would be allocated for 2006/07 and 2007/08 for this purpose. It must also be noted that the conversion of fully-subsidised medical aid contributions to a two-thirds subsidy reduced medical aid expenditure in 2005/06 from R790 million to R540 million, a considerable saving to the department (see <http://www.pmg.org.za/viewminute.php?id=7255>, accessed on 31.03.06).

12 The figures, as at August 2005, reflect a total prison population of 155 858 of whom 44 864 were unsentenced and 110 994 were sentenced. The comparable figures before the special remission were a total of 186 823 as at February 2005, of whom 135 743 were sentenced and 51 080 were unsentenced (*CSPRI Newsletter* 15, January 2006). By December 2005, however, the total number had climbed again to 157 402 prisoners (*CSPRI Newsletter* 16, March 2006).

13 This was the conclusion of a large number of judges, magistrates, criminologists and other experts who attended a conference hosted by the Department of Justice and Constitutional Development, Justice Training College and the DCS in Pretoria in October 2005.

14 The computation does not relate to actual incarceration unit costs, but is achieved by dividing the entire Correctional Services budget by the total number of prisoners. Since the largest component of the budget is devoted to staff salaries, which do not diminish if fewer prisoners are sent to prison, it is somewhat artificial to imagine that there would be serious cost savings if the prison population shrunk.

15 DCS Annual Report 1997.

16 See Roux (2005)

17 The departmental website gives the number as 58 699 youth, after the amnesty implemented from May 2005 reduced the prison population to around 155 000.

18 This is based on figures prior to the special remission of 2005. In August 2005 the number of female prisoners was 3 214, which is nevertheless in the region of 2 per cent of the overall prison population.

19 Johnny Steinberg's (2004) book *The Number*, detailing the life of a prison gangster, is a commendable first step in the exploration of the complex dynamics of youth gangs and criminality in the Western Cape, where the so-called coloured population by and large reside. See also Programme towards the Elimination of Child Labour and Community Law Centre, University of the Western Cape (2006).

20 During February 2006, Grootvlei prison in the Free State province was the first prison to be designated an approved health facility for the purposes of dispensing antiretroviral treatment (*Mail & Guardian* 24.03–03.04.06).

21 *S v Magida* (SCA case no 515/04) discussed in *CSPRI Newsletter* 13, September 2005.

22 In particular, *TAC v Minister of Health and others* (CCT 08/2002).

23 A prisoner's access to services is usually linked to the term of incarceration, with prisoners serving less than a two-year term not being eligible for such services in the past. The Act now specifies (in Section 38) that assessment and the development of a sentence plan must occur in respect of prisoners serving a sentence of more than 12 months.

24 At the time of writing, it has been rumoured that amending legislation has been prepared and will be introduced into the parliamentary process in 2006. Many of the amendments are allegedly technical in nature, or reverse unwelcome alterations that crept in during the original debates in Parliament.

25 It is not known whether the department has as yet undertaken a detailed costing of the White Paper, as has been promised. However, Treasury notes a request for R2 billion to implement the White Paper, a request which they argued could not be met with a once-off payment. White Paper-related outputs have only been mainstreamed in annual budgets to a limited extent (for more detail see *CSPRI Newsletter* 16, March 2006), and this in turn could mean that the fiscal aspects of preparedness for implementation of the White Paper have not kept pace with other initiatives.

26 Thus, the department has no effective control over average or specific detention cycles regarding awaiting-trial detainees, and in respect of sentenced prisoners, has no control over the incoming numbers or the length of time that they may be sentenced for. In only two respects does the DCS play a role in respect of managing its inmate population, namely via the parole system and through conversions of sentences into community corrections (correctional supervision). However, legislative inroads have been made even into this arena of administrative action, as the legislature commenced with establishing fixed, longer, non-parole periods in respect of persons sentenced in terms of the minimum sentences legislation (Act 105 of 1997). It is submitted that general amnesties,

bursting and the like are largely political decisions, in respect of which support far beyond the immediate departmental circle has to be engineered.

27 For further detail on corruption see the website of the Special Investigating Unit which has a fact sheet describing their ongoing investigation into corruption within the DCS, available at <http://www.siu.org.za/index.asp?include=about/dcs.html>, accessed on 28.02.06.

28 As indicated, for example, by the exceptionally high number of – within the public service generally – days' sick leave claimed by departmental officials, allegedly the highest of all sectors in the public service.

29 See, for example, the paper entitled 'Revitalising the Department of Correctional Services' written by the provincial commissioner of the Western Cape, Mr B Gxilishe, and reproduced on the DCS website, available at <http://www.dcs.gov.za>, accessed on 15.02.06.

30 See the sections devoted to court and case-flow management and to increased security cluster spending in the president's 'State of the Nation' address, February 2006. The same is evident in the Budget speech, presented later in the month. Quantifying this further, the Minister of Safety and Security reported that the police staff complement was expected to reach 165 850 by March 2008, up from 152 236 in 2005, and further that an additional 890 prosecutors' posts would be created. See <http://www.news24.com/South_Africa/Politics/0,,2-7-12_1878473,00.html>, accessed on 10.02.06.

31 At a round table convened by the Open Society Foundation of South Africa in January 2005, the beginnings of opposition to routine renewal were voiced (see Sloth-Nielsen & Ehlers 2005). This occurred at the same time as the Department of Justice and Constitutional Development invited comment on the proposed extension of the legislation, an opportunity which many from the judiciary and other stakeholder groups (the National Prosecuting Authority offices) evidently seized. In September 2005, Justice College together with a large group of government officials, non-governmental organisations, academics and others, convened a conference on the theme of the overcrowding of prisons, which seems to have resulted in an emerging consensus that some order of sentencing reform needs to be put on the table.

References

Altbeker A (2005) Positive trends – The 2004/05 Crime Statistics. *SA Crime Quarterly,* 14: 2–7.

Berg J (2001) Accountability in private corrections: Monitoring the performance of private prisons in South Africa. *South African Journal on Criminal Justice,* 14(2): 327–43.

DCS (Department of Correctional Services) (2005) *White Paper on Correctional Services.* Pretoria: Government Printers.

DCS (2006a) Department of Correctional Services: Strategic Plan 2006/07–2009, 10 March.

DCS (2006b) Department of Correctional Services Budget Vote. Available at <http://www.pmg.org.za/docs/2006/060307.budgetvote20.doc>.

De Vos P (2005) Prisoners rights litigation in South Africa since 1994 – a critical evaluation. *Law, Democracy and Development,* 9(1): 89–112.

Dissel A (2004) Submission to the Portfolio Committee on Correctional Services on the White Paper on Corrections (copy on file with the author).

Dissel A (2005) Submission to the Portfolio Committee on Correctional Services on the Correctional Services Budget (copy on file with the author).

Gallinetti J (2005) Civilian oversight and South African prisons: An examination of the Independent Visitor system. *Law, Democracy and Development,* 9(1): 67.

Giffard C (1997) Out of step? The transformation process in the South African department of correctional services. MSc dissertation in Criminal Justice Studies, University of Leicester.

Jagwanth S (2005) A review of the Judicial Inspectorate of prisons of South Africa. *Law, Democracy and Development,* 9(1): 45.

Judicial Inspectorate of Prisons (2006) Annual Report of the Office of the Inspecting Judge of Prisons 2005/06.

Law Society of South Africa (2005) *Report on prison visits 2004/05.* Pretoria: Law Society of South Africa.

Luyt W (2001) The transformation of Corrections in the new South Africa. *Acta Criminologica,* 14(3): 27.

Muntingh LM (2005) Surveying the prisons landscape – what the numbers tell us. *Law, Democracy and Development,* 9(1): 21–44.

Muntingh LM (2006) The Correctional Services budget – Some trends and observations. *CSPRI Newsletter,* No. 16, March.

Office of the Judicial Inspectorate (2006) Submission on Budget Vote 20 to the Parliamentary Committee on Correctional Services, 14.03.06 (copy on file with author).

Programme towards the Elimination of Child Labour and Community Law Centre, University of the Western Cape (2006) *Consultation with children on their use by adults in illicit activities.* Bellville, Cape Town: UWC.

Roux A (2005) *Everyone's guide to the South African economy* (8th edition). Cape Town: Zebra Press.

Sloth-Nielsen J (2003) *Overview of policy developments in Correctional Services 1994–2002*. Civil Society Prison Reform Initiative (CSPRI) Research series No. 1. Kenilworth: CSPRI.

Sloth-Nielsen J (2004) What does the new Correctional Services Act say about children in prison? *Article 40*, 6(3): 1–30.

Sloth-Nielsen J (2005a) Policy and practice in South African prisons: An update. *Law, Democracy and Development*, 9(1): 1–19.

Sloth-Nielsen (2005b) Parole pandemonium. *CSPRI Newsletter* No. 14, November.

Sloth-Nielsen J & Ehlers L (2005) *A Pyrrhic victory? Mandatory and minimum sentences in South Africa*. Occasional Paper No. 111, Institute for Strategic Studies, Pretoria.

Steinberg J (2004) *The Number*. Johannesburg: Jonathan Ball Publishers.

Steinburg J (2005) *Prison overcrowding and the constitutional right to adequate accommodation in South Africa*. Occasional Paper, Centre for the Study of Violence and Reconciliation, University of Cape Town.

Tapscott C (2005) *A study of best practice in prison governance*, CSPRI Research Paper No. 9.

Van Zyl Smit D (2005) Swimming against the tide – Controlling the size of the prison population in South Africa. In B Dixon & E van der Spuy (Eds) *Justice gained?* Cape Town: UCT Press.

16 'Truck and trailer': rugby and transformation in South Africa

Ashwin Desai and Zayn Nabbi

> Transformation and racism have been the contentious issues in South
> African sport – and in South African rugby in particular – since before
> the country's first democratic election. The process of integration and
> transformation is perfectly understandable and justified, given the
> years of exclusion of black and coloured athletes under apartheid.
> As Nelson Mandela has said, if South Africa is to move forward as a
> unified country, as it must, equal opportunities should be available to
> all. That is the theory, and highly commendable it is. But the trouble
> has been its implementation. The fact remains that, after more than
> 40 years of apartheid, a huge disparity had arisen between the sporting
> standards of black and white. That much was inevitable. But how to
> address the problem and close the gap? It is a question many South
> Africans have disagreed on. (Corne Krige, former Springbok captain,
> with Bills 2005: 147)

The twentieth-century history of 'white' rugby is closely linked to the emergence of
Afrikaner nationalism. Through the 1930s and 1940s rugby 'became part of a clus-
ter of cultural symbols closely associated with a resurgent Afrikanerdom'
(Grundlingh 1995a: 107).

It was not surprising that Tommy Bedford, one of the few 'English' Springbok captains of the apartheid era, was moved to say in 1989 that for over two-and-a-half
decades the primary agenda of rugby administrators was 'mainly to promote the
Afrikaner, his Church, his Party, his Government and the Broederbond...' (quoted
in Grundlingh 1995a: 131). Bedford responded with his own form of jingoism,
representing Natal as the last outpost of the former British Empire.

Black people began playing the game in the late nineteenth century with clubs
emerging in the coloured community in the Western Cape and among Africans in
the Eastern Cape. In time two national associations emerged: the South African
African Rugby Board and the South African Coloured Rugby Football Federation.
The latter became the South African Rugby Union (Saru) in 1966. In 1971 the
Kwazakhele Rugby Union (Kwaru) joined Saru, bringing in a large group of
African players. This move also encouraged defections in other areas to Saru,
including a few white players, most notably the Watson brothers from Port
Elizabeth who played for Kwaru.

As Saru became stronger and more overtly anti-apartheid in its stance, joining the South African Council on Sport (Sacos) as a founding member in 1973, the 'collaborationist' African and coloured administrators consolidated their links with the white rugby body, the South African Rugby Board (SARB), and relied on their patronage. White rugby through the apartheid years remained a member of the International Rugby Board (IRB).

Coming into the early 1990s there were two rugby teams in South Africa: 'On the one side were the status quo-supporting proponents of multinationalism and on the other the non-racial Saru which closely aligned itself with the struggles of the resurgent liberation movements' (Odendaal 1995: 59). It was these two sides that met in 1992 unification efforts with equal representation on both sides. In early 1992, a new body was formed – the South African Rugby Football Union (Sarfu).

In August 1992, the Australian national team, the Wallabies, and the New Zealand national team, the All Blacks, toured the country. The first test match took place on 15 August 1992 at Ellis Park against the All Blacks. An agreement had been reached that the erstwhile apartheid anthem, *Die Stem*, would not be sung, the South African flag would not be raised, and there would be a minute's silence for the victims of the Boipatong massacre. All these agreements were breached.

The fallout was mitigated by ongoing political negotiations at one level and a development programme at another. In March 1993 Sarfu committed a sum of R13 million rand for the first year and some 6 000 coaches fanned out across the country to bring rugby to disadvantaged communities (Grundlingh 1995b). However, all these developments were superceded by the holding of the 1995 World Cup.

The 1995 Rugby World Cup

The 1995 World Cup caused an orgy of sports and political writing. Most of it promoted the idea of the value of a unified nation and celebrated rugby's role in fostering and symbolising this notion. It led to one of the abiding images of the 'new' South Africa: President Nelson Mandela appearing at the final in the number 6 jersey of the Springboks, the South African team. The media rushed to outdo themselves. Writing in the *Cape Times*, David Miller gushed:

> For Nelson Mandela, it was a touch of genius. To take hold of the very colours of your historic enemy, of your cultural, social and political oppressor, and to raise them aloft as a symbol of brotherhood, was more powerful than a million words. With a mere green and yellow cloth on his back, instead of resorting to guns and bombs, this unique statesman's gesture has overturned a former hated bastille of racist privilege and created a talismanic club of equality. (*Cape Times* 27.06.95)

The interesting thing about the article, besides the messianic iconography of Mandela substituting the sackcloth of oppression '[W]ith a mere green and yellow cloth on his back', is that it encapsulated, in one piece, the Janus-faced nature of the arguments that are used by the African National Congress (ANC) to appeal to different constituencies. To white people (in this case Afrikaners in particular) it is argued that the retention of the Springbok is a mark of reconciliation, a concession to former foes. On the other hand, the retention of the Springbok is expressed to its black constituency as the appropriation of the enemy's symbols or, to put it more colloquially, a 'one in your face' kind of thing. More subtly, it could be taken as a dry run for African nationalist seizure of the commanding heights of Afrikaner sporting institutions, foreshadowing the promised capture of economic and political ones. However, the only black player wearing the green and gold was Chester Williams. Williams had played for the coloured federation allied to Danie Craven's rugby union and served in the apartheid defence force. Yet the actual content of the colours on show did not matter; what was crucial according to most political commentators was the symbolism that signified a nation united across racial lines.

The Luyt show

By 1996 the goodwill generated by the rugby Boks had begun to wilt. With Chester Williams injured, the Boks re-assumed a completely all-white complexion. A white player, Henry Tromp, a hooker, was selected: 'In 1993 Tromp and his father had beaten a sixteen-year-old black employee to death on their farm. They were both convicted and served a short sentence in prison' (D McRae, quoted in Eaton & Alfred 2005: 46). Trevor Manuel, a Cabinet member, revealed that he was an All Black supporter as he could not identify emotionally with an all-white team. Mandela did not attend any of the test matches against New Zealand and Australia. The mascot had decided to speak without raising his voice. Then, in April 1998, Toks van der Linde, the Western Province Stormers' prop, called a South African woman living in Christchurch a 'kaffir'. Earlier, a spat between Sarfu President Louis Luyt and Nelson Mandela ended in a court battle. Luyt was challenging a government-ordered commission of inquiry into rugby. On the field there were only four black players out of a possible 100 black players who played in the 1998 Super 12 series in which South Africa's leading teams participated (Booth 1999).

In other developments, rugby turned professional in the immediate aftermath of the World Cup. The first television deal was signed with Rupert Murdoch for the Tri-Nations contest between South Africa, Australia and New Zealand and the Super 12, worth $555 million over ten years (Luyt 2004). Suddenly the game was injected with huge amounts of cash. Crucially, television rights were sold to a pay-for-view channel, M-Net, for the Super 12 and test matches between Australia and New Zealand, cutting off a large mass market. While this move was criticised, the justification was that there would be more money for the enhancement and provision of facilities in disadvantaged areas. As one rugby commentator pointed out, 'More than 60 per cent of SA Rugby's annual income of more than R320 million comes from broadcasting' (Keohane 2004: 155). If politicians thought they were going to dominate the pace of change, clearly there were new competing interests.

In their analysis of newspaper articles of the time, Farquharson and Majoribanks (2003) see a change from an emphasis on symbolic reconciliation in 1995 to an increasing focus on institutional changes in the run-up to 1999. A major discussion point was the composition of the national team. Whereas the discordant voices in the build-up and aftermath of the 1995 World Cup were largely marginalised, this was not the case in the run-up to the successor event in 1999.

The erstwhile leading government supporters of rugby sounded warning shots with the Minister of Sport and Recreation, Steve Tshwete, talking about how the lack of change in the 'physical chemistry' of the team was creating 'disillusionment in the black community' (*The Star* 13.02.98). The frustrations were starkly revealed by the old National Sports Council/Congress (NSC) warhorse and ANC 'enforcer' Bill Jardine. The NSC was established in the early 1990s as a challenge to Sacos. It was closely allied to the United Democratic Front and the ANC. In a speech to the NSC in March 1998, Jardine outlined a litany of complaints. The old Saru, he declared, had been decimated:

> What has unity meant for us? Where are the 22 Saru union affiliates today? What happened to the more than 200 volunteer rugby administrators and technical personnel? Our school rugby programme, the building blocks of Saru – where has it gone? Our rugby culture in the black community has been destroyed in the wave of euphoria of nation building and reconciliation. (Van Wyk 1993: 233)

Jardine then went on to propose:

> …an agenda for the transformation of rugby…The immediate resignation of the president of Sarfu and his cronies…The convening of an urgent rugby sponsors' summit to discuss their association with the current Sarfu executive, and to plan the future involvement in rugby sponsorship especially as it relates to development…The halting of international tours and competition pending a satisfactory resolution to the crisis…The freezing of all Sarfu's assets. (Van Wyk 1993: 233)

There was some irony in Jardine's critique. His biography illustrates how he had been determined to break Sacos. Formed in the early 1970s under the banner 'No normal sport in an abnormal society', Sacos came to be closely allied to the Non-European Unity Movement that had an antagonistic relationship to the Charterist movement. Jardine and the NSC were criticised by Sacos because of the haste with which unity in South African rugby at both the local and international levels was carried out. Jardine's view was that he was there to follow the dictates of the ANC, and the NSC was there to implement its dictates while seeing off any opposition from other organisations with a base among the oppressed. But what is probably more crucial is the naïveté revealed in Jardine's position. In many senses the horse had bolted. By this time, television rights had been sold, players had individual contracts and sponsors were expecting 'performance'. There was no way to suddenly stop the juggernaut, even though Jardine called on the 'international community, local trade unions, churches and organs of civil society…to join a campaign to isolate Sarfu' (Van Wyk 1993: 233), for by now the international community had been demobilised and those that tried to hold out for a while had been bludgeoned into submission by the ANC. Nowhere in Jardine's analysis did the 'capitulation' of black administrators, their abandoning of 'grassroots' rugby or the ANC's own drift to the right in terms of economic policies and their increasing lack of principle and integrity in international relations feature.

Alongside this, Sarfu's core institutional policies of throwing resources into developing black players, the support for 'development players' as a specific interest group, and racial team quotas came under critical scrutiny. The divide broadly was around those who saw the need for affirmative action while others argued that one must be colour-blind in the selection of sports teams. The latter group was able to appropriate the very slogan of the anti-apartheid movement, 'merit selection', and use it for its own conservative ends.

Things reached a head in a warm-up game against Wales before the 1999 World Cup. The player at the centre of the storm was Breyton Paulse, one of two black players in the squad of 26. Nick Mallet, the coach, indicated that he was going to omit Paulse from the side. Paulse had already earned plaudits for his performances in the green and gold but, despite this, his 'dropping' was played out in terms of needing to pick your best team and the need to win (Farquharson & Majoribanks 2003). Nick Mallet entered the scrum, making the case for merit selection:

> I will not be pushed around. I feel strongly about it. There is no way
> I will ever take part in anything that can be construed as window
> dressing. The changes need to be made at grassroots, through the age
> groups and at provincial level. When you get to international level, you
> have to be the best there is. That is what international sport is all
> about. (*The Star* 23.06.99)

However, for once there were voices that challenged this approach. Journalist Gavin Rich wrote that he was perturbed about the lack of opportunities afforded black players and raised the question of whether the 'fourteen white provincial coaches and their bosses were free of prejudice' (*The Sunday Independent* 14.08.99). Rich drove home his point by focusing on individual selection choices:

> The fact that not everyone in South African rugby is a racist does not
> change my perception that a black player has to conquer many negative
> mindsets to be recognised for his true value. Let's illustrate the point

with a question: Would Dave von Hoesslin (a white player), given his inexperience at the top level and the rough edges to his play, have played scrum half for South Africa were he born black? Breyton Paulse (a black player) would never have played in Dunedin were it not for the pressure from those campaigning for transformation. Some of us were told in Cardiff he was not going to play, the reason being that Carisbrook was considered a tough place for a young player to play his first big test. When I asked management why they did not see the same criterion with Von Hoesslin, I did not receive an answer. Probably because there is no really satisfactory one.

For white coaches, according to Keohane (2004: 49), 'small' was 'a euphemism for "too black"'.

While purporting to reject the idea that anyone but the best player at the time for any position must be selected, ironically Mallet then picked Kaya Malotana for the Tri-Nations which immediately followed the Cardiff test. Malotana had not appeared in any of the four South African Super 12 squads and was an example of the very window dressing that Mallet had earlier railed against. Was this an example of picking players knowing they would fail and so reinforcing one's ideological predispositions?

As the clamour continued about black participation the Springbok manager for the 1999 World Cup, Arthob Petersen, was unphased: 'At this stage let's not get into a debate about who should play where, but we should go out and select the best side to represent South Africa on Saturday' (*Cape Times* 10.08.99).

The development programme

Barely a year and a half after the highly publicised launch of the development programme, Grundlingh pointed to how 'appearances proved to be deceptive. Certain developments bordered on fiascos as a result of poor organisation…Indeed, in 1993 some observers were of the opinion that with the World Cup in the offing, the development programme has lost much of its former urgency' (1995a: 6). However, although the winning of the World Cup was seen as a 'spark' to galvanise the development programme, the much-stated commitment to the latter rapidly became mired in who took ownership of it. Provincial unions called on Sarfu, while Sarfu was caught up in diverting resources into winning at international level. The promise of 'Operation Rugby', encouraging mass participation by building or upgrading over 40 grounds by using 40 per cent of World Cup profits, ground to a halt. The arrival of professionals also meant that players could command financially lucrative contracts.

By the time Mark Keohane arrived on the scene as communications manager of the Springboks in 2000:

> Sarfu's development programme…was a big farce. Millions of rands were ploughed into the game in black areas. But those responsible for black player development would draw up a different list of players every year, and provincial, Super 12 and national coaches would rarely communicate with this department. (Keohane 2004: 50)

Furthermore, by 2002, and in response to the slowness of demographic representivity, quotas had become the central mechanism for giving black players a chance. For Chester Williams, the downside of a quota system was that it labelled black players:

> It creates the perception that if it were not for the quota system then a player would not be good enough to take his place in the team. It can have a negative effect on black players, who can become unsure about the coach's true opinions of them. Such doubts can include whether the coach really rates the player or whether he is being forced to pick the black player. (Williams cited in Keohane 2002: 157)

Nonetheless, at the same time Williams appreciated that:

> Quotas are necessary in South African rugby. Without the quota system there would still be limited opportunities for black players. Black players, for the next few years, will have to learn to deal with the stigma and they will need to focus on the positive aspect that they now have a chance to show what good rugby players they really are…If it was not for a quota system at provincial level, the likes of Breyton Paulse, Bolla Conradie, Quinton Davids, Conrad Jantjies, Adrian Jacobs, Ricardo Loubscher and Deon Kayser would not have been given sufficient exposure in which to prove their worth as rugby players. Lawrence Sephaka and Gcobani Bobo are more recent examples of players who have benefited from the quota system at provincial level. They were both good enough talents to make provincial teams, but they suffered because of a belief that white players were better, purely by virtue of their skin colour. (Williams cited in Keohane 2002 : 157–8)

Corné Krige, former Springbok captain, opposes quotas because for him opportunities should be provided for all people regardless of their race or colour:

> With quotas, is there not a danger of denying some highly talented young white players their place in a team because room must be found for a specified number of black players? I dislike that idea as much as I dislike the idea of excluding players from previously disadvantaged backgrounds. We should not forget the white element in future South African rugby sides, because they have much to offer. There are potentially talented white players who live in the country, for example,

who might need funds and facilities to break through. (Krige with Bills 2005: 150)

Krige ignores the political fact that, put simply, it is hard luck for such white players since the purpose of affirmative action measures is to provide benefits to persons or groups disadvantaged by past political inequalities. Put differently, and in starkly political terms, if a white player needs a leg-up to become the best, he is not worthy of that title.

Mark Keohane is unequivocal. He is convinced that black players would not have come through if it was not for the quota system. However, according to Keohane, at senior level by 2000, the quota system was in a mess because there was no coherent system for identifying talented black players 'and the implementation of the system has for too many years relied on the selection of two black wings plus 13 white players' (Keohane 2004: 50).

In all of this, black players became an 'unnatural' category, white players natural. So a whole gamut of terminology was used ranging from 'non-whites', 'players of colour', 'development players', 'quota players', 'players from previously disadvantaged backgrounds' and 'them' (Keohane 2004: 50); and for at least one national coach, one may add, the 'kaffirs'.[1]

The labelling often boomeranged on the very players that the policy was supposed to help. Hanyani Shimange only became the category 'quota' or 'development player' when he entered senior rugby. Until then he was simply the best hooker and captained his school's team, but 'the moment he reached provincial level, coaches identified him as a quota player from a previously disadvantaged background. They saw black, added one and one together, and came up with three. This type of maths and logic dominated all discussion on transformation within South African rugby' (Keohane 2004: 50). Indeed, the label 'development player' remained despite the individual circumstances of the player. Long after Williams and Thinus Lee had become Springboks, they were still referred to as development players, with coaches using this label to argue that they had implemented quotas.

The balance sheet in 2002–03

An innovation just after the 1995 World Cup was the formation of a black elite squad of players who had displayed potential to go on to the highest levels of the sport. Of the 15 players in the squad named by Keohane, by 2003 not one of them had established a place in the Super 12.

Between 1997 and 2003 there were 17 black Springboks. However, Keohane raises some pertinent questions: 'How many of these 17 black test Boks played regular test rugby? How many did not even make their provincial or Super 12 teams when they returned from international duty? How many are still playing?' (Keohane 2004: 50).

In the 2003 Super 12, 25 of the 126 South African players were black. Of these, just 10 played more than 50 per cent competition game time. The only black player involved in every Super 12 match in 2003 was Ashwin Willemse. The following year, 10 of the 60 regular starting Super 12 players were black. Of the tournament total of 120 players, 26 were black.

By the end of the season in 2001, of the 694 registered professional rugby players in the country, 130 were black. However, these figures have to be read in the context of 300 000 rugby players in the country of whom over 120 000 are black. While more black players were making it into the Springbok squad, at lower levels, black player representation was low.

The reaction was the imposition of quotas in the Vodacom Cup, the Currie Cup and the Super 12. The first two competitions are played by provincial unions within South Africa while the Super 12 consists of teams from South Africa, New Zealand and Australia. Irked by the lack of black players in the Super 12, the authorities imposed an 'unofficial' quota of 4 black players in the squad. In 2002, no team went beyond the quota. In the Currie Cup, the numbers were gerrymandered with the coastal teams requiring 3 black players in a squad of 22 and the northern teams 2 players. More crucially there was no quota system for senior club rugby. In the 2002 national club championships no black players featured in the semi-finals (Keohane 2002). Despite this, by 2003 black players were emerging. But according to Keohane, senior coaches continued to act as crucial gatekeepers not only in selection choices but also in providing game time to black players.

The issue of racism was to rear its head in more spectacular form in the build-up to the 2003 World Cup. The Geo Cronje/Quinton Davids saga made international headlines when it was revealed that Cronje refused to share a room with Davids, a coloured player, at a training camp prior to the 2003 World Cup. Both were thrown out of the squad and Cronje eventually cleared of racism. But subsequent evidence has shown that there was a cover-up.

The revelations came amidst the story of *Kamp Staaldraad* (loosely translated it means Camp Barbed Wire), a military-style 'training' camp conducted over four days in preparation for the 2003 World Cup. It achieved notoriety when pictures were released of naked players forced to assault each other in a pit. Subsequent revelations have been chilling (Krige with Bills 2005).

After the heady heights of 1995, South African rugby had plunged back into the depths. But as we have seen and will see, the incidents were symptomatic of a deeper malaise. If Springbok rugby was all brawn and no brain again, could one expect any finesse or any progressive impulses in team selection in this or any other team?

Unpacking the statistics

On an annual basis since 1994, South African under-21 teams have been selected to assist in player development and to allow national selectors to identify emerging talent. These teams have competed in tournaments against international opponents where the strength of the South African youth could be gauged. South Africa has won three under-21 championships.

To date there have been 319 players who have come through the South African under-21 ranks. Fifty-eight (18.2%) of these players have graduated to international rugby at the senior level with 55 (17.2%) becoming Springboks and 3 players who later went on to represent other countries. There have been 13 (23.6%) black players and 42 (76.4%) white players who have played for the Springboks. When all the test caps of the black players were added together by the end of 2005, there were a total of 149 while the combined figure for white players equalled 747 appearances. Wing Breyton Paulse was by far the most capped black player with 55 games, and second to him is prop Lawrence Sephaka with 19 matches.[2] For white players, hooker, John Smit (48 tests) heads the table followed by lock Victor Matfield (42 tests) and number 8 Joe Van Niekerk (40). There are a host of retired players in their 30s, including flank Corne Krige, number 8 Andre Vos and prop Robbie Kempson.

From this sample, it was found that black players are on average given 11.5 games compared to 18 tests for white players. This means, on average, that white players are given 6.5 more games than black players to prove their mettle. In fact, if Paulse's 55 games were removed, black players would average 7.8 tests. Does this statistic reveal a potential racial bias by Springbok coaches and selectors against black players?

While the numbers do tell a story, discussions of this sort are all too often not sensitive to qualitative factors. In research conducted into sport in the United Kingdom and North America, it was found that black players did not hold key positions or positions of 'centrality' in certain team sports. In other words, positions that directly affect the pattern of play are the terrain of whites (Maguire 1991). Conversely, black players found homes on the periphery. This phenomenon has been termed 'stacking'. Chester Williams was the only black player in the 1995 World Cup. He played on the wing. 'Willemse [a wing] was the only black player to make the match 22 in the 2003 World Cup quarter-final against the All Blacks... In 1999, Breyton Paulse was the only black player in the Bok team in the World Cup play-off for third and fourth. He played on the wing' (Keohane 2004: 63).

The pattern of stacking exposes racial biases by coaches where black athletes are selected to play in secondary positions. According to Maguire, the key decision-making positions, which require 'leadership, intelligence, emotional control and a cool temperament under pressure, are left to whites' (1991: 990). While Maguire was writing about American football in the main, given the similarities with rugby it is a worthwhile exercise to examine if similar patterns exist in South African rugby.

The theory of stacking is based on the 'centrality' of a position and how a player or players would influence the pattern and structure of the team. Even after an indifferent game or two, no one would think of replacing these players because of the overall super-positional roles they played – in terms of leadership, strategy and 'understandings' with other key players: 'The qualities associated with those positions where blacks were over-represented involved strength, speed, quickness, high emotion and good "instincts"' (Maguire 1991: 99). Maguire surmised that 'ideal type, "central" positions are those where high levels of interaction occur' and 'the degree to which the team member must co-ordinate tasks and activities with other members' (Maguire 1991: 97).

During an analysis conducted on stacking in rugby in Britain in 1986, it was revealed that of 169 first-division players 5 per cent were black. Few black players operated in 'central' positions like hooker, number 8, scrum half, fly half or fullback. Out of a possible 26 wings in the league, 7 (27%) were black players. From interviews conducted with players evidence of racial stereotyping was gathered. Players said that they would not have been given a second look if they played a central position and most were shunted onto the wing during their formative years (Maguire 1991).

Chester Williams writes of his own experience and how he ended up on the wing: 'In 1993 I thought I was good enough to play for Western Province and to be a regular. Opportunities were limited. I had played at centre, but was deemed too small, too slow and not aggressive enough in the tackle. Oh, I think my passing was also not up to standard' (Keohane 2002: 64).

If we are to accept Maguire's definition of central positions in rugby, it appears that black players have been kept out of key positions. Of the 13 black players who graduated from national under-21 level it is fullback Conrad Jantjies, scrum halves Norman Jordaan and Enrico Januarie and hooker Hanyani Shimange who have played in central positions. However, Jantjies has only played eight games at national level while Shimange, with seven caps, is the second-choice South African hooker at the moment behind Captain John Smit. Shimange has never started a game for South Africa and has been used sporadically to replace Smit with only a few minutes, sometimes seconds, remaining in the game. Jordaan has made a single appearance for South Africa while Januarie (eight caps) alternates with Fourie du Preez (21 caps) for the number 9 jumper.

Five black players have played on the wing, a periphery position that requires speed and good instincts, with Paulse and new kid on the block Bryan Habana (12 caps) the outstanding performers to date. There have been no black number. 8s or fly halves.

Nonetheless, there are some positive signals to build on. The 2005 national under-19 and -21 'squads have broken through the transformation "ceiling" of unspoken quotas' (Colquhoun 2006: 14). The under-19 team had seven black players in the starting line-up for the final of the world championships, while the under-21 team had eight black players in the starting line-up. Of the four black players who played in Jake White's under-21 IRB 2001 title winning team, three – Enrico Januarie, Ashwin Willemse and Guthro Steenkamp – have gone on to win Springbok caps. It is that level of 'coming through' that was missing in the immediate post-1995 period that will need to be sustained.

We leave the level of national/international rugby developments and provide a 'fine-grained analysis' (O'Brien & Slack 2004: 169) of the impact of the last decade on one rugby club in the 'coloured' area of Durban.

Jaguars: the pride of Sydenham

Ask anyone in the area about the rugby club and they will happily point you down Randles Road to the Capell Road Ground, the den of Jaguars Rugby Club. When compared to the plush club rugby teams based in Durban North with several well-manicured pitches, it is hard to believe that the modest Sydenham club has managed to be competitive in the KwaZulu-Natal Premier Division.

In 2005 Jaguars underlined their nickname as the sabre-toothed minnows when they finished joint-third in the Premier league (Moor Cup) and lost in the semi-finals of the Murray Cup knockout cup competition. They remained undefeated at home and it is no secret that opponents find it extremely uncomfortable at Capell Road, which has come to be known as the 'House of Pain' like the famous Carisbrook Stadium in Dunedin, New Zealand.

The relative success of 2005 has inspired the club to map out an ambitious three-year plan to win the league by 2007. However, owing to the club's success, this optimism actually might turn out to be quite detrimental because Jaguars have become a victim of their own success. This stems from the transformation policies implemented by the South African Rugby Union/KwaZulu-Natal Rugby Union (KZNRU), which result in the club's best players being plucked away for provincial call ups, as well as in a lack of human, land and financial resources available to the Sydenham-based side.

To understand the current blockages that continue to impede the club's progress, it is important to have an understanding of the roots of Jaguars and its relationship with the KZNRU. Officially founded in 1987, Jaguars was born out of the amalgamation of four coloured clubs. Between 1960 and 1988, black rugby in the province of Natal was under control of the Natal Rugby Board (NRB, known as the Natal Rugby Union at one stage) and was affiliated to the non-racial body Saru. Saru followed the tenets of Sacos, which called for the dismantling of apartheid, as there could be 'no normal sport in an abnormal society'.

To avoid any confusion it must be pointed out that the white rugby fraternity in the province was also known as the NRB and was an affiliate of SARB, which controlled white rugby. Even though SARB and the white NRB tacitly supported the National Party by following the government's racist sports policies, the IRB, which governs the sport of rugby union globally, still acknowledged SARB as the ruling rugby body in South Africa. In 1992, SARB and Saru fused together to unify as one organisation. The new body was called Sarfu and in 2004 was renamed Saru.

During the period preceding the merger of SARB and Saru, the black NRB reported to Saru. Although competitive leagues were run in Durban and Pietermaritzburg, the standard of rugby played by the local black players was not as strong as that in the areas of Eastern and Western Cape. Even so, the local black players played the game with gusto. However, in the mid-to-late 1980s black rugby in Natal went through a rut. For several reasons the player base had been eroded and there were only three active clubs left. With so few teams operating, interest in the game waned while most of the games turned into 'grudge matches' and were not played with the best interests of the game at heart.

With the local leagues crumbling, the NRB sought guidance from mother body Saru. However, there was no resolution and the Saru officials left the NRB in a state of limbo.

Moving from one cage to another

At the end of 1987, a meeting was chaired in St Anne's Church Hall, and in the presence of representatives of the four amalgamating clubs, the decision was made to form one black rugby team and participate in the white-controlled NRB club competition from 1988 onwards. Thus it was that Jaguars was founded. However, Saru did not give this initiative its blessing. When Jaguars became an affiliate of the Durban Rugby Sub Union, all organised black rugby under the banner of Saru ceased. (This is a salient point because when there were unification talks between Saru and SARB in 1991–92 and the process of unification was taking place at a national and provincial level in other parts of the country, there was no actual unification in KwaZulu-Natal. This was to result in the current state of rugby in the province where the black clubs remain a very small minority and have very little influence in the running of the local game.)

The NRB officials had suggested that all the black players be absorbed by the white clubs but the founding members of Jaguars, Dekker Govender and Malcolm Groome, scoffed at the notion: 'The point of forming one club was to keep the culture of rugby alive in coloured community' (Groome, interview 04.01.06). Eventually a decision was made to include Jaguars in the NRB's lowest league, the fifth division, and the club entered one team in 1988.

In their inaugural season, Jaguars found themselves on the receiving end of some cricket scores but the following year (1989) two teams were entered into the club competitions. Jaguars now fielded sides in the fourth and fifth divisions. However, the club initially found it hard to find their footing because the fifth division was the stomping ground of many former Natal and club first-team players, who were now enjoying social rugby:

> Yes there were many former Natal and first XV club players in those
> fifth division teams so the games were tough. We also battled because
> our pack was smaller than the other forwards so we used to have a
> hard time up front. We had such a potent backline but sometimes we
> were unable to unleash them. (Govender, interview 03.01.06)

Both Groome and Govender also highlighted what they perceived as biased refereeing against them. This is something that, according to them, would intensify as the scores became closer during their rise to the Premier Division. In addition, players were subjected to verbal abuse:

> We also started being verbally abused. We were called 'Coolies, Kaffirs,
> Bushman, Bushies and Hottentots' on many occasions. People would
> say 'what do you know about the game?' and 'why are you playing this
> white sport'. But, we never complained to the Union [NRB] because we
> didn't take those comments seriously. The way I looked at it if
> somebody was calling me a Coolie I was one up on him. (Govender,
> interview 03.01.06)

In 1989 the Jaguars' first team was able to win the fourth division knockout cup – much to the surprise of all and sundry. That year the father of white rugby, Doc Danie Craven, made a trek to Durban after hearing about the growth of black rugby in the province. Craven was impressed with the club being in the heart of coloured community and with the fact that there were decent, albeit modest, facilities at the ground. Craven gave the Jaguars' executive an undertaking that he would support them and eventually cajoled the NRB into giving the club a R120 000 loan to build the clubhouse. As noted below, this loan would eventually become an albatross for the club and Jaguars are still paying it off.

While overt racism is one challenge the club has had to face, another problem is the lack of support Jaguars receives from the KZNRU. While the provincial body is quick to laud Jaguars as a positive exponent of their development programme (even though this is a misnomer because the club has been around since long before the catchphrase 'development' was coined), this has hindered the club's progress.

The KZNRU has always romanticised Jaguars' rise in the media and in Saru/Sarfu yet has done very little in terms of providing land, money and human resources. The transformation policy also works to the detriment of the club because, whenever provincial teams are selected, several Jaguars' players are usually to be found in the junior and senior KwaZulu-Natal squads. Although some players are in the team on merit, the others are there to meet quota requirements.

While the selection of these players does reflect positively on the club, in practice their departure weakens the team substantially and kills the momentum that has been established for it to move forward and upward. With none of the other eight clubs in the Premier Division selecting more than a paltry three players of colour in their starting XVs, Jaguars has been called upon constantly to provide the cream of black talent. Even though there are 17 other black clubs in the province, the next best black club is Wentworth, which plays in the third division.

With Jaguars seen as the home of black rugby in KwaZulu-Natal, players from various coloured and black townships have joined the club. However, many of these players do not have their own transport or cannot afford to pay for public transport. Accordingly, the club forks out money to run taxis (minibuses) to Wentworth, Newlands East, Ntuzuma and Marianridge. This comes out of the Jaguars' budget and costs the club about 40 per cent of its grant and sponsorship money. This cost is not carried by any of the other Premier Division clubs whose player bases are mainly middle-class white and black players.

Jaguars also spend a large chunk of their budget on the clubhouse, which was built in 1996 with a loan of R120 000 from the NRB. At the time, chairman Martin Newell agreed to pay off the money in instalments. However, with extremely limited resources, Jaguars have sat with this loan for 11 years, and because of the KZNRU's refusal to write it off, the club is forced to siphon off money which could be spent on the players and on investing in new resources. Jaguars is also given the smallest budget out of Premier Division clubs yet they have the highest expenses and historically have never received funding from the union. The current system of allocating funding in KwaZulu-Natal is geared towards maintaining the top clubs – the more teams you have, the more funding you get. While at one level this seems fair, the allocation affects Jaguars adversely. Here we see the poverty of the approach that sees non-racialism as denoting the denial of race and the historical privileges that have been accumulated over time. In fact, until recently, some of the white clubs were able to make a killing because they were able to rent parking space and collect the money for their own coffers when big games were played at the Absa Stadium.

The poaching of the Jaguars

The Jaguars' success has also led to several of its players migrating to other clubs within and across provincial boundaries. Even though local club rugby is meant to be fully amateur, Govender says that it is commonplace for under-the-table payments to be made.

With the lure of more money and with the 'development' or 'small club' label attached to them, the Jaguars have steadily lost players to the other bigger and wealthier clubs. For instance, fly half Andy 'Kaiser' Fynn and fullback Lungisa Kama have sought success at College Rovers, even though this has meant their stepping down from the first team at Jaguars to the second XV at their new club. Indeed, even when there have been injuries in the first team in the positions that Fynn and Kama have occupied, more often than not other white players have been called up to fill the gaps. Meanwhile, talented black players elsewhere have been negatively affected by racial bias, with coaches using players in provincial representative teams, as one Jaguars official put it, 'as pawns'.

According to Francois Louis, a Jaguars official, the problem with white clubs is that: 'they only want the finished product. They don't want to invest money or resources into developing black players. That's why it's easy for them to poach players from us' (Louis, interview 06.01.06). As if to emphasise this point, in April 2006 the Jaguars' outstanding 'coloured' fly half Ryan de la Harpe was signed by the Mpumalanga Pumas after strenuous overtures by local white clubs.

Meanwhile development initiatives are also undermined by racial bias. For instance, in about 1993, Beacon Sweets sponsored a development club initiative that saw Francois Louis and Gerald Pyoos running mini-rugby (usually played barefoot by children) in Sydenham. The programme became so successful that droves of black players flocked to Capell Road to learn the game. In fact, the Junior Jags, as they were nicknamed, became so good that they started to roll over the traditionally strong white clubs at under-6 to under-13 level. But, inexplicably, the sponsorship was suddenly withdrawn and the initiative died with it.

Concerns about tokenism, dealing with the lack of resources and inequitable distribution of income to the clubs, remain contested issues. Even though Louis chairs the transformation committee of KZNRU, by his own admission the committee has its limitations:

> We can't enforce anything because all our proposals have to be
> approved by council and the KZNRU executive. With the majority of
> the officials at the KZNRU being white, transformation is seen as a
> dirty word and an attack on white hegemony. There have been
> insignificant changes, even though the Sharks/KZNRU are meant to
> be the most transformed rugby body in the country. (Louis, interview
> 06.01.06) [Sharks are the professional arm of rugby while the KZNRU
> takes care of club rugby in the province.]

Meanwhile, black representation has also been minimal in the boardroom. Even though Oregan Hoskins, who is 'coloured', was the president of KZNRU as the study unfolded and chaired the Sharks Board of Directors between 2002 and 2003, there had been no black CEO of either the amateur or professional arms of rugby in the province. Indeed, when the senior vice-presidency position at the KZNRU fell vacant in late 2005, the man in line for the job was junior vice-president Francois Louis. However, Louis, who Jaguars official, Ludwig Bessig described as 'a born administrator', was challenged for the position by a junior administrator, Gary Meyer (Bessig, interview 06.01.06). In his time on council Louis has been seen as a radical by the conservative element. If one was to measure terms of service to the game, Louis had served on KZNRU council since unification in 1992 and even President Hoskins admitted that Louis was senior to him. However, Louis lost at the ballot box to Meyer. On a council of 42 members, with a meagre 8 black officials, it became common knowledge that the vote was not about competency but rather about preserving the upper echelons of power in white hands. Reflecting on the 'shock' that the voting took such an overtly racial bias, one of the Jaguars' officials reflected: 'Indeed the last outpost stands in the province and the message from the election blared out like a klaxon: the only Jaguars we want are ones without teeth.' (interview 06.01.06)

Jaguars without teeth?

What this case study demonstrates is the lack of a clear development programme for black rugby, how voting power (skilfully manipulated) blocks black administrators with a vision of change from rising through the ranks, how the transformation agenda is abused so that provinces and white clubs are able to use money to buy 'the finished product', and how this impacts negatively on clubs like Jaguars. Eleven years after winning the World Cup and 14 years after 'unity', there is still only one club from a disadvantaged background in the Premier league of rugby in the province. It would appear that the agenda is to create an elite group of players while the broadening of the game has fallen off the list of priorities.

Despite this, what remains so impressive about the Jaguars, apart from their sound administrative base and their success in producing top-class players, is the manner in which they have mutated from a 'coloured' club to a truly non-racial club. Today some seven of the players in the first team are African and the captain for 2006 is white. Furthermore, watch them play at home and you get a distinct sense of carnival: a small club battling against the odds, playing overwhelmingly 'white' sides with greater resources and longer traditions. Spectators are involved in the game – turning it into a spectacle full of drama. The administrators of the club are all ex-players. The clubhouse is a place of entertainment for the people of the area during the week.

In the pursuit of greater success, the club is looking for bigger sponsors. Yet even with the club's present success and track record, it encounters difficulties in securing commercial backing because of the limits of the impoverished market in which it is geographically and socially located. Thus in 2005 it managed to secure the sponsorship of a company, ChemSpec, selling spray-paint to panel beaters. A white firm, it hoped to break into the panel-beater market, traditionally a place with considerable 'coloured' influence. However, by 2006, having established a name, the company has proved hesitant to follow through on earlier promises. Despite such problems, the Jaguars remain determined to secure a lucrative sponsorship deal that will allow them to retain good players and even attract players from other clubs.

Will this change the club? If today the Jaguars can be defined as a 'co-operative club', will sponsorship change them into a 'commercial enterprise' (Howe 1999)? What effects will this have on the sense of community, on the way ex-players stay in the game and the environment created where black players in an overwhelmingly white rugby culture 'find their feet'? Will not these be sacrificed as the Jaguars embark on their hunt for increased sponsorship and silverware? Will not the very values upon which the Jaguars have built their success be undermined – and their teeth pulled?

Conclusions and recommendations

'Truck and trailer' is a metaphor that can be used to understand transformation in South African rugby.[3] The national team and the running of the game that flows from this are increasingly de-linked from the rest of rugby at local level. Measuring the success of transformation in rugby by reference to representation at national level is important because of its high public profile and because it allows for the creation of role models and so on. However, it can also be a poisoned chalice. It can cover up the lack of fundamental change at lower levels. This means that the base of the game is not broadened; the number of black players coming through is limited, placing incredible pressure on a few black players at the top and on the coach and selectors if top black players get injured. Transformation then becomes a roller coaster, with some provinces, Super 12 teams and the national squad showing progress – and then suddenly moving backwards with fewer and fewer black players available in the team. Furthermore, as we have seen, if qualitative factors are also not properly attended to and stacking is allowed to continue, those black players who do present themselves do so only as speedsters out on the wing.

The ideal situation would be for the transformation agenda to have a seamless web from bottom to top. As in the rules of the game, allowing one component of a loose maul to pull or push another along is not illegal per se – for 'truck and trailer' to be effective and not penalised, the entire loose maul must be in tandem, connected and bound to each other. But when the players in the front are acting as shields for the ball carrier behind, preventing him from being tackled, then a truck and trailer situation arises. This is, metaphorically, what is happening in South African rugby. The relative, if by no means adequate, representation of players of colour in the top echelon of the game disguises the fact that, behind them, all is not well at all. At that level, the ball carriers remain overwhelmingly white.

Chester Williams makes a number of suggestions. For him the coach of a team is crucial: 'The only person who can erase doubt is the coach. If our coaches are committed to selecting the best possible players in South African rugby, then there would not be a colour issue and the matter of quotas would disappear in time' (Williams cited in Keohane 2002: 157). There has to be a broader base of black players 'competing at provincial and Super 12 level on a regular basis. From this pool those good enough to make the national team will do so. You will never need a quota system applied to the test team if the quota system is effective at provincial level. The black players will stand up and be picked at the highest level because they are good enough.' All this, according to Williams, is predicated 'on a new order' administering the game.

Mark Keohane places great emphasis on changes that need to be made at domestic level and on the dangers of 'window dressing':

> Those politicians who were eager to see some progress in transformation, but who were frustrated by the slow pace of change, started playing the numbers game. But their good intentions were misdirected; instead of focusing on the domestic structures of the game, their emphasis was on the national level. This only harmed the fight by black players for equality in South African rugby and it abetted the absurd notion that blacks could not play test rugby. Black players were used as political pawns in the middle and late 1990s to deflect government pressures – and those players were the ones who suffered most. (2002: 153–4)

Stanley Raubenheimer, who played briefly for Western Province in 1993 as scrum half and who was a product of the anti-apartheid Sarfu, focuses on the fact that black administrators simply fitted into the 'system' and lacked courage: 'We can blame the provincial presidents and coaches until we are blue in the face, but our own people have let us down since unity. The administrators are only looking after themselves' (Keohane 2002: 107).

What Raubenheimer is alluding to is the need to rethink the kind of administrators needed in rugby. Is it simply about managing in the same way that previous white administrators did – seeing things in technical ways rather than in political and technical ways? Or is it about adopting a more patient route of building a solid foundation, from the school level upwards? Clearly, it means rather more than just taking the lead from government, and it will entail challenging the government to free up resources to fund a solid cohort of coaches at school level, identifying schools in townships that serve as well-endowed centres of excellence, forcing the hand of sponsors to look downwards for success rather than upwards, and creating the conditions for innovation rather than for the imitation of global trends.

There are also 'new' race issues to deal with in these new times. Mark Keohane points out how the 'black versus coloured power struggle has almost grown as prominent as provincialism...Black is not coloured and coloured is not black. While this debate continues, the white conservatives sit back and play the role of puppeteer' (2004: 236–7).

Nick Mallet, the former Springbok coach and present director of rugby at Western Province, weighed in with his own views on how to change South African rugby in early 2006. For Mallet, the 14 provincial unions would need to be reduced to 6 professional franchises that would each contract 35 players:

> SA rugby cannot afford to have 600 professional players because there's no strength in depth and because it costs too much money. I propose we pay fewer players – around 200 – more money. This way the Boks would stay in SA because they would receive good Super 14 and national contracts. (*Sunday Times* 02.04.06)

At the moment, the drain on South African players to all parts of the globe is significant, with some 300 players plying their trade overseas. If ever there is an indication that sport is work this is it. Good players abroad can earn between a million and a million-and-a-half rand a year. South African players in the Super 12 earn just over half that at best.

Mallet further argued that the Vodacom Cup should be jettisoned and replaced by a national club competition. The clubs, via a grant from Saru, would be run on a semi-professional basis. Mallet builds in a transformation element at this level with clubs only receiving:

> the grant if they met quotas – no transformation equals no money. You could perhaps say three white players must start for 'black' teams and five black players start for 'white' teams. This would guarantee broad-based transformation. (*Sunday Times* 02.04.06)

Mallet also favours a draft system for the six franchises and believes that this would provide a blueprint for more competitive games demanded by spectators and create the conditions for change because, in his words, 'the market forces will force it to change' (*Sunday Times* 02.04.06)

Sports journalists have, on the whole, received Mallet's proposals with acclaim. Yet if every union was to have six clubs, they would all require substantial resources to sustain more than one top black rugby club. And white clubs would simply raid black clubs for 'the finished product'. The game itself would become confined to fewer players and it would prove difficult to have a draft system grafted onto a quota system. Mallet's proposals would create the basis of the complete uncoupling of professional rugby from amateur. Yet the 'business model' for rugby keeps growing in influence.

Oregan Hoskins became Saru president in 2006. In a telephonic interview on 3 March 2006, he offered the following answers to questions of transformation and leadership:

> Q: Do you have any ideas about developing the game in areas where there are scarce resources?

OH: Let me say this: for transformation to take place the development of the game will have to work hand in hand. SA Rugby can provide the skills but government must provide the resources. We can't do that.

Q: But, don't you think given our past SA Rugby should be doing something extra to help previously disadvantaged areas/schools/clubs gain access to resources?

OH: We don't have the money to invest in resources. That must come from government. We can provide the skills, leadership and knowledge – like coaching and organising competitions. SA Rugby is not here to build infrastructure in the townships – that is government's job. We simply don't have the capacity or finances to do that. Government and SA Rugby must work hand in hand to develop the sport and I can tell you that the ministry of sport want to work with us to grow the game.

Q: What type of leadership model do you envisage for SA Rugby?

OH: I want the executive staff to handle the day-to-day running of the company and the Springboks. The CEO [Johan Prinsloo] would handle the goings-on at the head office of SA Rugby in Cape Town and ensure that everything is running smoothly. The president's council [made up of the 14 provincial heads, vice president, deputy president and president] would act as a check and balance on the executive staff. The President's Council would formulate policy and the executive staff would ensure that this policy is carried out. In no way do I see the President's Council becoming redundant or around just to rubber-stamp decisions. It is important to run our company like a professional business with the players the most valued assets.

There are some honest but worrying signals coming from Hoskins that stem from his view that he is running a business. He maintains that SA Rugby is not going to build infrastructure from the tens of millions it derives from television rights and sponsorship deals. For Hoskins, that is the job of government. He is right. But this is a government that has not thrown significant resources into disadvantaged areas. In fact, with Soccer 2010 looming, the emphasis will be on the 'big' developments – huge stadiums and the Gautrain and Dube-tradeport. Nor does the new macro-economic plan, the Accelerated Shared Growth Initiative for South Africa, signal any new development path.

Hence it is that as the rugby officials pass the ball to the politicians, they in turn look to the private sector, which looks to the disadvantaged areas and sees no market for their goods. And so intricate patterns are weaved across the field but there is no one taking the ball beyond the gain line into disadvantaged areas.

In 1995, two somewhat contradictory forces took to the playing field: the professionalism of the game that has as its centre profit, and an African nationalism that saw a progressive change of the game away from white dominance. African nationalism, beyond the power of Mandela's moral legitimacy at the time, was appeased by the singing of *Shosholoza* (a song ironically sung by migrant mineworkers to reflect on their difficult lives), and the renaming of the national team as 'the *Amabokoboko*'. This 'Africanised the team and gave blacks a stake in the Springboks for the first time' (Booth 1999: 189). In 2006, African nationalism demands more than renaming. But South African rugby players expect to be paid the same amounts as New Zealand and Australian players, leaving few resources for the development of the game in disadvantaged areas. The South African government is at the same time tied into an economic programme that places a premium on developing facilities in these areas. The emphasis rather is 'a cycle of events-driven development' (Booth 1999: 179).

At present the emphasis is on ensuring black representation at national level, but this is accompanied by a concomitant decline in broad-based development. Part of the reason for this comes from the heady days of 'unity'. Tommy Bedford, who played a pivotal role in the initial negotiations, reflected ruefully recently on how officials fed off the gravy delivered by Springbok rugby and the neglect of club rugby:

> Black and white rugby administrators had the undoubted responsibility to treat full integration [through the clubs, at club level competition] as their greatest priority for South Africa when they formed Sarfu. They singularly failed in this because they concentrated on getting the Springboks back into action; then on getting the IRB professional status; followed by the Super 12 and Tri-Nations. They allowed club rugby to go to pot and unable to produce the number of black players necessary for a new South Africa. So a quota system is a poor substitute but understandable 14 years on. (*Sunday Tribune* 19.03.06)

Without a kick from government or rugby officials, the truck of professional rugby could be un-coupled from the trailer of what is left of amateur club rugby in black areas.

Notes

1   The word was used by the then Springbok coach Andre Markgraff.

2   Many of these players are still playing and these figures discerned from yearbooks and interviews are valid for the second part of 2005.

3   Truck and trailer is rugby jargon used to explain obstruction at an attacking maul. What happens is that the ball carrier at the tail of the maul becomes de-linked from the maul by either detaching completely or by not being bound to a teammate at the shoulder. By detaching from the maul the player is using other team members as a shield to obstruct opposition from being able to fairly contest for possession. This is illegal and results in a penalty being awarded to a defending team.

References

Booth D (1999) Recapturing the moment? Global rugby, economics and the politics of nation in post-apartheid South Africa. In T Chandler & J Nauright (Eds) *Making the rugby world*. London: Frank Cass.

Colquhoun A (2006) Notes by the editor. In *SA Rugby Annual*. Cape Town: MWP Media.

Eaton T & Alfred L (2005) *A compendium of South African sports writing*. Cape Town: Double Storey Books.

Farquharson K & Majoribanks T (2003) Transforming the Springboks: Re-imagining the South African nation through sport. *Social Dynamics*, 29(1): 27–48.

Grundlingh A (1995a) Playing for power. In A Grundlingh, A Odendaal & B Spies (Eds) *Beyond the tryline*. Johannesburg: Ravan Press.

Grundlingh A (1995b) The new politics of rugby. In A Grundlingh, A Odendaal & B Spies (Eds) *Beyond the tryline*. Johannesburg: Ravan Press.

Howe P (1999) Professionalism, commercialism and the rugby club: The case of Pontypridd RFC. In T Chandler & J Nauright (Eds) *Making the rugby world*. London: Frank Cass.

Keohane M (2002) *Chester: A biography of courage*. Cape Town: Don Nelson.

Keohane M (2004) *Springbok rugby uncovered*. Cape Town: Zebra Press.

Krige C with Bills P (2005) *The right place at the wrong time*. Cape Town: Zebra Press.

Luyt L (2004) *Walking proud*. Cape Town: Don Nelson.

Maguire J (1991) Sport, racism and British society: A sociological study of England's elite male Afro/Caribbean soccer and rugby union players. In G Jarvie (Ed) *Sport racism and ethnicity*. London: The Falmer Press.

O'Brien D & Slack T (2004) Strategic responses to institutional pressures for commercialisation: A case study of an English rugby union club. In T Slack (Ed) *The commercialisation of sport*. London: Routledge.

Odendaal A (1995) 'The thing that is not round': The untold history of black rugby in South Africa. In A Grundlingh, A Odendaal & B Spies (Eds) *Beyond the tryline*. Johannesburg: Ravan Press.

Van Wyk C (1993) *Now listen here: The life and times of Bill Jardine*. Johannesburg: STE publishers.

Interviews

Malcolm Groome and Dekker Govender, Jaguars officials, January 2006

Ludwig Bessig, Jaguars' official, January 2006

Francois Louis and Gerald Pyoos, Jaguars officials, January 2006

Oregan Hoskins, president of Saru, March 2006

17 Violence against women in South Africa

Lisa Vetten

A praise song to the 'winning nation' that is South Africa, President Mbeki's 2006 'State of the Nation' speech is forward-looking and optimistic. He moves between past and present to measure the country's 'hectic pace' of progress post-1994 and makes it clear that we need to speed up efforts 'towards the day when they [the South African people] will be liberated from the suffocating tentacles of the legacy of colonialism and apartheid'. The president proposes a variety of economic and developmental interventions, carried out by partnerships amongst all sectors of the population,[1] to usher in this age of hope when we 'shall go out with joy/And be led out in peace'.

Women too feature within this vision. Specifically, they are noted for their contributions to the dismantling of apartheid, while their current circumstances are to be addressed by strengthening their economic prospects and paying the 'necessary attention' to their participation at decision-making levels of the public service. In this way they are fitted within an approach which foregrounds race and economic marginalisation but is silent on their oppression as women, as well as on measures intended to transform women's position in relation to men. For this state of the nation to be delivered, we had to wait another four weeks – when former Deputy President Jacob Zuma went on trial for rape and President Mbeki was silent on masculine power, this trial was eloquent on it.

The contrast between Mbeki's 'State of the Nation' speech – with its visions, plans and priorities – and Zuma's rape trial is instructive. Arguably, it illustrates what is, for many, the contradiction of post-apartheid South Africa: a woman-friendly state with its vision and plans for the achievement of gender equality – including a constitutional commitment to such equality and some of the highest numbers in the world of women holding public office – yet marked by the intractable, stubborn persistence of violence against women. However, as this chapter argues, there is no necessary connection between a progressive legislative framework and a reduction in violence against women. If anything, seeing a contradiction between these two sets of facts perhaps says more about the assumptions we hold about the power of the law and rights, than about their ability to deliver in practice. The argument in this chapter then is that this state of affairs represents not so much a contradiction as an illustration of the contingent, conditional and contested nature of gender equality in South Africa.

The argument proceeds in three parts. The first sets out what is seen as the contradiction: state responses to violence against women and a Bill of Rights enabling the advancement of women's rights, and the statistics for such violence. The section concludes by analysing how these particular responses have constructed the problem of violence against women and also critically examines the relationship between law and policy reform and the incidence of violence. The next section begins setting out the conditions and contingencies through a focus on the implementation of the Domestic Violence Act (No. 116 of 1998). What is contested is explored through the debates that have erupted around rape: in particular, the Charlize Theron advertisement against rape, rape statistics, as well as the judgment in the Zuma trial. These examples illustrate how while a good many changes may be achieved at the institutional level, this does not necessarily alter people's everyday behaviours, beliefs and values. The Zuma rape trial in particular highlights how resistant sections of the populace remain to discourse and practices intended to promote women's rights. Indeed, these contests point to another whole set of conditionalities whose operation ensures that only some women are treated as deserving of the protection of the law, and only some men are thought capable of rape.

The contradiction

Since coming to power in 1994, the African National Congress (ANC) government has introduced a range of measures intended to advance women's rights. These have included setting up the national gender machinery (comprising the Commission on Gender Equality [CGE], the Office on the Status of Women and the Parliamentary Joint Standing Committee on the Improvement of the Quality of Life and Status of Women), reforming a variety of discriminatory laws and introducing quotas to increase the numbers of women holding political office. Individual women and their advocates have also sought to promote a women's rights agenda through the courts and Constitution (Gouws 2005).

State responses

In line with a number of commitments made to addressing gender inequalities,[2] the National Crime Prevention Strategy of 1996 established crimes of violence against women and children as a national priority (a status such crimes have continued to enjoy in subsequent national policing strategy documents) and instituted a number of legislative reforms in this area. In relation to rape these included mandatory minimum sentences for certain rapes (the Criminal Law Amendment Act [No. 105 of 1997]); tightening bail conditions for those charged with rape through the Criminal Procedure Second Amendment Act (No. 85 of 1997); and, in 1998, introducing the National Policy Guidelines for the Handling of Victims of Sexual Offences.[3] National Management Guidelines for Sexual Assault Care and the National Sexual Assault Policy were also released by the Department of Health in 2005. Specialist facilities such as sexual offences courts and Thuthuzela centres[4] have also been set up. Still outstanding, however, is new sexual offences legislation, which has been mooted for reform since 1998.

The five family courts[5] set up around the country represent the specialist legal facilities established to address domestic violence. In relation to policy, the Policy Framework and Strategy for Shelters for Victims of Domestic Violence in South Africa was released in 2003, while the Domestic Violence Act (DVA) (No. 118 of 1998) provides women with protection from such violence.

The Domestic Violence Act

The DVA, which replaced the Prevention of Family Violence Act (No. 133 of 1993), is widely regarded as being one of the more progressive examples of such legislation internationally (Combrinck 2005).

The Act introduces South Africa's first definition of domestic violence and includes both a broad range of behaviours,[6] as well as a variety of familial and domestic relationships[7] within its ambit. Powers vested in the court by the DVA include being able to order the abuser (or respondent) not to commit any act of domestic violence (nor engage anyone else to perpetrate such behaviour), nor enter the family home or his/her partner's workplace. Respondents may also be instructed to leave the residence while continuing to pay rent or mortgage as well as providing money for food and other household expenses. In some circumstances, respondents may be prevented from having contact with a child or children. In addition, courts may order the police to remove the respondent's guns or other dangerous weapons, as well as provide a protective escort to the victim (or applicant) while she fetches clothing or other personal items from the home.

Because victims of domestic violence have long been on the receiving end of an ineffectual criminal justice system (Artz 1999; Human Rights Watch 1997), the DVA attempts both to place a number of obligations[8] upon the police in particular, as well as to provide for mandatory oversight of their adherence to the Act. Police officers' failure to comply with either the Act or its regulations constitutes misconduct which must be reported to the Independent Complaints Directorate (ICD), the civilian oversight body established in terms of the 1995 South African Police Service Act. The ICD primarily fulfils a monitoring and oversight role with the police obliged to institute disciplinary proceedings against recalcitrant officers (unless the ICD directs otherwise). Additionally, the ICD is required to submit six-monthly reports to Parliament recording the number and nature of complaints received against the police, as well as the recommendations made with regard to such complaints. The National Commissioner of the South African Police Services (SAPS) must also submit six-monthly reports to Parliament detailing the number and nature of complaints against the police for failing to adhere to their statutory obligations; the disciplinary proceedings instituted; and steps taken as a result of recommendations made by the ICD.

Many would appear to be seeking the Act's protection, with some 157 391 applications for protection orders made at 70 per cent of courts around the country in 2004 alone (Vetten 2005).

Advancing women's rights through the Constitution

Beginning with *S v. Baloyi*,[9] a number of Constitutional Court cases have begun exploring and outlining the duties imposed upon the police and courts in terms of the Bill of Rights. These cases have primarily centred on state duties in relation to rape and have begun establishing a delictual duty upon state agents.

In *S v. Baloyi* the Constitutional Court held that the Constitution imposes a direct obligation on the state to protect the right of all persons to be free from domestic violence. In *Carmichele v Minister of Safety and Security*[10] the high court held that the common law of delict required development in order to reflect the constitutional duty on the state and, in particular, the police and the prosecution, to protect 'the public in general, and women in particular, against the invasion of their fundamental rights by the perpetrators of violent crime'. The court ruled that the police and prosecution thus owed 'the plaintiff a legal duty to protect her against the risk of sexual violence' in the circumstances of the case.[11] In *Van Eeden v. Minister of Safety and Security* the Supreme Court of Appeal (SCA) held that the respondent owed a legal duty to the appellant to take reasonable steps to prevent an escaped serial rapist from causing her harm.[12] The case of *K v. Minister of Safety and Security*[13] concerned the gang rape by three on-duty policemen of a young woman whom they had offered a lift home after she was left stranded without transport in the early hours of the morning. This case turned on whether or not the Minister of Safety and Security was vicariously liable for the actions of the three officers. Ultimately the Constitutional Court found that the minister was indeed liable.

Criminal matters that have sought to draw on the Bill of Rights have centred on women who killed abusive partners. In *S v. Ferreira*[14] the SCA was asked to arrive at a suitable sentence for Ms Ferreira that balanced her right to be free from all forms of violence against her common-law partner's right to life. Taking all the facts of Ms Ferreira's abuse into account, the SCA substituted her life sentence with one of six years, with the portion she had not yet served to be suspended.

The second case concerning a woman who killed her abusive partner was that of *S v. Engelbrecht*.[15] This case attempted to reformulate the law of self-defence in a way that took into account women's experiences of violence and the gendered nature of self-defence. In considering Mrs Engelbrecht's actions, the court was also asked to take into account the efforts she had made to evade or stop the abuse before she finally killed her husband.[16] Ultimately, while the judge in this matter decided that Mrs Engelbrecht had made all reasonable attempts to end the abuse, she was over-ruled by her two assessors and Mrs Engelbrecht was convicted of murder. However, even if the arguments advanced did not succeed in having Mrs Engelbrecht acquit-ted, they played a significant part in determining her sentence: to be detained until the rising of the court. This meant that once Judge Satchwell stood up to leave the courtroom after completing her judgment, Mrs Engelbrecht was free to go.

The statistics

Police figures for rape post-1994 have consistently shown an upward trend. Between the period April 1994 to March 1995, 44 751 rapes were reported to the police. By 2004–05 the figures had risen to 55 000. However, because these statis-tics reflect only the number of rapes reported to police, the true extent of sexual violence in South Africa is currently unknown. Statistics South Africa (Stats SA) found that one in two rape survivors reported being raped to the police (Hirschowitz et al. 2000), while the Medical Research Council (MRC) found that one in nine women reported being raped (Jewkes & Abrahams 2002). Although their findings differ as to the extent, both studies clearly find rape to be under-reported. On the basis of the above studies it can be extrapolated that the 55 000 rapes reported by the SAPS in the data released for 2004–05 are more accurately calculated as falling somewhere between the region of 110 000 and 490 000 actual rapes having taken place.

At present, there is no data available from the police on the number of domestic violence cases reported to them, primarily because there is no crime specifically termed 'domestic violence'. When women do report attacks by their partners against them, these incidents will be captured within a variety of crime categories including common assault, assault with intent to cause grievous bodily harm and pointing a firearm (to name but a few).

Community-based prevalence studies find that domestic violence, in one form or another, affects as many as one in two women in some parts of South Africa. A 1997 study conducted in three of South Africa's nine provinces found that 27 per cent of women in the Eastern Cape, 28 per cent of women in Mpumalanga and 19 per cent of women in the Northern Province (now Limpopo) had been physically abused in their lifetimes by a current or ex-partner (Jewkes et al. 1999). The same study also investigated the prevalence of emotional and financial abuse experi-enced by women in the year prior to the study. This was found to have affected 51 per cent of women in the Eastern Cape, 50 per cent in Mpumalanga and 40 per cent in Northern Province. A study of 1 394 men working for three Cape Town municipalities found that approximately 44 per cent of these men were willing to admit to the researchers that they abused their female partners (Abrahams et al. 1999). At its most extreme, domestic violence may lead to women killing their abusive partners. However, the number of such killings is small in comparison to the number of women who become the victims of homicide (Ludsin & Vetten 2005). Approximately half of all South African women murdered in 1999 were killed by their intimate partners, translating into a prevalence rate of 8.8 per 100 000 of the female population aged 14 years and older – the highest rate yet reported by research anywhere in the world (Mathews et al. 2004).

In conclusion, a number of significant gains in relation to violence against women have been made at the level of law and policy. Nonetheless, at first glance these gains do not appear to have meaningfully reduced the high incidence of rape and domestic violence in the country, despite these figures often forming part of the rationale justifying such interventions in the first place. However, this assumption betrays confusion around what statistics actually tell us, as well as the role of law and policy in preventing social problems.

First, the state of South African crime statistics often makes it impossible to distinguish a rise in reporting rates from a rise in the actual incidence of a particular crime. Both the MRC and Stats SA surveys mentioned earlier date back to at least 1997 and have not been repeated, so it is impossible to know whether the extent of under-reporting in relation to rape has changed in any way, as well as whether the incidence of domestic violence has been impacted upon in any way. Indeed, law and policy intended to increase women's access to justice and punish behaviour that was formerly tolerated may well encourage more women to come forward, as may policies intended to bring about an improvement in police and prosecutorial treatment of women – particularly when a good deal of publicity advertises the introduction of such policy and law. On this basis one might even argue that the success of these various interventions is being signalled through the increase in police statistics. Indeed, police statistics in particular are a better indication of women's access to criminal justice mechanisms than the prevalence of rape and domestic violence.

Second, violence against women is a complex and multifaceted problem requiring a range of different interventions both to combat and prevent its occurrence. However, as this section illustrates, state responses to rape and domestic violence have been primarily confined to the criminal justice system and the Department of Social Development, framing violence against women primarily as a problem of crime and welfare. While rape, to some extent, is also seen as a problem warranting policy for the health sector, domestic violence is not – despite research indicating that women in abusive or controlling relationships are twice as likely to be infected with HIV than women in non-violent relationships (Dunkle et al. 2003).[17] Further, the policies, laws and legal decisions described earlier primarily provide for the better treatment of women by the criminal justice and health systems and are thus concerned with the consequences of such violence, rather than the conditions which give rise to it. This is not to suggest that these interventions have no deterrent or preventative value – certainly the DVA is intended to discourage the recurrence of abuse – but rather to argue that their role in achieving this is somewhat more indirect. Recognising that women have a right to be free from all forms of violence and putting in place measures to ensure that they are treated with dignity and equality indicates that what was formerly tolerated, overlooked and invisible is now a matter of serious social concern. Such interventions also signal a challenge to accepted norms and conduct. However, for such challenges to become more than symbolic statements of intent, the law must follow through and intention must be matched with action. However, as the next section will describe, the implementation frequently does not meet the intentions.

Conditions and contingencies: the implementation of the DVA

The preamble to the DVA states:

> It is the purpose of this Act to afford the victims of domestic violence the maximum protection from domestic abuse that the law can provide; and to introduce measures which seek to ensure that the relevant organs of state give full effect to the provisions of this Act, and thereby to convey that the State is committed to the elimination of domestic violence.

Since the operationalisation of the DVA in December 1999, three studies (Mathews & Abrahams 2001; Parenzee et al. 2001; Schneider & Vetten 2006) have assessed its implementation in parts of the Western Cape and Gauteng.

Effective implementation of the Act has been undermined by a range of factors, with police perceptions of domestic violence figuring prominently as obstacles to women seeking help (Mathews & Abrahams 2001; Parenzee et al. 2001). Parenzee et al. suggest that unwillingness to intervene in 'household disputes' remained pervasive in the SAPS and that domestic violence was rife among police officers. They concluded that progressive legislation, combined with unprogressive attitudes among law-enforcement agents, created negative attitudes towards complainants, resulting in secondary victimisation of abused women and/or a failure to act according to the legal obligations set out in the legislation. Negative attitudes towards complainants were found to be related to complainants' withdrawal of charges. Indeed, in December 2004 the KwaZulu-Natal MEC for Safety and Security, Bheki Cele, announced that police officers would, in future, be instructed to charge all women withdrawing domestic violence complaints with defeating the ends of justice (*The Mercury* 10.12.04).

Compounding these problems is the fact that oversight of the police's implementation of the DVA is not being satisfactorily accomplished. The ICD would appear to have submitted only two reports (ICD 2001; 2002) to Parliament since the Act's operationalisation in 1999,[18] while the SAPS have submitted no reports at all. Parliament does not appear to have requested these reports either – so failing to exercise its statutory oversight function.

The under-resourcing of courts and police stations emerges as another factor hampering implementation of the Act (Parenzee et al. 2001; Vetten 2005). Too few personnel, in combination with a lack of police vehicles, fax machines and photo-copiers are cited as placing additional burdens on law-enforcement agents. Magistrates have also expressed frustration with their resource constraints, point-ing to increases in all components of legal work without corresponding increase in staff numbers (Artz 2003).

It is not as if the police or Department of Justice and Constitutional Development (DoJCD) are unaware of their resource constraints. In its briefing on Budget 2001 to the portfolio committee, the DoJCD stated that the implementation of new leg-islation such as the DVA has placed 'severe pressure' on its offices. Officials went on to say that the 2001/02 budget for personnel 'appears to be less than that required for the number of approved posts; fewer persons can therefore be employed'.[19] In the same year national Police Commissioner Jackie Selebi was quoted as saying that the DVA was neither practical nor implementable and was 'made for a country like Sweden, not South Africa' (*The Star* 14.08.01; *The Mercury* 22.08.01).

Vetten's 2005 analysis of the budget votes for justice, the police and the ICD for the period 1999–2005 points for the most part to a lack of planning for the imple-mentation of the DVA. In the case of the police budget, the DVA is clearly under-prioritised and less planned for in comparison with legislation around firearms control.

Contrasting the police's budget for the Firearms Control Act with the budget allo-cated to the DVA is instructive, given that both are recognised policing priorities. The policy developments' section of the police's budget vote for 2000 contains the first reference to the DVA. It announced that the DVA had come into effect in December 1999 and required the police to offer a range of services to victims of domestic violence. The next paragraph stated that the firearms legislation was due in Parliament before the end of 2000 and in preparation for its implementation, new allocations of R35 million, R51 million and R36 million were earmarked over the next three years, in addition to existing allocations (National Treasury 2000: 185). There was no similar anticipation of the DVA in the 1999 budget vote. In 2003, the police budget vote stated that, 'Spending on firearm control will receive particular attention in the medium term' (National Treasury 2003: 575) and in his 2004 budget vote address, the Minister of Safety and Security committed R63.2 million to the firearms control project (covering expenditure on 458 vehicles, 1 153 desktops, 728 scanners and 573 printers, amongst other things).[20]

Training also appears to constitute the police's primary response to the Act (although no specific amounts are ever allocated towards such training). Within the justice budgets, sexual offences enjoy far greater prominence than domestic violence does, suggesting that it is also under-prioritised. In relation to the ICD budgets, their monitoring function has been located in the smallest and least-funded of its sub-programmes. Where research (Goldman & Budlender 1999; Vetten 2005) has been able to identify specific budget allocations towards the DVA, they primarily relate to ad hoc once-off projects around training and publicity, some of which have been funded by international donors rather than government. Clearly there is place for such activities, both to familiarise criminal justice system personnel with the content and application of a new Act, as well as to inform the public of the existence of the Act and its protection. But these are activities which should support the actual daily and ongoing enforcement of the Act, yet budget documents are silent on the costs associated with these activities.

There is also no guarantee that women will be granted the protection needed. For example, in Schneider and Vetten's (2006) study of applications for protection orders, weapons were used in more than one in three cases but orders for the police to remove those weapons were made in a scant 2 per cent of cases. To a large degree, this low number of orders may be attributed to the fact that very few applicants (3%) actually asked that the weapon be removed. Parenzee et al. (2001) also found that magistrates rarely ordered seizure of weapons in comparison to the number of times applicants referred in their applications to the use of weapons against them. It was also noted that applicants did not often request the seizure. Further, while the DVA allows for the eviction of abusers from the joint home under 'extreme circumstances', in practice magistrates have shown themselves reluctant to grant this provision (Parenzee et al. 2001).

Women's personal circumstances and capabilities make seeking protection from domestic violence a particularly contingent affair. While South Africa has 11 official languages, the application forms for the protection order are available in only 2 of these languages – English and Afrikaans. In addition to the difficulties this may pose to women who are not familiar with either language, the written completion and reading of the application forms challenge women with varying degrees of literacy. Further, the forms are not available in Braille, and sign language interpreters for deaf women are not readily available at courts.

Women's financial constraints also affect their access to justice. Typically applicants must pay the sheriff to serve the order unless a means test indicates that the applicant cannot afford the sheriff's fee, in which case the state must bear the costs of service. In practice it would seem there is little consistency around the criteria applied in conducting such tests. Thus, at some courts impoverished women will receive state aid while at others they will not benefit from this provision in the Act (Parenzee et al. 2001). The legacy of apartheid legislation such as the Group Areas Act, as well as the under-resourcing of rural areas, shifts further costs onto women. In 1994, for instance, 74 per cent of the country's police stations were located in white suburbs or business districts. The consequence of this is to impose what are often prohibitive travel costs upon black women. These costs are further added to when women are not attended to on the same day they arrive at court (usually due to a shortage of court personnel), and are required to return to court. At the least, this results in additional travel costs, childcare costs, loss of income and time off work, costs some women cannot afford.

This combination of difficulties may well be why at least one writer has asserted that a court order represents most abused women's last hope (Fedler 1995). A national survey of 1 000 women who had experienced abuse (Rasool et al. 2002) provides some support for this claim. Only 11 per cent of women in this study sought legal advice around the most serious incident of abuse they experienced, making legal assistance the form of help women sought least often. Recourse to legal assistance was also dependent upon geographical location, with 6 per cent of rural women, 13 per cent of women living in townships and 28 per cent of women living in suburban areas seeking such help (Rasool et al. 2002).

This review of the implementation of the DVA raises questions around the degree to which the state undermines its own efforts, – it seems that whatever sanctions or checks on abusive men's behaviour are promised by the law, the laws are simultaneously weakened by ineffectual implementation. This may have the effect of worsening abusive men's behaviour and encouraging a sense of impunity as they come to see that they may indeed be above the law.

Most of those accused of rape would also appear to be above the law if the performance indicators set by the police in their 2006 budget vote are anything to go by. The percentage of reported cases which should result in the arrest of suspects is set at 47 per cent (and 60% of indecent assaults), with 38 per cent of rape cases to court going for prosecution (32% in the case of indecent assault). Of this proportion proceeding to court, 70 per cent are targeted for convictions by the National Prosecuting Authority (National Treasury 2006). This target is for the specialist sexual offences courts; the regional magistrates' courts would appear to perform worse than these courts.[21]

Figures for some years back would suggest that these targets were not being met. A report compiled by the interdepartmental government management team tasked with developing the National Rape Prevention Strategy found that in 2000, 8.9 per cent of reported child rapes and 6.8 per cent of adult reported rapes resulted in convictions. Mpumalanga province recorded the lowest number of convictions (3% and 4% respectively), followed by Gauteng which secured convictions in 7 per cent of reported child rape cases and 4.9 per cent in adult cases. In the same year, perpetrators could not be traced in 30 per cent of cases nationally. The percentage of cases where the suspect could not be traced has been increasing by 10 per cent every year since 1996, with an 11 per cent increase having been recorded between 1999 and 2000. Forty-three per cent of reported rape cases were withdrawn in 2000, with less than half of these withdrawals occurring at the request of the victim (*Mail & Guardian* 15–21.11.02). No information is available to show whether or not there has been any improvement to these figures over the last few years.

Contests: challenging rape

A comprehensive history of sexual violence in South Africa has yet to be written. Nonetheless, where snatches of such a history may be glimpsed, they point to a long and ugly relationship between rape and race. Further, they illustrate how public outrage about rape has less often been motivated by pure concerns with women's rights than efforts to control and regulate both black men and white women.

Etherington (1988) documents a series of rape scares in Natal in the 1870s that prompted a host of calls for the increased control of the black population, including the British Secretary for Native Affairs, Theophilus Shepstone's argument for the creation of a rural black police force to check and control the movement of black men about the countryside without their employers' knowledge. A further rape scare in the province in 1886 resulted in the colonial government legislating a system of 'native' registration as well as the imposition of the death penalty for rape (Martens 2002). Those white women who neglected their domestic duties and employed black male 'houseboys' came in for criticism, as did the women's subsequent familiarity with their employees. Young, single white women's preference for employment outside of the domestic sphere (which then resulted in the employment of 'houseboys' in their stead) was also bemoaned (Martens 2002). Van Onselen (1982) documents a similar series of such scares on the Witwatersrand between 1890 and 1914, the last of which resulted in the Union of South Africa's 1913 Report of the Commission Appointed to Enquire into Assaults on Women, which proposed a variety of measures aimed at regulating and controlling black male domestic workers. Further, not only did the commission conclude with a recommendation to segregate 'natives in urban areas' (van Onselen 1982: 53), but as author Sol Plaatje pointed out, it also provided at least some of the ideological justification for the Native Land Act (van Onselen 1982). (There was no parallel discussion by the commission of the 'white peril', or white men's assaults upon, and seductions of, black women, as black intellectuals, Lerothodi Ntyweyi and RV Selope Thema, were quick to argue.) Berger (1992) also charts how concern to 'protect' white women from black men sparked a campaign in the 1930s to enact legislation prohibiting white women from working under the supervision of black men. Uglier still is the fact that until the abolition of the death penalty, more black men were hanged for raping white women than white men hanged for raping black women (Dugard in Chidester 1991)

Thus calls for the increased protection of helpless, vulnerable and defenceless women have in the past served not only to cast white men in the role of white women's 'protectors', but also to justify the oppressive treatment of black men. In the process, the violence done to black women has been utterly neglected and downplayed, while white men's violence towards women has been made invisible (unless those white men happened to fit another social stereotype – that of the white Afrikaans man who kills his entire family). Much research on men who rape has unintentionally reinforced this problem. While these studies (see Bhana 2005; Mokwena 1991; Vogelman 1990; Wood & Jewkes 1998) make valuable contributions to our understanding of rape, their focus on black men ensures that they remain seen as the problem while white men's violence continues to be rendered invisible. This racialised approach to sexual violence, whether intended or not, makes certain that race remains an important element of many of the contests over rape that have erupted in South Africa. This section explores two such contests: the upset generated by the Charlize Theron advertisement, and the Smith–Mbeki debacle over South Africa's rape statistics.

In 1999, South African-born actress Charlize Theron made an advertisement on behalf of Cape Town Rape Crisis. Looking directly at the camera (and viewer), she said: 'Many people ask me what South African men are like', and then responded by reciting South Africa's rape statistics. Following a complaint by 28 men and 1 woman that the advertisement discriminated against men, in October 1999 the Advertising Standards Authority withdrew the advertisement. This prompted public debate over what constitutes discrimination, as well as whose rights require protection. Following an appeal against the banning by Rape Crisis (joined by the CGE) the advertisement was reinstated (Vetten 2000).

In 2004, some five years later, it was the release of the SAPS' annual crime statistics that triggered debate. These figures recorded a slight decline in the number of reported rapes. Using these statistics as her starting point, journalist and rape survivor Charlene Smith then wrote an article highlighting not only the sub-standard treatment of rape survivors by the health-care system (amongst others), but also arguing that this neglect was driving HIV infection amongst women and children (*Sunday Independent* 26.09.04). Entitled 'Rape has become a sickening way of life in our land', her article also cited a number of statistics which, amongst other things, included the claim that South Africa has the highest rate of rape in the world.

President Mbeki's response was swift and irate. Writing in his regular on-line column, his counter-argument made two points: first, that many South Africans appeared incapable of acknowledging the police's success in combating crime; and second, their willingness to turn good news into bad was a symptom of racism. This element of Mbeki's argument drew upon an article Smith reportedly wrote for the *Washington Post* in June 2000. He quoted Smith as having written: 'Here [in Africa], [AIDS] is spread primarily by heterosexual sex – spurred by men's attitudes towards women. We won't end this epidemic until we understand the role of tradition and religion – and of a culture in which rape is endemic and has become a prime means of transmitting disease, to young women as well as children' (cited in *ANC Today* 4(39), 7 October 2004: 2). Mbeki responded: '[S]he was saying that African traditions, indigenous religions and culture prescribe and institutionalise rape. The "internationally recognised expert" was saying that our cultures, traditions and religions as Africans inherently make every man a potential rapist' (*ANC*

Today 4(39), 7 October 2004). Mbeki continued: 'I…will not keep quiet while others whose minds have been corrupted by the disease of racism, accuse us, the black people of South Africa, Africa and the world, as being, by virtue of our Africanness and skin colour – lazy, liars, foul-smelling, diseased, corrupt, violent, amoral, sexually depraved, animalistic, savage – and rapist.'

A subsequent column written just three weeks later further developed this line of argument with a quote attributed to one Dr Edward Rhymes: 'We are portrayed as oversexed or lascivious…It is African-Americans that get accused of being rampant sexual beasts, unable to control our urges, unable to keep our legs crossed, unable to keep it in our pants' (cited in *ANC Today* 4(42), 22–28 October 2004).

What both debates share is a focus on men and race, as will be argued in relation to the Theron advertisement.

Much public discussion and representation of rape typically emphasises the awful nature of the crime as well as the damage and trauma it inflicts upon its victims. Because it encourages sympathy for the plight of women and children, while simultaneously concealing who is responsible for rape, presenting the problem in this way is unthreatening. The Theron advertisement stepped outside of this tradition by unequivocally holding men to account for this harm. Arguably, what was also different and challenging about this advertisement is that it may well have achieved the novel result of including white South African men in the category of 'rapist'. This was achieved through the choice of Theron as spokesperson for this message.

Charlize Theron is widely considered an attractive and desirable woman, making it considerably more difficult to dismiss her statements as those of a man-hater made bitter by her unattractive state. Further, in her description of what South African men are like, it is probable that many viewers assumed Theron to be speaking of the kind of South African men she is most likely to have grown up with and been familiar with: white, middle-class men. To a 'respectable' group which has traditionally cast itself in the role of 'protector' and has been invisible in much public discourse around who rapes, suddenly finding itself implicated in the problem was clearly both dismaying and unfamiliar.

The Mbeki–Smith disagreement followed more familiar and predictable racial terrain. Outlined very crudely, Smith is a white woman who was raped by a black man and then criticised by another black man (the president), which then led to a white man coming to her defence (Ryan Coetzee of the Democratic Alliance). The point being made here is not that Smith and Coetzee specifically were racist, but that their comments may unintentionally have fed into long-standing racialised perceptions of who rapes and who, therefore, needs to be protected from whom.

Given the brief history outlined earlier, the president was entirely correct in pointing out how racism underpins some white people's outrage about rape. However, the fact that an ostensible concern with protecting women from sexual violence can and has been used to advance racist ends does not do away with the need to combat and eradicate rape. Instead, this history should make us mindful of the need to not split race from gender, but rather to begin exploring the complex inter-actions between race and gender which not only influence violent masculine behaviours, but also shape responses to the victims and perpetrators of such violence. Clearly such discussion is both painful and sensitive but necessary if the debate is to move beyond the paralysis or polarisation that results when race is introduced into public debate. Were this to happen, then it might also be easier to discuss the contributions of culture, tradition and religion to either preventing or encouraging rape – debates also likely to founder on racialised assumptions about whose culture and traditions are superior and civilised and whose backward, barbaric and primitive.

Nowhere was this need to critically examine culture and tradition at a range of levels made more apparent than in the Zuma trial.

The prosecution of Jacob Zuma for rape

On 2 November 2005, a 31-year-old family friend 'Kwezi', (as she chose to be pub-licly known), charged that Jacob Zuma, the former deputy president, had raped her at his home in Forest Town, Johannesburg. The trial began on 6 March 2006 and was concluded on 8 May when judgment was handed down acquitting Zuma of the charge. The case was considerably complicated by its political context – the suc-cession battle within the ANC – and the claims that Zuma is the victim of a polit-ical conspiracy intended to deny him the leadership of the ANC. With the rape charge depicted as one more example of the plot against Zuma, it was guaranteed that the trial would pit political sympathies against a women's rights agenda. This section, however, concentrates on the role of tradition in this case. By tradition, I mean widely accepted ways of behaving or doing things, developed over time and typically passed from one generation to the next. In this case, tradition operated on at least two levels – Zuma's explanation of his conduct, as well as in the legal tra-ditions employed to interpret and test the complainant's evidence.

From the outset, Zuma established himself as an adherent to his culture and tradi-tions by testifying in isiZulu. Next he situated his belief that Kwezi had consented within the context of Zulu norms around sexual relations. Thus, the fact that Kwezi discussed her frustrated sexual needs with him; wore a wrap-around sarong or kanga (but apparently no underwear) during some of her conversations on the night of the incident; and sat in a particular way, all led Zuma to believe that she was indicating a desire to have sex with him. Once he had started his sexual encounter with her, he also could not stop because to leave Kwezi in a state of arousal would be tantamount to rape. While many commentators derided this presentation of Zulu culture (with one going so far as to describe it as 'Zuma cul-ture'), at the same time it clearly struck a chord with others. This, perhaps, is the group for whom he embodies a particular way of life which they perceive as being under threat – particularly in relation to social arrangements concerning men and women. This reading is suggested by some of the forms of support for Zuma that took place outside the Johannesburg high court, many of which have traditionally been used to punish women for stepping out of place.

When Zuma emerged from court at the end of the first day of the trial, he and his supporters burst into singing 'Umshini wami' ('bring me my machine gun'). While there may be place for such sentiments in the context of an armed struggle, their use in the context of a rape trial is considerably more sinister and threatening, given the long association between guns and penises. Both symbolise power, while the act of ejaculating has also been likened to shooting or firing. Penises can thus be equated to weapons, and so share weapons' power to threaten, subdue or destroy. This song then carried a dual threat, which included rape.

On that very same first day of the trial, stones were thrown at a woman wearing a headscarf similar to that of the complainant. Those at court also said they heard the woman described as a slut. Both the insult and the action evoke echoes of the stoning of women for adultery. The following week, a woman arrived with a placard bearing the complainant's name and the claim that she shamed all South African women. Not only were flyers with a photograph of the complainant, as well as her name and address made available for sale, but her picture was publicly burned, an action which led some journalists to draw parallels with the burning of witches.

However, it was not only Zuma's supporters who wished to see women put back in the places they have traditionally occupied. Indeed, what many missed in their analyses of Zuma's cultural defence was how closely aspects of it tallied with long-standing preoccupations in Roman-Dutch law with women's dress and conduct. From the judgment it is clear that in deciding whether or not Kwezi had consented, the judge also took into account her clothing and conduct on the night in question. In other words, Zuma's explanation of why he assumed consent drew less on uniquely Zulu cultural norms than on shared cross-cultural masculine norms.

Scrutiny of the complainant's clothing and conduct was far from being the only method employed in this case to discredit the complainant. In rejecting Kwezi's version of events, the judge also measured her behaviour against the behaviour that he imagined 'real' rape survivors exhibit. Thus the fact that she did not bath immediately, did not suffer from depression after the rape, was not physically threatened, did not have clothing torn, failed to scream for either Zuma's daughter or the policeman stationed outside, did not 'immediately phone the world to tell them about it' and did not leave Zuma's home immediately after the incident all made her story implausible. She was either 'a sick person who needs help' – because so traumatised in the past that she perceives 'any sexual behaviour as threatening' – or a woman who changed her mind, feeling 'guilt, resentment, anger and emotional turmoil' after the event.[22]

A third long-standing legal tradition that this trial explicitly drew on, was the cautionary rule around sexual offences. Essentially, this rule stated that women who laid rape charges were particularly unreliable witnesses (being frequently motivated to lay false claims out of malice, vindictiveness, vengefulness and neurotic fantasy)[23] and that their evidence thus needed to be approached with caution. The 1998 Supreme Court case of *S v. Jackson*[24] effectively abolished the application of this particular cautionary rule to rape complainants generally, finding it to 'unjustly stereotype' this particular group of women, as well as to be both 'irrational' and 'outdated'. Nonetheless, the Jackson decision still left judges to apply a 'cautionary approach' to particular cases at their discretion. In the judge's opinion, the Zuma matter illustrated the need for just such a selective application of a cautionary approach.

The fourth means of disqualifying the complainant's version of events turned on a very particular interpretation of her previous sexual history. This hinged around the claim that she had a history of making false rape accusations, beginning from the time when she was 13 years old and exiled in an ANC camp. This particular episode appears to have triggered a period in Kwezi's life of troubled relationships with men, as well as blackouts. However, a reading of the evidence suggests these difficulties ceased in 1995 and no further claims of rape were made by the complainant in the ten years thereafter – until the charge against Zuma. Clearly, this behaviour begged further explanation and contextualisation and, at the conclusion of the state's case, three organisations attempted to enter the trial as *amicus curiae* to present such an alternative reading of Kwezi's history. They proposed to lead evidence around the sexual exploitation and abuse that occurred in the camps during the liberation struggle, as well as evidence around the impact of childhood sexual abuse. While such evidence in and of itself was unlikely to have convicted Zuma, it may have helped the court to arrive at a different understanding of the destructive consequences of childhood sexual abuse. The application was, however, dismissed as 'sidetracking' the courts and a bid for self-promotion and international publicity by the organisations concerned. It also provided a basis for the judge to criticise women's organisations for prejudging elements of the case.

It is telling that the judge chose to upbraid women's organisations for questioning and challenging the conservative legal traditions of criminal law – but was silent on the conduct of Zuma supporters outside court whose behaviour at times bordered on the criminal. Indeed, for this particular judge, challenging the law was, apparently, a more noteworthy threat than threatening or intimidating a witness. But this may be due to the fact that the judge, like Zuma's supporters, was also engaged with putting women back in their place – albeit using very different and entirely more sophisticated methods. In terms of his reasoning, complainants such as Kwezi, who are not the 'unfortunate victims of rape', have no place in the court, any more than do women's groups who 'bombard' a court 'with political, personal or group agendas and comments'. Expanding on this point, the judge quoted, with approval, the unnamed newspaper contributor who wrote: 'This trial is more about sexual politics and gender relations than it is about rape.'[25] Given that rape is a manifestation of a particular type of gender relations and thus cannot be separated from sexual politics, this quote reveals the extent to which both the unknown commentator and the judge not only fundamentally misunderstand the nature of sexual violence, but also seek to impose a mask of neutrality on the law – so denying how law is implicated in the politics of rape.

What gives rape its political dimension is power: to impose one's will upon another (whether by violence, force, threat, coercion, manipulation or obligation) as well as to rewrite such injury as harmless or imaginary. While such power is most obviously enacted upon individual women's bodies, it is also validated by communities and further legitimated by state institutions. Law is implicated in this politics for how it excuses or justifies such impositions, invalidates or diminishes the harm that subsequently arises, and upholds particular social arrangements concerning men and women. In this case the decision endorsed a conservative approach to gendered social relations and also sought to exclude particular women from the protection of the law. As such, it is also an illustration of the double-edged nature of the law. On the one hand, women and their advocates have successfully used the law to claim their constitutional rights, but at the same time the law has also been used to deny women rights to dignity, privacy and a fair trial in relation to rape. The extent to which this decision will reassert legally conservative approaches to future rape cases over the medium to long term can only be guessed at.

Finally, both the conduct outside the court as well as the commentary on this case point to a country divided on a range of issues. There are clearly many in South African society who do not support the profound changes to the status of women that have been introduced post-1994. At the same time, the consequences of this trial may not be entirely negative. Kwezi's treatment in court opened up important debates around the need to improve the criminal justice system's response to rape complainants and made apparent and urgent the need to reform rape law. In addition, the fact that a senior political figure was charged with and prosecuted for a crime is testament to the rule of law in South Africa.

Conclusion

This chapter has highlighted the enabling framework put in place by the state to address violence against women. It has also begun to point to where this framework remains incomplete and a more comprehensive approach is required. The components of such an approach in future could include further developing the health sector's contribution to addressing violence against women, both in terms of its response to the health-related consequences of such abuse, as well as its early detection of sexual and intimate partner violence. A comprehensive approach would also need to take into account how women's lack of access to tangible and material resources entraps them within abusive and sexually exploitative relationships and, following on from this recognition, what steps need to be taken to reduce women's economic dependency upon abusive men. This could include expanding current housing policy to accommodate abused women's housing needs, as well as examining how effective poverty-alleviation and job-creation measures – such as the Expanded Public Works Programme – are in assisting women to live more independently. Further it would need to seriously consider what other forms of social sanctions could be developed that do not make women's safety dependent upon their willingness to press criminal charges against their partners. At this point, many women do not utilise the protection of the law because, while they want the violence to stop, they do not necessarily wish to see their partners imprisoned.

The statistics currently used to measure the various forms of violence towards women have also been shown to be dated and incomplete, and thus inadequate to understanding and tracking the problem. Were community-based victimisation surveys to be run routinely to monitor under-reporting, then we would be in a much better position to understand what the numbers reported to the police actually reflect. And if on the basis of knowing the under-reporting rate, the police were then to set themselves a target of seeing reports increase (rather than decline), this may result in fewer stand-offs around the statistics. It is equally as important for both the police and courts to start publicly releasing statistics for their performance as a whole, ranging from the time a report is made all the way through to whether a withdrawal, conviction or acquittal is secured. Such figures are an important means of holding the state to account for its implementation of law and policy.

But whatever the form such expanded responses ultimately take, they will continue to be undermined by the conditional and contingent implementation of their various components. Indeed, when access to justice is reduced to the level of a contingency, it indicates the extent to which commitment to addressing gender-based violence is not consistently embedded in all spheres of the state. Such commitment would not appear to be embedded in sectors of South African society either. In part this is because understandings of gender and gender oppression do not adequately integrate the intersections of race, gender and economic marginalisation in individual men's and women's lives but treat them as separate, compartmentalised discriminations instead. This may have the effect of setting up a hierarchy of oppression where different forms of social disadvantage may be made to compete against, or even trump, each other. Further, while frameworks, plans and priorities may effect macro-level changes, they do not necessarily translate into changes at the micro level. Perhaps it is here, at the level of the everyday and routine, where change has been most difficult to achieve. This is where examination of traditions and cultures, whether expressed at the level of law or in the mundane, daily encounters between men and women, becomes so important. In conclusion, much still needs to be done if all of the nation, women and men, are to enter 'their season of joy'.

Notes

1   Other goals include strengthening the functioning of the criminal justice system and promoting effective and efficient government structures (particularly at local level).

2   The former National Party government signed the Convention on the Elimination of all Forms of Discrimination Against Women in January 1993. It was subsequently ratified without reservations by the ANC government in December 1995. The government also committed itself to the Beijing Platform of Action adopted at the Fourth World Conference on Women in 1995, which highlighted violence against women as one of its critical areas of concern. In 1996 the government also invited Ms Radhika Coomaraswamy, the United Nations Special Rapporteur on Violence Against Women, to visit the country and compile a report and recommendations based on her findings.

3   These guidelines are applicable to police officers, health workers, prosecutors, social workers and lay counsellors, as well as parole boards and institution committees of the Department of Correctional Services.

4   These centres act as a 'one-stop shop' for rape-care management, streamlining a network of existing investigative, prosecutorial, medical and psychological services in the hospital where they are located.

5   Family court centres include a divorce court, a maintenance court, children's court and family violence court. Five such pilot projects have been established in four provinces in South Africa.

6   Acts constituting domestic violence include physical, sexual, emotional, verbal and psychological abuse; economic abuse; intimidation; harassment; stalking; damage to property; entry into the complainant's residence without consent, where the parties do not share the same residence; and any other controlling or abusive behaviour where such conduct harms, or may cause imminent harm to the safety, health or well-being of the complainant.

7   Domestic relationships covered by the DVA include: married, divorced or separated couples; couples living together (including gay or lesbian couples); parents of a child; family members (including the extended family); people who are or were engaged or dating one another – including those circumstances where one party (but not the other) perceives some form of romantic, intimate or sexual relationship to be in existence; children; and people who share or have recently shared the same residence (such as flatmates, housemates).

8   Briefly, the police are required to explain to complainants that they are there to provide whatever assistance the circumstances require, which may include helping the complainant to find suitable shelter or obtain medical treatment. In addition they should inform the complainant of her right both to apply for a protection order, as well as lay criminal charges. Where reasonably possible this information should be provided to the complainant in the form of a notice. The notice also sets out the steps required to apply for a protection order, explains what the complainant should do in the event of a breach and sets out the type of relief or protection the complainant may request from the court.

Where complainants cannot read the notice, police officers should read it to them in the language of their choice. They are also obliged to arrest the abuser if he does not obey the protection order.

9   2000 (2) SA 425 (CC)

10   *Carmichele v. Minister of Safety and Security* 2001 (4) SA 938 (CC); 2001 (10) BCLR 995 (CC)

11   Having found that the police and prosecution had failed to discharge this duty, had done so negligently, and that the element of causation was satisfied, the high court held the defendant liable for delictual damages. The high court's finding was confirmed by the Supreme Court of Appeal in *Minister of Safety and Security v. Carmichele* 2004 (3) SA 305 (SCA).

12   The respondent had failed to discharge this duty and was thus delictually liable. It had admitted the elements of negligence, vicarious liability and causation. *Minister of Safety and Security v. Carmichele* 2004 (3) SA 305 (SCA).

13   2005 (9) BCLR 835 (CC)

14   [2004] 4 All SA 373 (SCA)

15   2005 (2) SACR 41 (W)

16   Evidence before the court showed that Mrs Engelbrecht had moved nine times to escape her abusive husband; made three attempts to divorce him (the sheriff failed on six occasions to serve the divorce summons, while the Family Advocate never compiled some of the documentation required to decide custody of a child); attempted on three occasions to obtain a protection order (on two occasions she failed to be informed of the court date and on the third the magistrate suggested that the couple go for coffee and resolve their differences); and made numerous calls to the 10111 police emergency service (these were played in court and clearly captured police dispatchers arguing with her about why they were not going to assist her). Police personnel also irregularly withdrew her charges, or refused to accept them, failed to comply with numerous aspects of the DVA and on one occasion advised her husband to obtain a protection order against her.

17   Domestic violence is also implicated in women's unlawful conduct. A survey carried out at the three women's prisons in Gauteng found a significant statistical correlation between the experience of being economically abused and being convicted of theft, as well as a significant correlation between being sexually abused by an intimate partner and being convicted of murder or attempted murder (Haffejee et al. 2005).

18   This report revealed that eight police stations visited in KwaZulu-Natal failed to submit a record of complaints received from the public regarding police action (or lack thereof). In addition, over the second six-month period in 2000, there were 115 reports to the ICD of police not fulfilling their obligations in terms of the Act. The same report to Parliament states that protection orders were left to pile up in the Community Service Centres of police stations visited in Gauteng, KwaZulu-Natal and the Eastern Cape due to a shortage of police vehicles and the refusal of the sheriffs to assist the police in serving protection orders.

19 The department did not appear to consider how the broader definition of domestic violence, as well as the more inclusive understanding of family and domestic relationships, was going to impact upon the courts. (Briefing to the Portfolio Committee on Justice: Budget 2001.)

20 Minister of Safety and Security, Charles Nqakula (2004) Budget Address Vote 25 Safety and Security, and Vote 23 Independent Complaints Directorate, 22 June. URL (consulted August 2004) <www.info.gov.za/speech.php/>.

21 During the department's 2004 budget briefing to the justice parliamentary portfolio committee, it was said that such courts had a 68 per cent conviction rate for rape in contrast with the 42 per cent conviction rate achieved by unspecialised courts. The chair of the portfolio committee, Fatima Chohan, was quoted as saying, 'There's a huge problem, clearly, at the regional court' (*Mail & Guardian* 17.06.04).

22 *S v. Zuma* 2006 JDR 0434 (W)

23 See for example, *S v. Balhuber* 1987 (1) PH H22 (A); also *S v. F* 1989 (3) SA 847 (A).

24 *See S v. Jackson* 1998(1) SACR 470 (SCA)

25 *S v. Zuma* 2006 JDR 0434 (W)

References

Abrahams N, Jewkes R & Laubsher R (1999) *'I do not believe in democracy in the home':*
Men's relationships with and abuse of women. Tygerberg: CERSA (Women's Health)
Medical Research Council.

Artz L (1999) *Violence against women in rural Southern Cape: Exploring access to justice through*
a feminist jurisprudence framework. Cape Town: Institute of Criminology, University of
Cape Town.

Artz L (2003) *Magistrates and the Domestic Violence Act: Issues of interpretation.* Cape Town:
Institute of Criminology, University of Cape Town.

Bhana D (2005) Violence and gendered negotiation of masculinity among young black school
boys in South Africa. In L Ouzgane & R Morrell (Eds) *African Masculinities.* New York:
Palgrave Macmillan.

Berger I (1992) *Threads of solidarity: Women in South African industry, 1900–1980.* Indiana:
Indiana University Press.

Chidester D (1991) *Shots in the streets: Violence and religion in South Africa.* Boston: Beacon
Press.

Combrinck H (2005) The dark side of the rainbow: Violence against women in South Africa
after ten years of democracy. In C Murray & M O' Sullivan (Eds) *Advancing women's*
rights. Cape Town: Juta.

Dunkle K, Jewkes R, Brown H, McIntyre J, Gray G & Harlow S (2003) *Gender-based violence*
and HIV infection among pregnant women in Soweto. Johannesburg: Gender and Health
Group, Medical Research Council.

Etherington N (1988) Natal's black rape scare of the 1870s. *Journal of Southern African Studies,* 15(1): 36–53.

Fedler J (1995) Lawyering domestic violence through the Prevention of the Family Violence Act 1993 – An evaluation after a year in operation. *The South African Law Journal,* 112: 231–51.

Goldman T & Budlender D (1999) *Making the Act work: A research study into the Budget allocation for the implementation of the Domestic Violence Act.* Cape Town: Gender Advocacy Project.

Gouws A (2005) The state of the national gender machinery: structural problems and personalised politics. In S Buhlungu et al. (Eds) *The State of the Nation: South Africa 2005–2006.* Cape Town: HSRC Press.

Haffejee S, Vetten L & Greyling M (2005) Exploring violence in the lives of women and girls incarcerated at three prisons in Gauteng Province, South Africa. *Agenda,* 66: 40–7.

Hirschowitz R, Worku S & Orkin M (2000) *Quantitative research findings on rape in South Africa.* Pretoria: Statistics South Africa.

Human Rights Watch (1997) South Africa – Violence against women and the medico-legal system. *Human Rights Watch,* 9(4A).

ICD (Independent Complaints Directorate) 2001. *Domestic violence report to Parliament,* 15 March. Available at <http://www.icd.gov.za/reports/rparliam.htm>.

ICD (2002) *Independent Complaints Directorate Media Statement* 13 November. Available at <http://www.info.gov.za/speeches/2002/02111314461001.htm>.

Jewkes R & Abrahams N (2002) The epidemiology of rape and sexual coercion in South Africa: An overview. *Social Science & Medicine,* 55(7): 1 231–44.

Jewkes R, Penn-Kekana L, Levin J, Ratsaka M & Schrieber M (1999) *'He must give me money, he mustn't beat me': Violence against women in three South African provinces.* Pretoria: CERSA (Women's Health) Medical Research Council.

Ludsin H & Vetten L (2005) *Spiral of entrapment: Abused women in conflict with the law.* Johannesburg: Jacana.

Martens JC (2002) Settler homes, manhood and 'houseboys': An analysis of Natal's rape scare of 1886. *Journal of Southern African Studies,* 28(2): 379–400.

Mathews S & Abrahams N (2001) *An analysis of the impact of the Domestic Violence Act (No. 116 of 1998) on women.* Cape Town: GAP and MRC.

Mathews S, Abrahams N, Martin LJ, Vetten L, van der Merwe L & Jewkes R (2004) *'Every six hours a woman is killed by her intimate partner': A national study of female homicide in South Africa.* MRC Policy brief No. 5, June.

Mbeki T (2006) 'State of the Nation', Address by the President of South Africa, Thabo Mbeki, to the joint sitting of Parliament, Cape Town, 03.02.06.

Meintjes S (2003) The politics of engagement: Women transforming the policy process – domestic violence legislation in South Africa. In AM Goetz & S Hassim (Eds.) *No shortcuts to power.* London: Zed Books.

Mokwena S (1991) *The era of the jackrollers: Contextualising the rise of youth gangs in Soweto*. Johannesburg: Centre for the Study of Violence and Reconciliation.

National Treasury (2000) *National medium term expenditure estimates, Vote 24, SA Police Service*. Pretoria: National Treasury.

National Treasury (2003) *National medium term expenditure estimates, Vote 25, Safety and Security*. Pretoria: National Treasury.

National Treasury (2006) *National medium term expenditure estimates, Vote 25, Safety and Security*. Pretoria: National Treasury.

Parenzee P, Artz L & Moult K (2001) *Monitoring the implementation of the Domestic Violence Act: First research report 2000–2001*. Institute of Criminology, University of Cape Town.

Rasool S, Vermaak K, Pharaoh R, Louw A & Stavrou A (2002) *Violence Against women: A national survey*. Pretoria: Institute for Security Studies.

Schneider V & Vetten L (2006) *Going somewhere slowly? A comparison of the implementation of the Domestic Violence Act (no. 116 of 1998) in an urban and semi-urban site*. Johannesburg: Centre for the Study of Violence and Reconciliation.

Van Onselen C (1982) *Studies in the social and economic history of the Witwatersrand 1886–1914, Volume 2, New Nineveh*. Johannesburg: Ravan Press.

Vetten L (2000) Paper promises, protests and petitions: South African state and civil society responses to violence against women. In YJ Park, J Fedler & Z Dangor (Eds) *Reclaiming women's spaces: New perspectives on violence against women and sheltering in South Africa*. Johannesburg: Nisaa Institute for Women's Development.

Vetten L (2005) 'Show me the money': A review of budgets allocated towards the implementation of South Africa's Domestic Violence Act. *Politikon*, 32(2): 277–95.

Vogelman L (1990) *The sexual face of violence: Rapists on rape*. Johannesburg: Ravan Press.

Wood K & Jewkes R (1998) *'Love is a dangerous thing': Micro-dynamics of violence in sexual relationships of young people in Umtata*. Pretoria: Medical Research Council.

18 Kingdom deferred? The churches in South Africa, 1994–2006

Anthony Egan

When Nelson Mandela was elected president of a democratic South Africa many felt that salvation – in theological terms the 'kingdom of God' – had come on earth. Though welcoming the end of apartheid, realistic Christians recognised that a new era in church–state relations had begun. This chapter cannot do justice to the multidimensional nature and multiple strands that have made up the Christian community's response to 12 years of democracy, not least since the Christian community is denominationally diverse and, within each denomination, there is a complex mixture of race, social class, gender attitudes, sexual diversities, educational levels and theological persuasions. Though there are many developments within the churches after 1994 that are not examined,[1] the focus of this chapter is on three main areas: the overall demographic state of the churches after 1994; the churches' responses to the challenges of reconciliation, HIV/AIDS and poverty; and (using brief case studies) three religious forms of response to church–state relations – withdrawal, opposition and critical co-operative engagement.[2]

The state of the churches

Before presenting an overview of the state of the churches in South Africa since 1994, it is necessary to clarify a few points.

Firstly, the term 'church' has a variety of meanings, from the local community of Christian worship, the parish, through to a universal designation for all individuals and denominations that identify themselves as Christians. Within this, secondly, there is a range of structures ranging from loose networks to hierarchies in different denominations and at local parish level. The significance of this lies in the way such authority structures generate opportunities and limitations for political activism, social and cultural involvement, and the possibilities for divergent theological opinions.

In addition, Christianity's role in the struggle for democracy in South Africa was ambivalent (Chidester 1992). Christianity has had a very complex political history (Elphick & Davenport 1997). While sections of 'prophetic Christianity' (Walshe 1995) gave their all for the struggle – very often expressing ideological and partisan preferences – large sections of the churches were either neutral or supportive of apartheid.

Though typologies are problematic, in a diverse Christian religious field like South Africa with no single denominational majority or 'state church', it is important to note the various 'tendencies and emphases' (see Turner 1979: 80) that exist:

- Arriving with Dutch colonialism in 1652, the *Reformed churches* have been internally divided along race lines. Although never the 'state church', the white Reformed churches endorsed segregation and apartheid (De Klerk 1976; Moodie 1975), while black, coloured and Asian 'sister churches' resisted apartheid and were instrumental in getting apartheid declared a heresy by the World Alliance of Reformed Churches in the 1980s. Many of the white churches have acknowledged this, particularly after 1994, and there have been recent attempts to unite the Reformed tradition.

- *'Mainline' Protestant* churches grew in the nineteenth century after British colonisation. Occupying an ambivalent position – part of the colonial system yet also helping to create an educated black middle class that would be part of the base of African nationalism – they were divided over their response to apartheid, producing many faith-based activists but often equivocating over direct and systematic opposition politics (see Cochrane 1986; De Gruchy & De Gruchy 2004; Villa-Vicencio 1988; Worsnip 1991).

- The *African Initiated Churches* (AICs), sometimes called Independent churches, began as splinter groups from colonial mainline churches, and comprise three subgroups. The *Ethiopian churches* were theologically very close to the denominations from which they separated (mainly over the failure of these churches to provide leadership opportunities for black ministers). The *Zionist* or *Spirit-based churches* emphasising healing and spiritual power arose out of western Pentecostal roots and incorporated many African traditional beliefs (Anderson 2000, 2001; Gunner 2004; Makhubu 1988; West 1975). The *African Pentecostal/Charismatic churches* were African-initiated Pentecostals. Collectively they are today the largest single Christian bloc in South Africa. The largest AIC, the Zion Christian Church (ZCC) – with 1 in 11 South Africans as a member – is the largest single church in South Africa (De Gruchy & De Gruchy 2004). Although seen initially, through its emphasis on African dignity and self-reliance (Pretorius & Jafta 1997), as a political threat and one of the founding elements of African nationalism, the AICs were largely silent on political matters. Some churches, like the ZCC, openly courted the apartheid regime, as seen in the visit of President PW Botha to their Easter celebration at Moria in 1985, a policy that has continued.[3]

- Prohibited under Dutch rule, the *Roman Catholics* arrived in South Africa during British rule, establishing churches in both the colonial and indigenous communities. Fearing anti-Catholic hostility and economically dominated by conservative white Catholics the church was politically cautious until the late 1950s (Abraham 1989; Brown 1960) but grew bolder in the 1960s under the leadership of Durban's Archbishop Denis Hurley. Grassroots organisations like the Young Christian Workers and Young Christian Students helped train generations of political activists, many of whom moved into mainstream struggle and labour movements.

- In the wake of the charismatic revival in the 1960s (Cox 1996; Hollenweger 1972), the *Evangelical–Pentecostal* movement grew within South African churches in the 1970s (Thompson 2004). Though some politically active groups like the Concerned Evangelicals used varied approaches to anti-apartheid politics (see Balcomb 1993; Walker 1993), mainstream charismatic–evangelicals eschewed politics for personal salvation, direct ecstatic experience and often the promise of prosperity for being the 'saved' (Moran & Schlemmer 1984; Verryn 1983). Popular among white people who were disaffected with the 'political' stance of their churches, some of these churches later acknowledged complicity in apartheid. After 1994, these churches have grown, particularly among the newly empowered black middle class.

- A number of *other churches* exist in South Africa, whether among ethnic immigrant communities (for example, Greek Orthodoxy) or as theologically 'fringe' sects (for example, the Quakers, Unitarians, Seventh Day Adventists and Mormons). Though increasing, their public significance is limited.

The new idea: secular democracy

After 1994 South Africa embraced a secular, democratic Constitution. Although non-religious in nature, the 1996 Constitution acknowledged the religious plurality of the country and the new African National Congress (ANC) government – a secular party comprising persons of all faiths and none – invited the religious sector to participate in the newly constituted National Religious Leaders' Forum to work with government and civil society on matters of common public concern (Cochrane 2000). Although avowedly secular, the new political dispensation was permeated with religious views. Numerous Christian clergy were members of government at every level and most political leaders had at least some form of religious upbringing. Inevitably perhaps, religious discourse found itself entering public debate, for example prayers beginning meetings at almost every level of government, constitutional prohibitions notwithstanding. Many different views of Christianity (Botha 1998) were presented in parliamentary debates at the service of the various party-political positions mirroring the observation that '[a] politician who lavishes attention on the spirit world may at the same time show a Machiavellian talent for political manoeuvre' (Ellis & Ter Haar 2004: 4).

Whatever the religious convictions of its members, the government pursued a modern secular liberal agenda informed by what it saw were the best social policies available, often from western states. Conservative Christians were distressed to see liberalisation of abortion policy, greater tolerance of pornography, legalisation of homosexuality, the secularisation of state education and the end to Christian civil religious hegemony in public events. Some, however, see it more positively:

In the old dispensation…Christians did not have to make a choice on certain issues, the unspoken 'rules' dictated. In the new 'human rights' dispensation…Christians need to be morally and ethically fit in order to make decisions about new choices. (Hendriks 2001: 67)

For them, the new order was an opportunity to construct faith in 'a world come of age'.

Contemporary Christian faith: the numbers game

The most reliable statistics on current trends in religion in South Africa are recent, from the 1996 and 2001 national censuses (see Table 18.1).

Table 18.1 *Christian denominations in South Africa by size, Census results*

Denomination	Christians 1996		Population 1996	Christians 2001		Population 2001
	(N)	(%)	(%)	(N)	(%)	(%)
Reformed churches	3 913 523	13.0	9.6	3 232 194	9.0	7.2
Roman Catholic	3 372 481	11.0	8.3	3 181 336	8.9	7.1
Mainline Protestant	7 081 185	24.0	18.0	7 846 034	22.0	16.5
Pentecostal/Charismatic	2 683 314	8.9	6.6	2 625 942	7.3	5.9
Other churches	2 139 344	7.1	5.3	4 275 942	12.0	9.5
African Initiated Churches	10 668 515	35.5	26.3	14 598 922	40.8	32.6
Christians as % of SA population			74.1			78.8

Source: Hendriks & Erasmus (2005)

From the figures in Table 18.1 we can see the considerable growth of the AICs and the dramatic decline of the Reformed churches. The statistics confirm the point made earlier in the chapter on the AICs by De Gruchy and De Gruchy (2004) – as Hendriks and Erasmus show, the 'market share' of the AICs is (as of 2001) collectively 40.8 per cent (2005: 99). They, combined with the Pentecostal/Charismatic and other churches (7.3% and 12%), now effectively constitute the new 'mainline' churches in contemporary South Africa, even though they are made up mainly of numerous small churches. The decline in the Pentecostal/Charismatic 'market share' might be on account of 'realignment' of some of these churches into the AIC bloc: 'African Pentecostalism' is very often much closer in character to the AIC than to 'historically white' Pentecostalism (see Anderson & Otwang 1993). Similarly, many of the latter might now find a home within the Mainline Protestant category, many of whose churches have taken on strongly evangelical and even Pentecostal worship characteristics. These charismatic–expressive shifts might be rooted in a general concern for healing in a time of AIDS, and – for the AICs – function as part of a renewed discovery of African identity among newly liberated South Africans.

A second significant fact that we can extrapolate from the recent censuses is the high level of South Africans falling into the category 'no religion/refused/not stated': 18.3 per cent in 1996 and 16.4 per cent in 2001. Although there may be other reasons for this – *inter alia* reticence, confusion on the part of those polled, sole adherence to African traditional religion (but not recorded under the category 'other') – it may also be a sign of the degree of secularisation of South African society. Particularly significant is the high percentage of white people in this category. As the part of South Africa most historically and culturally connected to secularised European culture, this trend – together with the rise of a materialist culture within the old and new South African middle class – may not be too surprising.

Compared to many other countries in the developed and developing world these statistics still do not seem to bear out complaints that religion is dying in the new South Africa. Nor is Christianity necessarily in decline; rather, there seem to be religious realignments. The implications for what we might call the 'formerly mainline churches' clearly need further study.

New challenges, new directions

Creating a future for the churches after 1994

After the end of apartheid in 1994, the churches were faced with a new set of challenges over how to engage with the state and the new society in a manner appropriate to the church's mission.

But what was the church's new mission? In the early 1990s two distinguished theologians of the struggle period proposed that the church's task should include the promotion of democracy and democratic values (De Gruchy 1995) and participation in reconciliation and nation building (Villa-Vicencio 1992). Together with other like-minded theologians, they saw the church's task as the midwife of democracy in the transition period and a strong defender of democratic values and institutions. The underlying assumption was that the churches would be partners with the state in the creation and propagation of democratic values and practices. Beyond that, a theology of reconciliation was needed to heal the wounds of apartheid.

Theologians and ANC activists alike reacted fiercely against any proposed blanket amnesty for atrocities under apartheid. Reconciliation became a key task as a result. Another problem facing South Africa was the HIV/AIDS epidemic, a new challenge to the church on two fronts: as part of the traditional Christian ministry of care for the sick and dying; and, more controversially, a challenge to the church to confront many taboos and prejudices about sexuality. A third crucial area – closely linked to the previous two – was the problem of socio-economic inequality, including questions of poverty, inequality of distribution of wealth, and landlessness in a profoundly unequal society entering a globalised economy.

Reconciliation

The churches had always called for reconciliation – at times it seemed to those on its left as an alternative to revolution or confronting the past (ICT1986). The complex political and theological meanings of reconciliation that were generated by the establishment of the Truth and Reconciliation Commission (TRC) were different from any 'cheap reconciliation' of the past. The ANC government and civil society drew on experiences of truth commissions in Latin America and Eastern Europe to create the TRC. The Christian community was less directly involved in the actual process leading to the creation of the TRC (with the exception of a few notable individuals), though, as the commission commenced in February 1996, theologians and psychologists started to reflect on what the process might mean (see Botman & Petersen 1996).

The theologians, from a variety of traditions, took traditional Christian ideas of suffering, pain, grace, confession and reconciliation and tried to apply them to the prospect of establishing the truth of what had happened under apartheid. It was acknowledged that the TRC, though a secular institution of the state, was indeed a theological issue for the churches. Many admitted that the church should (and did largely) testify before the TRC regarding its 'sins of omission', its collaboration (endorsement or acquiescence) with apartheid in many cases, and its failure to do enough to end apartheid.

Although a secular commission, the church played a considerable role in the actual conduct of the TRC. Given that the TRC's brief was to investigate all atrocities of the apartheid era, a balance had to be struck between political parties and interest groups so as to give the TRC as wide a legitimacy as possible. The commissioners were therefore selected to represent a broad spectrum of political opinion. For the chairperson and deputy chair two non-ANC churchpersons were chosen. Desmond Tutu, Anglican Archbishop of Cape Town and an anti-apartheid activist, would chair many of the most traumatic hearings. His deputy was Alex Boraine, a former superintendent of the Methodist Church, a former Member of Parliament and co-founder of the Institute for a Democratic South Africa. Numerous persons from the religious sector were brought into the TRC – as commissioners, administrators, members of the various committees, and in the research department.

The TRC commenced with an interfaith service of dedication and prayer at St George's Cathedral in Cape Town on 13 February 1996, and its hearings more often than not began with prayers, saw occasional outbursts of hymn singing, and sometimes ended with prayers. Many secular observers were critical of this phenomenon, some feeling that the process had been 'colonised' by Christian discourse. While there is some truth in this, it must be considered in its proper context.

Firstly, Christianity was the majority religion in the country. Most victims and perpetrators were rooted in Christian tradition, many of them deeply religious people who believed firmly that what they were doing (defending or opposing apartheid) was literally God's will. The primary means of dealing with grief in South Africa is religious – psychotherapy, where available, is the preserve of the wealthy. Thus stories of trauma – and confessions of atrocity – are primarily told within a religious 'language game' (to put it in Wittgenstein's terms). To expect victims to speak in a cool and clinical descriptive language, though more 'objective', would undermine the very language of truth that was being sought to 'heal' the nation.

The churches themselves participated in a series of 'faith community' hearings. For some the process had a sense of continuity, even *déjà vu*: a continuation of a self-evaluation that had started with the Rustenberg Declaration of Guilt (1991) and the self-critical statements of the South African Council of Churches (SACC). Churches and individuals made institutional statements and interventions. The institutional statements, many of them recorded in the chapter on the religious sector in the TRC Final Report (TRC 1998), follow a certain pattern. While a few churches – and a number of individuals – confessed to direct support for apartheid, most churches acknowledged what they had failed to do: complacency with apartheid rule, fear of disturbing the status quo and economically dominant white church people not supporting Christian activists sufficiently, and not putting the churches solidly behind non-violent civil disobedience.

However, the 'church hearings' were not without controversy. Though the literature (for example, Chapman & Spong 2003) has focused on those who participated in the hearings and endorsed them, the reality is more complex. Many Christians resented such collective confessions of guilt, whether not believing apartheid was wrong or by suggesting that the church – their church – had nothing to confess. Many non-activist white Christians could not or would not see that even though they had never supported apartheid they had been beneficiaries of the system. This might be explained in terms of their theology – one that saw 'sin' as personal, not 'social', or that believed no human mediation was either possible or necessary for forgiveness.

Most surprisingly, the ZCC refused to acknowledge its acquiescence with the system, despite its official silence during the apartheid period. ZCC Bishop Edward Lekganyane's rationale was that it was the church of the oppressed and therefore had nothing to confess about being oppressors. Lekganyane's refusal was 'a statement which [said] "I will not be reduced to your categories, even to your language. I do not have to justify myself to you in your terms"…an act of resistance, of "independency" at its most dramatic' (Petersen 1999: 120), and the conviction, all traditional arguments (and empirical evidence) to the contrary, that silence on political matters might itself be construed as political resistance.

Churches and individual Christians recognised that the TRC was a process rather than an event and a start rather than an end in itself. While churches talked about implementing reconciliation, many individual initiatives began (see du Toit 2003). These were varied in size, locality and focus, their scope acknowledging that social reconciliation entailed many aspects.

Christian community-based groups recognised, though black and white elites co-existed and cooperated in the pursuit of wealth, that at grassroots levels very little interaction, co-existence and understanding existed between black and white people. Throughout the country localised Christian groups tried to open up communication between races to make the 'other' familiar. From some groups, more aware of the economic roots of apartheid, self-help schemes, sharing of resources and economic development groups also emerged.

Though the TRC opened up many memories of atrocity and trauma, it did little to heal and learn from such memories. A survivor of an apartheid death squad, Anglican priest Father Michael Lapsley, started the Institute for the Healing of Memories that brought people from different sides of the struggle together to tell their stories to each other and, through ritual, to come to terms with their experiences.

More examples could be presented. As institutions the churches continued to talk of the work of reconciliation, each doing what it could – though with little overall co-ordination of work or resources.

HIV/AIDS

In southern Africa during the colonial period, care of the sick had been a major 'corporal work of mercy' of the churches. With the advent of HIV/AIDS, particularly in rural areas largely neglected under apartheid, this tradition has continued. Primary among church-based health-care providers today is the Catholic Church, through its network of hospitals and clinics, most of them rural or peri-urban, serving the largest number of persons with HIV/AIDS in the country outside state institutions. In addition, many churches have become involved in a range of works (often with the public sector and non-governmental organisations [NGOs]) including pastoral care to those with HIV/AIDS; ministry to HIV-infected women, AIDS orphans and children with HIV; advocacy work for antiretroviral (ARV) roll-out and theological reflection and advocacy within the churches. Many help facilitate new projects, providing information about setting up parish-level groups, where to find donors and even how to plan grassroots campaigns, often drawing upon the methods of social analysis developed by justice and peace organisations during the struggle era (Gennrich 2004).

The most important role of the churches is perhaps in challenging prejudices. Anglican Archbishop Njongonkulu Ndungane sees social stigma as one of the greatest problems fueling HIV/AIDS crisis, a stigma fuelled by shame, fear, ignorance and denial of the facts and further complicated by a false perception that it is a 'uniquely African disease'.

There is a problem, however. To varying degrees most churches in South Africa find sexuality problematic (De Gruchy & De Gruchy 2004). Historically, two hegemonic sexual ethical systems – traditional African culture and the western

Calvinist–missionary–Victorian culture – have collapsed. 'Whether or not these ethical systems did actually command the allegiance of the majority of the country is perhaps debatable…but what is not debatable is that neither shapes the contours of public discourse any longer' (De Gruchy & De Gruchy 2004: 237). New sexual mores dominate. Instead of engaging in dialogue with these new values the churches tend to hold fast to traditional sexual morality (see De Gruchy & De Gruchy 2004; Germond 2004).

In a time of AIDS this is problematic. Even pragmatic church leaders like Ndungane speak of the need to 'respect…the ancient wisdom of the Church about monogamy as being crucial for our survival' (Ndungane 2003: 61), though the evidence suggests the message is ignored. The question of using condoms to prevent the spread of HIV is controversial within many of the churches, particularly the Catholic Church, which rejects the use of condoms. Partly out of concern for increased sexual promiscuity, its major reason, rooted in universally-held institutional moral teaching, stems from the belief that any sexual act should be open to the possibility of the transmission of life. Debate continues in Catholic circles over the matter, particularly how to apply Catholic teachings pastorally (see Bate 2003). Though some church leaders and theologians have broken ranks and advocated condom use, and church-founded hospitals by no means apply their institutions' moral teachings uncritically, urgently needed dialogue about sex in South Africa that takes into account the widespread reality of gender violence (Denis 2003; Haddad 2002) remains nearly totally absent.

In this light, and given the reality of widespread homophobia in South Africa despite its rejection in the 1996 Constitution and Bill of Rights, hostility to proposed same-sex union legislation discussed at the SACC seminar in February 2006 makes considerable sense. Though the SACC preparation documents and most of the speakers were broadly sympathetic, a narrow majority of delegates to the Kempton Park meeting were hostile. The hostility was most obvious in the group discussions and some questions in plenary sessions, where more than a few delegates observed that the moral laxity of the Constitution needed changing.[4]

Poverty and socio-economic inequality

The problems of the new South Africa – poverty, unemployment, inequality and the complexities of land rights – have been another focus for the churches after 1994. The churches have addressed these problems in a number of ways. Charity is a Christian virtue practised by the churches, sometimes to the point of overlooking another virtue, justice. In the post-1994 era, as before, churches have run soup kitchens and self-help schemes, in some places networking between churches and other institutions. On regional and national levels religious charities operate – with reduced funds since the donor money that once flooded into church-based organisations in the apartheid era has, if not dried up, been drastically reduced.

More significant nationally is the degree of church-based lobbying of government on the issue of poverty. Although far from being the only issue they address, the SACC and Southern African Catholic Bishops' Conference (SACBC) parliamentary liaison offices have made numerous interventions to parliamentarians, committees and ministers of the government on poverty issues. Since 2000, the SACC together with the Congress of South African Trade Unions and the South African NGO coalition have drafted an annual 'People's Budget', a set of economic proposals that put poor people first and promote policies and state spending aimed at meeting basic needs, unemployment reduction, job creation, revitalised public services, and economic equity through better wealth distribution. Finance Minister Trevor Manuel has noted the initiative and made the People's Budget 'required reading' for his staff. In addition the Finance Ministry has asked the team to submit the annual People's Budget before the official Budget so that useful insights and ideas might be taken into consideration by the ministry. The 2006 Budget, though by no means a 'people's Budget', was received by some as a sign of at least the beginnings of a shift to a more people-friendly economic policy (Tindall, interview 25.02.06).

Closely linked to poverty is the issue of globalisation. The churches in South Africa display a manifest, but unsurprising, ambivalence to globalisation. Many churches are 'products' of nineteenth-century globalisation, and are part of global associations like the World Alliance of Reformed Churches, members of 'global religious federations' like the Anglican Communion, or the Catholic Church. Within each denomination, there are rich and poor, beneficiaries and victims of economic globalism.

Moral principles of economic justice have guided these churches' position on South Africa's role in the global economy. Whether guided by their reading of the Bible, by reason (natural law) or by other theological principles (and often a subtle combination), the churches have evolved a complex set of values by which they judge economic policy. While some church people and groups at the grassroots have endorsed liberation theology (a complex theology that is normally broadly sympathetic to some or other form of humane socialism), the churches' leadership has tended towards a form of people-centred social-democratic welfare capitalism. In South Africa after 1994 this has led to many churches endorsing the ANC's initial Reconstruction and Development Programme policies, and concern that the shift to the Growth, Employment and Redistribution strategy backtracked into a less people-friendly neo-liberalism. A guiding principle is the notion of 'economic justice for all' (the title of the SACBC's 1999 statement). Justice and the avoidance of South Africa becoming a neo-liberal 'imperial state' in Africa were central to the joint SACC/SACBC (2002) statement Unblurring the Vision: An Assessment of the New Partnership for Africa's Development by South African Churches.

Though an 'establishment' figure, Anglican Archbishop Ndungane exemplifies a churchperson who is willing, when necessary, to work with the new social movements of the poor in matters of common interest, particularly the Treatment Action Campaign (TAC) in its campaign for government ARV roll-out to poor people with HIV. On occasion, too, the SACBC has come out in support of the TAC's campaigns, though the established churches as organisations have been less high profile in supporting other new poor people's movements.

Support for these new grassroots movements has come from local church communities most affected by the problems – access to electricity, water, essential services, HIV medication and so on – that the new movements address. Some of these groups, for example Jubilee South Africa, originated in religiously motivated campaigns; others are secular in origin, led by mostly secular, often Marxist intellectuals, though some individual clergy and theologians work with groups like the Anti-Privatisation Forum. Grassroots meetings of these groups frequently begin with prayers, include hymns as much as 'struggle songs', and often interpret their activism as God's will. Secular activists and intellectuals have had to come to terms with this phenomenon (see *Sunday Independent* 27.11.05).

Churches and the South African government: withdrawal, opposition or critical co-operation?

Given the (albeit ambivalent) support of most South African churches for the struggle for a non-racial democracy, the response of the churches to the new government has been far from uniform. In this section church strategies for dealing with government will be examined.

As institutions (particularly traditional religious institutions) tend to be socially conservative, it is often difficult for them to adapt to a new socially liberal culture. In addition, the haemorrhaging of the 'vanguard' of the activist leadership of the religious sector into government or well-deserved retirement, combined with the changing (global and local) political environment that has made the 'liberation' discourse of the past seem irrelevant, what we are seeing in contemporary South African churches are a number of withdrawal or opposition options, as well as renewed emphasis on critical engagement with the state.

Withdrawal: spiritual healing and social connection

'Withdrawal' of churches from the political arena is complex. On one level, Christians, and South Africans as a whole, have withdrawn significantly from politics – that is, electoral voting, membership of parties, and so on – apparently validating the claim made by some churches (quite often the ZCC) that the way to salvation lies through faith and membership of the church. On another level, the churches as institutions have drawn even further away from the public sphere.

Local churches in all denominations have become less 'political', not least because their individual members are either non-aligned or are members of different parties. Most of all, the majority of churches (particularly AICs and Evangelical–Pentecostals) eschew 'politics' to focus on worship, personal ethics and healing.

Healing and deliverance from evil spirits is based on widespread belief in witchcraft (among mostly black people) and 'satanic influences' (among white and black people). Belief in sorcery is common in urban and rural African communities: sickness, economic failure or the success of relatives while others remain poor are all seen as signs of it. Envy and resentment of neighbours' success is widespread (Ashforth 2000, 2005: see 86–7 in particular), and bewitchment is dealt with mainly through counter-magic or through spiritual healing and exorcism offered particularly by the AICs. This language of 'spiritual warfare' is also common among white-originated Pentecostal churches where belief in the devil, demonic possession, evil spirits and 'satanic influences' is common. Sickness is often seen as demonically inspired and curable by prayers of exorcism.

Beyond such healing, many white-founded Evangelical–Pentecostal churches have attracted sections of the new, suburban black middle class. Separated socially from those they left behind, living behind the security fences of suburbia, they are drawn to the spiritual and emotional community offered by churches like Rhema Ministries. Highly organised, these churches cater to a range of languages and age groups (children, teens, young adults, singles and families), offering emotionally-charged worship and the possibility to network between new and old elites on the common basis of faith. Combining fairly literalist theology and high-tech communication (television broadcasting, Internet, and so on) with services that mingle old-fashioned revivalism with the atmosphere often of a rock concert, Rhema has also encouraged members to give of their time to worthy social causes – from soup kitchens to health clinics. Like the AICs, Rhema largely does not engage with the state, following the (selective) biblical injunction of obedience to the state while exhorting its members to live out its socially conservative commitment to 'biblical values'.

Opposition: the African Christian Democratic Party

Although it may be unusual to use a political party as a case study for the church option of opposition to the new social order, I have consciously chosen the African Christian Democratic Party (ACDP) for two reasons. It is a self-consciously Christian party, opposed to the allegedly godless secularism of the new ANC-led South Africa, one that openly and explicitly campaigns on a conservative ticket to create a faith-based state. It is, secondly, a broadly ecumenical coalition of like-minded Christians. In a sense it is a kind of 'anti-SACC', hostile to the ANC (which the SACC broadly supports), as well as to theological liberalism and interfaith religious pluralism. It is also, and to varying degrees, anti-socialist.

To this one must add a caveat. As with churches, so with political parties: political parties normally contain within them diversity of opinion, dissenting voices, differences of emphasis on policy and practice. What is used in this chapter to analyse the ACDP are its own *official* documents: election manifestos, policy statements and speeches of its elected representatives.[5] The private opinions of party members may vary.

The ACDP was founded by the independent church pastor Reverend Kenneth Meshoe in December 1993. He believed that a Christian political party was essential to promote the interests of Christians and create an explicitly Christian state. Convinced that the party had the support of 20 per cent of voters (Nyberg 1994), it polled 0.5 per cent in the 1994 general election – sending two Members of Parliament (MPs) to the National Assembly. By 2004 it had about 1.6 per cent popular support and six MPs, more than a number of opposition parties with longer political track records such as the Azanian People's Organisation and the Pan Africanist Congress. Though broadly ignored or dismissed by secular political analysts (sometimes as little more than a 'joke' or 'spoiler' party or as the resurgence of the religious right wing of the 1980s under a new guise [Cochrane 2000]), whatever one thinks of its theological views and social conservatism, many ACDP public office-holders – MPs, members of provincial legislatures, city and town councillors – are hard working, dedicated politicians faithfully participating in the procedures of government.

The primary issue for the ACDP is Christian government, 'a constitutional state that promotes Christian moral values and as such rejects the concept of South Africa as a secular state' (Election Manifesto 2004). It was the only party to vote against adopting the 1996 Constitution for that reason – making it look ridiculous to many church people as well as the general public. Supporting a non-racial, federal, free-market society rooted in Christian values and norms – 'the proper foundation for personal freedom, national unity, reconciliation, justice, peace and security' (Election Manifesto 2004) – the ACDP presents itself as the party of conservative Christianity, rooted in 'biblical principles'. Divine law, as ACDP understands it, mandates that society is built on the (heterosexual nuclear) family and although the state should not privilege any one church or religious group, governance should be based on Christian biblical values.

There are at least two basic problems with this reasoning. First, to found oneself on 'biblical principles' presupposes these principles are clear and universal. However, hermeneutically there is simply no such thing as a 'pure', 'literal' reading of a text, no matter how much some Christians (or Jews or Muslims) might imagine or wish it to be so. Secondly, this chapter has shown that there is no such thing as a single 'Christian' public in South Africa. Even the largest bloc, the AICs, is institutionally and doctrinally diverse. Complete Christian consensus on any matter seems virtually impossible.

These reservations notwithstanding, it is instructive to consider the political vision of the ACDP. It can be summed up in brief as radically pro-life (though not against 'discretionary' capital punishment), pro-family (specifically the heterosexual nuclear family), pro-morality (including traditional Christian sexual morality), pro-free market capitalism (including private ownership, with strong 'willing buyer, willing seller' land reform) and committed to values-based education, strong policing and strict anti-corruption policies (ACDP Election Manifesto 2004).

A reading of this list and a perusal of the speeches and press releases of the party over the last five years or so[6] suggests that there is not that much distinguishing it from any other conservative, free market political party. Consistent with its principles, the ACDP weighs in against the ANC (as any opposition party should), criticising the government for its perceived mismanagement of resources, 'softness' on crime, failure to deliver on its promises on education, health, social service delivery, and sometimes on foreign policy (for example, not taking a stronger stand on Zimbabwe). The tone of these interventions is restrained yet direct, seldom *ad hominem*; nor are they particularly couched in theological language. ACDP language gets more forceful when it addresses questions of abortion, homosexuality and matters pertaining to family. The rhetorical structure of such statements usually contains three elements:

*   The ANC are pursuing this secular liberal agenda (liberal abortion laws; redefining marriage to include same sex unions) without giving it due process in Parliament;
*   The majority of the people in South Africa are opposed to it;
*   It goes against the Christian faith as revealed in the Bible. (ACDP press release, 28.10.04)

The truths of ANC political wrangling within Parliament and public opinion aside, the problem is that although most South African churches might agree with the ACDP on some of these matters, many individual Christians do not. Nor do Christians agree on what the Bible says, how it is interpreted or the degree to which it is normative. Many Christians also flinch at the bluntness of ACDP rhetoric.

Why has ACDP support not grown beyond 2 per cent, when in theory at least it should rake in the votes of socially conservative Christians? A case could be made for the claim that the ANC remains the party of liberation for the majority of citizens and that tradition plays a major role in maintaining old political loyalties. In theological terms, the ANC remains the party of liberation – of national salvation. Whatever the quality or level, the ANC has also apparently delivered sufficiently to satisfy its voters – or is seen as the only party capable of doing so.

However, it is not the case that the churches have lost favour with the public. As in many countries the church is still the most trusted institution in South Africa – more than the ANC government, police or the business community. What may then be the cause of the ACDP's limited appeal is its religious rhetoric. It is too strident, too literalist, and though many may support aspects of its social conservatism, Christians broadly welcome our new democracy and seem to prefer critical co-operation.

Critical co-operation: parliamentary liaison offices

In modern secular liberal democracies when religious groups want to influence legislation they lobby. How they lobby varies according to the texture of the parliamentary democracy. In South Africa it is necessary to try to influence the parliamentary committees. In this section I examine the SACC and SACBC parliamentary liaison offices. There has long been a working relationship between the SACC and SACBC. During the struggle, as Borer (1998) has observed, the SACC was more radical because – ironically – its resolutions were not binding on its member churches, while the SACBC in effect had to 'clear' any potentially controversial action with Rome first. Since 1994, both organisations have acknowledged that the most effective way to pursue a working relationship with the state is through critical co-operation.

As a result of a 1996 resolution, motivated by the pleas of progressive Christian theologians and activists not to withdraw from the public arena after liberation, the SACC set up a small office in 1998 to monitor parliamentary activity. Led by a former Washington lobbyist, Doug Tindall, the policy unit – later renamed the parliamentary office – soon decided to focus in five areas:[7] policy and legislation development; advocacy of church concerns; informing churches on policy; conducting advocacy training workshops for churches; and pastoral care to MPs (Tindall, interview 25.02.06).

Advocacy and pastoral care became major focuses: 'building democratic institutions' required by the Constitution; 'securing justice for the poor' (through what became the People's Budget Campaign); children's and families' rights, including childcare and protection legislation, health and welfare directed towards families and challenging domestic violence; domestic and foreign peace and security issues, including support for gun control – something that surprised some MPs whose previous experience of Christians had led them to mistakenly think that the churches were universally 'pro-gun' (Tindall, interview 25.02.06). Noting the complexity of much legislation and the unpreparedness of congregations to deal with it, the SACC parliamentary office analysed legislation, particularly new tax laws, and put together manuals to help clergy and churches deal more proactively with the state.

Proactivity was also behind the founding of the SACBC liaison office. Originally mooted after the 1994 elections as a way in which a faith community might positively help to shape policy and legislation (Rassool 2006), Father Peter-John Pearson, a Capetonian activist priest and former law lecturer, set up the office in Cape Town in 1999 with a fairly large staff, eight members plus a number of interns, under the leadership of Bishop Kevin Dowling who supervised the national Justice and Peace Commission at the SACBC.

Like its SACC counterpart and frequent co-operator, the Catholic Parliamentary Liaison Office (CPLO) did not see its task as making 'Christian' or 'Catholic' legislation. As Pearson commented, its role was primarily to create a 'ripple effect': presenting ideas, responding to others, helping clarify the thought of parliamentarians. 'The idea was to open up in MPs' minds what theologian David Tracy calls discursive possibilities, Pearson remarked, 'it was not, was never intended to be, occasion for Bible-thumping' (Pearson, interview 27.02.06).

The engagement of the CPLO with Parliament has involved interaction on a number of levels. Through participation in portfolio committees, where most of the work of law making is done, the CPLO has, together with their SACC counterparts (admittedly tiny by comparison – never more than two members), made presentations and interventions on key policy matters. The office has built up good working relationships with MPs and Cabinet ministers, often drawing on these relationships to organise meetings between legislators and bishops. Starting a system of 'round tables', the CPLO has engaged with legislators, church people and others from civil society and NGOs. Here the CPLO has been deliberately selective in who they have chosen:

> It is no use to invite anyone interested in an issue, for example child pornography. Round tables are not the places for enraged ministers to sound off at government. We choose people who are familiar with the issues, with what Parliament has been doing, and are actually working on the documents and proposals under discussion'. (Pearson, interview 27.02.06)

Unlike the SACC parliamentary office, the CPLO has an important role in reporting back to a denomination. It participates in the SACBC Joint Agency Meeting, which meets three times a year to discuss the work of specialised agencies like the national Justice and Peace Commission, the national AIDS office, the Siyabhabha National Development Trust, the Denis Hurley Peace Institute, the Catholic Institute of Education, Catholic Health Care Association, the Rural Education Access Program and Rural Development Access Program – all organisations of the Catholic Church engaged in 'public' and 'secular' matters. In contrast, the SACC parliamentary office, which has no 'church' as such to report to, relies on SACC print and online publications to disseminate its work. Sometimes the task is one of reporting on new legislation, explaining its background, rationale and possible impact on churches. A recent example of this is a tax-policy update (SACC 2005), detailing how changes in public benefit organisation (PBO) registration might affect congregations – and how such congregations might maintain their PBO status.

On other occasions the updates are commentaries with recommendations for interventions by interested parties. An illustration of this was an update (SACC

2000) on the Conventional Arms Control Bill. As it stood the Bill, controlling the sale of conventional arms by South African companies, was moving towards passage without the inclusion of human rights criteria – particularly the human rights record of buyer countries. The update urged concerned Christians to contact the parliamentary defence portfolio committee and call for wider public debate on its lacunae.

Such then are the limitations on the SACC parliamentary office. While its members are perhaps freer agents in their engagement since they are not directly answerable to a church as such, their space for effective action backed up by the churches is more constrained. Theological as opposed to political contributions of the SACC parliamentary office depend on the theological interests and education of its members.

When, on the other hand, members of the CPLO attend parliamentary portfolio committees, they present Catholic insights into social issues informed by the grassroots practice of the church and the sophisticated philosophical–theological system of Catholic social thought (CST) – a part of Catholic moral theology dealing with political and economic issues. As such it draws upon the Aristotelian –Thomistic form of natural law that stresses reason rather than the appeal to scriptures that presumes Christian faith. Rather than ask questions like 'What does the Bible say?' or 'What does God command?' CST asks primarily 'What does this issue mean to the dignity of the human person?' Over the last century and a half CST has stressed human dignity, political participation, subsidiarity, the right to work and – if there is a fundamental conflict of interests – the priority of labour rights over capital. As a result the CPLO has made interventions on issues as varied as the arms trade, black economic empowerment, virginity testing, child rights, child pornography, religion–state relations, the Budget, the basic-income grant, intergovernmental relations and open democracy.[8]

Both the CPLO and the SACC parliamentary offices have been influential. As mentioned above the People's Budget Campaign has shown signs of bearing fruit. In a statement on the 2006 Budget (SACC 2006) the 13 per cent growth in spending on basic services and on land reform was welcomed, but it was noted that 'as the Budget itself recognises, South Africa cannot achieve sustainable, pro-poor growth unless the government and our people do far more to transform the economy and government spending in that context'. The way of critical co-operation continues.

What are the implications of these two organisations for this study? The first is that religions in general and Christianity in particular can dialogue with a secular state without somehow 'losing out'. It is easier for some than for others, particularly forms of Christianity that have an inbuilt philosophical ethical system that is not posited on religious revelation alone. Second, the rich experience of the two organisations gives the lie to some Christian claims that the ANC government is antireligious, ideologically rigid and not open to constructive dialogue on policy matters. Third, all those involved recognise that the process is dialogical and continuing. No easy victories, but no utter defeats.

Finally, it should not be suggested that these churches are somehow the tails 'wagging the dog'. These offices are contributory participants to policy-making in the new South Africa. The ANC government ultimately makes its own laws and develops its own policies. Certain of these policies – such as abortion and, very likely in the future, same-sex unions – will never gain the approval of some churches. Similarly, one must not assume too much about the churches behind the CPLO and SACC parliamentary office; there are probably many church people who still reject the idea of critical co-operation.

Conclusion

Though it seems an anti-climax to suggest that what has gone before in this chapter is in some way superficial, in a sense this is true. Twelve years in the life of a range of diverse organisations that together support, spiritually nourish, influence or fail to influence almost three-quarters of South Africa's population could hardly be covered adequately in a book, let alone a chapter. Vast areas of importance – theological education, religious publications, religious media, trends in spirituality, internal church struggles over leadership transformation, struggles over women's ordination, and so on – have been omitted. One crucial area deserving a study in itself is the relationship between religious belief and moral behaviour: South Africa remains religious while as a society it manifests disturbingly high levels of violent crime. This relationship, between faith and crime and the high degree of cognitive dissonance such a situation must entail, deserves further attention.

What has hopefully been shown is how the churches nationally have tried to face the challenges of post-apartheid South Africa. In facing them the churches have displayed much continuity with their practice in the past – and have tried to adjust to a new, more secular, yet ultimately more equal and just democratic political culture. Theologians often distinguish between a future fulfilled kingdom of God and the signs of its embryonic presence in the struggles of human history. The dialectic between continuity and change, between the kingdom's advance and its obstruction, is called salvation history, a history lived out in the secular world and manifested not simply in the church but in all human progress. Here is the clue and the impetus to many of the churches' continued engagement with the new South Africa.

Notes

1 I shall not examine the various mergers of churches that have occurred nor the political developments in the governance of individual churches (that is, the decline in some denominations of white middle-class leaderships and the rise of more representative church administrations); nor, indeed, the struggles for the ordination or leadership advancement of women in some churches. Though all these issues are an important part of the life of the church in South Africa, particularly in the denominations concerned, fairness to their complexity demands more detailed study by theologians, sociologists and historians of religion.

2 My thanks, too, to clergy, theologians, political activists and lay Christians whose conversations – acknowledged and 'background', formal and off the record – have added depth and humanity to my survey.

3 In 1994, the ZCC hosted Nelson Mandela (ANC), FW de Klerk (National Party) and Mangosuthu Buthelezi (Inkatha) at Moria. Also present, according to the Dutch newspaper *Trouw* (12.04.94), were Clarence Makwetu (PAC) and Zach de Beer (Democratic Party) (Ellis & Ter Haar 2004).

4 Personal observation at the event.

5 All documents used are available on the ACDP website <http://www.acdp.org.za>. Similarly, the SACC parliamentary office and SACBC parliamentary office references are, unless otherwise stated, also available online at <http://www.sacc.org.za>; and <http://www.sacbc.org.za>.

6 Accessible on <http://www.acdp.org.za>.

7 See <http://www.sacc.org.za>.

8 The scope of the CPLO involvement can be gauged by the columns Pearson writes fairly regularly for the Cape Town archdiocese's bimonthly newsletter *Archdiocesan News*.

References

Abraham G (1989) *The Catholic Church and apartheid: The response of the Catholic Church in South Africa to the first decade of National Party rule, 1948–1957*. Johannesburg: Ravan Press.

ACDP (2004) *Election manifesto – 2004*. Available at <http://www.acdp.org.za>.

Anderson AH (2000) *Zion and Pentecost: The spirituality and experience of Pentecostal and Zionist/Apostolic Churches in South Africa*. Pretoria: UNISA Press.

Anderson AH (2001) Types and butterflies: African Initiated Churches and European typologies. *International Bulletin of Missionary Research*, 25(3): 107–13.

Anderson AH & Otwang S (1993) *Tumelo: The faith of African Pentecostals in South Africa*. Pretoria: UNISA Press.

Ashforth A (2000) *Madumo: A man betwitched*. Cape Town: David Philip.

Ashforth A (2005) *Witchcraft, violence, and democracy in South Africa*. Chicago: University of Chicago Press.

Balcomb A (1993) *Third way theology: Reconciliation, revolution and reform in the South African church during the 1980s*. Pietermaritzburg: Cluster Publications.

Bate SC (Ed) (2003) *Responsibility in a time of AIDS: A pastoral response by Catholic theologians and AIDS activists in South Africa*. Pietermaritzburg: Cluster Publications.

Borer TA (1998) *Challenging the state: Churches as political actors in South Africa, 1980–1994*. Notre Dame: University of Notre Dame Press.

Botha J (1998) Appeals to religious authority in the South African Constitutional Assembly. *Scriptura*, 4: 309–34.

Botman HR & Petersen RM (Eds) (1996) *To remember and to heal: Theological and psychological reflections on truth and reconciliation*. Cape Town: Human & Rousseau.

Brown WE (1960) *The Catholic Church in South Africa, from its origin to the present day*. London: Burns & Oates.

Chapman AR & Spong B (Eds) (2003) *Religion and reconciliation in South Africa: Voices of religious leaders*. Pietermaritzburg: Cluster Publications.

Chidester D (1992) *Religions of South Africa*. London: Routledge.

Cochrane JR (1986) *Servants of power: The role of English-speaking churches 1903–1930*. Johannesburg: Ravan Press.

Cochrane JR (2000) Religious pluralism in post-colonial public life. *Journal of Church and State*, 42/3: 443–65.

Cox H (1996) *Fire from heaven: The rise of Pentecostal spirituality and the reshaping of religion in the twenty-first century*. London: Cassell.

De Gruchy JW (1995) *Christianity and democracy*. Cambridge: Cambridge University Press.

De Gruchy JW & De Gruchy S (2004) *The church struggle in South Africa* (25th anniversary edition). London: SCM.

De Klerk WA (1976) *The puritans in Africa: A history of Afrikanerdom*. Harmondsworth: Penguin.

Denis P (2003) Sexuality and AIDS in South Africa. *Journal of Theology for Southern Africa*, 115: 63–78.

Du Toit F (Ed) (2003) *Learning to live together: Practices of social reconciliation*. Cape Town: Institute for Justice & Reconciliation.

Ellis S & Ter Haar G (2004) *Worlds of power: Religious thought and political practice in Africa*. Johannesburg: Wits University Press.

Elphick R & Davenport R (Eds) (1997) *Christianity in South Africa: A political, social and cultural history*. Cape Town: David Philip.

Erasmus JC & Hendriks HJ (2003) Religious affiliation in South Africa early in the new millennium: Markinor's World Values Survey. *Journal of Theology for Southern Africa*, 117: 97–109.

Gennrich D (Ed) (2004) *The Church in an HIV+ world: A practical handbook*. Pietermaritzburg and Durban: Cluster Publications.

Germond PA (2004) Sex in a globalizing world: The South African churches and the crisis of sexuality. *Journal of Theology for Southern Africa,* 119: 46–68.

Gunner L (Ed/Tr) (2004) *The man of Heaven and the beautiful ones of God*. Pietermaritzburg: University of KwaZulu-Natal Press.

Haddad B (2002) Gender violence and HIV/AIDS: A deadly silence in the Church. *Journal of Theology for Southern Africa,* 114: 93–106.

Hendriks HJ (2001) Religion in South Africa: Census '96'. In *South African Christian Handbook 2001/2002*. Tyger Valley: Christian Network Media & TM.

Hendriks J & Erasmus J (2005) Religion in South Africa: The 2001 census data. *Journal of Theology for Southern Africa,* 121: 88–111.

Hollenweger WJ (1972) *The Pentecostals: The charismatic movement in the Churches*. London: SCM.

ICT (Institute for Contextual Theology) (1986) *The Kairos Document: Challenge to the Church: A theological comment on the political crisis in South Africa* (2nd edition). Johannesburg: Institute for Contextual Theology.

Makhubu P (1988) *Who are the Independent Churches?* Johannesburg: Skotaville Press.

Moodie T Dunbar (1975) *The rise of Afrikanerdom: Power, apartheid and Afrikaner civil religion*. Berkeley: University of California Press.

Moran ES & Schlemmer L (1984) *Faith for the fearful? An investigation into new churches in the Greater Durban Area*. Durban: Centre for Applied Social Studies.

Ndungane N (2003) *A world with a human face: A voice from Africa*. Cape Town: David Philip.

Nyberg R (1994) Evangelicals await a time of testing. *Christianity Today,* 7 March: 5–10.

Petersen RM (1999) The AICs and the TRC: Resistance redefined. In J de Gruchy et al. *Facing the truth: South African faith communities and the Truth and Reconciliation Commission*. Cape Town: David Philip.

Pretorius H & Jafta L (1997) 'A branch springs out': African Initiated Churches'. In R Elphick & R Davenport (Eds.) *Christianity in South Africa: A political, social & cultural history*. Oxford and Cape Town: James Currey/David Philip.

Rassool M (2006) The Catholic voice in Parliament. *Southern Cross,* January: 25–31.

SACC (2000) *Public policy update: Disastrous Arms Control Bill omits human rights criteria,* September. Available at: <http://www.sacc-ct.org.za/policy updates.html>.

SACC (2005) *Tax policy update*. Available at: <http://www.sacc-ct.org.za/taxup305.html>.

SACC (2006) *People's budget response to the 2006 national budget,* March. Available at: <http://www.sacc-ct.org.za/campaigns.html#peoples>.

SACC & SACBC (2002) *Unblurring the vision: An assessment of the New Partnership for Africa's Development by South African Churches*. Johannesburg and Pretoria: South African Council of Churches/Southern African Catholic Bishops Conference.

Thompson G (2004) 'Transported away': The spirituality and piety of charismatic Christianity in South Africa (1976–1994). *Journal of Theology for Southern Africa*, 118: 128–45.

TRC (Truth and Reconciliation Commission) (1998) *Final report* (5 volumes). Cape Town: Juta & Co.

Turner HW (1979) *Religious innovation in Africa*. Boston: G K Hall.

Verryn T (1983) *Rich Christian, Poor Christian: An appraisal of Rhema teaching*. Pretoria: Ecumenical Research Unit.

Villa-Vicencio C (1988) *Trapped in apartheid: A socio-theological history of the English-speaking churches*. Johannesburg and New York: Ravan/Orbis.

Villa-Vicencio C (1992) *A theology of reconstruction: Nation-building and human rights*. Cambridge: Cambridge University Press.

Walker DS (1993) *Challenging evangelicalism: Prophetic witness and theological renewal*. Pietermaritzburg: Cluster Publications.

Walshe P (1995) *Prophetic Christianity in contemporary South Africa*. Pietermaritzburg: Cluster Publications.

West M (1975) *Bishops and prophets in a black city: African Independent Churches in Soweto, Johannesburg*. Cape Town: David Philip.

Worsnip ME (1991) *Between the two fires: The Anglican Church and apartheid 1948–1957*. Pietermaritzburg: University of Natal Press.

Interviews

Doug Tindall, former Director of the SACC Parliamentary Office, Cape Town 25.02.06.

Fr Peter-John Pearson, Catholic Parliamentary Liaison Office, Cape Town, 27.02.06.

19 Improving learner achievement in schools: applications of national assessments in South Africa

Anil Kanjee

The application of national assessment studies for monitoring the education system comprises a critical function within any education ministry. Used appropriately, relevant assessment systems can provide the impetus to transform an education system so that government's desired goals can be attained (Schiefelbein & Schiefelbein 2003). In the South African education sector, however, despite numerous national assessments[1] and a massive investment in human and financial resources, the full value and impact from these studies has yet to be realised. In particular, there has been limited use of information derived from national assessments for improving the performance of learners, especially those from rural and poor backgrounds. The current reality is that the education sector in South Africa is data rich but information poor. Thus, a major challenge is to obtain relevant information from these studies that depict accurately the disparities that characterise education in South Africa and ensure that this information meets the specific needs of decision-makers to effect appropriate policies and practices for improving learner achievement.

This review of the state of national assessments is based on experiences in a number of national and international studies. In particular, this chapter examines the value of information obtained from national assessments to derive conceptual, methodological and practical lessons for use in improving learner achievement. The chapter begins by outlining the definition, role and use of national assessments followed by an overview of the context of assessment in South Africa, highlighting the current policy context and the range of assessments conducted. A brief overview of the three national assessments conducted thus far follows with a listing of some results, and of their strengths and shortcomings. A number of emerging issues pertaining to the impact of policy and practice, and methodology and design, are then noted. The chapter concludes by listing suggestions to policy-makers, teachers and researchers for improving practices pertaining to national assessments so that relevant information can be applied to improve the achievement levels of all learners within our education system.

Defining national assessments and how they are used

National assessments are defined as 'regular and systematic measurement exercises designed to determine what students have learned as a result of their educational experiences' (Unesco 2000: 14). They are different to public examinations in that their goal is to inform policy for the education system as a whole, rather than to certify individual learners. In national assessments, learner achievement levels and the context within which learning takes place serve as critical indicators for evaluating the impact of policies in the education system. Data are obtained by means of learner tests, questionnaires, interviews and/or observations pertaining to the functioning of learners, teachers, parents, school principals and education officials.

Kellaghan and Greaney (2001) and Lockheed (1996) note that the reasons for conducting national assessments include monitoring the functioning of the education system, evaluating effectiveness and efficiency of specific policies, aiding in decisions about resource allocation, holding schools accountable for learner performance, and diagnosing individual learner needs. The latter two reasons require that an entire cohort of schools/learners be tested, that is, census testing as compared to sample testing where the study is administered to a statistically selected group.

The context of assessment in South Africa

In this section, I provide an overview of the different types of assessments that are currently conducted at the different levels of the education system. However, to contextualise how assessments are conducted in practice, a synopsis of the relevant legislations and policies that impact on the education assessment system in South Africa is provided.

The policy context for national assessment in South Africa is prescribed by the National Education Policy Act of 1996, *Assessment policy in the General Education and Training Band: Grade R to 9 and ABET* (DoE 1998) and the *Framework for Systemic Evaluations* (DoE 2001). In addition, assessment practices at the school level are also determined by the *Curriculum 2005 assessment guidelines for inclusion* (DoE 2002), and *The national protocol on assessment for schools in the General and Further Education and Training Band (Grades R–12)* (DoE 2005).

Section 8(1) of the National Education Policy Act of 1996 mandates the Minister of Education to 'direct standards of education provision, delivery and performance throughout the Republic...'. As per the Act, this monitoring and evaluation is to be carried out with a view to assessing progress in compliance with the provisions of the Constitution of the Republic of South Africa and national education policy. To carry out this Act, Section 48 of the assessment policy for General Education and Training (DoE 1998) makes provision for 'systemic evaluations' to be conducted on a nationally-representative sample of learners and learning sites to evaluate all aspects of the school system and learning programmes. Furthermore, the policy stipulates that systemic evaluations be conducted on a regular basis in grades 3, 6 and 9 of the education system (DoE 2001). According to the *Framework for Systemic Evaluations*:

> The main purpose of systemic evaluation is to benchmark performance
> and track the progress made towards the achievement of the
> transformational goals of the education system in respect to access,
> redress, equity and quality. In so doing, Systemic Evaluation aspires to
> promote and ensure accountability and thus gain the confidence of the
> public in education. (DoE 2001: 5)

In particular, this framework stipulates that systemic evaluations seek to answer
the following questions:
* What is the context in which learning and teaching are taking place?
* What is the level of achievement of the learners at key points of the
  education system (grades 3, 6 and 9)?
* What factors affect learner performance?
* How can the level of achievement be improved?

Overview of assessment practices

The education assessment system in South Africa consists of:
* School-based assessments;
* Public examinations;
* Provincial/district assessments;
* National assessments;
* International assessments; and
* Assessments conducted to evaluate programmes or projects.

School-based assessments include regular classroom tests as well as end-of-term
and end-of-year examinations. These are usually devised and administered by
teachers, are typically aligned with the delivered curriculum and play an important
role in improving learning within the classroom and in the promotion of learners
to the next grade. In the context of Curriculum 2005, school-based assessments are
seen as critical components of the teaching and learning process. In this regard, the
National Protocol on Assessment is intended to regulate recording and reporting in
all schools and to reduce the workload of teachers (DoE 2005). Effected from the
beginning of 2006, the *National Protocol on Assessment* is intended to:

> standardise recording and reporting for schools (Grades R–12) within
> the framework of the National Curriculum Statements for Grades R–9 &
> 10–12. It also provides a regulatory framework for the management of
> school assessment records and basic requirements for learner profiles,
> teacher and learner portfolios, report cards and schedules. (DoE 2005: 4)

Public examinations are usually conducted at the national/provincial level for cer-
tifying completion of formal schooling and used in admission to tertiary education
and/or the world of work. In South Africa, the only public examination conducted in the school system is the matriculation exam. This examination is designed,

developed and administered centrally, has an exclusive focus on school subject areas, and meagre feedback (on learners' scores and pass rates) is provided to schools. For the final matric grade, classroom-based assessments contribute 25 per cent of the final result. Learner performance is thus measured through both the end-of-year examinations and their ongoing performance throughout the final years of schooling.

The purpose of the matriculation examination is to certify completion of 12 years of schooling and to test for admission into higher education. In the absence of any form of regular national monitoring of the education system, the matriculation examination has also been used as a signal of the quality of the country's education (Reddy 2006). However, there is no consensus on the accuracy of the matriculation results as an indicator of education quality (Seekings 2002). Matriculation results have also been used by the national Department of Education (DoE) to hold schools accountable for the performance of their learners. This accountability policy still continues even though the success of this policy has been questioned. Proponents point to the significant increase in pass rates over the last eight years as evidence that the policy of holding schools accountable is working. However, critics such as Jansen note that the improved results are attributable more to other factors that include holding unprepared learners back in Grade 11, subject choice of Grade 11 learners, change in criteria for passing and so on (*Sunday Times* 04.01.04).

Provincial/district assessments are similar to national assessments although these studies are conduced within the bounded education system defined by provinces or districts; for example, the system-wide district assessment conducted by one of the districts within the Gauteng DoE (Makgamatha et al. 2000). At present, only the Western Cape Education Department (WCED) has conducted any provincial assessments, that is, at Grade 3, Grade 6 and Grade 8 levels (WCED 2003a, 2004, 2005b). However, unlike the national assessments, instruments were administered in all schools at the targeted grade levels, where samples of all Grade 3, 6 or 8 learners were assessed respectively. The primary purpose for conducting the Grade 3 and 6 assessment was to obtain information for effecting appropriate intervention strategies to address the poor performance levels of learners (WCED 2003a, 2004, 2005b), while the purpose of the Grade 8 study was 'to inform study and career guidance for learners entering Grade 9' (WCED 2005a) and 'to analyse and report on the results of the tests in order for the WCED to benchmark learners, prioritise learners with potential and develop and support learning and teaching processes' (WCED 2005d).

Information about the provincial assessments of the WCED was obtained from media releases, tender documents and the 2004–05 annual report since none of the reports (nor data) from the different assessment studies have ever been made public. Thus, no information was available on the purpose of the provincial assessment, nor on specific approaches adopted and the processes employed. However, the documents reviewed point to:

- Some system of holding schools (that is, principals and perhaps even teachers) accountable for improving performance since results are reported to all schools and support is provided for improving learner performance (WCED 2003a);
- The identification of schools for additional support by using learner results (WCED 2003b);
- Using information from the assessments to develop interventions and to optimise the allocation of human and physical resources (WCED 2003b, 2004); and
- Reporting results to individual Grade 8 learners to enhance their subject selection process before entering Grade 9 (WCED 2005d).

International assessments are those studies that assess learners in multiple countries, with the principal aim of providing cross-national comparisons that can illuminate a variety of educational issues. While the design and methodology employed in these studies is similar to that of national assessments, international studies focus on common aspects pertaining to the curriculum or learning outcomes and are typically conducted by international organisations and/or research consortia (Kellaghan & Greaney 2001; Unesco 2000). It must be noted, however, that in many developing nations, international assessments are the only type of assessment studies conducted and are typically used in lieu of national studies (Braun & Kanjee 2006). Table 19.1 provides an overview of the international/ regional assessments that include participation from South Africa.

Assessments for evaluating education programmes in South Africa have generally been conducted at either the national, provincial or district level by a number of different service providers and/or consultants. Due to space constraints, detailed descriptions of these cannot be presented. They have, however, made significant contributions to the development and application of national assessments – for example similar test development, administration and analysis procedures have been applied. This cross-fertilisation of ideas and practices is certain to continue in

Table 19.1 *Participation of South Africa in international/regional studies*

Name of study	Area of focus	Grade	Current cycle/duration	Participating countries
TIMSS	Maths and science	4	3rd (1995, 1998, 2002)	Over 50 worldwide
PIRLS	Reading and writing	4	1st (2005) 4 years	Over 40 worldwide
SACMEQ	Maths and language	6	1st (2000) variable	15 southern African
MLA	Numeracy and literacy	4	1st (1999)	35 developing

Notes: For more information on TIMSS (Trends in International Maths and Science Study) and PIRLS (Progress in International Reading Literacy Study), see <http://www.timss.bc.edu>. In 2003, a sample of Grade 9 learners was also assessed in TIMSS. For more information on SACMEQ (Southern African Consortium for Monitoring Education Quality), see <http://www.sacmeq.org>. For more information on MLA (Monitoring Learning Achievement), see Chinapah et al. (2000).

the future as the limited technical and practical expertise in the country dictates that support for the national DoE in conducting national assessment is most likely to be sourced from the same (small) group of service providers. In addition, these studies also provide a rich source of information pertaining to learner achievement levels in the country. Some of the intervention programmes/projects that used assessment studies to measure impact include the Quality Learning Project (Kanjee & Prinsloo 2005), the Learning for Living project (Schollar 2005), the District Development Support Program (Claassen et al. 2004), the Systemic Wide Reading Assessment Project (Makgamatha et al. 2000), the Molteno Project (Makgamatha & Masehela 2005) and the Integrated Education Programme (JET Education Services 2005).

National assessment studies conducted in South Africa

In this section I review briefly the different national assessment studies conducted to date, that is, the Monitoring Learning Achievement (1999), the Grade 3 Systemic Evaluation (2001) and the Grade 6 Systemic Evaluation (2004). The focus of this review is to identify conceptual, methodological and practical lessons for informing future national assessments.

Monitoring Learning Achievement

The Monitoring Learning Achievement (MLA) project was a joint Unesco and Unicef initiative established to support developing nations report on indicator 15 of the Education for All 2000 assessment. Indicator 15 refers to the 'percentage of learners having reached at least Grade 4 primary schooling who master a set of nationally defined basic learning competencies' (Unesco 2000: 20). The MLA project focused on assessing the performance levels of Grade 4 learners in literacy, life skills and numeracy. In Africa, all instruments were developed jointly by representatives of participating countries and, where necessary, modified to address the specific country context (Chinapah et al. 2000). While the MLA can be regarded as an international study, in South Africa a different design was applied in collecting data, the instruments were adapted to reflect the South African context, all tests were translated into the 11 official languages, the analysis conducted differed from that in other African countries, and the results were not included in the Africa report for the Dakar EFA forum in 2000. Thus in practice, the South African MLA study was really a national assessment study, using adapted instruments developed by Unesco and Unicef.

The MLA study was conducted by the DoE with the assistance of the Research Institute for Educational Planning at the University of Free State (Strauss & Burger 1999). A total of 400 schools were selected. In each selected school, the instruments were administered to learners in an intact Grade 4 class comprising at least 30 learners while contextual questionnaires were administered to parents, teachers and principals. Results were presented on learner achievement and the context of learning and teaching in a series of ten reports (one national and nine provincial).

Learner achievement results

The learner achievement results were aggregated by province and reported as percentage mean scores as well as by the per cent of learners in each quartile. Figure 19.1 lists the results for the literacy task by province. The national mean was 48 per cent with approximately 13 per cent of learners scoring below 25 per cent and above 75 per cent while most learners (that is, 47%) scored between 25 and 50 per cent. The lowest scores were reported for Mpumalanga, Limpopo, North West and Free State provinces. It is worth noting that in all these provinces a large percentage of schools are located in the rural areas.

Figure 19.1 *Literacy results by province for the South African MLA study*

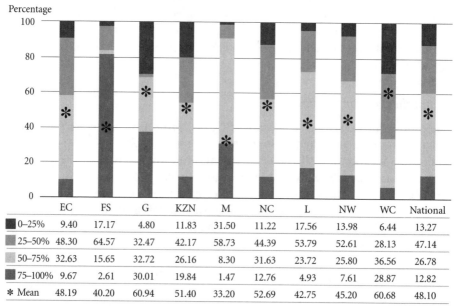

Percentage

	EC	FS	G	KZN	M	NC	L	NW	WC	National
■ 0–25%	9.40	17.17	4.80	11.83	31.50	11.22	17.56	13.98	6.44	13.27
■ 25–50%	48.30	64.57	32.47	42.17	58.73	44.39	53.79	52.61	28.13	47.14
■ 50–75%	32.63	15.65	32.72	26.16	8.30	31.63	23.72	25.80	36.56	26.78
■ 75–100%	9.67	2.61	30.01	19.84	1.47	12.76	4.93	7.61	28.87	12.82
✱ Mean	48.19	40.20	60.94	51.40	33.20	52.69	42.75	45.20	60.68	48.10

Source: Strauss & Burger (2000: 7)
Note: EC = Eastern Cape, FS = Free State, G = Gauteng, KZN = KwaZulu-Natal,
M = Mpumalanga, NC = Northern Cape, L = Limpopo, NW = North West, WC = Western Cape.

The results were also disaggregated for each content area. For example, Table 19.2 provides average learner scores at the national level by sub-domain for literacy. The two domains in which learners obtained the highest scores were word recognition and providing information while performance was lowest in the writing skills domain.

Additional analysis was also conducted on the achievement of learners by geographical region. As noted in Figure 19.2, the average scores of learners from the urban and semi-urban areas were significantly higher.

Table 19.2 *Analysis of the literacy task at national level by different domains*

Competencies and domain	Mean score (%)	Std deviation	Maximum (%)	Minimum (%)
Literacy (total)	48.1	21.0	100.0	0.0
Word recognition	67.7	11.9	84.6	56.4
Detail content	43.4	6.2	52.1	35.7
Writing skills	23.8	8.3	38.5	18.6
Spelling and grammar	47.2	2.6	49.9	44.6
Info. retrieval	47.5	12.1	69.5	31.8
Info. provision	65.5	26.0	87.1	34.0

Source: Strauss & Burger (2000: 9)

Figure 19.2 *Literacy results by location of schools*

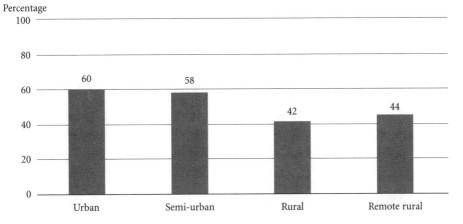

Source: Strauss & Burger 2000: 10

Context of learning and teaching

The contextual data reported by Strauss and Burger (2000) was based on the context-input-process-outputs model. Information was reported for different variables using frequencies and graphs, while detail responses were noted in the appendices. For example, Table 19.3 lists the responses of learners, teachers and principals pertaining to the total instruction time (in number of schools days) lost during the year as a result of lessons not starting on time, absenteeism and cultural activities.

Another example taken from Strauss and Burger (2000) is presented in Figure 19.3, which indicates that approximately 13 per cent of principals reported having Grade 4 classes with more than 60 learners, with the problem most acute in the

Table 19.3 *Total number of days lost across sample schools during the school year, by percentage*

Days lost	Learners' views (%)	Educators' views (%)	Principals' views (%)
6–10	8	44	34
11–20	4	34	27
21–30	29	15	14
30+	59	6	24

Source: Strauss & Burger (2000: 33).

Limpopo and Mpumalanga provinces. In addition, 46 per cent of the principals across all provinces reported class sizes of between 40 and 49, which exceeded the recommended 40 learners per class.

Figure 19.3 *Learner–classroom ratio by province*

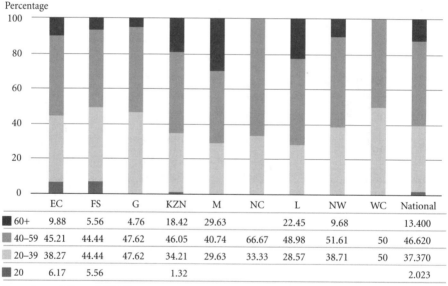

Percentage

	EC	FS	G	KZN	M	NC	L	NW	WC	National
■ 60+	9.88	5.56	4.76	18.42	29.63		22.45	9.68		13.400
▨ 40–59	45.21	44.44	47.62	46.05	40.74	66.67	48.98	51.61	50	46.620
░ 20–39	38.27	44.44	47.62	34.21	29.63	33.33	28.57	38.71	50	37.370
■ 20	6.17	5.56		1.32						2.023

Source: Strauss & Burger (2000: 25)

Findings and conclusions

The findings and conclusions of the study are presented as summaries of the contextual information (that is, under the headings socio-economic background, inputs, school endowment, process and final conclusion) and are too numerous to report. No conclusions were reported on learner achievement levels nor were any policy implications and recommendations noted.

Strengths and shortcomings

The MLA study was the first national assessment study conducted in South Africa and has served as the basis for other similar studies in terms of capacity development, methodology, design and reporting. Other strengths include:

- Its use of a model-based approach for analysing the data in the context within which learners function;
- The reporting of learner achievement results by sub-domain which provides detailed information on learner performance;
- The use of information from the national Census to compare similar information obtained from the contextual questionnaires; and
- The inclusion of additional details in the appendices to supplement information reported in the main body of the report.

However, several shortcomings should also be noted:

- No analyses were conducted to identify factors affecting learner performance;
- Learner achievement scores were only disaggregated by geographical location while scores for gender were noted in the appendix. No information was provided on other critical variables like home language or socio-economic status, and so on;
- The report did not contain any analysis on implications for policy and practice nor list any recommendations (although it must be acknowledged that the latter could be as a result of the terms of reference).

Grade 3 Systemic Evaluation Study

In September 2001, the Grade 3 national assessment study was conducted by the DoE with the assistance of an education research and policy consortium comprising a number of local service providers. The goal was to: '(a) serve as a baseline for future systemic evaluation studies, and (b) make appropriate recommendations regarding national education policy implementation' (DoE 2003: 7). The study assessed the performance of Grade 3 learners in literacy, numeracy and life skills. In addition, questionnaires soliciting information on the context of learning and teaching were administered to learners, teachers, principals and parents. All instruments administered to learners were translated into the 11 official languages. A 5 per cent sample was drawn from all primary schools comprising more than 30 learners. In each school, a random sample of all Grade 3 learners was assessed. Analyses were conducted to determine learner achievement, the context of learning and teaching and the factors associated with learner achievement. The results were reported at the national level as well as for each of the nine provinces.

Learner achievement results

The learner achievement results, presented in Figure 19.4, indicate extremely poor performance for mathematics (an average of 30 per cent) with higher average scores recorded for both literacy (reading and writing – 39 per cent; listening comprehension – 68 per cent) and life skills (54 per cent). The patterns of performance for each of the three learning areas were similar across the different provinces. Additional results were also reported by gender, geographical location, home language of the learner and by item type, that is, multiple choice or free response.

Figure 19.4 *Grade 3 systemic evaluation results by learning area and province*

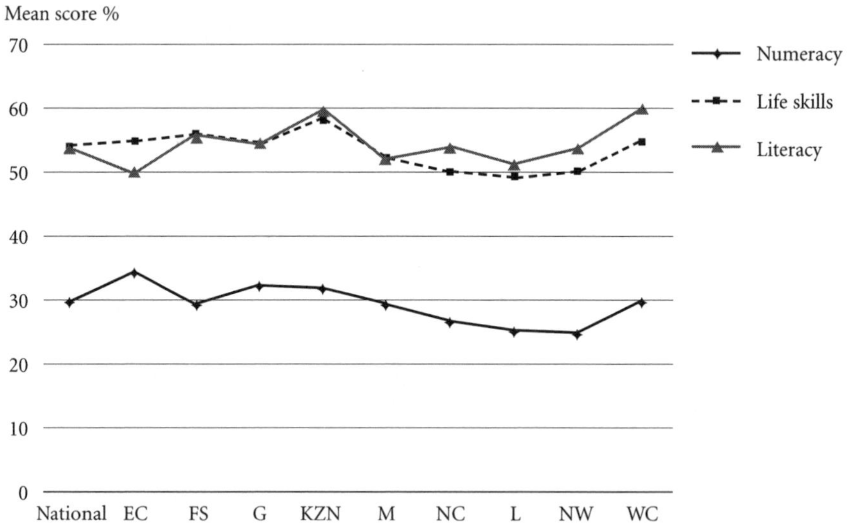

Source: DoE (2003: 62)

Context of learning and teaching

Analysis of the contextual data was based on a framework of 26 indicators arranged in a matrix according to the context-inputs-process-outputs model and policy goals of access, equity, redress and quality (see the appendix to this chapter). For example, the 'access to resources' indicator refers to whether learners had access to newspapers, books, radio, television and a computer at home, and is reported under the policy goal: access. From Figure 19.5, it is clear that access to learning resources was reported as being low in all provinces.

Factors affecting learner performance

Separate regressions analyses were conducted to identify the access, equity and quality indicators associated with learner achievement. The key access indicators identified as having the strongest association with the performance of Grade 3 learners were resources at home, ease of access to schools, repetition rate; the

Figure 19.5 *Access to resources at home by province*

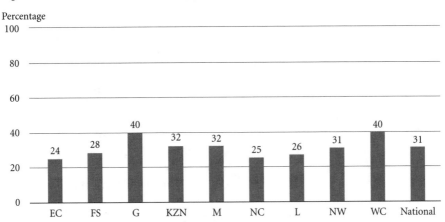

Source: DoE (2003: 15)

equity indicators identified were discipline, safety and learning atmosphere, private contributions and utilisation of funds; while the quality indicators identified were facilities at school, learning and teaching materials and teaching practices. A number of policy suggestions were noted based on these key indicators.

Findings and conclusion

The Grade 3 national assessment study found low achievement levels in numeracy and literacy with performance levels similar across all the provinces in all of the three learning areas assessed. In addition, learners performed better on tasks that required them to identify and select a correct response than on tasks that required them to produce their own response, while learners who undertook tests in their home language obtained significantly higher scores across all learning areas.

Access indicators accounted for 20 per cent of the variation in learner scores while equity indicators accounted for 9 per cent and quality indicators accounted for 22 per cent. However, it was noted that it is still unclear why critical indicators that are known to influence learner performance (for example, assessment of learners, homework and so on) did not display any or greater influence on learner scores. It is vital that specific reasons for these findings be determined in follow-up studies.

Strengths and shortcomings

The strengths of the Grade 3 systemic evaluation were:
- The use of indicators based on the key policy goals of access, equity and quality to describe the context of learning and teaching;
- The identification of specific indicators affecting learner achievement;

- The reporting of learner achievement scores by gender, item type and home language; and
- The provision of policy suggestions based on the key indicators.

However, a number of shortcomings need to be noted:

- The analysis of the context of learning and teaching and the presentation of the results were conducted separately for each of the policy goals (access, equity and quality). This provided an inaccurate picture as in practice these policy goals are intricately related and impact upon each other;
- The framework used to conceptualise and report on the context of learning and teaching comprised a number of indicators that were defined under different policy goals (see appendix to this chapter). This meant that the unique contribution of these indicators on learner achievement scores could not be identified;
- The learner scores were not reported by geographical location;
- The contextual information was obtained from self-reported measures with no verification conducted on its authenticity;
- The analysis of the factors affecting learner performance did not account for the hierarchical nature of the education system, thus the specific impact of classroom or school factors could not be determined; and
- No meaningful interpretations were provided to understand the practical impact of the indicators.

Grade 6 Systemic Evaluation Study

In September 2004, the DoE conducted the second national assessment study, this time focusing on Grade 6 (DoE 2006). Similar to the Grade 3 study, the DoE managed the study with the assistance of three different service providers assigned to do the piloting, sampling and data entry, cleaning, analysis and reporting. The study assessed the performance of Grade 6 learners in the language of learning and teaching (LOLT), mathematics and natural sciences, while questionnaires soliciting information on the context of learning and teaching were administered to learners, teachers, principals and parents. The contextual questionnaires were based on the same framework used in the Grade 3 study with a few modifications. All instruments used in the study were translated into the two official languages of learning and teaching, English and Afrikaans. A 5 per cent sample of all Grade 6 learners was selected, stratified by both provinces and districts. The results of the study were reported in one national and nine provincial reports.

Learner achievement results

The learner achievement results were reported by each learning area and disaggregated by achievement levels, learning outcome, gender, geographical location and language. Learner performance scores for each learning area were relatively low, with learners obtaining a national score of 38 per cent in LOLT, 27 per cent in mathematics and 41 per cent in natural sciences. Across most provinces, similar performance trends were observed, with the highest scores recorded in natural sciences, followed by language and mathematics. In all three learning areas, the highest mean percentage scores were recorded in the Western Cape, Gauteng and the Northern Cape provinces.

Learners from urban areas obtained significantly higher scores than their counterparts from rural areas in all three learning areas with a 35 per cent difference noted in language, 25 per cent for maths and 23 per cent for natural sciences. Substantial differences were noted between learners whose home language was the same as the LOLT and those for whom the home language was different (see Figure 19.6).

Figure 19.6 *Language achievement by home language and province*

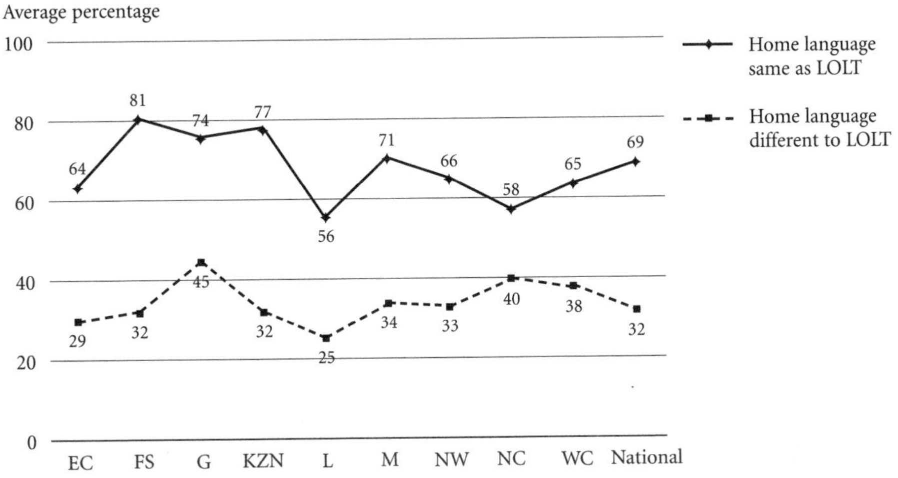

Source: DoE (2006: 81)

For each learning area, scores were also reported according to the four achievement levels to determine how learners were functioning (see Figure 19.7). An extremely high percentage of learners across all three learning areas were found to be functioning at the 'not achieved' level, that is, scores below 40 per cent, while a relatively small percentage of learners – 28 per cent in language, 12 per cent in mathematics and 31 per cent in natural sciences – were functioning at or above the required Grade 6 level, that is, 'achieved' (scores above 50 per cent) and 'outstanding' (scores above 70 per cent) combined.

Context of learning and teaching

The analysis of the contextual data was based on the 'AQEE (pronounced a-key) to improve learning' model to address a number of shortcomings identified with the

Figure 19.7 *National achievement levels for LOLT, mathematics and natural sciences*

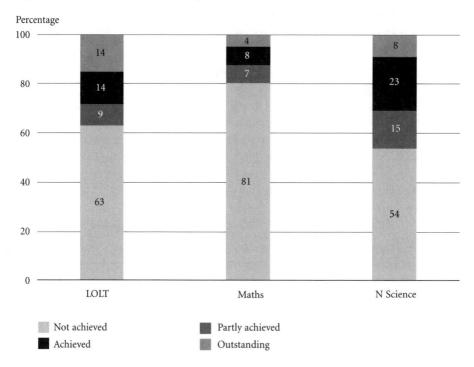

context-input-process-outputs model (see appendix) used to develop the instruments, that is, 'a number of indicators were categorised into more than one transformation goal, information on "efficiency" was not included in the framework, and the transformation goals were not represented as discrete and disjointed' (DoE 2005: 21). The AQEE model is a comprehensive evidence-informed decision-making model based on the four policy goals of access, quality, efficiency and equity. Each policy goal shown in Figure 19.8 comprises a framework that is defined and operationalised by indicators and indices. This makes it possible to adapt the model to the specific context that defines different national or local education systems and to focus on particular measures for monitoring and evaluating the attainment of relevant policy goals.

A number of indices were developed to report on each policy goal of the AQEE model. In addition, index scores were standardised on a scale of 0 to 10 and categorised to provide appropriate interpretations. For example, the learner participation index refers to the frequency of learner interaction and the nature of learner participation in the learning process, and comprises the following indicators: learner attitude; learner morale; learner participation in the mathematics, language and natural sciences class; library use; language of learning and teaching in the classroom; and extramural activities provided by the school. Learner participation was

Figure 19.8 *'AQEE to improve learning' model*

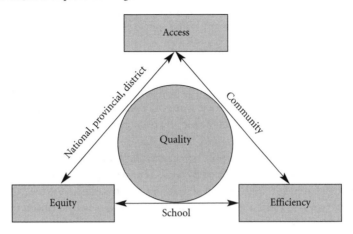

Source: Kanjee 2004

reported as 'limited' (that is, scores between 5.1 and 7) in all provinces, with a national average of 6.3.

The school resources index comprised the following indicators: classroom furniture, physical resources, school amenities, learning resources, sports resources, and vegetable gardens. As evident in Figure 19.9, the availability of resources is similar for all three learning areas across the provinces (thus the graphs appear as a single line), with school resources reported as 'largely problematic' in two provinces

Figure 19.9 *School resources by province and learning area*

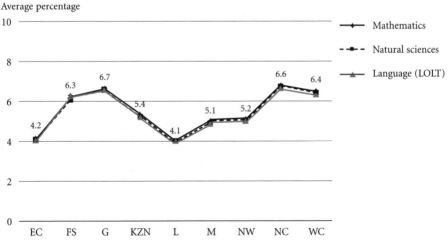

Source: DoE (2006: 36)

(Eastern Cape and Limpopo provinces where index scores were between 3.1 and 5), and 'limited' for the other seven provinces (scores between 5.1 and 7).

Factors affecting learner performance

Additional regressions and CHAID (Chi-squared Automatic Interaction Detector) analyses were also conducted to identify indicators affecting learner performance. Some of the key indicators identified were the socio-economic status (SES) of the learner, access to information at home, learner participation in class, resources available to teachers, school safety, access to information at school, parental involvement and disciple at school. For example, Table 19.4 lists the learner percentage scores for each learning area by SES. The average percentage language and mathematics scores for high SES learners are approximately three times higher than that of 'very low SES' learners. For natural sciences, the difference is more than double.

Figure 19.10 lists the relationship between learner participation and learner achievement. For all three learning areas, higher scores were associated with greater participation. In addition, there were significant differences in scores between

Table 19.4 *Learner percentage scores by socio-economic status*

Levels of SES	LOLT (average %)	Mathematics (average %)	Natural sciences (average %)
Unacceptable/very low	24	19	32
Largely problematic/poor	29	21	35
Problematic/inadequate	40	27	42
Satisfactory	66	48	60
High	80	63	71

Source: DoE (2006: 98)

those learners reporting unacceptable and poor participation compared to learners reporting satisfactory and high participation.

Findings and conclusion

The findings of the Grade 6 study point to relatively low levels of performance in all three learning areas with a relatively small percentage of learners functioning at the appropriate level for Grade 6. In addition, a number of indicators across the four policy goals were found to have a significant impact on learner achievement, for example, information at home or learner resources available to teachers, a trend that was evident across all provinces.

This study proposed several recommendations categorised by: home and community context (those factors outside the DoE's sphere of influence); resource inputs for

Figure 19.10 *Learner performance by participation in class*

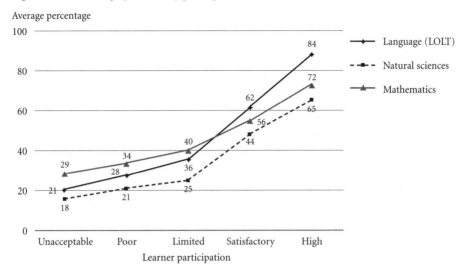

Source: DoE (2006: 107)

improving learning; and teaching and learning practices (both categories directly with-in the DoE's ambit of influence). Many of these recommendations called for more resources to be directed at schools, for existing policies to be implemented and moni-tored more stringently, for a fresh examination of the existing policy on the LOLT, and for consideration to be given to the special circumstances prevailing in schools in rural areas (DoE 2005). In particular, this study highlighted the central role of the educator and principal in raising the quality of education.

Strengths and shortcomings

The strengths of the Grade 6 study were:
- The reporting of learning outcomes using the four achievement levels stipulated in the official curriculum to gain an in-depth understanding of learner performance;
- The use of a systems model for analysing and reporting on the context within which learning takes place. This model is especially relevant given that it is based on the key policy goals of access, quality, equity and efficiency;
- The application of a scale for interpreting the indicators used to portray the context within which learning and teaching take place;
- The sample was stratified by province and district, thus enabling analysis to be conducted at the district levels as well;
- The use of advanced analysis techniques to obtain relevant information on the factors associated with learner performance; and

- The identification of recommendations that address the home and comunity contexts, as well as the resources needed to improve learning and teaching.

The shortcomings of the Grade 6 study were:
- The achievement levels applied did not provide relevant information on what learners know and can do. These had been arbitrarily set and are not linked to specific skills and competencies that learners are required to master;
- The assessment instruments used comprised a small number of items for each learning area and thus detailed analysis by learning outcome (and assessment standard) was not possible;
- The contextual information was obtained from self-reported measures with no verification conducted on its authenticity; and
- The analysis of the factors affecting learner performance did not account for the hierarchical nature of the education system, thus the specific impact of classroom or school factors could not be determined.

Emerging issues pertaining to national assessment in South Africa

A number of issues emerging from the above analysis are discussed in this section. These issues relate primarily to the impact on, firstly, methodology and design, and secondly, policy and practice.

Methodology and design

The various methodologies and designs applied to national assessments in South Africa have undergone significant improvements since the MLA project was conducted in 1999. The improvements in data collection, data entry and cleaning as well as the analysis and reporting of information have been manifested in a number of ways. First, there have been greater attempts to improve our understanding of how learning occurs through the identification and development of key indicators to explain the context within which teaching and learning takes place. However, there is no national consensus as to what constitute key indicators. Given the range of interpretations and understandings of indicators, their different conceptualisations, calculations, reporting and applications, as well as the lack of a national framework on key indicators for determining how the education system functions, it is unlikely that this issue will be addressed adequately in the near future.

Second, the use of the achievement levels specified to report on learner achievement points to a concerted effort at providing relevant interpretations of what learners know and can do. However the various scores that define these achievement levels (for example, between 50 and 69 per cent) have been arbitrarily set and the respective interpretations (that is, 'not achieved', 'partly achieved', 'achieved' and 'outstanding') do not provide detailed information on what learners know and can do.

Third, the focus on determining the factors associated with learner achievement indicates a commitment to providing explanations for the learner levels of achievement. However, the limited availability of high-level statistical expertise within the education sector as well as the restricted time frames within which to complete analysis and relevant reports have dictated the application of rudimentary procedures that are easy and quick to apply, but which cannot account for the complex nature of the education system. For example, the use of linear regressions cannot account for the fact that education systems are defined by structures that are embedded in specific hierarchies, that is, learners and teachers are an integral part of a classroom, which in turn forms part of a school, which in turn forms part of a district. In this context, especially where relevant data are available, the use of hierarchical linear models provides an appropriate alternative. Fourth, the application of a holistic approach to understanding how the education system functions, represents an attempt to take a systems approach. In this respect, the use of the AQEE model provides a basis for applying a systems approach to understanding the impact of relevant interventions and policies within the education sector.

There are also a number of methodological and design aspects that have not been adequately addressed. The first is the exclusive reliance on quantitative data. Given the limitations of large-scale surveys, the need to obtain reliable and valid qualitative information is vital to obtain a detailed understanding of the specific nuances that define how different role-players function within the complex structures and processes of the education system. While the collection of qualitative data is extremely costly, it is possible to reduce some costs by synchronising the Whole School Evaluation exercises (where qualitative data are collected through a school visit) with the Systemic Evaluation studies (Seekings 2002). It is encouraging to note that qualitative approaches have formed part of the design of a number of large-scale studies conducted in South Africa, for example the Quality Learning Project (Kanjee & Prinsloo 2005), and the Integrated Education Program (JET Education Services 2005). The second issue is the absence of information on key variables to provide detailed analysis of how learners from different backgrounds perform. In this respect, the reporting of learner achievement by race, gender and socio-economic status of learners, and the classification of schools into poverty quintiles should be prioritised. The third issue is the lack of consensus on appropriate indicators that define education systems, in particular indicators of access, quality, equity and efficiency. This aspect needs to be addressed urgently to ensure that all role-players do not use different data sources to report on similar issues.

Impact on policy and practice

Given the tenuous links between research and practice, the difficulty of measuring successful education reform, and the fact that national assessments in South Africa are still a relatively new phenomenon, it is not surprising that there is limited direct evidence to determine the impact of national assessment studies. However, there is evidence that policy-makers are using information from national assessment studies to develop interventions for improving learner achievement. For example, the national DoE is currently using the results of the Grade 6 systemic evaluation to develop appropriate mechanisms to support teachers in improving the learning and teaching process (personal communication, Mr Q Moloi, Director, Quality Assurance Directorate, national DoE). At the provincial level, the North West DoE recently included specific intervention targets in its education strategy based on the results of the recent Grade 3 and Grade 6 systemic evaluations. In Gauteng, on the other hand, the Grade 3 study was replicated in all their Presidential Nodal Initiative schools[2] to obtain relevant information for prioritising areas in need of intervention. The Western Cape DoE used the Grade 6 systemic evaluation results to provide detailed profiles to all schools that participated in the study for use in planning.

There has been a marked improvement in the reporting of information to reflect the wide disparities that characterise the South African system. For example, the 2005 Grade 6 results included details analysis disaggregated by SES, home language and geographical location and included recommendations that accounted for the home and school contexts that impact on learners. While additional analysis is still required, for example by race and poverty quintiles,[3] the key challenge still remains the effective use of information to implement policies and practices for improving the learning and teaching conditions of poor and rural schools.

At both the national and provincial levels, teacher testing has not been undertaken as part of national assessments even though it is generally accepted that low levels of teacher competencies pose a significant problem within the system. It must be acknowledged that this is a complex issue that needs a lot more consultation between the education department and teacher unions before such a system is effected as part of the national assessments. In this regard, it is possible to draw on experiences gained in the District Development Support Programme and the Integrated Education Programme (JET Education Services 2006), where teacher testing comprises one aspect of the strategy to improve the knowledge and skills of teachers.

There has been insufficient focus on schools themselves, both in terms of the analysis as well as the reporting of information. If effective policies are to be implemented to improve learner achievement, it is critical to know the specific contribution of schools to the performance of learners in different contexts. In the reports reviewed, no information was reported on how schools perform or the factors that affect schools. In addition, it is not standard practice to provide participating schools with detailed reports (although this has been done by the WCED for the Grade 6 systemic evaluation study) for use in improving practice.

Suggestions for improving practice

Notwithstanding the increased recognition of the role of national assessment studies and the use of information from these studies, a number of improvements need to be effected to ensure more reliable and valid data in future, as well as the greater use of information to enhance the decision-making process pertaining to improving policy and practice. To this end, the following suggestions should be considered for future applications of national assessments in South Africa. They are listed to highlight their implications for policy-makers, teachers and schools as well as researchers and academics. However, it must be acknowledged that these suggestions are not meant to be prescriptive nor are they exhaustive but should rather be seen as a starting point for further debate and discussion, and indeed some of the suggestions may have been addressed already.

Implications for policy-makers

A number of implications for policy-makers need to be noted. First, there is an urgent need for a coherent, strategic and unambiguous national policy on the use of information from assessment studies at all levels of the system (national, provincial, district and school). The policy should provide clear guidelines on appropriate structures, systems and processes for improving the achievement levels of all learners with a specific focus on learners with the greatest need, that is, those from rural and poor backgrounds. In addition, the strategy should guide decisions on participation in international and regional assessment studies as well. For example, there is a need to synchronise the national and international assessment studies. In this regard, the DoE has taken a strategic decision to simultaneously conduct the Grade 6 SACMEQ and Grade 6 national assessment study in the future (personal communication, Dr S Sithole, Chief Director, Quality Assurance Directorate, national DoE).

Second, the information obtained from national assessments should provide relevant and updated information that reflects the enormous disparities that currently define the education system. In the studies reviewed above, no analysis was provided by poverty index or ex-department, even though these indicators provide a vital source for deciding on appropriate interventions. For example, Reddy (2006) reports significant differences on the 2003 international mathematics test scores (in the order of 2.5 standard deviations) between ex-Department of Assembly schools (previously for white learners only) and ex-Department of Education and Training (DET) schools (previously for African learners only). Similarly, the results of the Grade 9 national assessment conducted by the Human Sciences Research Council (HSRC) (Kanjee & Povey 2006) indicate that African learners attending ex-House of Assembly (HoA) schools obtained significantly higher scores than African learners attending ex-DET schools. However the same African learners score significantly lower that their white colleagues in the ex-HoA schools. The results of both these studies provide evidence of the continued legacies of the apartheid education system and point to the value of reporting information in national assessments by both the ex-department as well as school type. Third, the approach applied in the Uruguayan education system merits further investigation, that is, the explicit use of national assessments for improving the functioning of poor schools (Benveniste 2000). It is, however, acknowledged that in the current system in South Africa responsibility for the delivery of education resides with the provincial departments and that the limited availability of resources provides unique challenges.

Implications for managers and administrators

In the South African context, the management of national assessment resides with education department officials while independent service providers usually administer the study. For these individuals, the following implications are worth noting. After three national assessments conducted since 1999, it is appropriate to:
- Review how these studies have been conceptualised, administered and applied;
- Identify the benefits and costs to the system; and
- Derive lessons for use in the planning and implementation of future studies.

Ideally, a team of specialists should conduct this review in collaboration with education department officials before the next national assessment is conducted.

In the absence of any formal review, however, some implications are worth noting. First, data-collection designs and methodologies should be improved to address the following:
- Obtain both qualitative and quantitative data, thereby addressing the problems related to the reliability of the data. For example, the Systemic Evaluation and Whole School Evaluation data-collection exercises should be conducted on the same schools (Seekings 2002), or at least a sample of the same schools, using instruments that have been synchronised to obtain a 'richer' picture of how the education system functions. In addition, data from the different instruments applied could be triangulated to assess the reliability of the data;
- Increase the number of items assessed in order to provide detailed reports of learner achievement on different aspects of the curriculum, for example reporting by different learning outcomes;
- Include diagnostic-assessment items to identify specific learner strengths and weaknesses as well as typical errors made when responding to specific questions. This information is extremely valuable for teachers and curriculum planners;
- Analyse and report information by schools, that is, how do schools in rural areas perform compared to schools in urban areas, or identify factors that affect the performance of schools, and so on;
- Apply appropriate data-analysis techniques that account for comparing schools over time (e.g. item response theory) and for the hierarchical nature of the education system when identifying factors affecting learner achievement (e.g. hierarchical linear modelling techniques);

- Ensure that the analyses conducted take into account the systemic nature of the education system within which learners function (for example, application of the AQEE model). It is also possible to collect comprehensive data on intact education systems like a specific district or all nodal schools, and to conduct analysis to account for these sub-systems as well;
- Conduct panel studies that track specific learners at different points within the system to obtain detailed information on how learners develop as they move through the education system. For example, the performance of Grade 3 learners can be assessed again in the Grade 6 national assessment, the Grade 9 Common Tasks of Assessment and the Grade 12 matric examinations. It is even possible to track these learners after they leave school. These panel studies, however, require careful and long-term planning as well as effective implementation if information obtained is to prove relevant and valid.

Implications for teachers and schools

For national assessment studies to be effectively and efficiently applied to improve the performance of all learners, the active participation of teachers and schools is essential. In this regard, a number of interventions merit further consideration. First, teachers need relevant and timeous information from national (as well as international) assessment studies, as well as support on how to use this information to improve learning and teaching practices. Thus a critical challenge would be to introduce appropriate policies and systems to disseminate information to teachers. For example, teacher-support materials could be developed using test items administered in national assessments. This can be accomplished by, for example, appropriately increasing the number of items administered in the national assessment. A percentage of these items could then be packaged in the form of short assessment tasks for teachers to use to gauge learner strengths and weaknesses at regular intervals, for example, after the completion of a learning outcome. The support materials should also provide guidelines on the administration of the tasks, interpretation of scores, recording of learner performance as well as information on specific intervention strategies based on learner-performance scores. For this approach to work, it is critical that the support materials reduce teacher workloads substantially to encourage its effective implementation. Alternatively, relevant software should be provided that:

- Develops required assessment tasks according to teacher specifications;
- Provides detailed analysis of learner scores;
- Lists suggestions for future interventions; and
- Records and tracks learner scores for all tasks administered.

At present, a project is under way within the HSRC to develop such software for use in schools.

Second, teachers need to be assessed to obtain relevant information for use in improving teacher competencies and skills. While the sensitivities pertaining to this matter are acknowledged, it is possible to develop a system where teachers are assessed anonymously, identify their own levels of competencies, and are encouraged to take steps to address any weaknesses identified. Education departments should then provide relevant support to encourage teachers to attend targeted training courses (for example, perhaps by linking training to the teacher performance appraisals).

Third, teachers need information on what learners know and can do. The interpretations of each performance level must be linked to specific curriculum outcomes and standards. However, these standards of performance must still be developed. Thus, the DoE should engage in a consultative and empirical process to determine appropriate standards, their respective meanings and their application in practice.

Fourth, results emanating from national assessments should be widely disseminated to all schools as well as to parents and learners. In particular, the provision of appropriate reports to all schools should be standard practice, while additional details should be provided to all sampled schools.

Implications for researchers and academics

A central database comprising all national assessment studies should be developed and made available to researchers, academics, university students and the public at large for further analysis. In this context, there is an urgent need to:
- Identify a suitable organisation for managing and making relevant datasets publicly available;
- Improve current methods of data collection and storage; and
- Ensure the availability of detail documentation that explains how the data were obtained and how they should be used.

Note on appropriate terminology

The term 'systemic evaluation' does not accurately reflect the goals of national assessment studies and thus should be revised because:
- National assessment studies focus on learners within a specific grade level at a specific point in time;
- The assessment of learner performance comprises a defining factor of these studies;
- The tracking of learner achievement and identifying factors that affect learner achievement are core objectives; and
- Information can be used by policy-makers and teachers, as well as parents and learners.

Systemic evaluation studies, on the other hand, focus on the 'entire' education system, generally have regular sources of data (that is, a ten-day survey of schools), use national indicators like 'net enrolment rate', 'expenditure per pupil', and so on, and are primarily only applicable for use by policy-makers and researchers. Ironically, the *Framework for Systemic Evaluation* correctly identifies the main purpose of systemic evaluation, that is, 'to benchmark performance and track the progress made towards the achievement of the transformational goals of the education system in respect to access, redress, equity and quality' (DoE 2001: 5), but erroneously stipulates questions that address issues pertaining to national assessments. It is proposed that the term 'systemic evaluation' be changed so that the name of the surveys is reflective of the purpose of national assessments – for example, National Assessment of Learner Achievement Grade 3 (NALA–3).

Conclusion

The provision of quality education in South Africa has been the stated goal of the new government since its installation in 1994 and has been the primary focus of all education stakeholders in the country over the last decade. In this respect, learner-achievement scores have been a significant indicator. The results from the three national assessments conducted provide a gloomy picture – marked as they are by low levels of learner achievement across the learning areas assessed. Despite the large number of interventions in the last decade, there has been little improvement in achievement levels. The specific reasons for this are unclear and there is little consensus on the exact nature of the problem and the likely solution for improving levels of achievement.

In this regard, national assessments provide essential information to identify areas in need of interventions, to allocate resources where they are needed the most and to develop and monitor appropriate intervention programmes. However, the provision of relevant and timeous information to policy-makers and other education role-players, especially teachers, to effect appropriate change has been a long and slow process. In particular, there is an urgent need for information to assit with the identification of the most vulnerable schools and learners and to inform interventions to address their needs. The primary challenge remains the effective use of information in making appropriate decisions to improve learner achievement, especially learners from rural areas and poor backgrounds. While this has been recognised by government and other education stakeholders, it remains to be seen whether their collective responses can effectively rise to the challenge.

Appendix

Matrix outlining the conceptualisation of the Systemic Evaluation Project

	Context (socio-economic environment)	Input HR, other resources, policies, etc.)	Process (learning, teaching, management and governance)	Output (pass rates, behaviours)
Access Language School Information Curriculum	• Location (transport) • Reading material (home) • Language of learner • Household income • Literacy levels of parents • Distance/time to school • Affordability of school fees	• Attendance • Admission policy • Buildings (and ramps for people with disabilities) • Curriculum policy • Language policy • Early childhood development experience • Out-of-school learners • Media centres • Access to books • Prohibition of learners to enter school	• Use of material at school • Implementation of language, admission policy • Implementation of Curriculum 2005 • Transition rate	• Pass rates
Redress Rural/urban/ squatter Race Special needs Gender		• School fees • School fund • District support • School feeding scheme • Racial composition • Development of educators • Implementation of norms and standards for financing	• Use of school fund • School management and governance	• Book loan scheme • Financial support
Equity NB: equity is a function of redress therefore concerns all redress issues		• School fees • Dress code • Language policy • Admission policy	• Relief from school fees • Other/used clothes	• Analysis of performance against gender, race, urban/rural, special needs will give equity levels
Quality		• Availability of learning/teaching materials • TV/radio/computers, etc. • Support/role of district officials • Discipline at school • Functional school days	• Regular testing • Classroom management and administration • Management issues like policies, code of conduct and administration, Section 21 schools, development plans • Teaching practices • Parents' support of learners • Utilisation of learning/teaching materials • Educators practising OBE	Performance of Grade 3 on: • Literacy • Numeracy • Life skills • Listening skills
Other		• School facilities • Training of School Governing Body • Safety at schools	• Attitudes of learners towards school, educator, learning programmes	• Attitudes of staff, learners, governors • Participation of parents, school governing bodies

Source: DoE (2001: 9)

Notes

1   Generally referred to as Systemic Evaluations in South Africa.

2   Nodal schools refer to those schools prioritised as part of poverty-reduction strategies known as the Presidential Nodal Initiative.

3   Each school has been characterised into one of five categories based on their resource needs.

References

Benveniste L (2000) Student assessment as a political construction: The case of Uruguay. *Educational Analysis Policy Archives*. 8 (32). Available at <http://epaa.asu.edu/epaa/v8n32.html>.

Braun H & Kanjee A (2006) Using assessment to improve education in developing nations. In H Braun, A Kanjee, E Bettinger & M Kremer (Eds) *Improving education through assessment, innovation and evaluation*. Cambridge: American Academy of Arts and Sciences.

Chinapah V, H'ddigui M, Kanjee A, Falayojo W, Fomba C, Hamissou O, Rafalimanana A & Byamugisha A (2000) *With Africa for Africa: Towards quality education for all*. Pretoria: HSRC.

Claassen N, Makghamaths M & Diedricks G (2004) *Grade 3 learner assessment results. Report submitted to the District Development Support Program*. Pretoria: HSRC.

DoE (Department of Education) (1998) Assessment policy in the General Education and Training Band: Grades R to 9 and ABET. *Government Gazette*, 402 (19640). Pretoria: Government Printer.

DoE (2001) *Framework for systemic evaluations*. Pretoria: DoE.

DoE (2002) *Curriculum 2005 assessment guidelines for inclusion*. Pretoria: DoE.

DoE (2003) *National report on systemic evaluation: Mainstream education – Foundation Phase*. Pretoria: DoE.

DoE (2005) *The national protocol on assessment for schools in the General and Further Education and Training Band (Grades R–12)*. Pretoria: DoE.

DoE (2006) *Grade 6 National systemic evaluation report*. Pretoria: DoE.

Greaney V & Rojas C (1996) Lessons learned. In P Murphy, V Greaney, ME Lockheed & C Rojas (Eds) *National assessments: Testing the system*. EDI Learning Resources Series. Washington DC: World Bank.

JET Education Services (2005) *Follow-up study 1: Results measurement of Grades 3 and 6 learners in IEP schools*. Available at <http://iep.rti.org/documents/index.cfm?fuseaction=pubDetail&ID=47>.

JET Education Services (2006) *Teacher baseline report*. Available at <http://iep.rti.org/documents/index.cfm?fuseaction=pubDetail&ID=50>.

Kanjee A (2004) Evaluation model and trends in South African education. Presentation to the Gauteng Department of Education, Office for Standards in Education Conference, Johannesburg.

Kanjee A & Povey J (2006) Monitoring trends in education quality: Technical manual. Unpublished report. Pretoria: HSRC.

Kanjee A & Prinsloo C (2005) *Improving learning in South African schools: The Quality Learning Project summative evaluation*. Report submitted to the Joint Education Trust. Pretoria: HSRC.

Kellaghan T & Greaney V (2001) *Using assessment to improve the quality of education*. Paris: Unesco.

Linn RL (2001) Assessments and accountability (condensed version). *Practical Assessment, Research & Evaluation,* 7(11). Available at <http://PAREonline.net/getvn.asp?v=7&n=11>.

Lockheed M (1996) International context for assessments. In P Murphy, V Greaney, M Lockheed & C Rojas (Eds) *National assessments: Testing the system.* Washington DC: World Bank.

Makgamatha MM, Kanjee A & Kivilu JM (2000) Systemic wide reading assessment project. Report submitted to the Gauteng Department of Education District S1. Pretoria: HSRC.

Makgamatha MM & Masehela K (2005) Impact study of the Molteno Project programmes. Report submitted to the Molteno Project. Pretoria: HSRC.

Reddy V (2006) *Marking matric: Colloquium proceedings.* Cape Town: HSRC Press.

Schiefelbein E & Schiefelbein P (2003) From screening to improving quality: The case of Latin America. *Assessment in Education,* 10(2): 141–54.

Schollar E (2005). Final report: The evaluation of the Learning for Living project. Report submitted to the Business Trust and READ.

Seekings J (2002) *Indicators of performance in South Africa's public school system.* CSSR Working Paper No. 10.

Strauss JP & Burger MA (1999) *Monitoring Learning Achievement Project: Report of a survey.* Bloemfontein: Research Institute for Education Planning, University of the Free State.

Unesco (2000) *Assessing learning achievement. Education for all: Status and Trends 2000.* Paris: Unesco.

WCED (Western Cape Education Department) (2003a) Gaum tackles challenges of literacy and numeracy manual. Available at: <http://wced.wcape.gov.za/comms/press/2006/index_press.html>.

WCED (2003b) WCED launches literacy and numeracy manual. Available at <http://wced.wcape.gov.za/comms/press/2006/index_press.html>.

WCED (2004) WCED studies Grade 6 reading, maths skills. Available at <http://wced.wcape.gov.za/comms/press/2006/index_press.html>.

WCED (2005a) *Annual report 2004/05.* Available at <http://www.capegateway.gov.za/Text/2006/1/wced_ar_2004.05_eng.pdf>.

WCED (2005b) *Grade 8 announcement of results of provincial tests in English/Afrikaans and mathematics in 2004* (EA/2005/0001). Available at <http://curriculum.wcape.school.za/site/21/pol/view/>.

WCED (2005c) *Grade 6 Literacy and numeracy assessment tests: October and November 2005* (ER 2005/0001). Available at <http://curriculum.wcape.school.za/site/21/pol/view/>.

WCED (2005d) Service: To develop instruments to assess the language and mathematical skills of Grade 8 learners in all WCED schools and analyse and report on the results of the tests. Tender document: B/WCED 385/05.

Part IV: South Africa in Africa

South Africa in Africa: introduction

Roger Southall

In this year's concluding section dealing with South Africa's external relationships, the focus is exclusively upon aspects of the nation's role in the African continent. Alas, this may not satisfy critics who feel that we have hitherto paid insufficient attention to South Africa's position in the wider world: its engagements with multilateral institutions, the US, Europe, the Middle East, emerging powers such as India and China, and more generally, how its foreign policy is linked to the country's search for domestic wealth and security. At one level, these are fair criticisms, for as Schoeman (2006) has observed, South Africa's bid to become a developmental state is intimately entangled with its changing relationships with diverse regions, markets and momentous issues in a rapidly globalising world. Yet given the inevitable shortage of space amidst a wealth of important potential topics, we make no apology for our selection in this year's review because of its centrality to South Africa's evolving diplomacy. We maintain the tradition, through the contribution of John Daniel, Jessica Lutchman and Alex Comninos, of examining South Africa's growing economic footprint in Africa, the fourth in this series of studies which, taken together, undoubtedly represent the most comprehensive set of published analyses of their topic. Secondly, we zoom in on one aspect, which Daniel et al. have already highlighted, that is, South Africa's developing relationship with the Democratic Republic of Congo (DRC). We examine this through the eyes of Claude Kabemba, a national of the DRC, whose interests are thus personal as well as political and academic, and who concludes that, notwithstanding various dilemmas, South Africa's role in the DRC provides solid grounds for optimism. However, our third chapter – by Elinor Sisulu, Bhekinkosi Moyo and Nkosinathi Tshuma on the Zimbabwean community in South Africa – sounds a very different note, and rather gives grounds for despair, frustration and, for South Africans who look back on their own struggle for freedom from oppression, a sense of shame.

The depth of previous analysis provides Daniel et al. with a valuable opportunity for retrospect. Whereas it was shown previously that South African business had been able to take rapid advantage of South Africa's emergence from apartheid isolation to become the largest source of new foreign direct investment (FDI) in Africa, some four or five years later these selfsame corporates are facing much stiffer competition from both western powers (whose enthusiasm for African investment had declined in the 1990s) and, increasingly, new investors from Asia, notably China, but also Japan, Malaysia, South Korea, and India. The bulk of this new investment is flowing into the oil and mineral sectors, as looming global shortages and a commodities upswing foment a 'new scramble for Africa', and as

Africa itself steadily opens up to become much more friendly and welcoming territory for foreign investors.

As Daniel and Lutchman (2006) demonstrated in a previous edition of *State of the Nation*, South African corporations, both private and public, have not been backward in joining the scramble for minerals and energy, and face some considerable danger of being seriously squeezed by the wealthier and weightier players (notably the US and China). However, South African corporations have gained a substantial and significant lead in one of the most rapidly expanding markets in Africa, that of telecommunications. Daniel et al. in this volume note in particular the 'extraordinary success' enjoyed by MTN – the cellphone company – in penetrating the large yet immensely challenging (because chaotic) market in Nigeria. This has made a significant contribution to South Africa retaining its status as the leading source of FDI in Africa, something which will not surprise visitors to the continent who see the rapid invasion of shopping malls by such regular South African brand names as Checkers, Game, Makro, Truworths, Woolworths and Standard Bank, and of middle-class living rooms and hotel bars by DSTV and the English Premier League. Yet Daniel et al. point out that whilst investments in the banking, retail, hotel/leisure sectors as well as farming and food production constitute the most visible aspects of the South African presence, they account for only 13 per cent of South African investment in Africa, with the overwhelming proportion of investment continuing to be made by the seriously large players (like MTN, Transnet, Eskom, AngloGold Ashanti, Randgold Resources, Sasol and PetroSA) in telecommunications, mining and energy. However, they also sound a warning in arguing that South African penetration of the African market may be reaching its limits, with 2002 representing the high mark so far in terms of Africa's share of South Africa's global exports, while in response, Africa today provides only 4.9 per cent of South Africa's imports. By contrast, South Africa's sales to the larger Asian and European markets continue to grow, while the African market is constrained by its wretched poverty, the small consumer market, and the lack of 'trickle down' from the current boom in oil and commodity prices. South Africa's present rapid expansion of its diplomatic presence in African countries may be good for politics, they conclude, but not so good for business.

Daniel et al. note that a recent change by the Treasury, which has increased the amount that South African companies can invest in Africa without prior approval from R750 million to R2 billion, could propel a further round of South African involvement in the continent, particularly in the financial sphere. Boldly, too, they provide a set of ten predictions regarding the South African business presence in Africa over the rest of the present decade. In future years, doubtless, they will be proven to have been wrong with regard to specifics, yet the depth and longevity of their work suggests that it will come as a surprise if there is significant deviation from their major conclusion: that while the presence of South African capital in Africa will continue to grow in the years ahead, the potential of Africa as an export market for South African products has levelled out and is unlikely to grow significantly in the period ahead, and will in no way challenge the primacy of the Asian and European arenas.

Although they predict that the DRC will become increasingly central to South Africa's evolving African strategy, Daniel et al. conceivably underestimate the potential for investment growth that this vast country represents. As Kabemba indicates, the significance of the DRC for Africa's development is huge, and if its potential is to be realised, South Africa appears destined to play a large part in its unravelling story. The DRC is set at the heart of the continent, it is vast in size and population, and it possesses an embarrassing abundance of natural resources – water, hydroelectrical power, land, forests, numerous minerals, timber, rubber and more. Yet if ever there was a country which, historically, has suffered from a 'resource curse', it is the DRC, the brutality and depth of exploitation to which it was subjected historically, under Leopold and then Belgian imperialism, being rivalled by the cynical abuse of its political economy by western multinationals and US support for the brazenly rapacious Mobutu during the cold war. Worse, when the US effectively pulled the rug from under Mobutu's feet once he was no longer any use to them after the collapse of Soviet power, he was ejected by a rebel invasion backed by two of the DRC's eastern neighbours. However, this was merely a prelude to later mayhem and ultimately a devastating war in which the new government of the DRC under Joseph Kabila called upon Angola, Namibia and Zimbabwe to help him fend off yet new rebels backed by his own former allies, Uganda and Rwanda. It was from this vicious imbroglio, in which between three and four million people lost their lives (largely ignored by the international community), that South Africa was to play a major role in extricating the DRC through the Inter-Congolese Dialogue and in helping to set it on the road to stability, peace and, hopefully, democracy of a sort following elections late in 2006.

Given this desperately unhappy history, it is not surprising that Kabemba writes with considerable enthusiasm and optimism concerning South Africa's involvement in the DRC. True, he takes us through 'realistic' and 'idealistic' perspectives which, in essence, debate whether South Africa's determination to gain profitable access to Congolese wealth and resources will not outstrip the loftier motivations of the Mbeki government's foreign policy. Yet the thrust of his analysis is that while there is a potential antagonism between South Africa's evident concern to secure the DRC as a major source for energy and minerals and Mbeki's pan-African intent to help construct a democratic state which can make a major contribution to continental development, there is ultimately a complementarity between South Africa's economic and diplomatic objectives. Yes, it is important that South African corporations should be closely monitored and constrained to behave in a socially responsible manner. Equally, there is a danger that growth of the South African economic and political presence will give rise to accusations of its subjecting the DRC to a local sub-imperialism. However, perhaps it is not surprising that a

Congolese author should opt for hope rather than cynicism as the DRC moves towards what many judge to be its best chance yet for peace, progress and even a modicum of prosperity.

Unfortunately, reasons for optimism regarding Zimbabwe have long been trammelled underfoot. Few serious analysts dispute the arguments of Zimbabwean nationalists and the ruling Zimbabwe African National Union–Patriotic Front itself that the deep roots of the present political and economic crisis in that land lie in the soil of colonialism, of an underfunded political settlement in 1980, of broken promises by Britain, and of the disastrous impact of the structural adjustment programmes imposed in the 1990s. Yet equally, only the deliberately willful can today ignore how the crisis has been provoked, manipulated and deepened by a liberation movement which now every day demonstrates its contempt for democracy, economic rationality and human rights. As Sisulu, Moyo and Tshuma indicate, the Mugabe government has pursued disastrous economic policies that have propelled the country into a calamitous downturn, so that it currently exhibits the highest rate of inflation and the lowest life expectancy in the world. Throw in the persecution of the government's political opponents and of even those who dare simply to be poor, and you have a massive outflow of Zimbabwean citizens to the outside world, probably the bulk of them coming to South Africa.

Just as Mark Anthony declared with crocodile tears that Brutus was an honourable man, so today the South African government declares that there is no crisis in Zimbabwe. It is here that what Sisulu et al. have to say intersects with a major theme of this volume – the dysfunctionality of the South African state. The sheer number of Zimbabweans who have migrated or fled to South Africa tells its own tale. The Central Bank of Zimbabwe admitted that some 1.2 million Zimbabweans had left for South Africa as early as 1990, well before the present crisis got going. It is scarcely surprising, then, that informal estimates suggest that there are between two and three million Zimbabweans in South Africa at the present time. Many of these are skilled and educated, their departure further hastening Zimbabwe's economic implosion. Yet can they find suitable work in South Africa? Sisulu et al. indicate conclusively that probably the majority of them cannot.

There is clearly a major contradiction here in South African government policy. On the one hand, Deputy President Phumzile Mlambo-Ngcuka, who is heading the Accelerated and Shared Growth Initiative of South Africa, regularly deplores South Africa's growth prospects as being hampered by a lack of skills. On the other, we have the willful refusal of the South African government to utilise the skills of so many Zimbabwean professionals – thousands of teachers, nurses, doctors, dentists, pharmacists, journalists and engineers. Why? Because the majority of them are deemed to be 'economic migrants' who are in South Africa illegally and thus need to be deported, whilst those who file applications for political asylum are turned down on the grounds that there is no political crisis in Zimbabwe. The reason is that to acknowledge that there is a political crisis would force the ANC to confront a fellow liberation movement with abusing human rights, and the government to admit that its policy of 'quiet diplomacy' has proved to be a dismal failure. Not surprisingly, the Zimbabwean community – although tragically divided, fearful and subject to considerable xenophobia – is organising itself into self-help groups such as Concerned Zimbabweans Abroad and the Zimbabwe Exiles' Forum. Not surprisingly, too, they are receiving solidarity and assistance from those who extended their help to the victims of apartheid: churches, trade unions, progressive lawyers, and human rights associations.

As this introduction was being written (June 2006), former Zimbabwean MP Roy Bennett – previously jailed by the Zimbabwean government and now dubiously accused of involvement in a plot to overthrow the government – was appealing against Home Affairs declining his application for political asylum. Statistics provided by Sisulu et al. suggest that his appeal will be rejected: only 86 out of 8 000 applications by Zimbabweans for political asylum have been granted, and the South African government may fear that Bennett's high profile status means that to concede his case would open up the floodgates. Thus Foreign Minister Nkosazana Dlamini-Zuma, in answering to the matter in Parliament, said it is up to Zimbabweans to sort out their own problems by themselves (*The Star* 30.05.06), defiantly ignoring the evidence that when the opposition seeks to oppose in Zimbabwe, as with the ANC in South Africa under apartheid, they are beaten up, tortured, persistently harassed, some murdered and many of them forced to flee the country.

It is not surprising that, with the ANC government so blatantly ignoring the lessons of its own history, the daughter-in-law of ANC hero Walter Sisulu should join her colleagues in concluding their chapter on a strong note of advocacy: for South Africa to recognise its responsibilities to Zimbabwean exiles under international law and to take a more forceful stand against the government of Robert Mugabe.

References

Daniel J & Lutchman J (2006) South Africa in Africa: Scrambling for energy. In S Buhlungu et al. (Eds) *State of the Nation: South Africa 2005–06*. Cape Town: HSRC Press.

Schoeman M (2006) Review of S Buhlungu et al. (Eds) State of the Nation: South Africa 2005–06. *Politikon* (forthcoming).

20 South Africa in Africa: trends and forecasts in a changing African political economy

John Daniel, Jessica Lutchman and Alex Comninos

Tell Shoprite they must come here.
(Tanzanian district official to South African High Commissioner,
interview 26.03.06)

We want to expand to projects throughout Africa, as this is in South
Africa's best interest. If other African countries are doing well they have
more resources with which to purchase South African goods and
services…not only is a stable continent beneficial for South Africa but
the IDC earns financial and developmental returns on its investments.
(Abel Malinga, head of mining and beneficiation strategic business
unit, Industrial Development Corporation quoted in *Business Day*
14.02.06)

This is the fourth *State of the Nation* chapter focused on the broad theme of South
Africa's post-apartheid economic involvement in Africa. The first, in 2003, surveyed the emergence of a post-apartheid phenomenon – South African businesses
operating in all parts of the continent. It detailed the growing significance of the
African market to the local economy and identified the dominant trends in South
Africa's interaction with this 'new' world. The second and third chapters were
narrower in scope, examining the South African–Nigerian business nexus in 2004,
while in 2005 we looked at the growing centrality of Africa's mineral and other
resources as a means to alleviating South Africa's emerging energy deficit. In this
chapter, we return to the 2003 format. Looking at the continental marketplace as a
whole, we discuss the trends – established and new – and offer some predictions as
to how South Africa's economic engagement with Africa will unfold through the
rest of this decade.

Reviewing the African political economy today, one is struck by certain important
differences, as well as some depressing continuities, from that of the late 1990s. In
our 2003 chapter, we commented that in the context of a process of post-cold war
western divestment from Africa, South African corporates seemed often to be the
'only show in town' and that by the late 1990s South Africa had become the single

largest source of new foreign direct investment (FDI) in Africa overall. Much in the FDI arena has changed in the last five years.

In 2006, in what is a more investor-friendly environment, new and would-be investors are to be found in all corners of the continent, including some of its least appealing spots like Equatorial Guinea, the Sudan, Zimbabwe, and Cote D'Ivoire. For example, despite the latter two's collapsing-state status of recent years, their lucrative diamond (in the case of Cote D'Ivoire), gold and platinum resources have attracted the interest of foreign mining groups while Zimbabwe's so-called 'look-east' policy has resulted in the Chinese developing a foothold in that economy. In short, in this latest post-colonial 'scramble' for Africa's resources, the field has become more crowded and more competitive. South African corporates can no longer expect to have everything their own way, as Vodacom and South African Airways discovered recently in Nigeria and Tanzania respectively.

In the African FDI arena, there have been two developments of significance in the course of this decade. One is that some former colonial powers (the United Kingdom in particular) and the United States have 'rediscovered' their appetite for doing business in Africa and reversed their retreat of the 1990s. In the case of the United States, this has involved considerable activity along Africa's oil-rich west African coast and the restoration of full economic ties with Libya. The second has been the emergence of a number of new largely Asian investors. The Chinese are the most prominent but increasingly active too has been Indian capital, along with the Japanese, Malaysians, and South Koreans. Joining them has been Brazil which is emerging as a significant player in former Lusophone Africa, Angola in particular.

The upward escalation in FDI flows into Africa is illustrated by the 50 per cent increase in the value of new external investment (including that into South Africa) from $18.7 billion in 2004 to $28–30 billion in 2005.[1] The bulk of that new money has been concentrated in the oil and minerals sector (copper, platinum, gold, zinc and silver, all the prices of which – bar gold – have surged to record highs in the last year), attracted, according to Mills, by 'a cyclical commodity upswing driven especially by Chinese demands' (2006: 4). Other factors, such as the desire of the United States to reduce its dependence on Middle-Eastern oil sources, have played a role too.

What this new investment activity has contributed to is a continental growth rate which now exceeds the world average. The modest and sluggish rates of the late 1990s have given way to a 5.1 per cent increase in Africa's real gross domestic product in both 2004 and 2005, exceeding the world average of 3.3 per cent by nearly 2 per cent. The Organisation for Economic Co-operation and Delevopment has predicted a growth rate of 5.8 per cent in 2006, driven primarily by Africa's oil producers where growth is likely to be in the region of 6.9 per cent (*Business Day* 19.05.06). Concurrent with this growth has been an improvement in Africa's external debt situation brought on by windfall oil profits, rising commodity prices and a more lenient attitude to both aid and debt relief by the G-8 and rich nations in general.

The African economic environment today is, therefore, somewhat different from that of the turn of this century. It is both more user-friendly and more efficient. The new investors have brought with them the sophisticated and tougher management methods of neo-liberalism and have bulldozed aside the slow, cumbersome and excessively bureaucratic ways of the first post-independence era. It is here, according to Neuma Grobbelaar, that South African corporates have contributed significantly. She argues that:

> South African investment is clearly leading the growth of the private sector in Africa, by increasing revenue generation for governments; improving economic growth and exports; transferring technology; ensuring the re-industrialisation of some economies through the acquisition and revitalisation of moribund state-owned enterprises; formalising the market, thereby ensuring greater price stability…and improved consumer choice; creating employment; transferring business skills; introducing good corporate practice; and boosting investment confidence from other foreign investors. (Grobbelaar 2006: 9–10)

Concurrent with these promising economic developments, there have been some positive political moves. Effectively the military has been driven from the political arena while the unrolling of the African Peer Review Mechanism has boosted accountability provisions. These developments should not be exaggerated, however, and should be balanced against the fact that decades of authoritarian rule persist in Angola, Egypt, Libya, Morocco, Swaziland, Gabon and Zimbabwe, to name a few, while the democratic advances of the 1990s in places like Uganda and Namibia appear to be on the retreat. Likewise, in the economic sphere corruption remains endemic to Africa, numerous economies remain as mono-culturally dependent on the export of single commodities as they were at the dawn of independence and hence are still vulnerable to the inevitable downturn in commodity prices while a few others, notably Malawi, remain essentially donor-driven. Then, finally, we should not forget the failed or collapsing states of Somalia and Zimbabwe.

The African market as an investment destination

Despite the emergence (and re-emergence) in recent times of other investors, in 2005 South Africa remained the largest single source of new FDI on the continent. It also continued its upward curve in terms of the value of new FDI, as Figure 20.1 illustrates.

The point needs to be made here, however, that the value of South African FDI reflected in Figure 20.1 includes those by some corporates which arguably are no longer South African companies. Major groups like Anglo American, Dimension Data and SABMiller have moved offshore in recent years and now have their primary listings in London. However, even if the value of their African investments is

Figure 20.1 *South African investments in the rest of Africa, 1997–2004*

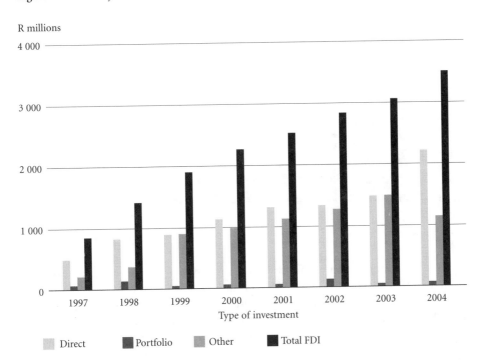

Source: Statistics derived from the *Quarterly Reports* of the South African Reserve Bank, 1997–2004.
Available at <http://www.reservebank.co.za/>

stripped out, South Africa remains Africa's largest supplier of new FDI (see Figure 20.2), followed by the United Kingdom and the United States. Australian and Canadian involvement in Africa is almost exclusively in mining and involves multinational giants like the Australian-based BHP Billiton. Given its long involvement in Africa, France's position may seem low but it reflects the fact that French business limits itself almost exclusively to France's former colonial possessions and the fact that the economy of the one-time 'jewel in their crown', Cote D'Ivoire, has self-destructed in the last decade.

Consultants Business Map have rated China ninth in their top ten investors in Africa. This is certainly an under-reflection of the extent of China's involvement on the continent. According to Reg Rumney, Business Map's chart reflects 'announced investments' and often times, he argues, China does not go public with many of its ventures, especially those in countries with poor human rights records – for example, Sudan (interview, February 2006).

Figures 20.3 and 20.4 show that by country Mozambique leads the way as South African capital's most favoured investment destination, followed by the Democratic Republic of Congo (DRC), Nigeria and Namibia. Since 1994, Mozambique has attracted 34 per cent of all South African FDI into Africa. This

Figure 20.2 *Selected investing countries in Africa, 1994–2004*

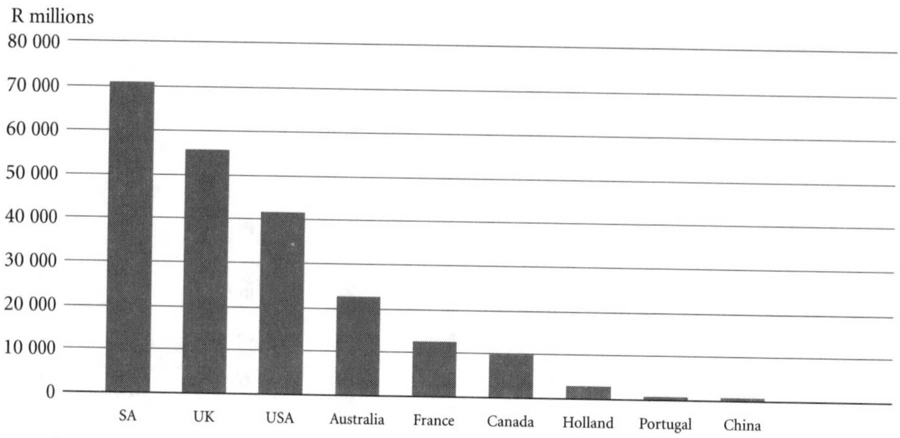

R millions

Source: Rumney 2006

level of investment in an economy which 10–15 years ago was a 'basket case' has been driven by two factors. First, Mozambique has been the site of two huge industrial projects in which South African investors have been prominent. One has been the Mozal aluminium smelter project in which the IDC has 24 per cent equity while the other involved Sasol in the construction of an 865 kilometre pipeline from onshore natural gas fields in central Mozambique to Secunda in Mpumalanga.

The second factor is that alongside these two giant schemes it is estimated that about 300 South African companies have opened up in the country. These are located in every sector of the economy and employ at least 50 000 Mozambicans. This involvement in its eastern neighbour's economy has contributed to Mozambique's transformation from its classification as Africa's poorest performing economy by the UN's Human Development Report in 1991 to growth rates in recent years in the region of 8 per cent.

The DRC's second place needs to be qualified. As noted above, Business Map's investment tables are based on 'announced intentions' and not on monies actually spent. South African capital's largest investment in the DRC will be in the Grand Inga hydroelectric-power project but it is a long-term scheme, the realisation of which will take another 10–15 years. If one strips Inga out, then the DRC slips behind Nigeria into third spot and equal with Namibia.

Given its image as a site of economic chaos and corruption, the level of South African involvement in Nigeria may surprise some. The key has been cellular network operator MTN's extraordinary success in that market and its demonstration that business can be done and money made in Nigeria. In its wake, a host of South African companies have set up shop in Nigeria, selling commodities and providing

Figure 20.3 *South African investment in Africa by country*

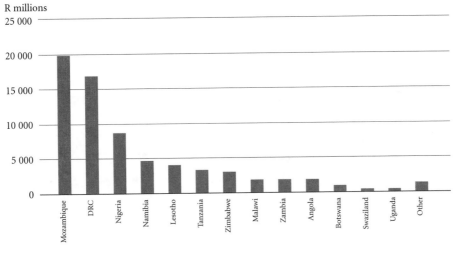

Source: Rumney (2006)

Figure 20.4 *South African foreign direct investment by country (without the Grand Inga)*

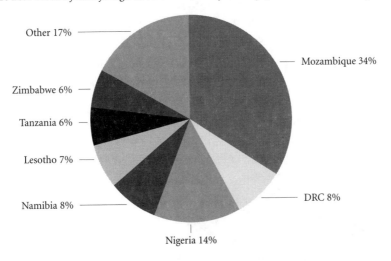

Source: Rumney (2006)

services to Africa's largest consumer market and one which was starved of quality products for years. South African investors have developed waterfront-type shopping malls in which groups like Game, Shoprite, Pep Stores, Truworths and Woolworths, Exclusive Books and Nu Metro cinemas have located. Leisure groups like Protea Hotels have taken over and refurbished run-down hotel establishments and built new ones.

Figure 20.5 *Sectoral breakdown of South African foreign direct investment in Africa*

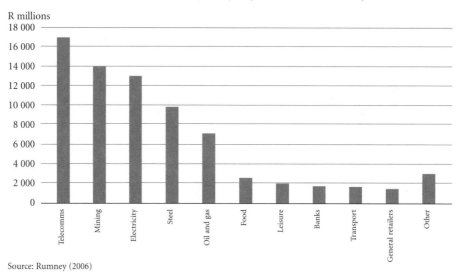

Source: Rumney (2006)

As Figures 20.5 and 20.6 show, telecommunications is the sector that has attracted the largest chunk of South African FDI into Africa, followed by mining, electricity, steel and other matters, and oil and gas. The remaining 13 per cent covers the banking, retail, hotel/leisure sectors as well as farming and food producers. Thus, while Checkers, Game and Makro, Protea Hotels, Debonairs, Nandos and Steers, Truworths and Woolworths, Standard Bank/Stanbic and Multichoice appear in ever greater numbers across the African economic landscape, the value of their investments is modest in comparison to the really big players – MTN, Vodacom, Transnet, Eskom, AngloGold Ashanti, Randgold Resources, Sasol and PetroSA.

Figure 20.6 *Sectoral view of South African foreign direct investment into Africa*

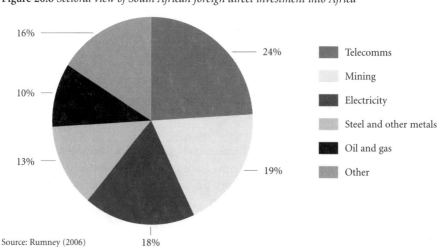

Source: Rumney (2006)

Two factors suggest that the telecommunications sector will for the foreseeable future remain South Africa's priority investment area. One is the massive growth in mobile telephony worldwide and the other is the comparative lack of penetration of the African market. By far the majority of African consumers do not have a cellphone and they want one and some African markets are potentially huge. The DRC is a case in point where Vodacom has signed only about 2 per cent of consumers. For Vodacom, peace and stability in the future will be lucrative.

The economic salience of the African market

Exports

In our 2003 chapter for *State of the Nation*, we commented upon the rapid growth post-1990 of an African export market for South African capital, noting how in a decade (1991–2001) Africa's share of South Africa's export market had grown from 4 to 12 per cent. At the time we predicted that it would continue to grow, a view seemingly borne out by the 2002 figure of 16.7 per cent. It was also in that year that Africa overtook the Americas to become South Africa's third largest export region. What we did not anticipate, however, was that 2002 might turn out to be this decade's high-water mark in terms of Africa's share of South Africa's global trade.

Whether that will be the case or not time will tell, but it is significant. As Table 20.1 indicates, in 2002 – and for the three consecutive years since – Africa's share of South Africa's global exports has either fallen or only risen slightly and not sufficiently to match the peak 2002 figure. This is not to suggest that the rand value of South Africa's exports into Africa has not risen. It has but only by a modest R7.1 billion over the period 2003–05. By contrast, the larger Asian and European markets rose by R21 billion and just under R25 billion respectively. What this suggests is that after an initial decade of growth for South African capital, the African export market might have peaked and is unlikely to grow even in the context of the

Table 20.1 *Rand value of South African exports by region and percentage change, 2002–05*

Region	Exports (R millions)				% change 2002–03	% change 2003–04	% change 2004–05	% of global exports 2002	% of global exports 2004	% of global exports 2005
	2002	2003	2004	2005						
Africa	44 580	39 000	39 037	46 135	−13	0	18	16.7	15.0	15.5
Americas	42 936	34 161	36 571	38 345	−20	7	4	16.1	14.1	12.9
Asia	67 412	65 176	73 200	86 403	−3	12	18	25.3	28.2	29.0
Europe	105 699	92 019	102 969	116 895	−13	12	13	39.7	39.7	39.3
Pacific	5 767	6 331	7 921	9 878	10	25	24	2.2	3.1	3.3
Total	266 394	236 687	259 698	297 656	−11	9.5	14	100.0	100.0	100.0

Source: Derived from the Department of Trade and Industry's economic database and the South African Revenue Services' preliminary trade statistics

increased African economic growth rate noted earlier. What this is indicative of is the level of poverty in Africa, the small size of its consumer market, and the lack of 'trickle down' from the commodities' boom.

A second conclusion is that for the foreseeable future the Asian and European markets will remain South Africa's most important in trade terms (in fact, the gap between Africa and the other two regions is widening) and this calls into question the wisdom of the Departments of Foreign Affairs and Trade and Industry's current priority of opening missions and trade offices in Africa. It may make for good politics but may also not be the best deployment of resources in business terms.

Imports

In regard to South Africa's imports, we noted last year the modest increase in imports from Africa, the surge in imports from Asia and the fact that between them Asian and European imports made up 80 per cent of South Africa's total imports. The picture for 2005 is little different in that imports from Africa rose by only 0.6 per cent, Asian import volumes continued to mount reaching 40 per cent of the total while by combination the European and Asian totals continued to be in the region of 80 per cent.

Table 20.2 *Rand value of South African imports by region and percentage change, 2003–05*

Region	Imports (R millions)			% change 2003–04	% change 2004–05	% of global imports 2004	% of global imports 2005
	2003	2004	2005				
Africa	8 217	13 000	17 250	58	33	4.3	4.9
Americas	36 436	40 158	43 670	10	9	13.1	12.6
Asia	89 131	114 806	139 308	29	21	37.6	40.0
Europe	116 597	129 398	139 564	11	8	42.4	40.1
Pacific	6 765	8 118	8 346	20	3	2.7	2.4
Total	257 146	305 480	348 138	18	13	100.0	100.0

Source: Derived from the DTI's economic database and SARS' preliminary trade statistics

Trade balances

In terms of trade balances, the downward curve in South Africa's positive balance with Africa (from 5:1 in 2001 to 3:1 in 2004) persisted in 2005 with the ratio falling to 2.67:1. Again, as in recent years, the narrowing gap was the product of Africa sourcing more oil and natural gas from African supplies. In 2005, fuels made up 42.4 per cent of all imports from Africa.[2]

Table 20.3 reflects the volumes of total trade (imports and exports combined) between South Africa and its African trade partners outside of the Southern African Customs Union (SACU). It reveals that this country's top ten African trade partners remain the same ten countries they have been over the past half decade, although there have been some shifts up and down in their 'league places', so to speak (but not in the past two years in the case of the top seven). What is extraordinary about this table is the continuing resilience of South African–Zimbabwean trade relations and the fact that in rand value terms the volumes of both imports and exports are rising. With the completion in 2003 of the first two phases of the Mozal smelter scheme, as well as the gas pipeline from Mozambique to Secunda, Mozambique has dropped two places to fourth. However, we expect trade volumes to increase again in the immediate period ahead, a point we return to later in the chapter. It is also worth highlighting the continuing miniscule levels of imports from seven of these top ten counties; in fact, in one or two cases import volumes have actually declined in the last two years or, in the case of Mozambique, for the last three years.

The one country in the top ten which has seen a sharp increase in its exports to South Africa is Angola, rising from R28 million in 2002 to R1.7 billion in 2004 and R1.9 billion in 2005. As in the case of Nigeria, almost all of this is accounted for by oil imports. Exports to Angola over the same period held steady in the region of R3.3 to R3.5 billion.

Table 20.3 *South Africa's top ten African trading partners*

Country	Exports (Rbillion) 2005	Imports 2005	Total trade 2005	Position 2005	2004	2003	2002
Zimbabwe	7.49	3.13	10.62	1	1	1	1
Nigeria	3.39	4.16	7.56	2	2	3	3
Zambia	5.44	1.30	6.75	3	3	4	4
Mozambique	6.40	0.20	6.60	4	4	2	2
Angola	3.54	1.89	5.43	5	5	5	5
Kenya	2.98	0.20	3.18	6	6	6	8
Tanzania	2.76	0.25	3.01	7	7	9	9
Mauritius	2.19	0.17	2.36	8	9	7	7
Malawi	1.64	0.46	2.09	9	8	8	6
DRC	1.81	0.26	1.83	10	10	10	10

Source: Derived from the DTI's economic database and SARS' preliminary trade statistics

Trends and prospects in South African–African trade relations

We have noted, by way of summary, that South African FDI into Africa is rising steadily, that export volumes are sluggish while import volumes are increasing – fuelled mainly by fuels. So what can we say of the period ahead? In looking ahead, we have factored into the equation the likely impact on South African FDI in Africa of the liberalisation of the Treasury's exchange control regulations.

In the 2005 Budget, the Treasury lifted the maximum amount that companies could invest in Africa without prior approval from R750 million to R2 billion. In the 2006 Budget, the equity threshold for South African companies and parastatals investing on the continent was lowered from a majority interest (50 per cent plus one share) to 25 per cent. The liberalisation has been welcomed by corporates with expansionary interests. Commenting on this, Loyiso Jiya, Ernst & Young's corporate finance partner, noted that the 'regulations have placed a major constraint on any designs that domestic companies have had regarding foreign direct investment capacity' and that 'the relaxation…will make a big difference to local companies that have wanted to invest in Africa' (*Business Day* 29.03.06).

With regard to the rest of the decade, we offer the following predictions:
- The lucrative African private telecommunications sector will continue to open up and expand, remaining thereby the most active site of new South African FDI. Within it, the two main South African players – MTN and Vodacom – will remain deeply involved but MTN will outperform its rival and develop into a formidable multinational operator. It will soon overtake Egypt's Orascom as Africa's biggest player.
- South Africa's mining sector will continue to expand into the African market, a process in which a number of so-called 'junior' mining companies will be active alongside the established majors.
- The South African energy sector (oil, gas and electricity) will intensify its 'scramble' to acquire African oil, gas and hydro/water resources as a core strategy to overcome South Africa's developing energy deficit. We predict, however, that South Africa's desire to acquire a greater share of Africa's oil resources will not easily be realised.
- The above notwithstanding, we predict that Sasol – with its technological edge in turning coal and gas into liquid fuels – will be the next South African company to develop into a global player and that its current 'love–hate' relationship with the South African government will persist so that the possibility of it moving offshore and delisting from the JSE cannot be discounted.
- Despite the DRC's current status as South Africa's tenth largest trade partner in Africa, we predict that the country will continue to be a site of considerable South African political/diplomatic and military activity. More than the DRC's minerals potential, this continuing high level of activity will be driven by the long-term importance of the Grand Inga hydroelectrical-power project.
- Zimbabwe will remain as South Africa's most important African trade partner, but under current conditions there will be little or no new South African FDI in that country. Indeed, if the Mugabe government carries through with its black economic empowerment legislation directed at the mining sector, there is a prospect of a shutdown or divestment of South African mining operations in that country.

- We anticipate growing levels of South African economic involvement in the Nigerian, Tanzanian, Zambian and Mozambican economies. In regard to the latter, we expect Mozambique to move up the trade-partner league table with the possible expansion of the Mozal aluminium smelter project and the development of Mozambique's offshore natural gas fields.
- In contrast to Mozambique, we anticipate that South African capital will continue to encounter difficulties in its attempts to obtain a foothold in the potentially lucrative Angolan economy. Cultural and linguistic factors, the bitter legacy of apartheid South Africa's involvement with Unita and the crippling 20-year-long civil war and the corruption of Angola's ruling class will continue to work against South African interests and to the advantage of outsiders like China, Brazil and India.
- Shoprite Checkers and Massmart will continue their steady expansion into Africa, consolidating their domination of the continent's retail sector and their position as the two largest distributors of consumer goods.
- We anticipate an increased role and presence in the African market of South Africa's state-backed financial institutions (the Development Bank of Southern Africa [DBSA] and the IDC) and its private banking sector. The current modest South African banking footprint in Africa will grow into a considerable network with Stanbic, First Rand and Barclays/Absa populating the Anglophone African landscape in ever increasing numbers.

We expand on these predictions below.

Telecommunications

If there were an award for the best performing post-apartheid South African corporate in Africa, it would likely be won by MTN. Given its second ranking to Vodacom in the domestic market where it has only a 35 per cent share, what MTN has achieved in Africa and beyond is remarkable.

Given the appalling state by the late 1990s of Africa's fixed-line and telecommunications' networks, the sector was ripe for privatisation and MTN was the first South African operator to take advantage of the market opportunities then opening up in Africa. In 1998, it launched commercial operations in Uganda, Rwanda and Swaziland and within three years had signed up one million customers. Its real African breakthrough, however, came in Nigeria when in 2001 it was awarded one of Nigeria's Global Systems Mobile licences for a fee of US$285 million. At the time this was MTN's biggest investment outside South Africa and was a move regarded in local corporate circles as a huge gamble given the perception that Nigeria was not a place where outsiders could do business profitably.

MTN entered Nigeria projecting that it would take five years before it received any return on its investment, which by the end of 2003 had topped US$1 billion in infrastructural and other start-up costs. By then, however, its customer base had topped one million and in 2004 – two years ahead of schedule – it recorded an after-tax surplus of R2.4 billion, exceeding by R0.2 billion the profit it made in South Africa in that year. Since then the Nigerian operation has gone from strength to strength and as of early 2006 had some 7.6 million Nigerian subscribers. MTN's success in Nigeria jolted other South African companies into an awareness of the opportunities afforded by Africa's largest consumer market and by 2004 there were over 60 South African firms doing business in Nigeria. One which tried but failed, however, was its rival Vodacom which, through a series of mishaps – including a corruption and bribery scandal – has failed to gain a toehold in Nigeria.

In the same year that it launched operations in Nigeria, MTN purchased a majority share in Cameroon's national phone operator and by the end of 2005 had over one million subscribers and a 54 per cent market share.

2005 and early 2006 have been hyperactive periods for MTN. Through a new round of mergers and acquisitions, it acquired a 51 per cent majority share in Telecel Zambia and Telecel Cote D'Ivoire, a 44 per cent share in Mascom Wireless in Botswana and 100 per cent control of the national operator – Libertis Telekom – in the Republic of Congo (Brazzaville). In November 2005, MTN was shortlisted along with a Portuguese operator for a 34 per cent stake in Namibia's mobile operator but this was 'the one that got away' as the tender was awarded to Portugal Telecom.

In a further internationalisation of its operations, MTN made its first move into the extra-African market, acquiring in November 2005 a 49 per cent interest in Irancell for which it paid an upfront licence fee of EUR3 000 million. In investment terms, many regard Iran as politically risky but this has not daunted the company in the past and its other risky investment domain, Nigeria, has turned into a 'cash cow' (*Sunday Times* 07.05.06).

The boldness of its Iranian venture was matched in May 2006 when MTN purchased the Lebanon-based Investkom group for R33 billion, giving it thereby a presence in 11 further African and Middle-Eastern countries. With the finalisation of this deal, MTN will be operative in 21 countries, 15 of them African, and will have a customer base of over 28 million subscribers. With such growth, perhaps the real risk the company now faces is the possibility of a takeover bid by one of the global players like China Telekom (*Mail & Guardian* 02–08.06.06).

By contrast, Vodacom's efforts in Africa have been modest. To be fair, its comparative lack of success has not all been due to managerial failings or timidity. Unlike MTN, which is a wholly owned South African company, Vodacom is a subsidiary of Britain's financially-troubled Vodaphone group and it has at times acted as a brake on its South African partner. It was not until 2002 that Vodacom was able to move into the African market – acquiring rights in Tanzania, Mozambique, Lesotho, Zambia and the DRC. Contract issues plagued the Zambian operation and the deal collapsed. Start-up problems also delayed its Lesotho venture for two years.

Vodacom's stuttering efforts beyond the Limpopo are reflected in its customer numbers, which at the end of 2005 stood at only 3.89 million in the above four markets. The contrast with the company's successes in South Africa is stark. It now has 17.6 million customers in South Africa, considerably more than MTN. However, beyond South Africa Vodacom is a small player.

Mining

Africa's minerals and energy commodities boom has seen mining groups, big and small, from all parts of the world converge on the continent. This has included the South African mining giant AngloGold Ashanti – one of the world's two largest gold producers – and the medium-sized Randgold and Exploration. Both are involved in mining gold in Mali, Ghana and Tanzania while AngloGold has interests in Namibia and Randgold in Senegal and Burkina Faso. At the same time as it is investing heavily in its two Malian mines, Randgold is engaged in an aggressive exploration drive elsewhere in Mali and Senegal where it is evaluating 31 sites, as well as in Burkina Faso, Ghana and Tanzania. The options it holds in Cote D'Ivoire are currently on hold pending the restoration of stability. The caveat needs to be noted here that Randgold is a part of the 'empire' of companies run by the recently slain Brett Kebble, and which are currently under investigation for wholesale fraud and corruption. The future of this group of companies could be said to be uncertain.

AngloGold, by contrast, is investing heavily in upgrading its Ghanaian mines acquired through the merger with Ashanti Gold. The other major South African gold mining group, Gold Fields, has also entered into the Malian mining sector by funding the exploration ventures of an Irish group, Glencar Mining, which has three options in Mali. Should any of these prove to be viable, Gold Fields reserves the right to acquire participation rights in the venture. Current indications are that at least one of these mines will come on stream (*Business Day* 25.04.06).

While South Africa's major miners are focused on west Africa, smaller or so-called 'junior' South African mining groups are concentrating their efforts in central southern Africa and east Africa. By and large the juniors have moved to take up options in some of Africa's high-risk trouble spots, like Zimbabwe and the eastern DRC, where it seems the majors fear they have too much to lose while the juniors are prepared to run the risk. Foremost amongst these juniors is Metorex, which has specialised in buying 'hot spot' options from companies immobilised by or looking for an exit option due to security concerns. Its biggest involvement is in the Ruashi Etoile copper and cobalt venture in Katanga province in the southern DRC where it is a majority partner (67%) with the DRC state mining group, Gecamines. Linked to this venture, Metorex has acquired a copper and cobalt processing facility in Zambia where it will refine the ore extracted in the DRC. This was due to come on stream in late-2006. It also has copper interests in Zambia.

Metorex purchased the Ruashi concession from another of the South African juniors, Mvelaphanda Holdings. This latter group owns shares in the diamond group

Trans Hex, which is active in Angola, and in an oil and gas exploration company, Ophir, which has drilling rights in both west and east Africa. In the case of the latter, these are off the coasts of Tanzania and the internationally unrecognised Republic of Somaliland.

Other South African juniors involved in African mining are the Metallon group of Mzi Khumalo with its five gold mines in Zimbabwe and Patrice Motsepe's African Rainbow Minerals (ARM) operating in conjunction with its Toronto-listed partner, TEAL Exploration and Mining. TEAL (in which ARM has a 65 per cent share) functions as a vehicle to house ARM's offshore assets including a copper mine in Zambia, copper and cobalt mines in Zambia and the DRC, and a gold mine in Namibia. TEAL also has a secondary listing on the JSE. A third junior is the TanzaniteOne Group, which operates the world's only tanzanite mine in a remote area near Arusha in Tanzania. Though Bermuda listed, the company is actually a reincarnation of the South African group African Gem Resources that was listed on the JSE. TanzaniteOne has several South Africans on its board, its mine management team is largely South African and a South African security group protects it.

Impressive though this may all seem, the tough pre-2006 foreign exchange regulations pertaining to FDI in Africa have hurt the South African mining sector in particular. One commentator noted (ironically on the day when the Minister of Finance announced the relaxations) that South Africa 'is losing in the scramble for Africa' due to 'the lack of capital...available to local companies to explore and establish operations' (*Mining Weekly* 20.01.06). He went on to note that Canadian and Australian companies now dominated the majority of mining operations in Africa because the cost of capital in those two countries is much lower than in South Africa. Some commentators regarded the government's liberalisation of foreign exchange regulations pertaining to FDI in Africa as a case of closing the gate after the horse has bolted. There was, however, a positive reaction from some junior miners. Neil Gardyne, executive director of the New Africa Mining Fund (NAMF) (which funds junior mining projects), commented that NAMF had lost 'out on many opportunities as a result of the regulations' and that there were 'a couple of deals we [NAMF] can now resuscitate'.[3]

Oil and energy

In our 2005 chapter, we reported on how South Africa was resorting increasingly to Africa's oil, gas and hydropower resources as a means of meeting its growing energy demands. We noted also how in regard to oil, South Africa was focusing on both the upstream (exploration and production) and downstream functions (refining and retailing). In regard to this latter, we commented on the establishment of the Cape Oil and Gas Supply Initiative as an initiative to acquire a larger share of the supply-side of the oil industry (rigs, equipment, clothing, food and so on). Now subsumed into the South African Oil and Gas Alliance, the initiative has scored some successes in the downstream market. These include an investment by Germany's MAN Ferrostaal to create an offshore oil and gas fabrication yard at Saldhana Bay which will employ up to 14 000 workers (*Africa Investor* April 2006: 21). Other service and supply contracts to the west African oil industry have been secured but this area is becoming increasingly contested as more west African oil-producing states impose heavy local content requirements on those bidding for tenders.

Besides PetroSA's acquisition in April 2006 of a 10 per cent stake in an oil exploration block off the coast of Namibia, we are aware of only one explorative concession being acquired on the continent by a South African concern in the last year. Again this was PetroSA which acquired 100 per cent of the rights to an oil block in Egypt's Gulf of Suez (*Business Report* 05.05.06).The Namibian project by contrast is not South African-led; here PetroSA is in partnership with Russian (70%) and Canadian companies (10%).

We do not expect South Africa to have much future success in the arena of concessions, unless perhaps as a junior partner with multinationals. This is because the scramble for Africa's oil concessions has become ever more competitive and is attracting the attention of global players whose resources South African groups cannot match. Furthermore, an increasing proportion of the bids on offer are for deep-level offshore fields and South African bidders cannot match the technological resources available to the oil multinationals in this niche area. A further complication is that as oil prices soar, African governments are becoming more aware of their strengthened bargaining position. Thus, not only are they demanding ever higher prices (which only the giants like Chevron and ExxonMobil and the state-owned oil companies of the west and their Chinese and Indian counterparts can afford), but they are also demanding larger offset deals. Thus, for example, the Angolan government has made it clear that it will look most favourably at those bidders for sites in seven offshore blocks who are also willing to invest in its new refinery in Lobito, a project seen by many in the oil trade as economically unviable. In March 2006, the Chinese energy company, Sinopec, agreed to invest $3 billion in the refinery as well as pay $2.4 billion for oil concessions in two blocks off the Angolan coast while ExxonMobil announced it would spend $2 billion annually in the exploration, development and production of oil and gas reserves in Nigeria. These are amounts no South African company can match.

Sasol

If the above is correct, then Sasol, which already plays a central role in South Africa's energy sector, will become even more important. Established as a state-subsidised entity to develop oil from coal, Sasol has in the last decade become a world leader in the production of synthetic liquid fuel from both coal and natural gas. Liquid fuels from gas are cheaper and cleaner and will be used increasingly in the years ahead to power the electric power plants South Africa is going to need. Consequently, Sasol's expertise is in increased demand worldwide and the company has become involved in mega gas-to-liquid schemes in Qatar, China, the United States and Nigeria. The first of these in Qatar came on stream in June 2006.

Once an apartheid-cosseted corporation and the beneficiary of all sorts of subsidies and tax breaks, the now-privatised Sasol is developing into a global giant earning profits on such a scale that government is contemplating imposing a 'windfall' tax regime on the company. This suggestion has been met with hostility from Sasol and a thinly disguised threat to move offshore. We predict that Sasol's relationship with government will continue to be volatile. We predict, too, that while Sasol's role and importance in the local economy will grow, it will find increasingly that the international market offers it far more lucrative opportunities and this will cause tensions around issues like loyalty and core interests. The possibility that Sasol might relocate abroad in the next decade should not be discounted, its current protestations notwithstanding.

The DRC

Given the energy considerations above, we predict that in the years ahead the DRC will become central to South Africa's evolving African strategy. This will be less a product of the DRC's considerable mineral resources than because its hydropower potential offers a possible long-term solution to South Africa's emerging energy crisis. In each of our three previous *State of the Nation* chapters we drew attention to the importance of the Grand Inga project. We will not repeat the details here except to reassert that its success over the planned 15–20 year construction phase will depend greatly on the achieving and maintenance of peace and stability in this conflict-ravaged country. Some progress has been made in recent years under the second Kabila regime but much more needs to be done and this will require a heavy dose of South Africa's diplomatic energy.

If this is achieved, there will be other spin-offs. In a *Business Day* article (02.03.06), Dianna Games noted that in recent years 'hundreds of companies have made the trek to Kinshasa and Lubumbashi to look for opportunities there'. With peace and stability, we would expect the same mushrooming of South African businesses in Kinshasa and other major centres, as has occurred in Mozambique and Nigeria. In short, Grand Inga could be the big 'South African show' in Africa over the next 15 or so years.

Claude Kabemba's chapter in this volume highlights the increasingly important political and economic role being assumed by South African in the DRC.

Zimbabwe

By contrast and assuming a continuance of the political status quo in Zimbabwe, we predict that that country will continue as the site of a great human tragedy with negative consequences for all its neighbours – South Africa more than any other. While as of February 2006 there were still 26 South African companies operative in Zimbabwe,[4] we predict an eventual decline in Zimbabwean–South African trade. Most of these companies are operating at less than full capacity and some are little more than holding operations pending an eventual change of situation in the country. In the interim, the continuing disintegration of the Zimbabwean economy will ultimately impact on its ability to import South African products while the anticipated semi-nationalisation of the Zimbabwean mining sector will lead to a slow down – and eventual shutdown – of the one sector of that economy still functional and reasonably profitable. South Africa's gold and platinum mines in Zimbabwe will cease to operate if the Zimbabwean government pursues its 'copy-cat' black economic empowerment-type legislation and, in time, the whole Zimbabwean mining industry could grind to a halt.

As an importer, this would largely have the effect of South Africa having to source potash from a new outlet. Potash is currently South Africa's biggest import from that country. Without discounting the human tragedy and the resultant inflow into South Africa of desperate economic refugees, we predict that Zimbabwe will become less and less relevant to South Africa's evolving economic strategy in Africa. It is already beginning to move off the radar screen.

Mozambique, Nigeria, Zambia and Tanzania

This will not be the case in regard to the above four countries where we will see continued growth and ever closer ties. In regard to Mozambique, this will continue to be largely one-way traffic with South African companies becoming ever more active inside Mozambique. These will be pan-sectoral but will be fuelled largely by those willing to invest in Mozambique's abundant mineral resources.

In regard to Nigeria, the picture could be similar provided political stability prevails and the government does not lose control of events in its oil-rich Delta. This could become a big 'if' factor, however. Likewise, key is Nigeria's continuing reform of its financial regulatory system. If these factors materialise positively, not only will Nigeria supply increasing amounts of oil to South Africa but its banks and industrial giants will enter the local market in larger numbers, some initially by way of listings on the JSE. Recently, for example, the so-called integrated energy-solutions firm, Oando (listed on the Nigerian stock market with a market capitalisation of US$400 million), applied for a listing on the JSE. It has set up office in Sandton and is interested in teaming up with Sasol and PetroSA in pursuit of gas-to-liquids opportunities in west Africa.

Simultaneously, we predict that South African companies will continue to mushroom across the Nigerian economic landscape, deriving benefits from a market starved for decades of quality consumer products.

Almost unnoticed, Tanzania has in the last decade become the site of considerable South African economic activity. Indeed, the estimated South African expatriate population in Tanzania – of between 4 000 and 5 000 – is the largest such cluster of South Africans in Africa. Located primarily in Dar es Salaam and Arusha, it operates in the retail, banking, construction, mining, leisure and tourism, and telecommunications sectors. While Shoprite is clearly the supermarket of choice amongst local shoppers, there is also some resentment at the growing presence of South Africans, dubbed by those hostile to them as the 'kuburu' (a derivative of the word 'boer'). Particular resentment is directed at the rough and tough labour regime operative at the TanzaniteOne mine, a facility described by one researcher as being run along the lines of a nineteenth-century frontier company in the American west (Schroeder, interview 24.03.06). The recent fatal shooting of some alleged local trespassers by the South African security company guarding the mine was illustrative of this and generated considerable local criticism. However, with the Tanzanian government keen to expand its economic ties with South Africa, there is little doubt that the volume of trade between what are two old allies will soar in the decade ahead.

South Africa's corporate presence in Zambia dates back to colonial times with Anglo-American's involvement in the copper industry. That presence shrank after independence with the partial nationalisation of the copper sector but never entirely disappeared. The dwindling South African business presence post-independence was more than compensated for by the fact that after 1964 Zambia became 'home from home' for a vast community of South African exiles, one which by the 1980s numbered several thousand. By 1991 all bar a handful had returned home and the South African footprint further dwindled until the late 1990s when the retail and tourism sectors re-entered what was by then a crumbling economy. That trickle of investors has in recent times turned into a flood attracted by the startling price recovery of Zambian copper on the world market and the general minerals' sector boom. By 2006, South Africa had overtaken Britain as the largest investor in the local economy, pouring some $373 million into agriculture, manufacturing, tourism, retail and services sectors, creating in the process, according to the *Chicago Tribune* (20.04.04), nearly 22 000 new jobs. With the minerals boom likely to hold up for as long as the Chinese and Indian buying sprees continue, South African capital will continue to look at Zambia as a site of opportunity.

Angola

For some years now we have predicted a surge in South African–Angolan trade relations but this has not materialised. While there has been some growth in both imports and exports and a number of South African companies have set up shop in Angola since 2002, we had anticipated higher volumes given the mineral wealth of Angola, the dire need to reconstruct its war-crippled infrastructure, and the reasonable proximity of Angola to the Northern and Western Cape provinces. We have now concluded that in the case of Angola there is going to be no 'big-bang' take-off as occurred with Mozambique. The reasons for this are essentially political, exacerbated somewhat by cultural and linguistic factors.

A large part of the problem with Angola is that it is, as Pearce (2005) put it, less a country than a ruling class happening. What he is referring to is the fact that the political class which took power at independence 30 years ago has clung to it ever since, brooking no challenge to its hegemony, unwilling even to test the will of the electorate in anything remotely like a free or fair contest. In the course of its rule, or perhaps reign would be a more apt term, this class has become fabulously wealthy, living palatially behind ever higher barricades while all around them most of Luanda and much of the rest of the country has fallen apart. Now the oil and commodities boom has afforded this self-perpetuating oligarchy the opportunity to accumulate ever greater wealth and to thumb its collective nose at attempts to pressurise it into even the mildest of reforms.

However, to take full advantage of the current oil and minerals bonanza, Angola's rulers need to engage with outsiders, some of whom, like South Africa, have democratic scruples, and others of whom, like the International Monetary Fund and the World Bank, have strict rules of accountability. Fortunately for this elite there are other powers with fewer scruples willing to 'turn the other cheek' and do business with Angola's rulers – none more so than the Chinese who are prepared to pay handsomely for their right to do business. As the *Financial Times* journalist John Reed has put it, 'the state-owned Chinese corporate presence is growing on the back of a blossoming political relationship between Angola and China which in 2004 extended a $2bn credit line to rebuild the country's war-ruined infrastructure' (*Financial Times* 01.03.06).

In a second report in the same newspaper, Reed quotes Human Rights Watch researcher Alex Vines who has for years focused on Angola. Vines argues that 'data transparency in Angola has not improved over the last couple of years' and that in recent years it has actually 'stagnated'. He points out that the only modest improvement came about at the end of the 1980s, which coincided, with 'a period of cheap crude'. Now, in a time of high oil prices, Vines notes that 'foreign governments and institutions are realising they have little leverage' (*Financial Times* 01.03.06).

It is this political context, along with decrepit infrastructure, poor economic management and endemic corruption, which leads us to suggest there will be little blossoming in the near future in the Angolan–South African relationship.

Shoprite and Massmart

In each of our previous chapters we have commented on the astonishing expansion of Shoprite into the African market to the point where – with 135 stores in 17 African countries outside of South Africa – it had by 2004 become South Africa's largest multinational retailer and Africa's busiest retail outlet. We noted, however, in the last edition that in 2004 it had only opened one new outlet in Africa (Nigeria) while also for the first time moving beyond the continent and into India. We speculated at the time as to whether this suggested that Shoprite felt the African market was saturated and that it would in the future look to Asia for further expansion. Our speculation was wrong.

In February 2006, Shoprite announced that turnover in its non-South African stores (that is its African and one Indian) was up by 18.9 per cent in the first three months of the 2005–06 trading year, exceeding that of its South African stores by just over 1 per cent. It also announced that the company planned to open 12 new stores in Africa in the coming years. Without naming the countries of site, CEO Whitey Basson announced that they intended to 'focus on oil-producing West African countries which have high gross domestic product growth'. He also announced that the company would be closing its Egyptian stores 'due to supply-line problems' (*Business Day* 23.03.06).

For a number of years, Massmart has operated Macro, Game and Jumbo stores in the inner-periphery SACU member states of Botswana, Lesotho and Namibia. More recently it has expanded its operations into Mozambique, Uganda, Zambia, Zimbabwe, Mauritius and Nigeria. In the latter, it opened no less than four Game stores in 2005. The full range of its African operations, however, also includes such suppliers as Federated Timbers and Builders Warehouse. Massmart is thus positioning itself as a supplier of a range of consumables well beyond those carried by a supermarket like Shoprite.

The Massmart group alone is now the third largest distributor of consumer goods in Africa, its South African operations included. Together with Shoprite, these two companies dominate the African consumer goods environment.

Banks and financial institutions

The 'big four' South African banking groups are Nedbank, FirstRand (which has First National Bank [FNB] as a subsidiary), Standard Bank and Absa. The first three all have colonial origins, while Absa originated as a so-called 'Afrikaans' bank.[5] In 1969 Nedbank became wholly South African-owned and in 1986 and 1987 both Barclays and Standard Chartered divested of their South African operations. When the big four began their post-1990s push into Africa, they faced a market largely dominated by the HSBC Bank, Citigroup, Standard Chartered and Barclays. Their own extra-South African presence was minimal with Standard[6] having operations in Namibia and Swaziland while the other three were limited to Namibia. In the last decade, each has expanded their African presence significantly. Standard is the largest with operations in 16 countries outside of South Africa while Nedbank has 6 African outlets, Absa 5 and FNB 3. Standard's thrust into the continent began in 1992 with the purchase of the African operations of the Australian-based ANZ Grindlays in Botswana, Ghana, Kenya, Nigeria Uganda, Zambia, Zaire and Zimbabwe. Between 1995 and 1997, Standard acquired operations in Tanzania and Malawi, some of Barclays' assets in Lesotho and Swaziland, and a privatised bank in Lesotho. Between 2001 and 2003, Standard purchased banks in Malawi and Uganda, established offshore operations in Mauritius and raised its shareholding in its Mozambican bank.

Absa entered Africa by acquiring stakes in privatised banks: a minority shareholding in 1998 in the Commercial Bank of Zimbabwe (trading as Jewel Bank) and majority shareholdings in the Tanzanian National Bank of Commerce (2000) and Mozambique's Banco Austral (2002). Between 1991 and 1994, FNB listed in Botswana and acquired three banks. In 1995, it made an acquisition in Swaziland while in 2004 FNB launched a subsidiary in Lesotho. The Nedbank group began its foray into the continent in 1993 with a merger in Namibia and an acquisition in Zimbabwe. Between 1995 and 1999 it made acquisitions in Lesotho, Swaziland, Mauritius and Madagascar. Nedbank, however, has also shed operations in Africa. In 1999, it acquired a 40 per cent stake in BNP Mozambique but then sold it to the Zimbabwean African Banking Group. In 2006, it divested of its share in the State Bank of Mauritius. Its only new acquisition in recent years has been a 50 per cent interest in Banco Commercial Angolano, becoming the first South African bank to establish a foothold in that difficult economic terrain.

Despite all of the above activity, Africa's contribution to the big four's bottom line is modest. In 2005 their combined African operations contributed only 10 per cent to their overall earnings with First Rand's, Absa's and Nedbank's African assets contributing only 4 per cent, 1.7 per cent and 0.05 per cent respectively to headline earnings.

So, the question then is why do these banks bother with the African market? The answer is likely a combination that includes the fact that they see the market as having potential, albeit modest by comparison with their local operations, while also serving the banking needs of many of their major South African corporate clients as they move into new and sometimes unfamiliar operating environments.

Perhaps the most significant development in recent times in South African banking circles has involved Britain's Barclays Bank taking a 60 per cent shareholding in Absa. This will also impact on the African banking scene as the second phase of the merger, which is to be realised in the period 2005 to 2007, will involve Absa taking control of all of Barclays' current African operations bar that of Egypt (which in operational terms Barclays regards as part of its Middle-Eastern cluster). Barclays is currently active in 11 African countries outside of South Africa. Given Absa's current location in Tanzania and Zimbabwe, the deal will boost the bank's profile from 5 to 13 countries and will vault it into the big league of African banks. A feature of the merger is that Absa's investment vehicle (the Corporate and Merchant Bank) will merge with Barclays' investment arm, the combination of which will create a major new funding force on the continent, one which it claims will focus on mining projects.

Operating alongside the private banks has been South Africa's two state-owned development finance institutions, the IDC and the DBSA. Both were apartheid-era creations and limited to the local market but both have since 1994 been unshackled and allowed to move into the African interior. The IDC's mandate is to fund private projects that are commercially viable (produce returns) and which will have a development impact. To these ends, the IDC relates to Africa through equity investments, commercial loans and export finance. The DBSA has a three-pronged role as 'financier' of debt and equity commitments, a 'partner' in knowledge-sharing and equity commitments and an 'advisor' on projects and other developmental issues.[7]

In the 2004/05 financial year, 24 per cent of the DBSA's investment and lending operations were in the Southern African Development Community (SADC) arena. To date, it has committed to over 120 projects in Africa. These have included the Lesotho Highlands Water Project; the Mozambique to South Africa Natural Gas project, which entailed a loan to Sasol; the Mozal aluminium smelter; and the N4 toll-road component of the Maputo Corridor. Elsewhere in Africa, the DBSA has focused on water and electricity energy projects, telecommunications, housing, agriculture and agro-processing. Sixty-six per cent of its investments in 2004 were geared at energy-related infrastructure.

In 2005, new DBSA projects included a US$8 million loan to the Speke Shipping Line, which operates on Lake Victoria between ports in Tanzania, Kenya and Uganda; a US$20 million advance to an East African Development Bank credit facility aimed at boosting economic development in Tanzania and the surrounding region; a US$9.5 million/R62 million contribution to the co-funding of a Tanzanian paper mill; a US$10 million loan to the Development Bank of Zambia; a R131 million loan to the privatised Zambian electricity utility ZESCO and a R81 million loan to the DRC's national power utility for the rehabilitation and stabilisation of the power distribution network in Kinshasa.

With regards to its African operations, the IDC is mandated to assist in the development of projects, as well as acquisitions and expansion. With regard to equity investments, the IDC is restricted to no more than a 50 per cent stake in SADC-based projects and a 25 per cent stake in projects in Africa outside of SADC. The IDC also requires that projects must in some way stimulate South African exports.

By June 2004, the IDC had 89 projects and export-financing schemes in 28 African countries, including several significant mineral projects, like the Corridor Sands titanium project in Mozambique, the Kanshansi copper mining project in Zambia, and the Kolwezi Tailings project in the DRC, which extracts copper and cobalt from tailings (waste material from previous mining ventures). The IDC's top eight countries by exposure as of September 2005 were Mozambique ($577 million), Nigeria ($23 million), Zambia ($32 million), Lesotho ($31 million), Swaziland ($17 million), Malawi and Mauritius (both $13 million) and Namibia (US$10 million).

Important to our analysis is another development in the National Treasury's exchange-control liberalisations. In 2006, Treasury repealed the restriction on the IDC and the DBSA which stipulated that loans issued needed to involve South African projects or companies that have a 50 per cent South African content. We predict that this will facilitate more South African investment on the continent. Whether this will have a negative impact on the ancillary activities and inputs from South African companies that accompany IDC and DBSA-related loans remains to be seen. The Treasury's view is that a relaxing of these conditions will contribute positively to South African employment and growth.

Conclusion

Clearly, South African capital has emerged as a significant economic force in Africa since 1990 and its presence will continue to expand in the years ahead. Yet, we return again to the points made earlier in the chapter, namely, that as an export destination, the African market has levelled out and is unlikely to grow significantly in the period ahead. Certainly it will in no way challenge the primacy of the Asian and European arenas. It will be these two markets that will constitute the engines of South Africa's future export growth.

Notes

1   See <http://www.unctad.org>.

2   Sources of South African crude oil in 2005 were: Nigeria (61%), Angola (28%), Gabon (9%) and Algeria (2%).

3   See <http://www.miningx.com>.

4   See IRIN@irinnews.org, 06.02.06.

5   Nedbank's origins are with the Dutch Nederlandsche Bank en Credietvereeniging. Standard Bank's origins lie with the Standard Bank of British South Africa; it merged in 1969 with Chartered Bank to become Standard Chartered. First National Bank's origins are a little more complex. Through a series of amalgamations of colonial and local banks, the Bank of Africa was established in 1879, which was acquired in 1912 by the National Bank of South Africa (established originally in the Boer Republic of the Transvaal).

In 1925, the African Bank amalgamated with the Anglo Egyptian Bank and the Colonial Bank (both British Banks) to become Barclays Dominion Colonial Overseas.

The Amalgamated Banks of South Africa (Absa) was established through amalgamation between 1991 and 1992 of the largely Afrikaans and formerly state-cosseted banks: Allied, United, Volkskas and Bankorp (TrustBank and Bankfin).

6   Standard Bank is called Stanbic in all countries in which Standard Chartered operates.

7   See <http://www.dbsa.org.za>.

References

Daniel J & Lutchman J (2005) South Africa in Africa: Scrambling for energy. In S Buhlungu et al. (Eds) *The State of the Nation: South Africa 2005–2006*. Cape Town: HSRC Press.

Daniel J, Lutchman J & Naidu S (2004) South Africa and Nigeria: Two unequal centres in a periphery. In J Daniel et al. (Eds) *The State of the Nation: South Africa 2004–2005*. Cape Town: HSRC Press.

Daniel J, Naidoo V & Naidu S (2003) 'The South Africans have arrived': Post-apartheid corporate expansion into Africa. In J Daniel et al. (Eds) *The State of the Nation: South Africa 2003–2004*. Cape Town: HSRC Press.

Grobbelaar N (2006) South African corporate engagement with Africa: Unpacking negative and positive perceptions. In SAIIA (Ed) *South African Yearbook of International Affairs 2005/06*. Johannesburg: SAIIA.

Mills G (2006) Ten things Africa can do for itself. Heritage Lecture, The Heritage Foundation, Washington DC, February.

Pearce J (2005) *An outbreak of peace: Angola's situation of 'confusion'*. Cape Town: New Africa Books.

Rumney R (2006) South Africa's FDI flows into Africa. Presentation to the National Treasury Interdepartmental Workshop, Johannesburg, 15 February.

Interviews

SG Mfenyana, South African High Commissioner in Tanzania, Dar es Salaam, 26.03.06

Reg Rumney, Business Map, telephonic interview, February 2006

Richard Schroeder, Associate Professor, Department of Geography, Rutgers University, interviewed in Dar es Salaam, 24.03.06.

21 *South Africa in the DRC: renaissance or neo-imperialism?*

Claude Kabemba

South Africa successfully mediated the Inter-Congolese Dialogue that in April 2003 brought about an end to one of Africa's most complex conflicts,[1] bringing hope of a smooth transition to democracy and stability to the Democratic Republic of Congo (DRC), a country long wracked by authoritarianism and war. While concerned western powers thought little of the chance for peace in the DRC and the Great Lakes region, President Thabo Mbeki was always confident that a solution to the DRC's crisis was possible. No wonder, then, that Congolese of all tendencies came to believe that 'there was no other country that was prepared to go an extra mile to accompany them in their endeavours in search of solutions to their political problems' (DRC Ministry of Mining, interview 02.2006).[2] Today, South Africa is widely considered to be the godfather of the Congolese transition, and a critical player in the future stability and development of the DRC. Even so, its motivations in mediating the peace are increasingly being subject to hard questions for the perception is growing that South Africa is primarily interested in the Congo for the wealth that it offers and by the prospect of displacing the western capitalist interests which have controlled and exploited the country's resources, with little or no regard for the interests of the country's nationals, since the time of King Leopold's Congo Free State. This chapter therefore seeks to address the issue of whether South Africa is behaving differently from the western capitalist interests that have dominated the DRC for so long. Is there a contradiction between keeping peace, on the one hand, and exploiting the country's resources, on the other? And how do Congolese perceive South Africa's foreign policy: as a genuine partner in development or as an imperialist power driven by its own interests?

The DRC's significance

The DRC shares the characteristics of poverty and political instability with the large majority of countries in Africa, and like them is engaged in a search for a development path which will lead it to stability and prosperity. However, the DRC is also a strategic state for the success of the New Partnership for Africa's Development (Nepad) for three main reasons. First, the DRC is huge, it is located at the heart of the continent, and it shares its borders with nine countries. Second, covering a total of 2 345 million square kilometres, it is the second largest country on the continent after Sudan, and the third largest in terms of population, estimated at some 60 million people. Third, and most important, is its natural wealth, for the DRC has an abundance of natural resources, including water, hydroelectrical power, arable land, forest, gold, coltan, diamond, zinc, copper, manganese, crude oil, coffee, timber, rubber and more. These resources have long been the *garde-chasse* of leading western powers, and have been the source of political tension and wars going right back to the Berlin Conference in 1885. The brutality of its exploitation as a personal fiefdom by King Leopold is notorious. In reality, it fared only marginally better under the successor administration of the Belgian state. And subsequently, during the post-independence period, the absence of an organised state has contributed to the continuing pillage of its rich resources.

Despite its riches, the people of the DRC remain amongst the poorest in the world. At independence, the hope of a better life was promised by Prime Minister Patrice Lumumba, the only leader who could command popular support across the entire country at the time of independence, but this has never materialised. However, Lumumba's fateful decision to call for Soviet assistance to bring a halt to the Belgian-backed secession of the minerals-rich Katanga province just a month after independence led to his American-inspired dismissal by President Kasavubu, his subsequent murder in detention, and a train of events – UN intervention, Katangese secessionist leader Moses Tshombe's exile and return as prime minister, his own call for Belgian assistance in quelling secessionism, and eventually his own dismissal from power by Kasavubu. In November 1965 Tshombe, too, was displaced – this time by a military coup led by Joseph-Desire Mobutu. Under American auspices, the latter erected a personalised dictatorship which lasted until it was eventually eroded by the end of the cold war and a wave of democratisation throughout Africa in the early 1990s.

By the mid-1990s, US support for Mobutu's puppet regime had been quietly withdrawn, Mobutu himself was seriously ill, and his ramshackle government and army were in no shape to withstand a rebellion by four militant groups from the east of the country. By 1996 these had come together as the *Alliance des forces démocratiques pour la liberation du Congo* (AFDL) under the leadership of Joseph Kabila, militarily supported by Uganda and Rwanda. With the large majority of the population wanting to see the back of Mobutu, there was little resistance to the rebels' advance. By early 1997, Kabila and his allies were already knocking on the door of Kinshasa, and were resistant to President Nelson Mandela's offer to negotiate a solution. They proceeded to take control of Kinshasa when in May 1997 a final stand by the Presidential Guard was avoided by South African mediation. Mobutu fled to Togo before moving on to exile in Morocco, where he died of cancer within weeks.

In the event, Kabila's installation as president brought little respite, for after banning political parties and erecting his own brand of authoritarianism (albeit while appointing a constitutional commission and promising elections for 1999), the AFDL itself became hugely unpopular, accused by many of being the instrument of his Ugandan and Rwandan allies. Yet by mid-1998, Kabila was chafing under the tutelage of his foreign allies, who had ambitions of dispensing with him. He proceeded to attempt to expel Rwandan and Ugandan forces from the DRC. They responded by bringing reinforcements from home whilst prompting a new rebellion against Kabila amongst disaffected domestic elites who had been excluded from influence to legitimise their invasion.

Kabila now turned for assistance to Angola and Zimbabwe. Acting under the mandate of the Southern African Development Community (SADC), the latter's intervention was decisive in securing his survival, even though Ugandan- and Rwandan-backed rebels – in something of an unholy alliance with fragments of Mobutu's army – continued to hold large swathes of territory in the north and east of the country. Complicated and vicious hostilities in what became known colloquially as 'Africa's world war' – during which all external warring parties on both sides funded their activities through, in essence, asset-stripping (UN 2001) – were subsequently only drawn to (a lingering) close following the signing of an agreement by the heads of state of the DRC, Rwanda, Uganda, Zimbabwe and Namibia, together with Angola's defence minister, in Lusaka on 10 July 1999. With a fragile situation barely held together by a UN peacekeeping operation, which was charged *inter alia* with overseeing the disengagement of foreign troops, the search for an uncertain peace was spearheaded by Sir Ketumile Masire, the former president of Botswana, who was mandated by the Organisation of African Unity to facilitate inter-Congolese political negotiations. Despite continuing military confrontations between the army and diverse rebel groups, notably in the eastern Kivu region, what became known as the Inter-Congolese Dialogue – in which South Africa came to play the principal mediating role – made steady if erratic progress towards the winding down of the war and the projected political transition to peace, stability and (at least formally) democracy, even surviving the assassination of Laurent Kabila and his replacement as president by his son, Joseph, in January 2001.

The success of the Inter-Congolese Dialogue holds out the prospect that the DRC may escape from its calamitous history of exploitation by western imperial powers, rapacious multinationals and their dependent and corrupt hangers-on who hitherto have constituted the Congolese political class. While the challenges are vast, the transition to a democracy offers hope not only that the exploitation of the DRC's resources can become of benefit to its own population, but that they can also become a catalyst for the development of the entire continent. However, in considerable part, realisation of that prospect will depend upon the motivations, responsibility and behaviour of external actors – amongst the most important of which, in this new era, is South Africa.

South Africa's interests in mediating peace in the DRC

There are two schools of thoughts concerning the real motives behind South Africa's foreign policy in the DRC. The first focuses on the idealist approach, which finds its roots in moral values. This perspective is based in South Africa's liberation tradition and its success in achieving a stable democracy since 1994. The African National Congress (ANC) acknowledges the support it received from a diversity of sources worldwide, not least from African countries and in particular from the frontline states, in its defeat of apartheid. Furthermore, post-apartheid South Africa has proclaimed a foreign policy that promotes human rights, peace and democracy across the continent. As Gelb argues, South Africa cherishes 'a visionary and principled foreign policy through which the ANC-led government would apply its human rights and state morality traditions' (2001: 1). Against this background, it could be argued that the country's policy towards the DRC is genuinely an attempt to support the creation of a stable and democratic society and is part and parcel of South Africa's wider peace efforts across the continent – in Burundi, Ivory Coast, Sudan (Darfur) and Zimbabwe. Ajulu captures this when he states, 'Mbeki has increasingly assumed the mantle of the African firefighter, dashing all over the continent putting out fires in theatres of conflict' (2005: 1). South Africa strongly believes that it is possible to bring peace to the entire continent, thereby shifting African efforts away from war towards development. It is for this reason that the South African president speaks boldly of the rebirth of the African continent, of the 'African Renaissance'.

South Africa's Minister of Foreign Affairs, Nkosazana Dlamini Zuma, has identified the country's foreign policy objectives as:
- The promotion of democratisation and the rejection of human rights abuses;
- The prevention of conflict and the peaceful resolution of disputes; and
- The advancement of sustainable development and the alleviation of poverty (Dlamini Zuma 1999).

This embodies the logic of the African Renaissance which Mbeki sees as being carried forward by Nepad (Gelb 2002), and for many observers provides the mainspring of South Africa's present role in the DRC. Landsberg, for instance, summarises South Africa's foreign policy towards the rest of the continent as follows:

> For the new post-apartheid rulers there can be no development without peace and security, and no peace and security without development. There can similarly be no development, peace and security without democratic governance and vice versa. Democratic peace at home is not sufficient for development; there is a need for broader democratic peace in the region. (2006: 124)

South Africa entered the DRC fray when the first war broke out in 1996. As has been noted already, President Mandela enjoyed only partial success in finding a solution to the DRC problem when, in bringing Mobutu and Laurent Kabila together, he negotiated Mobutu's departure into exile. Subsequently, Mbeki continued where his predecessor left off when the second war broke out in 1998, coming to play a key role in keeping the Inter-Congolese Dialogue alive. His commitment and dedication to the difficult and highly complex negotiations of the Inter-Congolese Dialogue are said by many observers to demonstrate South Africa's very real interest in promoting peace and democracy throughout the continent. The most important aspect of this commitment has been the fact that South Africa's policy-makers believe peace is possible in the DRC. They further believe that the Congolese, despite the structural and societal challenges they face, are capable of finding common ground.

The Congolese signed the All and Inclusive Peace Accords and adopted a transitional Constitution in Pretoria in 2003. President Mbeki has since been omnipresent throughout the transition, jetting into the DRC every time peace has been threatened and taking part in all the important events. He was present at the adoption of the Constitution of the Third Republic by the Parliament of transition in May 2005 and at the promulgation of the same Constitution by President Joseph Kabila on 18 February 2006. On many other occasions, he has dispatched teams constituted by government officials and members of his office to the DRC to assess the situation and facilitate further progress. Furthermore, South Africa now has troops in the DRC under the auspices of the United Nations peacekeeping mission (MONUC) and volunteered to print and transport ballot papers for the presidential and parliamentary elections held on 30 July 2006. Whereas previously many observers had deemed the balkanisation of the DRC as not only inevitable but the only viable way forward, the country now stands upon the verge of holding its first democratic elections in 40 years. No wonder then that Mbeki should have pronounced his strong satisfaction with the progress made and South Africa's continuing strong support for the transition (*ANC Today* 20–26.05.06).

The second school of thought regarding South Africa's involvement in the DRC views it as flowing from its economic interests. This perspective proposes that South Africa's mediation has had as its principal motivation the goal of situating South African players advantageously amidst increasing competition to exploit the DRC's resources. This view simply dismisses the moral argument based on human rights and promotion of democracy. Ian Taylor and Paul Williams make this point clearly when they argue that: 'the very neo-liberal principles that lie at the heart of Mbeki's vision of an African Renaissance have contributed to the erosion of the neo-patrimonial state in Africa and actually encouraged the growth of what William Reno described as "warlord capitalism"' (2001: 65). From this perspective, South Africa's refusal to join the other SADC countries in a military intervention to save President Laurent Kabila's government from being overthrown by Rwandan and Ugandan invading forces was not driven by a concern for neutrality but by economic reasons in that Kabila's reluctance to grant mineral concessions to two South African companies – De Beers and Anglo (both of which have long been involved in the Congo) – had provoked anger in Pretoria towards his government. Hence, according to this school, the ANC government's politico-diplomatic interests in the DRC, its stabilisation and its post-conflict reconstruction cannot be divorced from economic interests, notably its concern to secure access to minerals for South African corporations. Yet there agreement ends, for while radical realists view South Africa's motivations as imperialistic, more conservative realists view Pretoria's policy as merely nationalistic.

The implicit assumption of the radical realists is that South Africa's hidden agenda is to dominate the DRC; this view is largely justified by reference to the involvement of South African businesses in the exploitation of the DRC's resources. According to Patrick Bond, for instance, South Africa and the US are little different when it comes to doing business in the DRC: 'Pretoria and Washington back different corporations engaged in extraction and exploitation, but are agreed on the general framework for regional geopolitics, and for enslaving Kinshasa via multinational agencies' (2005: 6). Ajulu argues similarly that South African capital is behaving in no way differently from the way it has operated in the rest of the continent where 'the corporate sector has invariably pursued a minimalist and conservative agenda...[and] stifled the development of productive forces' (2005: 1). Furthermore, Ajulu continues, with their economic activities remaining largely in the realm of merchant capital, 'huge profits have been made not by revolutionising production, but rather by controlling the market.'

The corresponding conservative position is that, quite simply, it is government's role worldwide to create an environment for its corporate sector to invest outside the country. This is why, more often than not, the corporate sector has looked upon the politicians to provide solutions, and then moved in to reap the benefits. Even so, the South African government continues to call on its corporate sector entering the rest of the continent to respect business ethics and to work within the spirit of renewal of the African continent. Former Minister of Public Works, Jeff Radebe, has made this point clear with regard to the conduct expected of state-owned corporations (SOEs):

> It is imperative that SOEs involved in Africa...conduct
> themselves with probity...integrate commercial viability and returns
> on investment with appropriate policies of procurement, the
> empowerment of SMMEs, the employment of local labour and services
> that build up and, encourage sustainable development...We must
> ensure that SOEs do not operate in the manner of imperialist
> concessionaires. (Quoted in Ajulu 2005: 11)

From this perspective, South Africa is the regional leader by virtue of its economic muscle, and its mercantilist interest in the DRC is both normal and legitimate. Even in a situation where the ANC-led government had not become involved in mediating the peace process, South African businesses would still have been interested in the resources and the market the DRC offers. In today's world, 'Economics has become the new politics, and business is in the driving seat'(Hertz 2001: 85), and on the African continent, South Africa is the only country with the necessary infrastructure, know-how, finances and technology readily available to exploit the DRC resources. It makes economic sense, therefore, for South Africa to move into the DRC as long as Congolese citizens benefit in the process. This perspective also argues that South Africa preferred to stay out of the recent war in the Congo not only because of its disagreements with Kabila, but because its interests lay not in the illegal expropriation of resources as undertaken by the various belligerents (UN 2001) but in working towards the emergence of a stable environment favourable to orderly corporate investment. For South Africa, in other words, the bringing of peace, on the one hand, and the exploitation of the DRC resources, on the other, are closely linked. Indeed, in the eyes of the ANC leadership, the renaissance of a democratic DRC could go hand in hand with South Africa's own transformation (Braeckman 1999), a point echoed by Deputy Minister of Foreign Affairs Aziz Pahad (1996) when he observed: 'There is no Great Wall between us and the Great Lakes Region. The consequences of what happens there will have serious and disastrous consequences for all of us.' These consequences should not only be understood in terms of the number of 'Congolese refugees'³ who enter South Africa but also in terms of the missed opportunities for investment in the DRC's resources (minerals, markets and energy) that are critical for the growth and the sustainability of the South African economy.

Whatever the perspective that is adopted, it is clear that there is a strong connection between South Africa's mediation of peace and the opportunity for South African corporations to secure access to the Congo. And for the moment, at least, the South African-driven accord appears to be laying the basis for a sustainable peace. Furthermore, South Africa will not be alone in seeking to take advantage of the improved conditions for investment for it will have to compete with foreign actors, both multinationals and governments, which share similar interests and ambitions. Yet South Africa's involvements will be closely monitored by the Congolese themselves. For too long, the Congolese people have remained prisoners to their own resources – they have never had a say in how their riches should be exploited, by whom and far less how they should be shared. However, with the growing of the democratic space the Congolese are steadily gaining confidence to speak for themselves, and they will increasingly be prepared to stand up to anyone, and especially fellow Africans, who they see as robbing them of their wealth. How South Africa comes to be perceived by the Congolese will therefore determine the relationship between the two countries – and if South Africa chooses to act as an imperial power, it will meet the strong resistance of the Congolese people.

South Africa's ambiguous reputation

While the Congolese welcome South Africa in their country because of its present role in peacemaking and peacekeeping, they also have a negative image of the behaviour of the South African government and multinationals in the past. South

African corporations have been doing business in the DRC for many years. South African companies (such as De Beers, for example) have dominated the Congolese diamond industry for decades – yet many Congolese feel that De Beers has done little towards improving the standard of living of the Congolese in its area of operation. Indeed, the presence and privilege which De Beers enjoyed in the DRC previously had much to do with the good relations that existed between the apartheid and the Mobutu regimes. Both were aligned to and in different ways dependant upon the US and strongly allied to it in the struggle against communism; both supported Jonas Savimbi's *Uniao Nacional de Independencia Total de Angola* (Unita) rebel movement in Angola at the peak of the cold war, and when South Africa fought a bloody war in Angola alongside Savimbi, Mobutu's Congo served as the primary conduit for arms to Unita. Consequently, it is not surprising that when Mobutu asked for Zaire/DRC to become a SADC member in the early 1980s, the application was rejected. More recently, too, South African companies were also actively involved in the exploitation of resources during the two wars of 1996 and 1998, and were mentioned in the UN's report on the illegal exploitation of the DRC's resources. The report argued that South Africa, despite its political neutrality in the DRC conflict, was very much involved at the commercial level. Although it did not name companies, it stated that large South African mining conglomerates, such as Anglo-American, were active in the DRC at the height of the war (UN 2001). The report also made reference to various actors, some based in South Africa and others outside of the country, who were using the territory and facilities of South Africa to conduct illicit commercial activities involving the natural resources of the DRC. For all that the present South African government cannot be held responsible for such past sins, it remains the case that illegal and exploitative actions by South African business – whether in the past, present or future – are likely to give the country as a whole a bad name amongst the Congolese.

Meanwhile, South Africa's role during the most recent war in the DRC remains highly controversial. On the one hand, the government is much praised for what it achieved during the Inter-Congolese Dialogue; yet on the other, it is blamed by many for its ambivalence towards what they consider to have been an externally-driven war fomented by Uganda and Rwanda that left more than four million people dead. Indeed, there is widespread suspicion that South Africa covertly supported the rebel cause and deliberately supplied Rwanda, one of its foreign backers, with the means for pursuing the war. It is well known that South Africa did supply Rwanda with plentiful stocks of hardware – from ammunition to armoured vehicles – as was confirmed in Parliament by Kadar Asmal, chairperson of the National Conventional Arms Control Committee, when responding to a question from an opposition Democratic Party MP. However, Asmal was insistent that this happened before the war broke out (*The Star* 16.09.99) – while saying nothing about the country's willingness to export arms to one of the continent's most unstable hot spots.

In any case, South Africa's neutrality during the war also raises many questions amongst many Congolese. From the latter's perspective, this was far less a rebellion than an invasion launched by Rwanda and Uganda against a member of the SADC. Such Congolese consequently fail to understand why South Africa, which was at the forefront of arguing for the DRC's admission to the SADC, declined to protect one of its members. They argue that South Africa failed to understand that the reason why the second rebellion in 1998 failed to progress as smoothly as the first one had done was precisely because Congolese citizens rejected it. The ANC, it is said, failed to draw lessons from its own experience of struggle that no liberation movement can succeed without the support of the people. It is for this reason that Mahmood Mamdani, for example, has argued: 'For South Africa to stand against foreign military intervention – in the face of a rebellion already driven forwards by foreign intervention – is to be seen as opposing further foreign intervention, thereby condoning the existing intervention' (*Sunday Independent* 30.08.98). It is against this background that many Congolese have noted South Africa's retrospective change of attitude and approach towards the war, with Mbeki having recently indicated that he now considers it to have been precipitated by an invasion. 'After the murder of Patrice Lumumba,' he declared in the ANC's weekly newsletter, the Congolese people had for many decades been subjected to the rapacious rule of Mobutu Sese Seko. Yet after he died, 'the Congolese people were to be subjected to further torment of war, including invasions by some of their neighbours'(*ANC Today* 20–26.05.05).

South Africa's economic interests in the DRC

South Africa has economic interests in the DRC in a range of areas from mining, energy, agriculture, fishery, construction, communication through to information technology and trade. In the present era, South Africa's capital and expertise are expected to play a key role in bringing economic revival to the DRC. Indeed, South Africa has already increased its trade with the DRC considerably, with the latter having now become its tenth leading trading partner on the continent (see Daniel et al. in this volume) and, more generally, South African companies are competing fiercely with European multinationals. However, in this chapter the focus is exclusively on the mining and energy sectors.

South Africa's interests in mining

South Africa's interests in the mining and mineral processes are pursued by two groups of businesses – one operating largely independently of government, and another collaborating more closely with it.

The first group consists largely of established, overwhelmingly white-owned and dominated companies which are making private investments in the DRC, many of them in partnership with Australian, British or US multinationals (DRC Ministry of Mining, interview 2006). These companies are simultaneously very professional and aggressive. They are well informed about the country's mineral potential, they are conversant with its most recent mining legislation,[4] they also understand 'how to do business' in the DRC and are usually successful in their efforts to solicit mining concessions.

This group is large and diverse. It includes (the formerly South African but now London-registered) Ashanti Gold and De Beers, ANMERCOSA (Anglo Vaal), (the 49 per cent South African-owned) BHP Billiton, JIG Mining, Metorex Kumba Resources, and Mwana Africa. La Société Minière de Bakwanga and De Beers signed a joint venture agreement to exploit diamonds in the DRC on 23 November 2005, and BHP Billiton has signed an agreement with the Congolese government to invest US$2.5 billion in an aluminium plant in the Bas Congo province. Meanwhile, there are also five or six companies, led by Anglo Gold Ashanti's exploration of the kilo Moto gold belt, involved in gold mining. The present boom in the price of the precious metal is leading companies to 'hot' new destinations (*Financial Mail* 23.12.05).

Some of the companies in this group are accused of using foul as well as fair means to ease their access to minerals. A report by the British All Party Parliamentary Group on the Great Lakes Region and Genocide Prevention (2002)concluded that the exploitation of today is a continuation of the old pattern of corruption and personal enrichment at the expense of the majority of the people. The report further argued that in many instances multinational companies which have decided to operate in the country have forged relationships with those who lack legitimacy and accountability to the population and who systematically engage in human rights abuses. Meanwhile, allegations of corruption are widespread, as are suggestions that companies have been involved in supplying arms to rebel groups, with a recent report by Human Rights Watch (2004) accusing Anglo Gold of working closely with one such group in order to protect production at one of its mines in the Mongbwalu gold mining area. The report argues that: 'AngloGold Ashanti representatives established relations with the National and Integrationist Front (FNI), an armed group responsible for serious human rights abuses including war crime and who control the Mongbwalu area. In return for the FNI assurances of security for its operations and staff, AngloGold Ashanti provided logistical and financial support' (Human Rights Watch 2005: 2). While the extent of such activities is inevitably unknown, and subject to much rumour, the image which they project is one of pillage and exploitation of the DRC's resources. This suggests, therefore, that if South Africa is to secure and extend the good reputation inherent in the more lofty aspects of its foreign policy, then the government is going to have to become more active in monitoring and evaluating the activities of South African multinationals beyond its own borders.

The second group of South African institutions and businesses which are active in the DRC are those that have entered the country in harness with the South African government. The South African government has taken on the task of working with the Congolese government in order to create a better environment for the Congolese private sector in order to create confidence for foreign investors. Besides being involved in the political and security arena to bring sustainable peace to the DRC, the South African government has signed a bilateral co-operation agreement with its Congolese counterpart on economy, finances and infrastructure. This is backed up by a separate protocol whereby South Africa has committed itself to rebuilding the mining sector. Meanwhile, the co-operation agreement is deemed fundamental if the South African government is going to be able to convince the private sector to invest in the DRC as it provides for a protective legal instrument to cover their involvement.

The attitude of the Congolese Ministry of Mining towards this latter group of companies and institutions is considerably warmer than towards the independent multinationals. Most of them, notably the Council for Scientific and Industrial Research (CSIR), Mintek, which specialises in mineral and metallurgical technology, the Industrial Development Corporation (IDC) and the South African Diamond Board, are state-owned or related, and are regarded as possessing the technological capacity that will enable South Africa to play an influential role in the rehabilitation and further development of the mining sector.

The CSIR has been requested to study the possibility of putting in place geo-science laboratories in the DRC. The study is already under way and if accepted by the DRC's government, will go back to the South African government for loan funding. (The Belgian government apparently refused to grant this technology to the Congolese, citing a lack of confidence in DRC's capacity to maintain this high-tech infrastructure, although critics allege that its refusal was intended to perpetuate Congolese technological dependency [DRC Ministry of Mining, interview 2006].)

For its part, Mintek has been asked to explore the possibilities of rehabilitating the mining research centre of Bukavu. It is intended that an extension of such infrastructure in the eastern part of the DRC will allow the government to cross-check the results from mining companies' activities.

Meanwhile, the IDC has a 10 per cent equity in the $400 million Kolwezi copper and cobalt tailings project, a venture which is majority owned by Canada's Adastra. The Kolwezi project is ranked among the world's largest resources of primary cobalt and is a substantial source of copper. In addition, the IDC is also involved in a partnership with Kinyamwambi-Musonoyi Tailing in the Rwashi copper mining project (DRC Ministry of Mining, interview 2006).

The South African government is also committed to creating a dynamic partnership with the Congolese that builds capacity and facilitates the transfer of technology to the DRC. There is a tacit acceptance that unless a functional state administration is restored in the DRC, it will be difficult to sustain doing business there in the long run (South African embassy, DRC, interview 2006). For this to materialise, it is necessary to restore state capacities. This is why the two countries have insisted on signing memoranda of understanding concerning co-operation in the areas of mining, geology and metallurgy. In most of its involvement, the South African government attempts to emphasise the fact that Congolese must be encouraged and supported to build their own capacity to control and monitor the exploitation of their own resources. Meanwhile, Pretoria is also interested in positioning South Africa as the preferred source of mining equipment and other necessities.

Overall, Pretoria is primarily interested in helping the DRC to formalise the exploitation of its minerals. With regard to gold, there is already an initiative to support and formalise artisanal mining. Pretoria is proposing that small mines be organised in co-operatives. South Africa will provide them with the Igoli process, a technology that is used in exploiting gold without the use of mercury. The CSIR and Mintek are involved in this venture. South Africa has also promised to finance these co-operatives through the creation of a mineral fund to be managed by a non-governmental structure rather than by the Congolese government. The fund will be designed to assist in the creation of partnerships between Congolese and South African small mining companies, and to provide for training and the upgrading of Congolese skills and technology. Pretoria is also keen that more women should become involved in this sector.

Meanwhile, the South African Diamond Board, together with the South African Minerals and Energy Department, is to examine how to introduce a diamond bourse for precious and semi-precious materials in the DRC (DRC Ministry of Mining, interview 2006). There is also discussion around the promotion of small-scale mines in the diamond sector. At present, Congolese diamond miners are organised mostly in small informal groups dominated by men. While they seem effective, their products are smuggled out of the country, and the state loses enormous amounts of revenue (MacGaffey 1991). The artisanal production of diamond and gold was legalised in 1983, and licensed counters were set for their purchase in order to reduce such smuggling (MacGaffey 1991), but this only worked for a few years. South Africa is now proposing the reinforcement of the existing Congolese regulation in order to clamp down on illegal production and exports and the promulgation of legislation similar to South Africa's new diamond legislation, the Precious Metals and Diamonds Amendment Bill,[5] which was tabled in Parliament in September 2005. South Africa is also proposing that a diamond regulator be put in place in the DRC to encourage diamond cutting and polishing. As is proposed in the South African legislation, the Congolese regulator will have sweeping powers intended to promote regular supply and equitable access to, and local beneficiation of, unpolished diamonds. However, the challenge is how to ensure that such an industry can compete on an open market with already established low-cost Indian and Chinese cutting industries on the one hand, and higher cost-cutting centres like Antwerp and Israel on the other. Meanwhile, South Africa is also prepared to provide the DRC with new technologies in the diamond sector, mainly in the field of exploration and determination of grades.

In general, while South African mining companies have shown considerable interest in the DRC, many have been reluctant to invest because of political instability and economic insecurity (South Africa–DRC Bilateral Sub-Committee 2005; DRC Ministry of Mining, interview 2006). This applies particularly to South Africa's new breed of black-owned or -controlled mining companies. Black businesses are reluctant to take risks in an unfamiliar and unstable environment, and are often afraid to risk their relatively small capital in a country like the DRC where the risks are high. In contrast, established players in the sector tend to worry that by staying out of the DRC they may miss out on a new scramble for resources which, according to John Borshoff, Australian mining executive of Paladin Resources, 'is redefining Africa'(*Financial Mail* 23.12.05).

Yet South African black-owned companies are not only reluctant to go into the DRC for security reasons. They also lack the relevant information on which to base any such decision. In recognition of this fact, the Congolese and South African governments have agreed to work together to popularise the DRC's new mining legislation among (especially black-owned) South African businesses. Another factor inhibiting investment by black-owned companies is that, on the whole, they lack the financial resources to invest meaningfully in the DRC, despite the considerable advances that are being made in South Africa with regard to black economic empowerment legislation and strategy. South African mining investment in the DRC is therefore almost inevitably going to be dominated overwhelmingly by established, white-owned and -controlled companies, a factor which the government is seeking to counterbalance through its promotion of involvement in the mining sector by its parastatals.

South Africa's interest in hydroelectrical power

One resource that South Africa would like to secure in the DRC is energy from the Inga Dam. As in the case of mining, there exists a memorandum of understanding between the two governments on the exploitation of DRC energy with particular regard to the setting up of an energy commission structure. South Africa's industrial expansion and urbanisation will necessitate huge and stable energy provision in the coming years and the DRC offers a reliable source through its Grand Inga Hydro project. For the South African government, Inga is a strategic priority project.

There is a direct link between access to clean, cost-effective energy and economic growth. The 1995 Framework Agreement between business, labour and government for an extended public works programme views infrastructure development as a key driver of economic growth, job creation and the eradication of poverty (Sigcau 2003). Meanwhile, the Ministry of Housing has embarked upon an ambitious plan which will see houses provided for millions of its citizens and which aspires to doing away with shacks by the year 2015. The sustainability of this extended infrastructure programme will need to be supported by the provision of a stable source of electricity.

Although Eskom is involved in attempts to diversify energy sources internally, there is recognition that the expansion of the economy will necessitate looking beyond South Africa's borders for energy[6] (*Financial Mail* 03.02.06). The challenge is the high cost involved in moving away from coal,[7] which is in abundance in South Africa and remains the country's main source of energy.[8] South Africa already buys electricity from Cahora Bassa in Mozambique as part of the SADC's Southern African Power Pool (SAPP),[9] and there are many other planned projects across the region from which South Africa is hoping to secure its energy.[10] However, Inga stands out for its massive potential and its clean energy. Indeed, as Daniel et al. argue in this volume, it is central to South Africa's interest in the DRC for reasons which extend well beyond its own borders, for the revival of the continent, as envisaged by Nepad, will not be able to succeed without access to affordable and environmentally-friendly energy. Eskom therefore sees the Grand Inga project as central to a regional plan to establish an African grid.[11]

The flow rate of the Congo River is more than 40 000 cubic metres per second – four times greater than that of Niagara Falls. When harnessed the Congo River could produce 30 000 megawatts, equivalent to one-fifth of the total consumption of the United States, and three times that of Britain. Indeed, it is said that the cost of electricity will be even cheaper than the world's lowest price, achieved by the Tennessee Valley Authority, allowing for the transformation not only of the DRC itself but a large part of the continent as well. Not surprisingly, therefore, South African businesses are already setting up commercial activities in the proximity of the Inga Dam, including BHP Billiton signing a protocol with the Congolese Minister of Energy to start feasibility studies for a $2.5 billion aluminum smelter in the Bas-Congo region. This industry will be linked to the Inga Dam as it will need electricity for the coming 40 years (*Le Potentiel* 10.02.06). BHP Billiton is also in discussion with Eskom on how it could contribute to the construction of Inga 3. In addition, the South African government has proposed that Congo initiate an industrial corridor that will go from Banana-Boma-Matadi up to Kinshasa along the Congo River (DRC Ministry of Mining, interview 2006).

Given the above, Eskom is heavily committed to participating in the rehabilitation of Inga 1 and Inga 2. The DRC has to date failed to rehabilitate the smaller Inga 1 and 2 projects, which both require huge financial investment. With regard to Inga 1, negotiations between Eskom and the Congolese electricity company are advanced, although as yet there is still no funding for this project. However, the Congolese have secured $300 million from the World Bank for the rehabilitation of Inga 2, and South Africa is being encouraged to bid at the appropriate time (South Africa–DRC Bilateral Sub-Comittee 2005). The DRC has also asked South Africa to become involved in the rehabilitation of a power plant at Zongo, the construction of a132-KV line linking Boma to Muande, the construction of a second power line from Inga to Kinshasa and the electrification of rural areas around Bas-Congo and the areas surrounding Kinshasa. However, all this will necessitate the DRC obtaining extensive funding, to which end Eskom is assisting the DRC in drafting proposals for development finance from several sources including the Development Bank of Southern Africa and the World Bank. Meanwhile, the South African government, together with Angola, Namibia, Botswana and the DRC, has formed Westcorp, a company tasked with funding the proposed $5 billion, 3 500 megawatt Inga 3 hydroelectric-power project and transmission lines from the DRC to southern Africa (*Financial Mail Corporate Report* 03.02.06).

The Mbeki government clearly views Inga as a highly strategic project with huge potential advantages including providing an environmentally friendly and stable source of energy to underwrite the rapid pace of South Africa's industrial expansion and urbanisation. However, there are risks attached to the Inga project of which South Africa is uncomfortably aware.

The first risk is clearly that Inga is taking place in one of the most volatile regions of the continent, and the possibility of political instability interrupting the flow of energy is a serious threat to the project's viability. In 1997, when Rwanda together with Congolese rebels launched their attack to oust Laurent Kabila, the first thing they did was to seize control of the Inga Dam, which supplies electricity to the capital Kinshasa – and what the rebels did an alienated militia group might be able to do too. In short, the DRC's energy system and its various components are potentially vulnerable to attack by non-state actors as well as national armies. To complicate matters, most of the electrical cables will cut across potentially unstable countries such as Angola. Much of this line would have to traverse sparsely populated and largely inaccessible regions of the different countries, so the potential for these facilities to become the target of destabilisation is huge. As Scheffran and Singer (2004) have noted, access to physical power sometimes transforms into political power and the link between energy and security is multifaceted. Whilst welcoming Inga's development, therefore, customer countries are likely to diversify their supply, so as to prevent themselves becoming excessively reliant upon a potentially politically unstable source.

The second risk is that corruption is endemic in the DRC and this could undermine the project's efficacy. Finances for building the Grand Inga are estimated at US$50 billion. Given the DRC's recent rating among the top 15 most corrupt countries on Transparency International's corruption perception list, concerns are growing that the project will primarily benefit the powerful clique which runs the country in league with multinationals and will do little to ease the electricity or development needs of Africa's poor majority.

The third risk is political. The secretive approach that has accompanied the negotiations about the upgrading of the Inga Dam arouses considerable suspicion. The negotiations between the government of the DRC, South Africa, international bodies like the World Bank and multinationals take place behind doors that are kept firmly shut, and very little about the Inga project has been made public and there has been virtually no engagement with Congolese civil society. This is a worrying factor in a country supposedly moving towards democracy, and would represent a continuation of the project's unfortunate history, for in its origins the project was prompted by Mobutu's political needs rather than the interests of the nation as a whole.

When the project was proposed in the early 1970s, it was intended to pre-empt a shortage of energy in the Copper-mining area of the Katanga province as an energy deficit posed a serious threat to the extraction and processing of the ores and the ambitions of Gecamine for expanding production. A feasibility study at the time proposed that the best way to accommodate the copper industry's need for more power would be to construct a new hydroelectric station at Busanga, close to the heart of Katanga's mining complex. This would have been a far preferable option economically and much less risky than linking the Inga Dam with Katanga, a decision which will require stringing 2 000 kilometres of power line (Schatzberg 1984: 295). However, Mobutu went ahead with the Inga project for two reasons. The first was to ensure political control over Katanga, which was the economic engine of his government, contributing some 60 per cent of the state's budget. The second was to diversify and strengthen the DRC's bargaining position *vis à vis* western partners for it was expected that the creation of the Inga–Katanga line would lead to competitive bidding from firms representing many industrialised nations, this providing plenty of opportunities for profit for Mobutu and the avaricious elite with which he had surrounded himself (Schatzberg 1984). It is clearly important for the quality and legitimacy of the DRC's new democracy that this unfortunate history should not be repeated, and that Inga should not become a means for the enrichment of a fortunate few elite rather than a project for spreading wealth amongst the entire population.

Conclusion

This chapter has argued the complementarity of South Africa's encouragement of peace in the DRC with its growing economic interest in exploiting that country's most valuable resources. South Africa's engagements in the DRC are also consonant with the Mbeki government's commitments to Nepad and its promotion of the latter as a blueprint for the future development of the continent. Even so, many dilemmas attend South Africa's increasing presence in the DRC.

South Africa is widely viewed as wanting to challenge the domination that western interests have exercised over the DRC since the mid-nineteenth century. At one level, this is widely welcomed by the Congolese, yet at the same time, many query whether South Africa has the capacity to take the lead in the rehabilitation of the entire mining sector and in the upgrading of the Inga Dam. Many of the South African government's interventions have been geared to creating a favourable environment for corporate investment, while seeking to ensure that this is not achieved at any potential cost to human rights, peace and security. All this is indicative of good intentions, and runs contrary to the views of critics who dismiss South African involvements in the DRC as driven by imperialistic ambitions with lucrative spin-offs for its political and business elite. However, for these hopes to be realised, South African business, inclusive of parastatals such as Eskom, will not only need to exhibit the capacity for following through on the ambitions of the government, but will also need to demonstrate a high level of social responsibility and a determination to rise above the appalling record which foreign corporations have left behind them in the DRC to date. For the moment, there are some encouraging signs, with Vodacom, for instance, taking a prominent role in sponsoring major sports activities and in granting bursaries to students to pursue their studies in South Africa; similarly, BHP Billiton is making fulsome noises about providing a strong social responsibility component alongside its investment in the project aluminium plant. Yet corporate words come cheap, and only time will tell whether South African corporations are prepared to combine their pursuit of profit with corporate behaviour that is mindful of the social needs of their Congolese employees and host communities.

For the moment, at least, the South African presence in the DRC is welcome. Even so, its increasing involvement in the Congo is accompanied by a sense of unease throughout the region. This is scarcely surprising in a continent where in the present era many conflicts are driven by a struggle for control over scarce natural resources. In investing in the DRC, therefore, South Africa will not only have to engage with western interests, but will also increasingly meet fierce African competition – and jealousy. For instance, those countries that intervened militarily during the recent war – Angola, Namibia and Zimbabwe – will not meekly accept their isolation by the more economically powerful South Africa, and the latter will meet much resistance politically and diplomatically if it comes to be seen as bent on reducing the DRC to the status of a neo-colony.

This chapter has focused primarily on mining and energy – yet water is another resource of which the DRC has plentiful supplies in a region which in future years will be facing major scarcity of this life-giving vital commodity. South Africa is already said to be dreaming up projects for diverting the water of the Congo River before it reaches the sea in order to satisfy its increasing industrial thirst – yet in so doing, it could well foment major conflict with its equally thirsty, yet far less powerful, neighbours. Will there come a time when South Africa is prepared to use force to secure access to what it considers vital resources in a manner analogous to the way in which the US today links military adventures in the Middle East to the protection of its supplies of oil? If so, then such action would sound the death knell of South Africa's present best intentions and signal the rise of a dangerous sub-imperialism.

Notes

1   On 17 December 2002 in Pretoria, the main Congolese parties to the conflict – the DRC government, the rebel movements, non-armed opposition and civil society – signed the Global and Inclusive Agreement. The Final Act was signed at Sun City on 2 April 2003.

2   The author conducted interviews with the DRC Ministry of Mining and the South African embassy to the DRC in February 2006.

3   This explains South Africa's commitment to peace on the continent. Congolese streaming out of the country because of the war invariably sought to go to South Africa and stemming this flow was most certainly one of South Africa's motivations for intervention.

4   This legislation was drafted in 2003 in conjunction with the World Bank. It provides prospecting permit holders with broad access to explore its areas of prospecting or properties under transparent and efficient permit process.

5   The Bill is aimed at promoting the local beneficiation of South Africa's minerals.

6   Eskom has been developing its energy strategy around forecasts of 4 per cent economic growth per annum over the next few years, which it expects will be accompanied by growth in electricity demand of 3–4 per cent per year. This will translate into an additional 1 200 megawatts of capacity every year to add to its current supply capacity of about 42 000 megawatts.

7   At present coal accounts for more than 90 per cent of the primary energy used by Eskom. The utility wishes to reduce this ratio by 10 per cent by 2012.

8   For environmental reasons South Africa would like to move away from coal to using gas, nuclear, hydro and other renewable energy sources.

9   SAPP is a body established to enable SADC member countries to trade in electricity.

10 Namibia is planning to start producing energy from the 800 megawatt baseload CCGT power station which is being established by the Namibian Manpower at Oranjemund. It has been set to start in 2009/10. Coal power stations are also being planned in Botswana and Mozambique.

11 See <http://www.irn.org/programs/safrica/index.php?id>.

References

Ajulu R (2005) Stabilizing the Democratic Republic of Congo: The role of the state and the corporate sector. Paper presented at a symposium organised by the Institute for Global Dialogue on the Perspectives on the DRC Transition.

All Party Parliamentary Group on the Great Lakes Region and Genocide Prevention (2002) *Cursed by riches: Who benefits from resource exploitation in the Democratic Republic of the Congo*. London: APPG.

Bond P (2005) Is the New Partnership for Africa's Development already passé? Africa Dialogue Lecture, Centre for International Political Studies, University of Pretoria, 15.02.05.

Braeckman C (1999) *l'Enjeu Congolais: L'Afrique Centrale après Mobutu*. Paris: Fayard.

Dlamini Zuma N (1999) Address of the South African Foreign Minister to the South African Institute of International Affairs, Johannesburg.

Economy, Finance and Infrastructure, Mineral and Energy Sub-Committee (2006) *Review of the Bilateral Cooperation between South Africa and the Democratic Republic of Congo.*

Gelb S (2001) *South Africa's role and importance in Africa and for the development of the African agenda.* Johannesburg: EDGE Institute.

Gelb S (2002) The New Partnership for Africa's development (NEPAD): Collective action, commitment and Credibility. Unpublished.

Hertz N (2001) *The silent takeover: Global capitalism and the death of democracy.* London: William Heinemann.

Human Rights Watch (2005) *Democratic Republic of Congo: The curse of gold.* United States: Marcus Bleasdale.

Landsberg C (2006) South Africa. In GM Khadiagala (Ed) *Security dynamics in Africa's Great Lakes Region.* Boulder: Lynne Reinner.

MacGaffey J (1991) *The real economy of Zaire.* Philadelphia: University of Pennsylvania Press.

Pahad A (1996) Foreign Minister's Annual Address, given by the Deputy Foreign Affairs Minister, Aziz Pahad, at the South African Institute of International Affairs, Johannesburg, 07.11.96.

Schatzberg MG (1984) Zaire. In TM Shaw & O Aluko (Eds) *The political economy of African foreign policy, comparative analysis.* Aldershot: Gower.

Scheffran J & Singer C (2004) Energy and security: From conflict to cooperation. *International Network of Engineers and Scientists Against Proliferation*, Bulletin 24 on Energy and Security.

Sigcau S (2003) Public works contribution to human resources development and employment strategy. Speech to Parliament by the minister, 28.02.03.

South Africa–DRC Bilateral Sub-Committee (2005) Report on the review of the bilateral co-operation between South Africa and the Democratic Republic of Congo, 23–27.11.05.

Taylor I & Williams P (2001) South African foreign policy and the Great Lakes crisis: An African Renaissance meets vagabondage politique? *African Affairs* 100: 265–86.

UN (2001) *Security Report of the UN Panel of Experts on the illegal exploitation of the natural resources and other forms of wealth of the Democratic Republic of the Congo*, (S 2001/357), Final, including Addendum to the Report (S/2001/1072). Vienna: UN.

Van der Steen D (1979) Le Zaire Malade de sa dependence extérieure: Apercu Historique et diagnostic de la Crise de l'Economie Zairoise en 1978. *Geneve-Afrique*, 17(1): 127–8.

Van Nieuwkerk A (2005) South Africa's role in Africa: An overview. Unpublished.

22 The Zimbabwean community in South Africa

Elinor Sisulu, Bhekinkosi Moyo and Nkosinathi Tshuma

The tale of South Africa and Zimbabwe in the past decade has been one of contrasts. The fortunes of South Africa have been on the rise while those of Zimbabwe have taken a dramatic dive. Although South Africa still faces the challenges of poverty, unemployment and increasing income disparities, the country's steady growth since 1994 has consolidated its position as the economic powerhouse in the southern African region and in Africa generally. Correspondingly, South Africa has developed into a respected member of the global community, playing decisive roles in regional and international initiatives such as the New Partnership for Africa's Development and in institutions such as the African Union (AU) and the United Nations.

Zimbabwe, on the other hand, has been gripped by a series of interlocking crises. Since 2000, the government's unconstitutional assault on the independence of the media, judiciary, and civil society and its disregard for the rule of law and basic human rights has caused a political and constitutional crisis, which in turn has had a knock-on effect on the economy. Disastrous economic policies have also resulted in an economic downturn of staggering proportions, characterised by de-industrialisation, mass unemployment, chaotically administered and incomplete land reform, and a social/humanitarian crisis in which state-sanctioned political violence and violence against women have become endemic. High HIV-infection rates, AIDS-related morbidity and mortality, a dramatic increase in mortality rates as a result of the collapsing health system and a rise in other social problems exacerbate this.

Far from resolving the political crisis, the parliamentary elections of March 2005, whose 'freedom and fairness' was heavily contested by the opposition and observers, deepened it. In the wake of the elections, which constructed a two-thirds parliamentary victory for the ruling Zimbabwe African National Union–Patriotic Front (Zanu–PF), the humanitarian and social crisis was exacerbated by the extraordinary post-election actions of the government. In May 2005, the government of Zimbabwe launched Operation Murambatsvina (loosely translated it means 'Operation drive out the filth'). According to the government, this 'clean-up campaign' was aimed at enforcing city by-laws to stop illegal trading, remove illegal settlements and 'clean up' the cities and towns of Zimbabwe. From mid-May to July 2005, army and police units demolished thousands of shacks, informal vending and manufacturing operations and even brick and mortar houses in every major urban centre of Zimbabwe. The demolitions then extended to farming settlements and peri-urban and rural areas.[1]

So devastating was the destruction that UN Secretary-General Kofi Annan called upon the Zimbabwe government to halt the demolitions and sent housing expert Anna Tibaijuka as Special Envoy to Harare to report on the government blitz. Tibaijuka (2005) described what she saw as 'a humanitarian crisis of catastrophic proportions'. The Tibaijuka report confirmed that 700 000 men, women and children were rendered homeless, without access to food, water and sanitation, or health care at the height of winter. Massive displacements disrupted the education of over 30 000 children as well as the treatment and care of thousands of people living with HIV/AIDS. 'Murambatsvina' targeted the most materially deprived and marginalised sections of the population. People barely managing to eke out a living were rendered homeless, helpless and destitute, their meagre possessions swept away by a 'Zimbabwean tsunami' (Tibaijuka 2005).

Today Zimbabwe has the unenviable distinction of having the fastest shrinking economy, the highest rate of inflation and the lowest life expectancy in the world. The World Health Organisation reported in early 2006 that Zimbabwe's women now have a lifespan of 34 years, while that of men is a mere 37 years.[2]

Because of these harsh conditions, Zimbabweans have been leaving for 'greener pastures' elsewhere, particularly in South Africa. Yet for Zimbabweans in South Africa, life is not as good as they might have hoped for. They cite xenophobia, discrimination, police harassment, unemployment and lack of access to basic services as some of the challenges they face. More critical is the denial by the South African government that there is a serious crisis in Zimbabwe that demands urgent attention. Against the background of an increased influx of Zimbabwean illegal and legal immigrants to South Africa, this stance concerns those who expect President Thabo Mbeki to put pressure on the Zimbabwean government to normalise the political situation and rebuild the economy, yet Mbeki has not publicly acknowledged that there is a crisis in Zimbabwe. Because of the political turmoil and economic collapse, it is estimated that some three to four million Zimbabweans have left the country in the past decade. Migration studies on Zimbabwe show South Africa and the UK to be the most preferred destinations. Significant numbers of Zimbabweans have also emigrated to Australia, New Zealand and Canada, as well as to other countries in the Southern African Development Community (SADC) region. Many qualified professionals such as nurses, pharmacists, teachers and doctors go to the UK but both skilled and unskilled migrants seek sanctuary in South Africa.

Different groups have different reasons for leaving Zimbabwe, ranging from professional, economic, political, educational to linguistic and historic factors. Skilled professionals like doctors, nurses and pharmacists leave mainly for economic reasons while journalists, teachers and the youth tend to leave for political reasons. Since the 2005 elections, it has not been easy to draw this dichotomy because politics has had a knock-on effect on the economy. We return to the relationship between politics and the economy later in the chapter when we pose the question as to whether Zimbabweans in South Africa are political refugees or economic immigrants.

According to the Central Bank of Zimbabwe, about 1.2 million Zimbabweans have left for South Africa since 1990.[3] It is not surprising that South Africa should be a preferred destination of Zimbabwean migrants. It is not just its proximity but also South Africa's economic strength that makes it an attractive destination. Added to this is a long historical tradition of migration across the Limpopo in both directions, dating back to precolonial times. The migration of Mzilikazi and the subsequent establishment of the Ndebele kingdom across the Limpopo in the nineteenth century and the northerly scramble by white settlers in search of mineral riches laid the foundations for enduring cultural, linguistic and social ties between South Africans, black and white, and their northern neighbour. Labour migrancy further consolidated these ties. The labour needs of the South African mining industry ensured that, in the first half of the twentieth century, it was virtually a rite of passage for young men from colonial Rhodesia to have a stint working in South African mines.

Since Zimbabwe's independence in 1980, there have been three waves of migration of Zimbabweans to South Africa. The first consisted of white people who left Zimbabwe after Zanu–PF's victory in the 1980 elections. The ascendancy of the much-feared guerilla leader, Robert Mugabe, resulted in the emigration of large numbers of white people. The second wave was made up of Ndebele refugees who fled the *Gukurahundi* massacres that took place in the Matabeleland and Midlands provinces in the south-western areas of Zimbabwe between 1983 and 1987. These refugees entered South Africa illegally so there is little documentation of numbers. Their cultural and linguistic affinity with the Zulu community enabled them to settle largely unnoticed in South Africa and many took on South African identities, some of them through unlawful means. Simultaneously, small numbers of professionals also began leaving Zimbabwe to seek better-paying jobs in South Africa. Finally, the current wave of migration is of Zimbabweans who have left their homeland since 2000 as a result of economic collapse or political persecution or a combination of both (Solidarity Peace Trust 2004). This chapter focuses primarily on these recent arrivals in South Africa and examines the state of the Zimbabwean community in this country. Many terms are used to describe these Zimbabweans living abroad: 'exiles', 'the diaspora', 'refugees' and 'immigrants'. For this chapter, we use the term 'Zimbabwean community' as it is inclusive of all Zimbabweans in South Africa, including those who are in South Africa officially, for professional and economic reasons.

The size and composition of the Zimbabwean community in South Africa

There has been much debate about the numbers of Zimbabweans in South Africa and estimates have varied from three to four million. In the absence of a detailed census it is necessary to rely on estimates but one thing is certain – there has been a huge increase in the Zimbabwean presence in South Africa in the past five years. There are several indicators for this. One is a significant change in the ethnic composition of the Zimbabwean community in South Africa. As was pointed out, historically Zimbabwean migrants or refugees came mainly from Ndebele communities in Zimbabwe. However, in the past five years there has been a massive increase in Zimbabweans of Shona ethnicity. A few years ago, it was not common to hear Shona being spoken in Johannesburg or any other South African city. Nowadays it is rare to move around without hearing snatches of conversation in Shona, especially in restaurants and shopping centres. In Gauteng, it is not unusual to enter a restaurant to find a Zimbabwean waiter. Zimbabweans also seem to be very visible in the security industry.

Currently, Zimbabweans are living in all parts of South Africa, with large concentrations in Gauteng, Limpopo, KwaZulu-Natal and the Western Cape. The professionals are concentrated in the major cities, especially Johannesburg. The good quality of Zimbabwean education pre- and post-independence has stood Zimbabwean professionals in good stead and they enjoy considerable success in the corporate world, especially financial services. An indication of their presence has been the formation of the Batanai-Bambanani Zimbabwean Association, a non-profit social organisation registered in South Africa to bring Zimbabweans together in a non-political, non-religious community to assist each other in business or social affairs. In 2004 the organisation had over 200 members, most of them highly qualified professionals occupying senior positions in South African businesses and institutions. A charity dinner organised by Batanai-Bambanani in 2004 was attended by over 300 Zimbabwean professionals, obviously quite affluent, judging from the funds raised for local charities.

A study by the International Organisation of Migration (Bloch 2005) revealed that about 45 per cent of Zimbabweans in South Africa are in possession of a diploma in higher education. Men were more likely to have qualifications in engineering and women were more likely to be nurses. Prominent among Zimbabwean professionals in South Africa are health-care workers, teachers, media workers and journalists.

Zimbabwe's health-care sector has been particularly affected by the brain drain of recent years. According to Chikanda (2005), this has been two-dimensional. First, there has been a move of health professionals within the country from public institutions to the private sector. For example, in 1997, of the 1 634 doctors who were registered in the country, only 551 (33.7%) worked in the public sector while as many as 67 per cent of nurses in the public sector were considering a move to the private sector. Then there are the health professionals who have left Zimbabwe to work in the UK, South Africa, Canada, Botswana and Swaziland (Chikanda 2005). In 2000, the Ministry of Health in Zimbabwe estimated that it was losing about 20 per cent of its health-care professionals to emigration. The ministry also noted that between 1998 and 2000, about 100 doctors and 1 800 nurses had left Zimbabwe and in 2002, 2 346 UK work permits were issued to nurses from Zimbabwe (Chikanda 2005).

Reasons for leaving Zimbabwe cited by health-care professionals are economic, political, professional and educational. At least two studies on the health sector (Chikanda 2005; Gaidzanwa 1999) argue that economic factors are the major reasons for emigration. According to Chikanda (2005), a study of 59 doctors, 23 pharmacists, 15 dentists and 215 nurses (a total of 312 health professionals) revealed that 50 per cent were contemplating leaving the country for economic reasons. These included better remuneration in the country of their destination and the opportunity of earning an income to remit home. Other reasons included insufficient opportunities for promotion and self-improvement in Zimbabwe. Health-care professionals leaving the country also cited lack of good equipment in public hospitals and clinics. However, although most of these professionals in the health sector do not cite the political situation as their direct determinant to leave the country, it is certainly a major factor in their consideration. As these professionals argued in Chikanda's study, it is only in addressing the political crisis that economic recovery will be achieved. Many consider the collapse of democratic institutions, absence of the rule of law and the impasse between the ruling party (Zanu–PF) and the Movement for Democratic Change (MDC) as major factors contributing to the economic crisis. Indeed, about 45 per cent of Chikanda's respondents cited pessimism about the future and 23 per cent cited political violence and crime as their reasons for leaving the country. Furthermore, discussions with Zimbabwean health professionals in South Africa reveal that in the post-2002 era, health professionals – especially those who worked in rural areas – left mainly because of political persecution.

Anecdotal information and some research indicate that the same applies to teachers. In a research report commissioned by the Solidarity Peace Trust, the Reverend Nicholas Mukaronda (2005) found that in most rural areas in Zimbabwe teachers are regarded by the government as torch-bearers of the opposition MDC. Consequently they became targets of political violence so that many teachers fled to South Africa between 2000 and 2004. Loose networks of private schools and colleges in South Africa now employ a significant number of these teachers under very exploitative conditions. These include violation of contractual arrangements by employers, such as payment of scandalously low salaries or no payments at all. As most of these teachers are undocumented and do not have legal status, they have no legal recourse (Nyathi, interview 23.03.06). Some have been forced into menial jobs in the security and hospitality sectors. Others are jobless and destitute.

To address these challenges, teachers have established the Forum for Zimbabwean Teachers in South Africa. Some of their objectives include the organisation of exiled Zimbabwean teachers and lobbying for their recognition as political refugees in the country. Teachers' also intend registering with the South African Council for Educators. According to Magugu Nyathi, writing in *The Zimbabwean* (26.01.06), the South African chapter of the Progressive Teachers Union of Zimbabwe (PTUZ) registered 400 teachers in the month of January 2006 alone.[4] Bongani Nyathi, Interim Chairperson of the PTUZ in South Africa, claims that there are about 10 000 Zimbabwean teachers now in South Africa, 3 000 working for private colleges and 50 in state schools (Nyathi, interview 23.03.06). The PTUZ estimates that since 2000, about 4 000 teachers have left Zimbabwe per year. This suggests that about 26 000 teachers have left Zimbabwe since that date. The majority of these are in South Africa.

If teachers are seen as a threat by Zanu–PF, journalists are considered an even greater threat. Describing the state of the media in Zimbabwe in the period 2000–05, Professor Terence Ranger writes:

> I ought to be armored, then, against imagining that only recently have Zimbabwean newspapers become prejudiced and propagandistic. And I know very well, of course, that too many newspapers in Britain and the United States serve the national interests and imperial interests of those countries. Nevertheless, and despite all this, I do think that the rise of 'patriotic journalism' represents something qualitatively different. And I do not think that Zimbabweans ought to be asked to tolerate destructive journalism in their country today because the Rhodesians used to do much the same or because the Western press is prejudiced. Zimbabweans deserve better than this. (2005: 10)

The closure of media space through legislation like the Access to Information and Protection of Privacy Act and the Public Order Security Act, and the shutting down of critical publications like the *Daily News*, the *Tribune* and the *Weekly Times*, have made life very difficult for journalists who have also been arrested, detained, intimidated, imprisoned and deported. In February 2005, Zanu–PF's Department of Information and Publicity released a booklet listing what it called Zimbabwean traitors. Among those listed were journalists, Basildon Peta and Geoffrey Nyarota, as well as Trevor Ncube, publisher of the *Mail & Guardian* in South Africa.[5]

Consequently, media personnel are prominent among professionals leaving Zimbabwe. Most of these journalists – 34 of whom were interviewed in London and Johannesburg by the Committee to Protect Journalists (CPJ) in 2005 – cited political factors for leaving Zimbabwe. Journalists such as Abel Mutsakani, former manager of the banned *Daily News*, argued that they left Zimbabwe so that they could report freely and independently while others like Magugu Nyathi of *The Tribune* saw no job prospects in Zimbabwe (Witchel 2005).

There are approximately 100 Zimbabwean journalists in South Africa. Some are unemployed. Some have work permits and work in the mainstream South African media. Mutsakani and other journalists have set up an online paper in South Africa, *ZimOnline*. Others are now doing other jobs because they were unable to find employment within their profession (Chibaya, interview 23.03.06). Although a few journalists have found jobs with international media outlets, a significant number of them find it difficult to make ends meet. According to the study by CPJ, most make ends meet by working in factories, service jobs or clerical positions (Witchel 2005).

Unemployed journalists have formed the Cross Border Association of Journalists (CAJ) with a membership of over 30. CAJ creates opportunities for journalists by linking them with media institutions in South Africa and abroad for freelancing. CAJ also works closely with organised civil society formations in lobbying for media freedom.

Zimbabwean students constitute another significant part of the Zimbabwean community in South Africa. Research currently being carried out by Philani Zamchiya for the Crisis in Zimbabwe Coalition has established that over 75 per cent of these students are considering not returning home at the end of their studies. Instead, they want to seek employment in South Africa. Most of these students are supported by relatives in South Africa, UK and USA but there are others funded by the Zimbabwean government through presidential scholarships. In 2006 there were 500 Zimbabweans at Fort Hare University, 400 of whom had presidential scholarships.[6]

Students have established a range of associations to cater for their social, economic and political interests. Like other Zimbabweans, students complain of isolation and xenophobia. The Association of Zimbabwean Students in South African Universities (AZISSU) offers support in times of need. A study by Tevera (2005) showed that many students currently studying in Zimbabwe have decided to leave the country soon after they graduate. Their intended destinations are South Africa, the UK and other neighbouring countries. A study of 1192 students showed that while close to 60 per cent of them were proud to be Zimbabwean and would want to contribute to the economic development of the country, only 3 per cent were satisfied with their economic conditions. As a result, about 75 per cent of them wish to leave the country soon after their graduation (Tevera 2005). They are also encouraged by their families to leave the country so that they can remit money home.

At the other end of the economic spectrum are unskilled agricultural workers who work on farms in the Limpopo province along the border with Zimbabwe. This is a group that does not enjoy the same visibility as Zimbabweans in Gauteng and information on their numbers is not reliable. Anecdotal evidence, however, indicates that they are a major source of labour in the agricultural sector in Limpopo province and they may well constitute the largest proportion of Zimbabweans in

South Africa. It is difficult, however, to get exact figures because the majority of them are undocumented and many are seasonal workers who move back and forth across the border between Zimbabwe and South Africa.[7]

Among the unskilled and undocumented workers are a large number of disabled people, especially the blind. In the past two years there has been a dramatic increase of blind persons who survive by begging for money, often with the help of their young children, in the streets of Johannesburg. This group faces extreme difficulties in accessing decent accommodation and other basic services. A television programme on SABC 3's *Special Assignment* (07.03.06) established that over ten blind refugee families shared a single room. They have formed their own organisation, the Disabled People of Zimbabwe, to try to improve their plight.

Cross-border traders constitute another section of the Zimbabwean community in South Africa. Historically, cross-border migration between Zimbabwe and South Africa has been a male activity because it was deemed too far and too risky for women (Tevera & Zinyama 2002). Since independence in Zimbabwe, however, there has been an increase in the number of women pursuing cross-border trade in South Africa. The pattern was for them to sell crochet goods and other crafts in South Africa while purchasing South African goods to sell back home. However, with the decline of the Zimbabwean economy, increasing numbers of these women have opted to stay in South Africa permanently. Interviews with refugees indicate that Operation Murambatsvina has made it impossible to carry out their trade because of police harassment and the confiscation of their goods in Zimbabwe.

Socio-economic and political associational life

A clear indication of the increased presence of Zimbabweans in South Africa is the plethora of organisations that have emerged in the past five years, most of them specifically formed to assist increased numbers of asylum seekers and refugees fleeing from political persecution in Zimbabwe. There was a significant influx of refugees after the parliamentary elections in 2000 when, for the first time, Zanu–PF faced a stiff political challenge from the newly formed MDC. Opposition members were subjected to intense political harassment, persecution and torture. The pattern was repeated in the presidential elections in 2002 and to a lesser extent in the March 2005 parliamentary election. Every election and by-election in Zimbabwe has produced refugees fleeing from direct and indirect political violence. The Solidarity Peace Trust estimates that over 300 000 people have been victims of human rights violations of various kinds over the last four years (Solidarity Peace Trust 2004).

The MDC office set up in Johannesburg in 1999 was at the forefront of receiving and assisting Zimbabweans fleeing political repression. Realising that as a political party the MDC was unable to cope with the increasing demands for humanitarian assistance from its members, the party's leadership requested a group of

Zimbabwean professionals to facilitate the setting up of a special body to focus on the humanitarian needs of Zimbabwean refugees. The result was the Heal Zimbabwe Trust.

While the lengthy process of establishing the Trust was going on, Themba Lesizwe, the South African network of trauma service providers, was working with Amani Trust in Zimbabwe to provide a safe space and psychosocial assistance for Zimbabweans fleeing from political persecution. One of the organisations in the Themba Lesizwe network, the Centre for the Study of Violence and Reconciliation, provided trauma counselling for Zimbabweans. Themba Lesizwe also sponsored the Tree of Life workshops run by a group of Zimbabweans to promote psychosocial healing. The South African Council of Churches, the South African Catholic Bishops' Conference and other church-related organisations such as the Solidarity Peace Trust and the Jesuit Refugee Services also provided humanitarian assistance to the Zimbabwean refugee community. The churches also provided a powerful advocacy voice on human rights violations in Zimbabwe as well as being a source of information on the magnitude of the Zimbabwean refugee phenomenon. St Mary's Anglican Cathedral and the Central Methodist Mission came together to form an ecumenical refugee ministries service to provide a walk-in centre for refugees in Johannesburg.

While the centre at St Mary's Cathedral in downtown Johannesburg is a service to all refugees, the majority of its clientele are Zimbabweans. The Central Methodist Mission in Pritchard Street in Johannesburg has been swamped by Zimbabwean refugees and recently housed as many as 600 refugees (Ngenzi, interview 10.05.06). Meanwhile, Zimbabwean refugees use disused buildings around the metropolitan area of Johannesburg for shelter. In March this year, one such building was gutted by fire, killing two Zimbabwean and ten Malawian immigrants.

South African non-governmental organisations (NGOs) such as Lawyers for Human Rights, the Wits Law Clinic and Black Sash have provided legal assistance to refugees. Like other refugee service providers, the numbers of Zimbabweans seeking assistance have overwhelmed them. The Centre for the Study of Violence and Reconciliation has also provided counselling services to refugees and it currently houses the Zimbabwe Torture Victims' project.

Zimbabweans themselves have also formed a number of organisations to address the plight of refugees, asylum seekers and undocumented individuals. These include the Southern African Women's Institute of Migration Affairs (SAWIMA), the Zimbabwe Political Victims' Association, Concerned Zimbabweans Abroad and the Zimbabwe Exiles' Forum, among others. These organisations use their limited means to assist refugee communities by providing food, blankets, shelter, organising self-help projects, facilitating access to the asylum application process, and easing access to education and health facilities. However, they have limited capacity and resources, making it difficult for them to service their communities to the degree required. The Zimbabwe Research Initiative published research on the cost of the Zimbabwean crisis in the South African economy and sought to mobilise Zimbabweans in the corporate world. The Peace and Democracy Project (PDP) was established to mobilise young Zimbabweans to work for change. The PDP organised a number of forums on the crisis in Zimbabwe, which brought leaders of the MDC and civil society from Zimbabwe to address the plight of Zimbabweans in South Africa.

The establishment of the Crisis in Zimbabwe Coalition's South Africa office in the closing months of 2003 signalled the coming together of Zimbabwe's major civil society coalition with members of the Zimbabwean diaspora in South Africa to pursue the common goal of co-ordinating an effort to end the multi-ayered crisis in Zimbabwe and build a democratic social, economic and political order in that country. The Crisis in Zimbabwe Coalition is a network of civic organisations, with a mandate derived from a conference held on 4 August 2001 at which 250 civil society organisations met and outlined the major dimensions of the Zimbabwean crisis. The Crisis Coalition International/Regional Programme was set up in 2003 to conduct a sustained advocacy programme regionally and internationally to shift the debate on Zimbabwe, especially in Africa, from a narrow focus on the land question to the real causes of the current crisis, that is, the disastrous economic and political programmes pursued by the government.

In November 2004, the Crisis Coalition's South Africa office and the Heal Zimbabwe Trust organised a meeting of 22 Zimbabwean civil society bodies based in South Africa. The meeting resolved that closer co-ordination was necessary to avoid duplication and a wasting of resources and to foster increased co-operation between organisations. An example of the co-operation between the South African-based Zimbabwean organisations was the holding of a mock election at the Zimbabwean embassy in Pretoria on the eve of Zimbabwe's March 2005 election. About 1 000 Zimbabweans took part in the activity. Encouraged by this success, a handful of groups formed the Zimbabwe Civil Society Organisations' Forum, which aimed to bring all the civil society organisations together under one umbrella. The forum aims to hold an international conference for the entire Zimbabwean diaspora in Johannesburg. In the meantime it holds public meetings on topical issues relating to the Zimbabwean exile community.

South African organisations have also given solidarity to the Zimbabwean civil society organisations. The Zimbabwe Solidarity Forum, a network of South African civil society bodies, trade unions, student movements and faith-based organisations was established in 2004 to co-ordinate solidarity efforts and influence the South African government's policy towards Zimbabwe. The network has also facilitated dialogue amongst its South African constituencies to debate the Zimbabwean crisis more broadly.

More than 3 000 South Africans and Zimbabweans travelled to the Musina border post in 2005 to protest against violations of Zimbabweans' human rights. The Solidarity Rally was organised by Civicus, Amnesty International South Africa, World Alliance for Citizen Participation and the South African NGO Coalition. The rally highlighted problems faced by Zimbabwean refugees and conditions at the Lindela detention centre.[8] The Congress of South African Trade Unions and the Young Communists' League have also offered solidarity to the Zimbabwean organisations, organising pickets at the Zimbabwean embassy and dispatching fact-finding missions to Zimbabwe.

Despite all this activity, it is not possible to point to any major successes in mobilising the Zimbabwean diaspora. This amorphous diaspora, with its class and ethnic divisions, has failed to act in a concerted way to lobby for change in Zimbabwe. The lack of trust that is so much a feature of politics in Zimbabwe is unfortunately replicated in the diaspora groups. Most professional Zimbabweans prefer to stay away from politics, some because they have had a negative experience of political involvement in Zimbabwe, others because the demands of their jobs do not allow them the time to be involved in anything other than their professional work. Fear of arrest prevents many in the refugee community from actively participating in political activity (Muzondidya 2006). Sheer destitution within the refugee community is another inhibiting factor: people who do not know where their next meal is coming from find it difficult to raise funds for transport costs to take them to such public events as demonstrations.

Unfortunately the political rivalries and factionalism in the MDC in Zimbabwe were replicated in South Africa with the main party office aligning itself to Secretary-General Welshman Ncube and against leader Morgan Tsvangirai. In June 2005 tensions between rival MDC groups erupted into violence with fatal consequences. The deaths of four young Zimbabweans widened the already yawning chasm between the two groups. Divisions within the MDC, which culminated in the split over the senate elections in August 2005, have impacted negatively on interest in political engagement within all sections of the Zimbabwean community.

Between a rock and a hard place: harassments, arrests, detentions and deportations

> *Sibalekel' omnyama, sibalekela komnyama; South Africa usihlangabeza ngenduku, basithata basifaka eLindela, Thabo Mbeki ngabe sikwenzeni na?* (Ndebele song meaning, 'We are running away from a repressive black government to a well-governed black one; hoping to be assisted/accepted. However on our arival, we are sent straight into a frying pan. Thabo Mbeki, what wrong have we done?') (Nxumalo, interview 02.06.06)

The experience of Zimbabweans who cross the Limpopo to seek refuge and sustenance is poignantly expressed in the song *Lindela* by Zimbabwean musical group Abanqobi Bomhlaba. The song appeals to President Mbeki and Home Affairs Minister Nosiviwe Nqakula to understand the predicament of Zimbabwean exiles who are running away from terror only to be met by arrest, imprisonment and deportation when they arrive in South Africa.

Harassment, detention and the unlawful deportation of Zimbabweans are a common phenomenon. The *Herald* newspaper reported in January that 3 067 Zimbabweans were deported within a period of five days during the festive season (*Herald* 04.01.06). The process of arrest, detention and deportation of Zimbabweans by the South African authorities has been challenged by civil society organisations as unlawful. Zimbabweans who are legal residents have also been arrested. Conditions in the Lindela detention centre have also been deplored, resulting in Minister Nqakula establishing a commission of inquiry to investigate deaths of Zimbabweans in detention. Meanwhile, organisations such as the Southern African Women's Institute of Migration Affairs, Black Sash, Wits Law Clinic and Zimbabwe Torture Victims Project assist Zimbabwean asylum seekers to acquire legal status.

Xenophobia is another challenge that Zimbabweans regularly face. In Johannesburg, for example, a number of Zimbabweans who are in possession of asylum-seeker permits, work permits or other forms of permits have been denied the right to rent accommodation in certain flats. Locals use slang terms such as 'Makwerekwere' when referring to Zimbabweans and other foreigners. In January 2006, South African-based Zimbabwean civil society organisations in partnership with their South African counterparts commissioned a study on harassment, arrests, detentions and deportations of Zimbabwean immigrants (Moyo 2006). Some of the findings of interviews with 84 respondents (51 held Section 22 permits allowing them time to appeal for political asylum, 29 were undocumented, 3 held Section 24 refugee recognition status and 1 had an appointment letter issued by the Department of Home Affairs [DoHA]) are detailed in Table 22.1.

Political refugees or economic migrants?

The generally hostile treatment they face by the South African authorities arises because Zimbabweans are defined as economic migrants rather than as political refugees. By definition, economic migrants are people who leave their place of work and residence and go to another for better jobs and economic security (Cortes 2004). Political refugees are those who flee persecution in their home country.

South Africa has comprehensive legal instruments dealing with refugees. The South African Refugee Act defines a refugee as 'a person who has a well-founded fear of being persecuted on account of his or her race, religion, political opinion or

Table 22.1 *Experiences by Zimbabweans under various authorities*

Experiences	Number of respondents	Authority
Arrested/detained at least once	59	
Arrested/detained with valid Section 22 permit at time of arrest	10	SAPS, Lindela officials
Exposed to extortion (bribe solicited to stop having permit torn/being deported)	55	Beitbridge border SAPS, Lindela SAPS, DoHA staff, Johannesburg & Durban SAPS
Bribe solicited and paid	45	DoHA staff, SAPS
Deported (undocumented asylum seekers)	14	Lindela and Musina (Makhado) DoHA officials
Unprovoked physical assault	12	SAPS, security guards at refugee reception office (RRO), metro police
Harassed/verbally abused/threatened	21	SAPS, DoHA officials, security guards at RROs and Lindela
Threatened that Section 22 permit will be torn up if bribe is not forthcoming	6	SAPS officials
Asylum paper torn/confiscated (Section 22 permit)	3	SAPS in Johannesburg and Durban
Protection letter destroyed (issued by recognised refugee service provider)	2	SAPS in Johannesburg
Fell ill while at Lindela, Setshego, etc.	12	Lindela and Setshego (Musina) officials
Denied basic rights upon detention (eg. food, right to inform relatives/lawyers of arrest, over-detention, inhumane living conditions, right to appeal decision to be deported)	9	Lindela and Setshego (Musina) officials
Sexual favours solicited to secure release	2	SAPS police in Johannesburg
Attempt on life (eg. being shot at)	2	SA Army, SAPS
File missing or lost	2	DoHA, RROs & Refugee Status Determination officers

Source: Moyo (2006)

membership to a particular social group, or whose life, physical safety or freedom is threatened on account of external aggression, occupation, foreign domination, or other events seriously disturbing or disrupting public order in either part or whole of that country' (South Africa Refugee Act No. 130 of 1998). Asylum seekers are granted a Section 22 permit, which allows them to work and to apply for refugee status. If the application for refugee status is successful, the applicant is granted a Section 24 permit. According to the Refugee Act, many Zimbabweans currently in South Africa qualify for asylum and refugee status. Many have applied for asylum and refugee status but very few have been successful. The records of DoHA show that as of the beginning of 2005, only 86 of 8 000 Zimbabwean applications for political asylum had been successful.[9] A recent study on refugees commissioned by South African-based Zimbabwean civil society organisations and their South African counterparts shows that applicants spend a lot of time queuing outside RROs. They also show that Zimbabwean asylum seekers find it extremely difficult to obtain Section 22 asylum-seeker permits or the Section 24 refugee permits whose processing, anyway, can take between ten months and three years to be completed. Furthermore, some officials want to be bribed and many Zimbabwean immigrants have failed to raise the required amounts. The result is that many are not documented as refugees.

Political refugees, by definition, fear to return to their native countries because of the likelihood or threat of persecution. Economic migrants on the other hand are free to return to their homes as they wish. Indeed, their primary purpose in a 'foreign country is to make money and go back home to buy land, property and support their families' (Cortes 2004: 3). Yet this distinction is not relevant to the situation of the majority of Zimbabweans in South Africa, most of whom are illegal immigrants because of the complex nexus between the political crisis and the economic implosion in Zimbabwe. Most Zimbabweans who have come to South Africa in the past five years have been fleeing political persecution and economic collapse or a combination of the two. In addition, as a result of the porous nature of national borders, these illegal and undocumented Zimbabweans travel back to Zimbabwe clandestinely, especially during festive seasons. They do not need passports; they simply cross the borders. Thus, a classic definition of a refugee as someone who is not able to return home does not apply. Even so, we cannot easily dismiss this large group of Zimbabweans as simply economic migrants because they are in South Africa due to the interplay between the political crisis and the economic downturn in Zimbabwe. If there was political stability, good governance and observance of the rule of law, many Zimbabweans would still be in their country. Indeed, research has shown that Zimbabweans would want to return to their country when things normalise (Bloch 2005; Chikanda 2005; Tevera 2005).

Although there is no study currently of the impact of Operation Murambatsvina on migration figures from Zimbabwe to South Africa, it is likely that a significant proportion of the 700 000 individuals who were displaced crossed the border into South Africa.[10] Many are living in South African illegally as undocumented migrants. Operation Murambatsvina should be classified, in our view, as an event that seriously disrupted public order in most of Zimbabwe. Under the Refugee Act, victims of this controversial operation should automatically qualify for asylum and refugee status.

The reason most often given by home affairs for rejecting Zimbabwean asylum applications is that 'there is no war in Zimbabwe'. The South African government has never acknowledged the extent of the economic collapse in Zimbabwe nor the widespread human rights violations over the past five years. Consequently, Zimbabwe is not recognised as a refugee-producing country in the same way that the Democratic Republic of Congo (DRC), Somalia or Angola are. President Mbeki's 2006 'State of the Nation' address made no mention of Zimbabwe, despite making reference to troubles in the DRC, Ivory Coast and Sudan. This lack of political recognition is reflected in the attitudes to Zimbabwean asylum seekers of officials of the DoHA and the South African Police Services.

There is a need for the South African government to recognise the extent of the humanitarian crisis in Zimbabwe and accept that although what is occurring there may not qualify in official parlance as 'war', the consequences of government actions against the populace are as grave and damaging as those inflicted by any full-scale conflict. A report recently released by the Centre for Global Development revealed that:

> In mid-2005 the average Zimbabwean had fallen back to that [1953] level, wiping out the income gains over the past 52 years...The scale and speed of this income decline is unusual outside of a war situation. In fact, the income losses in Zimbabwe have been greater than those experienced during recent conflicts in Ivory Coast, Democratic Republic of Congo and Sierra Leone. (Clemens & Moss 2005)[11]

Charting the way forward
Why Zimbabwe?

Those advocating for a change in the South African government's attitude towards Zimbabwe are often met with an irritated response: 'Why Zimbabwe when there are more people dying in conflicts in other parts of Africa?' Such advocates are often rudely told by Zanu–PF sympathisers that the only reason Zimbabwe receives so much attention is because Robert Mugabe took the land from the white farmers, inviting the wrath of western powers on his head. Their argument goes on to accuse the white-dominated South African media of conducting an anti-Mugabe campaign under the influence of white Rhodesians who have settled in South Africa. 'What can South Africa do anyway? Do you expect South Africa to invade Zimbabwe?' they ask.

Why Zimbabwe indeed? The most compelling reason for South Africa to pay urgent attention to the Zimbabwean crisis is self-interest. No one should ignore a house that goes up in flames next door. It is abnormal and indeed 'inappropriate' to be concerned about fires in a distant suburb when the house right next door is burning and its residents are running to your house for shelter. Furthermore, the indications are that the political, economic and humanitarian crises in Zimbabwe will deepen. Consequently, the numbers of Zimbabweans filtering into South Africa will increase. There were reports in 2005 that in some villages in Limpopo province, the influx of Zimbabweans looking for food was so high that Zimbabweans could have 'outnumbered' the locals.[12] Clearly, such an influx is bound to place severe stress on communities in which resources are scarce and services are poor. The fact is that the most materially deprived communities are the ones most affected by the influx from Zimbabwe.

While many South Africans have recognised the suffering of their Zimbabwean brothers and sisters and opened their doors to them, there have also been xenophobic responses to the influx, with sometimes fatal consequences. Early in 2006, violent clashes broke out between South African nationals and Zimbabweans in Olivienhoutbosch, an informal settlement south of Pretoria, allegedly triggered by the allocation of housing to 'foreigners'. Two Zimbabweans died and several others were injured.[13] Recognising the scale of the Zimbabwean refugee problem and providing material assistance to communities that are flooded with large numbers of refugees would avoid such clashes.

Zimbabweans in South Africa are often victims of crimes such as rape, assaults, and police intimidation, but they are also sometimes the perpetrators of crime. Destitute, undocumented young people unable to find employment or further their education are vulnerable to the temptation to turn to crime. Organisations such as SAWIMA have long acknowledged this vulnerability and have campaigned for programmes to prevent young Zimbabweans from becoming involved in illegal activities.

Zimbabwean organisations have long sounded the warning that the lawlessness of the Zimbabwean government will have grave consequences for the region. Five individuals, two of whom were Zimbabweans, according to police reports, allegedly masterminded a robbery in March 2006 at the Johannesburg airport. This came in the wake of a series of cash-in-transit heists and a string of well-planned robberies at casinos towards the end of 2005. A senior Zimbabwe army officer recently commented that it was not surprising that serving and retired soldiers of the Zimbabwe National Army would become part of the spiralling crime wave in South Africa. In his words:

> The low pay, low morale and the fact that junior officers have been watching senior officers feathering their nests illegally since the DRC conflict has contributed in a big way towards crime in the service. So we now have retired and serving members who form themselves into groups that go around robbing.[14]

Crime prevention strategies have to take into account the impunity and lack of accountability of the armed forces in Zimbabwe as well as the implications of the massive influx of illegal immigrants into South Africa and other neighbouring countries.

South Africa's responses

The deaths of two Zimbabwean detainees in Lindela in July 2005 prompted a commission of enquiry into conditions at the centre by the Minister of Home Affairs.

The report produced by the commission acknowledged that conditions at Lindela, especially regarding medical care, were not as they should be. The minister declared the report 'a damning report and an indictment on her department'.[15] She refused, however, to accept allegations that Zimbabwean asylum seekers and refugees were among those detained in Lindela and that some had been at some stage deported to Zimbabwe. She was adamant that the only people detained in Lindela and deported to their countries of origin were people who were illegally in the country. She was insistent that the South African government is conscious of its obligations in international law and that it would not deport people who genuinely qualified for asylum. She welcomed further engagement with Zimbabwean organisations on the matter.

Clearly, the Zimbabwean influx into South Africa is a serious issue and it is encouraging that the Minister of Home Affairs has committed herself to addressing it in a more systematic and humane manner. She is, however, hampered by the lack of capacity of her department to deal with the magnitude of the influx. In August 2005, she told a parliamentary portfolio committee that her department would be launching a six-month programme to deal with the backlog of refugee applications estimated at 100 000. This undertaking was made against the backdrop of 50 000 Zimbabweans deported from South Africa in 2005, up from 45 000 in 2004 (Moyo 2006).

Improving the process of asylum seeking

What can South Africa do about the Zimbabwean refugee issue? A recent study by the Crisis Coalition (Moyo 2006) makes a number of recommendations to DoHA. These include improving access to RROs around the country for the more efficient processing of asylum applications, the determination of status, and the issuing of refugee identity documents; the establishment of information desks at all RROs to assist with the orientation of asylum seekers and refugees to the asylum-system process, as well as to attend to their queries, strengthen its anti-corruption unit and guarantee adequate resources.

The study urges the South African government to conduct objective and independent investigations urgently to ascertain the reasons why asylum seekers continue to hold Section 22 permits for more than three years when in law they ought to be held for a maximum of six months. Further, there should be provision for a clear complaint mechanism for asylum seekers and other clients to register complaints and to provide assurance that complaints will be considered without prejudice to refugee status claims, to ensure that the staff member about whom the complaint is directed is not involved in receiving or processing the complaint, and to assist illiterate clients to submit complaints. Corruption should be combated and there should be clear signs at RROs in the main languages of asylum seekers which state that all services are provided free of charge and that any request by reception office personnel for money, sexual or other favours should be reported immediately.

Further, the study calls upon the Independent Complaints Directorate to conduct a comprehensive investigation into the police's handling of foreign nationals in South Africa, as well as the education and sensitisation of the South African Police Services to issues of xenophobia and their role in protecting the rights and interests of foreigners. South African police, particularly those working at RROs and at immigration points, must be trained on the validity and availability of Section 22 permits in the hands of refugees, as it would seem that it is unclear to them that they are legal documents conferring certain rights on the holders. The Department of Community Safety and the South African Police Services are also urged to institute investigations and to take disciplinary steps against police officers who are implicated in the breaching of regulations. These practical recommendations will alleviate much suffering and make for a more humane and just process for asylum seekers.

Educational opportunities

Zimbabweans in the southern African region are more likely to return to Zimbabwe than those who have gone further afield to places such as the UK, Canada, North America, Australia or New Zealand. Some of the Zimbabwean refugees are young student leaders who have been expelled from Zimbabwean tertiary institutions, which have been the targets of a concerted campaign of state-sponsored violence. There is an urgent need for a scholarship programme for Zimbabweans to attend tertiary institutions in the region. Such a programme would simultaneously address several major needs of Zimbabwean society such as increasing support for human rights defenders, building the capacity of civil society organisations, developing leadership skills for future leaders and alleviating the brain drain by retaining the most gifted and capable young people within the region.

Humanitarian assistance to refugees

Currently, churches provide assistance to Zimbabwean refugees. However, this is uncoordinated, piecemeal and inadequate. When the scale of the Zimbabwean influx into South Africa is taken into account, it is surprising that the Zimbabweans present in the country have not been declared a 'vulnerable mobile population'. Such a declaration would allow for the development of a comprehensive humanitarian assistance programme for asylum seekers and refugees with inputs from relief agencies such as the International Organisation for Migration and the International Red Cross. Such a programme would cost the South African government nothing since international donors would fund it in much the same way as South African and Zimbabwean refugees and communities received support when they were in Zambia during the liberation struggle. It would not only be destitute refugees who would benefit but also the South African communities in which they find themselves.

One of the reasons that a comprehensive relief package has not been prepared for refugees is the reluctance on the part of the South African government and even some church bodies to create 'magnets' that might encourage even more Zimbabweans to leave the country. This view fails to take into account the fact that large numbers of Zimbabweans are already in South Africa and that the only way to reverse the influx is to address the political, social, economic and humanitarian crises in Zimbabwe. However, countries in the region have refused to acknowledge the scale of the crisis, even in the face of the overwhelming evidence. Manuel Barosso, the European Union Commission President, said as much when he met with President Mbeki in June 2005. Barosso specifically expressed disappointment with the AU's handling of Zimbabwe over its controversial clean-up operations.[16] Although Mbeki promised Barosso that he would respond to the UN envoy's report, we are still waiting for him and indeed any other head of state in the SADC region to act.

As long as the Zimbabwe government receives the moral support of its regional neighbours, it will continue with its gross violations of the rights of the most vulnerable of its citizens. These citizens will in turn respond by pouring into neighbouring South Africa and, to a lesser degree, Botswana.

So what *should* South Africa do? At the very least the South African government should acknowledge the magnitude of the crisis and stop trying to stave off international pressure on Zimbabwe. The South African and other governments of the region should encourage the Zimbabwean government to take comprehensive action to implement in full the recommendations of the report of the UN Secretary General's Special Envoy (Tibaijuka 2005), including:

- Compensating those whose property was unlawfully destroyed, creating an environment for effective relief, reconstruction and resettlement, and ensuring unhindered access of humanitarian workers and delivery of aid to victims of the operation;
- Holding to account those responsible for planning and executing the operation, including through prosecution where laws were broken; and
- Respecting its international obligations to protect the rights of refugees and granting full citizenship to former migrant workers residing for a long period in Zimbabwe, as well as their descendants.

The South African government should also hold Zimbabwe to its obligations under the African Charter on Human and People's Rights and the Constitutive Act of the AU. This would constitute a principled position that would apply to the present and future governments in Harare. Once Zimbabweans can enjoy the freedoms enshrined in these instruments, the direction of the human traffic across the

Limpopo will switch from a southerly to a northerly direction as the Zimbabwean diaspora makes the 'great trek' back home to rebuild their ruined country.

Conclusion

This chapter has argued that the Zimbabwean community in South Africa is comprised of many faces, ranging from professionals to illegal and unskilled immigrants. The contours of migration to South Africa have undergone many shifts over the years. Initially, young men from the southern part of Zimbabwe migrated to South Africa to work in the mines. These 'jelled' very well into South African communities due to commonalities in language, culture and history. The second 'trek' occurred in the 1980s with white people migrating to other countries, in particular, South Africa and the UK, for fear of being ruled by a black government. However, today the most talked-about 'trek' is that between 2000 and 2006 as a result of the political crisis and the economic meltdown in Zimbabwe.

The argument here is that the crisis faced by the Zimbabwean community in South Africa is likely to deepen if the South African government does not acknowledge publicly the enormity of the problem. This should be accompanied by comprehensive programmes that would take care of the community's educational, humanitarian as well as human rights needs. South Africa cannot do this alone; there is a need for international refugee assistance organisations to come on board as well. Meanwhile, the Zimbabwean government should also be required to implement and observe international instruments on human rights, to which it is a signatory. It is only by resolving the political crisis and the building and respect for democratic institutions that the disastrous economic meltdown will be addressed and the way opened for Zimbabweans living abroad to return to their home country.

Notes

1   See a joint report by the Department of Sociology, University of Zimbabwe, and Zimbabwe Lawyers for Human Rights on the impact of Operation Murambatsvina: The case of Hatcliffe Extension, May 2006. Available at <http://www.kubatana.net/docs/urbdev/zlhr_uz_impact_murambatsvina_hatcliffe_0506.pd>.

2   See <http://www.irinnews.org/subscriptions/subslogin.asp>.

3   See <http://www.news.bbc.co.uk/2/hi/africa/4416820.stm>.

4   See <http://www.afrika.no/Detailed/11332.html>.

5   See <http://www.cpj.org/attacks05/africa05zim_05.html>.

6   See <http://www.zimbabwesituation.com/may18_2003>.

7   These views are gained from the writers' interactions with Zimbabwean refugees as well as with civil society organisations such as the Nkunzi Development Association that work in the Limpopo province.

8   See <http://www.thezimbabwean.co.uk/18-march-2005/protests-mount.htl>.

9   See <www.irinnews.org/report.asp?ReportID=49890&SelectRegion=
     Southern_Africa:ahandfulofzimbabweansgrantedasylum>.

10   For more detail on Operation Murambatsvina see Tibaijuka 2005. Available at
     <http://www.unhabitat.org/documents/>.

11   See also Dzikamai Chidyausiku's article, 'Zimbabwe: Demolitions may be Mugabe's biggest
     mistake', *Africa Reports* 40, 14.08.05. Available at <http://www.kubatana.net/html/
     archive/demgg/0508141wpr1.asp?sector+hr&range_start=1>.

12   See an article published by *South Scan* entitled 'South Africa facing Zimbabwean
     Immigrant flood', on 02.10.05. Available at
     <http://www.queensu.ca/samp/migrationnews/article.php?Mig_News_ID=1918&Mig_Ne
     ws_Issue+104Mig_Cat=8. See also, Desperate Zimbabweans swamp Limpopo, SAPA
     18.09.05>.

13   See <http://www.news24.co.za:36heldforxenophobicviolence>.

14   See <http://www.irinnews.org/subscriptions/sublongin.asp>.

15   See 'Lindela horror revealed: 43 die in 4 months', *New Zimbabwe.Com* 28.10.05. Available
     at <http://www.newzimbabwe.com/pages/ASYLUMSA15.13376.HTML>.

16   See 'Barosso raise concerns over Zimbabwe situation'. Available at
     <http://www.english.people.com.cu/200506/26/eng20050626_192384.html>; see also 'AU
     stance "disappoints" EU chief', *Business Day* 27.06.05. Available at
     <http://www.businessday.co.za/articles/specialreports.aspx?ID=BD4A60983>.

References

Bloch A (2005) *The development potential of Zimbabweans in the diaspora*. Geneva: IOM.

Chikanda A (2005) *Medical leave: The exodus of health professionals from Zimbabwe*.
     Cape Town: Southern Africa Migration Project, Idasa.

Clemens M & Moss T (2005) *Dateline Zimbabwe: Who is to blame?* Available at
     <http://www.cgdev.org/contents/opinion/detail/3612/?print=1&id=3612&datatype=25>.

Cortes EK (2004) Are refugees different from economic immigrants? Some empirical evidence
     on the heterogeneity of immigrant groups in the United States. *Review of Economics and
     Statistics*, 86(2): 465–80.

Gaidzanwa R (1999) *Voting with their feet: Migrant Zimbabwea nurses and doctors in the era of
     structural adjustment*. Uppsala: Nordiska Afrikainstitutet.

Moyo W (2006) *The documented experiences of Zimbabweans refugees, asylum seekers and
     deportees in South Africa*. Johannesburg: Lawyers for Human Rights (SA) (forthcoming).

Mukaronda N (2005) Labour abuse of Zimbabwean teachers seeking asylum and migration
     status in South Africa. Unpublished. Johannesburg: Solidarity Peace Trust.

Muzondidya J (2006) Mobilising the diaspora for political activism. Paper presented at the
     South African Institute for International Affairs, Johannesburg, 28.02.06.

Ranger T (2005) The rise of patriotic journalism in Zimbabwe and its possible implications. London: University of Westminster. Available at <http://www.wmin.ac.uk/mad/pdf/zim_art1.pdf>.

Solidarity Peace Trust (2004) An account of the exodus of a nation. Unpublished. Johannesburg.

Tevera D (2005) *Early departures: The emigration potential of Zimbabwean students.* Cape Town: Southern African Migration Project, Idasa.

Tevera D & Crush J (2003) *The new brain drain from Zimbabwe.* Cape Town: Southern African Migration Project, Idasa.

Tevera D & Zinyama L (2002) *Zimbabweans who move: Perspectives on international migration in Zimbabwe.* Cape Town: Southern African Migration Project, Idasa.

Tibaijuka AK (2005) *Report of the fact-finding mission to Zimbabwe to assess the scope and impact of Operation Murambatsvina by the UN Special Envoy on Human settlement issues in Zimbabwe.* New York: United Nations.

Witchel E (2005) *Zimbabwe's exiled press: Uprooted journalists struggle to keep careers, independent reporting alive.* Available at <http://www.cpj.org/Briefings/2005/DA_fall05/zim/zim_DA_fall05_2.html>.

Zamchiya P (2006) Research on Zimbabwean students in South African universities. Unpublished.

Interviews

Zakeus Chibaya, exiled Zimbabwean journalist living in South Africa, Johannesburg, 23.03.06.

Emmanuel Ngenzi, volunteer programme director for Refugee Ministries,telephonic, 10.05.06.

Bongani Nxumalo, Project Coordinator, Abanqobi Bomhlaba, telephonic, 02.06.06.

Bongani Nyathi, Interim Chairperson, Progressive Teachers' Union, South Africa, Johannesburg, 23.03.06

Contributors

Doreen Atkinson
Visiting Professor,
Centre for Development Support
University of the Free State

Peter Barron
Specialist Technical Advisor
Health Systems Trust

Andries Bezuidenhout
Researcher, Sociology of Work Unit
Department of Sociology
University of Witwatersrand

Sakhela Buhlungu
Professor
Department of Sociology
University of Witwatersrand

Anthony Butler
Professor
Department of Political Studies
University of Cape Town

Alex Comninos
MA student
Department of Political Studies
University of Cape Town

John Daniel
Former Chair of the Editorial Board
HSRC Press

Ashwin Desai
Research Associate
Centre for Civil Society
University of KwaZulu-Natal

Anthony Egan
Jesuit Father and Lecturer
St Augustine's College

David Fig
Specialist Consultant
Environmental and Technology Issues

Sharon Fonn
Professor
School of Public Health
University of Witwatersrand

Heather Hughes
Senior Lecturer
Tourism and Heritage Department
Lincoln University, England

Zwelethu Jolobe
Lecturer
Department of Political Studies
University of Cape Town

Claude Kabemba
Chief Research Specialist
Society, Culture and Identity
Programme
HSRC

Anil Kanjee
Executive Director
Education Quality Improvement
National Priority Initiative
HSRC

Jessica Lutchman
Former Researcher
Democracy and Governance
Programme
HSRC

Neva Makgetla
Head, Policy Unit
Congress of South African Trade
Unions (COSATU)

Lephophotho Mashike
Lecturer
Department of Sociology
University of Witwatersrand

Bhekinkosi Moyo
Research Specialist
Africa Institute of South Africa

Mike Murphy
Specialist Consultant
Labour and Health Issues

Zayn Nabbi
Journalist
Independent Newspapers

Nicoli Nattrass
Professor
Department of Economics
University of Cape Town

Mcebisi Ndletyana
Senior Research Specialist
Democracy and Governance
Research Programme
HSRC

Helen Schneider
Senior Researcher
Centre for Health Policy
University of Witwatersrand

Collette Schulz-Herzenberg
PhD Candidate
Department of Political Studies
University of Cape Town

Elinor Sisulu
Media and Advocacy Manager
Crisis in Zimbabwe Coalition

Julia Sloth-Nielsen
Professor
Department of Law
University of Western Cape

Roger Southall
Distinguished Research Fellow
HSRC

Nkosinathi Tshuma
Director
Heal Zimbabwe Trust

Lisa Vetten
Researcher and Policy Analyst
Tshwaranang Legal Advocacy Centre to
End Violence Against Women

Karl von Holdt
Senior Researcher
National Labour and Economic
Development Institute

Index

A

abortion 302, 450, 461, 465
    laws 461
    legislation 302
    policy 450
absenteeism 330, 477
Accelerated and Shared Growth Initiative for
    South Africa (ASGISA), 227, 133–134,
    422, 506
acts
    Access to Information and Protection of
      Privacy Act 557
    Bantu Education Act (1953) 6
    Broad Based Black Empowerment Act
      (2003) 7
    Choice on Termination of Pregnancy Act
      (1996) 296
    Companies Act 214, 218
    Constitution 12th Amendment Act 65
    Correctional Services Act 388–390, 392
    Criminal Law Amendment Act (1997) 385,
      395, 426
    Criminal Procedure Second Amendment
      Act (1997) 426
    Demobilisation Act 356
    Domestic Violence Act (DVA) (1998) 348,
      427
    Domestic Violence Act (1998) 426
    Employment Equity Act (1998) 7, 253
    Firearms Control Act 432
    Group Areas Act 433
    Health 291
    Local Government Transition Act (1993)
      29
    Medical Schemes Act (1998) 296
    Medicines and Related Substances Control
      Amendment Act (1997) 300, 308
    Municipal Demarcation Act (1998) 30
    Municipal Finance Management Act
      (2004) 68–69
    Municipal Structures Act (1998) 30, 89
    Municipal Systems Act (2000) 30, 64, 85
    National Education Policy Act (1996) 471

    National Environmental Management Act
      (1998) 233, 275
    National Health Act (2003) 177, 291,
      295–296
    National Health Act (2005) 305, 307
    National Heritage Resources Act (1999)
      274
    Native Land Act 435
    Prevention of Corruption and Combating
      of Corrupt Activities Act (2003) 9
    Prevention of Family Violence Act (1993)
      427
    Promotion of Equality and Prevention of
      Unfair Discrimination Act (2000) 7
    Public Finance Management Act (PFMA)
      9, 68, 223, 297
    Public Health Act (1919) 291
    Public Order Security Act 557
    Refugee Act 564
    Regional Services Act (1985) 28
    Schools Act (1996) 390
    Skills Development Act 253
    Social Assistance Act (1992 & 2004) 181
    Social Pension Act 357
    South African Police Service Act 427
    Special Pension Act (1996) 356, 371
    Tobacco Products Control Amendment
      Act (1999) 296
affirmative action 8, 62, 210, 212, 380, 406,
    409
African Christian Democrat Party (ACDP)
    79, 91, 349, 459–462, 466
African Initiated church (AIC) 348, 449, 451,
    459
African Mineworkers Union (AMWU) 245,
    248
African Muslim Party (AMP) 79, 92
African National Congress (ANC) 2, 3–8,
    10–22, 27, 29, 32–33, 35–41, 43–49, 53,
    57, 64–67, 74–75, 78, 80, 82–84,
    87–107, 110, 111, 112, 114, 116, 117,
    119, 120, 121, 123, 125, 126, 127, 128,
    129, 132, 133, 134, 136, 137, 138, 139,